Roger Kerridge

School of Law, University of Bristol, BS8 1RJ

CONSTRUCTIVE AND RESULTING TRUSTS

Constructive and resulting trusts have a long history in English law, and the law which governs them continues to develop as they are pressed into service to perform a wide variety of different functions, for example, to support the working of express trusts and other fiduciary relationships, to allocate family property rights, and to undo the consequences of commercial fraud. However, while their conceptual flexibility makes them enormously useful, it also makes them hard to understand. In the twelve essays collected in this volume, the authors shed new light on various aspects of the law governing constructive and resulting trusts, revisiting current controversies, bringing new historical material to the fore, and offering new theoretical perspectives.

Constructive and Resulting Trusts

Edited by
Charles Mitchell

HART PUBLISHING

OXFORD AND PORTLAND, OREGON
2010

Published in North America (US and Canada) by
Hart Publishing
c/o International Specialized Book Services
920 NE 58th Avenue, Suite 300
Portland, OR 97213-3786
USA
Tel: +1 503 287 3093 or toll-free: (1) 800 944 6190
Fax: +1 503 280 8832
E-mail: orders@isbs.com
Website: http://www.isbs.com

© The editors and contributors severally 2009

The editors and contributors have asserted their right under the Copyright, Designs and Patents Act 1988, to be identified as the authors of this work.

All rights reserved. No part of this publication may be reproduced, stored in a retrieval system, or transmitted, in any form or by any means, without the prior permission of Hart Publishing, or as expressly permitted by law or under the terms agreed with the appropriate reprographic rights organisation. Enquiries concerning reproduction which may not be covered by the above should be addressed to Hart Publishing at the address below.

Hart Publishing Ltd, 16C Worcester Place, Oxford, OX1 2JW
Telephone: +44 (0)1865 517530 Fax: +44 (0)1865 510710
E-mail: mail@hartpub.co.uk
Website: http://www.hartpub.co.uk

British Library Cataloguing in Publication Data
Data Available

ISBN: 978-1-84113-927-2

Typeset by Forewords Ltd, Oxford

Printed and bound in Great Britain by
TJ International, Padstow, Cornwall

Preface

Constructive and resulting trusts have a long history, which we must understand if we want to know why these trusts are imposed and how they work. Many of the essays in this collection make extensive use of historical materials to cast some light on these difficult questions. Paul Matthews makes a series of telling points in his historical account of the formality and limitation rules by which constructive trusts are governed, and (in a discussion which reaches right into the present day) the relationship between the common intention constructive trust and the doctrine of proprietary estoppel. William Swadling revisits the decision in *Rochefoucauld v Boustead*, decided more than a century ago, and argues that the trust there was express, rather than constructive, a view which Matthews shares, and which affects our understanding of the extent to which equity uses the constructive trust as a mechanism to subvert formality statutes. Charles Mitchell and Stephen Watterson challenge the view that it means nothing to say that the knowing recipients of misdirected trust funds are 'personally liable to account as constructive trustees', and explain, by reference to a body of case-law from the last 200 years, how this liability corresponds to the liability of an express trustee to account for trust property to his beneficiaries. This affects the remedies awarded in knowing receipt cases, and also has implications for the question addressed by Matthew Conaglen and Amy Goymour, whether actions for knowing receipt lie against recipients of registered land. They convincingly argue, contrary to the view expressed by the Law Commission, that such actions do not lie.

John Mee mines the early law reports to show that there is more to the idea that the beneficiary of a resulting trust 'retains' an interest in the trust property than modern writers generally recognise. This idea is also discussed by James Penner in his review of the main controversies to emerge from the recent literature on resulting trusts. Meanwhile Jamie Glister traces the evolution of the presumption of advancement, and argues that recent extensions to the presumption relationships are misguided because they have lost sight of the question that should determine when the presumption applies, namely, whether a parent is under an obligation to establish a child as an independent economic actor.

In other chapters, Simon Gardner argues that many of the constructive trusts categorised by other writers as intention-based are best understood as operating to reverse reliance loss. His provocative analysis can usefully be read alongside Matthews's discussion of the common intention constructive trust. Robert Chambers considers the view that the presumption of resulting trust is a true presumption while the presumption of advancement is not, and argues for the opposite conclusion. Ben McFarlane observes that many constructive and resulting trusts might seem to be anomalous because they do not fit with a common view of trusts that understands them to come into existence only when a settlor exercises a power to create a new equitable property right. This problem disappears, in his view, once it is appreciated that all trusts arise when one person holds a right and is under a duty to another person in relation to that right.

Charlie Webb makes the point in his discussion of resulting trusts and mistake that a claimant's intention to transfer property is always conditional, in the sense that there are always circumstances to which it does not extend, so that in such circumstances he can genuinely say that he did not intend to make the transfer. Finally, Irit Samet examines the *locus poenitentiae* rule, under which property transferred for an illegal purpose can be recovered under a resulting trust (or, indeed, at common law) where the transferor withdraws from the transaction before any illegality has been committed. Writing from the standpoint of a moral philosopher, she asks what differences it makes whether a transferor sincerely repents of her wrongful intentions, and whether she withdraws before or after the date of her contemplated wrongdoing.

The chapters in this book were originally given as papers at a workshop held at King's College London in April 2009. On behalf of the authors I thank the King's Law School for its financial support, and all the workshop participants for their contributions to the discussion, most particularly Lord Walker, who kindly took time away from his judicial duties to join us.

Charles Mitchell
August 2009

Contents

Preface	v
Contributors	viii
Table of Cases	ix
Table of Legislation	xxix

	PART I: CONSTRUCTIVE TRUSTS	1
1	The Words Which Are Not There: A Partial History of the Constructive Trust PAUL MATTHEWS	3
2	Reliance-Based Constructive Trusts SIMON GARDNER	63
3	The Nature of the Trust in *Rochefoucauld v Boustead* WILLIAM SWADLING	95
4	Remedies for Knowing Receipt CHARLES MITCHELL and STEPHEN WATTERSON	115
5	Knowing Receipt and Registered Land MATTHEW CONAGLEN and AMY GOYMOUR	159
6	The Centrality of Constructive and Resulting Trusts BEN McFARLANE	183

	PART II: RESULTING TRUSTS	205
7	'Automatic' Resulting Trusts: Retention, Restitution, or Reposing Trust? JOHN MEE	207
8	Resulting Trusts and Unjust Enrichment: Three Controversies JAMES PENNER	237
9	Is There a Presumption of Resulting Trust? ROBERT CHAMBERS	267
10	The Presumption of Advancement JAMIE GLISTER	289
11	Intention, Mistakes and Resulting Trusts CHARLIE WEBB	315
12	*Locus Poenitentiae*: Repentance, Withdrawal and Luck IRIT SAMET	335

Contributors

Robert Chambers is a Professor of Property Law at University College London.

Matthew Conaglen is a Fellow of Trinity Hall, Cambridge, and a University Senior Lecturer at the University of Cambridge.

Simon Gardner is a Fellow and Tutor in Law at Lincoln College, Oxford, and a CUF Lecturer in Law at the University of Oxford.

Jamie Glister is a Lecturer in Law at the University of Sydney.

Amy Goymour is the Hopkins Parry Fellow in Law at Downing College, Cambridge, and a University Lecturer at the University of Cambridge.

Paul Matthews is a Visiting Professor of Law at King's College London and a consultant at Withers LLP.

Ben McFarlane is a Fellow and Tutor in Law at Trinity College, Oxford, and a Reader in Property Law at the University of Oxford.

John Mee is an Associate Professor of Law at University College Cork.

Charles Mitchell is a Fellow and Tutor in Law at Jesus College, Oxford, and a Professor of Law at the University of Oxford.

James Penner is a Professor of Property Law at University College London.

Irit Samet is a Lecturer in Law at King's College London.

William Swadling is a Fellow and Tutor in Law at Brasenose College, Oxford, and a Reader in Property Law at the University of Oxford.

Stephen Watterson is a Senior Lecturer in Law at the London School of Economics and Political Science.

Charlie Webb is a Lecturer in Law at the London School of Economics and Political Science.

Table of Cases

21st Century Logistic Solutions Ltd (in liq) v Madysen Ltd [2004]
  EWHC 231 (QB) 355
Abou-Rahmah v Abacha [2006] EWCA Civ 1492; [2007] 1 All
  ER (Comm) 827. 179
Actionstrength Ltd v International Glass Engineering SpA [2002]
  UKHL 17; [2002] 2 AC 541 . . . . 29, 30, 31, 43, 44, 61
Adamson, *ex parte* (1878) 8 Ch D 807 . . . . 124, 157
Agip (Africa) Ltd v Jackson [1990] Ch 265, *affirmed* [1991] Ch 547
  . . . . 118, 130, 157, 172, 179, 181, 242
Ahmed Angullia bin Hadjee Mohamed Salleh Angullia v Estate and
  Trust Agencies (1927) Ltd [1938] AC 624 124
Air Jamaica Ltd v Charlton [1999] 1 WLR 1399 . . . . 212, 259, 317
Ajayi v R T Briscoe (Nigeria) Ltd [1964] 1 WLR 1326 91
Alexander v Perpetual Trustees (WA) Ltd [2004] HCA 7;
  (2004) 216 CLR 109. 125
Algar v Middlesex County Council [1945] 2 All ER 243 25
Ali v Khan [2002] EWCA Civ 974 271
Aliakmon, The, see Leigh & Sillivan Ltd v Aliakmon Shipping Co Ltd
Allen v Rea Brothers Trustees Ltd [2002] EWCA Civ 85; (2002) 4
  ITELR 627 119
Allied Carpets Group plc v Nethercott [2001] BCC 81 132
Ambrazevicius Estate, Re [2002] MBQB 58; (2002) 164 Man R (2d) 5 . 127
Anderson Antiques (UK) Ltd v Anderson Wharf (Hull) Ltd [2007]
  EWHC 2086 (Ch). 27, 42
Andre et Cie v Ets Michel Blanc et Fils [1979] 2 Lloyds Rep 427 25
Andrews v Bousfield (1847) 10 Beav 511; 50 ER 678 118
Ang Toon Teck v Ang Poon Sin [1998] SGHC 67 309
Anglo-French Co-operative Soc, Re (1882) 21 Ch D 492 124
Anon (1718) 1 P Wms 495; 24 ER 487 154
Antoni v Antoni [2007] UKPC 10; [2007] WTLR 1335 . . . . . . 269, 274
Armitage v Nurse [1998] Ch 241 121
Armstrong v East West Airlines (Operations) Ltd, NSW Sup Ct
  (Eq Div) 3 February 1994 124
Armstrong v Sheppard & Short Ltd [1959] 2 QB 384. 26
Armstrong v Wolsey (1755) 2 Wils KB 19; 95 ER 662 6
Ashburn Anstalt v W J Arnold & Co [1989] Ch 1 . . . . 80, 89, 200
Ashby v Blackwell (1765) 2 Eden 299; 28 ER 913 126
Assets Co Ltd v Roihi [1905] AC 176 180
Attorney-General v Baliol College Oxford (1748) 9 Mod 407; ER 538 . . 26

x Table of Cases

Attorney-General v Trustees of the British Museum [2005]
EWHC 1089 (Ch); [2005] Ch 397. 157
Attorney-General of Hong Kong v Humphreys Estates (Queen's
Gardens) Ltd [1987] 1 AC 114 38
Attorney-General of Hong Kong v Reid [1994] 1 AC 324
. . . . 5, 112, 184, 185, 189, 190, 192, 199
Austin v Keele (1987) 72 ALR 579 50
B Liggett (Liverpool) Ltd v Barclays Bank Ltd [1928] 1 KB 48 135
Bacon v Clarke (1837) 3 My & Cr 294; 40 ER 938 124
Bahr v Nicolay (No 2) (1988) 164 CLR 604 . . . . 166, 180
Baillie, Re (1886) 2 TLR 660 19
Bairstow v Queen's Moat Houses plc [2001] 2 BCLC 531 127
Baker v Baker (1993) 25 HLR 408 53
Bank of China v Kwong Wa Po [2005] HKCFI 422 . . . . 133, 142
Bank of Credit and Commerce International (Overseas) Ltd v
Akindele [2001] Ch 437 . . . . 115, 160, 163, 164, 170, 196
Bank of New Zealand v New Zealand Guardian Trust Co Ltd
[1999] 1 NZLR 664 127
Banner Homes Group plc v Luff Developments Ltd [2000] Ch 372
. . . . 50, 72, 73, 74, 79, 81
Bannister v Bannister [1948] 2 All ER 133
. . . . 21, 53, 63, 68, 69, 82, 86, 89, 90, 96
Banque Financière de la Cité v Parc (Battersea) Ltd [1999] 1 AC 221 . . 171
Barclays Bank Ltd v Quistclose Investments Ltd [1970] AC 567 134
Barclays Bank plc v Boulter [1998] 1 WLR 1, *affirmed* [1999]
1 WLR 1919. 163
Barlow Clowes International Ltd v Eurotrust International Ltd
[2005] UKPC 37; [2006] 1 WLR 1476 . . . . 178, 179, 196
Barnes v Addy (1874) LR 9 Ch App 244 . . . . 100, 103, 130, 131, 158, 162
Barney, Re [1892] 2 Ch 265 . . . . 131, 169
Barrett v Barrett [2008] EWHC 1061 (Ch) 272
Barry v Heider (1914) 19 CLR 197 165
Bartlett v Barclays Bank Trust Co Ltd (No 2) [1980] Ch 515
. . . . 121, 124, 127, 157
Basham, Re [1986] 1 WLR 1498 . . . . 27, 33, 50, 52, 78
Batstone v Salter (1874) LR 19 Eq 250 298
Bawden v Bawden [1997] EWCA Civ 2664 54
Baylis v Newton (1687) 2 Vern 28; 23 ER 628 296
Beaney, Re [1978] 1 WLR 770 247
Beckford v Wade (1810) 17 Ves 87; 34 ER 34 100
Belchier, *ex parte* (1754) Amb 218; 27 ER 144 126
Bell Group Ltd (in liq) v Westpac Banking Corp (No 9) [2008]
WASC 239; (2008) 225 FLR 1 115
Bell's Indenture, Re [1980] 1 WLR 1217 124

Belmont Finance Corp v Williams Furniture Ltd (No 2) [1980]
  1 All ER 393 . . . . 115, 142, 145, 146
Bennet v Bennet (1879) 10 Ch D 474. . . . . 272, 285, 298, 300, 301, 302,
  303, 308, 310
Bigos v Boustead [1951] 1 All ER 92 . . . . 357, 365
Binion v Stone (1663) Nels 68, 21 ER 791; 2 Freeman 169;
  22 ER 1135 . . . . 11, 312
Binions v Evans [1972] Ch 359 . . . . 22, 80, 89, 90, 96, 107, 200
Birch v Curtis [2002] EWHC 1158 (Ch); [2002] WTLR 965 75
Birmingham v Renfrew (1937) 57 CLR 666 71
Birmingham and District Land Co v London and North Western
  Railway Co (1888) 40 Ch D 268 91
Birmingham Midshires Mortgage Services Ltd v Sabherwal (1999)
  80 P & CR 256 . . . . 25, 50
Blackwell v Blackwell [1929] AC 318 . . . . 65, 81, 82, 200
Blundell, Re (1888) 40 Ch D 370 . . . . 162, 163
Blyth v Fladgate [1891] 1 Ch 337. . . . . 130, 133, 134
Bodmin, Lady v Vandenbendy (1683) 1 Vern 179; 23 ER 399 163
Bond v Rosling (1861) 1 B & S 371; 121 ER 753 38
Bonny v Ridgard (1784) 1 Cox 145. 100
Boscawen v Bajwa [1996] 1 WLR 328. 116
Bostock v Blakeney (1794) 2 Bro CC 653; 29 ER 362 125
Bostock v Flyer (1865) LR 1 Eq 26 126
Bowmakers Ltd v Barnet Instruments Ltd [1945] KB 65 . . . . . . 337, 352
Box v Barclays Bank plc [1998] Lloyd's Rep Bank 185. 165
Boyd v Mayor of Wellington [1924] NZLR 1174 166
Bracken Partners Ltd v Gutteridge [2004] 1 BCLC 373 . . . . . . 132, 141
Brent's Case (1583) 2 Leonard 14; 74 ER 319. 232
Breskvar v Wall (1971) 126 CLR 376 166
Bridges v Mees [1957] Ch 475 . . . . 5, 51
Bridgman v Gill (1857) 24 Beav 302; 53 ER 374 100
Brightlingsea Haven Ltd v Morris [2008] EWHC 1928 (QB);
  [2009] 2 P & CR 11. 41
Bristol, Cardiff & Swansea Aerated Bread Co v Maggs (1890) 44
  Ch D 616 108
Bristol and West Building Society v A Kramer and Co (a firm)
  The Times 6 February 1995 125
British American Elevator Co v Bank of North America [1919] AC 658 . 124
Brogden, Re (1888) 38 Ch D 546 122
Brown v Brown (1993) 31 NSWLR 582 . . . . . . 272, 283, 284, 304, 313
Brydges v Kilburne (1792) *cited* 5 Ves Jun 689; 31 ER 807;
  6 Ves Jun 107; 31 ER 961 26
Bunt v Hallinan [1985] 1 NZLR 450 180
Burdick v Garrick (1870) LR 5 Ch App 233 . . . . 22, 103, 124

xii   Table of Cases

Burgess v Wheate (1759) 1 Black W 123; 96 ER 67 . . . . . . 217, 218, 231
Burns v Burns [1984] Ch 317 . . . . 190, 308
Burrowes v Lock (1805) 10 Ves Jun 470; 32 ER 927 25
Burrows v Sharp (1989) 23 HLR 82. . . . 52. 53
Butcher v Stapely (1685) 1 Vern 363; 23 ER 524 29
Butler v Fairclough (1917) 23 CLR 78 180
Buttle v Saunders [1950] 2 All ER 193 123
C (A Minor) (Contribution Notice), Re [1994] 1 FLR 111 . . . . . 293, 294
Caffrey v Darby (1801) 6 Ves Jun 488; 31 ER 1158 125
Calverley v Green (1984) 155 CLR 242 . . . . . . 303, 304, 305, 306, 307
Campbell v Griffin [2001] EWCA Civ 990; [2001] WTLR 981 . . 53, 54, 77
Campbell v Hogg [1930] 3 DLR 673 121
Canada Safeway Ltd v Thompson [1951] 3 DLR 295 151
Canson Enterprises Ltd v Boughton & Co [1991] 3 SCR 534 127
Cattley v Pollard [2006] EWHC 3130 (Ch); [2007] Ch 353 69
Cawdor, Lord v Lewis (1835) 1 Y & C Ex 427; 160 ER 174 26
Central London Property Trust Ltd v High Trees House Ltd [1947]
    KB 130 91
Chalmer v Bradley (1819) 1 Jac & W 51; 37 ER 294 102
Chalmers v Pardoe [1963] 1 WLR 677 . . . . 43, 52
Chaplin v Young (1864) 33 Beav 330; 55 ER 395 123
Chapman, Re [1896] 2 Ch 763. . . . 121
Charter plc v City Index Ltd [2006] EWHC 2508 (Ch);
    [2007] 1 WLR 26; *reversed sub nom* City Index Ltd v
    Gawler [2007] EWCA Civ 1382; [2008] Ch 313 . . . 115, 130, 161, 162
Chase Manhattan Bank NA v Israel-British Bank (London) Ltd
    [1981] Ch 105. 193
Chattey v Farndale Holdings Inc (1996) 75 P & CR 298 90
Chattock v Muller (1878) LR 8 Ch D 177 . . . . 73, 79
Chellaram v Chellaram (No 2) [2002] EWHC 632 (Ch); [2002] 3
    All ER 17. . . . . 122, 198
Chettiar v Chettiar [1962] 1 All ER 494. 364
Cheung v Worldcup Investments Inc [2008] HKCFA 78 . . . . . . 291, 306
Childers v Childers (1857) 1 De G & J 482; 44 ER 810 263
Christian v Christian (CA) 6 November 1980 50
Citadel General Assurance Co v Lloyds Bank Canada [1997] 3 SCR 805
    . . . . 156, 157
City Index Ltd v Gawler *see* Charter plc v City Index Ltd
City of London Building Society v Flegg [1988] 1 AC 54 159
Clark v Cutland [2003] EWCA Civ 810; [2004] 1 WLR 783 119
Cleaver (deceased), Re [1981] 1 WLR 939 69
Clough v Bond (1838) 3 My & Cr 490; 40 ER 1016 125
Cobbe v Yeoman's Row Management Ltd [2006] EWCA Civ 1139;
    [2006] 1 WLR 2964; *reversed* [2008] UKHL 55;

[2008] 1 WLR 1752 . . . 35, 38, 42, 43, 44, 55, 72, 73, 76, 77, 80, 191, 194, 201
Cocker v Quayle (1830) 1 Russ & M 353; 39 ER 206 124
Coleman v Bucks & Oxon Union Bank [1897] 2 Ch 243 159
Collier v Collier [2002] EWCA Civ 1095; (2002) 6 ITELR 270 271
Colling, Re (1886) 32 Ch D 333 51
Collings v Lee [2001] 2 All ER 332 229
Collins v Blantern (1767) 2 Wils KB 347; 95 ER 850 339
Collins v Brebner [2000] Lloyds Rep PN 587 127
Colour Control Centre Pty Ltd v Ty, NSW Sup Ct (Eq Div) 24 July 1995   127
Combe v Combe [1951] 2 KB 215 . . . . 92, 93
Coming, *ex parte* (1803) 9 Ves Jun 115; 32 ER 545 41
Commercial Bank of Australia v Amadio (1983) 151 CLR 447 340
Commissioner for Stamp Duties v Perpetual Trustee Co Ltd [1943]
    AC 425 . . . . 61, 62
Commonwealth of Australia v Verwayen (1990) 170 CLR 394 88
Commonwealth Oil & Gas Co Ltd v Baxter [2009] CSIH 75 158
Cook v Fountain (1676) 3 Swans 585; 36 ER 984
    . . . . 7, 8, 9, 10, 112, 249, 250, 251, 267, 276, 277
Cooper v Phibbs (1867) LR 2 HL 149 25
Coppard v Allen (1864) 4 Giff 497; 66 ER 802 122
Corin v Patton (1990) 92 ALR 1 . . . . 223, 224
Corporaçion del Cobre de Chile v Sogemin Metals Ltd [1997] 1
    WLR 1396 127
Corumo Holdings Pty Ltd v C Itoh Ltd (1991) 24 NSWLR 370 175
Costello v Chief Constable of Derbyshire Constabulary [2001]
    EWCA Civ 381; [2001] 1 WLR 143 336
Cottington v Fletcher (1740) 2 Atk 155; 26 ER 498 21
Coulthard v Disco Mix Club Ltd [1999] 2 All ER 457 121
Cowan v Scargill [1985] Ch 270 123
Cowan de Groot Properties Ltd v Eagle Trust plc [1992] 4 All ER 700 . . 160
Cowcher v Cowcher [1972] 1 WLR 425 46
CPT Custodian Pty Ltd v Commissioner of State Revenue [2005]
    HCA 53; (2005) 224 CLR 98 175
Crabb v Arun District Council [1976] Ch 179
    . . . . 35, 43, 51, 52, 53, 54, 78, 194, 195
Cressman v Coys of Kensington (Sales) Ltd [2004] EWCA 47;
    [2004] 1 WLR 2774 155
Criterion Properties plc v Stratford UK Properties LLC [2004]
    UKHL 28; [2004] 1 WLR 1846 169
Crosby v Wadsworth (1805) 6 East 602; 102 ER 1419 108
Cullen v AG for Ireland (1866) LR 1 HL 190 21
Currie and Others (Lamb's Trustees) (1901) 9 SLT 170 125
Cuthbertson v Swan (1877) 11 SALR 102 165

Dagle v Dagle Estate (1990) 70 DLR (4th) 201 311
Dale (deceased), Re [1994] Ch 31 . . . . 20, 75
Damberg v Damberg [2001] NSWCA 87; (2001) 52 NSWLR 492 . . . 290
D'Amore v McDonald [1973] 1 OR 845, *affirmed* (1973) 1 OR (2d) 370
. . . . 151
Dann v Spurrier (1802) 7 Ves Jun 231; 32 ER 94 26
Darkingjung Pty Ltd v Darkingjung Local Aboriginal Land
 Council [2006] NSWSC 1217. . . . . 130, 132, 146
David v Frowd (1833) 1 My & K 200; 39 ER 657. 154
Davies v Otty (No 2) (1865) 35 Beav 208; 55 ER 875. 21
Davies v Sear (1869) LR 7 Eq 427 26
Davis, Re [1902] 2 Ch 314 124
Dawson, Re [1966] 2 NSWR 211 124
De Beer v Kanaar & Co (a firm) [2002] EWHC 688 (Ch) 125
De Bussche v Alt (1878) 8 Ch D 286 27
De Tchibatschef v Salerni Coupling Ltd [1932] 1 Ch 330 25
DEG-Deutsche Investitions- und Entwicklungsgesellschaft mbH v
 Koshy (No 2) [2002] 1 BCLC 478 128
Derby & Co v ITC Pension Trust Ltd [1977] 2 All ER 850 38
Dextra Bank & Trust Co Ltd v Bank of Jamaica [2002] 1 All ER
 (Comm) 193. 327
DHN Food Distributors Ltd v Tower Hamlets LBC [1976] 1 WLR 852. . 90
Dillwyn v Llewelyn (1862) 4 De G F & J 517; 45 ER 1285
. . . . 36, 37, 38, 39, 41, 48, 52, 59, 77, 78
Diplock, Re [1947] Ch 716, *reversed* [1948] Ch 465, *affirmed sub
 nom* Ministry of Health v Simpson [1951] AC 251 . . . . . 44, 154, 155
Dixon v Dixon (1878) 9 Ch D 587 124
Dixon v Muckleston (1872) LR 8 Ch App 155 41
DKLR Holding Co (No 2) Pty Ltd v Commissioner of Stamp
 Duties (1982) 149 CLR 431, *reversing* [1980] 1 NSWLR 510
. . . . 187, 219, 221, 222, 223, 224
Docker v Somes (1834) 2 My & K 655; 39 ER 1095 124
Dodsworth v Dodsworth (1973) 228 EG 1115 53
Doneley v Doneley [1998] 1 QdR 602. . . . . 168, 175
Dowse v Gorton [1891] AC 190 126
Dubai Aluminium Co Ltd v Salaam [2002] UKHL 48;
 [2003] 2 AC 366 . . . . 150, 153, 155, 156, 157, 162, 178
Duckwari plc (No 2), Re [1999] Ch 268. 125
Duff v Duff (1988) 12 RFL (3d) 435 226
Duke of Marlborough, Re [1894] 2 Ch 133 21
Dullow v Dullow (1985) 3 NSWLR 531 249
Duncan v McDonald [1997] NZLR 669 166
Dunlop Pneumatic Tyre Co Ltd v Selfridge & Co Ltd [1915] AC 847 . . 106
Dyer v Dyer (1788) 2 Cox 92; 30 ER 42 . . . . . . 280, 296, 299, 311, 312

Eagle Trust plc v SBC Securities Ltd [1993] 1 WLR 484 . . . . . . 130, 161
Eaglesfield v Marquis of Londonderry (1876) 4 Ch D 693 25
East India Co v Vincent (1740) 2 Atk 83; 26 ER 451 26
Eaves, Re [1940] Ch 109. 26
Eaves v Hickson (1861) 30 Beav 136; 54 ER 840 126
Ebrand v Dancer (1680) 2 Chan Cas 26; 22 ER 829 . . . . 272, 297
Edge v Worthington (1786) 1 Cox CC 211; 29 ER 1133 41
Edgington v Fitzmaurice (1885) 29 Ch D 459. 318
Edlin v Battaly (1675) 2 Lev 152; 83 ER 494 25
Edwards v Bradley [1957] SCR 599. 291
Edwards v Warden (1876) 1 App Cas 281 22
Efstratiou v Glantschnig [1972] NZLR 594. 180
El Ajou v Dollar Land Holdings plc [1993] 3 All ER 717, *reversed*
   [1994] 2 All ER 685 . . . . 163, 242, 247, 249
El Ajou v Dollar Land Holdings plc (No 2) [1995] 2 All ER 213 . . 145, 146
Elder's Trustee and Executor Co Ltd v Higgins (1963) 113 CLR 426 . . 126
Elliot v Elliot (1677) 2 Chan Cas 231; 22 ER 922
  . . . . 12, 29, 272, 296, 297, 298, 299, 311, 312
ER Ives Investment Ltd v High [1967] 2 QB 379 24
Esso Petroleum Co Ltd v Kingswood Motors (Addlestone) Ltd
   [1974] QB 142. 166
Esteem Settlement, Re, 2002 JLR 53 156
Evans v Bicknell (1801) 6 Ves Jun 174; 31 ER 998 25
Evans v European Bank Ltd [2004] NSWCA 82; (2004) 7 ITELR 19
  . . . . 123, 132, 135, 139, 140, 142
Eves v Eves [1975] 1 WLR 1338 96
Explora Group Plc v Hesco Bastion Ltd [2005] EWCA Civ 646. . . . 72, 73
Falcke v Scottish Imperial Insurance Co (1887) 34 Ch D 234 26
Fales v Canada Permanent Trust Co [1977] 2 SCR 302 126
Farah Constructions Pty Ltd v Say-Dee Pty Ltd [2007] HCA 22;
   (2007) 230 CLR 89, *reversing* [2005] NSWCA 309 . . . . 130, 156, 158,
                                                    164, 171, 172, 175, 178
Farrow Finance Co Ltd (in liq) v Farrow Properties Ltd (in liq)
   [1999] 1 VR 584. 117
Fawcet v Lowther (1751) 2 Ves Sen 300; 28 ER 193. 218
Fenwicke v Clarke (1862) 4 De G F & J 240; 45 ER 1176. 154
Fish, Re [1893] 2 Ch 413 121
Fong v Sun [2008] HKCU 730 . . . . 310, 311, 313
Forest of Dean Coal Mining Co, Re (1879) 10 Ch D 450 123
Forster v Hale (1798) 3 Ves Jun 696; 30 ER 1226, *affirmed* (1800) 5
   Ves Jun 308; 31 ER 603 . . . . 98, 104
Foskett v McKeown [2001] 1 AC 102 . . . . 119, 163, 165, 198, 228, 229,
                                                              260, 261
Foster (No 2), Re [1938] 3 All ER 610 . . . . 25, 26, 27

Fowkes v Pascoe (1875) LR 10 Ch App 343 . . . . 250, 251
Fox v Fox (1870) LR 11 Eq 142. 123
Foxcroft v Lester, 2 Vern. 456 38
Frazer v Walker [1967] AC 569. . . . . 165, 166, 173
Freeman v Cooke (1848) 2 Exch 654; 154 ER 652 25
Fyffes Group Ltd v Templeman [2000] 2 Lloyd's Rep 643 151
Fyler v Fyler (1841) 3 Beav 550; 49 ER 216. 163
Gardner (No 2), Re [1923] 2 Ch 230. 64
Gardner v Hodgson's Kingston Brewery Co [1903] AC 229. 184
Gardner v Rowe (1828) 5 Russ 258; 38 ER 1024. . . . . 104, 105
Garrett v Wilkinson (1848) 2 De G & Sm 244; 64 ER 110. 298
George v Macdonald, NSW Sup Ct (Eq Div) 6 February 1992. 123
Gillespie v Alexander (1827) 3 Russ 130; 38 ER 525 154
Gillett v Holt [2000] EWCA Civ 66; [2001] Ch 210. . . . . . . 53, 54, 340
Gissing v Gissing [1971] AC 886
 . . . . 10, 45, 46, 47, 48, 49, 50, 96, 281, 282, 287, 308
Giumelli v Giumelli [1999] HCA 10; (1999) 196 CLR 101 . . . . . 88, 162
GL Baker Ltd v Medway Building Supplies Ltd [1958] 1 All ER 540. . . 175
Glazier Holdings Pty Ltd v Australian Men's Health Pty Ltd (No 2)
 [2001] NSWSC 6 121
Glenkco Enterprises Ltd v Keller (2000) 150 Man R (2d) 1 151
Godbold v Freestone (1695) 3 Lev 406; 83 ER 753 207
Godden v Merthyr Tydfil Housing Association [1997] EWCA Civ 780 . . 44
Gold v Rosenberg [1997] 3 SCR 767 . . . . 156, 157, 167, 171
Goldcorp Exchange Ltd, Re [1995] 1 AC 74. . . . . 165, 191
Goodchild (deceased), Re [1996] 1 WLR 694; [1997] 1 WLR 1216 5, 22, 71
Goodfellow v Robertson (1871) 18 Gr 572 . . . . 246, 247, 256, 283
Goodwyn v Lister (1735) 3 P Wms 387; 24 ER 1112 . . . . 5, 6
Goose v Wilson Sandford & Co (a firm) [2000] EWCA Civ 73;
 [2001] Lloyd's Rep PN 189 157
Gordon v Gonda [1955] 1 WLR 885 124
Grant v Baillie (1869) 8 M 77. 125
Grant v Edwards [1986] Ch 638 50
Gray v Johnston (1868) LR 3 HL 1 . . . . 130, 157
Gray v Richards Butler [2001] WTLR 625 155
Greasley v Cooke [1980] 1 WLR 1306. 52
Green v Weatherill [1929] 2 Ch 213 136
Gregory v Mighell (1811) 18 Ves Jun 328; 34 ER 341. . . . . 31, 32, 39, 41
Greig v Somerville (1830) 1 Russ & My 200; 39 ER 131 154
Grey v Grey (1677) 2 Swans 594; 36 ER 742
 . . . . 267, 272, 277, 278, 296, 297, 312
Grey v IRC [1960] AC 1 14
Grgic v Australian & New Zealand Banking Group Ltd (1994) 33
 NSWLR 202. 166

Griffiths v Williams (1978) 248 EG 947 52
Grimes (deceased), Re (1937) IR 470 . . . . 299, 302
Grundt v Great Boulder Pty Gold Mines Ltd (1937) 59 CLR 641 88
Guerin v Canada [1984] 2 SCR 335. 116
Gwembe Valley Development Co Ltd v Koshy (No 3) [2003]
    EWCA Civ 1048; [2004] 1 BCLC 131 127
Halifax plc v Curry Popeck (a firm) [2008] EWHC 1692 (Ch) . 42, 160, 167
Hallett's Estate, Re (1880) 13 Ch D 696 . . . . 52, 229, 260
Hardoon v Belilios [1901] AC 118 116
Harrison v Harrison (1740) 2 Atk 121; 26 ER 476 125
Head v Gould [1898] 2 Ch 250 123
Healey v Brown [2002] EWHC 1405 (Ch); [2002] WTLR 849 . . . . 5, 41
Hedley Byrne & Co Ltd v Heller & Partners Ltd [1964] AC 465 200
Hennessey v Bray (1863) Beav 96; 55 ER 302. 118
Heperu Pty Ltd v Belle [2009] NSWCA 252. 157
Hepworth v Hepworth (1870) LR 11 Eq 10 . . . . 290, 310, 311
Herbert v Doyle [2008] EWHC 1950 (Ch); [2009] WTLR 589. . . . 28, 42
Herdegen v Federal Commissioner of Taxation (1988) 84 ALR 271 . . . 175
Hewett v Foster (1843) 6 Beav 259; 49 ER 825 124
Hillsdown plc v Pensions Ombudsman [1997] 1 All ER 862. 122
Hinckly v Hinckly (1672-3) 73 Selden Soc 75 38
Hobday v Kirkpatrick's Trustees 1985 SLT 197 124
Hodgkinson v Simms [1994] 3 SCR 377 127
Hodgson v Marks [1971] Ch 892
    . . . . 21, 68, 69, 86, 109, 110, 183, 246, 247, 248, 257, 278, 279, 286
Hogg deceased, Re (Ch D, 11 July 1983) 308
Holiday Inns Inc v Broadhead (1974) 232 EG 951 73
Holland, Re [1902] 2 Ch 360. 108
Hollett v Hollett (1993) 31 RPR (2d) 251 . . . . 282, 283
Hollis v Edwards (1683) 1 Vern 159; 23 ER 385 29
Hollis v Rolfe [2008] EWHC 1747 (Ch) 160
Hollis v Whiteing (1683) 1 Vern 151; 23 ER 380. 29
Holman v Johnson (1775) 1 Cowp 341; 98 ER 1120 336
Holmes, Re [2004] EWHC 2020 (Admin); [2005] 1 WLR 857 132
Holt v Holt (1670) 1 Chan Cas 190; 22 ER 756 6
Hopgood v Brown [1955] 1 All ER 550 25
Houghton v Fayers [2000] 1 BCLC 511. 115
Hounslow LBC v Twickenham Garden Developments Ltd [1971]
    Ch 233 89
Hovenden v Lord Annesley (1806) 2 Sch & Lef 607 23
Hughes v Metropolitan Railway Co (1877) 2 App Cas 439 . . . . . . 91, 92
Hulbert v Avens [2003] EWHC 76 (Ch); [2003] WTLR 387 127
Huning v Ferrers (1711) Gilb Rep 85; 25 ER 59 26
Hunsden v Cheyney (1690) 2 Vern 150; 23 ER 703 26

Hunt v Carew (1629) Nels 46; 21 ER 786 25
Hutchison v B & DF Ltd [2008] EWHC 2286 (Ch); [2009] L & TR 12. . 43
Huxley v Child Support Officer [1999] EWCA Civ 3015; [2000] 1
    FLR 898. 294
Hyett v Stanley [2003] EWCA Civ 942; [2003] WTLR 1269 50
IDC Group Ltd v Clark [1992] 1 EGLR 187, *affirmed* (1993) 65
    P & CR 179. 89
Iliffe v Trafford [2002] WTLR 507 121
Island Realty Investments Ltd v Douglas (1985) 19 ETR 56 124
Jackson v Cator (1800) 5 Ves Jun 688; 31 ER 806 26
Jackson v Dickinson [1903] 1 Ch 947. 125
Jasmine Trustees Ltd v Wells & Hind (a firm) [2007] EWHC 38 (Ch);
    [2008] Ch 194. 150
Jefferys v Marshall (1870) 23 LT 548 120
Jenkins, Re [1903] 2 Ch 362 125
Jennings v Rice [2002] EWCA Civ 159; [2003] 1 P & CR 8
    . . . . 30, 37, 52, 53, 54, 55, 191
Jerome v Kelly [2004] UKHL 25; [2004] 1 WLR 1409 169
Jesse v Bennett (1856) 6 De G M & G 609; 43 ER 1370. 131
Job v Job (1875) 6 Ch D 562 126
Jobson v Palmer [1893] 1 Ch 71 126
John v Dodwell & Co Ltd [1918] AC 563 . . . . 130, 131, 163
John v James [1986] STC 352. 145
Jones v Badley (1868) LR 3 Ch App 362 20
Jones v Kernott [2009] EWHC 1713 (Ch) 60
Jones v Lewis (1750) 2 Ves Sen 240; 28 ER 155 . . . . 125, 126
Jorden v Money (1854) 5 HLC 185; 10 ER 868. . . . . . 33, 34, 38, 44, 92
JT Developments Ltd v Quinn (1991) 62 P & CR 33 78
K v P [1993] Ch 140 155
Kalls Enterprises Pty Ltd (in liq) v Balogalow [2007] NSWCA 191 . . . 146
Keane v Robarts (1819) 4 Madd 332; 56 ER 728 163
Keech v Sandford (1726) Sel Cas t King 61; 25 ER 223. 5
Keen, Re [1937] Ch 236 20
Kellaway v Johnson (1842) 5 Beav 319; 49 ER 601 124
Kelly v Solari (1841) 9 M & W 54; 152 ER 24 . . . . 171, 327
Kelly & Co, *ex parte* (1879) 11 Ch D 306. 124
Kemp v Burn (1863) 4 Giff 348; 66 ER 740. 120
Kemp v Sims [2008] EWHC 2579 (Ch); [2009] Pens LR 83 124
Kenney v Brown (1796) 3 Ridg PC 462. 26
Kennon v Spry [2008] HCA 56; (2008) 83 ALJR 145 175
Kilcarne Holdings Ltd v Targetfollow (Birmingham) Ltd [2004] EWHC
    2547 (Ch); [2005] 2 P & CR 105, *affirmed* [2005] EWCA Civ 45 . . 72, 73
Kinane v Mackie-Conteh [2005] EWCA Civ 45; [2005] WTLR 345
    . . . . 42, 48, 194

King's Wharf Coldstore Ltd Ltd (in rec) v Wilson [2005] NZHC 283 . . 142
Kleinwort Benson Ltd v Lincoln City Council [1999] 2 AC 349 326
Kleinwort Benson Ltd v South Tyneside MBC [1994] 2 All ER 972 . . . 145
Knox's Trusts, Re [1895] 2 Ch 483 123
Kolari, Re (1981) 36 OR (2d) 473 . . . . 226, 283
Koorootang Nominees Pty Ltd v Australia & New Zealand
    Banking Group Ltd [1998] 3 VR 16 . . . . 164, 171, 175
Laird v Birkenhead Railway Co (1859) Johns 500; 70 ER 519 . 34, 36, 38, 54
Lake, Re [1903] 1 KB 439. 125
Lamplugh v Lamplugh (1709) 1 P Wms 111; 24 ER 316 297
Lander v Weston (1853) 3 Drew 389; 61 ER 951 133
Lane v Dighton (1762) Amb 409; 27 ER 274. . . . . 226, 283
Langston, *ex parte* (1810) 17 Ves Jun 228; 34 ER 88 41
Laskar v Laskar [2008] EWCA Civ 347; [2008] 1 WLR 2695
    . . . . 274, 283, 301, 308
Lattimer v Lattimer (1978) 82 DLR (3d) 587 283
Lavelle v Lavelle [2004] EWCA Civ 223; [2004] 2 FCR 418 . 212, 255, 308
Leake v Morris (1682) 1 Dick 14; 21 ER 171. 29
Lee v Sankey (1873) LR 15 Eq 204 100
Leigh & Sillivan Ltd v Aliakmon Shipping Co Ltd, *The Aliakmon*
    [1986] AC 785. 187
Leroux v Brown (1852) 12 CB 801; 138 ER 1119 28
Lester v Foxcroft (1700) Colles 108; 1 ER 205; 2 Wh & TLC 460 29
LHK Nominees Pty Ltd v Kenworthy [2002] WASCA 291;
    (2002) 26 WAR 517. 175
Life Association of Scotland v Siddal (1861) 3 De G F & J 271;
    45 ER 882. 100
Lincoln v Wright (1859) 4 De J & G 16; 45 ER 6 21
Lipkin Gorman v Karpnale Ltd (1986) [1992] 4 All ER 331, *reversed*
    [1989] 1 WLR 1340, *reversed* [1991] 2 AC 548. . . . 127, 155, 171, 175
Llanover Settled Estate, Re [1926] Ch 626 16
Lloyd v Dugdale [2002] 2 P & CR 13. . . . . 78, 89
Lloyd v Spillet (1740) 2 Atk 148; 26 ER 493; *reported sub nom* Lloyd v
    Spillit (1740) Barn Ch 384; 27 ER 689 . . . . 13, 280
Lloyds Bank plc v Carrick (1997) 73 P & CR 314. . . . . 44, 51
Lloyds Bank plc v Rosset [1989] Ch 350, *reversed* [1991] 1 AC 107
    . . . . 9, 10, 22, 49, 50
Locke v Prescott (1863) 32 Beav 261; 55 ER 103 118
Locker's ST, Re [1977] 1 WLR 1323 123
Loffus v Maw (1862) 3 Giff 592; 66 ER 654 33
Loftus (deceased), Re [2005] EWHC 406 (Ch); [2005] 1 WLR 1890;
    affirmed [2006] EWCA Civ 1124; [2007] 1 WLR 591 148
Lohia v Lohia [2001] WTLR 101, *affirmed* [2001] EWCA Civ 1691
    . . . . 268, 271

London & Regional Investments Ltd v TBI plc [2002] EWCA Civ 355
. . . . 38, 72, 73
Longford, The (1889) 14 PD 34 29
Lonrho plc v Fayed (No 2) [1992] 1 WLR 1 . . . . 72, 73, 143
Lord Strathcona Steamship Co Ltd v Dominion Coal Co Ltd [1926]
  AC 108 89
Low v Bouverie [1891] 3 Ch 82. 123
Low Geok Khim (administratrix of the estate of Low Kim Tah,
  deceased) v Low Geok Bian [2006] SGHC 41. . . . . 309, 310, 311, 313
Low Gim Siah v Low Geok Khim [2006] SGCA 45. . . . . 310, 313
Lowry v Bourdieu (1780) 2 Doug 468; 99 ER 299 339
Lowson v Coombes [1999] Ch 373 308
Lysaght v Edwards (1876) 2 Ch D 499. . . . . 169, 193, 195, 199
Lyus v Prowsa Developments Ltd [1982] 1 WLR 1044 . . . . 89, 90
McCabe v Ulster Bank Ltd [1939] IR 1. . . . . 302, 303
McCann v Switzerland Insurance Australia Ltd (2000) 203 CLR 579 . . 125
McCausland v Duncan Lawrie [1997] 1 WLR 38. 42
McCormick v Grogan (1869) LR 4 HL 82 . . . . 64, 65
MacDonald v Hauer (1976) 72 DLR (3d) 110. 151
McDonnell v Loosemore [2007] EWCA Civ 1531 . . . . 292, 309
McGrath v Wallis [1995] 2 FLR 114. . . . . 255, 308
McGregor v Nichol [2003] NSWSC 332 305
McGuane v Welch [2008] EWCA Civ 785; [2008] 2 P & CR 24 . . . 41, 53
MacMillan Bloedel Ltd v Binstead (1983) 22 BLR 255 151
Macquarie Bank Ltd v Sixty-Fourth Throne Pty Ltd [1998] 3 VR 133
. . . . 174, 175
Maddison v Alderson (1883) 8 App Cas 467 . . . 10, 30, 33, 40, 41, 43, 108
Madsen Estate v Saylor [2007] SCC 18; [2007] 1 SCR 838. . . . . 299, 309
Magnus v Queensland National Bank (1888) 37 Ch D 466. . . . . 124, 125
Maintemp Heating & Air Conditioning Inc v Monat Developments
  Inc (2002) 59 OR (3d) 270. 121
Maitland v Bateman (1843) 13 LJ Ch 273. 122
Mansell v Mansell (1732) P Wms 678; 24 ER 913. 129
Mary Metledge t/as Metledge & Associates v Koutsouris & Anor
  [2005] HCA Trans 425 (17 June 2005). 223
Mason v Coleman [2007] EWHC 3149 (Ch) 120
Massingberd's Settlement, Re (1890) 63 LT 296 124
Master etc of Clare Hall v Harding (1848) 6 Hare 273; 67 ER 1169 . . . 26
Mathew v Brise (1845) 15 LJ Ch 39. 122
Maunsell v White (1854) 4 HLC 1039; 10 ER 769 . . . . . . 32, 33, 34, 38
MCC Proceeds Inc v Lehman Brothers (International) Europe [1998]
  4 All ER 675 187
M'Donnel v White (1865) 9 HLC 570; 11 ER 1454 . . . . 122, 127
Meech v Stoner, 19 NY 26 (1859). 339

Meehan v Glazier Holdings Pty Ltd [2002] NSWCA 22; (2002) 54
    NSWLR 146.................121
Mehta Estate v Mehta Estate (1993) 104 DLR (4th) 24 ...... 239, 269
Merchants Express Co v Morton (1868) 15 Gr 274............283
Metall und Rohstoff AG v Donaldson Lufkin & Jenrett Inc [1990] 1
    QB 391...................165
Metropolitan Properties Co Ltd v Purdy [1940] 1 All ER 188........55
Michaels v Harley House (Marylebone) Ltd [2000] Ch 104........192
Midland Bank plc v Cooke [1995] 4 All ER 562..............254
Midland Bank Trust Co Ltd v Green [1981] AC 513 ..... 105, 166, 181
Midland Bank Trust Co Ltd v Green (No 3) [1982] 1 Ch 529 166
Miller v Race (1758) 1 Burr 452; 97 ER 398 175
Mills v Stokman (1967) 116 CLR 61 180
Ministry of Health v Simpson *see* Diplock, Re
Mohamed v Alaga & Co (a firm) [2000] 1 WLR 1815.......... 365
Mohan v Broughton [1900] P 56 154
Mold v Wheatcroft (1853) 27 Beav 510; 54 ER 202 26
Mollo v Mollo, 8 October 1999 Ch D 24, 50
Monnickendam v Leanse (1923) 39 TLR 445 28
Montagu's Settlement Trusts, Re [1987] Ch 264 .... 118, 162, 164
Morgan v Stephens (1861) 3 Giff 226; 66 ER 392 ...... 130, 133, 134
Morlea Professional Services Pty Ltd v Richard Walker Pty Ltd (in liq)
    [1999] FCA 1820; (1999) 34 ACSR 371 .... 131, 132, 133, 141
Morley v Morley (1678) 2 Chan Cas 2; 22 ER 817 126
Morrison v Coast Finance Ltd (1965) 55 DLR (2d) 710.......... 151
Moss v Cooper (1861) 1 J & H 352; 70 ER 782 20
Mount Carmel Investments Ltd v Peter Thurlow Ltd [1988] 1
    WLR 1078..................220
Mountfort, *ex parte* (1808) 14 Ves Jun 606; 33 ER 653........... 41
Mountney v Treharne [2002] EWCA Civ 1174; [2003] Ch 135 . . 192, 199
Muller, Re [1953] NZLR 879.................... 270
Mulligan, Re [1998] 1 NZLR 181................... 127
Murless v Franklin (1818) 1 Swans 13; 36 ER 278 299
Nab v Nab (1718) 10 Mod 405; 88 ER 783............... 18, 19
Nabb Brothers Ltd v Lloyds Bank International (Guernsey) Ltd
    [2005] EWHC 405 (Ch) 120, 128
National Assistance Board v Wilkinson 1952] 2 QB 648.......... 294
National Bank of New Zealand v Waitaki International Processing
    (NI) Ltd [1999] 2 NZLR 211 135
Nationwide Building Society v Balmer Radmore (a firm) [1999]
    Lloyds Reports PN 241 125
Neale v Willis (1968) 19 P & CR 836 .... 22, 64, 71, 75, 79, 80, 200
Neesom v Clarkson (1844) 4 Hare 97; 67 ER 576 27

Nelson v Nelson [1995] HCA 25; (1995) 184 CLR 538; (1995) 132
   ALR 133 . . . . 272, 290, 304, 305, 306, 307, 337
Nelson v Rye [1996] 1 WLR 1378 22
Nestlé v National Westminster Bank plc [1993] 1 WLR 1260 127
Neville v Wilson [1997] Ch 144. 192
New Cap Reinsurance Corp Ltd v General Cologne Re Australia Ltd
   [2004] NSWSC 781; (2004) 7 ITELR 295 124
Newman v Barton (1690) 2 Vern 205; 23 ER 733 154
Niru Battery Manufacturing Co v Milestone Trading Ltd (No 1)
   [2003] EWCA Civ 1446; [2004] QB 985. 115
Niru Battery Manufacturing Co v Milestone Trading Ltd (No 2)
   [2004] EWCA 487; [2004] 2 All ER (Comm) 289 155
Nisbett & Potts' Contract, Re [1906] 1 Ch 386 163
Nocton v Lord Ashburton [1914] AC 932. . . . . 93, 157
Noel v Robinson (1682) 1 Vern 90; 23 ER 334 154
Nolan v Collie [2003] VSCA 39; (2003) 7 VR 287 148
Northen v Carnegie (1859) 4 Drew 587; 62 ER 225 218
Nunn v Fabian (1865) LR 1 Ch App 35 . . . . 38, 39
Nurdin & Peacock plc v DB Ramsden & Co Ltd [1999] 1 WLR 1249
   . . . . 325, 327
Oatway, Re [1903] 2 Ch 356 260
OBG Ltd v Allan [2007] UKHL 21; [2008] 1 AC 1 152
Ogle, *ex parte* (1873) 8 Ch App 711. 122
Oh Hiam v Tham Kong [1980] 2 MLJ 159 166
OJSC Oil Co Yugraneft (in liq) v Abramovich [2009] EWHC 161 (Ch)
   . . . . 157, 158
Olszanecki v Hillocks [2002] EWHC 1997 (Ch); [2004] WTLR 975 . . 127
Orgee v Orgee [1997] EWCA Civ 2650 54
Orr v Kaines (1750) 2 Ves Sen 194; 90 ER 125 154
O'Sullivan v Management Agency and Music Ltd [1985] QB 428 145
Ottaway v Norman [1972] Ch 698 . . . . 22, 69, 71
Ottey v Grundy [2003] EWCA Civ 1176; [2003] WTLR 1253 . . 52, 55, 77
Oughtred v IRC [1960] AC 206 12
Oxley v Hiscock [2004] EWCA Civ 546; [2004] 2 FLR 669;
   [2005] Fam 211 . . . . 10, 50, 59, 254, 255, 340
Pakistan v Zardari [2006] EWHC 2411 (Comm) 129
Pallant v Morgan [1953] Ch 43 . . . 64, 72, 73, 74, 76, 79, 80, 81, 200, 201
Pannell v Hurley (1845) 2 Coll 241; 63 ER 716 159
Paragon Finance plc v DB Thakerar & Co (a firm) [1999] 1 All ER 400
   . . . . 23, 69, 101, 128, 162
Parker v Mason [1940] 2 KB 590 . . . . 339, 358
Parker v Parker [2003] EWHC 846 (Ch) 53
Parkinson v College of Ambulance [1925] 2 KB 1 342
Partington v Reynolds (1858) 4 Drew 253; 62 ER 98 . . . . 121, 126

Partridge v Equity Trustees Executors and Agency Co Ltd (1947) 75
    CLR 149. 122
Parway Estates Ltd v IRC (1958) 45 TC 135 192
Pascoe v Turner [1979] 1 WLR 431. 52
Patel v London Borough of Brent (No 2) [2003] EWHC 3081 (Ch);
    [2004] WTLR 577. 122
Patten, Re (1883) 52 LJ Ch 787. 125
Paul v Constance [1977] 1 WLR 527 279
Pavey and Matthews Pty Ltd v Paul (1986) 162 CLR 217. . . . . . 108, 109
Peconic Industrial Development Ltd v Lau Kwok Fai [2009] 2
    HKLRD 537. 162
Pecore v Pecore [2007] SCC 17; [2007] 1 SCR 795
    . . . . 273, 291, 292, 299, 309, 310
Peffer v Rigg [1977] 1 WLR 285. . . . . 119, 160
Pennington v Waine [2002] EWCA Civ 227; [2002] 1 WLR 2075
    . . . . 190, 191, 256
Permanent Building Society (in liq) v Wheeler (1994) 12 ACLC 674. . . 137
Peterson v Peterson (1866) LR 3 Eq 111. 154
Pettitt v Pettitt [1970] AC 777. . . . . 10, 46, 282, 307, 308
Pettkus v Becker [1980] 2 SCR 834 . . . . 226, 282
Phillips v Phillips (1861) 4 De G F & J 208; 45 ER 1164 52
Pickard v Sears (1837) 6 Ad & El 469; 112 ER 179. 25
Pilmer v Duke Group Ltd (2001) 207 CLR 165 137
Plimmer v Mayor of Wellington (1884) 9 App Cas 699 . . . . 39, 55
Pocock v Reddington (1801) 5 Ves Jun 794; 31 ER 862 125
Pole v Pole (1747–48) Ves Sen Supp 54; 28 ER 454 . . . . 297, 298
Policy no 6402 of the Scottish Equitable Life Assurance Society, Re a [1902] 1
    Ch 282 290
Polloxfen v Stewart (1841) 3 D 1214 125
Polly Peck International plc v Nadir (No 2) [1992] 4 All ER 769. 163
Polly Peck International plc (No 4), Re [1998] 2 BCLC 185 165
Pooley v Budd (1851) 14 Beav 34. 51
Powell v Benney [2007] EWCA Civ 1283. . . . . 51, 53
Powell v Wilshire [2004] EWCA Civ 534; [2005] 1 QB 117. 123
Powys v Mansfield (1837) 3 My & Cr 359; 40 ER 964 299
Precision Instrument Manufacturing Co v Automotive
    Maintenance Machinery Co, 324 US 806 (1945). 340
Primlake Ltd (in liq) v Matthews Assocs [2006] EWHC 1127 (Ch);
    [2007] 1 BCLC 366 146
Pullan v Koe [1913] 1 Ch 9. 5, 51, 192
Pulvers (a firm) v Chan [2007] EWHC 2406 (Ch); [2008] PNLR 9 . . . 141
Pye, *ex parte* (1811) 18 Ves Jun 140; 34 ER 271. 185
Pye v Gorge (1710) 1 P Wms 128; 24 ER 323 129
Pym v Lockyer (1841) 5 My & Cr 29; 41 ER 283 299

Q v Q [2008] EWHC 1874 (Fam); [2009] 1 FLR 935 . . . 50, 52, 271, 355
Qayyum v Hameed [2009] EWCA Civ 352; [2009] 2 FLR 962 6
Quince v Varga [2008] QCA 376; (2008) 11 ITELR 939 158
R v Chester and North Wales Legal Aid Area Office *ex parte*
 Floods of Queensferry Ltd [1998] 1 WLR 1496 117
R (Kehoe) v Secretary of State for Work and Pensions [2005]
 UKHL 48; [2006] 1 AC 42 . . . . 292, 293, 294, 295
Ramsden v Dyson (1866) LR 1 HL 129 . . . . 26, 27, 33, 36, 39, 44
Rathwell v Rathwell [1978] 2 SCR 436 . . . . 250, 251, 282
Riddle v Emerson (1682) 1 Vern 108; 23 ER 348 6
Rivers, Re [1920] 1 Ch 320 154
RM Hosking Properties Pty Ltd v Barnes [1971] SASR 100 180
Robins v Incentive Dynamics Pty Ltd [2003] NSWCA 71; (2003) 45
 ACSR 244 . . . . 117, 164, 165
Rochdale Canal Company v King (1853) 16 Beav 630; 51 ER 924 26
Rochefoucauld v Boustead [1897] 1 Ch 196, *reversing* (1896) 65 LJ
 Ch 794. . . . v, 21, 63, 68, 69, 79, 80, 86, 95, 96, 97, 98, 99, 100, 101, 103,
     104, 105, 106, 107, 110, 113, 183, 200, 248, 286
Rolfe v Gregory (1865) 4 De GJ & S 576; 46 ER 1042 . . . . 131, 162, 170
Rose, Re [1952] Ch 499 . . . . 190, 191, 256
Ross v Davy 1996 SCLR 369 127
Rothko, Re, 43 NY 2d 305; 372 NE 2d 291 (1977) 138
Roxborough v Rothmans of Pall Mall Australia Ltd (2001) 208 CLR
 516 122
Royal Brunei Airlines Sdn Bhd v Tan [1995] 2 AC 378 . . . . 178, 179
Rushworth's case (1676) Freem 13; 89 ER 10 7
Russel v Russel (1783) 1 Bro CC 269; 28 ER 1121 41
Ryall v Ryall (1739) 1 Atk 59; 26 ER 39; Amb 413; 27 ER 276
 . . . . 226, 227, 247, 249, 283
St Vincent de Paul Society Qld v Ozcare Ltd [2009] QCA 335 158
Salmon, Re (1888) 42 Ch D 351 127
Salway v Salway (1831) 2 Russ & My 215; 39 ER 376 124
Samme's Case (1609) 13 Co Rep 54; 77 ER 1464 . . . . 208, 215, 224
Sandeman's WT, Re [1937] 1 All ER 368 123
Sanders v Parry [1967] 1 WLR 753 127
Sarat Chunder Dey v Gopal Chunder Laha (1892) LR 19 Ind App 203 . . 26
Satnam Investments Ltd v Dunlop Heywood & Co Ltd [1999]
 1 BCLC 385 157
Savage v Foster (1723) 9 Mod 35; 88 ER 299 26
Sawyer v Birchmore (1836) 1 Keen 391; 48 ER 357 154
Say-Dee Pty Ltd v Farah Constructions Pty Ltd [2005] NSWCA 309 *see* Farah
 Constructions Pty Ltd v Say-Dee Pty Ltd
Saylor v Madsen Estate [2007] SCC 18; [2007] 1 SCR 838 273
Sayre v Hughes (1868) LR 5 Eq 376 . . . . 281, 284, 298, 302

Scawin v Scawin (1841) 1 Y & CCC 65; 62 ER 792 310
Scott v Pauly (1917) 24 CLR 274 302
Sekhon v Alissa [1989] 2 FLR 94 308
Selangor United Rubber Estates Ltd v Craddock (No 3) [1968] 2 All
    ER 1073; [1968] 1 WLR 1555 . . . . 24, 128, 130, 134, 149, 162
Sempra Metals Ltd v IRC [2007] UKHL 34; [2008] 1 AC 561 146
Sen v Headley [1991] Ch 425 . . . . 36, 50
Shales v Shales (1701) 2 Freeman 252; 22 ER 1151 . . . . 297, 298
Sharma v Farlam Ltd [2009] EWHC 1622 (Ch) 124
Sharp v McNeil (1913) 15 DLR 73, *affirmed* (1915) 70 DLR 740 283
Sharpe, Re [1980] 1 WLR 219 . . . . 50, 55
Shaw v Applegate [1977] 1 WLR 970 26
Shaw v Foster (1872) LR 5 HL 321 . . . . 5, 51, 193
Shephard v Cartwright [1955] AC 431 212
Shepherd v Mouls (1845) 4 Hare 500; 67 ER 746 124
Sheridan v Joyce (1844) 7 Ir Rep Eq 115 . . . . 118, 131
Shih Shin Wang-Liu [2006] SGHC 196 310
Shippey v Derrison (1805) 5 Esp 190; 170 ER 782 108
Short v Taylor (c 1693-1700), *cited* 2 Eq Cas Abr 522; 22 ER 441 26
Sidmouth v Sidmouth (1840) 2 Beav 447; 48 ER 1254 . . . . 310, 311
Sikorski v Sikorski [2007] FamCA 487 306
Sinclair Investment Holdings SA v Versailles Trade Finance Ltd
    (in admin rec) [2007] EWHC 915 (Ch); [2007] 2 All ER
    (Comm) 993; (2007) 10 ITELR 58 . . . . 128, 142, 151, 162, 165
Sinclair v Sinclair [2009] EWHC 926 (Ch) 121
Singh v Ali [1960] AC 167 336
Singh v Beggs (1995) 71 P & CR 120 42
Sitt Tatt Bhd v Goh Tai Hock [2008] SGHC 220; [2009] 2 SLR 44 . . . 134
Sledmore v Dalby (1996) 72 P & CR 196 . . . . 52, 54
Smethurst v Hastings (1884) 30 Ch D 490 127
Smith v Acton (1858) 26 Beav 210; 53 ER 877 123
Smith v Cooke [1891] AC 297 3
Smith v Matthews (1861) 3 D F & J 139 98
Soar v Ashwell [1893] 2 QB 390 . . 69, 99, 100, 101, 102, 103, 121, 130, 132
Soar v Foster (1858) 4 K & J 152; 70 ER 64 299
Southern Cross Commodities Pty Ltd (in liq) v Ewing (1988) 14
    ACLR 39 . . . . 142, 146
Speight v Gaunt (1883) 22 Ch D 727, *affirmed* (1883) 9 App Cas 1 . . . 126
Springette v Defoe [1992] 2 FCR 561 . . . . 253, 254
Stack v Dowden [2007] UKHL 17; [2007] 2 AC 432 . . . . . 10, 46, 51, 52,
                55, 56, 57, 59, 60, 96, 254, 255, 274, 275, 282, 287, 308
Stallion v Albert Stallion Holdings (GB) Ltd [2009] EWHC 1950 (Ch) . . 53
Steadman v Steadman [1976] AC 536 . . . . 30, 31
Steed v Whitaker (1740) Barn C 220; 27 ER 621 26

Stevens, Re [1898] 1 Ch 162. . . . . 121, 126
Stileman v Ashdown (1742) 2 Atk 477; 26 ER 688 297
Stiles v Cowper (1748) 3 Atk 692; 26 ER 1198. 26
Stivactas v Michaletos (No 2), NSWCA, 31 August 1993 304
Stokes v Anderson [1991] 1 FLR 391. . . . 50
Stopher v National Assistance Board [1955] 1 QB 486 294
Street v Mountford [1985] AC 809. 89
Stuart v Kingston (1923) 32 CLR 309. 180
Super 1000 Pty Ltd v Pacific General Securities Ltd [2008]
   NSWSC 1222; (2008) 221 FLR 427. . . . . 142, 167, 175
Sutton v O'Kane [1973] 2 NZLR 304 (NZCA) 180
Sutton v Wilders (1871) LR 12 Eq 373 126
Tailby v Official Receiver (1888) 13 App Cas 523. 51
Tara Shire Council v Garner [2002] QCA 232; [2003] 1 QdR 556
   . . . . 167, 175
Target Holdings Ltd v Redferns [1996] AC 421
   . . . . 122, 123, 124, 125, 127, 132, 157
Tataurangi Tairuakena v Carr [1927] NZLR 688 166
Taylor v Bowers (1876) 1 QBD 291. 350
Taylors Fashions Ltd v Liverpool Victoria Trustees Co Ltd [1982]
   QB 133 . . . . 25, 26, 27, 28, 40
Templeton Insurance Ltd v Penningtons Solicitors LLP [2005] EWHC
   2885 (Ch) 121
Thomas v Griffith (1860) 2 Giff 504; 66 ER 211 154
Thomas v Sorrell (1673) Vaugh 330; 124 ER 1098. 89
Thomasset v Thomasset [1894] P 295 . . . . 294, 300
Thompson v Foy [2009] EWHC 1076 (Ch). 175
Thomson v Clydesdale Bank Ltd [1893] AC 282 159
Thorner v Major [2009] UKHL 18; [2009] 1 WLR 776
   . . . . 10, 25, 33, 40, 43, 44, 46, 51, 76, 77, 165
Thornton v Stokill (1855) 1 Jur 751. 125
Thorpe v HMRC [2009] EWHC 611 (Ch); [2009] Pens LR 139 5
Thynn v Thynn (1684) 1 Vern 296; 23 ER 479 21
Tidey v Mollett (1864) 16 CB (NS) 298; 143 ER 1143 38
Tinsley v Milligan [1992] Ch 310, *affirmed* [1994] 1 AC 340
   . . . . 240, 270, 271, 275, 290, 307, 335, 336, 337, 338, 352, 367
Tool Metal Manufacturing Co Ltd v Tungsten Electric Co Ltd [1955]
   1 WLR 761 91
Townshend v Townshend. 100
Transphere Pty Ltd, Re (1986) 5 NSWLR 309. 221
Tribe v Tribe [1996] Ch 107. . . . . 212, 271, 307, 337, 350, 351, 352,
                                                                               354, 355, 365
Trustor AB v Smallbone (No 2) [2001] 1 WLR 1177 . . . . 157, 169

Turner v TR Nominees Pty Ltd NSW Sup Ct (Eq Div) 3 November
    1995. 124
Twinsectra Ltd v Yardley [2002] UKHL 12; [2002] 2 AC 164
    . . . . 134, 156, 157, 178
Ultraframe (UK) Ltd v Fielding [2005] EWHC 1638 (Ch) . . 120, 121, 142,
    143, 150, 151, 164, 165
United Bank of Kuwait plc v Sahib [1997] Ch 107 40
Unity Joint Stock Mutual Banking Assoc v King (1858) 25 Beav 72;
    53 ER 563 27
Uzinterimpex JSC v Standard Bank plc [2008] EWCA Civ 819;
    [2008] Bus LR 1762. 115
Vajpeyi v Yusaf [2003] EWHC 2788 (Ch); [2004] WTLR 989. 308
Vandervell v IRC [1967] 2 AC 291, *affirming* [1966] Ch 261 . . . . 12, 112,
    184, 185, 191, 192, 199, 207, 209, 212, 213, 218, 222, 230, 244, 245,
    258, 259, 263, 268, 275, 290
Vandervell's Trusts (No 2), Re [1974] Ch 269, *reversed* [1974] Ch 269
    . . . . 209, 232, 241, 244, 246, 250, 251
Venture, The [1908] P 218 . . . . 239, 244
Vinogradoff, Re [1935] WN 68. . . . . 244, 252, 270
W J Alan & Co Ltd v El Nasr Export and Import Co [1972] 2 QB 189 . . 91
Waimiha Sawmilling Co Ltd v Waione Timber Co Ltd [1926] AC 101
    . . . . 179, 180
Walcott v Hall (1788) 2 Bro CC 305; 29 ER 167 154
Walker v Symonds (1818) 3 Swans 1; 36 ER 751 121
Walker v Walker [1984] CAT 173 (12 April 1984) 50
Wallersteiner v Moir (No 2) [1975] QB 373. 145
Wallgrave v Tebbs (1855) 2 K & J 313; 69 ER 800 20
Walsh v Lonsdale (1882) 21 Ch D 9. 262
Walton v Walton [1993] 2 FLR 47 . . . . 25, 40, 52
Waltons Stores (Interstate) Ltd v Maher (1988) 164 CLR 387 88
Ward v Snelling (CA, 20 April 1994) 313
Waxman v Waxman (2004) 7 ITELR 162 . . . . 120, 127
Waxman v Waxman [2008] ONCA 426; (2008) 240 OAC 18 145
Wayling v Jones (1993) 69 P & CR 170. . . . . 52, 77
Webb v Ledsam (1855) 1 K & J 385; 69 ER 508. 163
Webb v Stenton (1881) 11 QBD 518 124
Wells, Re [1962] 1 WLR 874 121
Westdeutsche Landesbank Girozentrale v Islington LBC [1996] AC 669. . 5,
    105, 117, 118, 119, 143, 145, 164, 165, 186, 193, 207, 213, 227, 229,
    251, 252, 255, 257, 262, 282
Westpac Banking Corp v Savin [1985] 2 NZLR 41 131
White v Tomasel [2004] QCA 89; [2004] 2 Qd R 438 . . . . 166, 174
Whitehouse, Re (1888) 37 Ch D 683 289
Wicks v Bennett (1921) 30 CLR 80 180

Wickstead v Browne (1992) 30 NSWLR 1 124
Wight v Olswang (No 2) [2000] WTLR 783, *reversed* [2001] WTLR
  291 127
Wiglesworth v Wiglesworth (1852) 16 Beav 269; 51 ER 782 123
Williams v Williams (1863) 32 Beav 370; 55 ER 145 . . . . 226, 283
Williams & Glyn's Bank Ltd v Boland [1981] AC 487 . . . . 173, 176
Willmott v Barber (1880) 15 Ch D 96 . . . . 26, 27, 59
Wilson, Re (1999) 27 ETR (2d) 97 310
Wilson v Moore (1833) 1 My & K 126; 39 ER 629, *affirmed* (1834) 1
  My & K 337; 39 ER 709 . . . . 100, 130, 163, 178
Windsor Steam Coal Co, Re (1901) Ltd [1929] 1 Ch 151 124
Winter Garden Theatre (London) Ltd v Millennium Productions Ltd
  [1946] 1 All ER 678 89
Wirth v Wirth (1956) 98 CLR 228 . . . . 303, 304, 306
Wright v Morgan [1926] AC 788 125
Wyman v Paterson [1900] AC 271 122
Yaxley v Gotts [2000] Ch 162 . . . . 27, 28, 41, 43, 50, 51, 58, 194
Yeoman's Row Management Limited v Cobbe *see* Cobbe v Yeoman's
  Row Management Ltd
Young, Re [1951] Ch 344 21
Young v Murphy [1996] 1 VLR 279 123
Youyang Pty Ltd v Minter Ellison Morris Fletcher (2003) 212 CLR
  484 124
Z v Z [2005] FamCA 996 . . . . 305, 306
Zielinski (deceased), Re [2007] WTLR 1655 . . . . 301, 308

Table of Legislation

Administration of Estates Act 1925
    s 45 218
    s 46. 4
    s 51 218
Administration of Justice Act 1982
    s 17 . . . . 18, 64, 86
    s 73(6) 18
Child Support Act 1991 . . . . 292, 295
Criminal Attempts Act 1981. . . . . 353, 354
    s 1 352
    s 1(3)(b) 365
    s 4 352
Family Law (Property and Maintenance) Bill 2005 312
    clause 2 . . . . 274, 312
    Guardianship of Minors Act 294
Human Rights Act 1998 65
    s 3. 65
Inheritance Act 1833, s 3 218
Insolvency Act 1986 189
    ss 238–240 190
    s 283(3)(a). 188
    ss 339–341 190
Judicature Act 1873 99
    s 25(2) 69
    s 25(3) 23
Land Charges Act 1925, s 13(2). 166
Land Charges Act 1972. 159
Land Registration Act 1925 . . . . 59, 173, 176
Land Registration Act 2002 . . . 56, 57, 159, 161, 166, 173, 175, 176, 220
    s 3. 263
    s 4(1)(a)(i) 160
    s 6(1) 160
    s 11(5) 166, 176
    s 26(3) 179
    s 27 169
    s 27(2)(b) 160
    s 27(2)(f). 160
    s 28 169

s 29 . . . . 160, 161, 164, 165, 168, 169, 170, 173, 174, 175, 176, 177, 178, 181, 182
s 29(1) 57, 58, 160
s 29(2) 160
s 29(2)(a)(i) 57
s 29(2)(a)(ii) 58
s 32(1) 57
s 33 . . . . 57, 58
s 116 . . . . 56, 58
Sch 1, para 2 160
Sch 3, para 2 . . . . 58, 100, 160, 176
Sch 4 160
Law of Property Act 1925 . . . . 14, 20, 21
  s 20 252
  s 34 4
  s 36 4
  s 40 . . . . 40, 109, 195
  s 40(1) 107, 108
  s 40(2) 28
  s 53 . . . . 12, 111
  s 53(1) 12, 247, 248, 278, 279
  s 53(1)(b) . . . 12, 20, 21, 68, 86, 97, 104, 106, 107, 109, 110, 111, 112, 113, 248, 253, 272, 278
  s 53(1)(c) 12, 186, 211, 248, 262
  s 53(2) 12, 14, 15, 21, 68, 111, 112, 113, 241, 278
  s 60(3) 271
Law of Property Amendment Act 1859, s 19 216
Law of Property (Miscellaneous Provisions) Act 1989 28
  s 2 . . . . 26, 40, 41, 42, 43, 195
  s 2(5) 41, 43, 58, 195
Limitation Act 1939, s 19 23
Limitation Act 1980, s 21 23
Limitation Acts 100, 102
Married Women's Property Act 1870 . . . . 293, 295, 301, 311
  s 13 293
  s 14 . . . . 293, 301
Married Women's Property Act 1882 . . . . 293, 295, 311
  ss 20–21 293
Matrimonial Causes Act 1857 293
Matrimonial Causes Act 1973 45
National Assistance Act 1948
  s 1 293
  s 42 293
  s 64(1) 293

Poor Law Act 1927, s 41 293
Poor Law Act 1930, s 14 293
Poor Relief Act 1601 293
Proceeds of Crime Act 2002
   s 6(4)(c) 336
   s 240 . . . . 336, 364
Settled Land Act 1925 15
Social Security Administration Act 1992 293
   s 78(6)(d) 293
Statute of Frauds 1677 . . . . 7, 8, 9, 11, 12, 20, 29, 30, 32, 35, 43, 98, 276,
                                                                                                                278, 280
   s 4 . . . . 28, 29, 44, 107, 108, 109
   s 5 17
   s 7 . . . . 12, 19, 20, 21, 97, 98, 104, 105, 107, 108, 109, 110, 111, 112,
                                                                                              113, 282
   s 8 . . . . 12, 13, 111, 112, 113, 282
   s 9 12
   ss 18-20 . . . . 17, 19
Statute of Uses 1536 . . . . 216, 217, 276
Trustee Act 1888 23
   s 8 . . . . 22, 69, 98, 99
   s 8(1)(b) 98
Trustee Act 1925
   s 44(vi) 123
   s 51(1)(d) 123
   s 61 135
Trusts of Land and Appointment of Trustees Act 1996 . . . . . 57, 194, 219
Wills Act 1837 . . . . 17, 19, 20, 21, 64, 65, 68, 86
   s 2 19
   s 9 . . . . 18, 20, 64, 86
Civil Procedure Rules 1998 (SI 1998/3132), Pt 40, r 40.20 123

Australia

Builders Licensing Act 1971 (NSW), s 45 109
Family Law Act 1975 (Cth) 304
   ss 31–32 273
   s 79 307

European Union

Regulation 44/2001 ('Brussels I') 19, 198
   art 5(6) 198

Israel

Contracts (General Part) Law (1973) 337
    s 3.142. 337
    s 21 337
    s 31 337

Malaya

Rubber Regulations 1934. 364

New Zealand

Land Transfer Act 1952
    s 62 179
    s 182. 180

United States of America

Model Penal Code 353, 354, 356
    s 5.01(a) 353
    s 5.01(4) 353, 356

International

Brussels Convention 1968 19
European Convention on Human Rights 274
    art 6 295
    Protocol 7 312
        art 5 . . . . 274, 312
Hague Convention on the Law Applicable to Trusts and on their
    Recognition 202, 203
    art 1 202
    art 3 202
    art 18 202
    art 20 202

PART I
CONSTRUCTIVE TRUSTS

1

The Words Which Are Not There: A Partial History of the Constructive Trust

PAUL MATTHEWS

If it is intended to have a resulting trust, the ordinary and familiar mode of doing that is by saying so on the face of the instrument; and I cannot get, out of the language of this instrument, a resulting trust except by putting in words which are not there.[1]

A. INTRODUCTION

History is many things. According to Dionysius, history is philosophy drawn from examples.[2] According to Thomas Carlyle, it is the biography of great men.[3] According to Sellar and Yeatman, it is what you can remember.[4] And, according to Henry Ford, it is more or less bunk.[5] It seems to me that all of these views have some truth in them, even the last.[6] But I have to deal with the history of a legal idea, rather than that of a nation, a place or a person. And unfortunately I am no historian, though I do claim to be (and at least earn my living as) some sort of lawyer.

The legal idea the history of which I am to attempt to describe is that of

---

* I have wanted to write this paper for many years, and am therefore very grateful to my colleague Charles Mitchell for the opportunity to do so now. I would also like to thank my former tutor Robert Venables (now QC), who first interested me in the subject when I was an undergraduate student.

[1] *Smith v Cooke* [1891] AC 297, 299 (Lord Halsbury LC).
[2] *Ars Rhetorica*, xi, 2.
[3] T Carlyle, *On Heroes, Hero-Worship and the Heroic in History* (London, Chapman & Hall, 1840).
[4] WC Sellar and RJ Yeatman, *1066 And All That* (London, Methuen, 1930) Compulsory Preface.
[5] *Chicago Tribune*, 25 May 1916.
[6] See the quotation at the head of this chapter.

the constructive trust. So the first task might be thought to be to ascertain the exact meaning of the phrase 'constructive trust'. This is, however, easier said than done. Indeed, the whole of this book is devoted to elucidating the concept of the constructive trust and its bedfellow the resulting trust. Waiting for a conclusive view before looking at the history would not only be potentially a lengthy process, but also a speculative one, indeed perhaps even existential as well. I need a shortcut.

According to Wittgenstein,[7] the meaning of a word is not what it stands for or designates, but the *use* that it has. Defining meaning is done by defining use. So what use is the phrase 'constructive trust'? Assuming that we know what we mean by the idea of the 'trust' in the first place, why do we need to distinguish between the 'constructive trust' and other sorts of trust?

B. THE DISTINCTION BETWEEN EXPRESS AND CONSTRUCTIVE TRUSTS

The usual answer that lawyers give to this kind of question is that different rules apply to things that are different in a legally relevant way. We know that express private trusts require a settlor who intends to create a trust, and a trustee (being a person of full age) who agrees so to act. The trust may require certain formalities in order to be validly created, the trustee has certain duties, and claims against the trustee for breach of those duties may or may not be subject to limitation periods. But already, as we think of these rules for express trusts, we can see that constructive trusts have—or at least may have—different rules from those for express trusts.

This is fundamentally because we think of the express trust as one where the settlor and the trustee (who may of course be the same person) expressly intend to create a trust structure, whereas the persons fulfilling those roles in a constructive trust may not. To put it another way, express trusts are created by the will of the parties, whereas constructive trusts are imposed by law. And, for example, it would not make much sense to provide that trusts imposed by law in response to wrongdoing could not be enforced unless proved by writing signed by the wrongdoer. In this chapter, we shall consider the development of the constructive trust idea by reference to some (but by no means all) of these points of distinction.

The main categories of purely constructive trust which may be recognised today (leaving on one side cases known as *resulting* trusts) are the following: (1) trusts created by statute;[8] (2) where an express trustee passes

---

[7] L Wittgenstein *Philosophical Investigations*, trans GEM Anscombe (Oxford, Blackwell, 1953) para 43.
[8] Eg on co-ownership of land under the Law of Property Act 1925, ss 34 and 36, and on intestacy under the Administration of Estates Act 1925, ss 46, etc.

trust property to a successor trustee; (3) where an express trustee pockets trust property for himself; (4) void distributions to beneficiaries, etc;[9] (5) where trust property is alienated in breach of trust to a third party who is not a bona fide purchaser for value of a legal estate without notice; (6) fruits of trust property;[10] (7) tracing into proceeds of express trust property; (8) property which a trustee has a duty to try to get for trust;[11] (9) property which a trustee has a duty *not* to get for himself;[12] (10) specifically enforceable contracts for the transfer of property rights[13] (including marriage settlements);[14] (11) mutual wills;[15] (12) proprietary estoppel;[16] and (13) common intention constructive trusts.[17]

In some of these cases (especially (2)–(5)) there is already an existing express trust. Where the legal ownership of the asset concerned does not change, it seems better to say that *that* trust continues in relation to the trust property, rather than that a new (constructive) trust is imposed on property which purports to leave the express trust. But where (as may happen in (4) and *ex hypothesi* does happen in (5)) the trust property is alienated in breach of trust to a person who is not the express trustee (and does not agree to become such), and who is not a bona fide purchaser of a legal estate for value without notice, that person may become a trustee and so far as he or she is concerned the trust will be constructive rather than express.[18] In other cases ((6)–(9)) there is property which never was the subject of any express trust but which comes into the hands of an express trustee in circumstances in which it should be treated as trust property. The remaining cases are not about existing trust property (or its products or substitutes) at all, but are about something which admittedly belongs (and has always belonged) to someone else and is merely *claimed* from that person because of obligation-generating conduct on his part or on that of a predecessor in title. They stand at the crossover between property and

---

[9] Eg *Thorpe v HMRC* [2009] EWHC 611 (Ch), [2009] Pens LR 139 [19].
[10] Cf M Graziadei, '*Tuttifrutti*' in P Birks and A Pretto (eds), *Themes in Comparative Law* (Oxford, Oxford University Press, 2002) 121.
[11] *Keech v Sandford* (1726) Sel Cas t King 61, 25 ER 223.
[12] Eg bribes: *AG for Hong Kong v Reid* [1994] 1 AC 324 (PC).
[13] *Goodwyn v Lister* (1735) 3 P Wms 387, 24 ER 1112; *Shaw v Foster* (1872) LR 5 HL 321, 349; *Bridges v Mees* [1957] Ch 475.
[14] Eg *Pullan v Koe* [1913] 1 Ch 9.
[15] *Re Goodchild* [1997] 1 WLR 1216, CA; *Healey v Brown* [2002] EWHC 1405 (Ch), [2002] WTLR 849.
[16] See below 25–45.
[17] See below 45–60.
[18] This is not the place for a discussion of Lord Browne-Wilkinson's remarks in *Westdeutsche Landsbank Girozentrale v Islington LBC* [1996] AC 669, about whether the innocent recipient is or is not a trustee, criticised by Sir P Millett, 'Restitution and Constructive Trusts' (1998) 114 *Law Quarterly Review* 399, 403–04, and W Swadling 'Property' in P Birks and FD Rose (eds), *Lessons of the Swaps Litigation* (Oxford, Mansfield Press, 2000) 242, 257–61. In my view this is a linguistic rather than substantive dispute: see P Matthews, 'All About Bare Trusts' [2005] *Private Client Business* 266, 271; and cf Charles Mitchell's and Stephen Watterson's chapter in the present volume: ch 4.B.

obligation. I have deliberately not tried to deal with cases arising from fraud or innocent misrepresentation, though there is a case for saying that they too involve a kind of constructive trust.[19]

I cannot deal with the history of all of these different manifestations of the constructive trust. So I am going to concentrate on three topics only: formalities, limitation, and the relationship between the doctrine of proprietary estoppel and the so-called common intention constructive trust. The third of these is the most topical, and occupies the greatest part of the chapter.

C. HISTORICAL MATERIAL

The distinction between express and constructive trusts is not easily visible in early legal materials. There are, for example, very few cases before the second half of the seventeenth century where a trust was held to exist which was not an ordinary express trust. Neil Jones refers[20] to three late-sixteenth-century cases of transfer to another which we might today regard as presumed resulting trusts (because of the absence of consideration for the transfer). But that really is about it. I have looked at (for example) St German's *Doctor and Student*,[21] and his *Replication* and *Little Treatise*,[22] but have found nothing on constructive uses or trusts. Yet it seems clear that, before the Statute of Uses, there were uses which resulted to the grantor by operation of law. This continued after the Statute,[23] even though in some cases such uses were 'executed' by the Statute so that the legal estate in the land did not pass at all.[24]

Perhaps this just goes to show the value of Wittgenstein's point. There was no reason to distinguish such cases. Either there was a use or a trust, or there wasn't.

In the second half of the seventeenth century we find constructive trust cases arising more frequently, even though the phrase 'constructive trust' itself does not appear in the reports until much later.[25] Thus, in *Holt v*

---

[19] See eg *Qayyum v Hameed* [2009] EWCA Civ 352 [41].

[20] N Jones, 'Trusts in England after the Statute of Uses: A View from the Sixteenth Century' in R Helmholz and R Zimmerman (eds), *Itinera Fiduciae: Trust and Treuhand in Historical Perspective* (Berlin, Dunkler & Humblot, 1998) 173, 177, n 30. Lionel Smith picked this up: LD Smith, 'Constructive Trusts and Constructive Trustees' [1999] *Cambridge Law Journal* 294, 297 n 17.

[21] TFT Plucknett and JL Barton (eds), C St German, *Doctor and Student* (Selden Society, vol 91, 1974)

[22] JA Guy (ed), *Christopher St German on Chancery and Statute* (Selden Society Supplementary Series, vol 6, 1985).

[23] See eg *Armstrong v Wolsey* (1755) 2 Wils KB 19, 95 ER 662.

[24] See Sir G Gilbert, *The Law of Uses and Trusts*, ed EB Sugden, 3rd edn (London, 1811) 117–25.

[25] See *Goodwyn v Lister* (1735) 3 P Wms 387, 24 ER 1112. The phrase 'resulting trust' is seen earlier: see eg *Riddle v Emerson* (1682) 1 Vern 108, 23 ER 348.

Holt[26] executors renewed a lease forming part of the deceased's estate for their own benefit, rather than for that of the beneficiaries, but 'it was agreed by the whole Court, that in case of an Executorship in Trust, the Renewal of such a Lease shall go to the Benefit of Cestuy que Trust'. [27]

The first judgment that I have been able to find apparently making use of the distinction between express and constructive trusts is that of Lord Finch of Daventry LC in *Cook v Fountain*.[28] Lord Finch later became Lord Nottingham,[29] and, since he is better known by that title to trust lawyers, I will anachronistically use it in referring to him even before he received it. The date of the judgment in the case of *Cook v Fountain*—1676—is important, because it pre-dates the enactment of the Statute of Frauds in 1677.[30] Nottingham was perhaps the first important lawyer to try to bring intellectual order to the trust institution and to the learning then available on it.

In *Cook v Fountain* the defendant held certain leases and a rentcharge, granted to him by the plaintiff's predecessor in title. The plaintiff claimed that they were held by the defendant on trust for him. After considering a mass of evidence, the Lord Chancellor (and other judges)[31] held that the plaintiff succeeded as to the leases but failed as to the rentcharge. But during the course of his judgment, he said this:

> I should now come to particulars, and consider where and in what part of the case a general or a qualified trust may be found, and where the case stands free and clear from being affected with any kind of trust at all; but before I do this, I hold it necessary to lay down some rules and distinctions touching trusts, which I must keep to and by which I must govern myself in all cases whatsoever.
>
> *All trusts are either, first, express trusts, which are raised and created by act of the parties, or implied trusts, which are raised or created by act or construction of law*; again, express trusts are declared either by word or writing; and these declarations appear either by direct and manifest proof, or violent and necessary presumption. These last are commonly called presumptive trusts; and that is, when the Court, upon consideration of all circumstances presumes there was a declaration, either by word or writing, though the plain and direct proof thereof

---

[26] (1670) 1 Ch Cas 190, 22 ER 756. See also *Rushworth's* case (1676) Freem 13, 89 ER 10.
[27] Ibid, 1 Ch Cas 191.
[28] (1676) 3 Swans 585, 36 ER 984; DEC Yale (ed), *Lord Nottingham's Chancery Cases*, vol 1 (Selden Society, vol 73, 1954) 362.
[29] Sir Heneage Finch Bt had been Attorney General from 1670 to 1673, Lord Keeper of the Great Seal from 1673 to 1675, and Lord Chancellor from 1675. He had been raised to the peerage as a baron, with the title of Lord Finch of Daventry, in January 1673/4. He was advanced to an earldom, with the (superior) title of Earl of Nottingham, only in May 1681, some 18 months before his death in December 1682. However, after his death, his son, the 2nd Earl of Nottingham, inherited the older title of Earl of Winchilsea from a second cousin, and hence his descendants have been known by that title rather than as Earls of Nottingham. Thus the first Earl of Nottingham is *the* Lord Nottingham.
[30] On the date of the Statute of Frauds, see GP Costigan, 'The Date and Authorship of the Statute of Frauds' (1913) 26 *Harvard Law Review* 329.
[31] Raynsford CJKB and North CJCP (later Lord Guilford LK).

be not extant. In the case in question there is no pretence of any proof that there was a trust declared either by word or in writing; so the trust, if there be any, must either be implied by the law, or presumed by the Court. There is one good, general, and infallible rule that goes to both these kinds of trusts; it is *Such a general rule as never deceives; a general rule to which there is no exception, and that is this; the law never implies, the Court never presumes a trust, but in case of absolute necessity.* The reason of this rule is sacred; for if the Chancery do once take liberty to construe a trust by implication of law, or to presume a trust, unnecessarily, a way is opened to the Lord Chancellor to construe or presume any man in England out of his estate; and so at last every case in court will become casus pro amico.[32]

The distinction drawn in the italicised passage above at first sight looks as though it is between (1) those trusts created by act of the parties, that is, intentional, and (2) those trusts imposed by the law, that is, irrespective of the intentions of the parties. To us in modern times that seems an obvious, indeed even banal, distinction.

There are, however, two points to make. The first point is that, if we go on to read the rest of the extract, it makes clear (1) that the first category of trust *includes* cases where the court finds a declaration of trust to have been made, but only by way of presumption from the circumstances (what Lord Nottingham calls 'presumptive' trusts), and (2) that the first category of trust *excludes* cases where there is no declaration to be presumed, but the court presumes a trust from the circumstances. In other words, the court presumes that the parties' intention was to create a trust, though it is unable to presume that there was a declaration. I will return to this point.

The second point is that, judged by the Wittgenstein approach to the meaning of words, at first sight this distinction appears to lack a useful purpose. The rules relating to formalities for the creation of trusts, which distinguished sharply between express and constructive trusts, were enacted only in the following year, in the Statute of Frauds 1677. The rules relating to certainty of intention to create a trust, to limitation of actions for breach of trust, and so on, had not yet been developed by the courts. So why did Lord Nottingham bother to distinguish express and constructive trusts?

So far as I can tell, there are two main reasons. First, the distinction was already present to his mind, both in the private collection of cases that he had made for himself called the *Prolegomena of Chancery and Equity* (discussed below), and also in the context of the law relating to formalities for trusts. There was no law requiring particular formalities for the creation of a trust at this time. The Statute of Frauds was only passed in 1677. But the first draft of the bill which eventually became the Statute of Frauds had been introduced in the House of Lords in February 1673.[33] That draft did

[32] *Cook* (n 28), 3 Swans 591–92 (original emphasis).
[33] On the authorship and passage of the Statute of Frauds, see Costigan (n 30); CD Hening, 'The Original Drafts of the Statute of Frauds (29 Car c 3) and Their Authors' (1913) 61 *Uni-*

not become law. But Lord Nottingham undoubtedly was the author of at least some of it. A further bill of 1675, which reproduced the text of that of 1673, was amended during its passage through Parliament, but did not pass because of the prorogation of Parliament. It was reintroduced into the House of Lords in February 1676–77, further amended during its Parliamentary passage, and finally received the Royal Assent in April 1677. So, even though at the time of the judgment in *Cook v Fountain* there were no rules of enacted law distinguishing express and constructive trusts from the perspective of formalities, nevertheless Lord Nottingham had the idea of such rules well in mind. They were contained in a bill which he had had a hand in drafting, and which was likely to become law sooner or later (and in fact did so).

The second reason is that the nature of the case itself rested on explaining why there was a trust in relation to the leases, but not in relation to the rentcharge. There was no direct evidence of a trust, such as a deed (or other writing), or even an oral declaration, of trust. The plaintiff did not even claim that there had been such a declaration. So the court could not presume from the circumstances that there had been one, for that would be to find a fact which was not alleged. It was therefore necessary to look at what the parties did and did not do, and to consider just how consistent each of these things was with the existence or non-existence of a trust. But it will be noted that the court was attempting nonetheless to ascertain the intentions of the parties. The question was how far the law would presume the intention to create a trust when there was no positive statement to that effect, and no pretence that there had been one.

This might at first sight be thought to correspond to the well-known distinction drawn in *Lloyds Bank plc v Rosset*[34] by Lord Bridge between (1) the case of a finding of an actual 'agreement, arrangement, or understanding', which had to be based on evidence of express discussions between the parties, and (2) the case where there is no evidence to support a finding of an agreement or arrangement, and the court relies on the conduct of the parties as to the basis on which to infer an common intention to share the property beneficially. In fact it does not, because the role of the agreement in that case—real or imputed to the parties—is not (as in Lord Nottingham's time) to act as a declaration of trust to which effect will be given,[35] but rather to act as the foundation for a constructive trust argument based on the detrimental reliance on that 'agreement' by the party claiming a share (or an increased share) in the property concerned.

versity of Pennsylvania Law Review 283; WS Holdsworth, *A History of English Law*, vol 6 (London, Methuen, 1924) 380–04.

[34] [1991] 1 AC 107, 132.

[35] At least in non-land cases, and in land cases too before the Statute of Frauds 1677 came into force on 24 June 1677.

Just as in the case of the old equitable doctrine of part performance,[36] the defendant is not charged upon the underlying agreement (because that is unenforceable by reason of non-compliance with statutory formalities rules), but upon the equity raised by the acts *done in reliance* on that underlying agreement. This is an important theme, to which I shall return.

In more modern times a trust accepted to exist in the kind of circumstances found in *Cook v Fountain* has been called an *implied* trust or a *presumed* trust (because the court was implying or presuming *in fact* what were the intentions of the parties). It would probably have been called a resulting trust too, because it would be a trust for the 'settlor' rather than for a third party.[37] It would not have been called a *constructive* trust, which would more properly refer to a trust imposed by the law where the 'settlor' and the 'trustee' do not so intend, or at any rate do not so agree (as in the cases now thought of as 'proprietary estoppel').[38] But in England, from the time of *Gissing v Gissing*[39] on, in these cases the courts have concentrated less on the presumed resulting trust model and much more on the constructive trust model, where there is detrimental reliance on an agreement or understanding, as found in decisions such as *Lloyds Bank plc v Rosset*.[40] But even so, as Lady Hale said recently in *Stack v Dowden*:

> [T]he search is still for the result which reflects what the parties must, in the light of their conduct, be taken to have intended . . . [I]t does not enable the court to abandon that search in favour of the result which the court itself considers fair.[41]

However, in the time of Lord Nottingham the line appears to have been drawn in a different place. As stated above, the first of his two categories includes cases where the court finds there was a declaration of trust without any direct evidence of one. This is obviously a case of an intended trust, and therefore may be classed as an express trust. The plaintiff has pleaded a fact—a declaration of trust—and the court had found it on the evidence. However, his second category (constructive trusts) includes, as well as cases where the parties never intended a trust at all, cases where the court holds that there never was a declaration but that the parties' intentions, judged from all the circumstances, were that there should be one. The plaintiff has not pleaded a fact, but a conclusion of law—that is, that in the circumstances there was a trust.

---

[36] See *Maddison v Alderson* (1883) 8 App Cas 467, 476 and 489, discussed in the text to n 140.
[37] See eg *Pettitt v Pettitt* [1970] AC 777.
[38] See, most recently, *Thorner v Major* [2009] UKHL 18, [2009] 1 WLR 776, discussed below in the text to n 210.
[39] [1971] AC 886.
[40] *Rosset* (n 34) 132. These cases are discussed below, in part H.
[41] [2007] UKHL 17, [2007] 2 AC 432 [61], commenting on *Oxley v Hiscock* [2004] EWCA Civ 546, [2005] Fam 211 [69], and the Law Commission, *Sharing Homes: A Discussion Paper* (Law Com No 278, 2002) para 4.27.

This view is borne out by reference to various cases decided before the Statute of Frauds, including one noted in Lord Nottingham's judicial *vade mecum*, his own *Prolegomena of Chancery and Equity*. This manuscript work appears to have been written by the judge for his own use in about 1674, though with some later additions. The original is lost, and it is known to us today only from a transcript by Francis Hargrave, now in the Library of Congress, and itself published only in modern times.[42] Chapter XIII is entitled 'Where trust shall be raised by construction and implication of law, and where not'. So it raises just the distinction with which we are dealing. Of the 15 cases it summarises or refers to, about half are cases where the court is deciding whether as a matter of fact the parties actually intended a trust. One (number 8) takes place in Hil 23 Car 2, that is, 1671. The facts are that A conveys to B (a stranger) property for payment of debts. The court holds that, if there is no covenant by B to pay the debts but A received the profits, then 'even though there be no express declaration of a trust, yet the law in this case shall imply a trust'.

Another, even earlier case is *Binion v Stone*.[43] There a man bought an estate in the name of his son, then five years old, probably to shield it from his Civil War enemies. As he feared, his estates were seized and sold. After the son came of age the purchaser of the estate paid the son (and his mother) a significant sum (but still an undervalue) for a further conveyance and a statement that they were not trustees for the father. The court held that this was nonetheless a trust for the father and the purchaser had to reconvey to him on being repaid the price he had paid.

D. THE IMPACT OF THE STATUTE OF FRAUDS

We must next consider the impact of the Statute of Frauds 1677. This contained three sections of particular importance to trusts, as follows:

> [7] AND bee it further enacted by the authoritie aforesaid That from and after the said fower and twentyeth day of June all Declarations or Creations of Trusts or Confidences of any Lands Tenements or Hereditaments shall be manifested and proved by some Writeing signed by the partie who is by Law enabled to declare such Trust or by his last Will in Writeing or else they shall be utterly void and of none effect.
>
> [8] PROVIDED always That where any Conveyance shall bee made of any Lands or Tenements by which a Trust or Confidence shall or may arise or result by the Implication or Construction of Law or bee transferred or extinguished by an act or operation of Law then and in every such Case, such Trust or Confidence shall be of the like force and effect as the same would have beene if this Statute had not been made. Any thing herein before contained to the contrary notwithstanding.

---

[42] DEC Yale (ed), *Lord Nottingham's 'Manual of Chancery Practice' and 'Prolegomena of Chancery and Equity'* (Cambridge, Cambridge University Press, 1965).
[43] (1663) Nels 68, 21 ER 791; 2 Freeman 169, 22 ER 1135.

12 The Words Which Are Not There

> [9] AND bee it further enacted That all Grants and Assignments of any Trust or Confidence shall likewise be in Writeing signed by the partie granting or assigning the same or by such last Will or Devise or else shall likewise be utterly void and of none effect.

In *Elliot v Elliot*[44] Lord Nottingham soon had the opportunity to comment on the reasons for and effects of the Statute. This was the case of a father who bought an interest in land in the name of his son. It was argued that the son held it as trustee for the father. Lord Nottingham so held, but (according to his own records) said this:

> [I]t being not a question of fact, but a question of law how far a trust was implied in this case, the point was not capable of being tried by a jury but of necessity to be determined by the judgment of this court; and this judgment was like to be of great example and consequence for the future, for, since by the late new Act for the prevention of Frauds and Perjuries all trusts not declared in writing are abolished, except such trusts as do arise by construction and implication of law, it is high time to set some bounds to such constructions and implications.

'Setting bounds' to the implication of trusts (except for those imposed by law) protects estate owners and their heirs. This furthers the policy of the Statute of Frauds. Trusts imposed by law, however, are required for the protection of different interests, judged to be of greater weight than those of estate owners and their heirs.

These provisions of the Statute of Frauds remained in force in England until 1 January 1926, when they were repealed and replaced by provisions in the Law of Property Act 1925, section 53. A reader familiar with the 1925 legislation will recognise section 7 of the earlier Act as corresponding to section 53(1)(b) of the later, section 8 as corresponding to section 53(2), and section 9 as corresponding to section 53(1)(c). In each case, however, the language has been shortened and simplified, and the spelling modernised.

In the case of section 53(2) of the 1925 Act, the changes in the language are particularly striking. That provision says simply: 'This section does not affect the creation or operation of resulting, implied or constructive trusts.' There is first of all an apparent difference in scope. In the Statute of Frauds, section 8 follows and seems to apply only in relation to section 7. But, in the 1925 Act, section 53(2) applies to *all three* provisions in section 53(1). This includes section 53(1)(c), relating to the assignment of equitable interests (corresponding to section 9 of the 1677 Act), which figured so heavily in *Oughtred v IRC*[45] and *Vandervell v IRC*.[46] But section 8 includes the words 'or bee transferred or extinguished by an act or operation of

---

[44] (1677) 2 Ch Cas 231, 22 ER 922; *Lord Nottingham's Chancery Cases* (n 28) cases 690, 751.
[45] [1960] AC 206.
[46] [1967] 2 AC 291.

Law',[47] which appears to cover the case of an assignment of an equitable interest by operation of law. Hence the difference in scope is more apparent than real.

More interesting from our point of view is the modernisation of the language in section 8, referring to trusts which 'shall or may arise or result by the Implication or Construction of Law'. Here we have three pairs of words: 'shall/may', 'arise/result' and 'implication/construction'. Each pair seems to reflect the old-fashioned draftsman's desire (still apparent in modern American legal drafting) to use two words where one will do. The first pair 'shall/may' means 'if it does', the second pair means 'come into existence' and the third pair 'implication/construction' means 'operation'. So on that basis the phrase refers to trusts which 'come into existence (if they ever do) by operation of law'. In other words, there is only *one* class of trust covered by these words in section 8, those imposed by the law rather than wished by the parties.

But although the wording of section 8 of the Act of 1677 remained in force until 1925, that is not how judges and commentators saw the phrase. Thus, in *Lloyd v Spillit*[48] Lord Hardwicke LC said that the trusts by operation of law within section 8 of the Statute of Frauds were only of two kinds, namely: (1) trusts where A purchased in the name of B, and (2) trusts where the settlor did not exhaust the beneficial interest. Both were what we would now call resulting trusts, though of different kinds, that is, (1) presumed and (2) automatic. There was no reference to what we would call constructive trusts at all.

In the nineteenth century lawyers separated out several classes of trust in addition to express trusts: these included implied, resulting and constructive trusts. But they were not consistent. For example, Story's *Equity Jurisprudence*[49] contained a chapter on 'Implied Trusts', covering both what we would now call constructive and resulting trusts (the latter including both presumed and automatic). Then Snell's *Equity*, in its first edition of 1868, contained chapters on 'Implied Trusts' and 'Constructive Trusts'.[50] The former chapter included resulting trusts (again, both presumed and automatic). The second edition of 1872 (not by Snell),[51] and subsequent editions, too, continued this approach, though by the time of the seventh edition, in 1884, the title of the former chapter was 'Implied and Resulting Trusts', more accurately describing the contents.[52]

---

[47] Apparently added to the original Bill of 1673 when it was reintroduced in 1675, by the House of Lords Committee: Hening (n 34) 294 and 307.
[48] (1740) Barn Ch 384, 27 ER 689.
[49] J Story, *Commentaries on Equity Jurisprudence*, 2nd edn (Cambridge, MA, 1839) vol 2, ch 22.
[50] EHT Snell, *The Principles of Equity* (London, Stevens & Haynes, 1868).
[51] EHT Snell, *The Principles of Equity*, 2nd edn, ed JR Griffith (London, Stevens & Haynes, 1872).
[52] EHT Snell, *The Principles of Equity*, 7th edn, ed A Brown (London, Stevens & Haynes,

However, Lewin's *Practical Treatise of the Law of Trusts and Trustees*,[53] at more or less the same time, took a different approach. There *was* a chapter on implied trusts, but this merely dealt with trusts created by precatory words, that is, trusts implied in *fact*. There were separate chapters on resulting and on constructive trusts, the former of which dealt with both presumptive and automatic resulting trusts. In the 13th edition, of 1928 (the first after the 1925 legislation), the separate treatment of 'implied trusts' was retained, but the two chapters on 'resulting' and 'constructive' trusts respectively were amalgamated into a single chapter called 'The Creation of Trusts by Operation of Law'.[54] This arrangement lasted until the 16th edition of 1964, by John Mowbray, which omitted the separate treatment of 'implied trusts', but retained the chapter on trusts by operation of law. The 1964 edition, perhaps revealingly, stated:

> Trusts arising by operation of law may be further divided into implied or presumptive, constructive and resulting trusts. . . . There is no generally agreed usage for *implied trusts*, which in previous editions was used to mean precatory trusts, but is in modern parlance generally used to include resulting trusts and other trusts arising from a presumed intention on the part of the settlor. Nor is there any agreed meaning for *constructive trusts*, which in its narrower meaning includes only trusts imposed by law against the settlor's own will . . . but which is sometimes used to include all trusts other than express trusts.[55]

Given that pre-1926 lawyers and judges did not treat section 8 as applying to only one class of trust, it is hardly surprising to find that modern commentators do not so read section 53(2) of the 1925 Act either. In any event, they do not treat the 1925 Act as a consolidation of the earlier legislation, but rather as an *amendment* of it.[56] Thus, like the nineteenth-century writers, they have tended to see the words 'resulting, implied or constructive' as disjunctive, referring to *three* classes of case. As a result, textbooks—and judges—have got themselves into all sorts of tangles trying to decide the difference between the three classes. Usually the bulk of the discussion centres on the distinction between resulting and constructive trusts, and there is some residual explanation of implied trusts

---

1884). By the 18th edition, in 1920, it had changed slightly, to 'Implied or Resulting Trusts': EHT Snell, *The Principles of Equity*, 18th edn, ed HG Rivington and AC Fountaine (London, Sweet & Maxwell, 1920). So it remains today: J McGhee *Snell's Equity*, 31st edn (London, Sweet & Maxwell, 2005).

[53] T Lewin, *A Practical Treatise on the Law of Trusts and Trustees*, 4th edn (London, W Maxwell, 1861).

[54] W Banks *Lewin's Practical Treatise on the Law of Trusts*, 13th edn (London, Sweet & Maxwell Ltd, 1928).

[55] WJ Mowbray, *Lewin on Trusts*, 16th edn (London, Sweet & Maxwell, 1964) 8 (footnotes omitted, emphasis in original).

[56] Eg *Grey v IRC* [1960] AC 1, 13–14 and 16–17.

as nowadays being implied in fact.[57] Indeed, one commentator goes so far as to say:

> In one sense an implied trust may be said to arise where the intention of the settlor to set up a trust is inferred from his words or actions, for example precatory trusts. Implied trusts in this sense are probably best regarded as express trusts, in that the trust is expressed, albeit in ambiguous and uncertain language.[58]

Against that, a popular Australian textbook says:

> An implied trust is a trust which arises by presumption of law in favour of the settlor or his representatives.[59]

It then goes on to describe the two classes of presumed resulting trusts, that is, transfers on trust failing to dispose of the entire beneficial interest, and purchase money resulting trusts.

Furthermore, just to make it absolutely clear, another English commentator says:

> Sometimes implied trusts are included as a further category of private trusts. This classification serves little purpose, and the examples commonly given might preferably be regarded as express, resulting or constructive trusts, as the case may be.[60]

As for resulting trusts themselves, they are commonly divided into presumed and automatic resulting trusts, the former being seen as a form of express trusts (because based on intention) and the latter as a form of constructive trust (because *not* based on intention).[61] A variant on this view is the following:

> [M]any, perhaps all, resulting trusts depend upon the implied intention of the settlor. Some accordingly treat resulting and implied trusts as synonymous though others consider implied trust as synonymous with constructive trust.[62]

This leaves us in some difficulty in construing section 53(2). Does it apply to *any* implied trusts? Does it apply to *all* resulting trusts? No one knows.

It is instructive to compare the problem of section 53(2) with the construction of a similar but different phrase in the Settled Land Act 1925.

---

[57] Eg DWM Waters, M Gillen and LD Smith, *Waters' Law of Trusts in Canada*, 3rd edn (Toronto, Carswell, 2005) 20.
[58] PH Pettit, *Equity and the Law of Trusts*, 10th edn (Oxford, Oxford University Press, 2005) 64.
[59] RP Meagher and WMC Gummow, *Jacobs' Law of Trusts in Australia*, 6th edn (Sydney, Butterworths, 1997) para 1201.
[60] JE Martin *Hanbury & Martin: Modern Equity*, 17th edn (London, Sweet & Maxwell, 2005) para 2–028.
[61] Eg W Ashburner, *Principles of Equity* (London, Butterworths, 1902) 124–25.
[62] Pettit (n 58) 64.

Re Llanover Settled Estates[63] was decided very shortly after the 1925 legislation had come into force. In that case, certain surplus rents accruing to will trustees were, in the events that happened, undisposed of to any beneficiary, and thus were held by the trustees for the heir of the testator. Astbury J had to decide whether the surplus rents were held during that period on an 'implied or constructive trust' within the meaning of that phrase in the Settled Land Act 1925, section 117(1)(xii). This phrase seems to have been new in 1925, as it did not appear in the predecessor legislation, the Settled Land Act 1882. The judge said:

> The will trustees contend that Mrs Herbert [the heir of the testator] did not take the surplus rents under an express trust, which is obvious, nor under an implied or constructive trust, properly so called. They contend that an implied trust means a trust declared by a party not directly but by implication. That no doubt is a strict and accurate statement, though not exhaustive. They also contend that a constructive trust is a trust that the Court elicits by a construction put upon certain acts of the parties, e.g., where a trustee renews a lease belonging to the trust in his own name. That again is perfectly accurate, but not, I think, exhaustive. They refer to *Lewin on Trusts*, 12th ed, p 124n, where the learned author states:
>
>> The terms Implied Trusts, Trusts by Operation of Law, and Constructive Trusts, appear from the books to be almost synonymous expressions; but for the purposes of the present work the following distinctions, as considered the most accurate, will be observed: An implied trust is one declared by a party not directly, but only by implication; as where a testator devises an estate to A. and his heirs, 'not doubting' that he will thereout pay an annuity of 20l. per annum to B. for his life, in which case A. is a trustee for B. to the extent of the annuity. Trusts by operation of law are such as are not declared by a party at all, either directly or indirectly, but result from the effect of a rule of equity, and are either: (1.) Resulting trusts, as where an estate is devised to A. and his heirs, upon trust to sell and pay the testator's debts, in which case the surplus of the beneficial interest is a resulting trust in favour of the testator's heir; or, (2.) Constructive trusts, which the Court elicits by a construction put upon certain acts of parties, as when a tenant for life of leaseholds renews the lease on his own account, in which case the law gives the benefit of the renewed lease to those who were interested in the old lease.
>
> Mrs Herbert's executors relied on two passages in *Underhill on Trusts*, 8th ed—namely, p 9, art 3:
>
>> Trusts are created either intentionally by the act of the settlor (in which case they are called express trusts) or by implication of a Court of equity where the legal title to property is in one person, and the equitable right to the beneficial enjoyment of it is in another, in which case they are called constructive trusts,

---

[63] [1926] Ch 626.

and p 147, art 26(1):

> Constructive trusts are either resulting trusts (in which the equitable interest springs back or results to a settlor or his representatives), or non-resulting trusts.

Those passages again are substantially accurate. It is true no doubt, as the trustees contend, that a resulting trust in ordinary circumstances is in one sense not really a trust at all. Where property is settled or devised upon limitations that do not exhaust it, a resulting use or trust of the unexhausted part is left in the settlor or devisor. But where, as in the present case, property is devised as a whole to trustees and the trusts declared do not exhaust the income during some particular period, although there is a resulting trust so called to the settlor or her heir at law, it is really a trust construed by the Court in the trustees of the income which they so hold, and which they cannot apply in accordance with any express trust in the settlement and which in the present case they hold on trust to pay to the person entitled thereto by reason of this so-called resulting trust. That, I think, is within the general meaning of implied or constructive trust.[64]

Thus the judge treated 'implied or constructive' as exhausting the whole ground of trusts by operation of law, including what we would now call 'automatic' resulting trusts (which was the kind of trust in fact the subject of that case).

E. THE IMPACT OF THE WILLS ACT 1837

Having considered the position of the Statute of Frauds (and the 1925 legislation which replaced it) on *inter vivos* transfers giving rise to trusts, it is necessary briefly to consider the impact of the Wills Act 1837 on transfers *mortis causa*. Section 5 of the Statute of Frauds had enacted:

> [5] AND bee it further enacted by the authority aforesaid That from and after the said fower and twentyeth day of June all Devises and Bequests of any Lands or Tenements deviseable either by force of the Statute of Wills or by this Statute or by force of the Custome of Kent or the Custome of any Burrough or any other perticular Custome shall be in Writeing and signed by the partie soe deviseing the same or by some other person in his presence and by his expresse directions and shall be attested and subscribed in the presence of the said Devisor by three or fower credible Witnesses or else they shall be utterly void and of none effect.

As can be seen, this applied only to gifts of land (that is, realty or leaseholds). The rules for wills of pure personalty were contained in sections 18–20 of the Statute:

> [18] AND for prevention of fraudulent Practices in setting up Nuncupative Wills which have beene the occasion of much Perjury Bee it enacted by the

---

[64] Ibid, 636–38.

authority aforesaid That from and after the aforesaid fower and twentyeth day of June noe Nuncupative Will shall be good where the Estate thereby bequeathed shall exceed the value of thirty pounds that is not proved by the Oathes of three Wittnesses (at the least) that were present at the makeing thereof, nor unlesse it be proved that the Testator at the time of pronounceing the same did bid the persons present or some of them beare wittnesse that such was his Will or to that effect, nor unlesse such Nuncupative Will were made in the time of the last sicknesse of the deceased and in the House of his or her habitation or dwelling or where he or she hath beene resident for the space of ten dayes or more next before the makeing of such Will except where such person was surprised or taken sick being from his owne home and dyed before he returned to the place of his or her dwelling.

[19] AND bee it further enacted That after six monethes passed after the speaking of the pretended Testamentary words noe Testimony shall be received to prove any Will Nuncupative except the said Testimony or the substance thereof were committed to writeing within six dayes after the makeing of the said Will.

[20] AND bee it further enacted That noe Letters Testamentary or Probate of any Nuncupative Will shall passe the Seale of any Court till fowerteene dayes at the least after the decease of the Testator be fully expired, Nor shall any Nuncupative Will be at any time received to be proved unlesse Processe have first issued to call in the Widow or next of kindred to the deceased to the end they may contest the same if they please.

Thus, even after 1677, and until 1838, it was possible to make a will of personalty orally, subject to certain procedural requirements as to witnesses and evidence[65]—and even these did not apply in the case of estates worth less than £30 (which would initially have been the case for a great many—perhaps most—people who did not own land).[66]

The 1837 Act replaced the earlier rules by a single rule in section 9:

No will shall be valid unless it shall be in writing, and executed in manner hereinafter mentioned; (that is to say), it shall be signed at the foot or end thereof by the testator, or by some other person in his presence and by his direction; and such signature shall be made or acknowledged by the testator in the presence of two or more witnesses present at the same time, and such witnesses shall attest and subscribe the will in the presence of the testator but no form of attestation shall be necessary.[67]

So whereas previously it had been possible to make a nuncupative will of personalty, that is, without any writing at the time, now a document was

---

[65] See eg *Nab v Nab* (1718) 10 Mod 405, 88 ER 783.

[66] By way of example, the diarist Samuel Pepys, at the beginning of his famous diary, estimated himself to be worth about £40 altogether: see entries for 29 January and 17 February 1659–60. He was then about 27 years old, and the son of a tailor, but he was well connected, had received a university education, and was now the clerk to important men.

[67] The section was replaced by a more modern form by the Administration of Justice Act 1982, ss 17 and 73(6), but without making any material change for our purposes.

needed. In a case where the testator wished to create a trust by will, he could use the will to transfer the property to the intended trustee. Plainly this now had to be done by signed and witnessed writing. The question was whether the will had to refer to the trust or not, and, if it did, whether it had to spell out all the terms of the trust. On the one hand, it could be said that the policy of the legislature was to require *all* dispositions of a testamentary nature to be in writing. But was a trust engrafted onto a legacy such a disposition of a testamentary nature within that policy?[68]

There is an important reference, in section 7 of the Statute of Frauds, to wills. That section requires all trusts of *land* to be proved 'by some Writeing signed by the partie who is by Law enabled to declare such Trust *or by his last Will in Writeing*'.[69] Thus the statute's policy was to require writing, or at least written evidence, for trusts of land. Why was the reference to the will necessary? Answer: because without it there would be no rule requiring a *will trust* of land to be in writing. Thus section 5 of the statute, requiring testamentary gifts of land to be in a written will, had to apply only to gifts of the legal estate. That is easily comprehensible: section 5 dealt with the legal estate; section 7 with the equitable.

But where did this leave gifts and trusts of personalty? As to *inter vivos* gifts and trusts, there was (and indeed still is today) no need for writing, whether as evidence or as the instrument (except where the law requires writing for a transfer of the legal interest). As for testamentary gifts and trusts, we can see that sections 18–20 imposed procedural requirements for the will, but allowed the testator to make his will orally. So prior to 1838 the testator could *orally* make a will leaving personalty to a legatee, on (oral) trusts affecting that legacy.[70]

After 1837, the testator of personalty had to make a written will to transfer the legacy to the legatee who was intended to be the trustee. But if section 9 was intended to require will trusts to be *in writing in the will*, that would render obsolete the reference in section 7 of the Statute of Frauds to trusts of land being in the will. That is not an impossible conclusion: after all, the Wills Act followed the Statute of Frauds by some 160 years. But although the later Act specifically repealed obsolete parts of the earlier statute,[71] it did not in terms touch these words. And, in *Re Baillie*,[72] where

---

[68] A similar question arises today in the context of the 'Brussels I' Regulation on the Allocation of Jurisdiction and the Enforcement of Judgments, Council Regulation (EC) 44 of 2001. That regulation—like its predecessor the Brussels Convention of 1968—includes special rules for allocating jurisdiction in the case of trust disputes, but excludes from its scope disputes about 'rights in property arising out of . . . wills and succession'. Are disputes arising from a will trust within or without the scope of the Regulation? See the Schlosser Report, 5 March 1979, OJ C59, para 112 (without); P Kaye *Civil Jurisdiction and Enforcement of Foreign Judgments* (Abingdon, Professional Books, 1987) 127–9 (within).
[69] Original emphasis.
[70] See *Nab* (n 63) (will in writing, oral trust of personalty held binding on legatee).
[71] See s 2 of the 1837 Act.
[72] (1886) 2 TLR 660.

a question arose as to a (half-secret) trust of land given by will, the judge relied on section 7 of the Statute of Frauds as the reason for its unenforceability, rather than section 9 of the Wills Act.[73]

This all suggests that the Wills Act 1837 had no impact on testamentary trusts. These were still governed by the Statute of Frauds, that is, section 7 for land and nothing for pure personalty. The 1925 legislation has since substituted the Law of Property Act, section 53(1)(b), for section 7, but otherwise the position is the same. And if that conclusion is right, then there is a significant knock-on effect on so-called 'secret' trusts.

F. SECRET TRUSTS

The doctrine of secret trusts and I are old friends.[74] In the conventional formulation it holds that a gift in a will which is intended by the testator to be held by the legatee on trust will be subject to the trust if certain communication requirements are satisfied. Secret trusts come in two flavours: fully secret and half-secret. In the former case, where the gift is apparently beneficial on the face of the will, the trust will be enforced against the legatee if the testator's intention is communicated to the legatee before the testator's death.[75] In the latter case, where it is clear from the face of the will that there is a trust (though not for whom), it must be communicated before or at the time of the making of the will.[76]

The justification for the doctrine is that not to enforce the 'secret' trust would enable the legatee to defeat the intentions of the settlor and facilitate a fraud.[77] It is notable that the doctrine draws no distinction between gifts of real and personal property. It is also notable (but perhaps connected to the first point) that the doctrine is formulated with reference to testamentary trusts. The doctrine, it is suggested by a recent commentator, 'has, therefore allowed testators to make informal, even oral testamentary dispositions in flat defiance of the Wills Act, to opt out, as it were'.[78] However, if I am right to suggest that it is not the Wills Act that requires formality for trusts, but originally the Statute of Frauds, and now the Law of Property

---

[73] But in *Wallgrave v Tebbs* (1855) 2 K & J 313, 321; 69 ER 800, 804, Page Wood VC said, obiter, that the Statute of Frauds had been superseded by the Wills Act in the context of secret trusts (though it is unclear if the judge actually had this point in mind). This statement was quoted with approval by Lord Cairns LC in *Jones v Badley* (1868) LR 3 Ch App 362, 364.

[74] P Matthews, 'The True Basis of the Half Secret Trust?' [1979] *Conveyancer and Property Lawyer* 360.

[75] *Moss v Cooper* (1861) 1 J & H 352, 70 ER 782.

[76] *Re Keen* [1937] Ch 236.

[77] Pettit (n 58) 127. See too DR Hodge, 'Secret Trusts: The Fraud Theory Revisited' [1980] *Conveyancer and Property Lawyer* 341; and cf D Wilde 'Secret and Semi-Secret Trusts: Justifying Distinctions between the Two' [1995] *Conveyancer and Property Lawyer* 366; the same applies to mutual wills: *Re Dale* [1993] 4 All ER 129, 142.

[78] J Penner, *The Law of Trusts*, 5th edn (Oxford, Oxford University Press, 2005) para 6.55.

Act, then the doctrine must be refocused, away from the Wills Act.[79] And indeed, there are a substantial number of cases of *inter vivos* transactions where the statutory formality rules have not been applied, on the same grounds as the testamentary rules have been said not to be applied, that is, that to do so would enable a fraud to be perpetrated. (They are not normally referred to as 'secret' trusts, but they might well be, as this would devalue the somewhat emotive use of the term to its true proportions: every trust is in some sense a secret, because it is engrafted onto the conscience of the legal owner, and it is an accident if the information about the existence of the trust is ever made public.)

These cases include *Cottington v Fletcher*[80] in the eighteenth century, *Lincoln v Wright*,[81] *Davies v Otty (No 2)*,[82] *Booth v Turle*,[83] *Re Duke of Marlborough*[84] and *Rochefoucauld v Bousted*[85] in the nineteenth century, and *Bannister v Bannister*[86] and *Hodgson v Marks*[87] in the twentieth. One of them, indeed, *Rochefoucauld v Bousted*, is the subject of a chapter in this book by William Swadling,[88] and so I will say very little about these cases. The most important thing is that I agree with him that these cases are not constructive trusts at all. They are *express* trusts, intended by the parties to create trusts, and are not prevented from achieving that aim by any requirement of formality, because the only possible such requirement—the Statute of Frauds, section 7, or now the Law of Property Act 1925, section 53(1)(b)—does not apply, on the basis that otherwise it would enable a fraud to be perpetrated.[89]

The disapplication of the statute is a relatively easy matter to justify when there are only two parties involved—as there were in all the cases just mentioned. A and B agreed that if A were to transfer land to B, B would hold it on trust for A. Since there is no compliance with the formalities rules, there is an implied understanding that B will not set up the statute against A. There is an estoppel-like principle at work, preventing B thereafter from setting up the statute. And the fraud in defeating the trust enures directly for B's benefit.[90]

---

[79] Secret trust cases often say that such trusts take effect '*dehors* the will': *Cullen v AG for Ireland* (1866) LR 1 HL 190, 198; *Re Young* [1951] Ch 344, 350. But cf Hodge (n 75).
[80] (1740) 2 Atk 155, 26 ER 498.
[81] (1859) 4 De J & G 16, 45 ER 6.
[82] (1865) 35 Beav 208, 55 ER 875.
[83] (1873) LR 16 Eq 182.
[84] [1894] 2 Ch 133.
[85] [1897] 1 Ch 197, CA.
[86] [1948] 2 All ER 133, CA.
[87] [1971] Ch 892, CA.
[88] See ch 3.
[89] It is a complication that in some cases the judges who rely on the principle that equity will not allow the statute to be used as an instrument of fraud sometimes go on also to rely on s 53(2) of the Law of Property Act 1925, on the basis that this is a 'constructive' trust: eg *Davies* (n 81); *Bannister* (n 85); *Hodgson* (n 86). However, that is just inconsistent and wrong. It is one or the other; it cannot be both simultaneously.
[90] For an early example, see *Thynn v Thynn* (1684) 1 Vern 296, 23 ER 479.

It is more difficult to see how the same principle can be applied in three party cases, that is, where A and B agree that A will transfer land to B to be held on trust for C. A and B may have an understanding, but C is no party to it. B may be 'estopped' against A from raising the statute as a defence, but not as against C. If B does not perform the trust, but keeps the property for himself, A loses nothing. As against him, there is no fraud. That has not stopped some judges, such as Lord Denning, from purporting to make use of the same principle in three party cases, such as *Neale v Willis*[91] and *Binions v Evans*.[92]

It is a question how far the same principle can apply in testamentary cases.[93] On the face of it, a testamentary ('secret') trust is a three-party case rather than a two-party one. But if I am right, the only cases where the testamentary secret trust doctrine—as opposed to the principle that equity will not allow, etc—needs to be applied is where there is a gift of land. Looking at the cases, this is actually very rare.[94] Most testamentary secret trust cases concern pure personalty. On the other hand, if the principle that equity will not allow, etc, can apply to three-party cases, then it also solves the testamentary trust cases, and so the separate testamentary secret trust doctrine is unnecessary.

G. LIMITATION OF ACTIONS: EXPRESS TRUSTS AND CONSTRUCTIVE TRUSTS

A further area in which, historically, the distinction between express and constructive trusts may have had a part to play relates to that of limitation of actions. In fact William Swadling has already surveyed this area too,[95] and there has also been a comprehensive Law Commission Consultation Paper.[96] So I can be brief.

As is well known, the statutes of limitation originally had no application to claims in respect of uses and trusts.[97] However, there was the equitable doctrine of laches to take into account.[98] This enabled the Court of Chancery on the grounds of severe delay to refuse relief to a plaintiff otherwise entitled to it.

The Trustee Act 1888, section 8, for the first time sought to govern the limitation of claims concerning trusts and trustees. It was replaced in

---

[91] (1968) 19 P & CR 836, CA.
[92] [1972] Ch 359, CA.
[93] See also *Re Goodchild* (n 15) 1230 (Morritt LJ), refusing to extend the *Rosset* principle to property owned by the second party to die in a mutual wills dispute.
[94] An example is *Ottaway v Norman* [1972] Ch 698, where the point was not mentioned.
[95] W Swadling, 'Limitation' in P Birks and A Pretto (eds), *Breach of Trust* (Oxford, Hart Publishing, 2002) 319.
[96] Law Commission, *Limitation of Actions* (LCCP No 151, 1998).
[97] Eg *Burdick v Garrick* (1870) LR 5 Ch App 233; *Edwards v Warden* (1876) 1 App Cas 281.
[98] A recent exposition is contained in *Nelson v Rye* [1996] 1 WLR 1378.

substance by the Limitation Act 1939, section 19, and then by the Limitation Act 1980, section 21, the statute currently in force.

The position was well explained by Millett LJ in *Paragon Finance plc v D B Thakerar & Co (a firm)* as follows:

> Before 1890, when the Trustee Act 1888 came into operation, a claim against an express trustee was never barred by lapse of time. The Court of Chancery had developed the rule that, in the absence of laches or acquiescence, such a trustee was accountable without limit of time. The rule was confirmed by s 25(3) of the Supreme Court of Judicature Act 1873, which provided that no claim by a cestui que trust against his trustee for any property held on an express trust, or in respect of any breach of such trust, should be held to be barred by any statute of limitation.
>
> The explanation for the rule was that the possession of an express trustee is never in virtue of any right of his own but is taken from the first for and on behalf of the beneficiaries. His possession was consequently treated as the possession of the beneficiaries, with the result that time did not run in his favour against them: see the classic judgment of Lord Redesdale in *Hovenden v Lord Annesley* (1806) 2 Sch & Lef 607 at 633–634.
>
> The rule did not depend upon the nature of the trustee's appointment, and it was applied to trustees de son tort and to directors and other fiduciaries who, though not strictly trustees, were in an analogous position and who abused the trust and confidence reposed in them to obtain their principal's property for themselves. Such persons are properly described as constructive trustees.
>
> Regrettably, however, the expressions 'constructive trust' and 'constructive trustee' have been used by equity lawyers to describe two entirely different situations. The first covers those cases already mentioned, where the defendant, though not expressly appointed as trustee, has assumed the duties of a trustee by a lawful transaction which was independent of and preceded the breach of trust and is not impeached by the plaintiff. The second covers those cases where the trust obligation arises as a direct consequence of the unlawful transaction which is impeached by the plaintiff.
>
> A constructive trust arises by operation of law whenever the circumstances are such that it would be unconscionable for the owner of property (usually but not necessarily the legal estate) to assert his own beneficial interest in the property and deny the beneficial interest of another. In the first class of case, however, the constructive trustee really is a trustee. He does not receive the trust property in his own right but by a transaction by which both parties intend to create a trust from the outset and which is not impugned by the plaintiff. His possession of the property is coloured from the first by the trust and confidence by means of which he obtained it, and his subsequent appropriation of the property to his own use is a breach of that trust. . . .
>
> The second class of case is different. It arises when the defendant is implicated in a fraud. Equity has always given relief against fraud by making any person sufficiently implicated in the fraud accountable in equity. In such a case he is traditionally though I think unfortunately described as a constructive trustee and said to be 'liable to account as constructive trustee'. Such a person is not in fact a trustee at all, even though he may be liable to account as if he were. He never

assumes the position of a trustee, and if he receives the trust property at all it is adversely to the plaintiff by an unlawful transaction which is impugned by the plaintiff. In such a case the expressions 'constructive trust' and 'constructive trustee' are misleading, for there is no trust and usually no possibility of a proprietary remedy; they are 'nothing more than a formula for equitable relief': *Selangor United Rubber Estates Ltd v Cradock (No 3)* [1968] 2 All ER 1073 at 1097, [1968] 1 WLR 1555 at 1582 per Ungoed-Thomas J.[99]

Thus although there has been a difference between the limitation rules for express trusts and constructive trusts, it applied only where the constructive trust was non-proprietary, that is, in the words of Ungoed-Thomas J 'nothing more than a formula for equitable relief'. Where the constructive trust bit upon a particular asset from the beginning, the position so far as limitation was concerned was the same as for an express trust.

H. PROPRIETARY ESTOPPEL AND THE COMMON INTENTION CONSTRUCTIVE TRUST

This part of the chapter—rather a cuckoo in the nest, I am afraid—is about the development of the doctrines of proprietary estoppel and common intention constructive trust. The phrase 'proprietary estoppel' itself appears to be of recent coinage. As far as I have been able to discover, it was first used in an English law context only in 1966, in a section (so headed) of chapter 7, itself entitled 'Equitable Estoppel', of the 26th edition of *Snell's Equity*, by RE Megarry QC and Paul Baker.[100] By that route it was then taken up in the well-known decision of the Court of Appeal in *ER Ives Investment Ltd v High*,[101] and its career was made. The phrase 'common intention constructive trust' is even more recent. It seems to have been first used in English academic writing only in 1988,[102] and in an English judicial decision only in 1999.[103] But in each case the label used is more recent

---

[99] [1999] 1 All ER 400, CA.

[100] EHT Snell, *Principles of Equity*, ed RE Megarry QC and P Baker, 26th edn (London, Sweet & Maxwell, 1966). The chapter was new in that edition. Megarry and Baker had in fact edited two earlier editions, and Megarry another before that. Curiously, the equally famous work on *The Law of Real Property* by Megarry and Wade for the first to fifth editions treated this area of law as part of the law of licences in relation to land, and it was left to Charles Harpum in the 6th edition of 2000 to introduce a chapter entitled 'Proprietary Estoppel'. Conversely, Kevin Gray (later Kevin Gray and Susan Francis Gray), *Elements of Land Law*, for the first two editions (1987 and 1993) had a chapter called 'Proprietary Estoppel', but in the third (2001) and subsequent editions treated the topic as part of a chapter on 'Informal Creation of Rights in Land'.

[101] [1967] 2 QB 379.

[102] DJ Hayton, 'Remedial Constructive Trusts of Homes: An Overseas View' [1988] *Conveyancer and Property Lawyer* 259.

[103] *Mollo v Mollo*, 8 October 1999, Chancery Division (Ian Hunter QC sitting as a deputy High Court judge).

than the principle at work. We must try to escape the straitjacket of arid terminological disputes, and concentrate on the substance behind the label. As Lord Walker said recently in *Thorner v Major*, 'the terminology and taxonomy of this part of the law are . . . far from uniform'.[104]

For reasons that will become apparent, we need to begin our discussion some distance away from those doctrines. I therefore ask the reader to be patient.

1. Proprietary Estoppel

Before dealing with the doctrine of *proprietary* estoppel, I must first say a few words about estoppel itself. The principle of representational estoppel at common law is one typically concerned with statements of fact. If A asserts a fact, intending B to rely on it, and B does so to his potential detriment, A will not be allowed to assert differently in subsequent proceedings, at least so long as the detriment cannot be removed.[105] But the same principle has also operated in relation to the assertion of the presence or absence of property rights. These may well amount to representations of *law*,[106] although, as judges sometimes used to say, a question of private rights is a question of fact.[107] Typically they involve the owner of an estate or interest in property positively representing to another person (intending that he should rely upon it) either that the representor has *no* interest, or that the representee in fact *has* an interest, in the same property.[108] The representee in fact relies on that representation to his detriment, and the representor is held to be unable later to assert his own interest as against—and in priority to—the representee, at least unless and until the detriment can be reversed. Because the representation is effected by a positive statement, it is not necessary that the representor know of his own rights. He should have stayed silent, or said he did not know, and not made

---

[104] [2009] UKHL 18, [2009] 1 WLR 776 [67]. See also, to the same effect, *Birmingham Midshires Mortgage Services Ltd v Sabherwal* (1999) 80 P & CR 256 (CA) [29]. In his lecture to the London Common Law and Commercial Bar Association on 9 June 2009, Lord Neuberger said (at para 35) that 'proprietary estoppel is often called equitable estoppel', as indeed Hoffmann LJ called it in *Walton v Walton*, CA 14 April 2004, [21].

[105] *Freeman v Cooke* (1848) 2 Exch 654, 154 ER 652.

[106] See *De Tchibatschef v Salerni Coupling Ltd* [1932] 1 Ch 330; *Algar v Middlesex County Council* [1945] 2 All ER 243.

[107] See eg *Cooper v Phibbs* (1867) LR 2 HL 149, 170; *Eaglesfield v Marquis of Londonderry* (1876) 4 Ch D 693, 703; *Andre et Cie v Ets Michel Blanc et Fils* [1979] 2 Lloyds Rep 427, 431 and 432; *Taylors Fashions Ltd v Liverpool Victoria Trustees Co Ltd* [1982] QB 133, 157–8.

[108] *Hunt v Carew* (1629) Nels 46, 21 ER 786; *Edlin v Battaly* (1675) 2 Lev 152, 83 ER 494; *Evans v Bicknell* (1801) 6 Ves Jun 174, 31 ER 998; *Burrowes v Lock* (1805) 10 Ves Jun 470, 32 ER 927; *Pickard v Sears* (1837) 6 Ad & El 469, 112 ER 179; *Re Foster (No 2)* [1938] 3 All ER 610 (common mistake involving cross-representations); *Hopgood v Brown* [1955] 1 All ER 550, CA.

the positive statement.[109] Even though they concern property rights, these are but sophisticated variations of ordinary estoppels, and do not help us.

There is then a related group of cases which operate in equity only. These are where the 'representor', knowing of his own rights, and knowing of the mistaken belief of the 'representee' that the former has no rights or that the latter has some, says nothing to the latter, but stands by and is aware that the 'representee' is acting to his detriment in reliance on that mistaken belief.[110] Of course the 'representor' makes no representation at all. But equity treats him as if he had, for it considers that in the circumstances he had a duty to speak.[111] Undoubtedly there is a relationship here with the equitable doctrines of laches and acquiescence.[112] But these cases—unlike those of laches and acquiescence—do not merely provide a defence to a claim. They actually enable a claim to be made which, were it not for the 'estoppel', could not have been made at all.

One of the most famous of the cases in this group is *Willmott v Barber*,[113] where Fry J set out five conditions (or 'probanda')[114] which had to be satisfied for this kind of estoppel to be raised. However, the classic statement usually quoted is that of Lord Cranworth LC in the earlier House of Lords case of *Ramsden v Dyson*:

> If a stranger begins to build on my land supposing it to be his own, and I, perceiving his mistake, abstain from setting him right, and leave him to persevere in his error, a court of equity will not allow me afterwards to assert my title to the land on which he had expended money on the supposition that the land was his own. It considers that, when I saw the mistake into which he had fallen, it was

---

[109] See *Sarat Chunder Dey v Gopal Chunder Laha* (1892) LR 19 Ind App 203, 216 (Lord Shand); *Re Eaves* [1940] Ch 109, 117–18; *Taylors Fashions* (n 106) 150–51.

[110] *Hunsden v Cheyney* (1690) 2 Vern 150, 23 ER 703; *Short v Taylor* (c 1693–1700), cited 2 Eq Cas Abr 522, 22 ER 441; *Huning v Ferrers* (1711) Gilb Rep 85, 25 ER 59; *Savage v Foster* (1723) 9 Mod 35, 88 ER 299; *Steed v Whitaker* (1740) Barn C 220, 27 ER 621; *East India Co v Vincent* (1740) 2 Atk 83, 26 ER 451; *A-G v Baliol College Oxford* (1748) 9 Mod 407, 88 ER 538; *Stiles v Cowper* (1748) 3 Atk 692, 26 ER 1198; *Brydges v Kilburne* (1792), cited 5 Ves Jun 689, 31 ER 807; 6 Ves Jun 107, 31 ER 961; *Kenney v Brown* (1796) 3 Ridg PC 462, 518; *Jackson v Cator* (1800) 5 Ves Jun 688, 31 ER 806; *Dann v Spurrier* (1802) 7 Ves Jun 231, 32 ER 94; *Lord Cawdor v Lewis* (1835) 1 Y & C Ex 427, 160 ER 174; *Rochdale Canal Company v King* (1853) 16 Beav 630, 51 ER 924; *Mold v Wheatcroft* (1853) 27 Beav 510, 54 ER 202; *Ramsden v Dyson* (1866) LR 1 HL 129; *Davies v Sear* (1869) LR 7 Eq 427; *Willmott v Barber* (1880) 15 Ch D 96, 105–06; *Falcke v Scottish Imperial Insurance Co* (1887) 34 Ch D 234 (CA) 242–43; *Re Foster (No 2)* (n 107) 613. Cf *Master etc of Clare Hall v Harding* (1848) 6 Hare 273, 67 ER 1169 (alleged 'representor' made claim to property before detriment incurred); *Armstrong v Sheppard & Short Ltd* [1959] 2 QB 384 (alleged 'representor' did not know of own rights).

[111] *Taylors Fashions* (n 106) 147.

[112] See eg *Shaw v Applegate* [1977] 1 WLR 970, CA.

[113] *Willmott* (n 109).

[114] In summary form these are: (1) mistake by the claimant as to his legal rights; (2) action by the claimant in reliance on the mistake; (3) knowledge by the owner of his own rights, inconsistent with those claimed by the claimant; (4) knowledge by the owner of the claimant's mistake; (5) encouragement of the claimant by the owner, or abstinence by the owner from alerting him to his mistake.

my duty to be active and to state my adverse title; and that it would be dishonest in me to remain wilfully passive on such an occasion, in order afterwards to profit by the mistake which I might have prevented.[115]

It was some of these 'failure to speak' cases that were cited by Megarry and Baker in the 1966 edition of *Snell's Equity* as exemplifying the newly coined doctrine of 'proprietary estoppel'.[116] It will, however, be seen that they are an extension of, though not different in principle from, the positive statement estoppels discussed above.[117] The critical difference is the need for the true owner to realise that he has rights which are being infringed. Hence Fry J's third and fourth probanda in *Wilmott v Barber*, which therefore are unnecessary in any case of *positive* representation.[118]

For myself, I would be reluctant to describe either class of case as giving rise to any kind of constructive trust.[119] Normally they do not split titles, as trusts do, but either leave the 'representee' with in effect the interest he thought he had, or prevent the 'representor' from asserting the interest he in fact had. At best, if they do split titles, they could give rise to rights secured by an equitable lien on the legal estate.[120] Robert Walker LJ may have been thinking of this distinction in *Yaxley v Gotts* where he said:

> Plainly there are large areas where the two concepts [ie estoppel and constructive trust] do not overlap: when a landowner stands by while his neighbour mistakenly builds on the former's land the situation is far removed (except for the element of unconscionable conduct) from that of a fiduciary who derives an improper advantage from his client.[121]

Modern practice seems, however, to use the phrase 'proprietary estoppel' in a different sense from that in the 1966 edition of *Snell*. This is to cover, not so much cases where the 'representation' (positive or negative) was about what rights a person *did or did not have*, but instead cases about whether or not the 'representee' *would acquire any in the future*.[122] In simple terms, the former group of cases were about *proposi-*

---

[115] *Ramsden* (n 109) 140–01. See, in very similar words, and to the same effect, Lord Wensleydale at 168; Lord Westbury (at 174) simply agreed with Lord Cranworth. Lord Kingsdown dissented on the facts, and hence did not deal with this point—his (equally famous) statement of law, focusing on his different view of the facts, is dealt with later.
[116] Snell, 26th edn (n 99) 629, n 33.
[117] See *De Bussche v Alt* (1878) 8 Ch D 286 (CA) 314; G Spencer Bower, *The Law Relating to Estoppel by Representation*, ed Sir AK Turner, 3rd edn (London, Butterworths, 1977) para 290.
[118] Spencer Bower and Turner (n 116) para 293.
[119] See also *Anderson Antiques (UK) Ltd v Anderson (Wharf (Hull) Ltd* [2007] EWHC 2086 (Ch) [30].
[120] See eg *Neesom v Clarkson* (1844) 4 Hare 97, 67 ER 576; *Unity Joint Stock Mutual Banking Assoc v King* (1858) 25 Beav 72, 53 ER 563; *Re Foster (No 2)* [1938] 3 All ER 610.
[121] [2000] Ch 162 (CA) 176.
[122] Although in *Taylors Fashions* (n 106) 150, Oliver J, and in *Re Basham* [1986] 1 WLR 1498, the deputy judge, Edward Nugee QC, used the expression to cover *both* situations. This was perhaps a transitional phase, as it corresponds to what I learned as a student during the late 1970s.

tions of property rights, and the latter about *promises* or *expectations* of rights. In the latter kind of case, the 'representee' (more properly, *promisee*)[123] is under no illusion as to what the legal position actually is. The 'error' (if that is an appropriate word) lies in his expectation as to what it will be in the future.[124]

Cases in the latter group are hard to find before the mid-nineteenth century. What are easier to find are cases dealing with what appears to be a very similar principle,[125] namely that of the old equitable doctrine of part performance. I have already[126] referred to this doctrine, preserved in 1925[127] but widely thought to have been consigned to oblivion in 1989.[128] It allowed a plaintiff bringing a suit in equity for specific performance of an alleged contract to escape the constraints of section 4 of the Statute of Frauds 1677. Given that a generation of lawyers in England has now grown up that knows nothing of this doctrine, it is necessary to spend a few moments on this.

Section 4 formerly provided that

> no action shall be brought to charge any person upon any contract or sale of lands, tenements, or hereditaments, or any interest in or concerning them, unless the agreement upon which such action shall be brought, or some memorandum or note thereof, shall be in writing, and signed by the party to be charged therewith, or some other person thereunto by him lawfully authorized.

It will be seen that the section required written evidence of the contract, before it could be enforced by action. Failure to comply did not make the contract void, merely unenforceable by *action*.[129] It could still be enforced in other ways, for example by forfeiting a deposit.[130] The doctrine of part performance, however, provided that the court could decree specific performance of a contract *not* complying with the formality requirements of section 4, *but* which had been 'partly performed'. A great deal of case-law was built up on exactly what constituted such 'part perfomance'. Thus, if the requirements of the doctrine were met, a plaintiff might sue and obtain specific performance not only of a contract in writing which the defendant had not signed, but even of an entirely oral contract.

But the doctrine was an entirely equitable construct. It allowed the

---

[123] In *Herbert v Doyle* [2008] EWHC 1950 (Ch), [2009] WTLR 589, the deputy judge rightly prefers 'promisor' and 'promisee' to the commonly used 'representor' and 'representee': see [16]–[17].
[124] *Taylors Fashions* (n 106) 147.
[125] In *Yaxley* (n 121) 176, Robert Walker LJ said 'At a high level of generality, there is much common ground between the doctrines of proprietary estoppel and the constructive trust, just as there is between proprietary estoppel and part performance.'
[126] See above 10.
[127] Law of Property Act 1925, s 40(2).
[128] That is, by the Law of Property (Miscellaneous Provisions) Act 1989.
[129] *Leroux v Brown* (1852) 12 CB 801, 138 ER 1119.
[130] *Monnickendam v Leanse* (1923) 39 TLR 445.

plaintiff to go to a court of equity to claim specific performance (if the requirements for that remedy were otherwise met). What it did not allow was for the plaintiff to sue for damages at law.[131] Some might have thought this distinction in treatment was down to a mere matter of statutory construction, coupled with a genuflection to the purpose of the Statute of Frauds, that is, to stop English juries being hoodwinked by lying witnesses. For section 4 famously begins[132] 'No *action* shall be brought . . .'. And the word 'action' was formerly apt only—especially in 1677—to describe originating civil process *at law*. The equivalent proceeding in equity was a 'suit', not an action at all. Indeed, the word 'action' in a nineteenth-century statute has been judicially construed as not extending to an admiralty suit.[133] And at that date a suit in equity was not heard before a jury, but instead before a professional judge, the Lord Chancellor (or his deputy) sitting alone. No hoodwinking there, obviously. So the courts of equity might well have said simply that section 4 did not apply to them in considering whether to decree specific performance.[134]

In fact—so far as we know—they did not say that.[135] Instead, they looked at whether the alleged contract had been in part performed. Had it been, in effect, *relied on*? If it had, then the matter was no longer one of pure agreement, covered by the statute. It was now one of fairness, of *equity*.[136] The earliest cases in the books on the subject after the statute date from 1682 onwards, just five years after the statute was enacted. The first cases are tentative, and are concerned with whether or not the oral agreement was to be put in writing.[137] In *Butcher v Stapely*,[138] however, the plaintiff succeeded in proving that he had taken possession of certain land in pursuance of an oral agreement for sale, and had tendered the purchase price, but that the vendor had refused to complete. Indeed, he had instead sold and conveyed the land to a third party, who, however, had had notice of the earlier transaction. The Lord Chancellor set aside the second agreement and decreed that third party to convey the land to the plaintiff upon payment of the price. The practice of the Court of Chancery was affirmed by the House of Lords in *Lester v Foxcroft*[139] in 1700, and continued down to 1989.

---

[131] See *Actionstrength Ltd v International Glass Engineering SpA* [2002] UKHL 17, [2002] 2 AC 541 [47] (Lord Walker).
[132] It is still in force in England in respect of contracts of guarantee (see *Actionstrength* (n 131)) and in other jurisdictions too.
[133] See *The Longford* (1889) 14 PD 34, CA.
[134] See Costigan (n 30) 343–45.
[135] Although cf Lord Nottingham's remarks in *Elliot* quoted in the text to n 40.
[136] Yet it seems that the practice was in fact the same before the Statute of Frauds, which did not effect any change in this respect. Lord Nottinghams's *Prolegomena* (n 42) (written before the statute) makes this clear, in ch 27, s 3.
[137] *Leake v Morris* (1682) 1 Dick 14, 21 ER 171; *Hollis v Whiteing* (1683) 1 Vern 151, 23 ER 380; *Hollis v Edwards* (1683) 1 Vern 159, 23 ER 385.
[138] (1685) 1 Vern 363, 23 ER 524.
[139] (1700) Colles 108, 1 ER 205; 2 Wh & TLC 460.

One issue that took some time to resolve, however, was *why* this worked. Was it that the part performance *proved* the agreement (so the requirement of writing under the Statute of Frauds was redundant and could safely be ignored)? Was it that the reliance on the oral agreement leading a party to change his position made it unconscionable for the non-performing party to insist on the statute? Or was it indeed that the statute was irrelevant, because the claim was not made on the contract at all, but upon a quite independent cause of action?

As I have already indicated, the House of Lords finally resolved this question in *Maddison v Alderson*.[140] In that case a housekeeper alleged after the death of her employer that he had promised to leave her an interest in land by his will, and that she had thereby been induced to remain in his service without remuneration for some years. Her claim failed. Lord Selborne LC, who gave the leading speech, said:

> In a suit founded on such part performance, the defendant is really 'charged' upon the equities resulting from the acts done in execution of the contract, and not (within the meaning of the statute) upon the contract itself. If such equities were excluded, injustice of a kind which the statute cannot be thought to have had in contemplation would follow.[141]

In answer to those who would ask whether this did not in effect set the statute at naught, Lord Selborne said that:

> [I]t is not arbitrary or unreasonable to hold that when the statute says that no action is to be brought to charge any person upon a contract concerning land, it has in view the simple case in which he is charged upon the contract only, and not that in which there are equities resulting from *res gestae* subsequent to and arising out of the contract. So long as the connection of those *res gestae* with the alleged contract does not depend upon mere parol testimony, but is reasonably to be inferred from the *res gestae* themselves, justice seems to require some such limitation of the scope of the statute, which might otherwise interpose an obstacle even to the rectification of material errors, however clearly proved, in an executed conveyance, founded upon an unsigned agreement.[142]

Thus:

> The present case, resting entirely upon the parol evidence of one of the parties to the transaction, after the death of the other, forcibly illustrates the wisdom of the rule, which requires some *evidentia rei* to connect the alleged part performance with the alleged agreement. There is not otherwise enough in the situation in which the parties are found to raise questions which may not be

---

[140] (1883) 8 App Cas 467.
[141] Ibid, 475, cited by Robert Walker LJ in *Jennings v Rice* [2002] EWCA Civ 159, [2003] 1 P & CR 8 [49], and Lord Hoffmann in *Actionstrength* (n 131) [23].
[142] Ibid, 476. In *Steadman v Steadman* [1976] AC 536, 559, Lord Simon said that Lord Selborne's speech achieved 'a complete reconciliation between the provisions of the statute and the doctrine of part performance'.

solved without recourse to equity. It is not enough that an act done should be a condition of, or good consideration for, a contract, unless it is, as between the parties, such a part execution as to change their relative positions as to the subject-matter of the contract.[143]

Lord O'Hagan and Lord Fitzgerald agreed with the reasons and conclusion of the Lord Chancellor.[144] The fourth (and final) member of the House on that occasion was Lord Blackburn. He was not an equity lawyer, but a common lawyer of some distinction. As sometimes happens with distinguished common lawyers, confronted with arcane equitable principle, he played the 'I am only a simple chap' gambit. He confessed to not understanding the principle upon which the cases of part-performance were based,[145] and, if the matter were *res integra*, would have refused to accept the doctrine of part-performance at all.[146] Nonetheless, even he accepted that the parties' conduct might be 'such as to make it inequitable to refuse to complete a contract partly performed', and that in such a case 'the contract may be enforced on the ground of an equity arising from the conduct of the party'.[147]

Thus the part-performance did not have to *prove* the contract, even though it had to be connected with and referable to it. Instead *it had to change the positions of the parties*, so as to raise the 'equity' referred to by the judges. The paradigm case was that of the purchaser of land who paid the purchase price and was let into possession.

The next and crucial aspect of the law is this. If a court of equity would decree specific performance of a promise contained in a bilateral contract unenforceable at law, because of the actions of the promise in relying on the promise by partly performing his side of the bargain, and so changing his position, the question was sure to arise: *was such a contract, or any contract, needed at all?* Now we are getting there. A number of nineteenth-century cases explored and developed this possibility.

First, another well-known part-performance case, *Gregory v Mighell*.[148] The parties agreed by parol for a lease of certain premises to be granted by the defendant to the plaintiff for 21 years at a fair rent to be settled by two independent arbitrators to be chosen by the parties. The plaintiff took possession and spent money on improvements to the land, not required by the terms of the contract. After some eight years, the parties failing to agree on the arbitrators to settle the rent, the defendant brought an action of ejectment at law. The plaintiff sought an injunction to restrain this action, and specific performance of the agreement. Grant MR held that the taking

---

[143] Ibid, 478. See also *Actionstrength* (n 131) [24] (Lord Hoffmann) and [47] (Lord Walker).
[144] Ibid, 483 and 491.
[145] Ibid, 488.
[146] Ibid, 489.
[147] Ibid, 489.
[148] (1811) 18 Ves Jun 328, 34 ER 341.

32 *The Words Which Are Not There*

of possession was a sufficient act of part performance to take the case out of the Statute of Frauds, and that the plaintiff succeeded. The rent could be directed to be assessed by the master on the same basis as the arbitrators. But he added this:

> I do not conceive, that the Defendant is now at liberty to say, it was a possession, that had no reference to the agreement; as he permitted the Plaintiff to remain in possession, and to make expenditure upon the land for eight years, before he brought an ejectment. He must have known, that the expenditure was made upon the faith of the agreement; and I cannot now permit him to turn round, and say, the Plaintiff bas been possessing merely as a trespasser as he must be, if his possession is not to be referred to the agreement.[149]

The references to expenditure being 'made on the faith of the agreement', to the knowledge of the defendant, were not relied on as acts of part performance. Nor could they be, as they were no part of the bargain. Yet they plainly weighed with the judge. A seed had been sown. Every good lawyer looking at leading part-performance cases would see this, and wonder if he could make use of it for his client.

Jump forward 40 years. The best young lawyers of the time of *Gregory v Mighell* were now senior judges. In *Maunsell v White*,[150] for example, a nephew looking to marry had sought from his rich uncle either a settlement or an assurance that he would leave part of his real estate to him. The uncle had refused to make a settlement, but represented to his nephew that he had already (some time before) made his will in the nephew's favour. This representation was communicated to the intended bride's guardians, who thereupon consented to the marriage. Uncle and nephew later became estranged, and the uncle changed his will, so that the nephew received nothing. On the death of the uncle, an attempt was made to hold his estate liable. It failed on the facts, as it was clear to all the judges that the uncle by making the representation as to having made the will was not engaging himself to leave any property to the nephew, and he was not aware that the nephew and his bride's guardians were treating it as an engagement.

But Lord St Leonards put forward this general proposition of equity, as though it were obvious, and even though not made out on the facts of this case:

> It is not my intention to go into the general question of equity. I do not dispute the general principle, that what is called a representation, which is made as an inducement for another to act upon it, and is followed by his acting upon it, will, especially in such a case as marriage, be deemed to be a contract. If a party will hold out a representation as a condition on which a marriage, may take

---

[149] Ibid, 18 Ves Jun 333.
[150] (1854) 4 HLC 1039, 10 ER 769.

place, and the marriage does take place upon it, he must give effect to that representation.[151]

It will be noted that Lord St Leonards used the word 'representation' to mean 'promise' or 'engagement'. He also put the doctrine in very general terms, and did not confine it to promises concerning land, or indeed any kind of property. However, the facts of that case concerned land, and it was also settled that the doctrine of part-performance was confined to cases concerning land. So it may be that Lord St Leonards was impliedly limiting himself in the same way. The important thing is that he saw a promise *intended to be and in fact relied upon* as being enforceable in equity as if it were a contract.[152]

Again, in *Jorden v Money*,[153] an attempt was made to enforce against the holder of a bond a 'representation' that she had no intention of enforcing it against the debtor, given at a time when the debtor was contemplating marriage (which he then undertook). Again the claim failed. There were in effect two grounds of claim. One was that the representation being relied on founded an estoppel *in pais*, or estoppel by representation, so that the bondholder had to make good her representation. The other was that the representation amounted to a promise, which should be enforced as a contract. In this case, however, we should notice that, whether this was a representation or a promise, it did *not* concern land. The majority of the House of Lords (three judges out of four) disposed of the case in two holdings. The first was that the doctrine of estoppel *by representation* only came into play when the representation was of an existing fact, and this was a representation not of an existing fact but of future conduct.[154] The second was that, properly understood, the bondholder had expressly declined to make any promise which could be relied on, insisting instead that the debtor *should trust her to her honour*.[155]

Lord St Leonards, however, dissented, both as to what the evidence

---

[151] Ibid, 4 HLC 1059–60. A curiosity of the case is that the appeal to the House of Lords was brought from a decree of Sir Edward Sugden (later Lord St Leonards) as Lord Chancellor of Ireland. The case took some ten years to come on before the House.

[152] The case may also be significant as the first case it which the proprietary estoppel principle was argued to involve an obligation to leave some or all of a deceased's estate to the plaintiff. *Loffus v Maw* (1862) 3 Giff 592, 66 ER 654, is also a case of this kind, where the plaintiff succeeded, albeit on the basis of faulty reasoning (ie that the 'promise' was a representation of fact): see *Maddison* (n 139) 473 and 483. Cf *Re Basham* [1986] 1 WLR 1498.

[153] (1854) 5 HLC 185, 10 ER 868.

[154] Ibid, 5 HLC 214–15 (Lord Cranworth LC) and 225–26 (Lord Brougham). Note that Lord Cranworth had been one of the Lords Justices in Chancery from whom the appeal was brought.

[155] Ibid, 221–22 and 223 (Lord Cranworth LC) and 228–29 (Lord Brougham). In *Thorner* (n 38) [53] Lord Walker suggested that *Ramsden v Dyson* contained 'the first references to the notion that an arrangement which is expressly and deliberately acknowledged to be a "gentleman's agreement" may not be capable of giving rise to an estoppel'. But *Jorden v Money* is older by more than a decade.

proved, and hence also as to what the case was about. As to the facts, he held that the bondholder *was* making a promise which was intended to, and therefore could, be relied on. As to the law, he argued for a wider principle, subsuming both representations of fact and promises as to future conduct, and applying not only to land but also (at least) to property other than land such as bonds:

> I think it is utterly immaterial whether it is a misrepresentation of fact, as it actually existed, or a misrepresentation of an intention to do, or to abstain from doing, an act which would lead to the damage of the party whom you thereby induced to deal in marriage or in purchase, or in anything of that sort, upon the faith of that representation. . . .
>
> What is the principle upon which the cases have proceeded? The principle is simply this, that you shall not be allowed, either in a court of equity or in a court of law, to misrepresent the state of circumstances in which property exists, so as to deceive parties and induce them to rely upon your statement, and to deal with matters of the utmost importance; for example, as in this case, with a marriage settlement, or in the purchase of property, which is a very common case. . . .
>
> [Y]our Lordships are asked to consider that a representation of an intention is not a binding act, and that you cannot misrepresent what you intend to do. But, if you declare your intention with reference, for example, to a marriage, not, to enforce a given right, and the marriage takes place on that declaration, I submit that, in point of law, that is a binding undertaking.[156]

As to the law, this was entirely consistent with his statement in *Maunsell v White*, quoted earlier. It was also not inconsistent with the statements of the other judges in this case. The difference with them was simply on the facts. Did the bondholder intend to make a promise intended to be binding on her and *on which the debtor could rely in future*? They held that she did not, and hence there was no factual basis for holding that she was prevented from suing on the bond. The question whether the law extended as far as Lord St Leonards considered, and in particular whether promises as to pure personalty stood on the same footing in equity as promises as to land when relied on, on their view simply did not arise for decision.

A further, tantalising step was taken in 1859 by Page Wood VC[157] in *Laird v Birkenhead Railway Co*.[158] The plaintiff, a shipbuilder, wished to connect his yard with the defendant's railway by building a private branch-line through a tunnel under a public roadway. The directors of the defendant approved his plans in principle. His detailed plans were submitted to the defendant's engineer, altered in part at his suggestion, and then approved by him. The shipbuilder constructed the tunnel according to the plans, and the defendant company laid rails through it. Once it was

---

[156] Ibid, 5 HLC 185, 248, 249 and 251–52.
[157] Later Lord Hatherley LC.
[158] (1859) Johns 500, 70 ER 519.

completed, however, the defendant company refused to allow the shipbuilder to run trains onto the defendant's railway until a detailed agreement had been entered into between the parties, covering inter alia the defendant's power of control over the traffic, the term of the agreement and the tolls to be paid. Negotiations took several weeks, at the end of which the plaintiff and the defendant's chairman and general manager were *ad idem* on the terms, and the general manager produced a memorandum. But no formal agreement was ever entered into between the plaintiff and the defendant company. For two and a half years the branch-line was used and the plaintiff made payments to the defendant for the use of the connection. In October 1859 the relationship broke down and the defendant refused to permit traffic over their line from the branch. The plaintiff claimed specific performance of the parol agreement between the parties and the grant of an appropriate right of way.

At first sight the case looks like an ordinary case of part performance of a parol agreement otherwise caught by the Statute of Frauds, and not signed on behalf of the defendant company by two directors, as required by company law. And that is how the case was framed, and pleaded. The defendant however pointed out that the acts of so-called part performance, that is, the construction of the tunnel and the laying of rails to join up to the defendant's railway, were not actually performing any agreement, since at that date none existed, even orally.[159] The defendant had agreed in principle to the connection, but much of importance remained to be agreed between the parties. It was similar to the position in *Crabb v Arun DC*,[160] where Crabb had been told by the council that he could in principle have the right of way, but no terms had been agreed by the time he sold off the land adjoining the highway, and so landlocked himself.[161]

Page Wood VC, however, said:

> In this state of things, when all the works were completed, the solicitor of the company writes the letter of the 2d. of February 1857, stating that he is instructed by the directors to say that the user of the branch is not to commence until a definite understanding should be come to respecting it. Here I pause to consider what were the rights of the Plaintiff at this moment. It might be very proper for the company to send such a letter as that of the 2d. of February, but I have great doubts whether it would have been competent for them, after all that

---

[159] Ibid, Johns 506 and 508.
[160] [1976] Ch 179, CA. It is perhaps surprising that *Laird* was not cited in *Crabb*.
[161] The recent case of *Yeoman's Row Management v Cobbe* [2008] UKHL 55, [2008] 1 WLR 1752, where a businessman failed in a claim for proprietary estoppel after relying on an agreement in principle (because it was indefinite) seems at first sight to be inconsistent with both cases: T Etherton, 'Constructive Trusts and Proprietary Estoppel: The Search for Clarity and Principle' [2009] *Conveyancer and Property Lawyer* 104, 118. Yet Lord Scott for the majority in *Cobbe* approved *Crabb* and *Laird*. The point, however, was that in *Cobbe* the promisor declined to give an assurance that could be relied on as a matter of law (as opposed to honour).

had taken place, to say, 'Unless we come to terms the rails must be taken up.' Where one set of persons have said to another, 'You desire to construct expensive works for purposes which will require our consent. We allow you to incur this outlay'—I have grave doubts, looking to the authorities, whether these persons, after having allowed the money to be laid out on the faith of the plan being carried out on reasonable terms, can be permitted to say, 'The terms must be such as we dictate; we are masters of the situation, and all your expenditure must go for nothing unless we can agree about the terms'.[162]

However, the judge did not rest his decision on this ground, for he held that the inchoate agreement of the parties had been rendered choate by the two and a half years of being put into effect, thereby settling the question of the reasonable terms on which the connection was to be permitted. So it was treated—perhaps rather unsatisfactorily—as a contract case after all.

It was left to Lord Westbury LC, three years later, to produce the definitive decision on the point, in *Dillwyn v Llewelyn*.[163] In this case a father made his will in 1847 leaving his real estate to trustees for his wife for her life, then to their son for his life, then for their son's son or sons, as the son should appoint, with further remainders over. In 1853 the father at the instance of the wife made an informal gift of a particular piece of land to the son, for the purpose of his building himself a house upon it. The son took possession, and, with the father's knowledge and approval, spent some £14,000 on building a residence there. But no conveyance of the land was ever made to the son. In 1855 the father died. The wife was willing that the son be regarded as the absolute owner of the particular land, notwithstanding the terms of the will. But since minors were also interested, the matter had to be 'narrowly examined' by the court.

Lord Westbury LC dealt with the matter in stages. First he set out the conventional view of an imperfect gift:

> A voluntary agreement will not be completed or assisted by a Court of Equity, in cases of mere gift. If anything be wanting to complete the title of the donee, a Court of Equity will not assist him in obtaining it; for a mere donee can have no right to claim more than he has received.[164]

Then he noted an important exception:

> But the subsequent acts of the donor may give the donee that right or ground of claim which he did not acquire from the original gift. Thus, if A. gives a house to B. but makes no formal conveyance, and the house is afterwards, on the marriage of B. included, with the knowledge of A. in the marriage settlement of B.

---

[162] *Laird* (n 158) Johns 510–11.
[163] (1862) 4 De G F & J 517, 45 ER 1285. In his 2009 lecture (n 104), Lord Neuberger said it was in *Ramsden v Dyson*. But he appears to have overlooked *Dillwyn v Llewelyn*, three years earlier. In *Sen v Headley* [1991] Ch 425 (CA) 439, Nourse LJ said that the doctrine of proprietary estoppel could not be dated before *Dillwyn*.
[164] Ibid, 4 De G F & J 521.

A. would be bound to complete the title of the parties claiming under that settlement.[165]

Next he moved to the facts of the present case:

> So if A. puts B. in possession of a piece of land, and tells him, 'I give it to you that, you may build a house on it,' and B. on the strength of that promise, with the knowledge of A. expends a large sum of money in building a house accordingly, I cannot doubt that the donee acquires a right from the subsequent transaction to call on the donor to perform that contract and complete the imperfect donation which was made.[166]

In support he cited a single authority, from the law of part performance, *but only by way of analogy*:

> The case is somewhat analogous to that of verbal agreement not binding originally for the want of the memorandum in writing signed by the party to be charged, but which becomes binding by virtue of the subsequent part performance. The early case of *Foxcroft v Lester* (2 Vern. 456), decided by the House of Lords, is an example nearly approaching to the terms of the present case.[167]

Next he pointed out that, as with part performance, the equity arose only on the detriment being suffered, and not earlier:

> The equity of the donee and the estate to be claimed by virtue of it depend on the transaction, that is, on the acts done, and not on the language of the memorandum, except as that shews the purpose and intent of the gift.[168]

Lastly he made plain his view that on the evidence the father's intention was to give the son the fee simple and not a mere life estate:

> The estate was given as the site of a dwelling-house to be erected by the son. The ownership of the dwelling-house and the ownership of the estate must be considered as intended to be co-extensive and co-equal. No one builds a house for his own life only, and it is absurd to suppose that it was intended by either party that the house, at the death of the son, should become the property of the father.[169]

Thus the son was entitled to a conveyance of the fee simple to make good the imperfect gift. It is important to notice that, although at certain points in his judgment Lord Westbury refers to 'contract' and to the language of contract, he is not suggesting that there actually was a contract in this case. (Nor do contemporary commentators, who generally look on it as

---

[165] Ibid.
[166] Ibid.
[167] Ibid, 521–22.
[168] Ibid, 522, cited by Robert Walker LJ in *Jennings* (n 141) [49], but unfortunately mistaking the reference to dependence on 'the transaction, that is, the acts done', as supporting an *evaluation of the detriment* going to proportionality of response, rather than as to the timing of the *accrual of the right* (which is on the incurring of detriment, and not the writing of the memorandum).
[169] Ibid, 4 De G F & J 522.

a case of imperfect gift.)[170] This is not a case of a promise, but of a failed gift. True, nineteenth-century lawyers construed a failed conveyance as an agreement to convey.[171] The proposition of Lord St Leonards in *Maunsell v White*, quoted above, though not cited in this case, is likely to have been well known to Lord Westbury, for he, as Sir Richard Bethell S-G, had been counsel for the unsuccessful appellant in that case. The structure of the judgment, and in particular the reference to *Foxcroft v Lester*, shows that Lord Westbury saw both part-performance and the principle at work in this case as proceeding from a common source. This was that where a promise to convey land was intended to be relied on,[172] and *was* relied on, that raised an equity in the intended transferee to have the promise made good. And this was quite distinct from the question whether there was a *contract* of which specific performance could be granted.[173]

The following year we see Lord Cranworth LC, sitting on appeal from the Master of the Rolls, in *Nunn v Fabian*.[174] A landlord verbally agreed with a yearly tenant to grant him a 21-year lease of the premises at an increased rent, with the option of purchasing the freehold. The landlord died before executing the lease, but after accepting rent at the increased rate. Unlike *Dillwyn v Llewelyn*, there was an oral contract here, and the case was argued and decided as a part-performance case. But there was another element. After the oral agreement, the tenant laid out about double his rent on improving the building, though—as in the case of *Laird*—this was no part of their agreement. He relied on this as part performance. Lord Cranworth said:

> Now, I do not think we can exactly call this part performance. The parol agreement was embodied in the lease, which is silent about the alterations. But although it was not part performance, it is important as showing that there was an agreement for a lease. No yearly tenant would have spent that amount of money in improving the front of his house without some such agreement as is here alleged. It is certainly evidence that there was some agreement; *I am not*

---

[170] PH Pettit, *Equity and the Law of Trusts* (London, Butterworths, 1966) 66–67 referred to it as a case of gift in the context of an exception to the principle of equity not assisting a volunteer; but in the 3rd edition (London, Butterworths, 1974) 6, he referred to the case for the first time as one of proprietary estoppel. DB Parker and AR Mellows, *The Modern Law of Trusts* (London, Sweet & Maxwell, 1966) did not refer to the case at all. The 2nd edn (London, Sweet & Maxwell, 1970) and the 3rd edn (London, Sweet & Maxwell, 1975) referred to it, but as an example of 'estoppel in equity'. Lord Walker in *Cobbe* (HL) (n 160) [49] treats the case as one of imperfect gift.

[171] *Hinckly v Hinckly* (1672–3) 73 Selden Soc 75; *Bond v Rosling* (1861) 1 B & S 371, 121 ER 753; *Tidey v Mollett* (1864) 16 CB (NS) 298, 143 ER 1143.

[172] Hence excluding the 'honour only' cases, such as *Jorden v Money*, and most recently *Cobbe* (HL) (n 160), and the 'subject to contract' cases, such as *AG of Hong Kong v Humphreys Estates (Queen's Gardens) Ltd* [1987] 1 AC 114 and *London and Regional Investments Ltd v TBI plc* [2002] EWCA Civ 355. See also *Derby & Co v ITC Pension Trust Ltd* [1977] 2 All ER 850, 896.

[173] As Lord Neuberger pointed (n 104) para 33.

[174] (1865) LR 1 Ch App 35.

sure that even beyond this the fact of a landlord standing by and seeing his tenant laying out money on the faith of a promise of a lease, might not raise an equity, though not in a strict sense part performance, by analogy to the equity which arises in the case of a person standing by and seeing his neighbour spending money on his land.[175]

And for this latter proposition Lord Cranworth referred to *Gregory v Mighell*,[176] which we briefly considered above. He then went on to hold that the payment of the increased rent *was* an act of part performance, and the plaintiff succeeded in his claim to specific performance of the oral agreement between the parties. The point is that Lord Cranworth saw that incurring expenditure in the improvement of land on the faith of a *promise*, even when not amounting to part performance of a contract, could give rise to an equity.

Three years later we find Lord Kingsdown saying exactly the same thing, in *Ramsden v Dyson*:

> The rule of law applicable to the case appears to me to be this: If a man, under a verbal agreement with a landlord for a certain interest in land, or, what amounts to the same thing, under an expectation, created or encouraged by the landlord, that he shall have a certain interest, takes possession of such land, with the consent of the landlord, and upon the faith of such promise or expectation, with the knowledge of the landlord, and without objection by him, lays out money upon the land, a Court of equity will compel the landlord to give effect to such promise or expectation. This was the principle of the decision in *Gregory v Mighell*, and, as I conceive, is open to no doubt.[177]

Yet another reference to *Gregory v Mighell*. Of course Lord Kingsdown was dissenting on the facts in *Ramsden*, which is why he alone put forward this proposition of law, but no one suggested, then or since, that he was wrong about that proposition, and it has been approved.[178] After all, Lord Cranworth LC, who gave the leading speech in *Ramsden*, had said much the same thing in *Nunn v Fabian*.[179]

Dillwyn v Llewelyn[180] was followed by the Privy Council in *Plimmer v Mayor of Wellington*,[181] where the local authorities' encouragement of the plaintiff in extending and maintaining a jetty in the harbour led to his reasonable expectation that his occupation of the jetty would not be disturbed. Thus he acquired such a right as qualified for compensation when by statute the jetty was taken over by those authorities for public purposes.

---

[175] Ibid, 40 (original emphasis).
[176] *Gregory* (n 148).
[177] (1866) LR 1 HL 129, 170.
[178] See *Plimmer v Mayor of Wellington* (1884) 9 App Cas 699, 711.
[179] (1865) LR 1 Ch App 35.
[180] *Dillwyn* (n 163).
[181] (1884) 9 App Cas 699.

Since then, an impressively long list of cases throughout the Commonwealth has applied the same principle.[182]

The classic modern formulation is that accepted by Oliver J from counsel in *Taylors Fashions Ltd v Liverpool Victoria Trustees Co Ltd*:

> [I]f under an expectation created or encouraged by B that A shall have a certain interest in land, thereafter, on the faith of such expectation and with the knowledge of B and without objection by him, acts to his detriment in connection with such land, a Court of Equity will compel B to give effect to such expectation.[183]

And this is the principle which in modern times we label 'proprietary estoppel'. It is not a contract, because the obligation arises, not when the promise is made or expectation created, but instead only when detrimental reliance occurs. As Hoffmann LJ once said, instead of looking forward, like a contract, it looks back, 'and asks whether, in the circumstances that have actually happened, it would be unconscionable for the promise not to be kept'.[184] Fifteen years later Lord Hoffmann, then on the brink of retirement, put the same idea more poetically, in saying that 'The owl of Minerva spreads its wings only with the falling of the dusk.'[185]

Unfortunately, in recent cases, concerned with the applicability of section 2 of the Law of Property (Miscellaneous Provisions) Act 1989, the crucial differences between contract and proprietary estoppel have been elided. The problem was first seen in the context of the equitable mortgage by deposit of title deeds. In the leading part-performance case of *Maddison v Alderson*, Lord Selborne LC, after stating the juridical basis of part-performance to be detrimental reliance on a promise leading to change of position, had simply said: 'The law of equitable mortgage by deposit of title deeds depends upon the same principles.'[186] This sentence followed a discussion of the doctrine of part-performance, which necessarily depends on the existence of a parol contract. Because of this, it was cited by the Court of Appeal in *United Bank of Kuwait plc v Sahib*[187] in support of its conclusion that the equitable mortgage by deposit of title deeds was contract based.[188] Hence (said the court) such a mortgage was no longer possible once the doctrine of part-performance had been abolished by the repeal of the Law of Property Act 1925, section 40 and its replacement by the Law of Property (Miscellaneous Provisions) Act 1989, section 2.

---

[182] RP Meagher, JD Heydon and MJ Leeming, *Meagher, Gummow and Lehane's Equity—Doctrines and Remedies*, 4th edn (Sydney, Butterworths, 2002) para 17–080, n 14.

[183] *Taylors* (n 107) 144.

[184] *Walton v Walton*, CA 14 April 1994, para 21, quoted by Lord Walker in *Thorner* (n 38) [57]. Lord Neuberger said the same thing in his talk to the London Common Law and Commercial Bar Association (n 104) para 28.

[185] *Thorner* (n 38) [8].

[186] *Maddison* (n 140) 480.

[187] [1997] Ch 107 (CA) 125.

[188] [1997] Ch. 107, 126–27.

However, Lord Selborne in referring to 'the same principles' might just as well have been referring to the notion of detrimental reliance on a promise leading to change of position.

It is certainly true that the earliest cases on equitable mortgage by deposit of title deeds (dating from the late eighteenth century) are contract based. But two points should be made. First, they pre-date the earliest statements about detrimental reliance raising an equity[189] by two or three decades. But, secondly, until about that time, all the reported cases appear to be cases, not of *new lending* on the faith of deposit of title deeds,[190] but of the later deposit of title deeds *to support existing indebtedness*.[191] And, as Lord Selborne LC himself said in *Dixon v Muckleston*, 'acts are much stronger in raising an equity than omissions can be'.[192] The argument about raising an equity against the depositor probably just did not occur to anyone so long as the only action in reliance that could be pleaded was in fact an *omission*, that is, the failure to take legal proceedings against the debtor.

But by the middle of the nineteenth century the law on detrimental reliance had established itself. It is not that there was, or might be, a contract involved. A mere contract on its own was neither sufficient, as Lord Selborne had said in *Maddison*, nor indeed necessary (as Lord Westbury had already held in *Dillwyn*). The point was—and still is—that an equity could be raised by *reliance by the creditor* on the debtor's promise to create or convey an interest in the land in favour of the creditor.

In the context of proprietary estoppel and contract generally, in *Yaxley v Gotts* Robert Walker LJ considered that the provision of section 2(5), disapplying the formalities requirements of section 2 to the case of a constructive trust

> would allow a limited exception, expressly contemplated by Parliament, for those cases in which a supposed bargain has been so fully performed by one side, and the general circumstances of the matter are such, that it would be inequitable to disregard the claimant's expectations, and insufficient to grant him no more than a restitutionary remedy.[193]

---

[189] Eg *Gregory* (n 108).
[190] The first case clearly in this class seems to be *ex parte Langston* (1810) 17 Ves Jun 228, 34 ER 88, where the leases were deposited, and 'the petitioners advanced £5000 upon the faith of the assurances and securities aforesaid'.
[191] *Russel v Russel* (1783) 1 Bro CC 269, 28 ER 1121; *Edge v Worthington* (1786) 1 Cox CC 211, 29 ER 1133; *Ex p Coming* (1803) 9 Ves Jun 115, 32 ER 545; *ex parte Mountfort* (1808) 14 Ves Jun 606, 33 ER 653.
[192] (1872) LR 8 Ch App 155, 160.
[193] *Yaxley* (n 121) [31], followed in *Healey* (n 15) [26]; *Brightlingsea Haven Ltd v Morris* [2008] EWHC 1928 (QB), [2009] 2 P & CR 11 [55]; *McGuane v Welch* [2008] EWCA Civ 785, [2008] 2 P & CR 24 [37].

The Court of Appeal in the post-1989 case of *Kinane v Mackie-Conteh*[194] applied similar reasoning, in an informal security case, to raise a proprietary estoppel claim in the absence of writing. According to Arden LJ:

> The security agreement demonstrates an intention to create a security interest. Mr Kinane made it clear in his witness statement and when giving evidence that he was not prepared to make a loan without security. Having obtained the security agreement, he made a loan which, to his detriment, is now irrecoverable. . . . He assumed that the security agreement was enforceable and thus he acted in the belief that he would be given a formal security. . . . Likewise, in my judgment, it is immaterial that the reliance consisted in the single act of making the loan. That act had significant consequences on its own, and is thus of itself sufficient to give rise to proprietary estoppel.[195]

But what about the 'escape hatch' of section 2(5) and the creation of a constructive trust? In *Yeoman's Row Management Ltd v Cobbe*, Lord Scott revisited the question, albeit *obiter*, saying:[196]

> Section 2 of the 1989 Act declares to be void any agreement for the acquisition of an interest in land that does not comply with the requisite formalities prescribed by the section. Subsection (5) expressly makes an exception for resulting, implied or constructive trusts. These may validly come into existence without compliance with the prescribed formalities. Proprietary estoppel does not have the benefit of this exception. The question arises, therefore, whether a complete agreement for the acquisition of an interest in land that does not comply with the section 2 prescribed formalities, but would be specifically enforceable if it did, can become enforceable via the route of proprietary estoppel. It is not necessary in the present case to answer this question, for the second agreement was not a complete agreement and, for that reason, would not have been specifically enforceable so long as it remained incomplete. My present view, however, is that proprietary estoppel cannot be prayed in aid in order to render enforceable an agreement that statute has declared to be void.[197] The proposition that an owner of land can be estopped from asserting that an agreement is void for want of compliance with the requirements of section 2 is, in my opinion, unacceptable. The assertion is no more than the statute provides. Equity can surely not contradict the statute.[198]

---

[194] [2005] EWCA Civ 45, [2005] WTLR 345. There had been earlier observations by Neill LJ in *Singh v Beggs* (1995) 71 P & CR 120 (CA) 122, and by Neill and Morritt LJJ in *McCausland v Duncan Lawrie* [1997] 1 WLR 38 (CA) 45 and 50, leaving the point open.

[195] Ibid, [31]. Thorpe LJ expressly agreed (at [52]) and Neuberger LJ agreed in substance (at [44]). See also *Halifax plc v Curry Popeck* [2008] EWHC 1692 (Ch), [15(d)].

[196] *Cobbe* (HL) (n 161) [29]. Lord Hoffmann and Lord Mance both agreed with the speech of Lord Scott.

[197] Cf Briggs J's comment in *Anderson Antiques* (n 119) [33], that 'if the defendant's case here [for a proprietary estoppel] was unaffected by section 2, it is hard to see how any oral contract for the sale of land cannot be enforced by way of proprietary estoppel once the promisee spends some time or money in reliance on the oral agreement, such as, for example, instructing solicitors to investigate title or surveyors to carry out a survey.'

[198] In *Herbert* (n 123) [15] the deputy judge (Mark Herbert QC) declined to follow this

The arguments are much the same as those made years ago against the doctrine of part performance. Up goes the cry: 'Equity is ignoring the statute.' But the answer today is the same as it was at the time of *Maddison v Alderson*:

> [T]he defendant is really 'charged' upon the equities resulting from the acts done in execution of the contract, and not (within the meaning of the statute) upon the contract itself. [199]

Or, in the words of Lord Walker in the more recent case of *Actionstrengh Ltd v International Glass Engineering SpA*:

> [T]he doctrine of part performance was developed not as the enforcement of a contract which Parliament had made unenforceable, but as an action on the equities arising out of what had been done towards performance of the oral contract. Granting relief on the strength of those equities was regarded as involving no inconsistency with the Statute of Frauds.[200]

In other words, the cause of action is not *contract* at all, and it is unnecessary to resort to section 2(5),[201] and to squeeze the proprietary estoppel into a constructive trust framework in order to escape the requirements of section 2. They simply never attach in the first place. Lord Neuberger in a recent lecture has made the same point:

> I suggest that section 2 has nothing to do with the matter. In cases such as those in *Crabb v Arun* and *Thorner v Majors*, the estoppel rests on the finding that it would be inequitable for the defendant to insist on his strict legal rights. . . . where there is the superadded fact that the claimant, with the conscious encouragement of the defendant, has acted in the belief that there is a valid contract, I suggest that section 2 offers no bar to a claim based in equity.[202]

Of course, even though contract and proprietary estoppel are not the same, it is still possible to ask (as Lord Scott does in *Cobbe*) the question whether, as a matter of public policy, a person who for lack of compliance with statutory formalities cannot make a contract claim can make a claim in proprietary estoppel for the same or similar relief.[203] But it is not obvious

---

statement. But in *Hutchison v B & DF Ltd* [2008] EWHC 2286 (Ch), [2009] L & TR 12 [85] Peter Smith J agreed with it and applied it to the case before him.

[199] *Maddison* (n 140) 475.

[200] *Actionstrength* (n 131) [47].

[201] Which makes it hard to understand why Robert Walker LJ said what he did in *Yaxley*.

[202] Neuberger (n 104) para 33, repeating views expressed in the annual ACTAPS lecture of 14 November 2006, para 38, and at least partially recanting views expressed in *Kinane* (n 194). See also to the same effect *Cobbe v Yeoman's Row Management Ltd* [2006] EWCA Civ 1139, [2006] 1 WLR 2964 [68] (Mummery LJ); M Dixon 'Invalid Contracts, Estoppel and Constructive Trusts' [2005] *Conveyancer and Property Lawyer* 247, B McFarlane 'Proprietary Estoppel and Failed Contractual Negotiations' [2005] *Conveyancer and Property Lawyer* 501; see also: Joanne Wicks's lecture to the Chancery Bar Association on 11 June 2009, 'Waiting for the Bus', para 18.

[203] See eg *Chalmers v Pardoe* [1963] 1 WLR 677, PC, where the dealing with the land was

that the policy that requires writing for contracts to be valid or enforceable from the very moment that they are made, and before any action has been taken in reliance on them, is necessarily determinative for cases where a person who has been encouraged to believe, and does believe, that he will acquire a property right in future is thereby induced to change his position to his detriment, in reliance on that belief.[204] On the other hand, there may be aspects of proprietary estoppel which should give rise to similar consequences as contracts do. One of them is that a person entitled to property as a result of detrimental reliance on a promise to convey, once the conveyance has taken place, will be regarded as a purchaser for value for the purpose of resisting an equitable tracing claim.[205]

The recent decision of the House of Lords in *Yeoman's Row Management Ltd v Cobbe*[206] is also seen as a milestone in the law of proprietary estoppel. Indeed some commentators have described it in apocalyptic terms.[207] But as with Mark Twain,[208] reports of the death of proprietary estoppel have been greatly exaggerated. The failure of the claimant in *Cobbe* rests on a single critical fact: he could not show that the assurance on which he said he had relied to his detriment had been intended by the defendant to be one on which he could rely as a matter of law.[209] It is *Jorden v Money* and *Ramsden v Dyson* all over again.

That proprietary estoppel is still alive and well in the House of Lords is amply demonstrated by its application, even more recently, in *Thorner v Major*.[210] A farm owner by a course of conduct over many years created an expectation in his cousin that the cousin would have the farm after the owner's death, on the faith of which he worked on the farm without pay and forewent the opportunity to establish himself in life in other ways. The owner had made a will in favour of the cousin but for unexplained reasons destroyed it and never made another. The House of Lords held that the judge had been entitled to find that the owner did intend to indicate to the cousin that he would inherit the farm. It was an assurance on which the cousin could and did rely, and not merely a statement about what his will said or might say in the future. Its significance lies in the fact that it is one

---

unlawful, *Lloyds Bank plc v Carrick* (1997) 73 P & CR 314, CA, in relation to an estate contract void as against a purchaser for non-registration, and *Godden v Merthyr Tydfil Housing Association* [1997] EWCA Civ 780, in relation to estoppel by convention.

[204] Cf *Actionstrength* (n 131), where the House of Lords held that part performance could not be used to escape the requirement of writing for contracts of guarantee in s 4 of the Statute of Frauds.

[205] *Re Diplock* [1947] Ch 716, 781–84 (Wynn-Parry J).

[206] *Cobbe* (HL) (n 161). It is interesting that the law reporters did not see it as worthy of inclusion in The Law Reports.

[207] Eg B McFarlane and A Robertson, 'Death of Proprietary Estoppel' [2008] *Lloyd's Maritime and Commercial Law Quarterly* 449.

[208] Cable to Associated Press from London, 1897.

[209] *Cobbe* (HL) (n 161) [81].

[210] *Thorner* (n 38).

of the few proprietary estoppel cases about promising to leave an estate or a share of estate on death.[211]

2. Common Intention Constructive Trusts

Proprietary estoppel is to be contrasted with the so-called doctrine of the 'common intention constructive trust'. The name given to the doctrine should indicate that it is at best a subset of the constructive trust, being that kind of constructive trust that (the reader might imagine) depends upon the common intention of the parties. The full phrase itself is very modern; the earliest use of it I have found dates from 1988.[212]

The doctrine does not have such a long pedigree as that of proprietary estoppel. All the sources lead only as far back as the speech of Lord Diplock in *Gissing v Gissing*.[213] Now this was a landmark decision of the House of Lords on the approach to matrimonial property in the days before the Matrimonial Causes Act 1973 conferred a free hand on divorce judges as to how they allocated family resources on the breakup of a marriage. The litigation concerned the beneficial ownership of the matrimonial home. This had been bought by the husband in his own name with monies loaned to him both by a building society and by his employers, which he was in the course of paying off. Although the wife had worked during the marriage, and had paid for some furnishings and laying a lawn, she had paid nothing towards the purchase of the house or the repayment of the mortgage. She originally claimed the whole beneficial interest, but by the time of the trial reduced her claim to one-half. Buckley J awarded her nothing. The Court of Appeal by a majority (including Lord Denning MR) gave her one-half. The House of Lords restored Buckley J's decision.

Given the importance to this area of trust law which the decision has subsequently assumed, perhaps the most unsatisfactory feature of the whole case is that, of the nine judges who heard it at the three levels, only the judge at first instance, Buckley J, was a chancery lawyer. None of the three judges in the Court of Appeal,[214] nor of the five judges in the House of Lords,[215] was experienced in the field of trust law. A second feature, nearly as curious, is that, although everyone knows of and cites from the speech of Lord Diplock (in fact the junior law lord on the appeal) as if he had given the leading speech, in fact *each* of the five law lords sitting delivered his own reasoned speech, and *none of them* stated his concurrence with any of

---

[211] Again, however, the law reporters did not think it worthy of inclusion in The Law Reports.
[212] See text to nn 101 and 102.
[213] *Gissing* (n 39).
[214] Lord Denning MR, Phillimore, Edmund Davies LJJ.
[215] Lords Reid, Morris, Dilhorne, Pearson, Diplock.

the others.²¹⁶ This does not make it very easy to determine exactly what the case stands for (and what it does not stand for). Nor are matters helped by the fact that the wife took no part in the argument, and the defence of the Court of Appeal's decision had to be undertaken by an *amicus curiae*.²¹⁷

The headnote in the Law Reports says that the House held

> that the wife had made no contribution to the acquisition of title to the matrimonial home from which it could be inferred that the parties intended her to have any beneficial interest in it.

In *substance* this is what Lords Morris, Dilhorne and Diplock held. They were looking for a basis for a constructive trust to be imposed on the husband, and did not find one. Lord Pearson simply held that the wife had made no substantial contribution to the purchase of the house, and therefore there was no *resulting* trust in her favour. Lord Reid's short speech, most unusually for him, was incoherent.²¹⁸ He began by agreeing with all the others that the appeal must be allowed. But he then posed two competing views of the law, one of which he thought unworkable and one of which he could live with. The problem is that it was the former and not the latter that was adopted by the other judges.²¹⁹ Ultimately, the decision in *Gissing* is much more about what counts as the facts (and what they were) than about big principles of law.

Nevertheless, in tracing the historical development of the common intention constructive trust idea, it is Lord Diplock's speech that counts.²²⁰ The passage that is *always* quoted is this:

> A resulting, implied or constructive trust—and it is unnecessary for present purposes to distinguish between these three classes of trust—is created by a transaction between the trustee and the cestui que trust in connection with the acquisition by the trustee of a legal estate in land, whenever the trustee has so conducted himself that it would be inequitable to allow him to deny to the cestui que trust a beneficial interest in the land acquired . . .²²¹

Sometimes the passage is quoted to the end of the paragraph (as of course it should be):

---

²¹⁶ One of them expressly agreed with the dissenting judge in the Court of Appeal, and two relied heavily on the speech of Lord Upjohn in *Pettitt v Pettitt* [1970] AC 777.
²¹⁷ Michael Fox QC (later Fox LJ): more perhaps of an amicus curiae than might be imagined; he had married Lord Denning's stepdaughter.
²¹⁸ Lord Walker, in *Thorner* (n 38) [22], politely calls it 'inconclusive'.
²¹⁹ A difficulty adverted to by Bagnall J in *Cowcher v Cowcher* [1972] 1 WLR 425, 433.
²²⁰ As Lord Walker acknowledged in *Stack* (n 41) [21] and *Thorner* (n 38) [21]. See also T Etherton, 'Constructive Trusts: A New Model for Equity and Unjust Enrichment' (2008) 67 *Cambridge Law Journal* 265, 274.
²²¹ *Gissing* (n 39) 905.

... and he will be held so to have conducted himself if by his words or conduct he has induced the cestui que trust to act to his own detriment in the reasonable belief that by so acting he was acquiring a beneficial interest in the land.[222]

Only rarely, however, are the next two paragraphs quoted:

> This is why it has been repeatedly said in the context of disputes between spouses as to their respective beneficial interests in the matrimonial home, that if at the time of its acquisition and transfer of the legal estate into the name of one or other of them an express agreement has been made between them as to the way in which the beneficial interest shall be held, the court will give effect to it—notwithstanding the absence of any written declaration of trust. Strictly speaking this states the principle too widely, for if the agreement did not provide for anything to be done by the spouse in whom the legal estate was not to be vested, it would be a merely voluntary declaration of trust and unenforceable for want of writing. But in the express oral agreements contemplated by these dicta it has been assumed sub silentio that they provide for the spouse in whom the legal estate in the matrimonial home is not vested to do something to facilitate its acquisition, by contributing to the purchase price or to the deposit or the mortgage installments when it is purchased upon mortgage or to make some other material sacrifice by way of contribution to or economy in the general family expenditure. What the court gives effect to is the trust resulting or implied from the common intention expressed in the oral agreement between the spouses that if each acts in the manner provided for in the agreement the beneficial interests in the matrimonial home shall be held as they have agreed.
>
> An express agreement between spouses as to their respective beneficial interests in land conveyed into the name of one of them obviates the need for showing that the conduct of the spouse into whose name the land was conveyed was intended to induce the other spouse to act to his or her detriment upon the faith of the promise of a specified beneficial interest in the land and that the other spouse so acted with the intention of acquiring that beneficial interest. The agreement itself discloses the common intention required to create a resulting, implied or constructive trust.[223]

The first passage quoted above is ripped from its context, and appears to justify a very wide, palm-tree justice approach to constructive trusts, depending on 'unconscionability'. But the remainder of the paragraph (the second quotation) shows that Lord Diplock had a very specific idea of what was unconscionable in this context. The next two paragraphs—the final quotation—put back (most of) the missing context. They make clear that, although Lord Diplock is talking about the common intention of the parties, what actually matters, and what makes the unwritten arrangement enforceable, is not the common intention at all. It is the *action in reliance* on the *expectation created* by the common intention.

The final paragraph also shows that the role of the common intention—

[222] Ibid, 905.
[223] Ibid, 905.

the agreement—is *evidentiary*: it proves the intention of the one party *to induce the other to rely on the promise*. The common intention or agreement is not an *element*, it is a *method of proof*. And the second and shortest of the three quotations above ('and he will be held', etc) is in fact nothing less than Lord Diplock's own formulation of the proprietary estoppel idea which we have already seen in *Dillwyn v Llewelyn* and elsewhere. It involves exactly the same elements as in *Dillwyn*, that is, (1) the promise or expectation created by words or conduct of an interest in property, (2) the intention that it should be relied on by the promisee and (3) detrimental reliance on the promise by the promisee. It is true that *Dillwyn* and the other cases are not cited, but that cannot change matters. Lord Diplock did not invent a new principle. He simply restated an old one.

It may be said that this cannot be so, because Lord Diplock referred to the 'common intention' of the parties, whereas proprietary estoppel depends on a *unilateral* promise or creation of expectation. But this is nonsense. We have already seen that the *Dillwyn* principle sprang from the same source as the part-performance doctrine, which involves agreement between the parties, and therefore *ex hypothesi* a common intention. And it is clear that the father and the son (and the mother too, come to that) in *Dillwyn* had a common intention. But, as Lord Diplock himself made clear, the 'common intention' in *Gissing* helped to demonstrate a crucial fact, namely that the promisor intended to induce the promisee to rely on the promise. This was as important in *Dillwyn* as it was in *Gissing*.

To prove the point, take a simple example. Suppose A says to B, 'Come and live with me and I will give you half my house', intending B to rely on that, and B does some significant acts in reliance, for example gives up another home, moves in, and spends money on major improvements to the property. It cannot seriously be suggested that if B says nothing, and simply does the actions in reliance, it is proprietary estoppel and only proprietary estoppel, but that, if B says 'Yes please' as well, it is common intention constructive trust, and only common intention constructive trust.[224]

The fact is that, at least according to their original formulations, *every* case of common intention constructive trust must include a proprietary estoppel, because an agreement between A and B that A will confer some property right on B must include a promise or other creation of expectation by A towards B, and the detrimental reliance that is good for the one is equally good for the other. It is not rational to suppose that a legal polymath like Lord Diplock would go to the trouble of inventing a completely new principle almost completely overlapping a perfectly good existing one.

---

[224] Although see Neuberger LJ in *Kinane* (n 194) [51]: 'the essential difference between a proprietary estoppel which does not also give rise to a constructive trust, and one that does, is the element of agreement, or at least expression of common understanding, exchanged between the parties, as to the existence, or intended existence, of a proprietary interest, in the latter type of case.'

There then followed much case-law on this kind of constructive trust. But we can jump forward 20 years. The doctrine of *Gissing v Gissing* (whatever it was) was revisited in the House of Lords, in *Lloyds Bank plc v Rosset*.[225] Lord Bridge gave the single reasoned speech, with which the other law lords agreed. A husband bought a house with monies provided by his family trust, and he was registered as sole proprietor. The wife made no financial contribution towards the purchase, but carried out decorating work and supervised renovation work, even before contracts were exchanged. The husband borrowed money from a bank on the security of a legal charge of the house, and did not repay it. The marriage broke up and he left. The bank claimed possession. It won at first instance, lost in the Court of Appeal, and succeeded in the House of Lords.

Much of the argument in the case was devoted to an important question in the law of registered land relating to the doctrine of 'actual occupation'. That does not concern us here. But there was also considerable argument put forward by the bank on the supposed distinction between proprietary estoppel (called 'detriment theory') and common intention constructive trust (called 'bargain theory'). Lord Bridge referred to them disparagingly as 'elaborate submissions'. After a long recital of the facts, he said that he had 'reached a conclusion on the facts which . . . does not seem to depend on any nice legal distinction'.[226] So distinguishing between competing theories of law was out. Instead, he then discussed what he called

> one critical distinction which any judge required to resolve a dispute between former partners as to the beneficial interest in the home they formerly shared should always have in the forefront of his mind.[227]

This was the distinction between (1) the case where there is a finding, based on *evidence of express discussions*, that the parties had reached an agreement or understanding as to the sharing of the property, and (2) the case where there was no evidence to support a finding of agreement or understanding to share, and the court had to rely on *the conduct of the parties* from which to infer the existence of a common intention to share the property. In the latter case the conduct which could support such an inference would probably have to be of the making of direct financial contributions to the purchase price or the payment of mortgage instalments, and it was 'extremely doubtful whether anything less will do'.[228]

Whatever its merits, this was a distinction, not about the *law*, but about the *facts*, and in particular about the evidence needed to support such facts. As he said, Lord Bridge regarded *Gissing* as an example of the second class of case. But what is very interesting about his speech is that Lord Bridge did

---

[225] [1991] 1 AC 107.
[226] Ibid, 132.
[227] Ibid, 132.
[228] Ibid, 133.

not even attempt to respond to the bank's counsel's arguments—detailed and lengthy as they were—that the doctrines of proprietary estoppel and common intention constructive trust *were different*. Indeed, he never once referred to either expression separately. It was always 'proprietary estoppel or common intention constructive trust' or 'common intention constructive trust or proprietary estoppel'. It was as if they were synonyms. It is true that he referred often to 'common intention'. But why should he not? It was an expression which Lord Diplock himself used in *Gissing*, and so did both sides during the argument in *Rosset*. And for good reason, on the authority of Lord Diplock: common intention showed the intention to induce reliance. Bingo.

3. The Overlap

In these circumstances, it is small wonder that judges for many years have expressed doubts as to whether there really was a difference between the two doctrines. There are lots of such doubts in the decided cases.[229] One example is that of Robert Walker LJ in *Yaxley v Gotts*, where he considered that proprietary estoppel and the *Gissing* kind of constructive trust might be the same thing. Thus:

> in the area of a joint enterprise for the acquisition of land (which may be, but is not necessarily, the matrimonial home) the two concepts coincide. Lord Diplock's very well known statement in *Gissing v Gissing* [1971] AC 886, 905 brings this out.[230]

And then further he referred to

> the species of constructive trust based on 'common intention' is established by what Lord Bridge in *Lloyds Bank plc v Rosset* [1991] 1 AC 107 at 132 called an 'agreement, arrangement or understanding' actually reached between the parties, and relied on and acted on by the claimant. A constructive trust of that sort is closely akin to, if not indistinguishable from, proprietary estoppel.

A further point of overlap relates not to functionality but to modality. It relates to the question whether proprietary estoppel *gives rise to* a constructive trust, as the means by which the law gives effect to the

---

[229] See eg *Re Sharpe* [1980] 1 WLR 219, 223; *Christian v Christian* CA 6 November 1980; *Walker v Walker* [1984] CAT 173 (12 April 1984); *Re Basham* [1986] 1 WLR 1498, 1503–04 (Edward Nugee QC); *Grant v Edwards* [1986] Ch 638, 656 and 657 (Browne-Wilkinson V-C); *Austin v Keele* (1987) 72 ALR 579 (PC) 587, (Lord Oliver); *Lloyds Bank plc v Rosset* [1989] Ch 350 (CA) 387 (Nicholls LJ); *Stokes v Anderson* [1991] 1 FLR 391 (CA) 399 (Nourse LJ; though see the same judge in *Sen v Headley* [1991] Ch 425 (CA) 440); *Mollo* (n 103); *Sabherwal* (n 104) [24]; *Banner Homes Group plc v Luff Developments Ltd* [2000] Ch 372 (CA) 384–85; *Oxley* (n 41) [66] (Chadwick LJ); *Q v Q* [2008] EWHC 1874 (Fam) [112] (Black J). Cf *Hyett v Stanley* [2003] EWCA Civ 942, [2003] WTLR 1269 [27].
[230] *Yaxley* (n 121) 176.

'estoppel'. In *Yaxley* Walker LJ thought that it did, at least on the facts of that case. As we have seen, Lord Neuberger seems to think that there is no need for this,[231] and he may well be right. But a further point, not I think so far noticed by any of the commentators, is this. Just as a specifically enforceable contract gives rise to a special kind of constructive trust,[232] because equity regards as done that which ought to be done, so too the same principle should apply to a proprietary estoppel where the remedy is a mandatory order to the defendant to perform his promise. Indeed, where in the case of the sale even of chattels the purchase price has been fully paid, a bare trust for the purchaser arises.[233] So too when proprietary estoppel is based on action in detrimental reliance *already performed*. Even if the availability of specific performance be the test, for contracts the existence in principle of the constructive trust is not affected by the fact that specific performance is an equitable, and therefore a discretionary, remedy.[234] If—as we shall see shortly—the 'minimum equity to do justice' is to perform the promise, the same should be true of proprietary estoppel.

4. The Contrast

However, Lord Walker at least is now beginning to row in the opposite direction. In the recent constructive trust case of *Stack v Dowden*, he said:

> I am now rather less enthusiastic about the notion that proprietary estoppel and 'common interest' constructive trusts can or should be completely assimilated. Proprietary estoppel typically consists of asserting an equitable claim against the conscience of the 'true' owner. The claim is a 'mere equity'. It is to be satisfied by the minimum award necessary to do justice (*Crabb v Arun District Council* [1976] Ch 179, 198), which may sometimes lead to no more than a monetary award. A 'common intention' constructive trust, by contrast, is identifying the true beneficial owner or owners, and the size of their beneficial interests.[235]

There is perhaps much to quarrel with here: the notion that proprietary estoppel involves an equitable claim against conscience, whereas (by implication) a common intention constructive trust does not; the idea that a common intention constructive trust gives rise to a full-bodied beneficial interest, but proprietary estoppel only to a puny *'interest-lite'* (the so-called

---

[231] See 43.
[232] See eg *Shaw v Foster* (1872) LR 5 HL 321, 349; *Bridges v Mees* [1957] Ch 475.
[233] *Pooley v Budd* (1851) 14 Beav 34; *Bridges* (n 232) 485; *Lloyds Bank plc v Carrick* (1997) 73 P & CR 314, 320.
[234] See *Tailby v Official Receiver* (1888) 13 App Cas 523, 547–49; *Pullan v Koe* [1913] 1 Ch 9. Cf *Re Colling* (1886) 32 Ch D 333.
[235] *Stack* (n 41) [37], cited by Sir Peter Gibson in *Powell v Benney* [2007] EWCA Civ 1283 [24]. See also S Gardner, 'Quantum in *Gissing v Gissing* Constructive Trusts' (2004) 120 *Law Quarterly Review* 541; MP Thompson, 'Constructive Trusts, Estoppel, and the Family Home' [2004] *Conveyancer and Property Lawyer* 496; *Thorner* (n 38) [20] (Lord Scott).

'mere equity');[236] the search for the 'minimum equity to do justice',[237] and so on. But others must deal with those things: my purpose is historical, and I must move on. It is enough to show that one original doctrine has, amoeba-like, split into two.

Of course, we know that law made by the courts changes over time as society itself changes,[238] and Lord Walker's loss of enthusiasm may simply reflect the changes over the last decade or so. Such changes do not, indeed cannot, alter the *origins* of the principles concerned.

Indeed, as I shall mention below, *Stack v Dowden*[239] itself may have changed the position even more fundamentally.

What are the current differences between the two doctrines? There seem to be four: (a) remedies; (b) retrospectivity; (c) the application of the two doctrines to registered land; and (d) negative entropy.

(a) Remedies

Historically, the plaintiff having established the promise or expectation induced, and proved the detrimental reliance upon it, the court simply decreed that the promise should be performed or the expectation made good.[240] In the comparatively recent case of *Chalmers v Pardoe*, for example, the Privy Council put it this way:

> There can be no doubt upon the authorities that where an owner of land has invited or expressly encouraged another to expend money upon part of his land upon the faith of an assurance or promise that that part of the land will be made over to the person so expending his money, a court of equity will prima facie require the owner by appropriate conveyance to fulfil his obligation.[241]

In more recent times this approach was criticised, as sometimes conferring upon the plaintiff a benefit that was disproportionate to the loss which he had suffered.[242] Now this might have been understandable in relation to the *propositional* estoppel cases. In such cases the plaintiff suffered loss by relying on a statement as to *the present position*. No one promised

---

[236] There is not space to argue it out now, but that 'doctrine' can be traced back to a single case (*Phillips v Phillips* (1861) 4 De G F & J 208, 45 ER 1164) which will not bear the weight.
[237] See 53–55 below.
[238] See eg *Re Hallett's Estate* (1880) 13 Ch D 696 (CA) 710 (Jessel MR); Lord Reid 'The Judge as Law-Maker' (1972) 12 *Journal of the Society of Public Teachers of Law* 22.
[239] *Stack* (n 41).
[240] *Dillwyn* (n 163); *Crabb* (n 160); *Griffiths v Williams* (1978) 248 EG 947, CA; *Greasley v Cooke* [1980] 1 WLR 1306, CA; *Pascoe v Turner* [1979] 1 WLR 431, CA; *Re Basham* [1986] 1 WLR 1498, *Walton v Walton* [1993] 2 FLR 47, *Wayling v Jones* (1995) 69 P & CR 170, *Burrows v Sharp* (1989) 2 HLR 82, 92, *Jennings* (n 141); *Ottey v Grundy* [2003] EWCA Civ 1176; *Q v Q* [2008] EWHC 1874 (Fam).
[241] [1963] 1 WLR 677, 681–82.
[242] See eg *Sledmore v Dalby* (1996) 72 P & CR 196 (CA) (Hobhouse LJ).

anything. The analogy is with *tort*, and the loss is the action in reliance. Requiring the defendant to disgorge the whole of a large property interest when the plaintiff had relied on the statement that he owned it (or that the defendant did not) by spending a few pounds only would indeed be disproportionate. But if the proceedings are brought to make good a promise relied on, then the analogy is not with tort; it is with *contract*. The loss is the loss of the performance of that promise, and not of the actions in reliance. Occasionally, of course, a promise might have to be satisfied by a lien for expenditure because of other, exceptional circumstances.[243]

But despite the historical origins, the position is now otherwise. The case-law of the last 10 or 15 years makes clear that the court has a discretion as to how to satisfy any equity arising through proprietary estoppel, and this remedy may not even be proprietary[244] but personal,[245] or indeed a mixture of proprietary and personal.[246] Indeed, it has been argued that there is always a personal liability of the promisor to the promisee, even if the property concerned has been transferred to a third party.[247] This is not consistent with the historical origins of the doctrine, but, as we have seen, the law does not stand still. Most, if not all, these developments appear to stem at least in part from a misreading of the decision of the Court of Appeal in *Crabb v Arun DC*.[248]

In that case the defendant's predecessor had given the plaintiff an assurance that he would be able to negotiate a right of way over their land to his, such that he could safely sell adjacent land which provided his only direct access to the highway. The plaintiff relied on this assurance and sold the land, thus landlocking himself. But negotiations broke down, and the council refused to grant the right of way. The Court of Appeal held that the plaintiff had established the elements of proprietary estoppel. The question was what remedy to award. In a famous phrase, Scarman LJ referred to 'the

---

[243] See eg *Dodsworth v Dodsworth* (1973) 228 EG 1115, where A owned a bungalow and B and C (A's brother and sister-in-law) were encouraged to spend money on it in the expectation fostered by A that they could live there the rest of their lives. But they fell out, and A claimed possession. At first instance the judge decided that instead of securing B's and C's expectation, they should instead have a lien for their expenditure. B and C appealed, but A died before the appeal was heard. The Court of Appeal would have allowed the appeal and given effect to the expectation, but for the fact that it would have created a Settled Land Act settlement, and so they declined to alter the remedy of a lien. It is interesting to note that in the earlier case of *Bannister v Bannister* [1948] 2 All ER 133 (CA) 137, the court had had no such qualms.

[244] See the cases cited in n 240.

[245] As in *Burrows v Sharp* (1989) 2 HLR 82, 92; *Baker v Baker* (1993) 25 HLR 408, CA; *Campbell v Griffin* [2001] EWCA Civ 990, [2001] WTLR 981; *Jennings* (n 141); *Parker v Parker* [2003] EWHC 846 (Ch); *Powell v Benney* [2007] EWCA Civ 1283; *McGuane v Welch* [2008] EWCA Civ 785 [44], [52] and [57].

[246] As in *Gillett v Holt* [2001] Ch 210; *Stallion v Albert Stallion Holdings* (GB) Ltd [2009] EWHC 1950 (Ch).

[247] S Bright and B McFarlane, 'Personal Liability in Proprietary Estoppel' [2005] *Conveyancer and Property Lawyer* 14; S Bright and B McFarlane, 'Proprietary Estoppel and Property Rights' (2005) 64 *Cambridge Law Journal* 449, part 3.

[248] *Crabb* (n 160).

minimum equity to do justice'. As we shall see, this seems to have been taken in subsequent cases as justifying an award to the plaintiff of *less* than was promised. But Scarman LJ in fact used it to refer to what should *normally* happen, that is, to order performance of the promise.

This case was unusual in that there was no promise of pure bounty: the assurance was that a right of way would be granted on commercial terms.[249] He said:

> There being no grant, no enforceable contract, no licence, I would analyse the minimum equity to do justice to the plaintiff as a right either to an easement or to a licence upon terms to be agreed.[250]

In a commercial case, this would indeed be the claimant's expectation. However, Scarman LJ went on:

> But, as already mentioned by Lord Denning MR and Lawton LJ, there has been a history of delay, and indeed high-handedness, which it is impossible to disregard. . . . [T]he effect of [the defendants'] action has been to sterilise the plaintiff's land; and for the reasons which I have endeavoured to give, such action was an infringement of an equitable right possessed by the plaintiff. It has involved him in loss, which has not been measured; but, since it amounted to sterilisation of an industrial estate for a very considerable period of time, it must surpass any sort of sum of money which the plaintiff ought reasonably, before it was done, to have paid the defendants in order to obtain an enforceable legal right. I think therefore that nothing should now be paid by the plaintiff and that he should receive at the hands of the court the belated protection of the equity that he has established.[251]

So the plaintiff in that case—because of the defendants' conduct making matters worse for the plaintiff—actually received *more* than the 'minimum equity to do justice'! But the phrase[252] was turned on its head in subsequent cases, and used to justify awarding *less* than the claimant's expectation,[253] that is, somewhere between the reliance loss and the expectation loss.[254] This then developed into a need for proportionality between the detriment incurred and the remedy awarded,[255] as if one were assessing the value of the consideration in a contract.

Robert Walker LJ in *Jennings v Rice*, however, accepted that there were cases where the claimant's expectation was the appropriate measure of the remedy:

---

[249] See also the strikingly similar case of *Laird* (n 158), which was not cited.
[250] *Crabb* (n 160) 198.
[251] Ibid, 199.
[252] In *Jennings* (n 141) [48] Robert Walker LJ quite rightly said that it 'must no doubt be read in the context of the rather unusual facts of that case'.
[253] *Bawden v Bawden* [1997] EWCA Civ 2664; *Gillett* (n 246).
[254] See Sir David Neuberger's lecture to ACTAPS of 14 November 2006, paras 65–66; *Orgee v Orgee* [1997] EWCA Civ 2650.
[255] See eg *Sledmore* (n 242) 208 (Hobhouse LJ); *Campbell* (n 245); *Jennings* (n 141) [36] and [56].

> [T]here is a category of case in which the benefactor and the claimant have reached a mutual understanding which is in reasonably clear terms but does not amount to a contract. I have already referred to the typical case of a carer who has the expectation of coming into the benefactor's house, either outright or for life. In such a case the court's natural response is to fulfil the claimant's expectations. [256]

On the other hand:

> [I]f the claimant's expectations are uncertain, or extravagant, or out of all proportion to the detriment which the claimant has suffered, the court can and should recognise that the claimant's equity should be satisfied in another (and generally more limited) way.

But no one has suggested such a restriction in relation to common intention constructive trusts. The parties agreed to share the property, and the legal owner's promise to do so is reflected in the court's order. No one suggests that giving the other party the agreed share is, say, disproportionate to the other party's detriment. The 'agreement' is to be performed.

The problem is that, once you abandon the performance of the promise as the remedy, and start to assess the 'worth' of the detriment, you embark upon the slippery slope to 'palm-tree justice'.[257] Moreover, you meet practical problems such as how to plead your case. In *Cobbe*, Lord Scott criticised the pleader for seeking a declaration that the promisor was 'estopped from denying that [the promisor] has such interest in the property and/or the proceeds of sale thereof as the court thinks fit'. But no one would criticise the pleader in a common intention constructive trust case for making a similar plea, *mutatis mutandis*, at least now that the House of Lords in *Stack v Dowden*[258] has accepted that the court may *impute* a common intention to the parties, and not merely *find* one.

(b) Retrospectivity

Originally it was accepted that a common intention constructive trust created a beneficial interest, not at the time of the formation of the parties' common intention, but at the time of the claimant's detrimental reliance on that intention, and even before any court order had been made in favour of the claimant. This meant that third parties might be affected in the period between the reliance and the litigation between the claimant and the legal owner. Historically, the same was true of proprietary estoppel.[259] However,

---

[256] *Jennings* (n 141) [50]. See too *Ottey* (n 240).
[257] See *Metropolitan Properties Co Ltd v Purdy* [1940] 1 All ER 188, 191.
[258] *Stack* (n 41).
[259] *Plimmer v Mayor of Wellington* (1884) 9 App Cas 699; *Re Sharpe* [1980] 1 WLR 219, 225.

it was later asserted[260] that a proprietary estoppel was different. It gave rise, not to a beneficial interest, but at best to a 'mere equity', a right to seek an equitable remedy from the court.[261] It could not bind third parties until the court ordered that the defendant should convey to the claimant or declared that the claimant had a certain interest. After all, it was argued, the court might not award a proprietary remedy at all, but a personal one such as payment of a sum of money. Both academic lawyers and judges were divided on the issue.[262] The Law Commission determined to resolve the issue, at least for registered land, in its Report and draft bill which later became the Land Registration Act 2002.

Section 116 of that Act accordingly provides:

> It is hereby declared for the avoidance of doubt that, in relation to registered land, each of the following—
> (a) an equity by estoppel, and
> (b) a mere equity,
> has effect from the time the equity arises as an interest capable of binding successors in title (subject to the rules about the effect of dispositions on priority).

As McFarlane rightly points out,[263] however, this provision is based on a certain view of proprietary estoppel as a two-stage process, involving, first, certain events taking place, and then, second, a decision by the court as to how to react to those events. He—again rightly—argues that this is a mistake, and that a better model for proprietary estoppel is unitary, as with all other methods of creating property rights, and looks simply at whether the events in question create or do not create proprietary rights. If they are proprietary, then they bind third parties (or not) in accordance with the application of the relevant rules of priority. If they are not proprietary, then they do not. Nevertheless, section 116 is helpful in settling the question of the point in time from which the rights created by the proprietary estoppel bind third parties (if at all).

Unfortunately, just as it looked as if a point of difference between proprietary estoppel and common intention constructive trust was about to be resolved, it has recently been argued that the decision of the House of Lords in *Stack v Dowden*[264] has had the opposite effect, that is, to make it possible for a common intention constructive trust to be prospective only. Writing extra-judicially, Sir Terence Etherton, the outgoing Chairman of the Law Commission, has argued:

---

[260] See eg P Ferguson 'Constructive Trusts—A Note of Caution' (1993) 109 *Law Quarterly Review* 114, 121.
[261] K Gray and SF Gray, *Elements of Land Law*, 4th edn (Oxford, Oxford University Press, 2005) para 10.212.
[262] The references are helpfully collected by B McFarlane, 'Proprietary Estoppel and Third Parties after the Land Registration Act 2002' (2003) 62 *Cambridge Law Journal* 661, 662 nn 4 and 5.
[263] Ibid.
[264] *Stack* (n 41).

The constructive trust imposed in *Stack*, not being an institutional trust, is a discretionary remedial trust. It need not be seen, and it should not be seen, however, as the full-blown retrospective remedial constructive trust of the US and Canadian model. That would be inconsistent with our jurisprudence and, in particular, our settled rules defining priorities between property interests. There is no difficulty, however, in a model analogous to the power of the court to award a property interest for proprietary estoppel. In that case, the right to the relief is a mere equity prior to judgment, which will take its priority in relation to other property interests in accordance with settled law and statute. This creates no difficulty in the *Stack* context so far as concerns dealings with the shared home in favour of third parties prior to judgment.[265]

This view depends on a careful analysis of *Stack*, which we have not time now to consider. Future judicial decisions will no doubt show whether it is the right one.

(c) Land registration

Here is a curiosity. The Land Registration Act 2002 appears to have introduced a subtle practical distinction between proprietary estoppel and common intention constructive trust cases. Assume that a registered estate in land is affected by a successful claim to a proprietary estoppel or a common intention constructive trust. Under section 32 of the Act:

> (1) A notice is an entry in the register in respect of the burden of an interest affecting a registered estate or charge.

But under section 33 of the Act:

> No notice may be entered in the register in respect of any of the following:
>   (a) an interest under
>   (i) a trust of land . . .

There is no definition of 'trust of land' in the Act, but there is no reason to doubt that it refers to a trust of land within the Trusts of Land and Appointment of Trustees Act 1996, which includes both a bare trust and a trust for the legal owner and another person, whether as joint tenants or as tenants in common. And there is equally no reason to doubt that this provision therefore includes any interest arising under a *constructive* trust of land, and therefore under a common intention constructive trust. Since the protection afforded by a notice on the register[266] is not available, the most practical form of protection against third parties which remains for such an interest is for the beneficiary to be in actual occupation of the land. For so long as he or she is in actual occupation of the land, and certain exceptions do not apply, the priority of the interest will be protected

---

[265] Etherton (n 220) 283.
[266] Land Registration Act 2002, s 29(1) and (2)(a)(i).

against third party purchasers.²⁶⁷ If he or she is not in actual occupation, however, then the only protection is to enter a *restriction*, intended to ensure that purchase money is paid to two trustees and thus overreach the interest.²⁶⁸

But what then is the position where there is a proprietary estoppel? As we have seen, it is clear, according to section 116, that 'an equity by estoppel . . . has effect from the time the equity arises as an interest capable of binding successors in title'. So it is an interest in the land. However, is it 'an interest under *a trust of* land'? In *Yaxley v Gotts*, Robert Walker LJ considered that the proprietary estoppel which was successfully claimed amounted to or created a constructive trust. This allowed the claimant to escape from the informality of the parties' agreement, under section 2(5) of the Law of Property (Miscellaneous Provisions) Act 1989.

As we have seen, however, that is not a universal view. Particularly interesting is the assumption, by Charles Harpum and Janet Bignell, that every claimed proprietary estoppel can and should be protected by entering a notice on the register. Referring to section 116, they say:

> If the court does grant [the claimant] a proprietary right, that interest can be protected in the register in the appropriate way. . . . Subject to the rules about the effect of dispositions on priority, the Act places the Registry's practice [of formerly allowing the entry of a caution or notice in respect of a claimed equity] on a statutory footing by declaring that in relation to registered land, an equity by estoppel has effect from the time when the equity arises as an interest capable of binding successors in title. A party can, therefore, protect his equity in the period after it has arisen but before a court has made an order giving effect to it, by entering a notice on the register.²⁶⁹

Harpum and Bignell do not mention section 33 in this connection. Harpum's view is of some importance, because he was the Law Commissioner responsible for the 2002 Act.²⁷⁰ Perhaps the authors meant to exclude from the purview of their remarks any proprietary estoppel which—as in *Yaxley v Gotts*—amounted to or created a constructive trust.

But as Joanne Wicks has justly observed,²⁷¹ it is not clear how easy the Land Registry staff will find it to distinguish constructive trusts which cannot be the subject of a notice from proprietary estoppels which apparently can be. And what of those estoppels which are *given effect to by way of* constructive trust, as in *Yaxley v Gotts*? Which box do *they* go in? Of

---

²⁶⁷ Land Registration Act 2002, s 29(1), (2)(a)(ii), Sched 3 para 2.
²⁶⁸ See C Harpum and J Bignell, *Registered Land: Law and Practice under the Land Registration Act 2002* (Bristol, Jordans, 2004) para 10.57.
²⁶⁹ Ibid, para 9.16. The same passage appears in para 3.41 of the same authors' earlier, introductory work, *Registered Land—The New Law* (Bristol, Jordans, 2002).
²⁷⁰ See also Law Commission, *Land Registration for the 21st Century: A Conveyancing Revolution* (Law Com No 271, 2001) paras 5.30 and 6.9, which are to the same effect.
²⁷¹ Wicks (n 202) n 32.

course, in any case where the claimant is in actual occupation of the land concerned (which may be most of them) the problem should not arise. Either way the priority of the claimant's interest will normally be protected. But it is strange that the new legislation—of conspicuously better quality than the Land Registration Act 1925 which it replaced—should have seemingly opened up such a division between proprietary estoppel and common intention constructive trust cases.

(d) Negative entropy?

Even if I have argued that proprietary estoppel and common intention constructive trusts spring from the same root, there is nonetheless a regrettable tendency in this area of the law to lump doctrines together, as all savouring of the same overarching idea, that is, to prevent unconscionable conduct. In a recent lecture Lord Neuberger put it this way:

> At the risk of sounding like some madly optimistic physicist seeking the unified field theory which eluded Einstein, may I suggest that there may be a general principle applicable to all estoppels? . . . At least in broad terms, may not estoppel now be seen to be a generic term for a claim by a claimant who has changed his position in the reasonable and foreseeable belief that a defendant's act, statement, silence or inaction has a particular consequence, so that it would now be unconscionable for the defendant to repudiate that consequence (wholly or to an extent) at least without giving te claimant some compensation.[272]

The trouble is that, put at such a high level of generality, such a formulation threatens to swallow up, not merely estoppel, but half of contract and tort law, as well as much of the law of restitution. If the distinction between, say, tort and contract is worth keeping, then it must equally be worth keeping the distinction between propositional and promissory forms of proprietary estoppel, that is, between *Willmott v Barber* and *Dilwyn v Llewelyn*. The first of each pair is about making good loss through misstatements, the second about allowing people to plan on the basis of their expectations. These are different legal objectives, requiring different rules.

On the other hand, a valiant attempt has recently been made to drive a further wedge between proprietary estoppel and common intention constructive trust. I have argued that the classical elements of both were and are the same: that is, promise, reliance, detriment. But Sir Terence Etherton now argues that *Stack v Dowden*[273] has destroyed all of that:

> This analysis of *Stack* helps to highlight why, contrary to the view expressed by Chadwick LJ in *Oxley*, there is no assimilation between the constructive trust in

[272] Neuberger (n 104) paras 36–37.
[273] *Stack* (n 41).

the *Stack* type of case and proprietary estoppel. They are performing quite different legal functions.

In the 2006 ACTAPS lecture Lord Neuberger described the essential requirements of proprietary estoppel as: (1) a statement or action (which can include silence or inaction) by one party, who ought to appreciate that the other party may act in reliance on it; (2) an act by that other party taken in reasonable belief that he has, or (more normally) will have, an interest in land, induced by the first party's action or statement ; and (3) detriment to the other party if the first party is able to resile from the belief so induced. The court will satisfy the equity by the minimum award necessary to do justice. None of those conditions is necessary for the claimant to succeed in a cause of action for unjust enrichment in the *Stack* type of case. Further, the remedy of a declaration of constructive trust for unjust enrichment performs a quite different function from relief for proprietary estoppel. As I have explained, the cause of action for unjust enrichment in *Stack* does not depend on any actual agreement, or common intention of the parties or any statement by the defendant or any detrimental reliance by the claimant on any such agreement, common intention or statement. [See *Jones v Kernott* [2009] EWHC 1713 (Ch), [4], [31].] The relief by way of constructive trust is not designed to compensate the claimant for any loss suffered, or to fulfil any expectation, since there may have been neither. It is designed quite simply to strip the defendant of his or her unjust enrichment. There is therefore no scope for any such concept as limiting the relief to the minimum necessary to do justice.[274]

Well, this may be the future. But it is certainly not the past.

I. CONCLUSION

At the end of the day, what does it mean to say that a trust has been imposed by law rather than intended by the parties? After all, it is the law that underpins the trust institution even when invoked by consent, and history tells us that the first uses as the forerunners of trusts were imposed on persons by the law in order to frustrate inequitable conduct by them. Later, persons would enter into such arrangements deliberately, knowing that the law would in those circumstances impose such uses or trusts. So at that stage we may say that they intend the consequences of their acts, and therefore *intended* those uses or trusts. How often do we say 'You brought it upon yourself'?

In cases where a presumption is supplied by the law, as in the law of resulting trusts, *ex hypothesi* there is no sufficient evidence of the parties' own intentions, and so without the rule of law which supplies the presumption there would be no trust. Does that make it a trust *imposed* by the law, or a trust which (according to the procedural and evidential rules) was *intended* by the parties? What fundamentally is the difference between

---

[274] Etherton (n 220) 286–7.

the case of A transferring land to B on express trust for A, and A transferring to B without saying anything, but in circumstances where there is presumed to be a trust for B? In each case rules of law impose consequences, like them or not, on the parties in the light of the facts which have occurred. The substantive result of each of these two cases is the same. Given the mischief intended to be remedied by the formalities rules, it may make little sense to say that the former trust must be evidenced in writing, but the latter need not. A better interpretation would say that writing was needed in both cases.

But in one case it might perhaps be thought worthwhile to distinguish the two situations. This is where A simply does not think about the matter at all, but would (if he *had* thought about it) have expressed the intention to create a trust for himself. *Ex hypothesi* he did not think about it, so we cannot expect him to have complied with the formalities rules. And—we might suppose—third parties are unlikely to be hurt, at any rate without their own fault, since they should take legal advice before buying from the apparent beneficial owner. The difficulty is twofold. First we must factor in extra legal costs for advice for those dealing with the apparent beneficial owner.

Second, in order to distinguish the two cases, we must allow the argument in every case to be made, with evidence adduced in support, that *this* case is *not* caught by the formality rule, whereas that case *is*, for the court cannot know, without hearing such evidence and argument, which case presented to the court is which. Yet the incurring of unnecessary legal costs, and the exposure of the apparent beneficial owner and the third party who deal with him to possibly vexatious, and certainly expensive, litigation, in order to decide who is telling the truth, constitute in large part the mischief against which the rule is directed.[275] Yes, says the legislator, the rule at the margins operates severely on some litigants with just claims. But it saves a whole lot more potential defendants with equally justified defences from unnecessary litigation.

A similar problem arises in cases of so-called automatic resulting trust. If A transfers land to B on trust for C for life, but, *knowing the rules*, is silent as to the remainder, how is that different from a transfer on trust for C for life, with an express remainder to A? The formalities rule should be the same in ether case. It is true that we would not describe a motorist who takes out his car on the road, and who becomes potentially subject to the operation of the tort of negligence, as thereby impliedly undertaking to compensate any pedestrian whom he negligently injures whilst driving. But that is very different. The legal consequences of the motorist's 'choice' are contingent on his own subsequent negligence, which is beyond his control. He intends to take his car out, but not to have an accident. The transferor

---

[275] See eg Lord Hoffmann in *Actionstrength* (n 131) [19].

of land, on the other hand, is making a deliberate choice which immediately translates into legal consequences. He may not get all the legal consequences right, but that *is* why he is doing what he is doing.

And if the transferor does not know the rules? Well, '[a] person who declares trusts of property only gives the beneficial interests covered by the trusts. Everything else he retains and does not give.'[276] It is not unfair for the law to suppose that what a man does not intend to give away, he intends to keep.

The history of constructive trusts is littered with anomalies of this sort. Partly as a result, categorisation disputes of the most sterile kind abound. But the policy reasons for distinguishing between different kinds of trust are or may be different in different areas of the law. What is right for formalities may not be right for limitation of actions, or for (say) international recognition of trusts.[277] If we are to move forward in this area of the law, we do not need a grand taxonomy conference. We need a clear view as to what policy rules we are trying to impose and why. Once we know what the policy is, and what kinds of case it applies to, the taxonomy will sort itself out. At that point, as Sellar and Yeatman[278] might put it, constructive trust history will come to a .

---

[276] *Commissioner for Stamp Duties v Perpetual Trustee Co Ltd* [1943] AC 425, 431.
[277] See J Harris, *The Hague Trusts Convention* (Oxford, Hart Publishing, 2002) 124–34.
[278] *1066 And All That*.

2
Reliance-Based Constructive Trusts

SIMON GARDNER*

A. INTRODUCTION

In a number of contexts, the law imposes a constructive trust in such a way as to produce an outcome which someone intended and which would not otherwise come about. For example, a secret trust tracks the testator's informally expressed wishes for the post-mortem disposition of his property. If we assume that the constructive trust arises *in order to* effectuate the relevant intention, the next question is: why should this be? Why, for example, should a testator's informally expressed wishes be given effect when, by definition, they do not comply with the law's normal requirements for such an outcome?

Much has been written on that question, both as regards specific contexts such as secret trusts, and generally. It seems to me fair to say that the question has, nevertheless, not yet been satisfactorily answered. In this chapter, I propose to come at the matter from a different direction. I shall examine the possibility that these types of constructive trust not only effectuate intention, but also correct a reliance loss—specifically, the loss that someone suffers when, acting in reasonable reliance on another's undertaking, he foregoes his opportunity to achieve the content of the undertaking in some other way. If these trusts can indeed be regarded in this way, it becomes much easier to see why the law should impose them.

The kinds of constructive trusts I shall consider are: secret trusts (both the fully and the half-secret varieties); trusts arising under the doctrine in *Rochefoucauld v Boustead*[1] and *Bannister v Bannister*,[2] and under principles

---

* I am indebted to those who had a hand, in their different ways, in the formation of the ideas contained in this contribution, in particular (as will appear) Charles Mitchell, Ben McFarlane and Mindy Chen-Wishart.

[1] [1897] 1 Ch 196 (CA).
[2] [1948] 2 All ER 133 (CA).

advanced in *Neale v Willis*[3] and *Pallant v Morgan*;[4] and those associated with mutual wills and proprietary estoppel.

Parts B–E are taken up with an examination of this material, to see whether it can indeed be successfully analysed along the lines of my hypothesis. Part F draws together the results of this examination, and considers the relationship between my approach and some of its cousins. Parts G and H glance at some further ideas to which my approach may point.

B. TRANSFERS IN RELIANCE ON UNDERTAKINGS GIVEN BY THE TRANSFEREE TO THE TRANSFEROR

We begin with some familiar material, which I believe can be analysed in the way I am suggesting. In this material, there is a transfer of the property in question to the person who emerges as trustee, and this transfer itself features in the action in reliance on the part of the recipient of the undertaking.

1. Secret Trusts

First I must establish that secret trusts belong in this study at all. I take it as self-evident that secret trusts effectuate testators' intentions. It seems to me also plain that they are constructive, rather than express, trusts.

If secret trusts are express trusts, it must be explained why they do not fail as testamentary dispositions which should have been made in conformity with the Wills Act,[5] but were not. One attempt at this avers that they are not testamentary: that they are formed *inter vivos*.[6] That is simply fallacious.[7] Another allows that they do indeed operate post mortem, and so are testamentary and thus on the face of it disallowed by the Wills Act; but maintains that they are saved because the Wills Act is itself disapplied, via the maxim 'equity will not permit a statute to be used as an instrument of fraud'.[8] This effort fares better: the authorities establish that there is such a maxim, and if 'fraud' covers all the ground of secret trusts (which is not wholly clear, however), it should save them from the Wills Act in this way. But although the maxim's existence is historically undeniable, it is not easy to reconcile with what we nowadays understand of parliamentary sovereignty. By what right does 'equity'—which means the judiciary, princi-

---

[3] (1968) 19 P & CR 836 (CA).
[4] [1953] Ch 43.
[5] Wills Act 1837, s 9, as amended by Administration of Justice Act 1982, s 17.
[6] *Re Gardner (No 2)* [1923] 2 Ch 230.
[7] P Critchley, 'Instruments of Fraud, Testamentary Dispositions, and the Doctrine of Secret Trusts' (1999) 115 *Law Quarterly Review* 631, 633–41.
[8] *McCormick v Grogan* (1869) LR 4 HL 82.

pally of the Chancery Division—decide whether or not to apply an Act of Parliament, on a basis ('fraud') of its own choosing and defining?[9] Perhaps the maxim is best seen as a metaphorical explanation for what actually occurs via a constructive trust.[10]

Regarding secret trusts instead as constructive trusts allows us to admit that they operate post mortem, but to explain how they escape the Wills Act: it simply does not apply to them. The Act applies to testamentary dispositions. Seen as constructive trusts, secret trusts are (unlike express trusts) not dispositions. I suspect that this is what Lord Sumner meant when, in his opinion in *Blackwell v Blackwell*,[11] he remarked that 'the whole topic is detached from the enforcement of the Wills Act itself'. That assertion is sometimes linked with the account which treats secret trusts as express trusts formed *inter vivos*, the common feature being the idea that the trust takes effect '*dehors* the will'. On the argument here, however, the two analyses use that idea in radically different ways: the one successfully, the other not.

So it seems to me clear that secret trusts are correctly seen as constructive. We can now move on to my argument that, although they give effect to the testator's wishes, they can also be analysed as calculated to correct a loss suffered in reliance on another's undertaking.

In this contribution, I shall call the recipient of the undertaking X, and its giver Y. In secret trusts, then, the law rules that if X, the deceased, leaves property to Y after an undertaking given by Y to hold the property on trust for Z, Y must comply with that undertaking. There appears to be reliance by X on Y's undertaking.[12] Further, it seems to me true to say that, were Y not to be held to his undertaking (that is, bound by the trust), X would

---

[9] Notice that not even the Human Rights Act 1998 allows the judges to disapply Acts of Parliament, though 'interpretations' under s 3 can come close to that. A judicial power to disapply a statute (or indeed declare it invalid) is asserted by some contemporary public law thinkers, but has not been put to the test in modern times. In any event, it depends for its justification on the statute's being constitutionally improper, and not, as the 'fraud' maxim does, on its botching a detail of interpersonal justice.

[10] Cf *McCormick v Grogan* (1869) LR 4 HL 82, 97 (Lord Westbury): 'The Court of Equity has, from a very early period, decided that even an Act of Parliament shall not be used as an instrument of fraud; and if in the machinery of perpetrating a fraud an Act of Parliament intervenes, the Court of Equity, it is true, does not set aside the Act of Parliament, but it fastens on the individual who gets a title under that Act, and imposes upon him a personal obligation, because he applies the Act as an instrument for accomplishing a fraud.'

[11] [1929] AC 318, 340. At 340 he also said 'there is no contradiction of the Wills Act'; and at 334: 'the doctrine of equity, by which parol evidence is admissible to prove what is called "fraud" in connection with secret trusts, and effect is given to such trusts when established, would not seem to conflict with any of the Acts under which from time to time the Legislature has regulated the right of testamentary disposition. . . . I do not see how the statute-law relating to the form of a valid will is concerned at all.'

[12] In part F, however, I shall argue that this appearance may be deceptive; and, therefore, that at least some secret trusts (anomalously among the types of constructive trust reviewed in this contribution) ought not to find support in the principle under discussion. For the moment, however, let us stick with the appearance.

suffer a loss; and that correcting that loss requires Y to be held to his undertaking.

To explain this latter assertion, I need to introduce and highlight an idea that will be central to this contribution. It is the idea of 'lost opportunity'. In a secret trust scenario, X loses the property in question. But reversing that loss would require only a resulting trust against Y, so cannot explain the law as we actually have it. It is not X's whole loss, however. He also loses the opportunity to provide for Z in the way he desires. Before he engages with Y, X has this opportunity. In reliance on Y's undertaking to take the property and apply it in the desired way, X leaves the property to Y. X thereby loses his opportunity to achieve what he wants via some other arrangement. Since, by definition, X is now dead, there is no recreating the opportunity. The only way to rectify its loss is by holding Y to his undertaking. It is in this way that the law on secret trusts can be seen not only to effectuate X's wishes, but at the same time to correct X's reliance loss.

Notice that the argument works as well for half-secret as for fully secret trusts: even though X here leaves the property to Y expressly 'on trust', he still relies on Y's undertaking to hold it *for* Z, and loses his opportunity to achieve a trust for Z unless Y is now held to that undertaking.

There may, however, be a problem. Commenting on an earlier draft of this chapter, Charles Mitchell objected that 'it seems meaningless to speak of X as having lost something [as I say he has lost his opportunity to make some other arrangement] after he has died'. The point clearly merits attention. On reflection, however, it seems to me not to overset my argument. I think I would answer it in two ways. (If it can be answered for the post-mortem context of secret trusts, it should, obviously, pose no problem for the remaining contexts with which this contribution deals, which are all in principle *inter vivos*.)

First, I am not sure that I agree with Mitchell's observation at all—or rather, more importantly, that the law agrees with it. It would mean, I think, that a deceased's estate cannot recover for a post-mortem breach of contract, when I believe the law of contract does allow such recovery. Closer to the present discussion, it would apparently obstruct all explanations of post-mortem dispositions centring on the protection of the disponor's interest. For example, it would mean we cannot support a will, or a secret trust, on the basis of upholding the testator's wishes, alias addressing his expectation loss.

Secondly, I am inclined to think that, even if right in principle, the observation does not quite bear on the idea I have in mind. The matter is subtle, and we need to think it through in careful steps. (1) X loses his opportunity to make other arrangements at the moment when, having chosen to put his faith in Y, he acts irretrievably upon that choice. In the context under discussion—that of secret trusts—this must be the moment when it becomes too late for X to alter his testamentary arrangements before he dies, leaving the property in question to Y. It is impossible to say exactly when that is, but it is plainly during X's lifetime, if only by a short while. (2) However, we do not readily think of this move as a loss unless and until Y resiles from his undertaking. That is probably because, until that time, there is a countervailing gain, in the form of the arrangement that X has with Y for the achievement of what he wants, which matters more to X than the loss. (3) But if and when Y does resile from his undertaking—in the practical sense that, having inherited X's property, he proposes or is obliged to use it otherwise than in accordance with his undertaking[13]—the picture changes. The gain disappears; the loss of the opportunity to make other arrangements remains outstanding, leaving the net effect one of a loss after all, such that we do start to use that word.

Certainly, Y's resiling from his undertaking is something that, in the secret trust context, necessarily occurs after X's death. But the loss which step (3) thus brings to the fore—X's loss of the opportunity to make other arrangements—has effect from the earlier time identified in step (1), which is necessarily during X's life.[14] This analysis connects with the point made above, that the law's correction of the loss has to operate with reference to the time identified in step (1)—which it does, in the shape of the constructive trust that arises as soon as, X having foregone his opportunity to make other arrangements on the faith of Y's undertaking, the property in question reaches Y's hands. Simultaneously, of course, this particular response pre-empts steps (2) and (3), that is, prevents those things occurring which make us want to speak of step (1) as a 'loss' at all; but that does not negate the truth that it is in step (1) that the loss, to which the law is responding, has its roots.[15]

For these two reasons, then, I believe it remains possible, despite Mitchell's objection, coherently to regard secret trusts as calculated to correct the loss of opportunity that, in reliance on X's undertaking, Y suffers when he foregoes his opportunity to make his intended provision for Z via other arrangements.

---

[13] The words 'proposes or is obliged' cover both the case where Y voluntarily repudiates his undertaking; and that where his own creditors, post mortem successors, etc, assert that the property he has inherited from X forms part of his personal estate, and is thus available to them.

[14] It is as if A contracts with B; then A incurs expenditure in reliance on the expectation of B's performance (= step 1); then A dies; then B repudiates (= steps 2 and 3). There seems no reason to doubt that the law allows A's estate to recover the reliance loss from B, exactly as A himself could have done had he survived. In other words, if (though, as I say in the text, I doubt this) the law constructs a 'loss' as something which must necessarily be suffered before death, A's expenditure here falls within that construction.

[15] The pre-emption is not, however, of the kind we see when the court issues an injunction to, for example, restrain the anticipated disclosure of confidential information. In that case, there is no loss in any sense unless and until the disclosure occurs; the pre-emptive response negatives everything.

2. *Rochefoucauld v Boustead* and *Bannister v Bannister*

Once again, to earn them a place in this study, I must first show that trusts arising under the doctrine in *Rochefoucauld v Boustead*[16] and *Bannister v Bannister*[17] give effect to the transferor's intention. This is indeed the case. We find it in *Bannister*,[18] where the transferor intended the transferee to hold the property in question on trust for the transferor herself, and that was the outcome; and in *Rochefoucauld*,[19] where the transferor (the Dutch company) intended the transferee (Mr Boustead) to hold the property on trust for the Comtesse de la Rochefoucauld, and that was the outcome.

I must also show that these trusts are constructive trusts at all, rather than express, as some contend. This seems to me quite clear. If they are express, at first sight they are covered by the Law of Property Act 1925, section 53(1)(b), and it must be shown why that is not in fact the case. Here there is no counterpart of the attempt to show that secret trusts are not covered by the Wills Act because they operate *inter vivos*: no such time-shift, taking the trusts in question outside the scope of section 53(1)(b), can conceivably be suggested. The only possible resort is to the maxim 'equity will not permit a statute to be used as an instrument of fraud'. As with secret trusts, that analysis is historically tenable, but theoretically objectionable. If these trusts are constructive, however, all is straightforward: by section 53(2) of the Law of Property Act 1925, section 53(1)(b) applies only to express trusts (just as the Wills Act applies only to express trusts because it applies only to testamentary dispositions).

It is sometimes said that *Rochefoucauld* itself declares these trusts to be express. That is a misreading of the case's reasoning, however. The key statement,[20] by Lindley LJ, is: 'The trust which the plaintiff has established is clearly an express trust within the meaning of that expression as

---

[16] [1897] 1 Ch 196 (CA).
[17] [1948] 2 All ER 133 (CA).
[18] Likewise *Hodgson v Marks* [1971] Ch 892 (CA).
[19] I had previously overlooked the fact that the intended beneficiary in this decision was not also the transferor; my error was brought home to me on re-reading T Youdan, 'Formalities for Trusts of Land, and the Doctrine in *Rochefoucauld v Boustead*' [1984] *Cambridge Law Journal* 306.
[20] *Rochefoucauld* (n 16) 208. Reference may also be made to another passage in Lindley LJ's reasoning, at 206: '[T]he Statute of Frauds does not prevent the proof of a fraud; and . . . it is a fraud on the part of a person to whom land is conveyed as a trustee, and who knows it was so conveyed, to deny the trust and claim the land himself. Consequently, notwithstanding the statute, it is competent for a person claiming land conveyed to another to prove by parol evidence that it was so conveyed upon trust for the claimant, and that the grantee, knowing the facts, is denying the trust and relying upon the form of conveyance and the statute, in order to keep the land himself.' This may follow the analysis whereby the formality statute is disapplied under the fraud maxim, allowing the original express trust to be informally proved; but it is certainly compatible with the analysis favoured here, whereby the fraud generates a constructive trust, which can be informally proved because the statute never applied to it anyway.

explained in *Soar v Ashwell*.'²¹ Lindley LJ's previous sentence makes clear that he is here considering whether the defendant had a defence of limitation. The statutory limitation provisions in force at the time²² distinguished constructive trusts, to which limitation applied, from express trusts, to which it did not. *Soar v Ashwell* interpreted that distinction, reviewing earlier authorities aimed at the same context. The decision's upshot is put thus by Kay LJ: 'The result seems to be that there are certain cases of what are, strictly speaking, constructive trusts, in which the Statute of Limitations cannot be set up as a defence'²³—that is, constructive trusts which, for limitation purposes, count as express trusts. So Lindley LJ's statement that the trust established in *Rochefoucauld* was 'an express trust within the meaning of that expression as explained in *Soar v Ashwell*' is in fact a confirmation that that trust was in truth a constructive trust; were it in truth an express trust, the reference to *Soar v Ashwell* would have been otiose. This reading of *Soar v Ashwell* is confirmed by the judgment of Millett LJ in *Paragon Finance plc v D B Thakerar & Co (a firm)*;²⁴ and the view that the principle in *Rochefoucauld v Boustead* generates a constructive, not express, trust is confirmed by *Bannister v Bannister*.²⁵

Now to think about these constructive trusts in terms of my analysis. In the cases concerned, X makes an *inter vivos* transfer of his land to Y, after an undertaking given by Y to hold the land on trust for Z (who may, as some of the cases show, be himself). X will normally rely on Y's undertaking, and will suffer a detriment in doing so. For before he engages with Y, X has the opportunity to establish the trust for Z. In reliance on Y's undertaking to hold the land for Z, X transfers it to Y. X thereby loses his opportunity to establish his desired trust for Z in some other way.²⁶ The law addresses that loss by requiring Y to honour his undertaking.

It is, however, less obvious here than in the post-mortem case of secret

---

²¹ [1893] 2 QB 390 (CA).
²² Judicature Act 1873, s 25(2); Trustee Act 1888, s 8.
²³ *Soar* (n 21) 405. Lord Esher MR, at 393–4, and Bowen LJ, at 396–8, express themselves less crisply, but to essentially the same effect.
²⁴ [1999] 1 All ER 400 (CA) 409. See further *Cattley v Pollard* [2006] EWHC 3130 (Ch), [2007] Ch 353.
²⁵ *Bannister* (n 17) 136. See too the analysis of counsel in *Ottaway v Norman* [1972] Ch 698, 701–02, adopted by Nourse J in *Re Cleaver (deceased)* [1981] 1 WLR 939, 947. The same area of law also received attention in *Hodgson v Marks* (n 18), but nothing relevant to the present discussion was added.
²⁶ It is fair to say that we do not know why, in *Rochefoucauld* (n 16) itself, X (the Dutch company) wanted Y (Mr Boustead) to hold the property on trust for Z (the Comtesse). The reported facts disclose no self-serving reason on X's part for wanting this outcome; it certainly appears not to have been X's idea (ibid, 197); but, however it occurred, it does indeed seem to have been a feature of a scheme, to which X was party, that the transfer to Y should be on the basis that Y be trustee for Z. If this was not the case—ie if X transferred the land to Y, unconcerned as to Y's plans for it—then I cannot see why the upshot was not simply an ineffective declaration of trust by Y. Y seems to have agreed with Z, before he took the transfer, that he would hold the land for her; but this surely makes no difference, at least if (as appears to have been the case) Z was in no position to help or hinder the transfer.

trusts that the constructive trust, imposed on Y from the time of the transfer, is needed to correct X's loss of opportunity. In the post-mortem case, since X has died, his loss of the opportunity to provide for Z can be corrected only by obliging Y to hold the property for Z. In the *inter vivos* case, by contrast, it might be objected that the lost opportunity to place the land on trust for Z can be restored by obliging Y to return the land to X (that is, by imposing a resulting trust of the land upon Y), whereupon X may once again—this time more successfully—set about establishing a trust of it in favour of Z.[27]

But this objection is too simplistic, in a number of ways. First, sometimes X will have died since making the transfer to Y; a resulting trust would then, far from allowing X to provide for Y, give the land to X's residuary legatee. Second, sometimes the transaction will be time sensitive: it will matter that the trust for Y should have been established when X transferred the land to Y on that understanding, rather than by a second, necessarily later, attempt—as for example where X has become insolvent in the meantime, or where his original attempt sought to take advantage of a tax break, subsequently closed. These remarks are, however, evidently true only in some circumstances, and if they were the whole story one would expect to see an inquiry in each case whether it should be so characterised, the outcome (constructive or resulting trust) depending on the answer to that inquiry. But there is a third point to be made, which shows that a resulting trust would never—even in this *inter vivos* case—operate precisely to restore X's lost opportunity, and that a constructive trust, holding Y to his undertaking, is always required to achieve that end. Returning the land to X would allow X now *not* to establish a trust of it for Z after all, but rather to keep it himself or to transfer it to or make a trust of it in favour of some other person. That outcome would not cleanly correct the loss that X suffered, when he relied on Y's undertaking, of the opportunity *to establish a trust of the land for Z.*

3. Mutual Wills

Usually,[28] in a mutual wills case, two people agree to make wills whereby the first of them to die leaves property to the survivor, on the footing that the survivor will in turn leave the property to a third person. The two testators must also agree not to revoke these wills. After the death of the first of the two, the property which he bequeaths to the survivor under this

---

[27] Cf B McFarlane, 'Constructive Trusts Arising on a Receipt of Property *Sub Conditione*' (2004) 120 *Law Quarterly Review* 667, 685: 'It is not immediately obvious why reliance by [X] should give rise to a right of [Z] which arises automatically, independently of [X's] current wishes.'

[28] For a variant, see part D.

agreement is immediately caught by a constructive trust[29] in favour of the third person, in accordance with the agreement—that is, with the first decedent's intentions.

The fit with my analysis seems straightforward. X (the first decedent) transfers the property in question to Y (the survivor) in reliance on Y's undertaking to in turn bequeath the property to Z (the third person). X thus loses the opportunity to provide for Z as he intended, say by leaving the property to Z directly. The constructive trust over the relevant property in Y's hands corrects that loss.

C. OTHER CASES OF LOSS OF OPPORTUNITY BY THOSE TO WHOM UNDERTAKINGS ARE GIVEN BY THE TRANSFEREES OF PROPERTY

So my argument is that, in the material discussed in Part B, we see a constructive trust arising over Y's property where that is necessary in order to correct the loss of opportunity—to achieve his intentions via some other route—that X suffers when he transfers the relevant property to Y in reliance on Y's undertaking to hold it in that way.

Under this argument, of course, the essential thing is that X, relying on Y's undertaking, suffers his loss of opportunity. In principle, it ought not to be important just how he does so: whether by transferring the property in question to X, or in some other way. So now I shall turn to material in which there is, once again, a transfer of the relevant property to Y; but this transfer does not itself form part of X's action in reliance.

1. *Neale v Willis*

In *Neale v Willis*,[30] a husband bought a house for £2,820. He borrowed £50 of this from his wife's mother. She lent him the £50 on the understanding that her daughter, his wife, should have a half share in the house. But the eventual conveyance was to him alone. The Court of Appeal, however, decided that he held the house on constructive trust for himself and his wife equally, thus effectuating the agreement.

It is not difficult to fit this decision to my analysis. X is the mother; Y, the husband; Z, the daughter. As I have noted, there is a difference from

---

[29] The characterisation of the trust as constructive seems not to be disputed. There is a concern, however, whether it is properly termed a 'trust' at all, since it may bind only such of the relevant property as remains undisposed of at the survivor's death. The cases treat this as possible, referring to the trust as a 'floating' one: *Birmingham v Renfrew* (1937) 57 CLR 666; *Ottaway v Norman* [1972] Ch 698; *Re Goodchild (deceased)* [1996] 1 WLR 694, affirmed [1997] 1 WLR 1216 (CA).
[30] (1968) 19 P & CR 836 (CA).

the material considered in Part B: although Y took a transfer of the land and gave an undertaking regarding it to X, the transferor of the land was not X, but a third party. Under my argument, however, this is unimportant. The key element is the fact that, when X made her loan, she relied on Y's undertaking to hold the land for Z, and so lost not merely her £50 but also the opportunity to make other arrangements for securing her desired provision for Z. The constructive trust which arose, holding Y to his undertaking, corrected this loss.

2. Pallant v Morgan

In a *Pallant v Morgan*[31] case, two people are interested in buying the same property. Rather than bid against one another, which would only raise the price, they enter into a 'joint venture' agreement: an agreement that one will buy the property, then share it with the other. The buyer cannot resile once he has obtained the property: a constructive trust arises obliging him to share it as agreed (though of course there is an allowance for his expenditure in acquiring the property). The constructive trust thus tracks the parties' intentions. There is a tradition to the effect that the doctrine applies even if the terms of the joint venture agreement are not fully settled, so that there is no enforceable contract, certainly not one capable of specific performance.[32]

Let me say immediately that this doctrine may be capable of explanation in another way: on the basis that when the buyer acquires the property, he does so as (*pro tanto*) a fiduciary for the other. That is how the idea seems to be put by Malins V-C in *Chattock v Muller*[33] and by Millett J in *Lonrho Plc v Fayed (No 2)*.[34] On this view, it would of course remain to be explained why acquisition by a fiduciary entails the fiduciary holding the property in question on constructive trust; I do not propose to investigate

---

[31] [1953] 1 Ch 43.

[32] As in *Pallant v Morgan* (n 31) itself; also in *Banner Homes Group plc v Luff Developments Ltd* [2000] Ch 372 (CA). Care is needed, however. More recent decisions have emphasised that the parties do at any rate need to be committed to a joint venture: *London & Regional Investments Ltd v TBI plc* [2002] EWCA Civ 355 [47]–[49]; *Kilcarne Holdings Ltd v Targetfollow (Birmingham) Ltd* [2004] EWHC 2547 (Ch), [2005] 2 P & CR 105 [229], affirmed [2005] EWCA Civ 45; *Cobbe v Yeoman's Row Management Ltd* [2008] UKHL 55, [2008] 1 WLR 1752 [30]–[37].

[33] (1878) LR 8 Ch D 177 (Ch D). Malins V-C speaks of the buyer as the other's agent. In *Explora Group Plc v Hesco Bastion Ltd* [2005] EWCA Civ 646 [47] it is observed that the buyer cannot be a true agent, otherwise there would be a contract between the parties, contrary to the tradition referred to in the text; see too McFarlane (n 27) 685 n 104. But the missing contract is that determining how the property is to be shared between the parties once acquired. *Quaere* whether its absence need prevent the buyer acting as agent; and certainly, a fiduciary relationship does not in principle require a contract.

[34] [1992] 1 WLR 1, 9–10.

that here. I wish instead to show that the *Pallant v Morgan* doctrine can alternatively be explained as an example of my analysis.

In the terms of that analysis, Y takes a transfer of the property after undertaking to X to allow a beneficial interest in it. The fact that the intended beneficiary is X himself, rather than a third party, Z, is unimportant. X is not the transferor of the property, but this too is unimportant. The key question is whether, in relying on Y's undertaking, X lost an opportunity to secure his intended beneficial interest in another way.

The answer is not straightforward. If X did suffer such a loss, it would obviously be correct also to say that he sustained a detriment: so, to fit my argument, this doctrine must involve a detriment. However, according to Chadwick LJ in *Banner Homes Group plc v Luff Developments Ltd*,[35] detriment is not required, because it is not always present, in a *Pallant v Morgan* case: it is enough if, through X's reliance on Y's undertaking, *either* X suffers detriment *or* Y gains an advantage. On this view, I could not claim this entire doctrine for my argument, though I might be able to claim its 'detriment mode'. But it seems to me that there is no warrant for Chadwick LJ's view, and that detriment—in the shape of loss of opportunity—is indeed a feature of all the doctrine's cases.

Chadwick LJ was led to his view by the observation that there was no detriment in *Pallant v Morgan* itself, yet a constructive trust arose. He then applied his view to the *Banner Homes* case, where, he thought, there may have been no detriment either.[36] The reason was that, in both cases, X would not have secured the property in question outside the joint venture.[37] In *Pallant v Morgan* this was because, although X would have bid for the property himself, Y would have outbid him.[38] In *Banner Homes*, it was because X would probably not have bid on his own account at all. So in neither decision did reliance on Y's undertaking cause X to lose the chance of acquiring the property outright. That seems to me correct. But it seems to me that X in both cases did lose, through reliance on Y's undertaking, the chance to secure a binding joint venture agreement with Y (or perhaps, though this may have been only a theoretical possibility, someone else), and so to take an interest in the property that way.

Remember the tradition whereby the terms of the joint venture agreement

---

[35] [2000] Ch 372 (CA) 388, 398–99 and 401.
[36] This was in fact the finding of the trial judge: ibid, 382. Chadwick LJ himself is less sure: ibid, 401.
[37] Which might sometimes be the case: as perhaps in *Holiday Inns Inc v Broadhead* (1974) 232 EG 951.
[38] Although Y ultimately bought the property for £1,000, X's bidding limit for it was £2,000, while Y's was £3,000. '[X's] claim rested on the fact that his agent had been kept out of the bidding by the arrangement which [Y] later repudiated. Since it was too late to restore [X] to his former position, [Y] was held to the arrangement he had made': *Lonrho* (n 34) 10 (Millett J).

need not be fully settled, meaning that there is no enforceable contract, certainly not one capable of specific performance. If there were such a contract, Y could of course claim his agreed interest via the conversion of this contract. The *Pallant v Morgan* doctrine operates where, in the absence of such a contract, Y assures X that he can nonetheless be trusted to acquire the property (if at all) for both of them as a joint venture. The fact that X would not have acquired the property solely for himself is then nothing to the point. It is enough if, relying on Y's assurance, X foregoes the chance to secure the joint venture arrangement after all.

It is of course insufficient that X merely fails to secure the arrangement: he must have had the chance to do so, and foregone that chance. And this is what we find in the relevant cases. Relying on Y's assurance, X refrains from playing a bargaining chip that might otherwise have helped him demand a proper contract before the start of bidding. X's bargaining chip in *Pallant v Morgan* was his ability, if he were to bid himself, if not to secure the property then nonetheless to force Y to pay at least £2,001 for it (remember that it in fact came to Y for £1,000). In the *Banner Homes* case, X's bargaining chip, though less clear cut, was nonetheless real: it was that, by bidding independently of Y, he would certainly have given Y a harder time. The advantage to Y that Chadwick LJ perceived in both cases was the correlative of this: the fact that, in reliance on Y's assurance that all would be well, X did not play his bargaining chip.[39]

If the doctrine is to fit my argument, I must finally show that the constructive trust is needed so as to correct X's loss. This is indeed the case. Under the promised joint venture agreement, X would have had a beneficial share in the property. Relying on Y's undertaking, he lost the opportunity to secure that share. The constructive trust, giving him his share after all, corrects that loss.

D. LOST OPPORTUNITY WHERE UNDERTAKINGS ARE GIVEN BY THOSE WHO HAVE PROPERTY ALL ALONG

Under my argument, the crucial thing is that X, by his action in reliance on Y's assurance, loses his opportunity to otherwise make the provision he wants to. It should not matter what form the action in reliance takes, so long as it has that consequence. Part C was aimed at beginning to verify that constructive trusts do indeed arise wherever that is the case, by finding instances of them in cases where Y takes a transfer of the property in

---

[39] Chadwick LJ himself appears to notice this: *Banner Homes* (n 35) 400–01. Ultimately, of course, my argument does not require that particular decisions such as those discussed are capable of explanation in this way: they may be explicable on some other basis, or even wrongly decided on their facts. The essential thing is that a case which does exhibit the characteristics I have described should generate a constructive trust in that way.

question, but not from X. Part D continues that work, by looking for further instances in cases where Y has the property in question all along.

Take, for example, the *Neale v Willis*[40] scenario. According to my argument, the key point is that X, the mother, relied on the undertaking given by Y, the husband, when she decided to lend him the money and to do so without formally securing the trust she wanted for Z, her daughter. It ought to be irrelevant that Y wanted the loan to buy the house. Imagine that he already owned the house, and sought the loan for some other reason. If, to obtain the loan from X, he gave the same undertaking to share the house with Z, and X relied on that undertaking in the same way, X would have suffered the same loss. If my argument is right, we should expect a constructive trust in Z's favour to arise against Y here too, correcting that loss on X's part. Is there any evidence that it will?

1. Mutual Wills Again

We looked at mutual wills in Part B. Usually, there is a transfer of the property in question from the first decedent to the survivor. But this is not essential. The mutual wills doctrine operates also where two people agree to make wills whereby each leaves property of his own directly to the third person. Again, so long as the two testators further agree not to revoke these wills, upon the death of the first a constructive trust arises over the relevant property in the hands of the survivor, in accordance with the agreement.[41]

In my terms, then: X makes his own bequest to Z, in the particular amount and form he does, in reliance on Y's undertaking also to make a certain bequest to Z. X thus loses the opportunity to adjust his own bequest so as to arrive at, or at least closer to, the overall provision for Z that he intended, or to extract a more effective (it would have to be *inter vivos*) engagement from Y. Just as in the more usual situation where X himself bequeaths the property in question to Y, a constructive trust arises over the relevant property in Y's hands, correcting that loss.

My pattern can, therefore, once again be found. The point to notice especially, however, is this. In the first version of mutual wills, considered in Part B, the property in question is transferred to the survivor, Y. But in this second version, there is no such transfer: the property is Y's own, all along. We thus find our evidence that constructive trusts will indeed arise, in the manner predicted by my argument, in that scenario too.

---

[40] *Neale* (n 30).
[41] *Re Dale (deceased)* [1994] Ch 31; *Birch v Curtis* [2002] EWHC 1158, [2002] WTLR 965 [6]. The authority base for this second version of mutual wills is thus quite slender. But the issue was very fully considered in *Re Dale (deceased)*, and decided in a judgment of Morritt J which follows the same path as my argument.

2. *Pallant v Morgan* Again

There is, however, a fly in the ointment. There is a case where the facts fit my pattern. If my argument is correct, we should expect to find a constructive trust, but the judges have in this case positively ruled out such a trust.

Say Y already owns property, and enters upon a joint venture with X to exploit the property, after undertaking, as an aspect of this joint venture (but not under an enforceable contract), to share the property with X. The facts fit my pattern: X, relying on Y's undertaking, fails to secure his right to his share in advance; that is, loses his opportunity to do so. So I should predict a constructive trust against Y to the extent of the share in question, correcting that loss. But if such a trust were to arise, it would be fair, given the way I have put the facts, to identify the doctrine in play as the rule in *Pallant v Morgan*. To be sure, the doctrine would be applied not in its familiar context where Y acquires the property in question after giving the undertaking, but in the context where Y has the property all along: but—this is the very point—on my argument, that ought not to matter. Despite earlier dicta to the contrary, however, it was held in *Cobbe v Yeoman's Row Management Ltd*[42] that *Pallant v Morgan* can operate only in the former context, not in the latter. This, then, stands as authority against my argument: as I say, the facts fit my pattern, so my argument would indicate a constructive trust, but the law rules this out.

There are two ways in which I might attempt to meet this difficulty. One is to aver that the ruling in *Cobbe* is simply wrong. While I dislike this approach in general, I confess to finding it tempting in the case of that particular decision. The second is to contend that, while a constructive trust does not arise in the circumstances I have described *under the name of Pallant v Morgan*, such a trust does, or might in principle, arise under some differently named doctrine, leaving the issue merely a trivial one about badging.

It is in fact possible to read *Cobbe* in the latter way. The ruling just mentioned meant that the claimant was unable to point to *Pallant v Morgan*, but he claimed also in proprietary estoppel, and no objection was raised in principle to his doing so. His claim eventually failed, but this was ultimately because, on the facts as the House of Lords saw them, the defendant had not cleanly undertaken to share the property in question with him.[43] This should likewise be fatal to the application of my analysis in its own terms. If Y does not cleanly undertake to X to allow X the right in question, X

---

[42] *Cobbe* (n 32) [33].
[43] Lord Scott's leading opinion in the decision itself clouds this, by invoking other supposed requirements (a 'certain', 'proprietary' interest) which the claimant failed to establish. But in *Thorner v Major* [2009] UKHL 18, [2009] 1 WLR 776 [96]–[99], these supposed requirements were forgotten, and the decision interpreted in the way suggested in the text.

cannot be said to forego the opportunity to secure the right (if, in these circumstances, he ever had such an opportunity) *in reasonable reliance on Y's undertaking*, so as to require Y to correct X's loss.

On this reasoning, then, *Cobbe* need not after all derail my argument. But I cannot yet firmly claim that my argument fits the law's response to this kind of situation, *sub nomine* proprietary estoppel. I need to look further at the latter, to see whether, if the facts as I require them are indeed made out, that doctrine will indeed generate a constructive trust in the way I predict. I turn to this now.

3. Proprietary Estoppel

Certainly, constructive trusts do sometimes arise via proprietary estoppel, that is, when the claimant emerges with a beneficial right (up to and including full ownership) in the defendant's property. Sometimes, too, these constructive trusts effectuate intentions. According (it seems) to Lord Scott in *Cobbe*,[44] they (and estoppel outcomes generally) must always do so; the 'always' should be doubted, for that would mean discarding a great deal of authority to which Lord Scott failed to attend, but it is certainly sometimes the case. To the extent, then, that proprietary estoppel does give rise to constructive trusts effectuating intentions, we can go on to ask whether these trusts also correct the loss, suffered by the claimant (X) in reliance on the defendant's (Y's) undertaking to allow the right, of the opportunity to secure the right more effectively. The answer, apparently, is 'sometimes'.

I will assume that reliance is indeed required for this doctrine.[45] The reliance clearly need not take the shape of the claimant's foregoing an opportunity he otherwise had to secure the right in question in some other way—even, crucially, where the outcome is a constructive trust. In *Dillwyn v Llewelyn*,[46] for example, the outcome was that the defendant (or his estate) had to convey the land in question to the claimant: in effect, then, the land was held on constructive trust for the claimant. Yet the defendant (Y) had surely not deprived the claimant (X) of the opportunity to secure

---

[44] *Cobbe* (n 32) [14], [16] and [28]: the defendant, having assured the claimant 'a certain interest' in his property, is estopped from denying that the claimant has that interest. The more recent decision of the House of Lords, *Thorner v Major* (n 43), implicitly (at [66]) restores the more widely held view that there is a discretion as to quantum; even Lord Scott seems to accept this, though preferring then to view the jurisdiction as a 'remedial constructive trust' rather than proprietary estoppel (ibid, [20]–[21]).

[45] Although in truth I am not convinced that it always is, for there is a tradition of at least fudging the point: eg *Wayling v Jones* (1993) 69 P & CR 170 (CA); *Campbell v Griffin* [2001] EWCA Civ 990, [2001] WTLR 981; *Ottey v Grundy* [2003] EWCA Civ 1176, [2003] WTLR 1253.

[46] (1862) 4 De G F & J 517, 45 ER 1285.

the right more effectively, if only because the defendant seems to have offered the right in question as a pure gift.

That, however, proves only that intention-effectuating constructive trusts can arise via proprietary estoppel even where there is no loss-of-opportunity pattern. I am comfortable with that; it seems to me likely that 'proprietary estoppel' is the title of a number of different projects,[47] so there is no problem in saying that decisions like *Dillwyn* may be aligned with some other of these projects. For present purposes, the question is whether intention-effectuating constructive trusts can arise via proprietary estoppel also where the claimant, relying on the defendant's undertaking, *does* forego the opportunity properly to secure the right in question.

I cannot very confidently point directly to a case in which this occurred, though it may be possible to view decisions like *Re Basham*[48] in this way: to say that the claimant, before doing so much for the defendant, might have demanded a firmer assurance of the promised bequest, but, relying on the defendant's assurance, forewent his opportunity to do so. I think, however, that we can certainly detect the loss of opportunity pattern in some estoppel decisions generating outcomes other than a constructive trust, and say that these must carry the point. This, for example, seems to be the way to look at *Crabb v Arun DC*.[49] Relying on the defendant's promise to allow him a way to the highway over its land, the claimant landlocked himself. He was awarded an easement over the defendant's land. This was the intended right, and it corrected the claimant's loss, in reliance on the defendant's undertaking, of his opportunity to secure the intended right more effectively. The outcome was not a constructive trust, but if this analysis holds good, that is simply because the intended right—the right which the claimant forewent his opportunity effectively to secure—was not a beneficial one. If we adjust the facts so that the intended right is of this kind, it ought to follow that a constructive trust emerges. This would be the instantiation of my argument that may perhaps otherwise be lacking.

E. REVERSAL OF RELIANCE LOSS AND FULFILMENT OF EXPECTATIONS

1. The Point

In Parts B–D we have considered a number of instances in which con-

---

[47] S Gardner, *An Introduction to Land Law*, 2nd edn (Oxford, Hart Publishing, 2009) § 7.4.
[48] [1986] 1 WLR 1498.
[49] [1976] Ch 179 (CA), and also *JT Developments Ltd v Quinn* (1991) 62 P & CR 33 (CA) and *Lloyd v Dugdale* [2002] 2 P & CR 13 (CA): see the analysis by S Bright and B McFarlane, 'Proprietary Estoppel and Property Rights' [2005] *Cambridge Law Journal* 449, esp 453 and 460–03.

structive trusts arise, effectuating intentions, but simultaneously obliging Y to make good the loss that X would otherwise suffer when, in reasonable reliance on Y's undertaking to allow a right in some property which is or comes to be in Y's hands, X foregoes an opportunity to bring this right about in some other way.

While these constructive trusts thus do effectuate intentions, it is far from obvious why the effectuation of intentions should be their raison d'être. In the material collected together in Part B—secret trusts, *Rochefoucauld v Boustead* and the first of the two versions of mutual wills—the key intention is presumably that of X, who as part of the transaction in question transfers the relevant property to Y: but there is a formality rule against the effectuation of that intention per se, that is, as the establishment of an express trust. In the material highlighted in Parts C and D, however—*Neale v Willis*, *Pallant v Morgan*, the second version of mutual wills and the relevant aspect of proprietary estoppel—the intention in question cannot be that of X. In this material, where Y acquires the property in question from a third party or has it all along, X is not the owner of the property at the moment before the trust has to arise, and so X has no right to say, by reference to his intention alone, that there should be such a trust. In principle, a trust could certainly arise (an express trust could be declared) on the basis of Y's intention, as articulated in his undertaking to X, but again there is a problem. Insofar as the property in question is land (as in *Neale v Willis* itself, all the leading *Pallant v Morgan* cases,[50] and usually in proprietary estoppel), or the trust is to arise by Y's testamentary disposition (as in mutual wills, and sometimes in proprietary estoppel), there is once again a contrary formality rule. In the Part C cases, too, although Y promises before acquiring the property that he will declare a trust of it as X wishes, when he actually does acquire it—which of course would be the relevant time, if the trust were to arise in that way—he fails to fulfil this promise.

We know that trusts—constructive trusts—do nevertheless arise in these cases. With sufficient effort and ingenuity, it may be possible to demonstrate that this should occur on the basis of X's or Y's intention, as the case may be. The object of this contribution, however, is to suggest that the correction of X's loss of opportunity, when he reasonably relies on Y's promise but is let down, offers an alternative, and more straightforward, explanation. In a nutshell, I have shown that in each type of case fitting my pattern, X does in fact suffer such a loss of opportunity; and that if the law is to correct this loss, it must in fact require Y to hold the property in question on a constructive trust along the lines of his undertaking. I have not shown, as a matter of principle, that the law ought to correct reliance losses; that could no doubt be shown, but I am assuming it. I recognise

---

[50] The others being *Chattock v Muller* (1878) 8 Ch D 177 and *Banner Homes* (n 35).

that, as the law stands, the principle for which I argue has taken effect in the guise of a number of nominally distinct doctrines (secret trusts, *Rochefoucauld v Boustead*, etc); but I contend, finally, that there is no good reason for this; that the principle may be recognised in the generalised form that I have described, yielding constructive trusts without further ado wherever the appropriate facts occur.[51]

2. McFarlane's View

Ben McFarlane too has published an article[52] considering the way to account for this material. Or, to be quite accurate, the bulk of this material, namely secret trusts, *Rochefoucauld v Boustead*, *Neale v Willis* and *Pallant v Morgan*.[53] He does not attempt to deal with mutual wills or proprietary estoppel. In his article, he not only advances his own thoughts, but also doubts the approach I am arguing for here.[54] I have the greatest respect for Ben McFarlane both as a scholar and as a colleague. Many of the positions I have assumed or adopted in this contribution are similar or identical to those put forward by him in his article. It is therefore with diffidence and regret that I find my thoughts to be ultimately at odds with his. I believe that in this contribution I provide the necessary defence of my own view, but I also think that there are difficulties with McFarlane's, to which I now turn.

To appreciate McFarlane's own statement of his account, it is necessary to note that, in all the material he seeks to explain, the person I am calling Y receives a transfer of the property in question: that is, he addresses only situations falling within my Parts B and C. He characterises the key facts as follows: 'first, . . . [Y] has made an undertaking to confer on another a right relating to the property [transferred]; secondly, . . . [Y] has, by means of this undertaking, acquired an advantage in relation to the acquisition of the property.' He continues:

> It seems that the law responds to this event by preventing [Y] from acting inconsistently with the undertaking, at least to the extent that the undertaking relates to the property in relation to the acquisition of which the purchaser has gained an advantage.[55]

---

[51] It follows, in particular, that I regard it as absurd for the House of Lords in *Cobbe* (n 32) to have held that the rule in *Pallant v Morgan* cannot apply where the facts are otherwise appropriate but Y already owns the property in question, when in such circumstances *the very same type* of constructive trust will arise 'via proprietary estoppel'.

[52] McFarlane (n 27).

[53] McFarlane also deals with what I call *Binions v Evans* [1972] Ch 359 (CA); he calls it *Ashburn Anstalt v W J Arnold & Co* [1989] Ch 1 (CA). For this, see part G.

[54] McFarlane (n 27) 685. I gave an earlier, less developed, account of my thinking in S Gardner, *An Introduction to the Law of Trusts*, 2nd edn (Oxford, Oxford University Press, 2003) 159–70; it is this account to which McFarlane is reacting.

[55] Ibid, 668. The final clause of this statement is intended to account for a detail of the deci-

Again,

> [A]ll the cases [which he seeks to explain] are based on the fact that [Y] has made an undertaking to confer on [Z] a new right in relation to property and as a result has acquired an advantage which assists his acquisition of that property, so that it can be said that [Y's] receipt of that property is coloured by his undertaking.[56]

McFarlane refers to a number of judicial dicta which, he says, put the rationale of this material in that way.[57] These dicta seem to me, on examination, simply to refer to the fact that, in the contexts in question, Y acquires the property after giving an undertaking. They do not add that the law is concerned specifically to prevent Y thereby securing an advantage; hence they stand neutrally as between us.[58] In the end, however, I am less concerned with what individual judges may have said than about the success or otherwise of the two theories in explaining the shape of the rules, and in holding theoretical water. It seems to me that McFarlane's account has three main weaknesses.

First, the account fails to cover quite all the material McFarlane claims for it. He does not distinguish between fully secret and half-secret trusts, seemingly regarding both types as within his account (indeed, he specifically cites *Blackwell v Blackwell*,[59] a half-secret trust decision). But there is surely no 'advantage' to Y in a half-secret trust case: the only possible outcomes are that Y holds on the trust he has undertaken, or that he holds

---

sion in *Pallant v Morgan*. There, X was awarded a half share in the land ('Lot 16') for which, in the absence of their joint-venture agreement, Y and he would both have bid, and which Y had now acquired. X was denied any right to further land ('Lot 15') which Y had also acquired, and for which X had not proposed to bid—but which the joint venture agreement would have substantially made over to him. McFarlane adopts the wording given in the text in an attempt to reflect the latter outcome as well as the former: ibid, 687–88. It seems to me, however, that the attempt fails. Lot 15 *was* 'property in relation to the acquisition of which [Y] . . . gained an advantage' by his undertaking to X. By inducing X not to bid against him, he was able to acquire Lot 16 more cheaply than he could otherwise have done, and was thereby helped to acquire Lot 15 too. It seems to me that the decision regarding Lot 15 was simply wrong. In my terms, X's reliance on Y's undertaking led him to lose his opportunity to insist on a binding agreement before the auction (or bid against Y). Such an agreement would have allowed him the intended rights to both Lot 16 and Lot 15. Correcting his loss should have meant giving him both rights.

[56] Ibid, 690.
[57] Ibid, 686 n 105.
[58] Two more particular comments are required. First, one of the dicta is by Viscount Sumner in *Blackwell v Blackwell* [1929] AC 318, 334–35. In fact—and of course unsurprisingly, given that the case concerns half-secret trusts—both Viscount Sumner and Lord Buckmaster (ibid, 329) make it quite clear that, at any rate in that context, advantage to Y is *not* required. Second, McFarlane could usefully add to his collection the dicta of Chadwick LJ in *Banner Homes* (n 35) 388, 398–99 and 401, that either detriment or advantage will suffice: advantage, because according to Chadwick LJ there was no detriment, only advantage, in *Pallant v Morgan* (n 31). I have already shown why I think Chadwick LJ was mistaken in so thinking: text at nn 35–39 above.
[59] *Blackwell* (n 38), cited in McFarlane (n 27) 677, 678 and 686.

on trust for the testator's residuary legatee. McFarlane could, however, meet this objection by hiving off half-secret trusts to join mutual wills in the category of material he does not seek to explain, though he would then have difficulty with the statements in *Blackwell* to the effect that both types of secret trust share a single foundation.

Second, McFarlane's account is under-ambitious. Perhaps it is true that, in all the cases he claims, minus half-secret trusts, there is indeed an advantage to Y. But if there is also a loss to X (as I say there is); and a loss to X, but no advantage to Y, is also to be found in adjacent material (as I say it is in half-secret trusts, the second type of mutual wills and sometimes in proprietary estoppel), then it seems to me right to focus on that, as pointing to a wider-reaching, and therefore more powerful, explanation.

Third, and perhaps most important, McFarlane's account does not explain itself. That is to say, it does not tell us *why* the fact that Y receives an advantage should mean that Y should be held to his undertaking, and no more and no less. There is a section of his article headed 'Does the event giving rise to the constructive trust justify the recognition of a right of [Z]?',[60] but it is hard to locate that question's answer. He tells us that the law 'responds to' Y's advantage 'by preventing [Y] from acting inconsistently with the undertaking'. No doubt this response negates Y's advantage, but there is no demonstration that it is *precisely what is needed* in order to negate the advantage. He also tells us '[Y's] receipt of that property is coloured by his undertaking'. But that is just a metaphor. One might try to progress by surmising that 'advantage' is actually a synonym for unjust enrichment, so accessing that concept's explanatory power. But the latter would not deliver the enforcement of Y's undertaking in favour of Z: only the restoration of the enrichment to its source.[61] For that reason, McFarlane eschews the equation with unjust enrichment.[62] But if 'advantage' is not unjust enrichment, what exactly is it, and why does it, when unjust enrichment does not, entail the enforcement of the undertaking?

In contrast, I believe my argument does explain itself. It maintains that the relevant rules operate to negate the loss that X will suffer, having reasonably relied on Y's undertaking (and for which Y is therefore responsible), if Y is able to resile from that undertaking. Y is held to his undertaking because that is precisely the response needed in order to correct X's loss, where that loss is the loss of the opportunity X otherwise had to secure more successfully the state of affairs that is the subject-matter of the undertaking.

[60] McFarlane (n 27) 683.
[61] Of course sometimes—as in *Bannister* (n 17)—the return of the enrichment and the enforcement of the undertaking may be the same thing, but that is a coincidence. Sometimes—as in secret trusts—they are not the same thing, yet the undertaking is still enforced.
[62] McFarlane (n 27) 677 and 683.

3. An 'Alternative'?

A moment ago, I referred to my reliance loss-based explanation for the material under discussion as an 'alternative' to an explanation centred on the effectuation of intentions. This may be the wrong way of viewing the two explanations' relationship.

Mindy Chen-Wishart has drawn my attention to the similarity between my account of these constructive trusts and the well-known article, 'The Reliance Interest in Contract Damages', by Lon Fuller and William Perdue.[63] Where I have been pessimistic about explaining these constructive trusts, which in fact operate to effectuate intentions, on that basis, Fuller and Perdue doubt that the usual measure of contract damages, which in fact tracks the claimant's expectations, can be satisfactorily explained simply on *that* basis.[64] They go on to consider other ways of accounting for the measure. One of these is a project of correcting the loss suffered by the claimant, in reliance on the defendant's promise, of the opportunity to secure the same gain elsewhere.[65] But their vision is not that the correction of this reliance loss is the authentic approach to recovery, while the vindication of the claimant's expectations is unauthentic. Rather, they take it that the law does indeed set out to vindicate the claimant's expectations, *for the very reason that it has to in order to correct this reliance loss*.[66] In other words, it is not that the two approaches happen to give the same outcome, but that they represent two ways of encapsulating what is the same essential project: the one describing its bottom line, the other addressing its underlying rationale. Perhaps the same is true for my reliance loss-based explanation of these constructive trusts, and that focusing on expectations.

Fuller and Perdue[67] go on to consider why, in contract, the project of correcting the claimant's loss of opportunity *where such a loss has occurred* should have turned into a generalised expectation measure, applicable even where, on the particular facts, the claimant cannot show a loss of opportunity. They make a number of interesting observations about that question, informed especially by the idea that the law has an aim of promoting trade. These observations may or may not resonate in the area(s) of trusts. While certainly not ruling out the possibility of a similar generalising phenomenon here, however, my argument in this contribution focuses on cases where Y has indeed suffered a loss of opportunity.

---

[63] L Fuller and W Perdue, 'The Reliance Interest in Contract Damages: 1' (1936–7) 46 *Yale Law Journal* 52.
[64] Ibid, 57–60.
[65] Ibid, 60–61.
[66] Ibid, 62.
[67] Ibid, 61–66, and further 66–71.

F. RELIANCE ON UNDERTAKINGS AND RELIANCE ON THE LAW

1. A Tale of Two Trusts

In a different way, however, I think my argument can do work beyond providing an explanation for the constructive trusts I have been addressing. I think it can be formed into a hypothesis as to the reason why the law has *express* trusts (originally, uses), and enforces them in (up to a point) the expectation measure—that is, by giving effect to the settlor's wishes. Consider the following tale. It seems to me plausible, though whether true as well, I have no idea.

Imagine Guy, a twelfth-century lord, about to go off on a crusade. He will be away for a considerable time; he may return, or he may not; and for a long time it will be uncertain whether he will return or not. Against this background, he is concerned to make sensible provision for his land-holdings. He devises an arrangement that he thinks will meet the case. He cannot give effect to it via an express use, because express uses do not yet exist. Nonetheless, having procured Richard's agreement to implement it, he transfers his lands to Richard; and leaves. Some time later, Richard reneges on his agreement to implement Guy's arrangement. Perhaps Guy returns; Richard was supposed, in this event, to restore the lands to Guy; but Richard refuses, standing upon his title at law. Guy approaches the Chancellor, arguing that, although Richard does indeed have an unqualified title to the lands at law, his conscience requires his compliance with the agreed arrangement. The Chancellor concurs, and orders Richard to comply. The result is that Richard holds what are now legally his lands to Guy's use.

We cannot know what was in the Chancellor's mind (early Chancery decisions are not reported), but the case displays the pattern in which I am interested. Relying on Richard's undertaking to hold the lands for Guy, Guy transfers them to Richard, and thereby foregoes his opportunity to effectuate his scheme in some other way (as for example by placing his faith in William rather than Richard). At all events, the resultant use is clearly what we would call constructive. It arises not, as an express use would, because the law offers a facility to make such a use, and Guy has availed himself of this facility. As I have already said, express uses do not yet exist: the Chancellor has not, before this time, announced the existence of such a facility. Guy's use arises (or so I rationalise it) as the Chancellor's reaction to Guy's decision, in reasonable reliance on Richard's promise, to neglect other ways of achieving his desired arrangement.

Now comes the interesting part. Word gets around about Guy's experience with Richard and the Chancellor's reaction to it. Reckoning on the Chancellor treating like cases alike, it occurs to other people that they can proceed in the same way as Guy and know that the state will assist them. They do, and (when necessary) it does. As this pattern takes shape, something significant has happened. Guys no longer rely on the personal trustworthiness of their Richards: they rely on the state's commitment to intervene, noticing the effect of that intervention to be the enforcement of such arrangements. The logic has become that, by making the right moves, Guys can if they so choose generate this legal effect. In a very English way, the express use has been born. In due course, since Guys thus rely on the Chancellor's response rather than on their Richards' undertaking, the same logic will indicate that it is unimportant whether they secure such an undertaking at all: they can generate their legal effect simply because they choose to (today, 'a trust will not fail for want of a trustee'). Later still, that will work out into the further idea that a Guy does not need to transfer the property to a Richard at all, but can generate the same effect, because he chooses to, while keeping the property himself ('declaring a trust').

As I say, I have no idea whether this tale is historically factual, but I do find it appealing. It also points a spotlight at a fundamental, but paradoxical, facet of the trust idea. Given the duties that the law imposes on trustees—starting with their obligation to hold the property not for themselves but for their objects, and continuing through more detailed directives—settlors and beneficiaries do not trust their trustees, as people, alone. Instead, or perhaps it is still more accurate to say as well, they trust the relevant law. Some of the implications of that line of thought are fascinatingly explored by Roger Cotterrell, in his essay 'Trusting in Law: Legal and Moral Concepts of Trust'.[68]

2. Challenging Subversion

Back to the constructive trusts under consideration. This idea of reliance on the law, rather than on Y's undertaking, solves an outstanding problem.

In the article to which I referred earlier, Ben McFarlane points to what he sees as a weakness in my argument. He says:

> There is . . . the question of establishing precisely what detriment [X] has suffered. In a secret trust case, for example, [X] may well have deliberately chosen not to go through the available mechanism of making a formal testamentary gift to [Z].[69]

I think McFarlane is right to see a difficulty here, but I do not think that that difficulty is over *detriment* (or loss, as I have tended to term it in this

---

[68] R Cotterrell, 'Trusting in Law: Legal and Moral Concepts of Trust' (1993) 46 *Current Legal Problems* 75.
[69] McFarlane (n 27) 685.

contribution). If indeed X relies on Y's undertaking to hold the property for Z, but Y can then renege on that undertaking, surely X has suffered a detriment, or loss, in the shape of the loss of the opportunity he otherwise had to provide for Z in some other way, whether by boxing Y in more effectively, or by choosing a different Y, or by taking a different approach altogether to providing for Z (for example by establishing, *inter vivos*, a bank account for himself and Z jointly). It seems to me that the difficulty is rather over *reliance*. X may be aware that, by engineering the secret trust scenario, he can give his wishes legal effect. He will then know, more particularly, that Y will have no option but to adhere to his undertaking. In that case, it seems to me possible to say—repeating the perception developed a moment ago—that he relies not on Y's undertaking itself, but on the law.

If this is right, we have found a conceptual tool by which to address an enduring problem: the fact that the constructive trusts under discussion can be used to subvert the rules applicable to express trusts. Let me begin by describing this problem.

Say Parliament enacts a rule, declaring it applicable to express but not to constructive trusts. If a would-be settlor of an express trust is repelled by the rule, he may try to find a way around it; and he will readily succeed. According to the principle I have explored in this contribution, all he needs do is, before transferring the trust property to his intended trustee, get the latter to agree to the terms of the projected trust. This done, he can make the transfer. We then have the familiar situation in which X transfers property to Y in reliance on Y's undertaking to allow Z an interest in it; to which the law responds, in order to correct the loss that X would otherwise suffer of the opportunity to make other arrangements, by holding Y to his undertaking. That is, the law generates a constructive trust with the same content as the express trust that our settlor would have liked to make, had it not been for the offensive rule. And the rule, remember, does not apply to constructive trusts. Our settlor, then, has succeeded in making the trust he wants, without attracting the rule. The rule is in effect optional.

The most familiar rules of this kind are the formality rules in the Law of Property Act 1925, section 53(1)(b), and in the Wills Act 1837, section 9.[70] There is no sign of settlors commonly hankering not to comply with the former; all it involves is writing, and settlors rarely prefer to keep their non-ambulatory dispositions oral; it would of course quickly be otherwise if a tax difference were perceived to be at stake. So we do not encounter cases where section 53(1)(b) is deliberately side-stepped, but only cases involving an accidental failure to comply with it.[71] But a number of settlors do seem to want to escape the Wills Act. Their aim is sometimes to make

---

[70] As amended by Administration of Justice Act 1982, s 17.
[71] *Rochefoucauld* (n 16); *Bannister* (n 17); *Hodgson* (n 18).

their ambulatory dispositions without the bother of writing and attestation (say, if they want constantly to change them), and sometimes to avoid the publicity that follows the admission of a valid will to probate. By making use of the phenomenon of the secret trust in the manner sketched in the previous paragraph, that is just what they are able to do.

We should find this problematic. We may indeed want the rule to apply to express but not to constructive trusts: a formality requirement, above all, may be a good idea for the former, but plainly cannot be applied to the latter. And we may feel that one who, innocent of the rule, relies on another's undertaking in the way we have been examining should indeed have the benefit of a constructive trust. But we may well jib at the thought of such constructive trusts being deliberately engineered by those who could, but prefer not to, obey the rule.

There is, however, a way of ensuring that settlors cannot engineer their way out of rules about express trusts in this manner. We should deny that, in the terms of my principle, X really does *rely on Y's undertaking*—so as to generate a constructive trust—when he in fact knows the law and uses it, in combination with Y's undertaking, to achieve his desired end. In such cases, X does not rely on Y's undertaking, but relies instead on the law. Given this, my formula for the constructive trust is not satisfied after all; so there can be no constructive trust, and thus no optional escape from the rule regarding express trusts. Constructive trusts will continue to arise, as is proper, only where X is innocent or at any rate unmindful of the principle's legal force, and therefore truly does rely on Y's undertaking itself.

Of the areas covered in this contribution, the greatest impact of this insight will thus be on secret trusts and mutual wills, areas where I suspect it is much commoner for X to rely on the law than on Y's undertaking itself. The insight will impact little, if at all, on the other areas examined, where surely X normally proceeds in ignorance of the law. And I realise, of course, that the necessary distinction between the two kinds of reliance might be hard to make in practice.

G. GOING WIDER?

The areas of law I have considered in this contribution all deal with different versions of the case where Y, the present or future owner of some property, undertakes to X that he will allow Z (who may be the same person as X) a right in that property, and X relies on this undertaking by foregoing the other opportunities he has to achieve the same end. According to my argument, the constructive trust that arises, delivering the right, can be explained as calculated to correct the loss that X would suffer if Y were to resile from his undertaking.

In all the material I have covered, the right that Y has undertaken to allow Z is—must be—a *beneficial* right. In the terms of my argument, that is why the response has to be a constructive trust over the property in question, as opposed to some other form of obligation upon Y: X's loss is of the opportunity to achieve his intended beneficial right in some other way, and so the response has to be to require Y to allow this very beneficial right, and that means his holding the property in question on trust to that effect. That is as wide as I need go for the purposes of this book, which concerns constructive (and resulting) trusts. But it may be worth considering, as a tail-piece, whether the principle to which I am pointing has a wider existence ... in particular:

1. Whether, where Y gives X an undertaking to allow Z (who may be X) some *non-beneficial* right over property which Y owns or expects to own, and X relies on this by foregoing his opportunity to achieve what he wants in some other way, the law will require Y to allow that right? If so, of course, the obligation on Y should not be a constructive trust, but should take the shape of the right in question.
2. Whether, further, the law will correct X's loss of opportunity by imposing an obligation on Y *where Y's undertaking did not relate to the use of property at all*? Again, the upshot—an obligation in the shape of the undertaking—will not be a constructive trust.
3. Whether the law will also correct *other forms of reliance loss* on X's part (that is, not the loss of his opportunity to achieve what he wants in some other way, but for example a simple loss of money), by generating other suitable obligations upon Y (such as an obligation to repay X the sum in question)?

English law[72] contains above all two pieces of evidence which, at any rate when taken together, indicate that the answer to each question is yes. They

---

[72] At one time it was argued that Australian law's doctrine of 'equitable estoppel' was a quite generalised vehicle for redressing reliance loss, which should have meant affirmative answers to the three questions. See especially M Spence, *Protecting Reliance* (Oxford, Hart Publishing, 1999); A Robertson 'Towards a Unifying Purpose for Estoppel' (1996) 22 *Monash University Law Review* 1; A Robertson 'Situating Equitable Estoppel within the Law of Obligations' (1997) 19 *Sydney Law Review* 32. The argument had judicial support in the form of statements in *Grundt v Great Boulder Pty Gold Mines Ltd* (1937) 59 CLR 641, *Waltons Stores (Interstate) Ltd v Maher* (1988) 164 CLR 387, and *Commonwealth of Australia v Verwayen* (1990) 170 CLR 394. The relief awarded in these and almost all succeeding decisions was, however, in the expectation measure (A Robertson, 'Satisfying the Minimum Equity: Equitable Estoppel after *Verwayen*' (1996) 20 *Melbourne University Law Review* 805 and A Robertson 'Reliance and Expectation in Estoppel Remedies' (1998) 18 *Legal Studies* 360), a trend culminating in *Giumelli v Giumelli* (1999) 196 CLR 101. In some cases, including *Waltons Stores* itself, this could be explained in terms of lost opportunity, but probably not in all. It seems more plausible, therefore, to regard the Australian doctrine as aimed (however inexplicably) at expectations per se, rather than reliance loss, after all: see J Edelman, 'Remedial Certainty and Remedial Discretion in Estoppel after *Giumelli*?' (1999) 15 *Journal of Contract Law* 179 (but cf A Robertson, 'The Reliance Basis of Proprietary Estoppel Remedies' [2008] *Conveyancer and Property Lawyer* 295).

are the doctrine described by Lord Denning MR in *Binions v Evans*, and—less securely, but more excitingly—the doctrine of promissory estoppel. Let us consider them.

1. Binions v Evans

In *Binions v Evans*,[73] Lord Denning MR asserted that, if a transferee of land undertakes to the transferor to honour a contractual licence that the transferor has previously granted over that land, a constructive trust arises against the transferee, obliging him to honour that undertaking. This assertion was approved by the Court of Appeal in *Ashburn Anstalt v W J Arnold & Co.*[74]

This principle can be fitted to my template as follows. The transferor, X, transfers the land to Y in reliance on Y's undertaking to honour the contractual licence that X has given Z. X will thereby have lost not only the land, but also the opportunity to provide as he wished for Z. To correct that loss, for which Y is responsible, Y must be required to keep to his undertaking. The constructive trust achieves this.

In fact, the principle seems to be wider than Lord Denning's statement of it. First, the undertaking need not be to honour a pre-existing right, rather than to allow a new right. Lord Denning[75] ascribes the principle to *Bannister v Bannister*,[76] and there the transferee's undertaking was certainly to allow a new right. Second, since a contractual licence over land is analytically nothing but a personal contract between licensor and licensee,[77] it making no difference that that contract applies to a piece of land, there seems no reason why the analysis should not apply to transfers of personalty as well as of land.[78] Third, the surrounding cases show that the principle is not confined to contractual licences, but extends to other kinds of right as well.[79] And fourth, the product of the principle need not be a constructive trust. In principle, it should be that right—whether a beneficial interest, some other right *in rem*, or some right *in personam*—which was the subject

---

[73] [1972] Ch 359 (CA) 368–69.
[74] [1989] Ch 1 (CA) 22–26. See too *IDC Group Ltd v Clark* [1992] 1 EGLR 187, affirmed (1993) 65 P & CR 179 (CA).
[75] *Binions* (n 73) 368.
[76] *Bannister* (n 17).
[77] *Thomas v Sorrell* (1673) Vaugh 330, 351; 124 ER 1098, 1109; *Winter Garden Theatre (London) Ltd v Millennium Productions Ltd* [1946] 1 All ER 678 (CA) 680; *Hounslow LBC v Twickenham Garden Developments Ltd* [1971] Ch 233, 246; *Street v Mountford* [1985] AC 809, 814; *Ashburn Anstalt* (n 74) 13–22.
[78] And McFarlane (n 27) 680–81, finds the principle being applied to the transfer of a ship in *Lord Strathcona Steamship Co Ltd v Dominion Coal Co Ltd* [1926] AC 108 (PC).
[79] *Lyus v Prowsa Developments Ltd* [1982] 1 WLR 1044, concerning an estate contract and a right to have a house built; *Lloyd v Dugdale* [2002] 2 P & CR 13 (CA), concerning a claim in proprietary estoppel.

of the undertaking. In *Bannister* itself, where the transferee undertook to hold on trust, it was a trust. In *Chattey v Farndale Holdings Inc*,[80] where the transferee undertook to respect a purchaser's lien, this—a non-beneficial right *in rem*—was the emergent right.[81] Likewise in *Lyus v Prowsa Developments Ltd*,[82] where the transferee undertook to allow an estate contract over the land, and the right to have the transferee build him a house on it, these were the emergent rights.[83] At first sight, Lord Denning's own judgment in *Binions v Evans* is out of step with this argument. The transferee's undertaking there was to respect a contractual licence, yet Lord Denning labels the emergent right a 'constructive trust'. But it is clear from a reading of his judgment as a whole that he did not mean this literally: that he intended only to say that the transferee was bound by the licence.[84]

Shorn of inessentials, then, the principle is that if a transferee of property undertakes to the transferor to allow a right concerning that property, an obligation arises against the transferee, requiring him to honour that undertaking. Or, in the terms of my argument, if X transfers property to Y in reliance on Y's undertaking to allow Z (who may presumably be X) a right over it, X loses the opportunity otherwise to secure his intended right in favour of Z. To correct this loss, an obligation arises—not necessarily a (constructive) trust, but whatever kind of obligation it may be—under which Y must allow the right. This firmly demonstrates that the answer to question (1) above is 'yes'.

---

[80] (1996) 75 P & CR 298 (CA). The transferee had also undertaken to respect an agreement for a lease of land, but this had gone off, and the claimant relied now on the undertaking to respect the lien securing his right, in these circumstances, to the repayment of his deposit.

[81] It is clear that the court regarded the emergent right as in rem. It observes (ibid, 315) that the right could have bound the second transferee in the case as a minor interest in the land, if only it had been registered as such: something only possible if it was in rem. Since it was not so registered, however, the second transferee would be affected only if he had made a fresh undertaking, which he had did not.

[82] *Lyus* (n 79).

[83] Such rights are by their nature respectively in rem and in personam; so the rights generated by the undertaking should likewise have been in rem and in personam. The ultimate issue in the case was whether a second transferee was bound, so the in rem quality of the one right might have mattered: but the reasoning gives it no attention. Doubtless, however, this was because the second transferee had given a fresh undertaking to honour all rights binding on the first.

[84] *Binions* (n 73) 366, where he expressly rejects the conclusion reached by the majority (Megaw and Stephenson LJJ) that the licensee had a beneficial interest (was tenant for life of a strict settlement). And ibid, 369, while labelling the licensee's right a 'constructive trust', he is clear that its effect was (only, therefore) to entitle her 'to reside [in the house] during her life, or as long as she might desire'. In *DHN Food Distributors Ltd v Tower Hamlets LBC* [1976] 1 WLR 852 (CA) 859, again, he follows his judgment in *Binions* to demonstrate that a licensee had a right to compensation for disturbance upon the compulsory purchase of the land in question; it being clear that the compensation was given on the basis that the licensee had an irrevocable licence, not a beneficial interest.

2. Promissory Estoppel

The best statement of the doctrine of promissory estoppel is by Bowen LJ in *Birmingham and District Land Co v London and North Western Railway Co*:

> [I]f persons who have contractual rights against others induce by their conduct those against whom they have such rights to believe that such rights will either not be enforced or will be kept in suspense or abeyance for some particular time, those persons will not be allowed by a court of equity to enforce the rights until such time has elapsed, without at all events placing the parties in the same position as they were before.[85]

Following our convention, call the representor Y, the representee X. The doctrine can be seen as correcting the loss X suffers when he relies on Y's undertaking not to enforce his contractual rights against X. The final clause of Bowen LJ's statement[86] is important. The estoppel cannot outlast the time stipulated in Y's undertaking, for X cannot reasonably have relied on Y's undertaking beyond that time. But Y can end the estoppel before that if X can return himself to the position he was in before the undertaking was given. This does not mean 'to the position of being able to perform the contract after all',[87] for when the undertaking was given he may not have been in such a position; indeed, he was probably not. Rather, it means 'to a position of being no less able to perform the contract, as a result of relying on the undertaking, than he was before he relied on it.' In other words, the estoppel lasts only so long as X's reliance on Y's undertaking *has taken him further away from* the ability to perform. The principle driving the law's intervention against Y, therefore, can be depicted as a wish to protect X from the detriment he suffers if, relying on Y's undertaking, he does so move further away, yet Y is able to renege.[88]

So we can see promissory estoppel as calculated, like the doctrines con-

---

[85] (1888) 40 Ch D 268 (CA) 286; interpreting the classic decision on the topic, *Hughes v Metropolitan Railway Co* (1877) 2 App Cas 439.

[86] Confirmed in *Tool Metal Manufacturing Co Ltd v Tungsten Electric Co Ltd* [1955] 1 WLR 761 (HL); *Ajayi v R T Briscoe (Nigeria) Ltd* [1964] 1 WLR 1326 (PC).

[87] Although if X does return to such a position, the estoppel certainly ends: *Central London Property Trust Ltd v High Trees House Ltd* [1947] KB 130.

[88] Some judges have said (though others have disagreed) that detriment is unnecessary in promissory estoppel: E Cooke, *The Modern Law of Estoppel* (Oxford, Oxford University Press, 2000) 100. The key statement is by Lord Denning MR in *W J Alan & Co Ltd v El Nasr Export and Import Co* [1972] 2 QB 189 (CA) 213: 'In none of [the] cases does the party who acts on the [undertaking] suffer any detriment. It is not a detriment, but a benefit to him, to have an extension of time or to pay less, or as the case may be. Nevertheless, he has conducted his affairs on the basis that he has that benefit and it would not be equitable to deprive him of it.' At first sight, this contradicts my argument; but on further examination I am not sure that that is so. Of course it is a benefit to X to be relieved of the need to perform. But the final sentence shows Lord Denning MR as agreeing (though his phrasing is imprecise) that the estoppel depends on the imperatives introduced by X's actions in reliance.

sidered earlier in this contribution, to correct the loss X suffers by relying on Y's undertaking. But it differs from the other doctrines in two ways. First, it does not require Y to be the (existing or prospective) owner of some property, nor—obviously, therefore—Y's undertaking to be that he will allow a right over that property. And second, X's loss can be the loss of his opportunity to remain no further away than he was from being able to perform his obligation. There is no requirement that it be the loss of an opportunity to secure the same arrangement in some other way. Indeed, in the kind of case where promissory estoppel is in point, X will rarely have been in a position to impose his own wishes.

Promissory estoppel shows, therefore, that an affirmative answer is possible to both questions (2) and (3) above. However, on the account given so far, it is itself limited to the case where Y has the benefit of a legal obligation—commonly, though not necessarily,[89] a contractual promise—and his undertaking is to forego performance of that obligation; and where X's loss is the loss of his opportunity to remain no further away than he was from being able to render that performance.

Can we go on to say that these limitations are inessential? And, therefore, that the true principle is, quite simply, that when one person suffers *any* loss by relying (in whatever way) on another's undertaking (of whatever import), the law will impose whatever obligation is needed to correct that loss? Meaning, for example, that if Y promises X £15,000, and in reliance on this X buys a car for £10,000, the law will require Y to pay X £10,000?

Combe v Combe[90] is usually understood to decide that promissory estoppel cannot go so far. According to Birkett LJ, promissory estoppel is 'to be used as a shield and not as a sword'.[91] According to Denning LJ, it 'does not create new causes of action where none existed before';[92] 'it may be part of a cause of action, but not a cause of action itself'.[93] These remarks are, however, wider than the decision in the case demanded. In the context of a divorce, a husband had made a non-contractual promise thenceforth to pay his wife £100 a year. When he failed to do so for several years, the wife sued him for the arrears, but the Court of Appeal held against her. Notice, however, that the wife's claim was not to the rectification of losses, if any, that she suffered through reliance on the husband's

---

[89] It certainly applies to a landlord's rights under a lease: *Hughes* (n 85). In principle, it should apply also to a creditor's right under a non-contractual debt, but that would involve direct confrontation with *Jorden v Money* (1854) 5 HLC 185, 10 ER 868.
[90] [1951] 2 KB 215 (CA).
[91] Ibid, 224.
[92] Ibid, 219.
[93] Ibid, 220. Presumably, in some such way as this: Y undertakes not to treat X's behaviour as the breach of contract it would otherwise be, and X relies on this; Y then repudiates the contract, as if for X's breach; X sues for Y's breach, relying on the estoppel to show that Y's repudiation is itself a breach rather than a disaffirmation.

undertaking: it was to the enforcement of that undertaking per se. In response to this, Denning LJ observed, as part of his argument, 'in none of [the] cases was the defendant sued on the promise, assurance, or assertion as a cause of action in itself'.[94] But the fact that *the undertaking* could not found a claim in its own right does not mean, as the broader dicta suggest, that *the losses suffered in reliance on the undertaking* could not and should not. The case did not put the matter to the test: Mrs Combe simply had not framed her claim that way.

It seems to me, then, that promissory estoppel[95] is less far than has commonly been supposed from being a rule obliging Y pay X £10,000 when, in reliance on Y's promise of £15,000, X buys a car for £10,000. I have no positive reason to say that it will go that distance, but if it will, we do indeed reach a quite generalised position where, if one person suffers a loss by relying on another's undertaking, the law will impose whatever obligation is needed to correct that loss.[96]

---

[94] Ibid, 220.

[95] Proprietary estoppel may occupy some of this territory too, but one cannot confidently say. Certainly it generates non-beneficial rights (question 1), but it appears that these must be rights over property (question 2). It seems to react to all forms of reliance (question 3) . . . but it does not always operate to protect the reliance interest at all. See Gardner (n 47) § 7.4.

[96] Further thought is, however, required regarding the relationship between this formula and the torts of deceit and negligent misstatement (and the form of liability in *Nocton v Lord Ashburton* [1914] AC 398). See Spence (n 72) 11–14.

3

The Nature of the Trust in Rochefoucauld v Boustead

WILLIAM SWADLING

A. INTRODUCTION

This chapter examines the nature of the trust recognised and enforced by the Court of Appeal in *Rochefoucauld v Boustead*.[1] Whilst the exact typology of the trust in similar cases, both before and after, has never been in issue, it was crucial in *Rochefoucauld* for the determination of a point of limitation. The court held the trust to be express, but the dominant view ever since has been that it was in truth constructive. This chapter explores the various explanations why the trust was constructive and finds them wanting. It concludes that the only tenable view, consistent both with the case itself and with the relevant statutory provision, is that the trust was indeed express.

Why is it important to show that the trust in *Rochefoucauld* was express and not constructive? The issue is vital because a number of commentators and judges have used a constructive trust analysis as the basis for a more general theory of constructive trusts. So, for example, McFarlane argues that there is in law what he calls a 'receipt after promise' principle generating constructive trusts,[2] and having as its foundation the *Rochefoucauld* doctrine and analogous case-law concerning secret trusts.[3] In the same way, Elias[4] has put forward an elaborate theory of constructive trusts as having, inter alia, 'perfectionary' functions, using *Rochefoucauld* as proof of its existence; and in the present volume, Gardner has similarly used

---

[1] [1897] 1 Ch 197.
[2] B McFarlane, 'Constructive Trusts Arising on a Receipt of Property *Sub Conditione*' (2004) 120 *Law Quarterly Review* 667; B McFarlane, *The Structure of Property Law* (Oxford, Hart Publishing, 2008) 382, 434–35. The thesis is discussed below, text to nn 47–51.
[3] The topic of secret trusts will not be addressed here, but it is submitted that, for the same reasons as will be argued below in relation to *Rochefoucauld*, they too involve express, not constructive, trusts.
[4] G Elias, *Explaining Constructive Trusts* (Oxford, Clarendon Press, 1990).

Rochefoucauld and the secret trusts cases to argue for a 'reliance-based' classification of constructive trusts.[5] More importantly, a classification of the *Rochefoucauld* trust as constructive has led to wrong turns being taken in the law. Thus, Lord Denning MR illegitimately circumvented the contractual privity rule in *Binions v Evans*[6] by relying on a doctrine of constructive trusts supposedly laid down by the Court of Appeal in *Bannister v Bannister*,[7] where that court purported only to follow *Rochefoucauld*. If the *Rochefoucauld* trust had been labelled express in *Bannister*,[8] then it would have been clear that it provided no authority for a case such as *Binions*, which concerned a different issue altogether, namely the ability of a stranger to enforce a contract made for his benefit. The same can be said of a dictum of Lord Diplock in *Gissing v Gissing*,[9] which Lord Denning MR took out of context to develop his 'constructive trust of a new model'.[10] If Lord Diplock had seen the type of trust involved in a case such as *Rochefoucauld* as express rather than constructive,[11] then Lord Denning's distortions of the law in the area of family homes might never have occurred.

At the outset, it is important to stress that this chapter is not concerned to defend the decision in *Rochefoucauld v Boustead*, merely to determine the type of trust to which the court thought it was giving effect. This is not the approach of those who argue that the trust was constructive, for it will be seen that the only way they can do so is by rejecting the reasoning of the court altogether.

B. THE *ROCHEFOUCAULD* DECISION

The facts of *Rochefoucauld v Boustead* are often misrepresented, and it is important that they be accurately portrayed. In 1868, the claimant, the Comtesse de la Rochefoucauld, held titles to some coffee plantations in Ceylon, the Delmar Estates. The plantations were managed for her by the defendant. Her titles had been used to secure substantial borrowings made by her, and the mortgagee was now seeking to enforce its security. Worried that her recently divorced husband, who had been awarded an interest in the estates by the courts, might buy up the mortgage and foreclose, the Comtesse, so she alleged, entered into an arrangement with the defendant

---

[5] See Gardner, ch 2 above.
[6] [1972] Ch 359 (CA). The case is discussed below, text to nn 50–51.
[7] [1948] 2 All ER 133 (CA).
[8] In an obiter comment, Scott LJ spoke of a 'constructive trust' being raised against a person who insisted on the absolute character of the conveyance: *Bannister* (n 6) 136, though citing *Rochefoucauld* as authority.
[9] [1971] AC 886, 904H–905D.
[10] As, for example, in *Eves v Eves* [1975] 1 WLR 1338 (CA).
[11] Cf *Stack v Dowden* [2007] UKHL 17, [2007] 2 AC 432, where at [23] Lord Walker spoke of Lord Diplock's 'insouciant approach to legal taxonomy' in *Gissing*.

manager under which he would buy the titles from the mortgagee at a price sufficient to cover the mortgage debt and expenses, and hold them for her on trust, subject to a lien for his expenditure. The reason the Comtesse did not simply borrow the money from her manager and pay off the debt herself is that she wanted to create the impression in her ex-husband that she no longer retained any interest in the estates. In 1873, the plan was put into action: the defendant bought the titles from the mortgagee as agreed, with the conveyance to him naturally enough saying nothing of the arrangement between the defendant and claimant. However, in 1876, 1877 and 1879, without the knowledge of the claimant, the defendant mortgaged various titles to the estates to secure his own heavy borrowings. Over 14 years later, in 1894, the claimant sought a declaration that the defendant had purchased the titles as trustee for her, for an account of his dealings as trustee with the estates, and of the balance due from him in respect thereof, and for payment of that balance.[12] The titles had in fact been sold many years previously, either by the defendant or by his mortgagees, but it was the claimant's case that the proceeds of sale were more than sufficient to repay the defendant all she owed him, and that a considerable surplus remained, which the defendant ought to have paid over to her.

The defendant denied that he had bought the titles as trustee for the claimant. In any case, he said, the trusts alleged by her could not be proved by any writing signed by him, and section 7 of the Statute of Frauds 1677, the predecessor of the modern section 53(1)(b) of the Law of Property Act 1925,[13] precluded the admission of oral evidence on her part to make good that allegation.[14] Section 7 provided that:

> All declarations or creations of trusts or confidences of any lands, tenements or hereditaments, shall be manifested and proved by some writing signed by the party who is by law entitled to declare such trust, or by his last will in writing, or else they shall be utterly void and of none effect.

The defendant also raised a defence of limitation, arguing that even if he was a trustee, he was only a constructive trustee, to whom a six-year time limit applied, rather than an express trustee, to whom no limitation period applied.[15]

At the trial of the action, Kekewich J appears to have heard the oral testimony but not admitted it into evidence on the ground that he was precluded from so doing by section 7.[16] He consequently found the allegation

---

[12] *Rochefoucauld* (n 1) 200.
[13] Section 53(1)(b) of the Law of Property Act 1925 provides that: 'A declaration of trust respecting any land or any interest therein must be manifested and proved by some writing signed by some person who is able to declare such trust or by his will.'
[14] *Rochefoucauld* (n 1) 201.
[15] *Ibid*, 203.
[16] This appears from the discussion of the trial in the Court of Appeal itself: *Rochefoucauld*

that the defendant had agreed to hold the estate titles on trust not proved and dismissed the claim. The Court of Appeal held that Kekewich J had been wrong to use section 7 to keep out the claimant's evidence. Lindley LJ, giving the judgment of a Court of Appeal which also included Lord Halsbury LC and A L Smith LJ, said:

> The section relied upon is s 7, which has been judicially interpreted in *Forster v Hale* (1798) 3 Ves 696 and *Smith v Matthews* (1861) 3 D F & J 139. According to these authorities, it is necessary to prove by some writing or writings signed by the defendant, not only that the conveyance to him was subject to some trust, but also what that trust was. But it is not necessary that the trust should have been declared by such a writing in the first instance; it is sufficient if the trust can be proved by some writing signed by the defendant, and the date of the writing is immaterial. It is further established by a series of cases, the propriety of which cannot now be questioned, that the Statute of Frauds does not prevent the proof of a fraud; and that it is a fraud on the part of a person to whom land is conveyed as a trustee, and who knows it was so conveyed, to deny the trust and claim the land himself. Consequently, notwithstanding the statute, it is competent for a person claiming land conveyed to another to prove by parol evidence that it was so conveyed upon trust for the claimant, and that the grantee, knowing the facts, is denying the trust and relying upon the form of conveyance and the statute, in order to keep the land himself.[17]

Applying that rule, the court held that the claimant's oral testimony was admissible.[18] Admitting that evidence, it held that it proved the claimant's case 'completely'.[19]

Pausing there, it would seem that the trust in question can only have been express. This is clear both from the fact that the claimant alleged an express trust, and that the court found, on the evidence held admissible under the rule that a statute enacted to prevent fraud could not be used as an instrument of fraud, that she had made good her allegations. However, the question as to the exact nature of the trust arose only later, when the court came to consider the limitation defence. The defendant sought to rely on the six-year limitation period in section 8(1)(b) of the Trustee Act 1888,[20] under which the defendant could only avail himself of the six-year

---

(n 1) 199. The first instance proceedings are reported at (1896) 65 LJ Ch 794, but on a different point.

[17] *Rochefoucauld* (n 1) 205–06.

[18] Ibid, 207.

[19] Ibid, 207. See also the first sentence of the passage cited below, text to n 21, where Lindley LJ said: 'Having come to the conclusion that the plaintiff has proved her case by evidence admissible by our law . . .': ibid, 207.

[20] Section 8 provided as follows: '(1) In any action or other proceeding against a trustee or any person claiming through him, except where the claim is founded on any fraud or fraudulent breach of trust to which the trustee was party or privy, or is to recover trust property, or the proceeds thereof still retained by the trustee, or previously received by the trustee and converted to his use, the following provisions shall apply: . . . (b) If the action or other proceeding is brought to recover money or other property, and is one to which no existing statute

limitation period therein provided if the trust under which he received the titles was constructive. The Court of Appeal held that it was express, so that no limitation period applied. Lindley LJ said:

> Having come to the conclusion that the [claimant] has proved her case by evidence admissible by our law, it is necessary to consider the other defences raised . . . [The court then considered and rejected the defence that the defendant was bankrupt.] The next defence is the Statute of Limitations. The trust which the [claimant] has established is clearly an express trust within the meaning of that expression as explained in *Soar v Ashwell* [1893] 2 QB 390. The trust is one which both [claimant] and defendant intended to create. This case is not one in which an equitable obligation arises although there may have been no intention to create a trust. The intention to create a trust existed from the first. The defendant is not able in this case to claim the benefit of s 8 of the Trustee Act 1888, and the statute which is applicable is the Judicature Act 1873, which enacts as follows: 'No claim of a cestui que trust for any property held on an express trust, or in respect of any breach of such trust, shall be held to be barred by any Statute of Limitations'. The Statutes of Limitation, therefore, afford no defence.[21]

There being no other valid defence, the court granted the relief sought in the following terms:

> It must be declared that the defendant purchased the Delmar estates as a trustee for the [claimant], but subject to a charge for the amount paid to the [mortgagee]. An account must then be directed of the defendant's dealings and transactions with the Delmar estates.[22]

So far, then, the decision would appear to be unequivocal: the trust was express. Although there was an initial question whether the claimant could adduce oral testimony to prove her allegation that a declaration of trust had been made in her favour, that issue was resolved against the defendant and her evidence admitted. The oral evidence was then found to prove her allegations 'completely' and, the defendant, having no recourse to any limitation period, was liable to account as the claimant sought. Given that the case involved a trust created by the parties, and not 'one in which an equitable obligation arises although there may have been no intent to create a trust',[23] it is difficult to see how it could be thought anything other than express.

---

of limitation applies, the trustee or person claiming through him shall be entitled to the benefit of and be at liberty to plead the lapse of time as a bar to such action or other proceeding in the like manner and to the like extent as if the claim had been against him in an action for money had and received, but so nevertheless that the statute shall run against a married woman entitled in possession for her separate use, whether with or without a restraint upon anticipation, but shall not begin to run against any beneficiary unless and until the interest of such beneficiary shall be an interest in possession.'

[21] *Rochefoucauld* (n 1) 207–08.
[22] Ibid, 212.
[23] Ibid, 208.

C. ARGUMENTS FOR CLASSIFYING THE *ROCHEFOUCAULD* TRUST AS CONSTRUCTIVE

1. The Classification Was Peculiar to the Law of Limitation

One argument for a constructive trust is that the trust in *Rochefoucauld* was only labelled 'express' because of certain peculiarities of the law of limitation, and that it was for all other purposes constructive. Thus, Youdan, picking up on the court's reference to *Soar v Ashwell*,[24] wrote:

> [T]he Court of Appeal's statement is complicated by the fact that the distinction between an express trust and a constructive trust had a decisive effect on the operation of the Statute of Limitations. The statement may possibly be explained as amounting only to a statement that the trust is an express trust for the purposes of the Limitation Acts. *Soar v Ashwell* was an authority on the effect of the Limitation Acts and in the context of these Acts there are other examples of trusts that are called express trusts although they would ordinarily be described as constructive trusts.[25]

Soar v Ashwell did indeed explain that there was an extended category of express trusts in the context of limitation, included within in it being such things as the personal liability of those who knowingly assist a breach of trust and the personal liability of a trustee *de son tort*. Thus, Bowen LJ said:

> [T]here has been some variety and inconsistency both in the language used about constructive trusts and in the line of demarcation that has been drawn between the cases of express and constructive trusts. First, the doctrine that time is no bar in the case of express trusts has been extended to cases where a person who is not a direct trustee nevertheless assumes to act as a trustee under the trust: *Life Association of Scotland v Siddal*. This extension of the doctrine is based on the obvious view that a man who assumes without excuse to be a trustee ought not to be in a better position than if he were what he pretends. Secondly, the rule as to limitations of time which has been laid down in reference to express trusts has also been thought appropriate to cases where a stranger participates in the fraud of a trustee: *Barnes v Addy*. Thirdly, a similar extension of the doctrine has been acted on in a case where a person received trust property and dealt with it in a manner inconsistent with trusts of which he was cognizant: *Lee v Sankey*. Fourthly, in some other cases, eg, in *Bridgman v Gill*, by Lord Romilly, and in *Wilson v Moore*, by Lord Brougham, language has been employed in regard to the question of limitations of time in certain instances of constructive trust which can scarcely be reconciled with the language held in *Bonny v Ridgard*; *Beckford v Wade*; *Townshend v Townshend*, and in other cases.[26]

---

[24] [1893] 2 QB 390.
[25] T Youdan, 'Formalities for Trusts of Land, and the Doctrine in *Rochefoucauld v Boustead*' [1984] *Cambridge Law Journal* 306, 331.
[26] *Soar* (n 24) 396–97.

Although the Court of Appeal in *Soar v Ashwell* included in their definition of express trusts things which are better classified as constructive trusts or not even trusts at all,[27] it does not therefore follow that all trusts falling within the category 'express' were to be seen as constructive, for if that were so, there would no longer be any express trusts at all. If a statute provides that for the purposes of the law on stray animals, the classification 'dog' is to include cats, it does not thereby turn every genuine dog into a false cat—there will still be some real dogs roaming the streets. The greater must include the lesser, and the court's statement in *Rochefoucauld* that the trust came within the definition of an express trust in *Soar v Ashwell* is therefore no guide whether it was a genuine express trust or one so classified for the purposes of limitation. Moreover, the reasoning seen in the passage extracted above[28] clearly shows that the court did not consider it an express trust so-called only for the purposes of limitation, for if it was, the statement that the trust arose because of the intention of the parties and not because of any obligation imposed by law[29] would have been both inexplicable and otiose. This conclusion is reinforced when it is seen that *Soar v Ashwell* itself concerned a conventional express trust, not one so named purely for limitation purposes. Indeed, apart from the passages dealing with trustees *de son tort* and the like, the case contains perfectly orthodox definitions of express trusts.

In *Soar v Ashwell*, a trust fund had been settled by Joseph Soar by will on trustees on trust for two persons in equal shares for their respective lives and, after the death of each, on trust as to his share for that person's children. The fund was entrusted by the trustees to a solicitor, Ashwell, employed by them as solicitor to the trust, and was by him invested, together with other moneys belonging to different trusts, on an equitable mortgage by deposit of title deeds, in Ashwell's name. The mortgage was paid off in January 1879. Ashwell received the money so invested from the mortgagor, and distributed one-half of it, one tenant for life having died, among that tenant's children, who by his death had become absolutely entitled to the same. However, he failed to account for the other half to the trustees, retaining it instead in his own hands. On 21 February 1891, an action was brought by the surviving trustee under the will, John Soar, against the personal representative of Ashwell, who had died in November 1879, claiming an account of the moneys so retained by him. Ashwell's personal representative argued that the claim was out of time.

Whether that contention was correct depended on the capacity in which Ashwell received the money from the trustees. If he received it beneficially, and under which his liability would have been described, somewhat confus-

---

[27] *Paragon Finance plc v D B Thakerar & Co* [1999] 1 All ER 400 (CA) 409 (Millett LJ).
[28] See the passage at text to n 21.
[29] *Rochefoucauld* (n 1) 207–08.

ingly, as a 'liability to account as a constructive trustee', the claim would have been barred through an application by analogy of the statutory limitation period for the common law action of account, the limitation period for which was six years. If, however, he received it as trustee, such trust arising because of a manifestation of intent to create a trust on the part of the trustees of the settlement, he would have been holding as express trustee, and could not take advantage of any statute of limitation. The Court of Appeal held that he was indeed an express trustee, and thus had no recourse to the limitation period. Lord Esher MR said:

> The moment the money was in his hands, he was in a fiduciary relation to the nominated trustees; he was a fiduciary agent of theirs; he held the money in trust to deal with it for them as directed by them; he was a trustee for them. He was therefore a trustee of the money before he committed, if he did commit, the alleged breach of trust, and was in possession of and had control over the money before he committed, if at all, the alleged breach of trust. . . . I am of opinion that the present case is within the description of that which is treated as and is called in equity an express trust, and that the inquiry as to the alleged breach cannot be stopped by the Statute of Limitations.[30]

Bowen LJ was also clear that this was an express trust, to which the statutes of limitation did not apply:

> It is not necessary in the present appeal to discuss the somewhat fluctuating expressions that can be discovered in equity authorities on the subject of constructive trusts. One thing seems clear. It has been established beyond doubt by authority binding on this Court that a person occupying a fiduciary relation, who has property deposited with him on the strength of such relation, is to be dealt with as an express, and not merely a constructive, trustee of such property. His possession of such property is never in virtue of any right of his own, but is coloured from the first by the trust and confidence in virtue of which he received it. He never can discharge himself except by restoring the property, which he never has held otherwise than upon this confidence: *Chalmer v Bradley*; *Marquis of Cholmondeley v Lord Clinton*; and this confidence or trust imposes on him the liability of an express or direct trustee. . . . On this simple ground, whatever other law or equity may or may not be applicable to the matter before us, whatever may be the limitations or definitions to be introduced into the doctrine of the Statute of Limitations and constructive trusts, this case (which is one of express or direct trust) lies outside them all. [31]

As to the definitions of express trusts referred to by Youdan, we have already encountered that of Bowen LJ.[32] Lord Esher MR's was as follows:

---

[30] *Soar* (n 24) 394.
[31] Ibid, 397. Disagreeing with the majority, Kay LJ held (at 405–06) that Ashwell became a trustee, not because he was entrusted with the money by the trustees, but because of his assumption of the duties of a trustee in respect of it. He was, in other words, a trustee *de son tort*, and for that reason unable to take advantage of the Limitation Acts.
[32] Ibid.

If there is created in expressed terms, whether written or verbal, a trust, and a person is in terms nominated to be the trustee of that trust, a Court of Equity, upon proof of such facts, will not allow him to vouch a Statute of Limitations against a breach of that trust. Such a trust is in equity called an express trust. If the only relation which it is proved the defendant or person charged bears to the matter is a contractual relation, he is not in the view of equity a trustee at all, but only a contractor; and equity leaves the contractual relation to be determined by the common or statute law. If the breach of the legal relation relied on, whether such breach be by way of tort or contract, makes, in the view of a Court of Equity, the defendant a trustee for the plaintiff, the Court of Equity treats the defendant as a trustee become so by construction, and the trust is called a constructive trust; and against the breach which by construction creates the trust the Court of Equity allows Statutes of Limitation to be vouched. There are cases not falling strictly within either of those thus enunciated, some of which have been treated by the Courts of Equity as within the class in respect of which a Statute of Limitations will not be allowed to be vouched, and some within the class in respect of which such a statute may be vouched. It must obviously be unnecessary on this occasion to state exhaustively all the different cases. It suffices to determine in which class is the present case. There is another recognised state of circumstances in which a person not nominated a trustee may be bound to liability as if he were a nominated trustee, namely, where he has knowingly assisted a nominated trustee in a fraudulent and dishonest disposition of the trust property. Such a person will be treated by a Court of Equity as if he were an express trustee of an express trust. The propositions thus enunciated seem to me to follow from the judgments of Lord Hatherley and Giffard LJ in *Burdick v Garrick*, and of Lord Selborne in *Barnes v Addy*.[33]

At best, therefore, the reference by Lindley LJ in *Rochefoucauld* to 'an express trust within the meaning of the expression as explained in *Soar v Ashwell*'[34] is ambiguous. It could be to an express trust properly so called, or one so named for the purposes of limitation. However, given what Lindley LJ says elsewhere in *Rochefoucauld* as to the nature of the evidence held to be admissible, the only fair reading of that phrase is to the parts of *Soar v Ashwell* wherein genuine express trusts are discussed, not the oddities deemed to be express trusts for limitation purposes.[35]

2. The Failure to 'Comply' with Section 7 Having Rendered the Express Trust Void, the Trust Enforced by the Court Must Have Been Constructive

Another argument for a constructive trust is that the lack of writing in *Rochefoucauld* rendered the express trust void, so that the trust eventually enforced could only have been constructive.

---

[33] *Soar* (n 24) 393–95.
[34] *Rochefoucauld* (n 1) 207–08.
[35] It is also worth noting that the facts of *Rochefoucauld* do not come within any of the exceptional cases described by either Lord Esher MR or Bowen LJ.

For a number of reasons, this approach is untenable. First, it misrepresents the nature of the rule in section 7. Despite speaking of a declaration of trust of land not manifested and proved by writing being 'utterly void and of none effect', words which, incidentally, no longer appear in the Law of Property Act 1925, section 53(1)(b),[36] it is well established that section 7 was not a rule of validity but of evidence. As the Court of Appeal itself recognised in *Rochefoucauld*, it was a rule describing how, if it came to litigation, an allegation that a declaration of trust respecting land must be proved.[37] It was not, as many text writers insist, a rule concerned with the 'creation' of a trust of land with which settlors need 'comply'.[38] Indeed, it was not addressed to settlors at all, but to litigants attempting to prove declarations of trust, who will generally be beneficiaries. That section 7 was concerned with proof rather than validity formed the basis of decision in a number of cases, including *Rochefoucauld* itself.[39] Typical in this regard is *Forster v Hale*,[40] a case relied on by the court in *Rochefoucauld*,[41] where Sir RP Arden MR said:

> It is not required by the *Statute*, that a trust should be created by a writing; and the words of the *Statute* are very particular in the clause (*sect.* 7) respecting declarations of trust. It does not by any means require, that all trusts shall be created only by writing; but that they shall be manifested and proved by writing; plainly meaning, that there should be evidence in writing, proving there was such a trust.[42]

A clear illustration of the application of such thinking is provided by *Gardner v Rowe*.[43] A lease was granted to Williams, allegedly on trust for

---

[36] The wording of which is set out above in n 13.
[37] *Rochefoucauld* (n 1) 205–06.
[38] See eg the confused discussion in relation to s 53(1)(b) in C Harpum, S Bridge and M Dixon, *Megarry and Wade: The Law of Real Property*, 7th edn (London, Sweet & Maxwell, 2008), where in para 11–037 there is a discussion of the provision under the heading 'Formalities Required for the Creation of a Trust' and talk of a trust of land before 1677 being able to be created orally, but then an acknowledgement of the evidential nature of the rule. Similar confusion between proof and creation can be found, inter alia, in EH Burn and J Cartwright, *Cheshire and Burn's Modern Law of Real Property*, 17th edn (Oxford, Oxford University Press, 2006) 903–04; R Chambers *An Introduction to Property Law in Australia* (Sydney, LBC Information Services, 2001) 251; S Gardner, *An Introduction to the Law of Trusts*, 2nd edn (Oxford, Oxford University Press, 2003) 84–93; D Hayton and C Mitchell, *Hayton & Marshall's Law of Trusts and Equitable Remedies*, 12th edn (London, Sweet & Maxwell, 2005) para 2–13; C Mitchell, 'Unjust Enrichment' in A Burrows (ed), *English Private Law*, 2nd edn (Oxford, Oxford University Press, 2007) para 18.135; A J Oakley, *Parker & Mellows: The Modern Law of Trusts*, 9th edn (London, Sweet & Maxwell, 2008) paras 4-008–4-016. K Gray and SF Gray *Elements of Land Law*, 5th edn (Oxford, Oxford University Press, 2009) paras 7.1.19–7.1.21 is better, though even its authors lapse into a discussion of the rule being concerned with preventing the 'creation of unsuspected trust relationships'.
[39] See the passage cited above, text to n 17.
[40] (1798) 3 Ves Jun 696, 30 ER 1226; affirmed (1800) 5 Ves Jun 308, 31 ER 603.
[41] *Rochefoucauld* (n 1) 205.
[42] *Forster* (n 40) 3 Ves Jun 707.
[43] (1828) 5 Russ 258, 38 ER 1024.

Rowe, though no words of trust appeared in the conveyance. Williams later became bankrupt, after which he executed a deed declaring that he all along held the lease on trust for Rowe. At trial, the jury found the document to be genuine. It was argued that even so, the writing came too late, that this was a trust created after bankruptcy and therefore void. The court rejected the argument. The provision was evidential only; no trust was created by the execution of the deed and the trust thus preceded the act of bankruptcy. Lord Lyndhurst LC said:

> It is true, that the property of a trader cannot be assigned by him after his bankruptcy: the property is no longer his; it is vested in his assignees. But property held in trust, is not the property of the bankrupt; it does not pass to his assignees. The only question therefore . . . is, whether the declaration contained in the deed was founded upon a previous trust, or was altogether fraudulent. That question, however, has been decided in substance by the jury upon the trial of the issue; for they have found that the name of Williams was used in the original deed as a trustee for Rowe.[44]

Moreover, even if section 7 was a rule of validity, it would not thereby make the *Rochefoucauld* trust constructive. As we have seen, the court held section 7 to be inapplicable. With the statute out of the way, there would be no 'requirement' that the declaration of trust be 'in writing', with the result that there would be nothing standing in the way of the express trust's 'validity'. Thus, the only way to get to a constructive trust through this line of reasoning is to ignore completely the reasoning of the court. The problem then, of course, is that we would no longer be concerned with the trust in *Rochefoucauld* but one arising in a different case altogether.

Assuming, however, that that could be done, and, further, that section 7 was a rule of validity, and, further still, that the court did not disapply section 7 but held the express trust void for want of writing, is there any basis on which a constructive trust might arise on the facts of *Rochefoucauld*? More specifically, what would be the trust's causative event? It is difficult to see it being the unjust enrichment of the defendant at the expense of the plaintiff, for the enrichment came not from the plaintiff but the mortgagee. Moreover, the award of a trust rather than a personal right as a response to unjust enrichment is fraught with difficulty.[45] Nor is it possible to see any wrong committed by the defendant, for all he would be doing in this imagined scenario would be taking advantage of a statutory rule of invalidity. As Lord Wilberforce, with whom all the other members of the House of Lords agreed, said in *Midland Bank Trust Co Ltd v Green*, in relation to a rule of invalidity for unregistered land charges, 'It is not

---

[44] Ibid, 5 Russ 261–2.
[45] As witness the decision of the House of Lords in *Westdeutsche Landesbank Girozentrale v Islington LBC* [1996] AC 669, rejecting a claim for a trust in respect of payments made under contracts subsequently found to be void.

fraud to rely on legal rights conferred by Act of Parliament.'[46] Is there then some event in the miscellany to which the Comtesse could appeal?

McFarlane thinks there is. He says that the raising of a constructive trust on the facts of *Rochefoucauld* is explicable by something he calls the 'receipt after promise' principle. In his description of *Rochefoucauld*, he says:

> A, due to the promise he made to A0 when acquiring his Freehold, was under a duty to keep that promise. As a result, A was under a duty to B not to use his Freehold for his own benefit and, as promised, to use his Freehold for B's benefit. As a result, the section 53(1)(b) formality rule did not apply: B's right did *not* arise as a result of a 'declaration of Trust'; instead, it arose by operation of law.[47]

McFarlane's thesis deserves a fuller treatment than it can be given here, but for the purposes of our analysis of *Rochefoucauld*, a number of problems can be identified. First, if, as he says, section 53(1)(b) did not apply in *Rochefoucauld*, then there was nothing standing in the way of the validity[48] of the express trust. Second, it misrepresents completely the reasoning in that case. As we have seen, the court there made it very clear that the trust did not arise by operation of law but because of a declaration of trust, the very opposite of McFarlane's assertion. Third, there is little, if any, authority for McFarlane's 'receipt after promise' principle. Indeed, he cites *Rochefoucauld* itself as authority, a *petitio principii* if ever there was one. Fourth, even if such a principle did exist, it does not describe the facts of *Rochefoucauld*, for no promise was made by the defendant to the person from whom he took a transfer of the right, the mortgagee: the promise was made to the claimant in the action, the Comtesse. Fifth, McFarlane gives no explanation why his 'receipt after promise' principle should generate a trust response from a court. Indeed, given that it contravenes the doctrine of privity of contract,[49] at least in those cases where the promise is contractual, it is difficult to see why any response at all is merited, least of all a trust. Sixth, McFarlane seems to misunderstand the *Rochefoucauld* doctrine, for he sees the fraud in that case as A's reneging on his promise to A0 to hold the right on trust for B. Yet as *Rochefoucauld* shows, this is not the fraud with which the court was concerned; it was instead the reliance on the statute. Indeed, given that the maxim is that a *statute* cannot be used as an instrument of fraud, it must have been the use of the statute which was in issue. However, in a case which McFarlane interprets in line with his

---

[46] [1981] AC 513, 531.
[47] McFarlane (n 2) 382 (original emphasis).
[48] Or 'enforceability': see the discussion below, text to nn 52–65.
[49] So, for example, it runs counter to the decision of the House of Lords in *Dunlop Pneumatic Tyre Co Ltd v Selfridge & Co Ltd* [1915] AC 847, for there title to tyres was sold to the defendant sub conditione but no right was thereby created in the third party in whose favour that condition was expressed.

theory, *Binions v Evans*,⁵⁰ where a purchaser of a fee simple agreed with the vendor to take 'subject to' the rights of a licensee, the problem was not one of the application of a statute, but the common law doctrine of privity, and there is no rule that a court will not allow the doctrine of privity to be used as an engine of fraud.⁵¹ It is therefore difficult to see what relevance *Rochefoucauld* could have to such a case. Finally, his theory attempts to prove too much, for it encompasses the vast majority of express trusts, for a conveyance of rights by A to B on condition that B will hold them on trust for either A or C will also be a 'receipt after promise' case. For McFarlane, therefore, there is in such cases no difference between express and constructive trusts, leaving him to explain why *Rochefoucauld* falls on the constructive side of the line. All in all, therefore, there is nothing to commend McFarlane's 'receipt after promise' doctrine as an explanation why the *Rochefoucauld* trust should be seen as constructive, rather than, as the court found, express.

3. The Lack of Writing Having Rendered the Express Trust Unenforceable, the Trust Enforced by the Court Must Have Been Constructive

A slightly different argument for a constructive trust is to say that the want of writing rendered the express trust in *Rochefoucauld* 'unenforceable' (rather than void), so that the trust which was enforced must have been constructive.

This thesis fares no better than the last. Once again, the obvious objection is that it is completely at odds with how the case was pleaded, argued and decided. As we have seen, the court disapplied section 7, and so whatever section 7 said, it could not have stood in the way of the 'enforcement' of the express trust. Moreover, section 7 is no more a rule of 'enforceability' than validity. Many commentators, however, treat it as such, stating that an orally declared trust of land is 'valid but unenforceable', an error seemingly caused by confusion with the operation of the now-repealed Law of Property Act 1925, section 40(1), which replaced the Statute of Frauds 1677, section 4. Typical in this regard is Pettitt, who says:⁵²

> Although the wording is somewhat different, the requirement of writing in s 53(1)(b) is generally thought to be the same as was required under s 40(1), now repealed, and reliance can accordingly be placed on decisions on the latter section. . . . Section 53(1)(b) does not contain any express sanction for failure to comply with its provisions. The assumption of most textbook writers is probably right: that since s 53(1)(b) merely requires writing as evidence, absence of writ-

---

⁵⁰ [1972] Ch 359.
⁵¹ Cf Sparkes (1988) 103 *Law Quarterly Review* 175, 178.
⁵² PH Pettitt, *Equity and the Law of Trusts*, 11th edn (Oxford, Oxford University Press, 2009) 88–89 (footnotes omitted).

ing does not make the declaration of trust void, but merely unenforceable as was previously the case under s 40(1).

The analogy is, however, false.

Section 4 of the Statute of Frauds 1677 provided as follows:

> No Action shall be brought . . . upon any Contract or Sale of Lands, Tenements or Hereditaments, or any Interest in or concerning them . . . unless the Agreement upon which such Action shall be brought, or some *Memorandum* or Note thereof, shall be in Writing, and signed by the Party to be charged therewith, or some other Person thereunto by him lawfully authorized.

Section 40(1), its successor in the 1925 legislation, provided in almost identical terms that:

> No action may be brought upon a contract for the sale or other disposition of land or any interest in land, unless the agreement upon which such action is brought, or some memorandum or note thereof, is in writing, and signed by the party to be charged or by some person thereunto by him lawfully authorised.

Section 4 of the 1677 statute does of course bear a superficial similarity to section 7, for it likewise lays down no rule of validity. It is not, in other words, a rule concerned with 'creation'. As Lord Selbourne LC explained in *Maddison v Alderson*, 'The Statute of Frauds does not avoid parol contracts, but only bars the legal remedies by which they might otherwise have been enforced.'[53] For that reason, as with section 7, the necessary writing can come into existence after the contract was made.[54] But this is where the similarity ends, for while section 7 lays down a rule of proof, section 4 says nothing about the type of evidence admissible to prove that a contract was made. It is instead concerned with the conditions for the *enforcement* of that contract, a different thing altogether. Of course, a declaration of trust which cannot be proved to have been made cannot be enforced, but a contract for which there is no memorandum or note thereof in writing, though it cannot be enforced, can at least be proved by oral testimony to have been made. Its existence, therefore, can be established in litigation not concerned with its enforcement, for example, claims in unjust enrichment.

A good example is provided by *Pavey and Matthews Pty Ltd v Paul*,[55] which concerned an unenforceability provision similar to section 4 of the 1677 Act but with its subject-matter building contracts rather than con-

---

[53] *Maddison v Alderson* (1883) 8 App Case 467, 474. See also *Bristol, Cardiff & Swansea Aerated Bread Co v Maggs* (1890) 44 Ch D 616, 622; *Crosby v Wadsworth* (1805) 6 East 602, 611; 102 ER 1419, 1423.
[54] *Shippey v Derrison* (1805) 5 Esp 190, 193; 170 ER 782, 783; *Re Holland* [1902] 2 Ch 360.
[55] (1986) 162 CLR 217.

tracts for the sale of land. By section 45 of the Builders Licensing Act 1971 (NSW):

> A contract . . . under which the holder of a licence undertakes to carry out, by himself or by others, any building work or to vary any building work or the manner of carrying out any building work, specified in a building contract is not enforceable against the other party to the contract unless the contract is in writing signed by each of the parties or his agent in that behalf and sufficiently describes the building work the subject of the contract.

The claimant builder entered into an oral contract with the defendant to renovate her cottage. On completion of the work, the defendant refused to pay the price demanded. Although unable to sue on the contract, the builder was nevertheless allowed by the High Court of Australia an unjust enrichment claim for the value of his services. Importantly, no issue was raised as to the existence of the contract, and more particularly, as to whether oral evidence was admissible to prove its making. Moreover, the existence of the contract was essential to the builder's claim. So, for example, Mason and Wilson JJ spoke of 'proof of the oral contract' forming 'an indispensible element of the plaintiff's success' in showing that the benefits were not intended as a gift and that the defendant had not rendered the promised exchange value,[56] while Deane J talked of the defendant being able to rely on the contract to place a ceiling on the unjust enrichment claim.[57] None of this would have been possible if the relevant provision had been evidentiary. It is likewise with section 4 of the 1677 Act/section 40 of the 1925 Act, for if they were framed in terms of evidence rather than enforceability, the court in such circumstances would not be able to see that there is a contract at all.

This insight is important, for both Birks[58] and Chambers,[59] albeit in a slightly different context, fall into the same trap as Pettitt in seeing section 7/section 53(1)(b) and section 4/section 40 as analogous.[60] They then argue that the trust in *Hodgson v Marks*,[61] where A conveyed to B on oral express trust for A, though it could not be express because section 53(1)(b) prevented its 'enforcement', was a constructive trust[62] arising because the evidence which proved the unenforceable trust demonstrated a 'non-

---

[56] Ibid, 227–28.
[57] Ibid, at 257.
[58] P Birks, 'Restitution and Resulting Trusts' in S Goldstein (ed), *Equity and Contemporary Legal Developments* (Jerusalem, Hebrew University of Jerusalem, 1992) 335, 363–64.
[59] R Chambers, *Resulting Trusts* (Oxford, Clarendon Press, 1997) 25.
[60] They are not the only restitution lawyers to do so. The same mistake is made by one of the fathers of the US Restatement, and indeed may be the source of their confusion: AW Scott 'Constructive Trusts' (1955) 71 *Law Quarterly Review* 39, 43; American Law Institute, *Restatement of the Law of Restitution* (St Paul, MN, American Law Institute, 1937) s 182.
[61] [1971] Ch 892.
[62] Chambers prefers to call it a 'resulting' trust, but there is no logical difference in this context.

beneficial intent' on the part of A, which non-beneficial intent triggered a trust arising by operation of law, which was not caught by the statute.[63] However, a correct reading of section 53(1)(b) destroys that argument *in limine*, for if the section really did apply on the facts,[64] the oral testimony of A as to the circumstances of the transfer would have been inadmissible for *all* purposes, not just those concerned with the 'enforcement' of the express trust. In other words, A would have been unable to prove an indispensable element of her cause of action, namely the fact that her transfer was accompanied by a 'non-beneficial intent'. Birks and Chambers are only able to make their argument by wrongly seeing section 7/section 53(1)(b) as a rule of enforceability.

But even if section 7 was a rule of enforceability, it is not easy to see how that would make the *Rochefoucauld* trust constructive. Once again, the argument ignores the fact that the court in *Rochefoucauld* held section 7 to be inapplicable, with the result that there could now be no obstacle to the 'enforcement' of the express trust. Moreover, even if the express trust was not being enforced, on what ground could a court impose a constructive trust? Once again, there seems to be none. There is certainly no unjust enrichment of the defendant at the expense of the plaintiff, for the reasons outlined above;[65] nor could a trust arise as a response to an alleged breach of trust on the part of the defendant, for that would be to enforce the unenforceable trust; nor is it possible to see any other wrong in play. Of course, there is the McFarlane 'receipt after promise' principle, but, as we have seen, that is flawed. So, even if we were to misread the statute and see it as concerned with enforceability, and misread *Rochefoucauld* as not disapplying the statute, the argument for a constructive trust is still weak.

4. The Oral Trust Being 'Ineffective' for Non-Compliance with Section 7, the Trust Enforced by the Court Must Have Been Constructive

Some commentators speak of section 7/section 53(1)(b) as a rule of 'effectiveness', with the consequence that a declaration of trust which is not in writing is somehow an 'ineffective' declaration of trust. This, for example, is the language (at times) of both Hayton and Mitchell[66] and Chambers.[67] It is, however, difficult to know what is being said here. If by 'ineffective' is

---

[63] Whether there can be such a thing as a 'non-beneficial' intent different from a transfer on trust is contentious: W Swadling 'Explaining Resulting Trusts' (2008) 124 *Law Quarterly Review* 72, 90–93.

[64] In fact, the court held that the plaintiff's oral testimony was admissible under the *Rochefoucauld* doctrine so that it was the express trust which was ultimately enforced: *Hodgson* (n 61) 933.

[65] Text to n 45.

[66] Hayton and Mitchell (n 38) para 2-12.

[67] Chambers (n 59) 25, 34 and 139.

meant 'void', then the argument is no different to that made in section 2 above.[68] If, however, they are saying that it cannot be enforced for lack of writing, then it is no different to the argument made in section 3. Either way, for the reasons addressed above, it is no argument for a constructive trust.

5. The Trust Was an Informal Trust, the Creation of which Was Sanctioned by Section 8 of the Statute of Frauds 1677

A further argument is that the court recognised a constructive trust created by the settlor exercising a power conferred on him by section 8 of the Statute of Frauds 1677/section 53(2) of the Law of Property Act 1925. This is the view of Battersby, who writes:

> Section 53(2) of the Law of Property Act 1925 provides that a trust relating to land may arise informally if it is an implied, resulting, or constructive trust. That provision allows for the wide-scale creation of informal interests, since the legislature has left it to the courts to decide exactly when an informal trust shall arise, and the justification in a particular case (or category of case) for allowing the normal formalities to be waived.[69]

This is an odd thesis indeed, for it appears to envisage rights-holders rather than courts creating constructive trusts. Moreover, it is hardly borne out by the wording of either section 8 or section 53(2).

Section 8 provided as follows:

> Provided always, That where any Conveyance shall be made of any Lands or Tenements by which a Trust or Confidence shall or may arise or result by the Implication or Construction of Law, or be transferred or extinguished by an Act or Operation of Law, then and in every such Case such Trust or Confidence shall be of the like Force and Effect as the same would have been if this Statute had not been made; any Thing herein before contained to the contrary notwithstanding.

Its successor, section 53(2), makes the same point, though rather more succinctly:

> This section [section 53] does not affect the creation or operation of resulting, implied or constructive trusts.

The essential point to note is that since neither section 7 of the 1677 Act nor section 53(1)(b) of the 1925 Act is concerned with rules of 'creation', the exceptions in sections 8 and 53(2) cannot allow for the 'creation of informal interests', wide-scale or not. The provisions are not power-

---

[68] This indeed would appear to be the usage of Chambers.
[69] G Battersby, 'Informally Created Interests in Land' in S Bright and J Dewar (eds), *Land Law: Themes and Perspectives* (Oxford, Oxford University Press, 1998) 487, 496.

conferring rules at all, but merely exempt certain types of trust from the primary evidentiary rule laid down in section 7/section 53(1)(b).[70] And in that respect, the provisions simply state the obvious. Leaving aside implied trusts on the ground that they seem to be nothing more than either resulting or constructive trusts, sections 7 and 53(1)(b) can have no application to constructive trusts because these are trusts which arise for reasons other than declarations of trust by rights-holders. Since they respond to events other than declarations of trust, a rule as to the type of evidence admissible to prove a declaration of trust is in their case redundant. Thus, in *A-G for Hong Kong v Reid*,[71] where claims to constructive trusts of titles to land bought with the proceeds of bribes received in breach of fiduciary duty were made, no appeal to section 53(2) was considered necessary. As to resulting trusts, one species, the 'automatic' resulting trust, is nothing more than a constructive trust, for it too arises for a reason other than a declaration of trust,[72] whilst the other, the so-called 'presumed' resulting trust, arises because of proof by presumption of a declaration of trust.[73] The reason section 7/section 53(1)(b) has no application in the latter case is that the operation of the presumption is to shift the onus of proof, so that no burden now rests on the person alleging a declaration of trust to bring evidence of the declaration, with the result that no question as to the type of evidence admissible to discharge any burden can arise. For these reasons, it is probably better not to describe sections 8 and 53(2) as laying down 'exceptions' to sections 7 and 53(1)(b) at all, but as simply detailing the situations to which the sections cannot possibly apply. In any case, what section 8/section 53(2) certainly does not do is give rights-holders the power to create informal trusts, and it is notable that no reference whatever was made to section 8 in the *Rochefoucauld* decision itself.

6. The Trust Must Have Been Constructive so as not to Contradict Section 53(1)(b)

A number of commentators argue that the trust in *Rochefoucauld* must have been constructive so as not to offend notions of Parliamentary supremacy. To disapply section 7, as did the court in *Rochefoucauld*, is said to offend basic notions of constitutional propriety. However, as Parliament has by section 8 exempted constructive trusts from the 'requirement' of writing, it is perfectly legitimate for the courts to create constructive trusts

---

[70] A similar misunderstanding occurs in relation to resulting trusts, with some commentators asserting that, by s 53(2), the legislature sanctioned the informal creation of resulting trusts: eg C Webb and T Akkouh, *Trusts Law* (London, Palgrave Macmillan, 2008) 214.
[71] [1994] 1 AC 324.
[72] *Vandervell v IRC* [1967] 2 AC 291.
[73] *Cook v Fountain* (1676) 3 Swanst 585, 591; 36 ER 984, 987 (Lord Nottingham LC).

on facts such as those in *Rochefoucauld*, whilst leaving section 7 intact. Typical in this regard is Penner, who writes:

> The constructive trust analysis may appear to be preferable to the express trust analysis simply because it gives an identical result without appearing to disregard the statute, since constructive trusts are specifically exempted from formality requirements by s 53(2).[74]

However, such a reclassification is purely instrumental, for Penner gives no other reason why the court should impose a constructive trust. Indeed, he seems here to fall into the same error as Pettitt identified above in using the language of 'exemption'. Moreover, it is hardly consistent with principles of Parliamentary supremacy for a court to do one thing but say it is doing another simply to hoodwink readers of the law reports.

D. CONCLUSION

If the subject-matter of the trust in *Rochefoucauld v Boustead* had been shares, there would be no doubt but that the trust was express. The question then is why the nature of the trust should change where the subject-matter is a title to land. The difference now, of course, is that section 7 of the Statute of Frauds 1677 is potentially in play, but, as we have seen, this was a rule of evidence which the court disapplied on perfectly orthodox and long-settled grounds. That in turn meant there was no barrier to the admission of the claimant's oral testimony to prove a declaration of trust by the defendant in her favour, and an ordering of accounts on the basis of the declared trust. That the trust was express can be tested in another way. Assume the legislature repealed section 7/section 53(1)(b). Were the facts of *Rochefoucauld* to recur, there could be no argument but that the trust was express. What in fact happened is that the Court of Appeal in *Rochefoucauld* did effectively repeal the statute, as least so far as the claimant was concerned, with the result that the trust there could likewise only be express.

The arguments that the trust was constructive either ignore the reasoning of the court altogether or mistake the nature of section 7 or both. Indeed, if the judges in *Rochefoucauld* thought that they were dealing with a constructive trust, why was no mention made of section 8? When properly analysed, the only possible categorisation of the *Rochefoucauld* trust which accords with both the *ratio* of the case and the wording of section 7 of the Statute of Frauds 1677 is that the trust enforced in the case was an express trust.

[74] J Penner, *The Law of Trusts*, 6th edn (Oxford, Oxford University Press, 2008) para 6.10.

4

Remedies for Knowing Receipt

CHARLES MITCHELL and STEPHEN WATTERSON*

A. INTRODUCTION

A defendant incurs an equitable liability for knowing receipt when he acts unconscionably by receiving trust property with the knowledge that it was transferred to him in breach of trust.[1] In this context, unconscionability is a measure of fault which includes, but is not limited to, dishonesty.[2] This chapter considers the nature of liability for knowing receipt and the basis on which this liability is assessed. To understand these matters we must investigate what the courts mean when they say that a knowing recipient is personally liable to account as a constructive trustee. First, though, we must stress that the question whether a knowing recipient owes a personal liability to the beneficiaries whose property he receives differs from the question whether they have an equitable interest in the property once it is in his hands.

B. PERSISTING EQUITABLE OWNERSHIP

When an express trustee wrongfully transfers the original trust property to a recipient who is not entitled to it, the property continues to be owned by

---

*We thank Steven Elliott, Simon Gardner, and Lionel Smith for their comments.

[1] *Bank of Credit and Commerce International (Overseas) Ltd v Akindele* [2001] Ch 437; *City Index Ltd v Gawler* [2007] EWCA Civ 1382, [2008] Ch 313, esp [8] and [32]. Liability for knowing receipt can also be incurred when property is transferred in a breach of fiduciary duty other than a breach of trust, eg by a company director. However, we shall focus our attention on misapplied trust property and the rights of trust beneficiaries. For discussion of the conceptual problems created by extending the rules on receipt of misdirected trust property to take in receipt of misdirected corporate property, see *Bell Group Ltd (in liq) v Westpac Banking Corp (No 9)* [2008] WASC 239, (2008) 225 FLR 1 [4750]–[4799].

[2] Ibid. See too *Belmont Finance Corp v Williams Furniture Ltd (No 2)* [1980] 1 All ER 399 (CA) 405; *Houghton v Fayers* [2000] 1 BCLC 511 (CA) 516; *Niru Battery Manufacturing Co v Milestone Trading Ltd (No 1)* [2003] EWCA Civ 1446, [2004] QB 985 [155]; *Uzinterimpex JSC v Standard Bank plc* [2008] EWCA Civ 819, [2008] Bus LR 1762 [43]–[46].

the beneficiaries in equity, whether or not the recipient knows of the breach of trust, unless he is a bona fide purchaser for value without notice of their equitable interest. The same rule applies when the trustee uses the original trust property to acquire substitute property which he then wrongfully transfers to the recipient. In the first case, the court does not need to impose a new trust on the property in order to create an equitable interest in the beneficiaries' favour, because they are already the equitable owners of the property under the express trust. In the second case, their equitable interest in the original trust property is transmitted to the substitute property,[3] and, as in the first case, the recipient cannot take this new property clear of the beneficiaries' interest under the express trust unless he is a bona fide purchaser without notice. When the substitute property is acquired in an authorised transaction, the source of the beneficiaries' interest in this property is the settlor's intention that they should have such an interest following the trustee's authorised exercise of his powers of sale and investment.[4] When the new property is acquired in an unauthorised transaction, the beneficiaries can choose whether to adopt or reject the transaction. If they adopt the trustee's purchase, then, again, the new property is impressed with an equitable interest arising under the express trust, by a process which looks like an ad hoc variation of the trust that gives the beneficiaries rights whose source, again, is the settlor's intention that they should have these rights, albeit in a form which is different from that which the settlor originally envisaged.[5]

Some courts have held that a trust necessarily comes into existence whenever the legal and equitable ownership of property is split,[6] suggesting that whenever a recipient of misdirected trust property takes it subject to the beneficiaries' persisting equitable interest he must immediately hold it on a constructive or resulting trust.[7] Other courts have said that a trust

---

[3] Cf C Rickett, 'Old and New in the Law of Tracing' in S Degeling and J Edelman (eds), *Equity in Commercial Law* (Sydney, Lawbook Co, 2005) 119, 140–44, observing that if their equitable interest in the original trust property were not transmissible in this way, then the equitable doctrine of overreaching would be unsustainable; see too D Fox, 'Overreaching' in P Birks and A Pretto (eds), *Breach of Trust* (Oxford, Hart Publishing, 2002) 95.

[4] R Chambers, 'Tracing and Unjust Enrichment' in J W Neyers et al (eds), *Understanding Unjust Enrichment* (Oxford, Hart Publishing, 2004) 263, 267.

[5] This does not explain why the beneficiaries should acquire an equitable proprietary interest in new property which has been acquired with misdirected trust property by a recipient other than a bona fide purchaser. In this case, if the recipient has knowledge of the breach, then it might be said that he acts unconscionably if he uses the trust property to acquire the new property, and that he holds the new property on constructive trust for this reason; alternatively (and necessarily in cases where he has no knowledge of the breach) the source of the beneficiaries' equitable proprietary interest in the new property is the law of unjust enrichment: P Birks, 'Property and Unjust Enrichment: Categorical Truths' [1997] *New Zealand Law Review* 623, 661; A Burrows, *The Law of Restitution*, 2nd edn (London, Sweet & Maxwell, 2005) 64–66 and 208–09.

[6] *Hardoon v Belilios* [1901] AC 118 (PC) 123; *Guerin v Canada* [1984] 2 SCR 335.

[7] *Boscawen v Bajwa* [1996] 1 WLR 328 (CA) 334–35 (Millett LJ). Cf R Chambers, *Result-*

does not necessarily arise whenever there is a split between legal and equitable title, because a trust cannot exist unless the legal owner of the property owes duties to the equitable owner.[8] We share Lord Millett's view that this is a semantic debate about the meaning of the word 'trust' which distracts attention from some more important questions that arise when misdirected trust property reaches the hands of a third party recipient:[9] namely, when does the beneficiaries' equitable interest in the property come into being; when does it come to an end; does the recipient owe duties with respect to the property; and if so, what is the content of these duties, and when do they arise? These are different questions, the answers to which are important for different reasons, and they should not be muddled together.[10]

The answer to the first set of questions is that the beneficiaries' equitable interest in the original trust property arises when the trust is created, and ends when the property is transferred pursuant to an authorised sale (in which case their interest is overreached), or is transferred in an unauthorised transaction to a bona fide purchaser for value without notice, or is consumed or otherwise destroyed. The beneficiaries' interest in the traceable proceeds of the original trust property arises when the substitute property is acquired, whether this transaction is authorised or subsequently ratified,[11] and comes to an end in the same circumstances as in the previous case.

The answer to the second set of questions turns on whether, and if so, when, the recipient knows of the breach of trust. If he knows about the breach at the time when he receives the property, then he is immediately fixed with a duty to return the property.[12] If he receives the property innocently, but later acquires knowledge of the breach while the property (or its traceable residue) is in his hands, then a duty to return the property

---

ing Trusts (Oxford, Oxford University Press, 1997) 202; Sir P Millett, 'Restitution and Constructive Trusts' in W R Cornish et al (eds), *Restitution: Past, Present, and Future* (Oxford, Hart Publishing, 1998) 199, 200. The recipient cannot be the *express* trustee of the property if he has never been properly appointed as such.

[8] *Westdeutsche Landesbank Girozentrale v Islington LBC* [1996] AC 669, 707.

[9] *R v Chester and North Wales Legal Aid Area Office, ex parte Floods of Queensferry Ltd* [1998] 1 WLR 1496 (CA) 1500 (Millett LJ).

[10] Cf M Bryan, 'Recipient Liability under the Torrens System: Some Category Errors' in R Grantham and C Rickett (eds), *Structure and Justification in Private Law* (Oxford, Hart Publishing, 2008) 339, arguing that the Australian courts have done precisely this in some recent cases where they have held that the creation of an equitable proprietary interest in misapplied property turns on the recipients' knowledge: eg *Farrow Finance Co Ltd (in liq) v Farrow Properties Ltd (in liq)* [1999] 1 VR 584 [161]; *Robins v Incentive Dynamics Pty Ltd* [2003] NSWCA 71, (2003) 45 ACSR 244.

[11] That is, where the trustee buys new property in an unauthorised transaction which is subsequently ratified by the beneficiaries, their equitable interest is retrospectively deemed to have arisen at the time of purchase.

[12] This duty, and other duties which the recipient may also owe, are discussed in parts D and E.

is imposed at that moment.[13] Conversely, a recipient who does not know of the breach before dissipating the property never owes any duty with respect to the property, although the beneficiaries have the power to place him under a duty, simply by informing him of the breach of trust before he disposes of the property. Whether or not the recipient acquires knowledge of the breach and thereby incurs a duty to the beneficiaries, they are the equitable owners of the property throughout the period when it is in his hands.

This summary of the law is supported by many English authorities including *Re Montagu's Settlement* where Megarry V-C considered that:

> [T]he doctrines of purchaser without notice and constructive trusts are concerned with matters which differ in important respects. The former is concerned with the question whether a person takes property subject to or free from some equity. The latter is concerned with whether or not a person is to have imposed upon him the personal burdens and obligations of trusteeship. I do not see why one of the touchstones for determining the burdens on property should be the same as that for deciding whether to impose a personal obligation on a man. The cold calculus of constructive and imputed notice does not seem to me to be an appropriate instrument for deciding whether a man's conscience is sufficiently affected for it to be right to bind him by the obligations of a constructive trustee.[14]

In *Agip (Africa) Ltd v Jackson* Millett J held that:

> Unless [a recipient of misdirected trust property] is a bona fide purchaser for value without notice, he must restore the trust property to its rightful owner if he still has it. But even a volunteer who has received trust property cannot be made subject to a personal liability to account for it as a constructive trustee if he has parted with it without having previously acquired some knowledge of the existence of the trust.[15]

In *Westdeutsche Landesbank Girozentrale v Islington LBC*, Lord Browne-Wilkinson held that:

> Once a trust is established, as from the date of its establishment the beneficiary has, in equity, a proprietary interest in the trust property, which proprietary interest will be enforceable in equity against any subsequent holder of the property (whether the original property or substituted property into which it can be traced) other than a purchaser for value of the legal interest without notice.[16]

In the same case, his Lordship also declined to hold that a recipient of misdirected trust property holds it on (constructive or resulting) trust for

---

[13] *Sheridan v Joyce* (1844) 7 Ir Rep Eq 115, 119; *Andrews v Bousfield* (1847) 10 Beav 511, 50 ER 678; *Locke v Prescott* (1863) 32 Beav 261, 55 ER 103; *Hennessey v Bray* (1863) 33 Beav 96, 102–03; 55 ER 302, 305.
[14] [1987] Ch 264, 272–73.
[15] [1990] 1 Ch 265, 290.
[16] [1996] AC 669, 705.

the beneficiaries where he does not know that it was transferred in a breach of trust, even though he is not a bona fide purchaser for value without notice of the beneficiaries' equitable interest. The relevant passage of his Lordship's speech runs as follows:

> The bank contended that where, under a pre-existing trust, B is entitled to an equitable interest in the trust property, if the trust property comes into the hands of a third party, X (not being a purchaser of the value of the legal estate without notice), B is entitled to enforce his equitable interest against the property in the hands of X because X is the trustee for B. In my view the third party, X, is not necessarily a trustee for B; B's equitable right is enforceable against the property in just the same way as any other specifically enforceable right can be enforced against the third party. Even if the third party, X, is not aware that what he has received is trust property B is entitled to assert his title in that property. If X has the necessary degree of knowledge, X may himself become a trustee for B on the basis of knowing receipt. But unless he has the requisite degree of knowledge he is not personally liable to account as a trustee.[17]

In *Foskett v McKeown*[18] Lord Browne-Wilkinson restated his view that where the traceable proceeds of trust property are wrongfully transferred to a recipient, the question whether the beneficiaries have a proprietary interest in these proceeds does 'not involve any question of resulting or constructive trusts' because their equitable proprietary interest under the express trust is 'enforceable against whoever for the time being holds those assets other than someone who is a bona fide purchaser for value of the legal interest without notice or a person who claims through such a purchaser'. In *Allen v Rea Brothers Trustees Ltd*,[19] Robert Walker LJ followed *Westdeutsche* to hold that the trustees of a pension scheme could recover the traceable proceeds of money wrongfully transferred into a second scheme, but that one of the trustees of the second scheme was not personally liable to account for this money because there was never a time when it had known that the transfer was invalid and had also had the means of ascertaining what sum should be returned or of raising this sum. Similarly, in *Clark v Cutland*[20] Arden LJ held that a claimant's concession that he has no personal claim against a recipient of misdirected trust property in respect of dealings with the property prior to the action does not equate to a concession that he has no persisting equitable interest in the property, nor to a concession that the recipient owes no duty to return the surviving property once the breach has been drawn to his attention. Likewise in

---

[17] Ibid, 707.
[18] [2001] 1 AC 102, 108–09. At 129 Lord Millett similarly said that the beneficiaries have 'a continuing beneficial interest not merely in the trust property but in its traceable proceeds also'. These dicta make it clear that Graham J was wrong to hold in *Peffer v Rigg* [1977] 1 WLR 285, 294, that a 'new' constructive trust is imposed on misdirected trust property in the hands of a knowing recipient.
[19] [2002] EWCA Civ 85, (2002) 4 ITELR 627 [44]–[46] and [52]–[55].
[20] [2003] EWCA Civ 810, [2004] 1 WLR 783 [30].

Nabb Brothers Ltd v Lloyds Bank International (Guernsey) Ltd[21] Lawrence Collins J held that a 'proprietary equitable claim' against a volunteer who has received misdirected trust money 'is not strictly dependent on the imposition of a constructive trust' and that 'it does not necessarily follow [from the recognition of such a claim] that the defendant is treated as a trustee of the money'.

C. PERSONAL LIABILITY TO ACCOUNT AS AN EXPRESS TRUSTEE

In parts D and E we shall argue that when the courts say that a knowing recipient is personally liable to account as a constructive trustee, they mean that he must account for the misdirected property in just the same way that an express trustee must account for property that is transferred to him by the settlor as part of an express trust arrangement. Before going any further, it may therefore be useful to remind readers of the rules governing an express trustee's duty to account for the trust property.

1. The Duty to Account

At the core of an express trust is the trustees' duty to produce accounts that are available for the beneficiaries to examine. The beneficiaries are entitled to the production of these accounts without any court order, but they can also obtain an order for an account as a means of enforcing their rights to performance of the trustees' primary duties and reparation for losses flowing from the trustees' breaches of duty.[22] Lewison J explained this process in *Ultraframe (UK) Ltd v Fielding*:

> The taking of an account is the means by which a beneficiary requires a trustee to justify his stewardship of trust property. The trustee must show what he has done with that property. If the beneficiary is dissatisfied with the way that a trustee has dealt with trust assets, he may surcharge or falsify the account. He surcharges the account when he alleges that the trustee has not obtained for the benefit of the trust all that he might have done, if he had exercised due care and diligence. If the allegation is proved, then the account is taken as if the trustee had received, for the benefit of the trust, what he would have received if he had exercised due care and diligence. The beneficiary falsifies the account when he alleges that the trustee has applied trust property in a way that he should not

---

[21] [2005] EWHC 405 (Ch) [69]. Further authorities in point are: *Waxman v Waxman* (2004) 7 ITELR 162 (Ontario CA) [583]; *Ultraframe (UK) Ltd v Fielding* [2005] EWHC 1638 (Ch) [1518].

[22] 'Trustees who indefensibly fail to produce accounts may be ordered to pay not only the costs of proceedings to obtain the accounts but also the costs of taking the account which is ordered': *Mason v Coleman* [2007] EWHC 3149 (Ch) [93]. See too *Kemp v Burn* (1863) 4 Giff 348, 66 ER 740; *Jefferys v Marshall* (1870) 23 LT 548.

have done (eg by making an unauthorised investment). If the allegation is proved, then the account will be taken as if the expenditure had not been made; and as if the unauthorised investment had not formed part of the assets of the trust. Of course, if the unauthorised investment has appreciated in value, the beneficiary may choose not to falsify the account: in which case the asset will remain a trust asset and the expenditure on it will be allowed in taking the account.[23]

As Austin J explained in an Australian case, *Glazier Holdings Pty Ltd v Australian Men's Health Pty Ltd (No 2)*,[24] there are two forms of account, with an order to pay any sum found to be due to the trust estate when the accounting process is complete: the common account and the account on the footing of wilful default. The order for a common account is available without any allegation of wrongdoing, and requires the defendant to account only for what has been received, what has been disbursed by way of expenses, and what has been distributed.[25] In contrast, an order for an account on the basis of wilful default is grounded on the trustee's misconduct, and requires him to account not only for what he has received, but also for what he would have received if he had not committed a breach of duty.[26] The term 'wilful default' is a misleading one in this context since it extends to all breaches of duty, running from negligence through to deliberate fraud.[27]

In all cases, the onus lies on the trustee to prove and justify his records, and evidential presumptions are made against him if he fails to do so.[28] Where the trustee can show that he disposed of trust property in an authorised transaction which entailed no breach of duty he will be discharged from his duty to hold the relevant property for the beneficiaries.[29] However, where the court decides, following its scrutiny of the

---

[23] [2005] EWHC 1638 (Ch) [1513].

[24] [2001] NSWSC 6. This was reversed on appeal, but nothing was said by the NSWCA that contradicted Austin J's description of the forms of equitable accounting: *Meehan v Glazier Holdings Pty Ltd* [2002] NSWCA 22, (2002) 54 NSWLR 146. For further discussion, see R Chambers, 'Liability' in Birks and Pretto (n 3) 1, 16–20.

[25] *Partington v Reynolds* (1858) 4 Drew 253, 255–59; 62 ER 98, 99–100; *Re Fish* [1893] 2 Ch 413, 421; *Re Wells* [1962] 1 WLR 874, CA; *Templeton Insurance Ltd v Penningtons Solicitors LLP* [2005] EWHC 2885 (Ch).

[26] *Re Stevens* [1898] 1 Ch 162 (CA) 175; *Bartlett v Barclays Bank Trust Co Ltd (No 2)* [1980] 515, 546; *Armitage v Nurse* [1998] Ch 241 (CA) 252; *Coulthard v Disco Mix Club Ltd* [1999] 2 All ER 457 (CA) 482; *Iliffe v Trafford* [2002] WTLR 507 [9].

[27] *Walker v Symonds* (1818) 3 Swans 1, 69; 36 ER 751, 776; *Re Chapman* [1896] 2 Ch 763 (CA) 776 and 779–80. See too JH Stannard, 'Wilful Default' [1979] *Conveyancer and Property Lawyer* 345, esp 348.

[28] *Campbell v Hogg* [1930] 3 DLR 673 (PC) (where the beneficiary represented herself in the Privy Council with remarkable success; for the interesting background to this case, see C Backhouse and N L Backhouse, *The Heiress vs The Establishment: Mrs Campbell's Campaign for Legal Justice* (Vancouver, UBC Press, 2004)); *Maintemp Heating & Air Conditioning Inc v Monat Developments Inc* (2002) 59 OR (3d) 270 (Ontario Sup Ct), esp [40]–[44]; *Sinclair v Sinclair* [2009] EWHC 926 (Ch) [39]–[41].

[29] *Soar v Ashwell* [1893] 2 QB 390 (CA) 394.

trust accounts, that he owes the beneficiaries a personal liability, different forms of order can be made, according to the nature of the trust. Where the trust is absolute and there is no need to reconstitute the fund, the court can simply order the trustee to transfer trust property or pay money directly to the beneficiaries.[30] In the more common case where the trust is still on foot, the trustee will be ordered to reconstitute the fund, or where he has been replaced by new trustees, to transfer property or pay money to the new trustees, to be held by them under the terms of the trust.[31]

The accounting process is the conceptual mechanism through which beneficiaries can bring two different types of compensation claim against trustees, which will be termed substitutive performance claims and reparation claims.[32] Substitutive performance claims are claims for a money payment as a substitute for performance of the trustees' primary obligation to account for and deliver trust property *in specie*. Claims of this sort are apposite when trust property has been lost or misapplied in an unauthorised transaction, and the amount claimed is the objective value of the property which the trustees should have been able to produce when called upon to do so. Reparation claims are claims for a money payment to make good the damage caused by a breach of trust, and the amount claimed is measured by reference to the actual loss sustained by the beneficiaries. Claims of this sort are apposite where, for example, the trustees have carelessly mismanaged trust property or failed to bring in trust income.

2. Substitutive Performance Claims

A trustee's 'paramount obligation' is 'recovering, securing and duly applying the trust fund'.[33] He must get in the trust property where the trust deed requires him to do so,[34] and if he or any other trustee misapplies the

---

[30] *Target Holdings Ltd v Redferns* [1996] AC 421, 435. The beneficiaries' right to payment generally arises in equity, but 'when there remains nothing to the trustee to execute except the payment over of money to the beneficiary, or the trustee admits the debt' then interestingly a common law action for money had and received also lies: *Roxborough v Rothmans of Pall Mall Australia Ltd* (2001) 208 CLR 516 [67] (Gummow J), explored in LD Smith, 'Simplifying Claims to Traceable Proceeds' (2009) 125 *Law Quarterly Review* 338.

[31] *Partridge v Equity Trustees Executors and Agency Co Ltd* (1947) 75 CLR 149; *Hillsdown plc v Pensions Ombudsman* [1997] 1 All ER 862, 897; *Chellaram v Chellaram (No 2)* [2002] 3 All ER 17 [159]; *Patel v London Borough of Brent (No 2)* [2003] EWHC 3081 (Ch), [2004] WTLR 577 [32].

[32] Terminology suggested by Steven Elliott in *Compensation Claims against Trustees* (Oxford DPhil thesis, 2002). Parts of this insightful work are published as: SB Elliott, 'Remoteness Criteria in Equity' (2002) 65 *Modern Law Review* 588; SB Elliott and C Mitchell, 'Remedies for Dishonest Assistance' (2004) 67 *Modern Law Review* 16, 23–34; SB Elliott and J Edelman, 'Money Remedies against Trustees' (2004) 18 *Trust Law International* 116.

[33] *Re Brogden* (1888) 38 Ch D 546 (CA) 571 (Fry LJ).

[34] *Maitland v Bateman* (1843) 13 LJ Ch 273; *Mathew v Brise* (1845) 15 LJ Ch 39; *Coppard v Allen* (1864) 4 Giff 497, 66 ER 802; *M'Donnel v White* (1865) 9 HLC 570, 584; 11 ER 1454, 1460; *ex parte Ogle* (1873) 8 Ch App 711; *Wyman v Paterson* [1900] AC 271.

property, then he must bring proceedings to recover it or otherwise obtain relief on the beneficiaries' behalf.[35] He must 'properly . . . preserve the trust fund', and 'pay the income and the corpus to those who are entitled to them respectively'.[36] The beneficiaries have corresponding primary rights to have the trust property collected, maintained and disbursed in accordance with the trust deed,[37] and the courts can give direct effect to these rights, without proof that the trustee has committed any breach of duty, in various ways—for example, by making a declaration setting out the nature of a beneficiary's interest,[38] or the trustees' duty;[39] by directing the trustees to exercise an obligatory discretionary power of appointment;[40] by directing them to transfer trust property to an absolutely entitled beneficiary;[41] or by issuing a prohibitory injunction, restraining them from acting inconsistently with their primary obligations.[42]

In just the same way, the court can also give direct effect to the beneficiaries' primary rights without proof of wrongdoing where a trustee cannot perform his primary obligation to deliver trust property *in specie* because he has lost or misapplied it in an unauthorised transaction. In such a case, the court can order the trustee to pay money as a substitute for performance of his primary duty. The amount due is calculated by requiring the trustee to produce accounts which omit no relevant incomings and record only authorised outgoings, by inspecting these to determine what property makes up the trust fund, and then, if the trustee cannot produce this property *in specie*, by ordering him to pay over a money substitute—either directly to the beneficiaries, or more usually, into the trust fund so that the trust can remain on foot. Thus, as Kekewich J stated in *Head v Gould*:

> As against a trustee who, on the accounts being taken, is shewn to have improperly applied part of the trust estate, the right of a *cestui que trust* is to have those accounts set straight—that is, to compel the trustee to pay such a sum as will make them balance.[43]

The amount due from the trustee to make the accounts balance may be

---

[35] *Re Forest of Dean Coal Mining Co* (1879) 10 Ch D 450, 453–54; *Young v Murphy* [1996] 1 VLR 279 (Victoria CA), esp 281–82; *Evans v European Bank Ltd* [2004] NSWCA 82, (2004) 7 ITELR 19 [116].
[36] *Low v Bouverie* [1891] 3 Ch 82 (CA) 99 (Lindley LJ).
[37] *Target Holdings Ltd v Redferns* [1996] AC 421, 434.
[38] *Smith v Acton* (1858) 26 Beav 210, 53 ER 877. The proper form of a declaration of equitable interest under CPR rule 40.20 is discussed in *Powell v Wilshire* [2004] EWCA Civ 534, [2005] 1 QB 117 [39]–[45].
[39] *Cowan v Scargill* [1985] Ch 270.
[40] *Re Locker's ST* [1977] 1 WLR 1323.
[41] *Re Knox's Trusts* [1895] 2 Ch 483; *Re Sandeman's WT* [1937] 1 All ER 368. See too the Trustee Act 1925, ss 44(vi) and 51(1)(d).
[42] *Fox v Fox* (1870) LR 11 Eq 142; *Buttle v Saunders* [1950] 2 All ER 193; *George v Macdonald* NSW Sup Ct (Eq Div) 6 February 1992.
[43] [1898] 2 Ch 250, 266. See too *Wiglesworth v Wiglesworth* (1852) 16 Beav 269, 272; 51 ER 782, 783; *Chaplin v Young* (1864) 33 Beav 330, 343; 55 ER 395, 400.

the value of misapplied (or wrongfully retained) trust income,[44] or of a misapplied capital sum plus interest.[45] Where some other property than money has been misapplied, he may be liable to pay the market value of the property at the date of misapplication plus interest,[46] or, if this is a higher sum, the market value of the property at the date of judgment,[47] along with the amount of any income that would otherwise have been generated by the property between the date of misapplication and the date of judgment.[48]

The courts have often said that substitutive performance claims resemble claims for 'an equitable debt' and that the trustees' liability is a 'liability in the nature of a debt'.[49] The point of this comparison is that the beneficiaries' claim is not like a common law claim for damages because it is not founded on an assertion that the trustees have committed a wrong.[50] Hence it makes no difference whether the beneficiaries have been caused a loss by the trustees' actions or omissions,[51] for the amount payable 'looks not so much to the loss suffered as to what is required to restore the trust fund',[52] and indeed beneficiaries cannot bring substitutive performance claims to recover loss which they have personally suffered through the trustee's un-

---

[44] *Sharma v Farlam Ltd* [2009] EWHC 1622 (Ch) [401] ff.

[45] *Docker v Somes* (1834) 2 My & K 655, 39 ER 1095; *Burdick v Garrick* (1870) 5 Ch App 233, CA; *Re Davis* [1902] 2 Ch 314; *Gordon v Gonda* [1955] 1 WLR 885, CA; *Kemp v Sims* [2008] EWHC 2579 (Ch); [2009] Pens LR 83.

[46] *Shepherd v Mouls* (1845) 4 Hare 500, 504; 67 ER 746, 747.

[47] *Re Massingberd's Settlement* (1890) 63 LT 296, CA; *Re Bell's Indenture* [1980] 1 WLR 1217.

[48] *Kellaway v Johnson* (1842) 5 Beav 319, 324; 49 ER 601, 603; *Hewett v Foster* (1843) 6 Beav 259, 49 ER 825; *Dixon v Dixon* (1878) 9 Ch D 587.

[49] *Ex parte Adamson* (1878) 8 Ch App 807 (CA) 819; *ex parte Kelly & Co* (1879) 11 Ch D 306 (CA) 311; *Webb v Stenton* (1881) 11 QBD 518, 530; *Wickstead v Browne* (1992) 30 NSWLR 1, 14–15; *Armstrong v East West Airlines (Operations) Ltd* NSW Sup Ct (Eq Div) 3 February 1994; *Turner v TR Nominees Pty Ltd* NSW Sup Ct (Eq Div) 3 November 1995.

[50] *Bacon v Clarke* (1837) 3 My & Cr 294, 298–99; 40 ER 938, 940; *Ahmed Angullia bin Hadjee Mohamed Salleh Angullia v Estate and Trust Agencies (1927) Ltd* [1938] AC 624, PC. See too Lord Millett, 'Proprietary Restitution' in Degeling and Edelman, *Equity* (n 3) 309, 310: 'If a trustee or fiduciary has committed a breach of trust or fiduciary duty, Equity makes him account as if he had not done so . . . [and he] is not allowed to say that he acted in breach of duty.'

[51] *Cocker v Quayle* (1830) 1 Russ & M 353, 39 ER 206; *Salway v Salway* (1831) 2 Russ & My 215, 39 ER 376; *Magnus v Queensland National Bank* (1888) 37 Ch D 466 (CA) 471–72; *British American Elevator Co v Bank of North America* [1919] AC 658 (PC) 663–64; *Island Realty Investments Ltd v Douglas* (1985) 19 ETR 56, 64; *Youyang Pty Ltd v Minter Ellison Morris Fletcher* (2003) 212 CLR 484 [63] and [69]. To the extent that parts of Lord Browne-Wilkinson's analysis in *Target Holdings Ltd v Redferns* [1996] AC 421 suggest otherwise, they are out of line with many previous authorities, including Street J's classic exposition of the law in *Re Dawson* [1966] 2 NSWR 211, which Lord Browne-Wilkinson himself endorsed in *Target* at 434 (and which was also approved by Brightman LJ, sitting as a first instance judge, in *Bartlett v Barclays Bank Trust Co Ltd (No 2)* [1980] Ch 515, 543).

[52] *New Cap Reinsurance Corp Ltd v General Cologne Re Australia Ltd* [2004] NSWSC 781, (2004) 7 ITELR 295 [55] (Young CJ in Eq). See too *Re Anglo-French Co-operative Soc* (1882) 21 Ch D 492, 506; *Re Windsor Steam Coal Co (1901) Ltd* [1929] 1 Ch 151, 166–67; *Hobday v Kirkpatrick's Trustees* 1985 SLT 197 (Court of Session, Outer House) 199.

authorised actions, for example because his disposal of trust property deprives them of income on the timely receipt of which they were relying.[53] For the same reasons it makes no difference whether the trustees have behaved negligently or dishonestly.[54] Nor do the concepts of remoteness[55] and contributory negligence[56] have any bearing on the beneficiaries' claim.

When deciding whether a trustee's payments are justified and should therefore be allowed to stand on the taking of the account, the court will generally disallow unauthorised disbursements, with the result that unauthorised purchases are treated as having been made with the trustee's own money.[57] However, there are exceptional cases where unauthorised disbursements will be allowed, and the trustee exonerated from performance of his duty to hold the relevant property for the beneficiaries. One such case is where the beneficiaries elect to adopt the trustee's actions and ask the court to treat these as though they had been authorised all along. Beneficiaries would wish to do this where the trustee has bought an unauthorised investment which has increased in value,[58] or where the trustee has wrongfully sold trust property whose current market value is lower than the value of the sale proceeds plus interest.[59] Sometimes the courts also relieve a trustee from the performance of his duty where they consider that this would be inequitable. For example, in *Jones v Lewis*, Lord Hardwicke LC held that: '[I]f a trustee is robbed, that robbery properly

---

[53] K Biedermann, *The Trust in Liechtenstein Law*, trans HG Crossland (Oxford, Alvescot Press, 1984) 136. It is possible that a beneficiary could recover for this kind of loss by making a reparation claim if he could show, for example, that the trustee's misapplication of trust property had been negligent.
[54] *Caffrey v Darby* (1801) 6 Ves Jun 488, 31 ER 1158; *Clough v Bond* (1838) 3 My & Cr 490, 496–97; 40 ER 1016, 1018; endorsed in *Target Holdings Ltd v Redferns* [1996] AC 421, 434.
[55] *Clough v Bond* (1838) 3 My & Cr 490, 40 ER 1016; *Magnus v Queensland National Bank* (1888) 37 Ch D 466; *Re Duckwari plc (No 2)* [1999] Ch 268 (CA) 272; *McCann v Switzerland Insurance Australia Ltd* (2000) 203 CLR 579, 621–22.
[56] *Alexander v Perpetual Trustees (WA) Ltd* [2004] HCA 7, (2004) 216 CLR 109 [44] and esp [104]: contributory negligence is inapt because of 'the basic principle that a fiduciary's liability to a beneficiary for breach of trust is one of restoration'. See too *Bristol and West Building Society v A Kramer and Co (a firm)* The Times 6 February 1995; *Nationwide Building Society v Balmer Radmore (a firm)* [1999] Lloyds Reports PN 241; *De Beer v Kanaar & Co (a firm)* [2002] EWHC 688 (Ch) [92].
[57] *Polloxfen v Stewart* (1841) 3 D 1214 (Court of Session, Inner House); *Jackson v Dickinson* [1903] 1 Ch 947, esp 951–52 (where the consequences of this rule are fully explored).
[58] *Grant v Baillie* (1869) 8 M 77 (Court of Session, Inner House); *Re Patten* (1883) 52 LJ Ch 787; *Currie and Others (Lamb's Trustees)* (1901) 9 SLT 170 (Court of Session, Outer House); *Re Jenkins* [1903] 2 Ch 362; *Wright v Morgan* [1926] AC 788 (PC) 799. If the beneficiaries choose to adopt the investment, they cannot *also* demand that the trustees pay in the difference between the current value of the investment and the (higher) current value of an authorised asset that was sold to make the purchase: *Thornton v Stokill* (1855) 1 Jur 751, which should be preferred on this point to *Re Lake* [1903] 1 KB 439.
[59] *Harrison v Harrison* (1740) 2 Atk 121, 26 ER 476; *Bostock v Blakeney* (1794) 2 Bro CC 653, 656; 29 ER 362, 364; *Pocock v Reddington* (1801) 5 Ves Jun 794, 800; 31 ER 862, 865.

proved shall be a discharge, provided he keeps [the trust property] so as he would keep his own'.[60]

It is tempting, but wrong, to conclude from the fact that trustees need not account for stolen trust property which they kept with reasonable care that the courts will never require trustees to reach into their own pockets unless they have committed a breach of duty.[61] Various cases have already been cited for the proposition that substitutive performance claims do not depend on the assertion that the trustee has committed a breach of duty. Another is *Eaves v Hickson*,[62] where Romilly MR declined to relieve a trustee who made unauthorised distributions on presentation of a forged document. No finding was made that the trustee had failed to examine this document carefully, and although counsel cited *Jones* and other robbery cases,[63] his Lordship concluded that the trustee was still 'bound to pay the trust fund to the right person'.[64] It follows that much can turn on the question whether a trustee's acts are unauthorised (in which case liability to perform his primary duties will subsist unless he is relieved) or authorised (in which case no liability will ensue unless he commits a breach of duty). This has sometimes led the courts to reclassify as authorised types of trustee action that were previously held to be unauthorised, with a view to moderating the law's severity. For example, in *Speight v Gaunt*[65] the Court of Appeal and House of Lords changed the law when they held that the delegation of a trustee's investment duties to a broker was not an unauthorised action, although it was an action that had to be done carefully.

3. Reparation Claims

Reparation claims are claims that trustees should make good the harm which the beneficiaries have suffered as a consequence of their breach of duty. In contrast to substitutive performance claims, they depend on the assertion that the trustees have committed a wrong,[66] and the award made

---

[60] (1750) 2 Ves Sen 240, 241; 28 ER 155, 155. See too *Morley v Morley* (1678) 2 Chan Cas 2, 22 ER 817; *Jobson v Palmer* [1893] 1 Ch 71. And cf *ex parte Belchier* (1754) Amb 218, 219; 27 ER 144, 145 (trustee not answerable for property lost on banker's bankruptcy); *Job v Job* (1875) 6 Ch D 562, 563–64 (similar rule for executors).
[61] As argued in R Chambers, 'Liability' in Birks and Pretto (n 3) 1, 9.
[62] (1861) 30 Beav 136, 54 ER 840. See also *Ashby v Blackwell* (1765) 2 Eden 299, 28 ER 913; *Bostock v Flyer* (1865) LR 1 Eq 26; *Sutton v Wilders* (1871) LR 12 Eq 373.
[63] Ibid, 139.
[64] Ibid, 141.
[65] (1883) 22 Ch D 727, CA, affirmed (1883) 9 App Cas 1; discussed in C Stebbings, *The Private Trustee in Victorian England* (Cambridge, Cambridge University Press, 2001) ch 5, esp 151–55.
[66] *Partington v Reynolds* (1858) 4 Drew 253, 255–56; 62 ER 98, 99; *Dowse v Gorton* [1891] AC 190, 202; *Re Stevens* [1898] 1 Ch 162, 170.

is calculated by reference to the loss suffered by the beneficiaries,[67] including the loss of a chance to avoid a detriment or make a gain.[68] The beneficiaries must prove that their loss has been factually caused by the trustees' breach of duty, using a 'but-for' causation test, regardless of whether the breach was innocent, negligent or fraudulent.[69] Canadian authorities also indicate that their claims are subject to the principle of *novus actus interveniens*,[70] and that where the beneficiaries have become aware that their trustees are not to be trusted, losses flowing from clearly unreasonable behaviour by the beneficiaries thereafter will be judged to have been caused by this behaviour and not by the breach.[71]

A reparation claim might be brought, for example, where a trustee negligently makes an authorised investment which declines in value or produces an unreasonably low income,[72] where he negligently fails to diversify the trust investments,[73] or to sell particular property,[74] or to collect rents payable on the trust property,[75] or to monitor the activities of a 99 per cent owned company.[76] A reparation claim might also lie where a trustee fails to strike a fair balance between the interests of a life tenant and a remainderman when investing the trust property.[77] Where the trustee has negligently bought an authorised investment that declines in value, no question can arise of the beneficiaries choosing whether to adopt or reject the transaction: the investment forms part of the trust estate, but the trustee may be personally liable to pay compensation for the loss caused by his negligence.[78]

---

[67] *Elder's Trustee and Executor Co Ltd v Higgins* (1963) 113 CLR 426, 453; *Fales v Canada Permanent Trust Co* [1977] 2 SCR 302, 320.

[68] *Sanders v Parry* [1967] 1 WLR 753, 767; *Nestlé v National Westminster Bank plc* [1993] 1 WLR 1260 (CA) 1269; *Colour Control Centre Pty Ltd v Ty* unreported NSW Sup Ct (Eq Div) 24 July 1995; *Bank of New Zealand v New Zealand Guardian Trust Co Ltd* [1999] 1 NZLR 664, 685–86.

[69] *Target Holdings Ltd v Redferns* [1996] AC 421, 436; *Collins v Brebner* [2000] Lloyds Rep PN 587; *Hulbert v Avens* [2003] EWHC 76, [2003] WTLR 387 [56]; *Gwembe Valley Development Co Ltd v Koshy (No 3)* [2003] EWCA Civ 1048, [2004] 1 BCLC 131 [147]. But cf *Bairstow v Queen's Moat Houses plc* [2001] 2 BCLC 531 [53]–[54]. On the question whether reparation claims are subject to a remoteness cap, see S B Elliott, 'Remoteness Criteria in Equity' (2002) 65 *Modern Law Review* 588; and also *Olszanecki v Hillocks* [2002] EWHC 1997 (Ch), [2004] WTLR 975.

[70] *Hodgkinson v Simms* [1994] 3 SCR 377, 443; *Waxman v Waxman* (2004) 7 ITELR 162 (Ontario CA) [663].

[71] *Canson Enterprises Ltd v Boughton & Co* [1991] 3 SCR 534, 554, endorsed in *Corporaçion del Cobre de Chile v Sogemin Metals Ltd* [1997] 1 WLR 1396, 1403–04. See too *Lipkin Gorman v Karpnale Ltd* [1992] 4 All ER 331, 361.

[72] *Smethurst v Hastings* (1884) 30 Ch D 490; *Ross v Davy* 1996 SCLR 369 (Court of Session, Outer House) 384.

[73] *Nestlé v National Westminster Bank* [1993] 1 WLR 1265 (CA) 1281.

[74] *Wight v Olswang (No 2)* [2000] WTLR 783, reversed [2001] WTLR 291, CA; *Re Ambrazevicius Estate* [2002] MBQB 58, (2002) 164 Man R (2d) 5.

[75] *M'Donnel v White* (1865) 9 HLC 570, 584; 11 ER 1454, 1460.

[76] *Bartlett v Barclays Bank Trust Co Ltd* [1980] Ch 515.

[77] *Re Mulligan* [1998] 1 NZLR 181 (NZ High Ct).

[78] *Re Salmon* (1888) 42 Ch D 351 (CA) 369 and 371.

D. PERSONAL LIABILITY TO ACCOUNT AS A CONSTRUCTIVE TRUSTEE

Having explained the nature of an express trustee's liability to account for property settled on an express trust, we now turn to the nature of a knowing recipient's liability to account as a constructive trustee of property received in breach of trust. Over the past 20 years it has become fashionable to say that nothing is added to our understanding of liability for knowing receipt by the language of constructive trusteeship, and indeed that this language obscures the true nature of the liability. This was a recurring theme in the work of Peter Birks,[79] which seems to have exercised a strong influence on the thinking of some members of the senior judiciary. For example, Lord Nicholls has written extra-judicially that:

> The traditional approach to [knowing recipients and dishonest assistants] involves interposing a deemed ('constructive') trusteeship between the wrongful conduct (dishonest participation) and the remedy (liability in equity). This intermediate step seems otiose and, indeed, confusing.[80]

Similarly, in *Paragon Finance plc v D B Thakerar & Co (a firm)*, Millett LJ observed of liability for both dishonest assistance and knowing receipt that:

> Equity has always given relief against fraud by making any person sufficiently implicated in the fraud accountable in equity . . . Such a person is not in fact a trustee at all, even though he may be liable to account as if he were. He never assumes the position of a trustee, and if he receives the trust property at all it is adversely to the plaintiff by an unlawful transaction which is impugned by the plaintiff. In such a case the expressions 'constructive trust' and 'constructive trustee' are misleading for there is no trust and usually no possibility of a proprietary remedy; 'they are nothing more than a formula for equitable relief'.[81]

---

[79] Although Birks's understanding of the relationship between knowing receipt and unjust enrichment changed (see n 194), he never shifted from his view that the language of constructive trusteeship was a 'mystifying label' that should be discarded: eg P Birks, *An Introduction to the Law of Restitution* (Oxford, Clarendon Press, 1985) 80–82; P Birks, 'Persistent Problems in Misdirected Money: A Quintet' [1993] *Lloyd's Maritime and Commercial Law Quarterly* 218, 236; P Birks, *Unjust Enrichment*, 2nd edn (Oxford, Oxford University Press, 2005) 293–95. Like views are expressed in C Rickett, 'The Classification of Trusts' (1999) 18 *New Zealand Universities Law Review* 305, 321–24; Burrows (n 5) 196–97; M Cope, *Equitable Obligations: Duties, Defences and Remedies* (Sydney, Lawbook Co, 2007) 224—although Cope also states at 224, n 39, that 'the personal liability [of a knowing recipient] is the same as the personal liability of an express trustee', a statement with which we broadly agree.

[80] Lord Nicholls, 'Knowing Receipt: The Need for a New Landmark' in Cornish (n 7) 231, 243.

[81] [1999] 1 All ER 400 (CA) 409, quoting *Selangor United Rubber Estates Ltd v Cradock (No 3)* [1968] 1 WLR 1555, 1582. The fact that Millett LJ meant to speak of knowing receipt as well as dishonest assistance in this passage is noted by Rimer J in *DEG-Deutsche Investitions- und Entwicklungsgesellschaft mbH v Koshy (No 2)* [2002] 1 BCLC 478 [288] and in *Sinclair Investment Holdings SA v Versailles Trade Finance Ltd (in admin recship)* [2007] EWHC 915 (Ch), (2007) 10 ITELR 58 [122]; also by Lawrence Collins J in *Nabb Brothers*

To the extent that these comments concern liability for dishonest assistance, their Lordships are right to say that a dishonest assistant need not receive property, with the result that his liability cannot depend on his owing duties as trustee in his own right. But even so their Lordships do not tell the whole story, because this form of liability can entail fixing the defendant with a duplicative liability which mirrors that of the trustee whose breach has been assisted. Hence it can meaningfully be said that he is 'constructively liable as a trustee' in the sense that he is deemed to be liable to pay over the same sums as the trustee.[82] Leaving that point to one side, and focusing our attention on liability for knowing receipt, their Lordships also miss something fundamental when they dismiss the language of constructive trusteeship when it is applied to knowing recipients.[83]

In our view, when the courts say that a knowing recipient is personally liable to account as a constructive trustee, this language accurately conveys the distinctive nature of liability for knowing receipt, which many modern accounts of the subject misunderstand or ignore.[84] Many of these accounts are motivated by a proper desire to rationalise equitable principles, but they are misguided to the extent that they attempt to characterise liability for knowing receipt in terms of common law models of liability. This project can only be accomplished at the cost of ignoring what the courts actually do—and explicitly tell us that they do—in knowing receipt cases. Liability for knowing receipt cannot be collapsed into a liability for unjust enrichment, nor a liability for primary equitable wrongdoing which mirrors the common law tort of conversion, nor a liability for secondary equitable wrongdoing which mirrors the common law economic torts. Liability for knowing receipt is a distinctive, primary, custodial liability, which closely resembles the liability of express trustees to account for the trust property with which they are charged.

Ltd v Lloyds Bank International (Guernsey) Ltd [2005] EWHC 405 (Ch) [70] and *Pakistan v Zardari* [2006] EWHC 2411 (Comm) [88].

[82] Liability for dishonest assistance is discussed in part F.2.

[83] They also appear to be motivated by the wish to merge dishonest assistance and knowing receipt into a single equitable wrong of 'dishonest participation in a breach of trust', something that we believe would be a false step, for reasons that we discuss in the text around n 187.

[84] But see S Gardner, *An Introduction to the Law of Trusts*, 2nd edn (Oxford, Oxford University Press, 2003) 281–82; S Worthington, *Equity*, 2nd edn (Oxford, Oxford University Press, 2006) 179–89, esp 180 and 188; Cope (n 78) 342–43. And cf R Nolan, 'Equitable Property' (2006) *Law Quarterly Review* 232, 239–40, who cites various old cases for the proposition that unless they give consideration even the innocent recipients of misdirected trust property are 'liable to the trust in the same manner as the trustees themselves were': eg *Pye v Gorge* (1710) 1 P Wms 128, 128; 24 ER 323, 324; *Mansell v Mansell* (1732) P Wms 678, 681; 24 ER 913, 914. We agree with Nolan that recipients can owe duties akin to those owed by express trustees, but we consider that he places insufficient emphasis on the fact that in all of the cases he cites the defendant still had the property when proceedings were brought, by which time he must have known of the breach of trust even if he had previously been unaware of it.

In short, when the courts say that a knowing recipient is 'personally liable to account as a constructive trustee', they mean exactly what they say: because of the circumstances in which knowing recipients acquire title to the misapplied property, Equity fixes them with custodial duties which are the same as some of the duties which are voluntarily assumed by express trustees. The accounting mechanisms through which a knowing recipient can be made liable for the performance of these duties, or their breach, are the same as those through which trust beneficiaries can take action against express trustees. We shall explain this further in part E, but first, we shall show that this understanding of the law is borne out by judicial statements which stretch back for many years.

The courts have frequently said that a knowing recipient is 'liable to account' for the misdirected trust property which he receives.[85] They have also used other expressions which evoke the accounting processes through which the duties of express trustees are enforced. Thus, the courts often talk of knowing recipients becoming 'accountable for',[86] or 'chargeable with',[87] the property that they receive. They ask whether a knowing recipient can claim to be 'discharged',[88] and in cases where he cannot, they state that he must 'restore' or 'replace'[89] the misapplied trust property, or 'make restitution' of this property.[90] Sometimes the courts have gone further, and have drawn out the parallels between the personal liabilities of trustees, and the personal liabilities of knowing recipients. So, for example, it is common to find statements that a knowing recipient is liable to account 'as a trustee', or 'as a constructive trustee'. For example, in *Morgan v Stephens*,[91] Stuart V-C said that 'when trust money gets into the hands of

---

[85] Eg *John v Dodwell & Co Ltd* [1918] AC 563 (PC) 569 (Viscount Haldane LC); *Agip (Africa) Ltd v Jackson* [1990] Ch 265, 291–92 (Millett J).

[86] Eg *Morgan v Stephens* (1861) 3 Giff 226, 237; 66 ER 392, 397 (Stuart V-C).

[87] Eg *Wilson v Moore* (1834) 1 My & K 126, 146; 39 ER 629, 636 (Sir John Leach MR); *Barnes v Addy* (1874) LR 9 Ch App 244, 251–52 (Lord Selborne LC); *Farah Construction Pty v Say Dee Pty Ltd* [2007] HCA 22, (2007) 230 CLR 89 [112] (per curiam).

[88] Eg *Blyth v Fladgate* [1891] 1 Ch 237, 351 (Stirling J). Cf *Soar v Ashwell* [1893] 2 QB 390 (CA) 394 (Lord Esher MR) and 405 (Kay LJ) (using similar language of a trustee *de son tort*).

[89] Eg *Charter plc v City Index Ltd* [2006] EWHC 2508 (Ch), [2007] 1 WLR 26 [13] (Morritt C); *Darkingjung Pty Ltd v Darkingjung Local Aboriginal Land Council* [2006] NSWSC 1217 [47]; *Selangor United Rubber Estates Ltd v Craddock (No 3)* [1968] 1 WLR 1555, 1591. Cf *Eagle Trust plc v SBC Securities Ltd* [1992] 4 All ER 488, 500 (Vinelott J): 'The question is whether the defendant can be made personally liable to make good the value of property which he no longer has.'

[90] *Gray v Johnston* (1868) LR 3 HL 1, 14. The term 'restitution' is not used here to denote a gain-based liability to return a benefit, but as a synonym for restoration of the trust estate either by returning the trust property *in specie* or by paying in its current value, whether or not this value was actually received by the defendant. This is discussed further in part F.4.

[91] (1861) 3 Giff 226, 237; 66 ER 392, 397. See too *Selangor Estates United Rubber Estates Ltd v Cradock (No 3)* [1968] 2 All ER 1073, 1097 (Ungoed-Thomas J): a knowing recipient 'is made liable in equity as trustee by the imposition or construction of the court of equity. This is done because in accordance with equitable principles applied by the court of equity it is equitable that he should be held liable as though he were a trustee.'

a person who, knowing the trusts, allows such money to be improperly dealt with, he is accountable', and he went on to declare that the defendant was 'bound to account as trustee for such portions of the [trust] assets as came into his hands'. In *Sheridan v Joyce*,[92] Sir Edward Sugden LC held that 'the moment [the defendant] had notice that the money [he received] was trust money, he became a trustee of it for the parties entitled'. In *Jesse v Bennett*,[93] Lord Cranworth LC referred to beneficiaries who knowingly received more than their share of the trust property as 'persons [who had] . . . participated in the breach of trusts and who by their conduct had put themselves in the situation of trustees'. In *Rolfe v Gregory*,[94] Lord Westbury LC said that:

> [T]he wrongful receipt and conversion of trust property place the receiver in the same situation as the trustee from whom he received it, and by the principles of this Court he becomes subject in a Court of Equity to the same rights and remedies as may be enforced by the parties beneficially entitled against the fraudulent trustee himself.

In *Barnes v Addy*,[95] Lord Selborne LC said that 'those who create a trust clothe the trustee with a legal power and control over the trust property, imposing on him a corresponding responsibility', but that this 'responsibility may no doubt be extended in equity to others who are not properly trustees', such as knowing recipients. Similarly, Kekewich J held in *Re Barney*[96] that 'undoubtedly there are persons who can be made responsible as trustees to the full extent of a trustee's responsibility, notwithstanding that they have never been properly appointed as trustees'. Finally, in *John v Dodwell & Co Ltd*,[97] Viscount Haldane said that any person who knowingly takes property from a wrongdoing fiduciary 'holds what has been transferred to him under a transmitted fiduciary obligation to account for it to the principal'.

E. DUTIES OF KNOWING RECIPIENTS

The duties of a knowing recipient are rarely stated, but one cannot fully understand the nature of his liability to account as a constructive trustee without identifying these duties and the mechanisms by which they are enforced.

---

[92] (1844) 7 Ir Rep Eq 115, 119.
[93] (1856) 6 De G M & G 609, 612; 43 ER 1370, 1371.
[94] (1865) 4 De G J & S 576, 578; 46 ER 1042, 1043.
[95] (1874) LR 9 Ch App 244, 251–52.
[96] [1892] 2 Ch 265, 271.
[97] [1918] AC 563 (PC) 569. See too *Westpac Banking Corp v Savin* [1985] 2 NZLR 41 (NZCA) 52; *Morlea Professional Services Pty Ltd v Richard Walker Pty Ltd (in liq)* [1999] FCA 1820, (1999) 34 ACSR 371 [57].

1. The Core Restorative Duty

(a) *The nature of the duty*

A knowing recipient's core duty, and generally his only duty of practical significance, is to restore the misapplied trust property.[98] His duty is to restore the property immediately, rather than to restore it on demand.[99] In this respect his position can be contrasted with that of an express bare trustee, who holds the trust property to the order of the beneficiary while the trust subsists, and whose continuing retention of this property is authorised, and therefore legitimate, until the beneficiary gives contrary instructions. In contrast, a knowing recipient's continuing retention of misapplied trust property is unauthorised and illegitimate, and so he owes an immediate restorative duty which does not depend on any demand for restoration having been made.

Although an action to enforce the knowing recipient's restorative duty can be brought by the beneficiaries,[100] it does not follow that performance of the duty necessarily entails transfer or payment to them. On the contrary, the duty is essentially to restore the misapplied property to the trustees, so that that the trust can be reconstituted and duly administered. However, much depends on the basis on which the property was held. If it was held on a bare trust, then, whilst the knowing recipient's duty is essentially a duty to restore the property to the trustees (assuming that the trust is still on foot), he could discharge his duty by restoring it directly to the absolutely entitled beneficiary instead.[101] But if the trust is a more elaborate continuing trust, where there is no single absolutely entitled beneficiary, then he cannot perform his duty in this way, and must instead restore the property to the trustees so that the trust can be reconstituted, and the trust fund administered for all of the beneficiaries.

When can a knowing recipient claim to have performed his duty to restore the trust property? Obviously, if he hands over the property *in*

---

[98] Cf *Re Holmes* [2004] EWHC 2020 (Admin), [2005] 1 WLR 857 [22]; *Darkingjung Pty Ltd v Darkingjung Local Aboriginal Land Council* [2006] NSWSC 1217 [47].

[99] Notwithstanding Colman J's dictum to the contrary in *Allied Carpets Group plc v Nethercott* [2001] BCC 81, 89–90.

[100] The trustees can also bring an action for knowing receipt in a representative capacity, as discussed in *Morlea Professional Services Pty Ltd v Richard Walter Pty Ltd* [1999] FCA 1820, (1999) 34 ACSR 371. In rare cases, a knowing recipient may also bring an action in knowing receipt against a knowing recipient from him, pursuant to his duty to get in the property so that the trust fund can be reconstituted: *Bracken Partners Ltd v Gutteridge* [2004] 1 BCLC 373 (CA); *Evans v European Bank Ltd* [2004] NSWCA 82, (2004) 7 ITELR 19. This is discussed in s 2(b) below.

[101] Cf *Soar v Ashwell* [1893] 2 QB 390 (CA) 395, where Kay LJ refers to a defendant who has 'concurred with the trustee in committing a breach of trust, and has taken possession of the trust property, knowing that it was trust property, and has not duly discharged himself of it by handing it over to the proper trustees or to the persons absolutely entitled to it'. And cf *Target Holdings Ltd v Redferns* [1996] AC 421, 435 (express trustees).

specie then he will have done what he was meant to do.[102] By analogy with the express trustee cases, he may also perform his duty by paying a money substitute for the property.[103] But what if he hands over different property in lieu of the property that he received? This question arose in *Morlea Professional Services Pty Ltd v Richard Walter Pty Ltd*,[104] where a corporate trustee, which had misapplied trust money by making sham loans to another company, accepted from the other company the transfer of a debt equal in value to the sham loans, with 15 per cent interest. According to the Full Court of the Federal Court of Australia, this 'did not effect actual (in the sense of precisely equivalent) restoration to the trusts'; rather its effect 'was to bring a new asset into the trusts by way of substitution for what was misappropriated', namely 'a debt equivalent in sum to the moneys misappropriated, [which] asset was treated by the trustees as being subject to the trusts and was dealt with accordingly'.[105] In the court's view, trustees who act in this way are bound by their actions vis-à-vis the knowing recipient, but the beneficiaries are not. They might disavow the trustees' actions and refuse to accept the new property as a substitute for the misapplied property. If they take this course, then the knowing recipient will be unable to say that he has performed his duty, and will remain liable for the current market value of the property that he received.[106]

Can the knowing recipient discharge his duty by returning the property to the wrongdoing trustee from whom he received it? In principle, the duty can generally be discharged in this way, consistently with the fact that, at least until he is replaced by another trustee, the wrongdoing trustee has a duty to recover the misapplied trust property.[107] More difficult, though, are cases where the knowing recipient knows that the wrongdoing trustee will misapply the property again if it is returned to him, and will not use it to reconstitute the trust fund as he should. It may be that in this case the knowing recipient's restorative duty would not be discharged if he re-transferred the property to the trustee. This is suggested by *Blyth v Fladgate*,[108] where solicitors acting for a set of trustees were held not to

---

[102] Although problems may arise if the property has been damaged, or has lost its value for some other reason, through his fault. In this case a reparation claim might lie for the beneficiaries' loss, as we discuss in 2(a) below.
[103] See part C.2.
[104] [1999] FCA 1820, (1999) 34 ACSR 371. Cf *Lander v Weston* (1853) 3 Drew 389, 394; 61 ER 951, 953 (Kindersley V-C): express trustees who wrongfully sell trust stock cannot obtain a discharge by replacing some other stock in the fund unless the beneficiaries adopt their transactions—'they are not discharged by substituting something different'.
[105] Ibid, [75].
[106] Ibid, [76].
[107] See the authorities cited at n 35.
[108] [1891] 1 Ch 337. See too *Morgan v Stephens* (1861) 3 Giff 226, 236–37, 66 ER 392, 397. Neither case concerned liability for knowing receipt, since the defendants did not initially receive the relevant property in breach of duty, but the result would have been the same if they had: *Bank of China v Kwong Wa Po* [2005] HKCFI 422 [90], where a recipient of moneys stolen from the claimant bank by ex-employees was not discharged when it repaid the

have been discharged from their liability to account for trust property which they had paid over at the direction of the trustees for the purposes of an investment which they actually or constructively knew to be improper. Another way of approaching this question, however, might be to say that, whether or not the knowing recipient's restorative duty is discharged, he may in any event incur an independent liability for dishonestly assisting the wrongdoing trustee's further breach of trust.

Can the knowing recipient discharge his duty by transferring the property to a third party? A transfer by the knowing recipient for his own purposes would obviously not be an acceptable means of performing his duty. But he might be better placed if he dealt with the property in accordance with instructions by the trustees from whom he received it, and to whom he has a primary duty to restore the property. Dealing with the property in this way might count as performance of the knowing recipient's duty, since it could be seen as a 'constructive' form of restoration, as effective in law as actual restoration. However, it is also clear that he cannot claim to be discharged if he knows that the relevant dealing constitutes a breach of the trustees' own duties, as in *Blyth v Fladgate*.[109]

What happens if the knowing recipient does not return the property, but applies it in a way that amounts to an authorised application of the property according to the trust deed, although the trustees have not instructed him to do this? It is not obvious that he has performed his restorative duty in these circumstances. Nevertheless in a recent case from Singapore,[110] a company which received money knowing that this had been lent to a borrower under a *Quistclose*-type arrangement[111] was discharged from its duty to restore the money to the lender, to the extent that it had actually been applied to the relevant purpose.[112] Similarly in *Selangor United Rubber Estates Ltd v Craddock (No 3)*,[113] Ungoed-Thomas J held that the liability of a knowing recipient of misapplied corporate funds should be reduced to the extent it could be shown that these had actually been applied to the company's purposes. However, it may be that the latter case can be explained in another way, on the basis that the funds were applied for the claimant's benefit, so that the reduction involved the setting-off of a counterclaim in unjust enrichment, analogous to the set-off

moneys, not to the claimant, but to one of these ex-employees and/or the company which was the vehicle for their frauds.

[109] [1891] 1 Ch 337. See too *Morgan v Stephens* (1861) 3 Giff 226, 236–37; 66 ER 392, 397.
[110] *Sitt Tatt Bhd v Goh Tai Hock* [2008] SGHC 220, [2009] 2 SLR 44.
[111] That is, the money was lent on the basis that it could only be used for a particular purpose, so that it was held on trust for the lender, subject to a power vested in the borrower to spend it on the specified purpose: *Barclays Bank Ltd v Quistclose Investments Ltd* [1970] AC 567, as interpreted by *Twinsectra Ltd v Yardley* [2002] 2 AC 164.
[112] Ibid, [73].
[113] [1968] 2 All ER 1073, 1120.

allowed to a bank in cases such as *B Liggett (Liverpool) Ltd v Barclays Bank Ltd*.[114]

Finally, the question arises whether the court might ever excuse the knowing recipient from performance, or relieve him from liability for non-performance, in the same way that it sometimes relieves express trustees under the Trustee Act 1925, section 61? Consider a case where the property is lost or destroyed or stolen before the knowing recipient can return it. If the loss would not have occurred but for a delay by the knowing recipient in performing his duty of immediate restoration, then it can usually be said that he was at fault and should not be excused.[115] However, this may not always be the case. Suppose, for example, that he cannot immediately restore the trust property, because he cannot identify or ascertain the whereabouts of the parties to whom restoration should be made—a rare situation, but one that arose in *Evans v European Bank Ltd*.[116] Or again, suppose that the parties to whom restoration should be made mistakenly deny that restoration is required and refuse to take the property back—another rare situation, but analogous to that which arose in *National Bank of New Zealand v Waitaki International Processing (NI) Ltd*.[117] In either case, if the knowing recipient takes reasonable steps to preserve the property pending performance of his duty, and yet it is unexpectedly lost or destroyed in the interim, then it would seem unfair to force him to pay a money substitute in lieu of delivering the property once all the relevant facts are known.

(b) Remedial implications

What remedy do the beneficiaries have if a knowing recipient fails to perform his primary restorative duty? By analogy with the express trustee cases, he can clearly be ordered to restore the property *in specie* if it is still in his hands. By the same analogy, if he disposed of the property, then he must show that this disposal was authorised, or else the account will be falsified, and an order for substitutive performance made, requiring him to pay the current monetary value of the property, or where the property is money, the capital sum plus interest.[118] As we have discussed,[119] the beneficiaries would not have to allege a breach of duty against an express trustee before they could obtain an order of either kind, and for exactly the same

---

[114] [1928] 1 KB 48.
[115] An express trustee would no doubt be in the same position, if it was the case that he had come under a duty immediately to transfer a particular asset to a beneficiary: cf cases cited in n 60. Bailees of chattels are similarly placed once they have come under a duty to deliver the goods: they are then strictly liable for the goods' loss or destruction.
[116] [2004] NSWCA 82, (2004) 7 ITELR 19. For discussion see text to n 132.
[117] [1999] 2 NZLR 211 (NZCA).
[118] On interest, see part E.3.
[119] See part C.2.

reasons they do not have to allege a breach of duty against the knowing recipient either. In other words, once they have established that he knowingly received the trust property and was therefore placed under a primary restorative duty, the beneficiaries need not show that he breached this duty by failing to return the property, as they are entitled without more to an order for specific or substitutive performance of his primary duty.

Authority for this is *Green v Weatherill*,[120] where a daughter received money from her father, to be held on trust for him, and transferred part of the money to her sister, who knew that this transfer constituted a breach of trust. The sister was ordered to pay the relevant sum into court, although there was no allegation in the pleadings that she had committed any breach of her duty as a constructive trustee of the money. Maughan J explained this as follows:

> In the present action [the defendant] is sued as a constructive trustee of the sum so paid to her with full knowledge of the action and of the nature of the claim was being made as to the sum deposited by her sister with Martin's Bank. In my opinion those facts having been established; she must be taken to be a trustee. It is not alleged in the action that she has committed any breach of trust, and counsel for the plaintiff would be entitled on the pleadings as they stand to ask for an account of the sum received by her with notice of the plaintiff's claim. It is not disputed that the sum paid to the defendant . . . is the sum of 135l, and an account against her is therefore unnecessary. This, therefore, is a case where the Court has ascertained to its satisfaction that the sum of 135l is in the hands of the defendant . . . as a constructive trustee, and I can see no reason why the Court should not order payment by the said defendant of that amount into Court.[121]

Because the main liability of a knowing recipient is to perform his primary duty of restoration in just the same way as an express trustee, it is a distinctive form of liability which cannot be collapsed into other forms of liability which arise in the law of wrongs or the law of unjust enrichment. Several points can be made in this connection. First, because the knowing recipient is liable to perform or render substitutive performance of his restorative duty, and this liability does not depend on an allegation of a breach of duty, it is easy to see why the knowing receipt cases look like plausible candidates for recharacterisation as claims in unjust enrichment. Claims of this sort also generate a 'restitutionary' liability which entails performance of a primary duty to pay the value of benefits received by the defendant, rather than performance of a secondary duty to pay money triggered by breach of a primary duty.[122] However, a liability to make resti-

---

[120] [1929] 2 Ch 213.
[121] Ibid, 222–23.
[122] Cf S Smith, 'Unjust Enrichment: Nearer to Tort than Contract' in R Chambers, C Mitchell and J Penner (eds), *Philosophical Foundations of the Law of Unjust Enrichment* (Oxford, Oxford University Press, 2009) 181.

tution of an unjust enrichment is a crucially different liability from a liability to effect restoration of misapplied trust property, and it is important that this distinction should not be obscured by the latent ambiguity in the term 'restitution'.[123]

Secondly, the fact that the beneficiaries can get a remedy against the knowing recipient without asserting that he has breached his duty as constructive trustee has some implications for the defences that he can raise. If claims for knowing receipt were wrong-based, in the sense that they depended on the knowing recipient's breach of duty, then this might suggest that he was entitled to the defence of contributory negligence.[124] One response might be that contributory negligence is not available as a defence to every wrong; that the courts have been prepared to deny the defence to particular types of wrongdoer on policy grounds; and that this defence may be unavailable against claims for breach of fiduciary duty, because admitting the defence might undermine the fiduciary's core duty of undivided loyalty.[125] However, this response assumes a particular answer to a different question, namely whether knowing recipients owe fiduciary duties.[126] And there is a different and better reason why contributory negligence cannot be pleaded against claims for actual or substitutive performance of their restorative duty.[127] Because the beneficiaries need not allege a breach of this duty in order to obtain an order for performance, there is no room for argument that they have been a partial cause of their own loss, because it makes no difference whether they have been caused a loss, whether by the knowing recipient's fault or their own. Where the beneficiaries were aware of the transfer to the knowing recipient, however, the knowing recipient might instead be able to escape liability by arguing that the beneficiaries acquiesced in the trustee's breach of duty, with the result that no claim lies against him at all because the case is effectively one of authorised transfer.

Thirdly, the measure of a knowing recipient's liability may be very different from the measure of other liabilities which he might owe on a

---

[123] This is discussed further below in part F.4.

[124] P Jaffey, 'The Nature of Knowing Receipt' (2001) 15 *Trust Law International* 151, 157–58.

[125] See *Pilmer v Duke Group Ltd* (2001) 207 CLR 165 [86] and [171]–[172], quoting His Honour Justice WMC Gummow, 'Compensation for Breach of Fiduciary Duty' in TG Youdan (ed), *Equity, Fiduciaries and Trusts* (Toronto, Carswell, 1989) 57, 86, and His Honour Justice KR Handley, 'Reduction of Damages Awards' in PD Finn (ed), *Essays on Damages* (Sydney, Lawbook Co, 1992) 113, 127.

[126] See further part E.2(c).

[127] This is not to rule out the possibility that a defence of contributory negligence might be raised against a knowing recipient where a reparation claim is made against him, for example where he has lost trust property through his negligence—a possibility we consider below. Cf *Permanent Building Society (in liq) v Wheeler* (1994) 12 ACLC 674 (Western Aus Sup Ct), where Ipp J correctly noted the difference between a trustee's duty to account, and his duty of care, which can bring issues of causation and relative fault into play.

different footing. Suppose, for example, that a defendant receives and then disposes of property that subsequently increases in value. If he owed a liability in unjust enrichment, then assuming that a change of position defence were disallowed, the measure of his liability would most probably be the value of the property at the time of receipt, and would certainly be no more than the value of the property when he disposed of it.[128] However, if he were chargeable with the property as a knowing recipient, then he would be liable as constructive trustee to pay its current monetary value. An example is an American case, *Re Rothko*,[129] where executors of the renowned painter, Mark Rothko, improperly transferred a large number of his paintings to third parties, who subsequently disposed of them. The value of Rothko's works then appreciated hugely, and in proceedings by the beneficiaries of his estate, the New York Court of Appeals held that the third parties were liable for the current market value of the paintings.

2. Other Duties

In some circumstances the law imposes additional, positive duties on a knowing recipient, over and above his core restorative duty.[130] Some of these assume special significance in cases where the person to whom the property should be returned cannot immediately be found, or if the knowing recipient simply fails to return the property immediately because he dishonestly chooses to keep it for himself.

(a) Duty to preserve and/or invest the property

A duty of restoration is not inconsistent with a duty to take care of the property while it is in the knowing recipient's custody, nor is it necessarily inconsistent with a duty to invest, and cases can be found in which such duties have been imposed.[131] Where the property is lost or destroyed at a time when the knowing recipient owed a duty to return it, the court might well hold that its loss or destruction is no reason for discharging him from his restorative duty. In that case, there would be no need for the benefi-

---

[128] It is a controversial question whether the English law of unjust enrichment permits claims for value surviving in a claimant's hands, or confines them to the recovery of value received. Reasons of space prevent discussion of this question here, but we take the latter view, which is consistent with the rule that a cause of action in unjust enrichment generally accrues at the date of receipt.

[129] 43 NY 2d 305; 372 NE 2d 291 (1977).

[130] Cf LD Smith, 'Transfers' in Birks and Pretto (n 3) 136–37: if a transferee of misapplied trust property 'really is a wrongdoer, it may well be appropriate to impose obligations in addition to' his core restorative duty.

[131] Cf the US authorities cited in W Fratcher (ed), *Scott on Trusts*, 3rd edn (Boston MA, Little Brown, 1967) vol 4, para 291.2.

ciaries to argue that the knowing recipient has breached a separate duty of care in order to recover the value of the property. But what if the property is damaged through the knowing recipient's negligence, and he then returns it in a damaged state? It would be surprising if he could escape liability simply by restoring the property in such a case, but to recover for their loss, the beneficiaries would have to establish that he owed a duty to take care of the property, breach of which entitles them to make a reparation claim. In our view the law should have no difficulty in finding that he owes a duty to take care of the property himself and to safeguard it from loss or damage by third parties. The former is a duty readily imposed by the common law on us all as regards property to which others have ownership or possessory rights, while the latter is a duty readily imposed by the common law on bailees, who voluntarily assume possession of goods which they know belong to another. It would be a small step for Equity to hold that knowing recipients owe similar duties. If it is asked why there is so little authority to support this conclusion, then the answer may be that in practice most knowing recipients are recipients of money, in relation to which these issues do not usually arise.

Turning to the question whether the knowing recipient might owe a duty to invest the misapplied trust property, the answer must often be a simple 'no' because this would be inconsistent with his immediate restorative duty. It could only be appropriate to impose an investment duty in cases where the knowing recipient cannot immediately restore the property, for example because he cannot identify the parties to whom restoration should be made. These were the facts of *Evans v European Bank Ltd*,[132] where a company knowingly received US$7.5m stolen from credit card holders. Unsurprisingly it was impossible for the company immediately to identify the tens of thousands of parties to whom restoration had to be made, and to calculate the amounts which they ought to be paid. The New South Wales Court of Appeal held that the company's duty was only to refund the money to the defrauded credit card holders 'as soon as they could be ascertained'. The court also held that until they could be identified the company was 'under a duty to properly invest the trust fund'. An interest-bearing deposit account with a bank in the currency of the fraud was 'perfectly appropriate'.[133]

Unsurprisingly, this case falls short of imposing an active 'managerial' investment duty on knowing recipients of the kind that is often assumed by express trustees, that is, a duty to maximise financial returns, diversify the trust portfolio, etc. Instead, the case can be read in one of two ways. On

---

[132] [2004] NSWCA 82, (2004) 7 ITELR 19.
[133] Ibid, [162]. On the facts, this conclusion had the effect of *exonerating* the bank, with which the money had been deposited, from liability for knowing receipt, on the basis that the deposit did *not* constitute a misapplication of the money of which the company was constructive trustee, and knowing recipient.

one reading it holds that where the trust property is money (so that *in specie* restoration is unnecessary) and immediate restoration is impossible, then he does not owe a duty to invest it, but he does have an implied authority to do so, and if he decides to do so, then he must undertake this task with reasonable care. A second approach is to say that whatever the nature of the property he receives, a knowing recipient who cannot immediately return it always owes a duty to preserve it from loss, and that this preservation duty encompasses a duty to take reasonable steps to preserve its value. Where the property is money, this means that he must at least place the money in an interest-bearing account to preserve its buying power. The practical effect of all this, however, is that a knowing recipient is unlikely ever to have to pay a sum by way of reparation that exceeds what he would have to pay by way of interest in any event.[134]

(b) Duty to get in the trust property

Express trustees have a well-established duty to get in the trust property, which manifests itself in two main ways.[135] First, they must obtain possession or control of assets or moneys due to the trust, in such a manner as the nature of the property admits—a duty that would, for example, require the trustee to claim and enforce debts due to the trust. Secondly, in cases where trust property has been misapplied, the trustees must bring proceedings to recover this property or otherwise obtain relief on the beneficiaries' behalf. For this purpose, it does not matter whether the property was misapplied by the trustee in question, by a co-trustee, or by a former trustee, who has since resigned or been replaced.

If the duties of a knowing recipient also include a duty to get in the trust property, then the first aspect of the duty would be material if, for example, he received property which yielded income—such as land which yielded rent, or shares which yielded dividends, or a debt which bore interest. If he actually received such income, then he would be accountable for this money as trust property (although it would also be possible to regard this as a claim for the disgorgement of wrongful profits[136]). However, if he failed to collect the trust income, then he would be liable to pay reparation for the loss caused by his breach of duty. We have found no clear authority holding a knowing recipient liable on this first basis. There is, however, important recent authority which unequivocally recognises that a knowing recipient who transfers the property to a third party has a duty to recover it. In *Evans v European Bank Ltd*,[137] receivers of a company brought proceedings against the defendant bank, which had received over $7.5m into a

---

[134] Interest awards are discussed below in part E.3.
[135] See the cases cited in nn 34 and 35.
[136] See part E.3 below.
[137] [2004] NSWCA 82, (2004) 7 ITELR 19. The receiving bank was not liable on the facts.

deposit account in the company's name. This money was the proceeds of frauds perpetrated by the company on credit card holders, and its receivers brought the proceedings to recover the money for the purpose of reimbursing them. The New South Wales Court of Appeal held that the company, as an active participant in the theft, was a trustee of the stolen money for the defrauded card holders—either resulting or constructive—and had the same duty to get in the trust property as an express trustee. The court explained:

> [The trust] that arises in this way . . . should be equated with an express trust for the purposes of the duty to get in the trust estate. In both instances, this duty is necessary to ensure that the objectives of the trust are achieved by what will often be the most efficacious means, i.e. proceedings by the trustee rather than the beneficiaries. In any event, the duty is fundamental to the performance of all other duties and does not vary in strength from one class of trust to another.[138]

In practice, a beneficiary will rarely need or wish to bring proceedings against a knowing recipient either to compel performance of this primary duty, or to obtain reparation for losses resulting from its breach. Generally, his needs will be met much more simply by forcing the knowing recipient to account for the trust property which he received, and with which he remains charged. Nevertheless, cases can be imagined in which it will still matter that a knowing recipient has a primary duty of this type. Principal amongst these is the case where a knowing recipient, even without compulsion from the beneficiaries, wishes to sue a fourth party to whom he transferred the trust property—for example because it has risen in value since the transfer. In such a case the knowing recipient may have his own right to recover the property, but he may not,[139] and in the latter case, if he wishes to bring proceedings, then this may need to be on the basis of a representative form of standing, relying on the cause of action which is primarily vested in the beneficiaries.

Morlea Professional Services Pty Ltd v Richard Walter Pty Ltd[140] seems to hold that where an express trustee misapplies trust property, his duty to get in the trust property provides the justification for giving him a form of representative standing to sue a knowing recipient on behalf of the benefi-

---

[138] Ibid, [116]. See too *Bracken Partners Ltd v Gutteridge* [2004] 1 BCLC 373 (CA), where the Court of Appeal also allowed a knowing recipient to bring proceedings against a third party, to whom the misapplied property was subsequently transferred. The Court of Appeal's reasoning in that case is, however, not uniform, and is somewhat more opaque: the duty to 'get in' the trust property is not explicitly given as the basis for recognising the knowing recipient's standing.

[139] Or his own cause of action may not bring all the advantages of a claim made on a different basis. Cf *Evans v European Bank Ltd* [2004] NSWCA 82, (2004) 7 ITELR 19, where the knowing recipient hoped to establish a proprietary claim to the traceable proceeds of the money paid to the defendant bank.

[140] [1999] FCA 1820, (1999) 34 ACSR 371. See too *Pulvers (a firm) v Chan* [2007] EWHC 2406 (Ch), [2008] PNLR 9 [380].

ciaries. *Evans v European Bank Ltd*[141] suggests that by analogous reasoning the courts will also allow a knowing recipient to sue a defendant who has knowingly received the property from him.

(c) Fiduciary duties and accountability for gains

Lord Walker has written extra-judicially that '[a knowing recipient] who is held liable as if he were a trustee . . . [is liable] to account for any profit'.[142] Many cases explicitly or implicitly support this view. For example, where a knowing recipient uses misdirected trust property for his own benefit (or perhaps where he cannot show that he has not done so), he will be liable for a disgorgement measure of interest, reflecting the interest that he earned or is presumed to have earned.[143] Moreover, the cases go further than this. In *King's Wharf Coldstore Ltd Ltd (in rec) v Wilson*,[144] knowing recipients of a company's business and cash were held liable to account for 'all profits or funds received'.[145] In *Super 1000 Pty Ltd v Pacific General Securities Ltd*,[146] it was contemplated that the knowing recipient of a mortgage granted by a company in circumstances involving a breach of fiduciary duty by its director might be liable to account for its profits,[147] and it was no objection that the mortgagor company had suffered no loss. Again, in *Bank of China v Kwong Wa Po*,[148] a knowing recipient of moneys stolen by the ex-employees of a bank was held liable to 'account for the profits he [had] made out of the use of [the moneys received, and with which he was charged as constructive trustee]'.[149] And in *Ultraframe (UK) Ltd v Fielding*,[150] Lewison J said that a knowing recipient can be made personally liable to account for 'any benefit he has received or acquired as a result of the knowing receipt',[151] and the judge also seems to have thought that if a defendant knowingly receives ownership of a business which generates profits, then he must account for those profits.

On what basis is a knowing recipient liable to account for profits? Two

---

[141] [2004] NSWCA 82, (2004) 7 ITELR 19.

[142] Lord Walker, 'Dishonesty and Unconscionable Conduct in Commercial Life—Some Reflections on Accessory Liability and Knowing Receipt' (2005) 27 *Sydney Law Review* 187, 202.

[143] *Belmont Finance Corp v Williams Furniture Ltd (No 2)* [1980] 1 All ER 393 (CA) 419; *Southern Cross Commodities Pty Ltd (in liq) v Ewing* (1988) 14 ACLR 39 (Full Ct of Sup Ct of South Australia). See too the discussion in the text to n 166 and n 173.

[144] [2005] NZHC 283.

[145] Ibid, [126]–[127].

[146] [2008] NSWSC 1222, (2008) 221 FLR 427.

[147] Ibid, [236]. This was the difference between what it recovered relying on its rights under the mortgage, and what it would have recovered had the relevant mortgage not been granted.

[148] [2005] HKCFI 422.

[149] Ibid, [90].

[150] [2005] EWHC 1638 (Ch).

[151] Ibid, [1577] ff. See too *Sinclair Investment Holdings SA v Versailles Trade Finance Ltd* [2007] EWHC 915 (Ch), (2007) 10 ITELR 58 [125].

positions need to be distinguished, although it may be that they can coexist in practice. The first is that his liability to account for his profits is a secondary gain-based liability for wrongdoing. This in turn raises the question: what is the wrong? One answer is that the knowing recipient is a fiduciary in the same full sense as an express trustee, and owes the same loyalty-based duties not to make an unauthorised profit from his position, and not to place himself in a position in which his interest and duty may possibly conflict. Any gain made in breach of those duties must, on this assumption, be disgorged. In his recent decision in *Ultraframe (UK) Ltd v Fielding*,[152] Lewison J seems to proceed on exactly this assumption. The defendant knowingly received a business transferred in breach of fiduciary duty, and the judge attributed his liability to account for the profits of the business to the 'fundamental rule that a fiduciary must not make any unauthorised profit from his position'.[153]

The second approach is to say that the knowing recipient's liability to account for profits is a primary liability, because his duty to account for the trust property takes in a duty to account for the fruits of the trust property. This approach is arguably consistent with the basis on which the courts have traditionally charged express trustees with the fruits of the trust property. However, it may be that this analysis cannot explain why the knowing recipient should be liable to pay over his entire receipts—particularly those which do not represent the traceable proceeds of the trust property, or its fruits, or perhaps earnings from its use. To the extent that it leaves other profits out of account, it then becomes important to understand whether the courts do indeed regard a knowing recipient as a fiduciary in the same full sense as an express trustee. Such a characterisation would bring with it a wide array of additional prohibitions and potential liabilities.

Legal writers have tended to deny that the trustees of trusts imposed by law owe fiduciary obligations.[154] However, some care must be taken with these accounts, for the reason that they are usually addressed to the general question whether such a trustee might owe fiduciary obligations merely by virtue of his status as trustee. All proceed on the assumption, at variance with Lord Browne-Wilkinson's findings in *Westdeutsche Landesbank Girozentrale v Islington LBC*,[155] that a trust exists whenever there is a separation of legal and equitable title. On that premise, a trust can arise without knowledge on the part of the trustee of the facts that generate it. It

---

[152] Ibid, [1577] ff.
[153] Ibid, [1587] and [1588].
[154] On constructive trusts, see eg LD Smith, 'Constructive Fiduciaries?' in P Birks (ed), *Privacy and Loyalty* (Oxford, Clarendon Press, 1997) 249, 262–67; Sir Peter Millett, 'Restitution and Constructive Trusts' in Cornish (n 7) 199, 205; LD Smith, 'Transfers' in Birks and Pretto (n 3) 136–37. For an illustration, see *Lonrho plc v Fayed (No 2)* [1992] 1 WLR 1. On resulting trusts, see eg R Chambers, *Resulting Trusts* (Oxford, Clarendon Press, 1997) ch 9.
[155] [1996] AC 669, 706.

should be no surprise, therefore, that these scholars are reluctant to accept that a constructive trust necessarily imports fiduciary obligations in all cases.[156]

Ultimately, the issue boils down to a general question: on what basis does the law generally impose fiduciary obligations? This is a difficult question to answer, partly because of the diversity of fiduciary relationships, and partly because of the diversity of the obligations imposed within them. Much ink has been spilt in the attempt to resolve this question.[157] However, a common assumption, unifying many or all of these accounts, is that fiduciary obligations depend, in some sense, on a voluntary undertaking by the fiduciary.[158] But even if these accounts are correct, it is not clear that they go so far as to preclude the possibility of some knowing recipients coming under fiduciary obligations, to prioritise the interests of the beneficiaries of the constructive trust above their own. Consider a case where a knowing recipient receives land, and is approached in his capacity as the new legal owner by a property developer with a valuable proposal for buying the land. He persuades the developer to buy some other land, which he also owns, knowing that an honest express trustee of the misapplied trust land would have taken this opportunity for the beneficiaries. Intuitively it seems unlikely that a court would excuse him from liability to account for these profits. Could one say that by voluntarily choosing not to return the trust land to the beneficiaries, the knowing recipient effectively chooses to assume responsibility to the beneficiaries, for managing the land to their best advantage?

3. Interest

The courts' understanding of the basis and measure of interest awards made against knowing recipients is not easy to fathom. As in other areas, questions of interest tend to be dealt with briefly, if at all, at the end of lengthy judgments addressed to other questions. The best that can be done is to explain what the courts *might be* doing in these cases. Probably the

---

[156] Eg Smith, 'Transfers' (n 154) 137.
[157] Eg A Scott, 'The Fiduciary Principle' (1949) 37 *California Law Review* 539; L Sealy, 'Fiduciary Relationships' [1962] *Cambridge Law Journal* 69; J Shepherd, 'Towards a Unified Concept of Fiduciary Relationships' (1981) 97 *Law Quarterly Review* 51; T Frankel, 'Fiduciary Law' (1983) 71 *California Law Review* 795; P Finn, 'The Fiduciary Principle' in T Youdan (ed), *Equity, Fiduciaries and Trusts* (Toronto, Carswell, 1989) 1; R Flannigan, 'The Fiduciary Obligation' (1989) 9 *Oxford Journal of Legal Studies* 285; J Gautreau, 'Demystifying the Fiduciary Mystique' (1989) 68 *Canadian Bar Review* 1; P Birks, 'The Content of Fiduciary Obligation' (2002) 16 *Trust Law International* 34; LD Smith, 'The Motive, Not the Deed' in J Getzler (ed), *Rationalising Property, Equity and Trusts: Essays in Honour of Edward Burn* (London, LexisNexis, 2003) 53; M Conaglen, 'The Nature and Function of Fiduciary Loyalty' (2005) 121 *Law Quarterly Review* 452.
[158] Eg Smith, 'Constructive Fiduciaries' (n 154) 263–65; Millett (n 154) 205.

key preliminary question, in uncovering this, is whether the interest awards made against knowing recipients are merely components or corollaries of the claimant's primary cause of action; or are independent awards, which are not shaped by the claimant's primary cause of action.

(a) Independent awards

'Independent' awards are awards that might in principle be made by a court against any defendant who is liable to pay a sum of money to another. Such awards are afforded by the general law, independently of the precise cause of action that generates the liability to pay, and are not coloured by it—they simply recognise that the defendant owes a duty to pay a sum of money, and by virtue of his delay in performing this duty, the claimant has suffered loss (yielding, uncontroversially, a compensatory measure of interest) and/or the defendant has been enriched (potentially yielding, more controversially, a restitutionary measure of interest).

Awards made under the courts' statutory jurisdiction to award pre-judgment interest, and a fortiori post-judgment interest, can be understood as 'independent' awards in this sense. It is certainly conceivable, too, that in making interest awards against trustees and other accountable parties, the courts of equity have also been making awards of this nature. But even assuming that this is so, it must be accepted that these awards are not wholly independent, in that the courts have unquestionably allowed the status of the defendant to effect the measures of independent award which they have made. Thus the fact that a defendant occupies a fiduciary position has been thought to justify an interest award against him where he uses his principal's property for his own benefit, as a means of forcing him to disgorge the interest that he actually or presumably earned.[159] At least until recently, it was also common to find cases which assumed that in the absence of fraud, compound interest would only be awarded in equity against a fiduciary who was accountable for profits which he earned from his position, apparently on the ill-founded assumption that an award of compound interest was inherently a disgorgement measure.[160]

If this is the proper way of understanding interest awards made against trustees and other parties accountable in equity, then the interest awards which the courts have made against knowing recipients assume some significance. Such as they are, these suggest that where a knowing recipient

---

[159] For this assumption, see *Westdeutsche Landesbank Girozentrale v Islington LBC* [1996] AC 669, 701. See too *Waxman v Waxman* [2008] ONCA 426 (2008) 240 OAC 18.

[160] *Westdeutsche Landesbank Girozentrale v Islington LBC* [1996] AC 669, 701; *Wallersteiner v Moir (No 2)* [1975] QB 373, 397 and 406. See too *Kleinwort Benson Ltd v South Tyneside MBC* [1994] 2 All ER 972, 990–95; *John v James* (1986) STC 352, 355; *O'Sullivan v Management Agency and Music Ltd* [1985] QB 428 (CA) 461 and 474; *Belmont Finance Corp v Williams Furniture Ltd (No 2)* [1980] 1 All ER 393 (CA) 419. But cf *El Ajou v Dollar Land Holdings plc (No 2)* [1995] 2 All ER 685 (compensatory compound interest).

cannot be proved to have used the property received for his own benefit (on one view),[161] or where the knowing recipient cannot prove that he has not used this property for his own benefit (on another view),[162] the award which will be made against him will be a compensatory measure of interest only; and there is support for the view that the measure is designed to address the loss suffered by the claimant through being denied the property which the defendant should have restored.[163] In some of these cases, this compensatory measure has only been awarded at a simple rate;[164] but cases can also be found which accept that such interest might be awarded at a compound rate.[165] Where, in contrast, a knowing recipient can be proved to have used the property received for his own benefit (on one view) or cannot prove that he has not used the property in this way (on another view), it would seem that the courts will award a disgorgement measure, reflecting the interest that the knowing recipient did or can be presumed to have earned, and that this interest will be at a compound rate.[166] The wider significance of these cases for this paper is that they provide a further clear illustration of knowing recipients being treated as, or as equivalent to, express trustees. On the basis of the law as generally understood before *Sempra Metals Ltd v IRC*,[167] it may be that that characterisation would have been the only clear basis on which such a defendant could have been charged with compound interest in equity.[168]

(b) Dependent awards

Despite what has just been said, it is not altogether clear that the interest awards made by courts of equity, against trustees and other accountable parties, can or must always be understood as 'independent' awards, which are not components (or corollaries) of the claimant's primary cause of action. What might the alternative analysis involve?

---

[161] *Belmont Finance Corp v Williams Furniture Ltd (No 2)* [1980] 1 All ER 393 (CA) 419.
[162] *Southern Cross Commodities Pty Ltd (in liq) v Ewing* (1988) 14 ACLR 39 (Full Ct of Sup Ct of South Australia).
[163] *El Ajou v Dollar Land Holdings plc (No 2)* [1995] 2 All ER 213, 224; *Darkingjung Pty Ltd v Darkingjung Local Aboriginal Land Council* [2006] NSWSC 1217 [47]. See too, implicitly, *Belmont Finance Corp v Williams Furniture Ltd (No 2)* [1980] 1 All ER 393 (CA) 419, where simple interest only was awarded on the basis that there was no evidence that any part of the money was used by the defendant for its own commercial advantage.
[164] *Belmont Finance Corp v Williams Furniture Ltd (No 2)* [1980] 1 All ER 393 (CA) 419.
[165] *El Ajou v Dollar Land Holdings plc (No 2)* [1995] 2 All ER 213, 224.
[166] See *Belmont Finance Corp v Williams Furniture Ltd (No 2)* [1980] 1 All ER 393 (CA) 419; *Primlake Ltd (in liq) v Matthews Assocs* [2006] EWHC 1127 (Ch), [2007] 1 BCLC 366 [343]. Cf *Kalls Enterprises Pty Ltd (in liq) v Balogalow* [2007] NSWCA 191 [200] (which, however, merely records that compound interest was claimed; the court did not in fact go on to quantify and award interest in the immediate proceedings). See too Walker (n 142) 202.
[167] [2007] UKHL 34, [2008] 1 AC 561.
[168] But quaere whether the knowing recipient's liability could be explained on the basis of fraud?

Looking at the matter from first principles, and by analogy with the treatment of express trustees,[169] it would seem that a knowing recipient might be charged with a compensatory measure of interest—as a component of the primary cause of action against him—on the assumption that he owed a duty to invest the property which he received. Assuming such a duty, a knowing recipient who failed to invest the property, in breach of this duty, could be held liable as a wrongdoer, to pay reparation for losses caused by his breach: the earnings that the knowing recipient would have made, but did not.[170] There is some authority, already examined, that a knowing recipient may exceptionally owe such a duty, where he is unable immediately to restore the trust property.[171] In such a case, difficult questions would inevitably arise as to the proper measure of compensation, since this would depend on what investments the knowing recipient, acting properly, should have made. A court, faced with this question, would need either to prescribe some minimum return which a knowing recipient would be duty-bound to obtain; or might be forced to adopt the solution that courts have adopted when dealing with express trustees, who have a duty to invest, but a wide discretion as to the appropriate investment. This involves cutting the Gordian knot by awarding, as a measure of compensation for their breach of trust, a conventional measure of interest which reflects average earnings from trustee investments.[172]

Turning finally to the basis on which a disgorgement measure of interest may be awarded against a knowing recipient, the proper answer seems rather clearer on the authorities. It seems that, at least where a knowing recipient can be shown to have used the property for his own benefit, the courts will hold him liable to account for the interest that he has in fact earned, or to pay a disgorgement measure of interest, at a compound rate, reflecting what he has presumed to have earned.[173] This is readily explained as a facet or corollary of the knowing recipient's primary duty to account for the trust property, and for profits accruing from it.

4. Rights of Knowing Recipients

An express trustee generally has a right to be indemnified for costs or expenses that he incurs in the due performance of his duties. If a knowing

---

[169] Cf S Elliott, 'Rethinking Interest on Withheld and Misapplied Trust Money' [2001] *Conveyancer and Property Lawyer* 313, dealing with express trustees. Although he does not explicitly draw out the distinction drawn above between 'independent' interest awards, and components of the primary cause of action, it is clear that he is implicitly approaching interest awards on the latter basis.
[170] Mediated via the account, this would presumably be by way of 'surcharge'.
[171] See part E.2(a).
[172] See Elliott (n 169) where this is drawn out with particular clarity.
[173] See the cases already cited at nn 159 and 160.

recipient were to owe one or more of the custodial duties described here, then the question arises whether he should similarly be entitled to an indemnity for costs incurred in their performance? The cases do not provide authoritative guidance on this point.[174] However, analogous guidance can be found in the courts' treatment of express trustees, who would ordinarily be disentitled from claiming an indemnity against costs or expenses which they incur as a result of their own breaches of duty, and against costs or expenses which are not otherwise occurred in the bona fide performance of their duties (or the bona fide exercise of their powers). Adopting this starting-point, the scope for a knowing recipient to claim an indemnity seems, at best, extremely narrow. In the normal case, the knowing recipient's primary duty is immediately to restore the trust property, and not to deal with it in any other way. If, in breach of this duty, the knowing recipient transfers the property to a third party, then he should have no basis for claiming an indemnity against costs or expenses incurred in seeking its recovery: this would be to require the trust and its beneficiaries to indemnify him against the consequences of his own breach of duty. The only obvious basis on which it seems even remotely arguable that the knowing recipient might claim an indemnity involves a very exceptional set of facts and assumptions. They are: that the knowing recipient was unable immediately to restore the trust property; that pending such restoration, the law holds that he has a duty to take steps to safeguard this property from loss, damage or destruction; *and* that the knowing recipient incurred costs or expenses in the bona fide performance of that duty.

F. LIABILITY FOR KNOWING RECEIPT CONTRASTED WITH OTHER LIABILITIES

1. Liability of Trustees *de Son Tort*

Many of the nineteenth-century cases draw no clear distinction between the custodial liabilities incurred by trustees *de son tort* and knowing recipients. Given the underlying nature of these two types of liability, this is unsurprising. Trustees *de son tort* and knowing recipients incur similar liabilities because the courts have used similar strategies to render them

---

[174] Cf *Nolan v Collie* [2003] VSCA 39, (2003) 7 VR 287 [32]–[34] (constructive trust arising under specifically enforceable contract of sale; alleged breach by vendor in granting new 'all moneys' mortgage, which the mortgagee subsequently enforced by sale of the property; unsuccessful contention that the vendor, as 'trustee', was entitled to indemnification for expenses incurred in carrying out this 'trust'); *Re Loftus (deceased)* [2005] EWHC 406 (Ch), [2005] 1 WLR 1890 [202], not considered on appeal [2006] EWCA Civ 1124, [2007] 1 WLR 591 (property transferred in breach of trust by executors; no reimbursement for costs expended in connection with the property which was required to be restored; but in so far as the recipient was held accountable for rents and profits, revenue expenditure might be deducted).

liable, namely to treat them as though they were duly appointed express trustees who are chargeable with the property they receive. If there is a difference between the two, it lies in the reason why the courts think it appropriate to treat them in this way, which in turn has consequences for the remedies available against them.

The custodial duties of a knowing recipient are imposed because he receives property which he knows, or comes to know, was transferred to him in breach of trust. His trusteeship of this property is of a very specific kind, and has a limited goal. He is not responsible for administering the misapplied trust property in accordance with the terms of the trust on which they were held. He is not a surrogate trustee in this sense. His primary duty, and generally his only duty, is to restore the property immediately, so that the trust can be reconstituted and duly administered. To the extent that his duties go beyond this, they arise only in service of his core restorative duty: for example, a duty to get in the trust property, by recovering it when he has wrongfully paid it away, and perhaps also a duty to safeguard the property when it cannot immediately be restored.

The duties of a trustee *de son tort* have a different basis, and thus a different content. They are not imposed because the property he receives has been misapplied, or because he intends to act against the beneficiaries' interests. They arise because he has voluntarily assumed responsibility for handling the trust property as though he were a duly appointed express trustee. Voluntary assumption of responsibility is a basis for imposing legal obligations for actions and omissions which is widely reflected in both equity and common law rules: fiduciary duties of loyalty and care have been readily recognised on this basis; and the same concept is now often used to justify the imposition of duties of care in the law of tort. Ungoed-Thomas J neatly captured the distinctive origin of the trusteeship of a trustee *de son tort* in *Selangor United Rubber Estates Ltd v Cradock (No 3)*, when he spoke of

> those who, though not appointed trustees, take on themselves to act as such and to possess and administer trust property for the beneficiaries, such as trustees *de son tort*. Distinguishing features for present purposes are (a) they do not claim to act in their own right but for the beneficiaries, and (b) their assumption to act is not of itself a ground of liability (save in the sense of course of liability to account and for any failure in the duty so assumed), and so their status as trustee precedes the occurrence which may be the subject of a claim against them.[175]

Some important consequences flow from this. First, the courts have no qualms about fixing the trustee *de son tort* with a more onerous set of duties than are owed by a knowing recipient. They are happy to say that a trustee *de son tort* owes fiduciary duties of the same full nature as an

---

[175] [1968] 2 All ER 1073, 1095.

express trustee. Lord Millett, who has insisted that constructive trustees do not all owe fiduciary duties, because these must be assumed voluntarily, is nevertheless content to describe trustees *de son tort* as 'true trustees' for this purpose:

> Substituting dog Latin for bastard French, we would do better today to describe such persons as de facto trustees. In their relations with the beneficiaries they are treated in every respect as if they had been duly appointed. They are true trustees and are fully subject to fiduciary obligations. Their liability is strict; it does not depend on dishonesty.[176]

Secondly, the knowing recipient's core duty is to restore the property to the trustees, and so it is uncertain whether he can discharge himself by spontaneously dealing with the property in a manner which would be authorised, if he were an express trustee.[177] In contrast, the trustee *de son tort* can almost certainly do this to some extent. Because he acts as though he were an express trustee with a full range of duties for the ongoing administration of the trust, he will be held liable, and may be discharged, on this basis. However, there are limits to this principle, and it seems, for example, that he cannot validly exercise dispositive discretions conferred on the trustees by the trust instrument.[178]

2. Liability for Dishonest Assistance

There are some obvious similarities between liability for dishonest assistance in a breach of trust and liability for knowing receipt, but there are also some important differences. Both are commonly said to be liable to account 'as a constructive trustee', but in the case of a dishonest assistant, this means that he is fixed with a 'secondary' or 'attributed' liability which duplicates the liability of the trustee whose breach of trust he assisted.[179] This has some important consequences. First, he may owe the same liability to account for the trust property as does the trustee, and so be subject to the same liability for substitutive performance, although he has never himself been a trustee of the property in question, and so has never himself owed custodial duties in respect of this property. Secondly, he owes the same liability to make reparation for loss caused by the trustee's breaches of duty as does the trustee, without any need for the claimant to prove a

---

[176] *Dubai Aluminium Co Ltd v Salaam* [2003] UKHL 48, [2003] 2 AC 366 [87].
[177] See part E.1(a).
[178] *Jasmine Trustees Ltd v Wells & Hind (a firm)* [2007] EWHC 38 (Ch), [2008] Ch 194.
[179] SB Elliott and C Mitchell, 'Remedies for Dishonest Assistance' (2004) 67 *Modern Law Review* 16. The argument made in this article was effectively accepted in *Ultraframe (UK) Ltd v Fielding* [2005] EWHC 1638 (Ch) [1506] where Lewison J held that 'liability as a dishonest assistant, as the law has developed, is a secondary liability akin to the criminal liability of one who aids and abets the commission of a criminal offence.'

causal connection between the dishonest assistant's actions and the relevant loss, beyond his assistance of the conduct that amounts to the breach. Thirdly, and more controversially, but by the same reasoning, he might also owe the same liability as the trustee to account for profits received by the trustee, although he has not had the benefit of these for himself.[180]

All of these liabilities look surprising, until it is noted that they are *attributed* liabilities. For this reason, it does not matter if the dishonest assistant never obtains custody of the property, and so never owes primary custodial duties in his own right. By a fiction, he is deemed to have incurred the same liabilities as the trustee. Of course, this attribution of liability must be justified, just like any other attribution of liability—for example, the vicarious liability of employers for their employees' torts. And the justifications that can be found for attributing a trustee's liabilities to a dishonest assistant may not justify the attribution of *all* the trustee's liabilities—just as the justifications for making an employer vicariously liable for compensatory damages may not also justify vicarious liability for gain-based or exemplary damages.[181]

The argument that dishonest assistants incur 'secondary' or 'attributed' liabilities might seem to create a problem because it does not explain why a dishonest assistant might be liable to disgorge his own profits. Such a liability is readily justified in principle and has the support of authority.[182] But how can this be squared with the idea that dishonest assistants owe a 'secondary liability'? One suggestion, offered by Steven Elliott and Charles Mitchell in 2004, is that dishonest assistance might need to be characterised in two different ways: as a parasitic wrong which generates a 'secondary civil liability' and also as an 'independent civil wrong which exposes [the dishonest assistant] to a primary obligation to pay over the amount of his own separate profits'.[183] They recognised that this 'dual characterisation' might seem anomalous, requiring the liability of the dishonest assistant to be viewed as secondary and duplicative for most purposes, but as primary in relation to this one head of recovery. However, they considered that this anomaly might be tolerated, to avoid leaving the dishonest assistant in

---

[180] This has been widely recognised in the Canadian case-law: eg *Canada Safeway Ltd v Thompson* [1951] 3 DLR 295 (BCSC); *MacDonald v Hauer* (1976) 72 DLR (3d) 110 (Sask CA); *Morrison v Coast Finance Ltd* (1965) 55 DLR (2d) 710 (BCCA); *D'Amore v McDonald* [1973] 1 OR 845 (Ontario HCJ), affirmed (1973) 1 OR (2d) 370 (Ontario CA); *MacMillan Bloedel Ltd v Binstead* (1983) 22 BLR 255 (BCSC); *Glenkco Enterprises Ltd v Keller* (2000) 150 Man R (2d) 1 (Manitoba CA). Recent English cases have refused to follow the Canadian cases in this regard: see esp *Ultraframe (UK) Ltd v Fielding* [2005] EWHC 1638 (Ch).

[181] Cf S Watterson, 'The Law of Damages in the 21st Century' [2004] *Lloyd's Maritime and Commercial Law Quarterly* 513, 527–28.

[182] See eg *Fyffes Group Ltd v Templeman* [2000] 2 Lloyd's Rep 643, 668; *Ultraframe (UK) Ltd v Fielding* [2005] EWHC 1638 (Ch) [1594]. But note that English law does not give a proprietary claim to capture the profits made by dishonest assistants: *Sinclair Investment Holdings SA v Versailles Trade Finance Ltd (in admin rec)* [2007] EWHC 915 (Ch), [2007] 2 All ER (Comm) 993.

[183] Elliott and Mitchell (n 179) 42.

possession of his ill-gotten gains. A different answer, given by Pauline Ridge, is to reject the secondary liability model and to say that all of a dishonest assistant's liabilities, including his liability to disgorge his own gains, should be seen as primary liabilities for his wrong.[184]

We are not persuaded by Ridge's arguments against the secondary liability model, but to meet the points that she makes, and also in the light cast by a helpful piece on this subject by Mysty Clapton,[185] we would now put Elliott and Mitchell's point in the following, rather different way. A dishonest assistant is liable for his own wrongdoing, no less than a person who commits the tort of procuring a breach of contract, but at the same time, dishonest assistance is a 'secondary' wrong in the sense that it is defined by reference to the commission of a wrong by another person. Just as there can be no tort liability for procuring a breach of contract unless a breach of contract has occurred,[186] so, too, there can be no liability for dishonest assistance, unless a breach of trust has occurred. However, the fact that the wrong can be described as a 'secondary' wrong, parasitic on the wrong of the trustee, does not change the fact the dishonest assistant is held liable for his own wrong.

The characterisation of conduct as a civil wrong does not dictate that the law must respond to the wrong in any particular way(s). And there is no logical objection to the law responding to the secondary civil wrong committed by a dishonest assistant by fixing him with a duplicative liability, which duplicates the compensatory and (more controversially) gain-based liabilities of the trustee, nor to the law's also fixing him with a separate, non-duplicative liability in his own right for the gains which he makes for himself. As a matter of observation, this may well be what the courts have done, and it can be supported in principle, because the policies that are likely to justify equity in imposing the duplicative liability on the dishonest assistant—most obviously, the concern to preserve the integrity of fiduciary relationships—are the same as those which make it desirable to force a dishonest assistant to surrender his own gains. In short, the proper understanding is that 'dishonest assistance' is an equitable secondary wrong, which attracts both a duplicative liability, duplicating that of the trustee, *and* a liability for his own gains.

In her article, Ridge denies that the law imposes any kind of duplicative liability on dishonest assistants, and argues that the dishonest assistant's compensatory liability is only a liability to compensate for losses caused by his own wrong, and that his gain-based liability should only be a liability for his own gains. However, she concedes that even if this model of

---

[184] P Ridge, 'Justifying the Remedies for Dishonest Assistance' (2008) 124 *Law Quarterly Review* 445.
[185] MS Clapton, 'Gain-Based Remedies for Knowing Assistance: Ensuring Assistants Do Not Profit From Their Wrongs' (2008) 45 *Alberta Law Review* 989.
[186] *OBG Ltd v Allan* [2007] UKHL 21, [2008] 1 AC 1.

'primary liability' were accepted, there might still be good policy reasons why the law *should* hold the dishonest assistant to liable to compensate losses caused by the trustee, and more exceptionally, *might* hold the dishonest assistant liable for gains made by the trustee.[187] We agree with this analysis, to the extent that we would now also say that the dishonest assistant is liable for his own wrong, albeit that this is a secondary wrong, parasitic on the trustee's wrong. However, a significant weakness of Ridge's account of the law is that she pays insufficient regard to the basis on which the courts have imposed liability, both on wrongdoing trustees and on those who dishonestly assist them. Trustees certainly owe a liability to make reparation for losses caused by their breaches of trust; and it is certainly possible to hold a third party liable to make good the same losses, as Ridge suggests, on the basis of a 'generous, claimant-favouring' approach to the assessment of the losses to be compensated. However, the limitations of her analysis appear once it is recognised that trustees do not merely owe a liability to make reparation for losses caused by their breaches of trust, but are also liable for substitutive performance of their primary duties to hold and deal with the property only in accordance with the terms of the trust. A dishonest assistant who has never been a trustee of the relevant property, and has never owed custodial duties in relation to it, can owe no primary liability for substitutive performance. No 'generous, claimant-favouring' approach to the rules of liability can explain how the beneficiaries might have a claim of this nature against the dishonest assistant. A claim for 'substitutive performance' ultimately makes sense only if there are primary duties whose performance can be ordered. Hence there is no way in which the courts might hold a dishonest assistant liable for substitutive performance except by deeming him to owe custodial duties which replicate those of the trustee, or else by holding that his liability duplicates the trustee's primary liability for substitutive performance of his custodial duties.

Whatever may ultimately be the right answer to these questions, it is clear that liability for dishonest assistance is very different from liability for knowing receipt: liability for knowing receipt is not a 'secondary liability', nor even a liability for a form of 'secondary wrongdoing'. Any attempt to reduce liability for knowing receipt to a mode of committing a larger wrong of 'dishonest participation in a breach of trust or fiduciary duty'[188] is therefore misplaced, and distorts the law, because it ignores this distinction. Knowing recipients do not owe a secondary liability, and are not liable as secondary wrongdoers, by reason of their involvement in the trustees' breach of their custodial duties. Knowing recipients owe primary duties, and incur liabilities for the performance or breach of these duties that they

---

[187] Ridge (n 184) 457–60.
[188] As contemplated in *Dubai Aluminium Co Ltd v Salaam* [2003] UKHL 48, [2003] 2 AC 366 [87] (Lord Millett). Cf J Edelman, *Gain-Based Damages: Contract, Tort, Equity and Intellectual Property* (Oxford, Hart Publishing, 2002) 193ff.

themselves owe in relation to the property that they themselves have received.

This can have significant remedial consequences. Consider the following example. A trustee misappropriates shares, converts them to cash, and gives the cash to a defendant, who knows that the transfer is a breach of trust. The value of the shares subsequently doubles. If the defendant's liability was for dishonest assistance in the breach of trust, then the defendant would be liable for the current value of the shares, because his liability would replicate the liability of the trustee to pay a money substitute for the shares which he can no longer produce when called upon to do so. In contrast, if the defendant's liability was as a knowing recipient, then the trustee's liability would not be attributed to him. His liability would be a primary liability for the substitutive performance of his own custodial duties, which only arose in respect of the property that he received. Thus his liability would be for the value of the cash received, plus interest.

3. Liability to Return Unauthorised Distributions from a Deceased Person's Estate

In *Re Diplock*[189] the executors of a will distributed cash to certain charities pursuant to an invalid residuary disposition. The testator's next of kin, to whom the money should have been paid, brought a combination of personal and proprietary claims against the charities. With respect to the personal claims, the Court of Appeal rejected the argument that the charities should be personally liable to account as constructive trustees of the money, since they had lacked the requisite degree of knowledge to make it appropriate to impose upon them 'the heavy obligations of trusteeship'.[190] Drawing on a line of cases starting in the eighteenth century,[191] however, the court held that they were personally liable to refund the capital value of the sums received (but not to pay any interest on these sums), subject to the proviso that the next of kin should first exhaust their claims against the executors. These findings were all affirmed by the House of Lords.[192]

[189] [1948] Ch 465.
[190] Ibid, 478.
[191] *Noel v Robinson* (1682) 1 Vern 90, 23 ER 334; *Newman v Barton* (1690) 2 Vern 205, 23 ER 733; *Anon* (1718) 1 P Wms 495, 24 ER 487; *Orr v Kaines* (1750) 2 Ves Sen 194, 28 ER 125; *Walcott v Hall* (1788) 2 Bro CC 305, 29 ER 167; *Gillespie v Alexander* (1827) 3 Russ 130, 38 ER 525; *Greig v Somerville* (1830) 1 Russ & My 200, 39 ER 131; *David v Frowd* (1833) 1 My & K 200, 39 ER 657; *Sawyer v Birchmore* (1836) 1 Keen 391, 48 ER 357; *Thomas v Griffith* (1860) 2 Giff 504, 66 ER 211; *Fenwicke v Clarke* (1862) 4 De G F & J 240, 45 ER 1176; *Peterson v Peterson* (1866) LR 3 Eq 111; *Mohan v Broughton* [1900] P 56; *Re Rivers* [1920] 1 Ch 320. For a survey of this historical background, see SJ Whittaker, 'An Historical Perspective to the "Special Equitable Action" in *Re Diplock*' (1983) 4 *Journal of Legal History* 3.
[192] *Ministry of Health v Simpson* [1951] AC 251.

There are two obvious differences between liability for knowing receipt and the personal liability recognised in *Re Diplock*. First, liability for knowing receipt depends on proof of knowledge, whereas the *Diplock* liability is strict. Secondly, the measure of liability for knowing receipt depends on the duty which the beneficiaries seek to enforce, but where they seek substitutive performance of the defendant's duty to restore property that has been dissipated he will have to pay its current market value; in contrast, the measure of the *Diplock* liability is the value received by the defendant (less whatever the claimant can recoup from the personal representatives). Although the court did not expressly say so, these two features of the *Diplock* personal liability mean that it can be readily characterised as a liability in unjust enrichment,[193] and for this reason the case is frequently often invoked as analogous authority by those who contend that the recipients of misdirected trust property should similarly owe a strict liability in unjust enrichment to the beneficiaries. We turn to this argument in the next section, but it should be stressed at this stage that these two features of the *Diplock* liability also mean that it fundamentally differs from liability for knowing receipt.

4. Liability in Unjust Enrichment

The argument that recipients of misdirected trust property should owe a strict liability in unjust enrichment to the beneficiaries has been made by Peter Birks and other scholars,[194] and accepted by some eminent judges

---

[193] Two aspects of the decision are hard to reconcile with principles of the law of unjust enrichment as they are now understood: (1) Lord Simonds's dismissal of the argument that the charities should have been entitled to a change of position defence (at [1951] AC 276) was queried in *Lipkin Gorman v Karpnale Ltd* [1991] 2 AC 548, 580, where Lord Goff attributed it to 'the mistaken assumption that mere expenditure of money may be regarded as amounting to a change of position'; however, Lord Simonds's finding has since been followed in *Gray v Richards Butler* [2001] WTLR 625. (2) The rule that recipients should be liable for no more than the balance remaining after recovery from the wrongdoing personal executors is out of line with many contribution cases in which the burden of common liabilities has fallen on defendants who have made a gain rather than those who have merely committed a breach of duty, even if the latter have acted dishonestly: eg *K v P* [1993] Ch 140, 149; *Dubai Aluminium Co Ltd v Salaam* [2002] UKHL 48, [2003] 2 AC 366; *Niru Battery Manufacturing Co v Milestone Trading Ltd (No 2)* [2004] EWCA 487, [2004] 2 All ER (Comm) 289; *Cressman v Coys of Kensington (Sales) Ltd* [2004] EWCA 47, [2004] 1 WLR 2774 [48]; and cf Nicholls (n 80) 241.

[194] Birks initially argued that liability for knowing receipt should be understood as a liability in unjust enrichment to which a fault element had been inappropriately attached (eg P Birks, 'Misdirected Funds: Restitution from the Recipient' [1989] *Lloyd's Maritime and Commercial Law Quarterly* 296), but came around to the view that the law should recognise concurrent heads of fault-based liability for knowing receipt and strict liability in unjust enrichment (eg P Birks, 'Receipt' in Birks and Pretto (n 3) 213). The view that a strict liability claim in unjust enrichment should lie is also taken by Burrows (n 5) 202–06 and by R Chambers and J Penner, 'Ignorance' in S Degeling and J Edelman (eds), *Restitution in Commercial Law* (Sydney, Lawbook Co, 2008) 253 (identifying 'want of authority' rather than 'ignorance' as

in obiter dicta and extra-judicial writings.[195] The argument comes in two versions. One version holds that liability for knowing receipt is in fact a liability in unjust enrichment and that it is only the obfuscating old language of constructive trusteeship which prevents us from seeing this clearly. In effect this was the view taken by the Supreme Court of Canada in *Gold v Rosenberg*[196] and *Citadel General Assurance Co v Lloyds Bank Canada*,[197] where the court held that the 'essence' of a knowing receipt claim is that the defendant has been unjustly enriched at the claimant's expense. The other version holds that liability for knowing receipt is not itself a liability in unjust enrichment, but that all recipients of misdirected trust property owe a strict liability in unjust enrichment, whether or not they know of the breach of trust, so that a knowing recipient owes concurrent liabilities in knowing receipt and unjust enrichment. A finding to this effect was made by the Royal Court of Jersey in *Re Esteem Settlement*.[198] An important difference between these decisions is that proof of fault is still required under Canadian law before 'restitutionary' liability for knowing receipt is imposed, whereas Jersey law holds that liability in unjust enrichment for receiving trust property is strict.

In our view the Canadian approach is misguided because it misunderstands the nature of the remedies that can be awarded in knowing receipt cases; we also believe that the English courts should think carefully before they follow the lead of the Jersey court.[199] This is not because we are persuaded by the High Court of Australia's reasons for refusing to take the same step in *Farah Constructions Pty Ltd v Say-Dee Pty Ltd*;[200] on the contrary, we believe that the court's discussion of this point was analytically weak and contrary to previous High Court authority recognising unjust enrichment as a source of rights and obligations in Australian law. Before they recognise a concurrent strict liability in unjust enrichment, however, we believe that the English courts should reflect on the nature of the remedies to which claimants would then become entitled, and recognise that these would be different from the remedies to which claimants are currently entitled under the law of knowing receipt. Failure to acknowledge

---

the reason for restitution). An argument against the recognition of a restitutionary claim is offered by LD Smith, 'Unjust Enrichment, Property, and the Structure of Trusts' (2000) 116 *Law Quarterly Review* 412, critiqued in M Bryan, 'The Liability of the Recipient: Restitution at Common Law or Wrongdoing in Equity?' in Degeling and Edelman, *Equity* (n 3) 327.

[195] *Twinsectra Ltd v Yardley* [2002] UKHL 12, [2002] 2 AC 164, 194 (Lord Millett); *Dubai Aluminium Co Ltd v Salaam* [2003] UKHL 48, [2003] 2 AC 366 [87] (Lord Millett). See too Nicholls (n 80) 231; Walker (n 142) 202; Lord Millett, 'Proprietary Restitution' in Degeling and Edelman, *Equity* (n 3) 309, 311.

[196] [1997] 3 SCR 767.

[197] [1997] 3 SCR 805.

[198] 2002 JLR 53 [148]–[161].

[199] As contemplated in Lord Walker, 'Fraud, Fault, and Fiduciary Liability' (2006) 10 *Jersey Law Review* [31].

[200] [2007] HCA 22, (2007) 230 CLR 89 [148]–[158].

these remedial differences could lead to a slide into the Canadian position where the two types of liability are muddled together and valuable remedial options are lost in the process.

Terminological problems will not make it easier for the English courts to avoid this pitfall. The word 'restitution' has now passed into common usage as a term to describe the gain-based remedy awarded to claimants in unjust enrichment, but in breach of trust cases it has often been used—and is still sometimes used—as a synonym for restoration of the trust estate as a compensatory device, either by returning the trust property *in specie* or by paying its current value, whether or not this value has ever been received by the defendant.[201] Similar difficulties arise in connection with statements that knowing receipt is a 'receipt-based' liability, a description which dates from Millett J's decision in *Agip (Africa) Ltd v Jackson*.[202] There is nothing wrong with saying this, to the extent that it correctly identifies receipt as one of the necessary ingredients of a claim for knowing receipt. However, in *Twinsectra Ltd v Yardley*,[203] Lord Millett used the term 'receipt-based' in opposition to the term 'fault-based' when expressing the (obiter) opinion that liability for knowing receipt is already a strict liability in unjust enrichment. In our view, his Lordship was mistaken in this opinion, although this does not mean that the courts could not now recognise a concurrent liability in unjust enrichment. Whatever the position they take on this point, however, we hope that they will use clear language to express their conclusions.

Returning to the requirement that a defendant must have received trust property before he can be liable in knowing receipt,[204] we would stress that the reason why this matters is not because the defendant must have been unjustly enriched,[205] but because liability for knowing receipt depends on

---

[201] See eg *Gray v Johnston* (1868) LR 3 HL 1, 14; *ex parte Adamson* (1878) 8 Ch D 807, 819; *Nocton v Lord Ashburton* [1914] AC 932, 952; *Bartlett v Barclays Bank Trust Co Ltd (No 2)* [1980] Ch 515, 543; *Target Holdings Ltd v Redferns* [1996] AC 421, 436; *A-G v Trustees of the British Museum* [2005] EWHC 1089 (Ch), [2005] Ch 397 [20].

[202] [1990] Ch 265, 292.

[203] [2002] 2 AC 264 [105]. Cf *Dubai Aluminium Co Ltd v Salaam* [2002] UKHL 48, [2003] 2 AC 366 [111] where he also contrasted 'fault-based liability' with 'receipt-based liability in unjust enrichment'. It is no coincidence that the Supreme Court of Canada also held that liability for knowing receipt is a 'receipt-based' liability in unjust enrichment in *Citadel* (n 197) [46] (followed in *Gold* (n 196) [41]), since the court derived this terminology from Lord Millett's article 'Tracing the Proceeds of Fraud' (1991) 107 *Law Quarterly Review* 71, 83.

[204] Eg *Satnam Investments Ltd v Dunlop Heywood & Co Ltd* [1999] 1 BCLC 385 (CA) 404; *Goose v Wilson Sandford & Co (a firm)* [2000] EWCA Civ 73, [2001] Lloyd's Rep PN 189 [88]; *Trustor AB v Smallbone (No 2)* [2001] 1 WLR 1177 [18]–[19] (Morritt V-C, citing ER Hewitt and JB Richardson (eds), *White & Tudor's Leading Cases in Equity*, 9th edn (London: Sweet & Maxwell, 1928) vol 2, 595); *OJSC Oil Co Yugraneft (in liq) v Abramovich* [2009] EWHC 161 (Ch) [372]; *Heperu Pty Ltd v Belle* [2009] NSWCA 252.

[205] Note that the requirement that receipt must be 'beneficial' is inconclusive as to the nature of the liability, because this rule simply operates to protect those who receive ministerially as agents, and does not compel the conclusion that the liability depends on proof of 'enrichment'. An agency defence could be afforded to a wrong-based claim, no less than a claim in unjust enrichment.

the defendant owing custodial duties as a trustee of the property. The strict insistence on receipt of property does not make sense, except on this assumption; and it helps to explain why knowing receipt should not be collapsed into either the wrong of dishonest participation in a breach of trust, or into a liability in unjust enrichment. If the only reason why it mattered that a defendant had received title to the property was to establish that the defendant had been enriched, then liability in 'knowing receipt' could be expected to arise in a much wider category of case, including, for example, cases where the defendant has never received any property, but has been enriched as a result of property having being used for his benefit, as in the discharge of his debts. Yet the courts have specifically denied that 'receipt' has this extended meaning.[206]

It has been suggested that if the law were to impose a strict liability in unjust enrichment for the receipt of misapplied trust property, then the beneficiaries could no longer derive an advantage from suing for knowing receipt, because the measure of recovery would be no greater, and yet the beneficiaries would have to surmount the additional obstacle of proving that the defendant was at fault.[207] However, once it is recognised that a knowing recipient owes an obligation to restore the property *in specie*, and that he can be ordered to make substitutive performance of this duty in cases where he no longer has the property, then there may well be circumstances in which the beneficiaries will do better to sue for knowing receipt, rather than unjust enrichment. For example, suppose that a knowing recipient of shares sells them and spends the cash on a holiday. The shares then triple in value. His liability in unjust enrichment would either be for the value of the shares at the time of receipt, or else (possibly) for the value of the cash realised by the sale, plus interest. But his liability in knowing receipt would be for the current value of the shares.

---

[206] *Quince v Varga* [2008] QCA 376, (2008) 11 ITELR 939 [48]-[53]; *OJSC* (n 204) [365]; *Commonwealth Oil & Gas Co Ltd v Baxter* [2009] CSIH 75; and cf *St Vincent de Paul Society Qld v Ozcare Ltd* [2009] QCA 335.

[207] See eg *Farah Constructions Pty Ltd v Say-Dee Pty Ltd* [2007] HCA 22 (2007); 230 CLR 89 [134]: 'recognising [strict liability in unjust enrichment as] a new and additional avenue of relief . . . is an avenue which tends to render the first limb [of *Barnes v Addy*] otiose.' See too LD Smith, 'W(h)ither Knowing Receipt' (1998) 114 *Law Quarterly Review* 394, 397; S Gardner, 'Moment of Truth for Knowing Receipt' (2009) 125 *Law Quarterly Review* 20, 24.

5

Knowing Receipt and Registered Land

MATTHEW CONAGLEN and AMY GOYMOUR

A. INTRODUCTION

This chapter explores the question whether a constructive trust arises following a breach of trust where the breach of trust comprises an unauthorised disposition by the trustee of registered land, as opposed to other forms of property.[1] In other words, where a trustee transfers trust property which is registered land in breach of trust, is the registered disponee of that property affected in some way by the trust?

Where the trust property is personalty, it is clear that the trust beneficiaries can assert their pre-existing equitable interests in the property against the disponee, unless he is a bona fide purchaser for value of the legal title to the property without notice of the breach of trust,[2] or unless the beneficiaries' interests under the trust were overreached by the transfer.[3] The same result follows where the relevant trust property is land, if title to the land was not registered at the time of the disposition.[4]

---

[1] This chapter focuses primarily on the regime for registered land in England and Wales. The same issues, and many of the same arguments, will be relevant in other common law jurisdictions that operate systems of land registration, but in order to avoid confusing analysis of the variety of different statutory provisions by which such registration schemes are implemented, attention is focused here on the provisions of the Land Registration Act 2002.

[2] The relevant notice is of the breach of trust, rather than of the trust itself: *Thomson v Clydesdale Bank Ltd* [1893] AC 282 (HL) 292; *Coleman v Bucks & Oxon Union Bank* [1897] 2 Ch 243 (Ch); *Pannell v Hurley* (1845) 2 Coll 241, 243; 63 ER 716, 718. See too PD Finn, 'The Liability of Third Parties for Knowing Receipt or Assistance' in DWM Waters (ed), *Equity, Fiduciaries and Trusts* (Scarborough, Ontario, Carswell, 1993) 199.

[3] A transaction concerning trust property can overreach the beneficial interests in some circumstances despite it being in breach of trust: see eg *City of London Building Society v Flegg* [1988] 1 AC 54; DM Fox, 'Overreaching' in P Birks and A Pretto (eds), *Breach of Trust* (Oxford, Hart Publishing, 2002) 95, 99–100; RC Nolan, 'Property in a Fund' (2004) 120 *Law Quarterly Review* 108, 113; RC Nolan, 'Understanding the Limits of Equitable Property' (2006) 1 *Journal of Equity* 18, 24–8.

[4] The registration scheme created by the Land Charges Act 1972 for interests in unregistered land does not apply to equitable interests under trusts. A transfer of the sort described in

Alternatively, where the trust property is personalty or unregistered land, the beneficiaries can sue the disponee in knowing receipt, if he has received trust property that has been transferred to him in breach of trust and his 'state of knowledge [is] such as to make it unconscionable for him to retain the benefit of the receipt'.[5]

Where, however, the relevant trust property is land and the trustee's title to that land has been registered with HM Land Registry, the position is different. Provided that the transfer was made for valuable consideration, the Land Registration Act 2002, section 29 ensures that once he has registered his title the purchaser takes that title free of the beneficiaries' interests under the trust, unless the beneficiaries were in actual occupation of the land at the time of the disposition to the purchaser.[6] This is so irrespective of whether the purchaser had notice of the breach of trust, and irrespective of whether his part in the transaction was in bad faith.[7]

The question addressed here is whether the trust beneficiaries have any claim in knowing receipt against such a purchaser where title to the land is registered. Knox J's decision in *Cowan de Groot Properties Ltd v Eagle Trust plc*[8] suggests that they do, although the point appears to have been assumed rather than taken directly. Addressing the point more directly, in

---

the text triggers the obligation to register the property: Land Registration Act 2002, ss 4(1)(a)(i) and 6(1). If the purchaser had notice of the trust interests, then he will continue to be bound by those interests after first registration (Land Registration Act 2002, s 11(5)), as he would also if the beneficiaries were in actual occupation (Land Registration Act 2002, sch 1, para 2).

[5] *Bank of Credit and Commerce International (Overseas) Ltd v Akindele* [2001] 1 Ch 437 (CA) 455.

[6] Land Registration Act 2002, s 29(1) and (2) and sch 3, para 2. This is also the case where the disposition involves the grant of a legal charge or lease over the trust property: see Land Registration Act 2002, ss 27(2)(b), (f).

[7] Law Commission, *Land Registration for the Twenty-First Century* (Law Com No 271, 2001) para [5.16]. Norris J's decision in *Halifax plc v Curry Popeck (a firm)* [2008] EWHC 1692 (Ch) might be read to mean that fraud will take a transaction outside s 29, on the basis that it is not for valuable consideration. Forgery can take a transaction outside s 29, on the basis that forgery renders the transaction void so that there is no registrable disposition: C Harpum, S Bridge and M Dixon *Megarry and Wade: The Law of Real Property*, 6th edn (London, Sweet & Maxwell, 2008) para 7-061. But fraud does not have that effect. Norris J's decision in *Curry Popeck* need not be read as broadly as has been suggested and can be limited to circumstances where the purported consideration was not in fact intended to be paid, so that there was no valuable consideration. This narrower reading would be preferable because the alternative effectively resurrects Graham J's widely discredited decision in *Peffer v Rigg* [1977] 1 WLR 285. In this chapter we do not address the situation that arises where the transfer was forged, or the transferee has committed a fraudulent misrepresentation to induce the transaction, as different mechanisms exist for arranging the return of the property in such cases, which do not depend on the law of knowing receipt: see Land Registration Act 2002, sch 4; and DM Fox, 'Forgery and Alteration of the Register under the Land Registration Act 2002' in EJ Cooke (ed), *Modern Studies in Property Law*, Vol III (Oxford, Hart Publishing, 2005) 25.

[8] [1992] 4 All ER 700 (Ch). It is not made clear in the judgment whether title to the relevant properties was registered in this case. See also *Hollis v Rolfe* [2008] EWHC 1747 (Ch) [172]–[174].

Eagle Trust plc v SBC Securities Ltd, albeit only in obiter dicta, Vinelott J indicated that he would consider it 'very anomalous if the [beneficiaries'] rights . . . were to depend on whether the land is registered or unregistered'.[9] Similarly, the Law Commission's 1998 Consultative Report on land registration explicitly envisaged the possibility of a knowing receipt claim being brought in such circumstances.[10] Given that the Law Commission's report ultimately led to the enactment of the Land Registration Act 2002, it is important to be clear about the correctness of its views on the viability of knowing receipt claims where registered land is concerned. In this chapter, we seek to explain why we respectfully differ from the view adopted by Vinelott J and the Law Commission, and suggest that a knowing receipt claim ought not to lie against a purchaser of registered land, even if he knew that title to the land was transferred in breach of trust.

B. KNOWING RECEIPT AS AN *IN PERSONAM* CLAIM

The first issue that falls to be considered is the nature of the claim in knowing receipt in terms of the result of such a claim. If it is a claim to a *proprietary* constructive trust over the property that has been transferred to the disponee in breach of trust, it can almost immediately be ruled out of contention where the trust property was registered land, because enforcement of the pre-existing beneficial interests in the trust property against the disponee of the property via the mechanism of a knowing receipt claim would be contrary to the terms of the Land Registration Act 2002, section 29.

But that is not the nature of a knowing receipt claim. Where the trust beneficiaries sue a transferee in knowing receipt, the claim is a *personal* claim which, if successful, results in the transferee being ordered to pay equitable compensation for the value of the property that was received.[11]

The difference between the personal claim in knowing receipt and the proprietary claim to recapture trust property can be seen in two related ways.[12] The first way of highlighting the difference between the two claims is to consider the circumstances in which each is most important. Where the trust property has been transferred in breach of trust and the trust property remains extant in the hands of the transferee, or if the transferee

---

[9] [1993] 1 WLR 484, 504.

[10] Law Commission, *Land Registration for the Twenty-First Century* (Law Com No 254, 1998) paras 3.48–3.49; see also Law Com No 271 (n 7) para 4-11.

[11] The remedies for knowing receipt may also include an account of profits: see *Charter plc v City Index Ltd* [2007] EWCA Civ 1382, [2008] Ch 313 [64]. In this chapter we confine our discussion to the compensatory measure. For discussion of some of the difficulties in assessing the measure of compensation in knowing receipt claims, see AC Goymour, 'A Contribution to Knowing Receipt Liability' [2008] *Restitution Law Review* 113.

[12] See also M Conaglen and R Nolan, 'Strict Liability for Receipt of Misapplied Trust Property—Confusion Abounds' [2007] *Cambridge Law Journal* 19, 20.

still holds the traceable substitute of the original trust property, the beneficiaries can assert rights over that property *in specie*. The claim in knowing receipt matters most where the trust property or its traceable substitute are no longer held by the transferee—for example, the property has been irretrievably dissipated, or it has been transferred onwards to a third party who can claim the benefit of a defence such as the bona fide purchaser defence. In this case, the beneficiaries are unable to force the original transferee to return the trust property *in specie* because he no longer holds that property, but they can bring a claim in knowing receipt, provided they can make out the requisite elements of such a claim. If they can so this, the defendant is liable as a 'constructive trustee',[13] but he cannot be a trustee of the trust property itself because he no longer holds that property or its traceable substitute. Rather, his constructive trusteeship

> is nothing more than a formula for equitable relief. The court of equity says that the defendant shall be liable in equity, as though he were a trustee. He is made liable in equity as trustee by the imposition or construction of the court of equity.[14]

In other words, the transferees 'are not trustees themselves, but are liable . . . to be made to account as if they were trustees'.[15] That liability is a personal liability to pay compensation, just as a trustee is personally liable to pay equitable compensation where he has disposed of trust property in breach of trust. In other words, notwithstanding the label of 'constructive trusteeship', the liability is personal: the defendant is described as a 'constructive trustee' but in 'such a case the expressions "constructive trust" and "constructive trustee" are misleading, for there is no trust and usually no possibility of a proprietary remedy; they are "nothing more than a formula for equitable relief"'.[16]

Thus, proprietary claims to recover trust property and 'the imposition of a constructive trust by reason of the knowing receipt of trust property are governed by different rules and must be kept distinct . . . the imposition of a constructive trust creates personal obligations that go beyond mere property rights'.[17]

---

[13] See eg *Barnes v Addy* (1874) LR 9 Ch App 244, 251.
[14] *Selangor United Rubber Estates Ltd v Cradock (No 3)* [1968] 1 WLR 1555, 1582.
[15] *Re Blundell* (1888) 40 ChD 370, 381. See also *Rolfe v Gregory* (1865) 4 De G J & S 576, 578–79; 46 ER 1042, 1043–44.
[16] *Paragon Finance plc v DB Thakerar & Co* [1999] 1 All ER 400 (CA) 409. See also *Giumelli v Giumelli* [1999] HCA 10, (1999) 196 CLR 101 [4]; *Dubai Aluminium Co Ltd v Salaam* [2002] UKHL 48, [2003] 2 AC 366 [135]–[142]; *Sinclair Investment Holdings SA v Versailles Trade Finance Ltd* [2007] EWHC 915 (Ch), [2007] 2 All ER (Comm) 993 [121]–[124]; *Peconic Industrial Development Ltd v Lau Kwok Fai* [2009] 2 HKLRD 537 [19]. And see *Charter plc v City Index Ltd* [2007] EWCA Civ 1382, [2008] Ch 313 [64]: 'the expressions "constructive trust" and "liable to account" are portmanteau expressions that can be used to define the remedies for different sorts of causes of action'.
[17] *Re Montagu's Settlement Trusts* [1987] Ch 264 (Ch) 285.

Secondly, the way in which each claim needs to be proven differs. As has been mentioned, where trust property is transferred to a third party in breach of trust, the beneficiaries can claim an interest in the asset in the hands of the third party, which is a proprietary claim in the sense that it is an equitable claim to the property itself, or to a share in it, or a charge over it.[18] In order to bring such a claim, the beneficiary must prove his equitable entitlement, but he need not establish notice on the recipient's part. In other words, proof of the equitable entitlement suffices to establish the proprietary claim and it then falls to the transferee to try to avoid the consequences of such a claim by himself proving that he was a bona fide purchaser of the legal estate without notice of the breach of trust. As Collins MR put it in *Re Nisbett & Potts' Contract*, the beneficiaries' claim

> may be defeated by a purchaser for value without notice; but the burden is upon the person who takes the land to shew that he has acquired it under such conditions as to defeat the right as against him, namely, that he has acquired it for value and without notice.[19]

In contrast, where the beneficiaries rely instead on the personal claim for knowing receipt, they must show that the transferee was 'a party to the breach of trust'[20] and in order to do that they must show 'knowledge on the part of the defendant that the assets he received are traceable to a breach of fiduciary duty'.[21] As Stirling J said in *Re Blundell*:

> a stranger to the trust receiving money from the trustee which he knows to be part of the trust estate is *not liable as a constructive trustee unless there are facts brought home to him which shew that to his knowledge* the money is being applied in a manner which is inconsistent with the trust; or (in other words) unless it be made out that he is party either to a fraud, or to a breach of trust on the part of the trustee.[22]

Furthermore, in *BCCI v Akindele*, Nourse LJ expressed doubt about the argument that knowing receipt should be a strict liability claim in unjust enrichment because that would reverse the burden of proof in such claims.[23] His doubt only makes sense on the basis that the burden of proof

---

[18] *Foskett v McKeown* [2001] 1 AC 201.
[19] [1906] 1 Ch 386 (CA) 403; see also 404 and 409–10. And see *Lady Bodmin v Vandenbendy* (1683) 1 Vern 179, 23 ER 399; *Barclays Bank plc v Boulter* [1998] 1 WLR 1 (CA) 8; *Barclays Bank plc v Boulter* [1999] 1 WLR (HL) 1919, 1924.
[20] *Keane v Robarts* (1819) 4 Madd 332, 357; 56 ER 728, 737. See also *Webb v Ledsam* (1855) 1 K & J 385, 387; 69 ER 508, 509; *Re Blundell* (1888) 40 ChD 370, 382.
[21] *El Ajou v Dollar Land Holdings plc* [1994] 2 All ER 685 (CA) 700; *Bank of Credit and Commerce International (Overseas) Ltd v Akindele* [2001] 1 Ch 437 (CA) 448. See also *John v Dodwell & Co Ltd* [1918] AC 563 (PC) 569–70; *Polly Peck International plc v Nadir (No 2)* [1992] 4 All ER 769 (CA) 777.
[22] (1888) 40 ChD 370, 381 (emphasis added). See also *Fyler v Fyler* (1841) 3 Beav 550, 567–68; 49 ER 216, 223; *Wilson v Moore* (1834) 1 My & K 337, 358; 39 ER 709, 717.
[23] See *Bank of Credit and Commerce International (Overseas) Ltd v Akindele* [2001] Ch 437 (CA) 456.

in such a claim currently rests with the claimant, rather than the recipient, to prove not only beneficial receipt of trust property but also knowledge that the property is traceable to the breach of trust. It is that knowledge which makes it unconscionable for him to retain the benefit of the receipt,[24] and which justifies the order that he pay equitable compensation for what he received but no longer has.

Hence, by way of example, as Lord Browne-Wilkinson explained in *Westdeutsche*, a donee of trust property which was transferred in breach of trust can be required to re-transfer the property if he still has it at the time of the action, even if he was previously unaware of the trust, but he cannot be made personally liable in knowing receipt unless knowledge is shown:

> [W]here, under a pre-existing trust, B is entitled to an equitable interest in trust property, if the trust property comes into the hands of a third party, X (not being a purchaser for value of the legal interest without notice) . . . B's equitable right is enforceable against the property in just the same way as any other specifically enforceable equitable right can be enforced against a third party. Even if the third party, X, is not aware that what he has received is trust property B is entitled to assert his title in that property. If X has the necessary degree of knowledge, X may himself become a constructive trustee for B on the basis of knowing receipt. But unless he has the requisite degree of knowledge he is not personally liable to account as trustee.[25]

The knowing receipt claim is thus most important where the trust property (or its traceable substitute) cannot be recovered *in specie* from the transferee, as the knowing receipt claim enables the trust beneficiaries to claim compensation for the value of the property notwithstanding that it cannot be recovered *in specie*.[26] The odd thing about knowing receipt claims where the trust property is registered land is that the transferee may well still have title to the property in his hands, but that title is protected from the beneficiaries by the priorities rules contained in the Land Registration Act 2002, section 29.

Contrary to the view that has been advanced here, some Australian cases seem to have treated knowing receipt claims as having proprietary consequences.[27] These are best understood, if they are to be accepted at all,[28]

---

[24] Ibid, 455.
[25] *Westdeutsche Landesbank Girozentrale v Islington LBC* [1997] AC 669, 707 (emphasis removed). See also *Re Montagu's Settlement Trusts* [1987] Ch 264, 271.
[26] *Ultraframe (UK) Ltd v Fielding* [2005] EWHC 1638 (Ch) [1486] and [1577].
[27] Eg *Say-Dee Pty Ltd v Farah Constructions Pty Ltd* [2005] NSWCA 309 [233] and [235]; *Robins v Incentive Dynamics Pty Ltd* [2003] NSWCA 71, (2003) 45 ACSR 244 [44]–[51]; *Koorootang Nominees Pty Ltd v Australia & New Zealand Banking Group Ltd* [1998] 3 VR 16, 75.
[28] The decisions are criticised by Michael Bryan on the basis, consistently with what we have said, that knowing receipt is a personal claim: M Bryan, 'Recipient Liability under the Torrens System: Some Category Errors' in CEF Rickett and R Grantham, (eds) *Structure and Justification in Private Law* (Oxford, Hart Publishing, 2008) 339.

on the basis that the trust which they have recognised is a remedial constructive trust, as Mason P said in the New South Wales Court of Appeal in *Robins v Incentive Dynamics Pty Ltd*.[29] The trust cannot be an ordinary institutional constructive trust[30] over the original trust property as that property cannot be traced; if it could, then the beneficiaries would simply claim that property without need of the knowing receipt argument. Remedial constructive trusts appear to have been accepted in Australian law, but, after some hints that English law might move towards recognition of such trusts,[31] the English courts have more recently indicated quite clearly that they are not prepared to do so.[32] That approach can be criticised,[33] but for present purposes it means, when coupled with the points already made, that our attention should be focused on the question whether a personal claim for compensation will lie against a knowing recipient where he can no longer be forced to reconvey the property *in specie* because his title is protected by section 29. As Michael Bryan has said, 'it is precisely because a proprietary claim is barred . . . that personal relief comes into its own'.[34]

C. *IN PERSONAM* CLAIMS CONCERNING REGISTERED LAND

Notwithstanding the protection that an owner of registered land obtains by registration of his title, the registered owner is not immune from *in personam* claims concerning that land. Simple examples of this proposition are found in the enforceable nature of contracts to convey the land into which the owner enters, and the enforceable nature of trusts that the owner may declare over his land.[35] As the Privy Council said in *Frazer v Walker*, the fact that a registered proprietor's title is

---

[29] *Robins* (n 27) [26] and [45]. See also M Harding, '*Barnes v Addy* Claims and the Indefeasibility of Torrens Title' (2007) 31 *Melbourne University Law Review* 343, 361.

[30] For the difference between institutional and remedial constructive trusts, see *Metall und Rohstoff AG v Donaldson Lufkin & Jenrett Inc* [1990] 1 QB 391 (CA) 478; *Westdeutsche* (n 25) 714–15.

[31] Eg *Metall und Rohstoff* (n 30) 479; *Re Goldcorp Exchange Ltd* [1995] 1 AC 74 (PC) 104; *Westdeutsche* (n 25) 716.

[32] Eg *Re Polly Peck International plc (No 4)* [1998] 2 BCLC 185 (CA) 201 and 205; *Box v Barclays Bank plc* [1998] Lloyd's Rep Bank 185 (Ch) 200; *Foskett v McKeown* [2001] 1 AC 102, 109 and 127; *Ultraframe* (n 26) [1597]; *Sinclair Investment Holdings SA v Versailles Trade Finance Ltd* [2007] EWHC 915 (Ch) [128]. Lord Scott's suggestion that remedial constructive trusts are part of English law in *Thorner v Majors* [2009] UKHL 18, [2009] 1 WLR 776 [14] and [20] is against the weight of authority on the point, and is based on reasoning with which the other Lords disagreed: see [62] (Lord Walker) and [101] (Lord Neuberger).

[33] See the discussion in M Conaglen, 'Thinking about Proprietary Remedies for Breach of Confidence' [2008] *Intellectual Property Quarterly* 82, 98–100.

[34] Bryan (n 28) 358.

[35] *Cuthbertson v Swan* (1877) 11 SALR 102 (SASC) 112; *Barry v Heider* (1914) 19 CLR

immune from adverse claims, other than those specifically excepted . . . in no way denies the right of a plaintiff to bring against a registered proprietor a claim *in personam*, founded in law or in equity, for such relief as a court acting *in personam* may grant.[36]

Midland Bank v Green[37] provides a potentially comparable example in the context of unregistered land in England and Wales. The facts are well known. In essence, the claimant's mother and father conspired to defeat the claimant's unregistered option over his father's farm by transferring the farm to the claimant's mother at 1.25 per cent of its market value. The House of Lords accepted that the mother was 'a purchaser . . . for money or money's worth' under the Land Charges Act 1925, section 13(2), so that the option was void as against her, notwithstanding that the purpose of the transfer had been to defeat the son's proprietary interest. The fact that the mother's title to the land was thereby taken free of the son's option did not, however, protect the mother and father from separate proceedings brought by the son for damages for the tort of conspiracy.[38] We have been unable to find any record of the claim for conspiracy having been determined judicially. However, the important point for present purposes is the fact that the Court of Appeal was prepared to countenance the possibility of such a claim being brought.

As the Privy Council emphasised in *Frazer v Walker*, these *in personam* claims must be 'founded in law or in equity',[39] and so must be brought on the basis of recognised causes of action.[40] There is no doubt that knowing receipt is a recognised cause of action. So the question is whether it is available in the circumstances under discussion. The Law Commission's Consultative Report 1998 on land registration, which ultimately led to the enactment of the Land Registration Act 2002, explicitly envisaged the possibility of *in personam* claims being brought.[41] The first such claim

---

197, 216; *Boyd v Mayor of Wellington* [1924] NZLR 1174 (NZCA) 1223; *Tataurangi Tairuakena v Carr* [1927] NZLR 688 (NZCA) 702; *Oh Hiam v Tham Kong* [1980] 2 MLJ 159 (PC).

[36] [1967] AC 569 (PC) 585. See also *Breskvar v Wall* (1971) 126 CLR 376, 384–85; *Bahr v Nicolay (No 2)* (1988) 164 CLR 604, 653; *White v Tomasel* [2004] QCA 89, [2004] 2 Qd R 438 [57] and [70]. And see generally A Mason, 'Indefeasibility—Logic or Legend?' in D Grinlinton (ed), *Torrens in the Twenty-first Century* (Wellington, LexisNexis, 2003) 12; E Cooke and P O'Connor, 'Purchaser Liability to Third Parties in the English Land Registration System: A Comparative Perspective' (2004) 120 *Law Quarterly Review* 640; B McFarlane, 'Constructive Trusts Arising on a Receipt of Property *Sub Conditione*' (2004) 120 *Law Quarterly Review* 667.

[37] [1981] AC 513.

[38] See *Midland Bank Trust Co Ltd v Green (No 3)* [1982] 1 Ch 529 (CA). See also *Esso Petroleum Co Ltd v Kingswood Motors (Addlestone) Ltd* [1974] QB 142, 156.

[39] *Frazer* (n 36) 585.

[40] *Grgic v Australian & New Zealand Banking Group Ltd* (1994) 33 NSWLR 202 (NSWCA) 222–23; *Duncan v McDonald* [1997] NZLR 669 (NZCA) 683; *White v Tomasel* [2004] QCA 89, [2004] 2 Qd R 438 [72].

[41] Law Com No 254 (n 10) paras 3.48–3.49. See also Law Com No 271 (n 7) para 4-11.

which it listed was a claim to make the transferee 'liable as constructive trustee for "knowing receipt" of trust property'.[42] In such a case, the Law Commission said that 'a purchaser may acquire the registered land free from the rights of the third party, yet find himself personally liable for the loss suffered by that third party or subject to some personal equity'.[43] This view influenced Norris J's analysis in *Halifax plc v Curry Popeck*,[44] and other commentators have taken a similar line.[45]

Without calling into question the possibility of *in personam* claims in general, for the reasons that follow we suggest that claims in knowing receipt ought not to be recognised where section 29 renders the purchaser immune to the beneficiaries' *proprietary* entitlement.

D. KNOWING RECEIPT AND PURCHASERS OF REGISTERED LAND

The question whether liability for knowing receipt ought to be available in the context of land registration systems has been described by Atkinson J in the Queensland Court of Appeal as bringing 'into sharp relief the great tectonic plates of law and equity as they grind against each other and struggle to settle in to a stable position on the substratum of the . . . legal landscape'.[46] While perhaps overly dramatic, this imagery usefully demonstrates that the availability of knowing receipt liability against a registered purchaser requires a careful examination of the intersection of two sets of rules—the principles governing liability for knowing receipt and the principles of land registration—which have developed largely independently of one another and in different contexts.[47]

1. Technical Compatibility

One way of approaching the question is to ask whether a knowing receipt claim is even coherent where a purchaser[48] of registered land can claim the

---

[42] Law Com No 254 (n 10) para 3.48.
[43] Ibid, para 3.49.
[44] *Halifax* (n 7) [49]–[51].
[45] Eg Bryan (n 28) 341 and 358; Harding (n 29) 352–53 and 357–59.
[46] *Tara Shire Council v Garner* [2002] QCA 232, [2003] 1 Qd R 556 [80].
[47] Knowing receipt claims have predominantly been brought in connection with dispositions of personalty rather than real property.
[48] Knowing receipt claims are normally based on transfer of ownership in the trust property. It may, however, be the case that acquisition of a security interest over the trust property will also suffice to generate liability in knowing receipt: *Super 1000 Pty Ltd v Pacific General Securities Ltd* [2008] NSWSC 1222, (2008) 221 FLR 427 [204]–[205]. The acquisition of a mere security interest has been held in Canada to be a sufficient 'receipt' of the trust property, and sufficiently 'beneficial' to the 'recipient', to qualify for knowing receipt liability: see eg *Gold v Rosenberg* [1997] 3 SCR 767 [54]–[55]. However, that decision was based on the view that

benefit of the Land Registration Act 2002, section 29. In particular, it is arguable that the purchaser is not in receipt of trust property where the very act that confers legal title on the purchaser—that is, registration—at the same time allows the purchaser to take that title free of the beneficiary's prior equitable interest. The property is no longer subject to the trust, and so the recipient cannot be said to have received trust property. On this view, section 29 is inherently and logically incompatible with knowing receipt. As Sarah Worthington has put it:

> [If] a defaulting trustee makes an unauthorized transfer of trust property to a third party, the third party may still acquire perfectly good title to the property. If this is the case, then the beneficiary cannot make any claim against the recipient, and the analysis can stop immediately.[49]

In other words, section 29 effectively eliminates the trust beneficiaries' interests in the property as against the registered purchaser, so that he cannot be said to have received trust property. Hence, no claim in knowing receipt of trust property can lie.

This argument has a great deal to commend it. However, there are two ways in which claimants might seek to avoid the effect of this analysis.

First, claimants might seek to rely on the fact that section 29 does not in terms extinguish the prior equitable interests of the trust beneficiaries, but rather postpones them to the purchaser's registered interest. Section 29 provides:[50]

> If a registrable disposition of a registered estate is made for valuable consideration, completion of the disposition by registration has the effect of *postponing* to the interest under the disposition any interest affecting the estate immediately before the disposition.[51]

The notion of postponement is explained by the doctrine of relativity of title, according to which there can be many different claims against one piece of property, which coexist but rank in order of priority.[52] Hence, 'postponement' of a beneficiary's interest under section 29 could be argued

---

knowing receipt is an unjust enrichment claim which, as we argue below, is not the case in England (see text accompanying nn 64–71). See also *Donely v Donely* [1998] 1 Qd R 602, 612.

[49] S Worthington, *Equity*, 2nd edn (Oxford, Oxford University Press, 2006) 179. See also B McFarlane, *The Structure of Property Law* (Oxford, Hart Publishing, 2008) 418–19.

[50] Emphasis added.

[51] This, of course, is not the case where the beneficiaries' interest is 'protected' by their actual occupation of the property in question: see n 6 above.

[52] See further D Fox, 'Relativity of Title at Law and in Equity' [2006] *Cambridge Law Journal* 330. See also Law Com No 271 (n 7) para 5.6, n 17: 'The Bill necessarily refers to the prior interest being postponed to the later registered disposition. The disponee will thereby take free of the unprotected interest. That does not mean that the interest is necessarily destroyed. It may still remain valid as against interests other than that of the disponee under the registered disposition.'

to mean that the beneficiary's interest persists but is relatively inferior in priority to that of the registered purchaser. That leaves room for the beneficiary to argue that the purchaser has received property which is still subject to the trust and all that has happened is that the priority of the trust beneficiaries' interests is subordinated to that of the purchaser. On that basis, it might be argued that the purchaser has received trust property for the purposes of a claim being brought in knowing receipt.

Secondly, claimants could seek to rely on the fact that section 29 only operates to protect a registered purchaser's interest once that interest has been registered. In the interim, the purchaser will have acquired an equitable title of some form: at exchange of contracts the purchaser obtains an equitable interest in the property,[53] which ripens into an interest under a bare trust upon delivery of the executed deed of transfer.[54] The beneficiaries' equitable interests under the trust are only postponed to the purchaser's interest once it is registered, which typically occurs at a time after both exchange of contracts and the disposition by delivery of the deed of transfer.[55] Until that point, the equitable title that the purchaser has obtained is held subject to the beneficiaries' prior interests.[56] On that basis it might be argued that the purchaser is a recipient of trust property until registration postpones the priority of the beneficiaries' interests.[57] In other words, a claimant might seek to bring a knowing receipt claim on the basis that the transferee 'received' an interest in the trust property before the trust's priority was lost.[58]

Whether such an argument would be effective is not clear. *Criterion Properties plc v Stratford UK Properties LLC* appears to hold that

> creation by the contract of contractual rights does not constitute a 'receipt' of assets . . . The question whether an executory contract is enforceable is quite different from the question whether assets of which there has been a 'knowing receipt' are recoverable from the recipient.[59]

---

[53] *Lysaght v Edwards* (1876) 2 Ch D 499; *Jerome v Kelly* [2004] UKHL 25, [2004] 1 WLR 1409 [29]–[32]. See further *Megarry and Wade* (n 7) paras 15-012–15-056.

[54] It is implicit in the requirement that the purchaser registers his interest in order to acquire legal title (Land Registration Act 2002, s 27) that until registration his title will be a full beneficial interest, but will only exist in equity: C Harpum and J Bignell, *Registered Land: Law and Practice under the Land Registration Act 2002* (Bristol, Jordans, 2004) para 8.2.

[55] When e-conveyancing is introduced, the date at which the deed is executed and registration will collapse into one stage, thus closing the so-called 'registration gap'. See further Harpum and Bignell (n 54) part 5.

[56] Land Registration Act 2002, s 28.

[57] Whatever interest the purchaser receives in the property prior to registration will rank in priority behind the trust beneficiaries' interests: Land Registration Act 2002, s 28.

[58] In *Trustor AB v Smallbone (No 2)* [2001] 1 WLR 1177 [18], for example, Morritt VC referred to liability for knowing receipt arising where the recipient 'has the trust property vested in him, *or so far under his control that he can require it should be vested in him*' (emphasis added). The authority cited for this proposition was, however, *Re Barney* [1892] 2 Ch 265, 273, which concerned liability for acting as a trustee *de son tort*, rather than liability for knowing receipt.

[59] [2004] UKHL 28, [2004] 1 WLR 1846 [27]. See also DJ Hayton and C Mitchell, *Hayton*

It is unclear whether this comment was intended to cover transactions involving the sale and purchase of land. Unlike many other contracts, such transactions normally generate equitable proprietary interests in the land prior to the conveyance of legal title, particularly once the deed of transfer has been executed and delivered.

Thus, while the argument that knowing receipt is technically incompatible with the Land Registration Act 2002, section 29 is a very strong one, for these two reasons it is not clear that it completely defeats the possibility of knowing receipt claims being brought against purchasers of registered land. To evaluate the viability of such claims, it is necessary to consider the underlying nature and function of each doctrine, in order to assess the degree to which they are, or are not, compatible. For the reasons that follow, we suggest that the nature of knowing receipt claims is such that they ought not to be permitted against a purchaser who can claim the protection of section 29.

2. The Nature and Function of Knowing Receipt

The nature of knowing receipt liability is itself unclear. The doctrine has been variously considered as a form of equitable wrongdoing, part of the law of unjust enrichment and a remedy to vindicate property rights.[60]

Traditionally, liability in knowing receipt has been treated as based on the defendant's wrongdoing. In *Rolfe v Gregory*, for example, the defendant argued that liability in knowing receipt is based on the fact that the recipient is treated as a trustee of the property he has received. Lord Westbury LC rejected this as involving 'a misapprehension of the true principles on which the action of this Court is founded . . . the relief is founded on fraud and not on constructive trust'.[61] Similarly, in *BCCI v Akindele*, Nourse LJ emphasised that 'the recipient's state of knowledge must be such as to make it unconscionable for him to retain the benefit of the receipt'.[62]

---

and Mitchell: *Commentary and Cases on the Law of Trusts and Equitable Remedies*, 12th edn (London, Sweet and Maxwell, 2005) para 11.20.

[60] For a recent analysis of the competing arguments, see D Sheehan, 'Disentangling Equitable Personal Liability' [2008] *Restitution Law Review* 41. See also P Birks, 'Receipt' in P Birks and A Pretto (eds), *Breach of Trust* (Oxford, Hart Publishing, 2002) 213.

[61] (1865) 4 De GJ & S 576, 579; 46 ER 1042, 1044. This does not mean that there is no constructive trusteeship in knowing receipt claims, as Lord Westbury also made it clear that 'when it is said that the person who fraudulently receives or possesses himself of trust property is converted by this Court into a trustee, the expression is used for the purpose of describing the nature and extent of the remedy against him'. Rather, the point was that the recipient does not become trustee of the property. See also text accompanying nn 13–16 above.

[62] *Bank of Credit and Commerce International (Overseas) Ltd v Akindele* [2001] 1 Ch 437 (CA) 455.

Thus, as has already been mentioned,[63] a donee of trust property who mistakenly but honestly believes that the property is his beneficially, and who dissipates the property irretrievably, is not liable to the beneficiary for having done so as he was not at fault in dissipating property that he did not realise belonged to another.

Knowing receipt has also been seen as a part of the law of unjust enrichment. This view has some support in other jurisdictions,[64] but has not yet been applied to a knowing receipt claim in an English case as a necessary explanation. Such an approach would be problematic. The requirement of fault for liability in knowing receipt jars with unjust enrichment liability, for which there is no distinct fault requirement. For unjust enrichment, a claimant need only show enrichment of the defendant at the claimant's expense, and the presence of an unjust factor.[65] Hence in *Kelly v Solari*,[66] for example, an insurance company could recover a payment that it mistakenly made to a widow pursuant to an expired life insurance policy, notwithstanding that the widow's receipt was entirely innocent. Had this case concerned trust property, knowing receipt would not lie against such a recipient.

Of course, fault is not entirely irrelevant in the law of unjust enrichment,[67] but it is by no means universal. For example, certain unjust factors require the defendant to have acted with some degree of fault (such as undue influence and duress). But the fact that fault clearly is a requirement for knowing receipt liability makes it less than obvious that it ought to be categorised as an instance of unjust enrichment. One of the main reasons why it is important to recognise claims as falling within the category of unjust enrichment is that such claims are generally subject to a change of position defence: as Andrew Burrows has said, 'change of position goes hand in glove with unjust enrichment'.[68] The defendant's wrongdoing where a claim in knowing receipt is viable means that such a defence will be unavailable,[69] which suggests that its classification as unjust enrichment

---

[63] See text accompanying n 25. See also PJ Millett, 'Tracing the Proceeds of Fraud' (1991) 107 *Law Quarterly Review* 71, 80.

[64] See eg *Kooratang Nominees Pty Ltd v Australia and New Zealand Banking Group* [1998] 3 VR 16, 99–105; and *Say-Dee* (NSWCA) (n 27) [233], although the court's unjust enrichment analysis was rejected by the High Court of Australia in *Farah Constructions Pty Ltd v Say-Dee Pty Ltd* [2007] HCA 22, (2007) 230 CLR 89. See also *Gold v Rosenberg* [1997] 3 SCR 767.

[65] *Banque Financière de la Cité v Parc (Battersea) Ltd* [1999] 1 AC 221 (HL) 277.

[66] (1841) 9 M & W 54, 152 ER 24.

[67] See GJ Virgo, 'The Role of Fault in the Law of Restitution' in A Burrows and Lord Rodger (eds), *Mapping the Law* (Oxford, Oxford University Press, 2006) 83. See also Birks, 'Receipt' (n 60) 227.

[68] A Burrows, 'The Relationship between Unjust Enrichment and Property' in S Degeling and J Edelman (eds), *Unjust Enrichment in Commercial Law* (Sydney, Thomson Reuters, 2008) 352. This is also implicit in *Test Claimants in the FII Group Litigation v HMRC* [2008] EWHC 2893 (Ch) [336].

[69] The change of position defence is reserved to those who act in good faith: *Lipkin Gorman v Karpnale* [1991] 2 AC 548, 579.

is analytically uninformative, and hence unimportant. An alternative approach has been to argue that knowing receipt liability ought to be strict, rather than fault based, in order to make it fit more comfortably with the rest of the law of unjust enrichment.[70] But such arguments just serve to emphasise that the claim is *not* currently a claim in unjust enrichment, and the High Court of Australia held in *Farah Constructions v Say-Dee* that no sufficient justification has been shown for changing that position.[71]

Given its emphasis on fault or wrongdoing on the part of the disponee, the claim in knowing receipt could be considered simply to be part of the law of wrongs. However, notwithstanding that the knowing receipt claim involves wrongdoing, the claim is inherently linked to the receipt of property. For example, Millett J said in *Agip (Africa) Ltd v Jackson* that knowing receipt is 'concerned with rights of priority in relation to property'.[72] Thus, although the claim for recapture of trust property from a transferee and the personal claim against him for knowing receipt are distinct claims with distinct modes of proof,[73] 'the source of his liability is the same, ie, the receipt of trust property to which he was not entitled'.[74] The *source* of the claim in knowing receipt is receipt of property that does not belong beneficially to the recipient and the 'wrong' lies in treating property that he knows is not beneficially his own as if it were, whether by dissipating it or otherwise putting it beyond the reach of those to whom it belongs beneficially.

It is not easy to categorise the fundamental nature of the claim in knowing receipt because it sits uncomfortably between, and partakes of aspects of both, claims to the recapture of property that are based on proprietary entitlement and claims for compensation based on wrongdoing. On balance, however, we suggest that although it involves an element of wrongdoing, which justifies the compensatory order in circumstances where the trust property cannot itself be returned, the fundamental purpose of the claim seems to be to vindicate the pre-existing property rights that have been lost as a result of the wrongful disposition.[75] In that sense, knowing receipt can be understood as a form of vindication of

---

[70] See eg C Harpum, 'The Basis of Equitable Liability' in PBH Birks (ed), *The Frontiers of Liability*, vol 1 (Oxford, Oxford University Press, 1994); Lord Nicholls, 'Knowing Receipt: The Need for a New Landmark' in WR Cornish et al (eds), *Restitution: Past, Present and Future* (Oxford, Hart Publishing, 1998) 231; Birks, 'Receipt' (n 60).

[71] *Farah* (HCA) (n 64).

[72] [1990] Ch 265, 293.

[73] See part B.

[74] Millett (n 63) 81. See also *Agip* (Ch D) (n 72) 292; C Harpum, 'The Stranger as Constructive Trustee (Part II)' (1986) 102 *Law Quarterly Review* 267, 290; C Harpum, 'Liability for Intermeddling with Trusts' (1987) 50 *Modern Law Review* 217, 220; Harpum (n 70) 19.

[75] This view is similar to that presented in ch 4 above. However, for the reasons given in part B above, we consider that there are important differences between claims to recover trust assets in specie and claims for knowing receipt.

property rights.[76] It is not vindication in the ordinary sense, as the property itself is ordinarily no longer there to be returned.[77] Nonetheless, as Graham Virgo has argued, 'the use of the word "vindication" does serve a useful function . . . because it describes, albeit in general terms, the nature of the remedies where property rights have been interfered with by the defendant'.[78] The knowing receipt claim is vindicatory in this sense, in that the transferee is made to compensate the trust beneficiaries for having dissipated, or put beyond their reach, property to which they would otherwise have had a claim while knowing that he ought not to have done so. The wrongdoing, on which the claim depends, arises because the transferee has knowingly acted wrongly in respect of property which belongs, at the time of receipt, beneficially to another.

3. The Nature and Function of Section 29

Section 29 of the Land Registration Act 2002 regulates the priority of proprietary interests over registered land. Hence it forms a crucial part of the system of land registration. As Lord Wilberforce explained in *Williams & Glyn's Bank Ltd v Boland*:

> The system of land registration, as it exists in England, which long antedates the Land Registration Act 1925, is designed to simplify and to cheapen conveyancing . . . Above all, the system is designed to free the purchaser from the hazards of notice—real or constructive—which, in the case of unregistered land, involved him in enquiries, often quite elaborate, failing which he might be bound by equities.[79]

Section 29 facilitates this policy aim by protecting the registered purchaser against adverse equitable interests irrespective of whether he has any knowledge or notice of those interests.

---

[76] The fact that the claim of knowing receipt is concerned with vindicating property rights does not mean that it must be strict liability. 'Property' can mean different things in different contexts (RC Nolan, 'Equitable Property' (2006) 122 *Law Quarterly Review* 232, 255–56; Conaglen (n 33) 88–90) and equitable property rights have always been protected in different ways from legal property rights (see LD Smith, 'Unjust Enrichment, Property and the Structure of Trusts' (2000) 116 *Law Quarterly Review* 412). Hence, the fact that legal property rights are vindicated by strict liability claims does not necessitate the view that equitable property rights must be vindicated in the same way.

[77] Bryan (n 28) 351. Even in Roman Law, the primary remedy for the 'vindicatio' claim was monetary compensation rather than return of the property *in specie*: B Nicholas, *Introduction to Roman Law* (Oxford, Oxford University Press, 1975) 101.

[78] GJ Virgo, *The Principles of the Law of Restitution*, 2nd edn (Oxford, Oxford University Press, 2006) 16.

[79] [1981] AC 487, 503. These comments were made regarding the Land Registration Act 1925, but there is nothing to suggest that they are not equally applicable with regard to the Land Registration Act 2002: see eg Law Com No 271 (n 7) para 5.16. See also *Frazer* (n 36) 582.

4. Conclusions Regarding the Compatibility of Knowing Receipt and Section 29

In the light of this functional analysis of knowing receipt claims and section 29 of the Land Registration Act 2002, we suggest that knowing receipt claims ought not to be permitted against a registered purchaser of trust property.

Knowing receipt claims vindicate the beneficiaries' property rights in the trust property. Such claims are therefore inherently inappropriate against a purchaser who can postpone the beneficiaries' interests under section 29. In other words, with one strike section 29 wipes out both the beneficiaries' property rights, and also the personal claim in knowing receipt, as the personal claim is parasitic upon that property right.

One of the important functions of land registration would be stultified if knowing receipt were allowed to operate against a registered purchaser. As McMurdo J said of *in personam* claims in the Queensland Court of Appeal in *White v Tomasel*:

> [T]hose rights of action which are not defeated by the registration of the defendant's title are cases where there is no inconsistency between the enforceability of the right of action and the policy and proper purposes of the Torrens system of title.[80]

It undermines the purposes of the land registration system to allow trust beneficiaries, whose beneficial interests in the trust property have been subordinated to the legal title of a transferee, nonetheless to sue the transferee for compensation on the basis of knowing receipt because he took title to the property with notice that the beneficiaries had a claim over it.[81] Cases from Australia are instructive in presenting the concern. As Tadgell JA said for the majority of the Victorian Court of Appeal in *Macquarie Bank Ltd v Sixty-Fourth Throne Pty Ltd*:

> [I]t might be possible to treat the holder of the registered proprietary interest as a constructive trustee arising from 'knowing receipt' of trust property [but] there is neither room nor the need, in the Torrens system of title, to do so. If registration . . . is not achieved by fraud the Act provides, subject to its terms, for an indefeasible interest. Those terms allow, it is true, a claim in personam founded in equity against the holder of a registered interest to be invoked to defeat the interest; and a claim in personam founded in equity may no doubt include a claim to enforce what is called a constructive trust. . . . However that may be, to recognise a claim in personam against the holder of a mortgage registered under the Transfer of Land Act, dubbing the holder a constructive trustee by application of a doctrine akin to 'knowing receipt' when registration of the mortgage

---

[80] [2004] QCA 89, [2004] 2 QdR 438 [71].
[81] See also Conaglen and Nolan (n 12) 517.
[82] [1998] 3 VR 133 (VCA) 156–57. Winneke P agreed at 135.

was honestly achieved, would introduce by the back door a means of undermining the doctrine of indefeasibility which the Torrens system establishes.[82]

Ashley AJA dissented, on the basis that the indefeasibility of the recipient's title is insufficient reason to render him immune from liability in knowing receipt,[83] and his dissent was preferred by a majority of the Queensland Court of Appeal in *Tara Shire Council v Garner*.[84] On the other hand, four of the five members of the Western Australia Court of Appeal in *LHK Nominees Pty Ltd v Kenworthy* held that Tadgell JA's decision in *Macquarie Bank* was to be preferred.[85] And in the *Farah Constructions* case, a unanimous High Court of Australia indicated, albeit obiter dicta, that a transferee of property transferred in breach of trust ought to be protected by the registration of title from any *proprietary* claim brought on the basis of knowing receipt.[86] It is not made explicit, but it is consistent with that view and with the court's approval of the analysis in *Macquarie Bank*,[87] that a *personal* claim in knowing receipt ought also to be barred in such circumstances in order that the purpose of the registration system is not undermined 'by the back door'.[88]

Caution is, of course, required when relying on Australian authorities (or those from any other jurisdiction) about knowing receipt claims in the context of registered land, as those decisions will be affected by the specific statutory provisions of the registration system within which they are decided,[89] which will differ from state to state and between the Australasian Torrens systems and the English registration system. However, the general purpose of registration systems for land does not differ between Australia and England. The intention of the Land Registration Act 2002

---

[83] Ibid, 166.
[84] [2002] QCA 232, [2003] 1 QdR 556 [80]–[89]. This view was also taken in *Koorootang* (n 64) and *Doneley v Doneley* [1998] 1 QdR 602.
[85] [2002] WASCA 291, (2002) 26 WAR 517 [185]–[186], [210]–[213], [273] and [278]–[292].
[86] *Farah* (HCA) (n 64) [190]–[198].
[87] Ibid, [196].
[88] See also *Super 1000* (n 48) [219]. The effect of this argument is that s 29 would then mirror the effect that overreaching and the bona fide purchaser principle have on claims against remote recipients. To our knowledge, a knowing receipt claim has not been successfully asserted after one of those defences has effectively extinguished the beneficiaries' proprietary interests. See *GL Baker Ltd v Medway Building Supplies Ltd* [1958] 1 All ER 540 (CA) 543, where Jenkins LJ applied (erroneously) a strict liability analysis to the claim but recognised that bona fide purchase would be an 'effective shield' against in personam liability. In an analogous fashion, the bona fide purchaser defence operates at common law in relation to money to vest legal title in the purchaser. At the same time, the defence extinguishes personal claims: see eg *Lipkin Gorman v Karpnale Ltd* [1991] 2 AC 548; *Miller v Race* (1758) 1 Burr 452, 97 ER 398.
[89] For the importance of statutory context when considering issues of general equitable principle, see *Herdegen v Federal Commissioner of Taxation* (1988) 84 ALR 271, 283; *Corumo Holdings Pty Ltd v C Itoh Ltd* (1991) 24 NSWLR 370, 398; *CPT Custodian Pty Ltd v Commissioner of State Revenue* [2005] HCA 53, (2005) 224 CLR 98 [14]–[15]; *Kennon v Spry* [2008] HCA 56, (2008) 83 ALJR 145, [52], [89], [154] and [162].

appears to be to continue the tradition that 'the doctrine of notice has no application to registered conveyancing'.[90] It undermines that purpose to require a purchaser of registered land to compensate trust beneficiaries for the loss of the land which the purchaser has bought where the purchaser knew that the transfer was taking place in breach of trust: the purchaser retains title free of the trust interests but the value of that title is removed, or substantially reduced, by the back door by requiring him to pay away in compensation the value of the equitable interests which have thereby been subordinated to the purchaser's legal title. The purchaser is left worse off as a result of the knowledge with which he entered into the transaction, which runs counter to the statutory purpose. Thus, knowing receipt claims must be sensitive to the manner in which section 29 orders priorities in registered land. As Charles Harpum has said:

> In *Williams & Glyn's Bank Ltd v Boland*, Lord Wilberforce stated more than once in his judgment that the doctrine of notice had no application to registered conveyancing, and that the only kind of notice recognised was by entry on the register. In registered conveyancing therefore, the liability of a recipient of trust property transferred in breach of trust must depend upon the provisions of the Land Registration Act 1925 and not upon questions of notice.[91]

The changes wrought by the Land Registration Act 2002 to the system of land registration in England and Wales do not provide any reason to take a different view.

To return to Vinelott J's argument, mentioned earlier, that it would be 'very anomalous'[92] if there were to be a distinction between the beneficiaries' rights depending on whether the land were registered or unregistered, the answer is that this is a consequence of the very difference which the introduction of registration systems is intended to create. No such registration system has been introduced regarding trust interests in unregistered land. Thus, where the land is unregistered, the traditional equitable doctrines of notice continue to govern not only the transferee's personal liability in knowing receipt, but also the beneficiaries' proprietary claims against the property. It is those notice-based doctrines that the registration system is designed to avoid,[93] with the consequence that one would expect there to be differences between the way in which a transferee will be

---

[90] *Boland* (n 79) 508; *Thompson v Foy* [2009] EWHC 1076 (Ch) at [134]. There are, of course, specific limited statutory exceptions to this proposition: see eg Land Registration Act 2002, s 11(5). See further n 93 below.

[91] Harpum (n 74) 271–72. See also text accompanying n 72 above.

[92] See text accompanying n 9 above.

[93] This is not to suggest that notice is entirely irrelevant in the registered land context. The Land Registration Act 2002 refers to notice in a number of places: see eg s 11(5). A narrower version of the doctrine of notice is also present in sched 3, para 2 which refers to 'actual knowledge'. However, in contrast to the approach that applies to unregistered land, notice is not the central criterion for determining the priority of trust beneficiaries' interests following a registered disposition for valuable consideration.

affected by the receipt of registered and unregistered land respectively. It undermines the registered land system to accept that the transferee's title is unaffected by pre-existing equitable proprietary interests where section 29 applies, but to hold nonetheless that the transferee must pay further compensation (that is, in addition to the price that he paid, which triggered the application of section 29) for having received the title free of those equitable interests.

In summary, knowing receipt should be inapplicable against a registered purchaser who can claim the benefit of section 29. In general terms, outside the context of registered land, the knowing receipt claim is parasitic on the proprietary nature of the beneficiaries' equitable interests in the trust property: it is a claim to vindicate those property rights once they are no longer able to be vindicated *in specie*. The purpose served by such claims runs directly counter to the purpose of section 29, which is to protect purchasers from the effect of pre-existing interests irrespective of whether the purchaser has notice of those interests. Although it seeks to achieve that purpose merely by 'postponing' the pre-existing interests to those of the registered purchaser, it would undermine the function of section 29 if that were used as a reason to allow the personal claim in knowing receipt where proprietary interests are no longer enforceable. As explained above, knowing receipt is sensitive to, and respects, the manner in which section 29 orders the priority of competing interests in land. To allow a knowing receipt claim to lie against the registered transferee would subvert the function that section 29 was designed to perform, even though it might be formally consistent with the language used in the section. Furthermore, it would also undermine the purpose which section 29 is intended to achieve if knowing receipt claims were to be recognised on the basis that the purchaser acquires a merely equitable interest in the property which is subject to the trust beneficiaries' interests before registration. Again, to allow knowing receipt to operate in such circumstances, against a purchaser who ultimately registers his interest, would stultify the aims of land registration and therefore, as a matter of principle, should be rejected.

E. DISHONEST ASSISTANCE

However, the argument that knowing receipt claims ought not to be permitted where the person to whom property has been transferred in breach of trust has received a registered title to land does not entail that all *in personam* claims are ruled out. As has already been mentioned in Part C, the registration system is not inconsistent with the availability of *in personam* claims per se. In particular, the argument that it would be inappropriate to recognise knowing receipt claims because they are concerned with protecting and vindicating proprietary interests that have been relegated by the statutory registration system does not entail that other claims, based on wrongdoing rather than the protection of proprietary interests, ought also to be rejected.

For example, if it can be shown that the disponee assisted in the breach of trust in a dishonest fashion, the trust beneficiaries ought still to be able to pursue a claim in dishonest assistance.

This is relevant in the context under consideration, because *receipt* of property that was been transferred in breach of trust can potentially be considered to be of *assistance* in the breach of trust, in the sense of putting the trust assets beyond the reach of the beneficiaries. As Lord Millett recognised in *Dubai Aluminium Co Ltd v Salaam*, receipt of trust property can constitute assistance in a breach of trust for the purposes of liability for dishonest assistance:

> Dishonest receipt gives rise to concurrent liability, since the claim can be based on the defendant's dishonesty, treating the receipt itself as incidental, *being merely the particular form taken by the defendant's participation in the breach of fiduciary duty*; but it can also be based simply on the receipt.[94]

The argument that liability for dishonest assistance ought to be possible against a registered purchaser, notwithstanding that the Land Registration Act 2002, section 29 applies, can be tested by reference to someone who assists in the commission of a breach of trust but who does not receive the trust property in any way. Assuming that such a person acted dishonestly in the assistance he provided,[95] he would be liable on the basis that he has dishonestly involved himself in the trustee's breach of duty.[96] While the trustee's duties are clearly connected with the trust property, in that the trustee's fundamental duty is to account for his stewardship of that property, a claim for dishonest assistance is not limited to assistance that involves unauthorised transfer of the trust property and is certainly not dependent on receipt of the trust property by the defendant.[97] In other words, the defendant's liability in a dishonest assistance claim arises squarely on the basis of his wrongdoing—in assisting a wrong committed by another—rather than on the basis that the liability is necessary to vindicate property interests which have been lost because the defendant

---

[94] [2002] UKHL 48, [2003] 2 AC [87] (emphasis added). See also *Wilson v Moore* (1834) 1 My & K 337, 353 and 362; 39 ER 709, 718; *Agip* (Ch D) (n 72) 291–93 (upheld on appeal: [1991] Ch 547 (CA)).

[95] *Royal Brunei Airlines Sdn Bhd v Tan* [1995] 2 AC 378 (PC) 392; *Twinsectra Ltd v Yardley* [2002] UKHL 12, [2002] 2 AC 164 [20] and [36]; *Barlow Clowes International Ltd v Eurotrust International Ltd* [2005] UKPC 37, [2006] 1 WLR 1476 [10]. The position differs in Australia, where the breach of trust must have been dishonest, but the assistant need not have acted dishonestly: *Farah* (HCA) (n 64) [163].

[96] See eg *Farah* (HCA) (n 64) [121].

[97] This point further emphasises the central importance of property to the claim in knowing receipt.

acted wrongly with respect to the property of another. As Millett J said in *Agip*, in a dishonest assistance case 'the basis of the stranger's liability is not receipt of trust property but participation in a fraud'.[98]

As the source of the claim is wrongdoing rather than property there is no reason to exclude such a claim merely because the trust property happens fortuitously to be registered land. Indeed, it would be extremely odd to hold that someone who dishonestly assists in a breach of trust is liable unless the trust property happened to be registered land in which case they are somehow protected by the land registration system notwithstanding that they never received the trust property. Further, there is no good reason for a defendant who dishonestly assists in a breach of trust to be exonerated from liability for his dishonest wrongdoing merely because he also happened to receive title to the trust property—it would be strange if that form of assistance in the breach of trust were to immunise the defendant from liability.[99]

However, if this view is adopted and dishonest assistance claims are permitted where the receipt of registered title to land can be said to have (dishonestly) assisted in the breach of trust, a difficulty will arise in determining what constitutes dishonesty. This difficulty arises because the concept of honesty, although objectively applied in dishonest assistance claims, 'does have a strong subjective element in that it is a description of a type of conduct assessed in the light of what a person actually knew at the time'.[100] Where the relevant assistance involves receipt of title to registered land, the dishonesty of the transferee's conduct will depend on what the transferee knew, which seems again to run counter to the purposes of the land registration system. For example, in *Barlow Clowes*, the Privy Council concluded that the defendant acted dishonestly when he 'consciously decided not to make inquiries because he preferred in his own interest not to run the risk of discovering the truth'.[101] On the other hand, in *Abou-Rahmah v Abacha*, general suspicions (as opposed to suspicions regarding particular transactions) were held not to provide a sufficient foundation for a finding of dishonesty.[102] The same difficulty arises in the Australasian Torrens land registration systems, which generally provide that a registered owner's title is indefeasible unless he acted fraudulently,[103] which is con-

---

[98] *Agip* (Ch D) (n 72) 292.
[99] This is also consistent with Land Registration Act 2002, s 26(3), which distinguishes between the existence of a breach of trust (or other ground of unlawfulness) and the effect that has on the transaction which constitutes the breach. In other words, there can be a breach of trust (and so assistance in it) even if the title of the counterparty to the transaction that constitutes the breach of trust is protected from the effect of that breach.
[100] *Tan* (n 95) 389.
[101] *Barlow Clowes* (n 95) [11]–[12].
[102] [2006] EWCA Civ 1492, [2007] 1 All ER (Comm) 827 [72].
[103] See eg Land Transfer Act 1952 (NZ), s 62.

strued as requiring 'some act of dishonesty',[104] while also providing that mere knowledge of the interests of others does not constitute fraud.[105]

> The determination of what is and is not fraud remains a troublesome problem, and one of the major factors in relation to the concept of fraud in the Torrens system statutes is to decide what factors must be present in addition to mere knowledge in order to constitute fraud.[106]

Something more than mere knowledge of the pre-existing interest is required, and knowledge that the interest is in existence and will be defeated by registration is not fraud,[107] but guidance on where the line is to be drawn has not been particularly clear.[108] The Privy Council said, for example, in *Waimiha Sawmilling* that:

> If the designed object of a transfer be to cheat a man of a known existing right, that is fraudulent, and so also fraud may be established by a deliberate and dishonest trick causing an interest not to be registered and thus fraudulently keeping the register clear. It is not, however, necessary or wise to give abstract illustrations of what may constitute fraud in hypothetical conditions, for each case must depend upon its own circumstances. The act must be dishonest, and dishonesty must not be assumed solely by reason of knowledge of an unregistered interest.[109]

Without entering into a detailed analysis of the nature of fraud under the Torrens systems of land registration, it is suggested that they illustrate the possibility that a legitimate distinction could be drawn in England between situations (1) where the transferee has knowledge of a pre-existing equitable interest, and even knowledge that the interest will be defeated by section 29 on registration, and (2) where the transferee deliberately set out, in combination with the trustee, to destroy those interests.[110] The transferee's knowledge in the first category of case ought not to amount to dishonesty for the purposes of bringing a claim in dishonest assistance. But where the only reason for the transaction having been instigated is as part of a deliberate contrivance to destroy the trust beneficiaries' interests, assis-

---

[104] *Waimiha Sawmilling Co Ltd v Waione Timber Co Ltd* [1926] AC 101 (PC) 106. See also *Assets Co Ltd v Roihi* [1905] AC 176 (PC) 210; *Butler v Fairclough* (1917) 23 CLR 78, 90; *Wicks v Bennett* (1921) 30 CLR 80, 91; *Stuart v Kingston* (1923) 32 CLR 309, 329.

[105] See eg Land Transfer Act 1952 (NZ), s 182.

[106] GW Hinde, DW McMorland, NR Campbell and DR Grinlinton, *Land Law in New Zealand* (Wellington, Butterworths, 1997) para 2.055.

[107] *Bahr v Nicolay (No 2)* (1988) 164 CLR 604, 653; *Mills v Stokman* (1967) 116 CLR 61, 78; *RM Hosking Properties Pty Ltd v Barnes* [1971] SASR 100, 103; *Bunt v Hallinan* [1985] 1 NZLR 450 (NZCA) 462.

[108] The Australian and New Zealand authorities have drawn the line in different places: *Sutton v O'Kane* [1973] 2 NZLR 304 (NZCA) 323 and 346; *Bunt v Hallinan* [1985] 1 NZLR 450 (NZCA) 459; A Mason, 'Indefeasibility—Logic or Legend?' in DR Grinlinton (ed), *Torrens in the Twenty-first Century* (Wellington, LexisNexis, 2003) 9; P Blanchard, 'Indefeasibility under the Torrens System in New Zealand' in Grinlinton, ibid, 29, 41–44.

[109] *Waimiha Sawmilling* (n 104) 106–07. See also *Stuart* (n 104) 359.

[110] See eg *Efstratiou v Glantschnig* [1972] NZLR 594 (NZCA).

tance in that scheme could legitimately sound in a compensatory claim for dishonest assistance, irrespective of whether the assister received title to the trust assets and irrespective of whether any title which he did receive is protected by section 29. Such a claim is an equitable analogue to the conspiracy claim that was brought in *Midland Bank v Green* (where the transaction was not itself a breach of trust, but rather a breach of the son's option).[111]

The consequence of this analysis may seem slightly odd, in that we argue that the recipient of registered land transferred in breach of trust ought to be able to avoid a personal claim in knowing receipt where section 29 of the Land Registration Act 2002 applies, but the same person may be held liable for dishonest assistance in the breach of trust. However, the reason for drawing that distinction is that dishonest assistance liability does not run counter to the fundamental principles of the land registration system. Systems of registered land are concerned to ensure that purchasers are protected from notice or knowledge of pre-existing interests other than those which are recorded on the register or otherwise specifically protected, but that is quite distinct from saying that purchasers ought also to be free dishonestly to assist trustees to commit breaches of trust where the trust property happens to be registered land. The facilitation of conveyancing which registered land systems are designed to bring about reduces the protection that trust beneficiaries would otherwise have, but there is no need for it to be reduced to the point where dishonest assistance in a breach of trust must be left unremedied. That distinction can be justified by reference to the differences in the fundamental nature of the distinct *in personam* claims for knowing receipt and dishonest assistance respectively: 'the basis of liability in the two types of cases is quite different'.[112]

F. CONCLUSIONS

In summary, in situations where trust property is registered land and the trustee transfers title to that land in breach of trust, if the disposition was made for valuable consideration so that the transferee can claim the benefit of section 29 of the Land Registration Act 2002 to avoid the beneficiaries' pre-existing equitable interests in the land, the transferee ought also to be immune from a personal claim for knowing receipt. This conclusion can be supported in two ways. First, the practical effect of section 29 is that the transferee receives title to the land free of the trust interests and so does not receive 'trust property', which is a necessary pre-requisite to the claim in knowing receipt of trust property. Secondly, the purpose of systems of

---

[111] See text accompanying nn 37–38 above.
[112] *Agip* (Ch D) (n 72) 292.

land registration is to avoid the pitfalls of equitable doctrine's traditional rules regarding notice of equitable interests. To allow a claim in knowing receipt subverts that purpose, because the knowing receipt claim is fundamentally a claim for compensation based on the recipient, once he receives trust property, acting wrongly in knowingly putting the property of another beyond the reach of that other person. It is a claim to vindicate equitable proprietary interests, and ought not to be permitted where those proprietary interests are no longer enforceable against the recipient by virtue of section 29. In other words, section 29 should be seen as the functional equivalent of doctrines such as overreaching and bona fide purchase: it protects registered purchasers against pre-existing proprietary interests and so ought to protect such purchasers against personal claims that are parasitic on those pre-existing proprietary interests. The difference between this and the situation that arises where the trust property is unregistered land is not anomalous, as it is simply a consequence of the fact that trust interests in unregistered land remain governed by the traditional equitable doctrines of notice. Finally, the argument that claims in knowing receipt ought not to be permitted where section 29 applies does not mean that other *in personam* claims are inapplicable. In particular, where the transferee can be said to have assisted in the breach of trust, and that conduct was dishonest by the standards of ordinary reasonable people, a claim can legitimately lie against the transferee for compensation for dishonest assistance, notwithstanding the protection that section 29 affords.

6

The Centrality of Constructive and Resulting Trusts

BEN McFARLANE

A. TWO PERSPECTIVES

How central are constructive and resulting trusts to the law of trusts? The answer given to this question, like any survey of a particular field, will depend on the observer's perspective. On a particular (and not uncommon) view of the law of trusts, constructive and resulting trusts are anomalies in special need of justification. On this view, the existence of an express trust can be simply explained: a party with a right (the settlor) has exercised a power to ensure that his right be held in a particular way. That power can be exercised either by the settlor transferring his right to a trustee to hold on trust for a beneficiary; or by the settlor declaring that he holds his right on trust for a beneficiary. This perspective does not depend on, but is often linked to, the equally common view that a beneficiary under a trust has a property right. The settlor is viewed in much the same way as a party with a freehold who gives another a legal lease or legal easement: he has simply dealt with his property in such a way as to give another a right in that property. Of course, a number of trusts, usually labelled as constructive or resulting trusts, cannot be accommodated within this model: they are so labelled precisely because their existence cannot readily be explained as dependent on a settlor's exercise of his power to set up a trust.

On this first view, it may be possible to rehabilitate at least some of these anomalous constructive and resulting trusts by explaining that, initial appearances notwithstanding, they also depend on a settlor's exercise of his power to set up a trust.[1] However, some such trusts simply cannot be

---

[1] See eg the explanation of *Hodgson v Marks* [1971] Ch 892 given at first instance by Ungoed-Thomas J and developed in WJ Swadling, 'A Hard Look at *Hodgson v Marks*' in PBH Birks and FD Rose (eds), *Restitution and Equity: Resulting Trusts and Equitable Compensation* (London, Mansfield Press, 2000) 61. See too Swadling's analysis of *Rochefoucauld v Boustead* [1897] 1 Ch 196 in the present volume (ch 3).

dressed up in that way: the constructive trust recognised by the Privy Council in *Attorney-General of Hong Kong v Reid*[2] provides one obvious example; the form of resulting trust recognised by the House of Lords in *Vandervell v IRC*[3] provides another. On the first view, then, such trusts remain unprotected and open to doubt; it may even be argued that our highest courts have been mistaken in recognising them.[4] After all, it seems that a legal lease or legal easement cannot arise unless a grantor has exercised his power to create such a right;[5] why should anyone acquire a right under a trust if a settlor has not exercised his power to create such a right? Further, even if such a trust arises to protect its beneficiary, why should that party receive an equitable property right rather than a personal right?[6]

The main purpose of this chapter is to argue against both that first view and the proprietary model of the trust to which it is linked. Building on the analyses of Professor Chambers and Professor Smith, as well as my own work in *The Structure of Property Law*,[7] it will be argued that resulting and constructive trusts are far from anomalous and that is a mistake to accord primacy to the express trust. This argument depends on surveying the field of trusts from a second perspective. On this view, the existence of a trust depends not on the creation of a particular form of property-holding but, instead, on the concept of a 'duty-burdened right'. To acquire a right under a trust, it is essential for the beneficiary (B) to show that the trustee (A) both holds a particular right and is under a duty to B in relation to that right. Those basic requirements apply to any situation in which B claims 'an equitable property right'; to show that such a right arises under a trust, B must also show that A is under the 'core trust duty': a duty to B not to use A's right for A's own benefit (unless and to the extent that A is also a beneficiary of the trust). From this second perspective, resulting and constructive trusts are not anomalous: they are simply cases in which the core trust duty arises not because of a settlor's exercise of a power to impose that duty on A but, instead, for some other reason.

---

[2] [1994] 1 AC 324 (PC).

[3] [1967] 2 AC 291.

[4] For arguments against the form of constructive trust recognised in *Reid* (n 2), see eg R Goode 'Ownership and Obligation in Commercial Transactions' (1987) 103 *Law Quarterly Review* 433, 441–45; R Goode 'Property and Unjust Enrichment' in AS Burrows (ed), *Essays on the Law of Restitution* (Oxford, Clarendon Press, 1991) 215. For the view that the form of resulting trust recognised in *Vandervell* (n 2) 'defies legal analysis', see W Swadling, 'Explaining Resulting Trusts' (2008) 124 *Law Quarterly Review* 72.

[5] It can be argued that the acquisition of a legal easement by prescription does not depend on a freehold owner of the servient tenement having exercised a power to grant an easement (see eg B McFarlane, *The Structure of Property Law* (Oxford, Hart Publishing, 2008) 864–70). However, the courts explain the doctrine of prescription as resting on an implied grant: see eg *Gardner v Hodgson's Kingston Brewery Co* [1903] AC 229, 239 (Lord Lindley).

[6] Swadling has drawn attention to this important question: eg Swadling (n 4) 98 and 101.

[7] McFarlane (n 5) esp parts B, C1, D2 and F3. See too B McFarlane, 'Equity, Obligations and Third Parties' [2008] *Singapore Law Journal* 308.

Indeed, on this second view, if we really have to pick on particular trusts, it can be said that express trusts are the true anomaly. For example, in *Reid*, the Privy Council advised that A, having received a bribe to act contrary to his duty to B, held that bribe on constructive trust for B. The existence of that trust depends on A's duty to B not to use the bribe received by A for A's own benefit; it is possible to see that duty as depending on A's fiduciary duty to B not to make a profit from his position. In *Vandervell*, the House of Lords held that an option to purchase shares, granted by the Royal College of Surgeons to the Vandervell Trustee Company (A), was held by the Trustee Company on resulting trust for Mr Vandervell (B), who had been solely beneficially entitled to the shares and had ordered that they be transferred to the Royal College. The existence of that trust depends on A's duty to B not to use the option for A's own benefit, where that option was viewed by the court as effectively acquired from B; it is possible to see that duty as depending on A's duty not to unjustly retain an enrichment received at B's expense.[8] So, in each of *Reid* and *Vandervell*, A's duty to B arises, and B thus acquires his right under a trust, due to a principle that is firmly established as a means by which A may come under a duty to B. By way of contrast, consider the case where A simply declares that he holds a right on trust for B. In a very general way, we can say that A's duty to B arises because of A's consent; but it is nonetheless remarkable that a gratuitous, oral declaration of A, on which B has in no way relied, can impose a duty on A to B. As Hackney memorably puts it:

> I can informally transfer to you my economic advantages in chattels of huge value by a few significantly chosen words, and once simply done the act cannot be revoked. No other device in the legal system approaches the massive power of these spoken words in Equity: 'I declare myself trustee of this for you.'[9]

Similarly, where a settlor sets up a trust by transferring a right to A to hold on trust for B, it may initially seem surprising that a gratuitous undertaking, made by A to the settlor, can lead to A's being under a duty to B. It is tempting to turn the tables in this way, and thus to reject the idea that any resulting or constructive trusts need rehabilitating in the emperor's new clothes of the express trust. However, such a move would obscure the

---

[8] See eg R Chambers, *Resulting Trusts* (Oxford, Clarendon Press, 1997) ch 2.

[9] J Hackney, *Understanding Equity and Trusts* (London, Fontana, 1987) 109. Langbein has also pointed to the seemingly anomalous nature of such self-declared trusts: J Langbein, 'The Contractarian Basis of the Law of Trusts' (1995) 105 *Yale Law Journal* 625, 628, 645 and 672–75. I am grateful to John Mee for pointing out to me that the self-declared trust was first recognised as valid only in *ex parte Pye* (1811) 18 Ves Jun 140, 34 ER 271. As noted by GS Alexander, 'The Transformation of Trusts as a Legal Category, 1800–1914' (1987) 5 *Law & History Review* 303, 329: 'No prior Equity decision had recognized the validity of a gratuitous declaration of trust, but [Lord] Eldon enforced [the] arrangement on that ground without even discussing the point.'

central point made here: no trust in which A is genuinely under the core trust duty to B should be treated as anomalous, as any such trust falls within the conceptual definition of the trust.[10]

B. MOVING TO THE SECOND PERSPECTIVE

The starting point in defining the trust must be the ability of B (a trust beneficiary) to assert a right not only against his trustee (A) but also against third parties. One way to explain this ability is to see B as having an 'equitable property right', or even as having 'equitable title to' or 'equitable ownership of' the right held on trust by A. However, as a number of commentators have pointed out, there are insuperable problems with the 'equitable ownership' analysis.[11] First, as Maitland noted 100 years ago, it is premised on the absurdity that, within one country, there exist two sets of rules and that under the first set, A has ownership, whereas, under the second, B has ownership.[12] Second, the 'equitable ownership' analysis suggests that the existence of a trust depends on the carving out of B's right from the right initially held by the settlor. Yet, if it were the case that any unencumbered holder of a right had both legal and equitable ownership, any express trust would involve a disposition by the settlor of a pre-existing beneficial interest and so, due to section 53(1)(c) of the Law of Property Act 1925, would require writing signed by the settlor. Certainly, the notion that a resulting trust may arise as a result of a settlor failing to give away a pre-existing equitable title has been rejected at the highest judicial level.[13] The better view, as has been noted by Professors Chambers and Smith,[14] is that, to adopt the phrase used by Dr Jones when examining the development of the trust in the seventeenth century, 'the creation of a trust is a process of cumulation, and not division'.[15] That view is certainly supported

---

[10] Eg Langbein (n 9) treats the self-declared trust in an appendix: this marginalisation of that form of trust reveals an important weakness in his contractarian analysis of the trust.

[11] See eg F Maitland, *Equity, Also the Forms of Action at Common Law: Two Courses of Lectures* (Cambridge, Cambridge University Press, 1909) chs 9–11; H Stone, 'The Nature of the Rights of the Cestui Que Trust' (1917) 17 *Columbia Law Review* 647; R Chambers, *An Introduction to Property Law in Australia*, 2nd edn (Sydney, Lawbook Co, 2008) para 13.90; L Smith, 'Trust and Patrimony' (2008) 38 *Revue Générale de Droit* 9, para 15.

[12] Maitland (n 11) chs 9–11.

[13] *Westdeutsche Landesbank Girozentrale v Islington LBC* [1996] AC 669, 706–07 (Lord Browne-Wilkinson). As noted by Mee in this volume (ch 7), the fact that an unencumbered holder of a right does not have a distinct equitable title to that right does not necessarily prevent the notion of 'retention' having some metaphorical purchase in explaining at least some resulting trusts.

[14] See eg Chambers (n 11) para 13.90; L Smith, 'Philosophical Foundations of Proprietary Remedies' in R Chambers, C Mitchell and J Penner (eds), *Philosophical Foundations of The Law of Unjust Enrichment* (Oxford, Oxford University Press, 2009) 281.

[15] N Jones, 'Trusts in England after the Statute of Uses: A View from the 16th Century' in R Helmholz and R Zimmerman (eds), *Itinera Fiduciae: Trust and Treuhand in Historical Perspective* (Berlin, Duncker & Humblot, 1998) 190.

by the analysis of Brennan J in *DKLR Holding Co (No 2) Ltd v Commissioner of Stamp Duties*: 'an equitable interest is not carved out of a legal estate but impressed upon it'.[16]

The notion that a beneficiary of a trust has an 'equitable property right' is also problematic for at least two further reasons. A standard usage of the term 'property right' focuses on the question 'against whom can the right be asserted?'[17] If B has a personal right against A, then such a right, by definition, can be asserted against A alone.[18] However, if B has a property right, that right imposes prima facie duties not only on A but also on the rest of the world. So, if A has sold his car to B, and X then takes the car, X (on the face of it) has breached a duty to B and thus committed a wrong against B. In contrast, if A has simply agreed to sell his car to B and X then takes the car, X (on the face of it) has breached no duty to B. On this view, then, a property right is a right that imposes a prima facie duty on the rest of the world. However, it is not true to say that all such rights are viewed as property rights. For example, B's right to physical integrity or to his reputation also imposes a prima facie duty on the rest of the world; yet such rights are not generally regarded as property rights. It therefore seems that a property right may be defined as a right, *relating to a specific physical thing separate from the right-holder,*[19] that imposes a prima facie duty on the rest of the world.

That definition draws a useful distinction between property rights on the one hand and personal rights on the other. However, it causes problems for the concept of an 'equitable property right'. First, it is clear that, if B has such a right, A and the rest of the world are *not* under the same prima facie duties to B. For example, if A holds A's ownership of goods on trust for B, and those goods are then stolen or carelessly damaged by X, X (on the face of it) breaches no duty to B.[20] In this sense, an 'equitable property right' does *not* impose a prima facie duty on the rest of the world. Second, it is clear that an 'equitable property right' need not relate to a specific physical thing. For example, if A holds a bank account on trust for B, there is no

---

[16] (1982) 149 CLR 431. For further consideration of the *DKLR* case, see ch 7 below.

[17] Birks uses the term 'exigibility' to refer to that question: eg PBH Birks, 'Five Keys to Land Law' in S Bright and J Dewar (eds), *Land Law: Themes and Perspectives* (Oxford, Oxford University Press, 1998) 457, 473.

[18] This is not inconsistent with the fact that the existence of A's duty to B may impose different, ancillary duties on the rest of the world (such as a duty not to procure a breach by A of A's contractual duty to B): see McFarlane 'Equity' (n 7).

[19] For discussion, see eg J Penner, *The Idea of Property in Law* (Oxford, Oxford University Press, 1997) ch 5. Penner's analysis allows property rights to exist in relation to non-physical things (provided they are separate from the rights-holder). For a more narrow analysis, see A Pretto-Sakmann, *Boundaries of Personal Property: Shares and Sub-Shares* (Oxford, Hart Publishing, 2005); McFarlane (n 5) 132–37.

[20] See eg *MCC Proceeds Inc v Lehman Brothers (International) Europe* [1998] 4 All ER 675 (CA); *Leigh & Sillivan Ltd v Aliakmon Shipping Co Ltd, The Aliakmon* [1986] AC 785; A Tettenborn, 'Trust Property and Conversion: An Equitable Confusion' [1996] *Cambridge Law Journal* 36.

specific physical thing to which B's 'equitable property right' relates. This point has been noted by Professor Chambers, who distinguishes between those property rights that relate to things (legal property rights) and those that relate to rights (equitable property rights).[21] An alternative position is that the term 'property right', to remain coherent, should be limited to rights relating to a physical thing that impose a prima facie duty on the rest of the world. On this view, the term 'equitable property right' is misleading and should be replaced.[22]

It is vital to note that this alternative position does not view an 'equitable property right' as no more than a personal right.[23] Such a view would be inconsistent with the additional protection against certain third parties enjoyed by a holder of an 'equitable property right'. Instead, the view offers a different explanation of the power of such rights to affect third parties. On this analysis, an 'equitable property right' is not a right against a thing, nor simply a right against a person: it is rather a right against a right. So, if A holds a right (whether it be a personal right or a property right) on trust for B, then B has a right against A's right. This means that, if B can follow that right into the hands of a third party (C), it may also be possible for B to show that C is under a duty to B, even if C, when acquiring his right, had no actual or constructive notice of B's prior right.[24] In particular, it means that B receives protection in A's insolvency: if the right held by A on trust were to pass to A's trustee in bankruptcy, B could in any case prevent the trustee in bankruptcy using that right for the benefit of A's general creditors.[25]

Analysing 'equitable property rights' as rights against rights has certain advantages. It can explain the fact that B can have such a right in relation to a personal right held by A; and it can explain why B can make a claim against a third party, such as C, who acquires a right that depends on A's right, but not against X, who acquires no such right. Further, the analysis, unlike an analysis which sees the separation of legal and equitable title as constitutive of an 'equitable property right', can account for cases in which A holds an equitable right on trust for B. For example, if Z holds a right on trust for A, it is clear that A can then hold his right on trust for B. Such a sub-trust arises because A holds a particular right (A's right under the head trust) and is under a duty to B in relation to that right.

---

[21] Chambers (n 11) para 13.90. W Swadling, 'The Law of Property' in A Burrows (ed), *English Private Law*, 2nd edn (Oxford, Oxford University Press, 2008) paras 4.140–4.147 also makes the point that the subject-matter of a trust is never a thing but rather a right held by the trustee.

[22] McFarlane (n 5) 25–32; McFarlane (n 7).

[23] It therefore differs from the views of eg Maitland (n 11) and Stone (n 11).

[24] Of course, if C has also given value in return for the right, he will be able to use the 'bona fide purchaser' defence and will therefore acquire his right free from any liability to B.

[25] It is for that reason that rights held by A on trust do not form part of A's estate on bankruptcy: see Insolvency Act 1986, s 283(3)(a).

C. OBJECTIONS TO CONSTRUCTIVE AND RESULTING TRUSTS

From the first perspective, B, a party claiming rights under a constructive or resulting trust, may be faced by an important objection: given that, by definition, no one has successfully exercised a power to set up a trust in B's favour, why should B acquire the benefits associated with a right under a trust? For example, in a case such as *Reid*, why should B (the Hong Kong government) enjoy the protection in A's insolvency denied to other parties against whom A has committed a wrong? From the second perspective, the method by which B can overcome that objection is clear. Let us imagine that V was carelessly injured by A. In such a case, A has breached a primary duty to V and, as a result, has come under a secondary duty to pay V a sum of money. It is clear that A's duty to V does not currently relate to any *specific* right held by A: if A is ordered to pay V £10,000, A need not take that sum from any particular source. In contrast, if A receives a bribe of £10,000 in breach of his fiduciary duty to B, it seems that A comes under a duty to B in relation to that very right to £10,000: A is not permitted to use that right for his own benefit. As a result, B, in contrast to V, acquires more than a personal right against A: B has a right against a specific right held by A. From a functional perspective, it may seem that the legal system has given B an advantage over V—certainly, B has less to fear from A's insolvency. However, from a conceptual perspective, the difference between B's position and V's position depends on the very nature of an 'equitable property right': it arises if, and only if, A's duty relates to a specific right held by A.

On this view, there is no reason to prioritise express trusts: such trusts may be functionally very important; but, conceptually, they simply constitute examples of a wider principle. That principle means that a trust *must* exist whenever A is under a duty to B in relation to a particular right held by A,[26] provided that A's duty includes the 'core trust duty': a duty not to use that right for his own benefit, unless and to the extent that A is also a beneficiary of the trust. The finding of a trust in *Reid*, therefore, does not depend on a specific policy of giving B extra protection in A's insolvency; rather, as soon as A comes under the core trust duty to B, there is no need or room for policy in justifying the existence of a trust. Indeed, if A would otherwise be under the core trust duty to B, the only role policy may play is to justify an exceptional rule *denying* B a right under a trust. This may occur, for example, where A's attempt to set up a trust in B's favour can be set aside under the provisions of the Insolvency Act 1986 as a transaction at

---

[26] McFarlane (n 5) 23–25. Professor Smith has drawn attention to the key idea that 'equitable property rights' depend on A's being under a duty in relation to a particular right: eg L Smith, 'Unravelling Proprietary Restitution' [2004] *Canadian Business Law Journal* 317; Smith (n 14); Smith (n 11) para 17.

an undervalue or as an unlawful preference.[27] Of course, in such cases, the relevant policy concerns are far more likely to be used as a means to invalidate an express trust rather than a constructive or resulting trust.

From the second perspective, therefore, constructive and resulting trusts need no special justification. In a case such as *Reid*, it is simply not possible both to accept that A was under a duty to B not to use the bribe for A's own benefit *and* to deny that B acquired a right under a trust. Whenever B claims that a trust has arisen, we need to ask: (i) if there is a good reason for A's being under a duty to B; and (ii) if that reason also demands that A's duty to B relates to a specific right held by A; and (iii) if that reason also demands that A is under a duty to B not to use that right for A's own benefit (unless and to the extent that A is also a beneficiary of the trust). On this view, there are three forms of objection that can be made when B claims a right under a trust.

1. The First Objection

B's claim to a trust should be rejected where there is no legally recognised reason for A's being under a duty to B. For example, in the somewhat notorious case of *Burns v Burns*,[28] Mrs Burns claimed that Mr Burns, whom she had lived with for almost 20 years, held his freehold on trust for both himself and Mrs Burns. The Court of Appeal found against Mrs Burns: the essence of their Lordships' reasoning was that, whilst Mrs Burns had made a number of contributions to her family life with Mr Burns and their children, there was no legally recognised reason for Mr Burns to be under any duty to Mrs Burns.

It is important to note that, whilst the second perspective reveals the centrality of resulting and constructive trusts, it does not necessarily lead to an expansion in the scope of resulting and constructive trusts. Indeed, it may lead to a contraction: for example, the second perspective casts doubt on the form of constructive trust recognised in *Re Rose*[29] and applied in *Pennington v Waine*.[30] In the latter case, the Court of Appeal found that A, as a result of her attempts to transfer shares to B (her nephew), held those shares on trust for B at the time of her death. Whilst the reasoning in the case is far from clear, both Arden and Clarke LJJ found that A had made an 'equitable assignment' of the shares to B. The reasoning seems to be that, whilst A's attempt to transfer the shares had failed at common law, it had succeeded in Equity. That reasoning is consistent with the first perspective and, in particular, the view that A, when simply holding the shares, had

---

[27] Insolvency Act 1986, ss 238–40 and 339–41.
[28] [1984] Ch 317 (CA).
[29] [1952] Ch 499 (CA).
[30] [2002] EWCA Civ 227, [2002] 1 WLR 2075.

both a legal and equitable interest in those shares. From the second perspective, however, the finding of a trust, like the finding of an equitable assignment,[31] depends on A's being under a duty to B in relation to a specific right held by A.[32] On this view, it is far harder to justify the finding of a constructive trust or equitable assignment in *Pennington*. There is no obvious reason why, simply as a result of her efforts to transfer her shares to B, A should come under a duty to B. The only possible grounds for such a duty might be B's reliance on A's unsuccessful attempts to make a gift (in *Pennington*, B had agreed to act as a director of the relevant company) but, as the law currently stands, it is difficult for B to found a claim on such reliance,[33] and it is not clear why it should necessarily lead to A's being under a duty to transfer the shares to B.[34]

2. The Second Objection

B's claim to a trust should be rejected where, although there is a legally recognised reason for A to be under a duty to B, that reason does not demand that A's duty relate to a specific right held by A. For example, in *Re Goldcorp Exchange Ltd*,[35] A had made a contractual promise to transfer ownership of gold bullion to B. As a result, B (unlike Mrs Burns) had a personal right against A. However, A had not promised to transfer any *specific* bullion to B: as a result, A's duty to B did not relate to a specific right held by A and B's claim to a trust failed.

Controversies over the scope of resulting and constructive trusts centre on this second objection. For example, in *Reid*, it can be argued that A's duty to B is adequately performed if A simply pays B a sum of money equal to any gains A has made by accepting the bribe.[36] On that view, A's duty to B, like the duty to pay damages to an accident victim, does not relate to any specific right held by A. Similarly, in a case such as *Vandervell*, it can be

---

[31] For an analysis of equitable assignment making use of the concept of a right against a right, see McFarlane (n 5) 27–8, 118–19 and 125–26.

[32] There is a further view: Chambers has argued that a trust arises where B has a *power* to acquire an asset currently held by A: eg Chambers (n 11) paras 24.95 and 29.145. That analysis can explain cases where, for example, A is under a duty to transfer a right to B and cases where, as in *Re Rose*, B is factually in a position to complete a transfer of a right initiated by A: eg R Chambers, C Mitchell and J Penner, 'Introduction' in Chambers et al (n 14) 1, 18. This analysis does, however, seem to collapse the distinction between trusts and mere equities: McFarlane (n 5) 226–27 and 513–14.

[33] For example, it is far from clear whether the doctrine of proprietary estoppel can apply in such a case: see eg the analysis of Lord Scott in *Yeoman's Row Management Limited v Cobbe* [2008] UKHL 55, [2008] 1 WLR 1752 [14] and [16].

[34] See eg *Jennings v Rice* [2002] EWCA Civ 259, [2003] 1 P & CR 100, where the court rejected the submission that a successful proprietary estoppel claim necessarily imposes a duty on A to keep a commitment made to B.

[35] [1995] 1 AC 74.

[36] As argued by Goode in the works cited in n 4.

argued that, to the extent that the Vandervell Trustee Company was enriched at Mr Vandervell's expense by the acquisition of the option, that enrichment can be adequately reversed by ordering the Company to pay a sum of money to Mr Vandervell.[37] If that argument is correct, there is no basis for Mr Vandervell to have a right against the option and so there can be no trust of that right.

For present purposes, it is unnecessary to evaluate the strength of the second objection in those particular cases. The crucial wider point concerns the general position of resulting and constructive trusts. It is whether it can *ever* be the case that: (i) A is under a duty to B not to use a right for A's own benefit; and (ii) A's duty has arisen for reasons other than someone exercising a power to set up a trust. The first point to make is that, given the varied grounds on which A can come under a duty to B, it would be very surprising to find that there are no such cases. Indeed, as Professor Chambers has noted,[38] where A is unjustly enriched at B's expense, and that enrichment consists precisely of A's receipt of a particular right from B, it would be no surprise if A came under a duty to B in relation to that very right. The second, and more important, point is that English law has undoubtedly recognised a number of such cases. The trusts recognised in *Reid* and *Vandervell* of course provide examples. Perhaps the simplest case is one noted by Professor Smith:[39] the trust recognised in *Mountney v Treharne*.[40] A court had made an order, in ancillary relief proceedings following a divorce, that one spouse (A) had to transfer particular rights to the other (B). As a result, a trust arose: the particular means by which A's duty to B arose (the court's order) was irrelevant; the key point was that, due to that court order, A came under the core trust duty to B. It should be noted that the finding of a trust in *Mountney* was important as it gave B additional protection in A's insolvency; however, as in *Reid*, that protection was simply the consequence of the fact that A's duty to B related to a specific right held by A. Further examples occur where A acquires a right having made a binding promise to hold that right on trust for B;[41] and where A makes a binding promise to transfer a right, currently held by A, to B. Where A's promise is to transfer a right to goods, it is almost always true to say that there is no room for a trust: A's right itself is transferred under the contract of sale. However, where A's contractual promise, by itself, cannot transfer A's right (as where further formal requirements must be met, as in the case of the transfer of shares,[42] subsisting equitable interests[43] or

---

[37] As argued in Swadling (n 4) 98 and 101.
[38] See esp R Chambers, 'Two Kinds of Enrichment' in Chambers et al (n 14) 242.
[39] Smith (n 14) 293.
[40] [2002] EWCA Civ 1174, [2003] Ch 135.
[41] See eg *Pullan v Koe* [1913] 1 Ch 9. Such a trust is not an express trust as it arises as soon as A acquires the relevant right, even in the absence of a declaration of trust by A.
[42] See eg *Parway Estates Ltd v IRC* (1958) 45 TC 135; *Michaels v Harley House (Marylebone) Ltd* [2000] Ch 104, esp 113–14.
[43] See eg *Neville v Wilson* [1997] Ch 144 (CA).

property rights in land)[44] that promise will give B a right against A's right: by his own contractual promise, A comes under a duty to B in relation to a specific right held by A.

The second perspective thus focuses on the nature of A's duty to B: a trust can arise only where A is under a duty to B not to use a particular right for A's own benefit (unless and to the extent that A is also a beneficiary of that trust). This requirement raises an important question about A's knowledge of the facts giving rise to A's duty to B. In the *Westdeutsche* case, Lord Browne-Wilkinson referred to the difficulty of imposing such a duty on A where A lacks sufficient knowledge of those facts.[45] For example, in a case such as *Chase Manhattan Bank NA v Israel-British Bank (London) Ltd*,[46] where B transfers a right to A in the mistaken belief that the transfer discharges a liability owed by B to A, it can be argued that, if A still holds that right when he learns of B's mistake, A comes under the core trust duty to B. However, it is more difficult to argue that A is under such a duty at a point when A does not know of B's mistake and has no reason to know of it. Certainly, if A, having received a right whilst sharing in B's genuine but mistaken belief that the transfer of the right from B to A discharged a liability owed by B to A, then proceeded to use that right for A's own benefit, it would be very difficult to say that A has breached a duty to B. Lord Browne-Wilkinson's analysis in *Westdeutsche* has not commanded general support,[47] but, judged from the second perspective, it correctly identifies an important limit on the scope of resulting and constructive trusts (and therefore on the scope of express trusts too): A's duty not to use a particular right for his own benefit cannot exist unless and until A has sufficient knowledge of the facts giving rise to that duty.

3. The Third Objection

It may be that there is a legally recognised reason for A to be under a duty to B; and that reason demands that A's duty relates to a specific right held by A. In these cases, B thus acquires an 'equitable property right': a right against A's right. However, as A is not under the core trust duty, B's right does not arise under a trust. An example occurs where A, in return for a loan from B, gives B a fixed equitable charge over a right held by A. A's contractual promise to hold that right as security for B means that A is

---

[44] See eg *Shaw v Foster* (1872) LR 5 HL 321; *Lysaght v Edwards* (1876) 2 Ch D 499. The third objection may, however, be relevant in these cases: see text at n 56 below.
[45] *Westdeutsche* (n 13) 714–15.
[46] [1981] Ch 105.
[47] Although, as discussed in part D.1, it is supported by the current test for liability in knowing receipt.

under a duty to B in relation to a specific right. However, A is otherwise free to use that right for his own benefit and so no trust arises.

This objection is clearly the least significant of the three: in many cases (such as where A has gone into insolvency), the crucial question is simply whether B has more than a personal right against A—it matters little whether or not B's right arises under a trust. Nonetheless, there may be practical situations where the correct characterisation of B's right does matter;[48] and it is in any case important to separate out trusts from other situations in which B has a right against a right of A. For example, in both *Yaxley v Gotts*[49] and *Kinane v Mackie-Conteh*,[50] A and B had entered into negotiations concerning the grant of a legal property right in land. In each case, no contractual agreement had been made, but B nonetheless performed his side of the planned deal, following encouragement from A that the deal would be completed. Under the doctrine of proprietary estoppel, at least as it stood before the House of Lords' decision in *Cobbe*,[51] A came under a duty to B in order to prevent B suffering a detriment as a result of his reasonable reliance on A.[52] In each case, A's duty was to perform his side of the planned deal: in *Yaxley*, this meant that A had to grant B a promised legal lease;[53] in *Kinane*, it meant that A had to grant B a promised legal charge. In each case, B must acquire an 'equitable property right': an equitable lease in *Yaxley* and an equitable charge in *Kinane*. B has more than a personal right against A as A's duty to B relates to A's power, as a holder of a legal estate in land, to grant B a particular form of legal property right. In each case, the Court of Appeal also described B's right as arising under a constructive trust. That terminology was adopted in order to reconcile B's acquisition of a right with the formality rule imposed by the Law of Property (Miscellaneous Provisions) Act 1989, section 2(5) of which acknowledges an exception for constructive trusts.

However, in each of *Yaxley* and *Kinane*, it is very difficult to see why B's right should arise under a trust.[54] A's duty was simply to grant B the promised legal property right; provided A complied with that duty, A was otherwise free to use his legal estate as he wished. It seems the court made a purely functional use of the constructive trust label as a means to justify B's acquisition of a right as a result of A's oral promise. However, there is no need for the term to be abused in that way. For example, in *Crabb v*

---

[48] Eg the rules set out by the Trusts of Land and Appointment of Trustees Act 1996 apply if, and only, there is a trust of land.
[49] [2000] Ch 162.
[50] [2005] EWCA Civ 45, [2005] WTLR 345.
[51] *Cobbe* (n 33).
[52] See further McFarlane (n 7) part E4.
[53] In *Yaxley*, the order of the court also gave A the choice of paying B a sum of money equal to the value of the promised lease: however, it seems that choice was not taken up by A.
[54] B McFarlane, 'Proprietary Estoppel and Failed Contractual Negotiations' [2005] *Conveyancer and Property Lawyer* 501.

Arun District Council,⁵⁵ the Court of Appeal also recognised that, even in the absence of a binding contract, A could come under a duty to grant B a promised legal property right. In that case, no mention was made of constructive trusts, nor of the doctrine of part performance. The point is that section 2 of the 1989 Act, like its predecessor (the Law of Property Act 1925, section 40, which applied in *Crabb*) simply relates to *contracts* for the sale or other disposition of interests in land. As a result, it has no relevance where A's duty to B arises not as a result of a contract but through different means, such as the doctrine of proprietary estoppel. So, as long as A comes under a non-contractual duty to B in relation to a specific right in land held by A, B can acquire an 'equitable property right', even if A's dealings with B have been purely oral. That is the case whether or not B's right arises under a resulting or constructive trust.

This third objection may also be relevant in those cases where A makes a contractual promise to transfer a right to B. For example, where A has made a contractual promise to transfer a legal estate in land to B, it is clear that B acquires a right against A's legal estate: as a result, B has more than a personal right against A.⁵⁶ If B has not yet performed a condition essential to the transfer (such as payment of the purchase price) there is, however, a question as to whether B's right is properly analysed as arising under a trust.⁵⁷ In particular, the terms of the contractual agreement between A and B may allow A some freedom to continue to use his legal estate for his own benefit, at least until B performs all conditions essential to the transfer. In such a case, it may be impossible for B to show that A is under the core trust duty to B. However, this objection, of course, does not undermine the crucial point that, as A's duty to B relates to a specific right held by A, B has more than a personal right against A: he has a right against A's right.

D. SUPPORTING EXPRESS TRUSTS

Any attempt to accord primacy to the express trust, at the expense of resulting and constructive trusts, will ultimately be self-defeating as resulting and constructive trusts play a crucial role in delimiting and protecting the rights of the beneficiary of an express trust. This dependence of express trusts on resulting and constructive trusts can be seen in two functional areas: the ability of B, the beneficiary of an express trust, to assert a claim against C, a third party who acquires a right from A; and the ability of B to assert a claim in relation to rights, held by either A or C, and acquired as a result of A or C's unauthorised use of rights held under an initial trust. The

---

⁵⁵ [1976] Ch 179.
⁵⁶ See eg *Lysaght* (n 44).
⁵⁷ See eg C Harpum, M Dixon and S Bridge, *Megarry and Wade's The Law of Real Property*, 7th edn (London, Sweet & Maxwell, 2008) 646–49.

1. Claims against Third Parties

Where A holds a right under an express trust, A may be under a number of duties to B. If anyone dishonestly assists A in breaching one of those duties, that party commits a wrong against B.[58] This makes it clear that the presence of A's initial duties has an effect on the rest of the world. In a similar way, if A is under a contractual duty to B, the rest of the world has a prima facie duty to B not to procure a breach by A of A's contractual duty to B. In such cases, the presence of a particular initial duty owed by A to B leads to the imposition of different, ancillary duties on the rest of the world. In the case of dishonest assistance, a party breaching such an ancillary duty is said to be liable to B as a 'constructive trustee'. However, that label should not lead us to think that the dishonest assistant need hold any right on trust for B; after all, his assistance may not involve the acquisition of any right.

A third party (C) may also be liable to B 'as a constructive trustee' where he knowingly receives a right initially held by A on trust for B. It is important to note that, as in the case of dishonest assistance, C's liability to B is not strict. The presence of B's initial right under the trust does *not* impose a prima facie duty of non-interference on the rest of the world. As discussed in Part B, the first perspective on the nature of trusts is therefore apt to mislead when used to explain the means by which a right under a trust may bind a third party. Where a third party is bound by B's legal property right, he is bound by the same duty as the rest of the world: a duty to B not to interfere with a particular thing. In contrast, where B has only an 'equitable property right', the rest of the world is under no such duty to B. So, we cannot explain C's liability to a beneficiary of an express trust as depending on the fact that B's initial right imposes a particular duty on C. Instead, as noted in Part B, C's duty depends on the crucial fact that he has acquired a 'duty-burdened' right: either the very right initially held by A on trust for B; or a right that depends on that initial right.

Further, as shown by the test for liability in knowing receipt,[59] C's duty does not arise *simply* because C has acquired such a right. For example, consider a case where A holds a right on express trust for B and then, acting beyond his powers as trustee, transfers that right, for free, to C. C then transfers the right, for free, to C2. At no point before the transfer to C2 did C know, or have reason to suspect, that A held the right on trust for

---

[58] As discussed in eg *Barlow Clowes International Ltd v Eurotrust International Ltd* [2005] UKPC 37, [2006] 1 WLR 1476.
[59] *Bank of Credit and Commerce International (Overseas) Ltd v Akindele* [2001] Ch 437.

B. In such a case, C is under no duty to B. When we say that B can assert his right under the initial trust against a third party, we mean that, *if* C acquires a right that depends on the right initially held on trust, and *if* A had no power under the trust to make that transfer, *then* C will come under a duty to B *if* C acquires sufficient knowledge of the initial trust *whilst* still holding the right acquired from A or its traceable product. This reveals a further difference from the position in which B has a legal property right: C's duty to B only arises where C has sufficient knowledge of B's initial right. The current test for liability in knowing receipt thus provides important support for the view, discussed in Part C, section 2, that a trust cannot arise unless and until the holder of a specific right has knowledge of the facts giving rise to his duty not to use that right for his own benefit.

Of course, if C still holds the right acquired from A, or its traceable product, it is possible for B to ensure that C acquires the requisite knowledge: he simply needs to inform C. In such a case, B can be viewed as having exercised a (factual) power to impose a duty on C. As noted by Nolan,[60] it is not then the case that C is bound by all the terms of the initial express trust. Rather, C is bound only by the core trust duty: a duty, owed to B, not to use the right he holds for his own benefit. As part of that core trust duty, C comes under a duty to account to B for the right held on trust. So, if B can show that C came under the core trust duty *before* disposing of a right received from A, B can enforce C's duty to account for that right. The courts describe such a duty to account as depending on C's 'knowing receipt' of the right acquired from A; however, it is clear that C's knowledge may arise after C's initial receipt, provided it coincides with C's holding of the right or its traceable product. In contrast to the case with dishonest assistance, C's liability *does* depend on a constructive trust: there must have been a point at which C both holds a particular right and is under a duty to B not to use that right for C's benefit.[61]

From this second perspective, then, it is clear that the means by which a right under an express trust is said to bind a third party is very different from the means by which a legal property right achieves that effect. If B has a legal property right, the rest of the world is under a duty to B not to interfere with a thing. If B has an 'equitable property right', the rest of the world is under no such duty. Rather than having a right against a thing, B instead has a right against a right. As a result, the rest of the world is under a Hohfeldian liability: *if* C acquires a right that depends on the right held by A on trust for B, *if* A has acted beyond his powers as trustee, and *if* C acquires sufficient knowledge of B's initial right under the trust whilst still holding the right acquired from A or its traceable product *then* C comes

---

[60] R Nolan, 'Equitable Property' (2006) 122 *Law Quarterly Review* 232.
[61] For extended discussion of all these points, see ch 4.

under the core trust duty to B. In such a case, it is clear that the trust on which C holds his right is very different from that on which A held: it has a different content and arises for a different reason. True, the initial creation of the express trust on which A held is a necessary element of the eventual trust which binds C. However, that initial creation, by itself, cannot explain the trust on which C holds. That trust can only be explained as constructive;[62] and, as we saw in Part C above, it can arise only where C has sufficient knowledge of the facts giving rise to C's duty to B. From the second perspective then, the key functional feature of the express trust, its ability to bind a third party, depends on the recognition of a particular form of constructive trust.

2. Claims in Relation to Unauthorised Substitutes

Where A holds rights under an express trust, A's initial acceptance of the trust may, at a stretch, be said to cover not just the rights initially held by A but also the authorised products of those rights. This is, at least, the view of those who see the fund as an important concept in English law, and the trust as an example of that concept.[63] However, it is not obvious that A's initial acceptance can be extended to rights acquired by A as a result of an unauthorised use of the rights initially held on trust for B. Nonetheless, it is clear that, in English law, such rights will also be held by A on trust for B.[64] Different explanations have been given for this phenomenon and each has its own weaknesses.[65] For present purposes, however, it is enough to focus on two points. First, the trust that attaches to such unauthorised substitutes is recognised in English law and forms an important part of the functioning of the express trust. Second, that trust cannot be explained without admitting the importance of non-express trusts. For example, even if, as suggested by Lord Millett,[66] the trust is seen as a necessary consequence of

---

[62] The characterisation of the trust as resulting or constructive (as opposed to express) can have significance in the conflict of laws. For example, A may hold a right on express trust for B, under a trust instrument which confers jurisdiction on the English court. If A transfers that right to C, B may claim that C now holds that right on trust for B. If Council Regulation (EC) 44/2001 applies, and B's claim is seen as arising under the initial express trust then, under Art 5(6), an English court will have jurisdiction to hear B's claim against C, even if C is not domiciled in the UK. However, if B's claim is seen as arising under a constructive trust, Art 5(6) will not apply: see eg *Chellaram v Chellaram (No 2)* [2002] EWHC 632 (Ch). [2002] 3 All ER 17 [162].

[63] See eg R Nolan, 'Property in a Fund' (2004) 120 *Law Quarterly Review* 108; J Penner, 'Value, Property, and Unjust Enrichment: Trusts of Traceable Proceeds' in Chambers et al (n 14) 306.

[64] See eg *Foskett v McKeown* [2001] 1 AC 102.

[65] For an explanation based on unjust enrichment, see eg R Chambers 'Tracing and Unjust Enrichment' in J Neyers et al (eds), *Understanding Unjust Enrichment* (Oxford, Hart Publishing, 2004) 263. For doubts about that explanation, see eg Smith (n 26).

[66] See *Foskett* (n 64) 129–32; Lord Millett, 'Proprietary Restitution' in S Degeling and J Edelman (eds), *Equity and Commercial Law* (Sydney, Lawbook Co, 2005) 309. See too Penner (n 63).

A's duty to account, it will still arise where B's initial right arises under a constructive or resulting trust, in which A's initial duty to account does not arise as a result of A's consent. In *Reid*, for example, B's claim related not to the bribe initially received by A but to freeholds later acquired by using that bribe. It was found that those freeholds were held on trust, even though the trusts of these unauthorised substitutes of the bribe could not possibly be based on any party's exercise of a power to set up a trust.

3. THE CONCEPTUAL BASIS OF THE EXPRESS TRUST

As noted in Part A above, an express trust, viewed from the first perspective on the nature of trusts, arises from a settlor's exercise of a power to set up a trust. As the law has developed, that is certainly a natural way to analyse the creation of an express trust. However, it is worth pausing to note that the initial development of the express trust cannot have depended on that analysis. This is not a point based on the early history of the trust;[67] rather, it is based on the logical impossibility of justifying the first express trust by pointing to a settlor's exercise of a power to set up such an arrangement. In a world without trusts, it is of course meaningless to claim that a trust exists because a settlor has exercised his power to create one.

First, we can consider the case of a trust established by a transfer: for example, S transfers a right to A subject to a duty to use that right wholly for B's benefit. If B then goes to court to complain when A begins to use that right for A's own benefit, how can that claim be put? From the second perspective on the nature of trusts, B needs to show why A is under a duty not to use that right for A's own benefit. As noted in Part A, B, in contrast to the beneficiaries of the trusts in *Reid* and *Vandervell*, faces a particular problem: his case is not covered by any independently recognised means by which A can come under a duty to B. In contrast to *Reid*, A's receipt of the right from S, in itself, cannot amount to a wrong against B. In contrast to *Vandervell*, A's receipt of the right from S, in itself, cannot amount to an unjust enrichment of A at B's expense. In contrast to cases such as *Lysaght v Edwards*,[68] A is under no contractual duty to B; and, in contrast to *Mountney v Treharne*,[69] there is certainly no court order which has been made in B's favour. How, then, can B make his claim?

Two possibilities present themselves. First, B could argue that, if A were under no duty, that would unduly interfere with S's freedom to dispose of his initial right: after all, S transferred his right to A on the faith of A's undertaking to hold that right for B's benefit. This view focuses on S's

---

[67] For speculation on the historical origins of the trust, based on the writings of St Thomas Aquinas, see Smith (n 14).
[68] *Lysaght* (n 44).
[69] *Mountney* (n 40).

reliance on A. Second, B could argue that, if A were under no duty, A would then be allowed to keep the benefit of a particular right that A received on the basis that he would use that right in a particular way. This view focuses on A's potential benefit. For present purposes, it is not necessary to make a choice between these arguments, as neither view depends on simply saying that S exercised a power to give B a particular form of right. Instead, each depends on the recognition of a new principle by which A can come under a duty to B. If either principle is accepted, that principle will clearly not be confined to cases in which B claims a right under a trust: it can also apply, for example, if A acquires a freehold from S having undertaken to allow B occupation of the land for a period.[70] Indeed, the debate as to why A comes under a duty to B is precisely the one that now exists in relation to a set of trusts often viewed as constructive:[71] those arising or discussed in cases such as *Rochefoucauld v Boustead*,[72] *Blackwell v Blackwell*,[73] *Pallant v Morgan*,[74] *Neale v Willis*[75] and *Ashburn Anstalt v Arnold*.[76] Of course, in the first mentioned case, the Court of Appeal held that the trust arising in favour of the Comtesse was an express trust.[77] For those who harbour doubts about the validity of constructive trusts, that interpretation offers the chance of clothing the Comtesse's trust in a more respectable mantle—even if the cost is to allow judges a constitutionally dubious power to alter statutory formality rules. However, for present purposes, the critical point is that, however such trusts are categorised, they must depend on a principle which, originally at least, identified a reason for A's being under a duty to B which did not depend simply on S's exercise of a power to set up a trust.

Second, we can consider the case in which A has a right and declares that he holds that right on trust for B. How we can justify A's being under a duty to B not to use that right for A's own benefit? We could explain A's duty as based on A's consent; but that explanation, in itself, is unsatisfactory. If A makes an oral, gratuitous declaration of trust, why is it that A cannot then change his mind and revoke the trust? It is true that, where it amounts to an assumption of responsibility for the carrying out of a task, an oral, gratuitous promise may impose a duty on A, owed to B, carefully to carry out that task.[78] Nonetheless, when compared with the limited

[70] See eg *Binions v Evans* [1972] Ch 359.
[71] Eg Simon Gardner adopts a reliance-based explanation for those cases in the present volume (ch 2); and in 'Constructive Trusts Arising on a Receipt of Property *Sub Conditione*' (2004) 120 *Law Quarterly Review* 667, I propose a benefit-based analysis.
[72] [1897] 1 Ch 196.
[73] [1929] AC 318.
[74] [1953] Ch 43.
[75] (1968) 19 P & CR 836.
[76] [1989] 1 Ch 1.
[77] See Swadling's contribution to this volume (ch 3).
[78] Eg as discussed by the House of Lords in *Hedley Byrne & Co Ltd v Heller & Partners Ltd* [1964] AC 465.

effects of such a promise, the onerous duties imposed by a declaration of trust seem anomalous. The closest equivalent lies in the so-called 'equitable assignment' of an existing right held by A. The term 'assignment' is misleading as there is no transfer of any right of A to B; instead, A retains a right and, as a result of an oral, gratuitous promise comes under a duty to B in relation to that right. The effect of such an 'equitable assignment' therefore closely resembles that of a declaration of trust.[79] Each case reveals the spectacular misunderstanding that lies behind the maxim 'Equity will not assist a volunteer'. In general, both common law and equity refuse to recognise that a gratuitous promise imposes a duty on A; yet, anomalously, that stance softens when we come to equitable assignments and declarations of trust.

It is worth noting that the arguments developed above, in relation to the establishment of a trust by a transfer of a right to a trustee, have no purchase where A simply makes a declaration of trust. In such a case, as A held the right in question before the declaration, it cannot be said that any party transferred that right to A in reliance on A's undertaking, nor that the undertaking led to A's acquisition of a benefit. Indeed, in *Cobbe*,[80] Lord Scott made precisely that distinction in explaining why the constructive trust principle exemplified by *Pallant v Morgan*[81] cannot apply in a case where A already holds a right when making a promise to use that right, at least in part, for B's benefit. It may therefore be that the recognition of A's power to make an oral, gratuitous declaration of trust has to be justified on functional or policy grounds. After all, if A can set up a trust by means of a transfer to A1 to hold for B's benefit, it may seem unnecessarily technical to deny A the power to impose the office of trusteeship on himself. Certainly, the purpose of the current analysis is not to question the validity of an oral, gratuitous declaration of trust. Rather, it is to point out that such express trusts, rather than constructive or express trusts, may be regarded as anomalous and so require a justification based on functional or policy concerns.

E. THE COMPARATIVE PERSPECTIVE

The first perspective on the nature of the trust is often adopted by those looking at the English trust from abroad. This is no surprise, as that perspective is closely linked to a functional view of the trust, and comparative analyses often adopt a functional approach, in large part to avoid the confusion that may result from assuming that a conceptual term, if used in

---

[79] This point has been noted by eg M Smith, *The Law of Assignment* (Oxford, Oxford University Press, 2007) para 6.10 and McFarlane (n 7) 125–26.
[80] *Cobbe* (n 33) [36].
[81] [1953] Ch 43.

the law of one jurisdiction, must have the same meaning in a different jurisdiction. Certainly, a focus on the express trust is evident in the Hague Convention on the Law Applicable to Trusts and on their Recognition. Article 1 of the Convention includes in its definition of the term 'trust' a requirement that there must be a legal relationship 'created—*inter vivos* or on death—by a person, the settlor, when assets have been placed under the control of a trustee for the benefit of a beneficiary or for a specified purpose'. Article 3 stipulates that the Convention applies 'only to trusts created voluntarily and evidenced in writing'.[82]

Lupoi has forcefully argued that the Hague Convention has little to do with the English trust; it instead creates a 'shapeless trust'[83] due to its emphasis on function and a lack of attention to the underlying concepts that can give the trust its form. The irony of the Convention may be that, even if it was conceived, at least in part, with the aim of allowing other jurisdictions to recognise the traditional English trust, one of its effects is to force English courts to recognise as trusts legal relationships far removed from the traditional English trust.[84] It may be countered that the principal practical aim of the Convention was to give some legal certainty to parties choosing to set up an express trust in circumstances where litigation in relation to that trust may occur outside England; and so there was no need to deal with non-express trusts. Nonetheless, a failure to attend to resulting and constructive trusts may also be significant in hampering the attempts of civil jurisdictions to introduce trust-like devices into their domestic legal systems.

For example, a civilian jurisdiction, envious of the practical usefulness of the trust, may permit a structure which mimics one or more of the functions of the trust: for example, to accord B protection in A's insolvency, a civilian system could allow for multiple patrimonies, in which a party simultaneously holds one set of rights and liabilities as his own patrimony and another such set for the benefit of B.[85] Through the principle of real

---

[82] Art 20 does allow a contracting state, by means of a declaration, to extend the Convention provisions to trusts 'declared by judicial decisions'. A current list of states to have made such a declaration is maintained on the website of the Hague Conference on Private International Law: the UK has made the declaration; but, for example (as of 24 June 2009), France, Italy and Australia have not. I am grateful to Professor Smith for referring me to this source.

[83] M Lupoi, *Trusts: A Comparative Study*, trans S Dix (Cambridge, Cambridge University Press, 2000) ch 6.

[84] Although see P Matthews, 'STAR: Big Bang or Red Dwarf?' (1998) 12 *Trust Law International* 98 for the argument that an English court may use Art 18 of the Convention to deny recognition, on grounds of public policy, to at least some arrangements which fall within the Convention definition of a trust but outside the definition adopted by English law. For a counter-argument see A Duckworth, 'STAR WARS: Smiting the Bull' (1999) 13 *Trust Law International* 158.

[85] See eg the analysis of the Scottish approach in G Gretton, 'Trusts Without Equity' (2000) 49 *International & Comparative Law Quarterly* 599. As discussed in Smith (n 11) the Quebec *fiducie* depends on seeing rights held on trust as an ownerless patrimony.

subrogation, such a device may also allow for a trust to operate as a fund.[86] However, such a model may fail to capture the two practical features of the trust examined in Part D: the ability of B's right under a trust to bind C, a third party acquiring a right from A; and the fact that A will come under a duty to B not just in relation to the initial rights held on trust and their authorised substitutes but also in relation to unauthorised substitutes of those initial rights.

Of course, if a civilian jurisdiction makes a deliberate decision that its trust-like devices should differ from the English trust, then such differences are unproblematic. However, if such a jurisdiction genuinely wants to allow for devices that provide B with the protection available to a beneficiary of an English trust, it can only do so by adopting a conceptual model of the trust, based on the central notion of a duty-burdened right. Such a model must accord an important role to resulting and constructive trusts. Indeed, it is worth noting that, in his study of the comparative law of trusts, Lupoi sees resulting and constructive trusts as at 'the heart of the trust'.[87]

F. CONCLUSION

It was noted in Part A that the second perspective on the nature of trusts builds on the analyses of Professors Chambers and Smith, as well as my own analysis. When analysing resulting and constructive trusts in *The Structure of Property Law*, I argued that, once it can be shown that: (i) there is a legally recognised reason for A's being under a duty to B; and (ii) that duty relates to a specific right held by A; then (iii) B necessarily acquires a right against A's right and so has, to use the orthodox term, an 'equitable property right'. On this view, resulting and constructive trusts require no special justification and do not depend on special policy concerns. As far as B's acquisition of an 'equitable property right' is concerned, the only relevant question is whether the reason giving rise to A's duty to B also demands that A's duty must relate to a specific right held by A. In a recent essay, Professor Smith makes a crucial point in response to the argument that resulting and constructive trusts require special justification: any attempt to undermine what has here been called the second perspective (that is, the view that the trust depends on the concept of a 'duty-burdened' right) must necessarily imperil the very thing it purports to promote: the express trust. As Smith has put it: 'That is because express trusts arise from promises, and promises as such only make obligations.'[88]

---

[86] See eg Gretton (n 85) 609–10.
[87] See Lupoi (n 83) ch 2. It is therefore unsurprising that Lupoi has serious reservations about the scheme of the Hague Convention: ibid, ch 6.
[88] Smith (n 14) 302–03.

This chapter has attempted to develop that point, and to show that a full understanding of the law of trusts, including the law of express trusts, is possible only if we stop worrying and learn to love resulting and constructive trusts.

PART II
RESULTING TRUSTS

7

'Automatic' Resulting Trusts: Retention, Restitution, or Reposing Trust?

JOHN MEE*

A. INTRODUCTION

This chapter examines the nature of so-called 'automatic resulting trusts',[1] focusing on a number of alternative conceptualisations of the process of their creation. The aim is to explain, as a matter of authority and principle, the justification for the substantive rules in relation to the creation of this type of resulting trust. One prominent explanation is that the beneficial interest under a resulting trust has been 'retained' by the settlor—in other words, it is 'never drawn out of him'.[2] It seems to have been assumed in the literature that this view is of relatively modern origin, stemming from the decision of the House of Lords in the leading case of *Vandervell v IRC*.[3] Chambers, for example, has argued that 'the passive concept of the resulting trust . . . requires a view of equitable ownership which is contrary to history and precedent'.[4] However, support for this idea in *Vandervell* was no novelty but rather reflected authority spanning hundreds of years. It will be pointed out in this chapter that the retention

---

*I am grateful to Dr Mary Donnelly for her comments on this chapter. Any errors which remain are solely my responsibility.

[1] This chapter adopts this convenient term to describe the category of resulting trust under discussion, notwithstanding the suggestion by Lord Browne-Wilkinson in *Westdeutsche Landesbank Girozentrale v Islington London Borough Council* [1996] AC 669, 708, that such trusts do not operate 'automatically' because of the possibility that the settlor may have intended to abandon the property. While the current author does not accept the validity of Lord Browne-Wilkinson's argument on this point, it is not proposed to pursue the matter in this chapter. On the label 'automatic', see further the text to nn 12–13.
[2] *Godbold v Freestone* (1695) 3 Lev 406, 407; 83 ER 753, 754.
[3] [1967] 2 AC 291.
[4] R Chambers, *Resulting Trusts* (Oxford, Oxford University Press, 1997) 104. See also W Swadling, 'Explaining Resulting Trusts' (2008) 124 *Law Quarterly Review* 78, 99.

approach to resulting trusts had direct practical consequences in English law right up to modern times.

The existence of this authority does not, of course, prove that the retention idea holds true or provides a satisfactory theoretical explanation for the existence of the automatic resulting trust. As well as seeking to correct the record in relation to the history of the retention idea, this chapter will seek to interrogate that idea more closely to determine whether it has any plausibility in theoretical terms. Having undertaken a Hohfeldian analysis of the position, it will be suggested that it is an exaggeration to contend that the settlor under a resulting trust retains *no* pre-existing rights. However, many of the rights under a resulting trust cannot, strictly speaking, be said to have been 'retained'. Therefore, the retention explanation, though strongly rooted in authority, does not appear to provide a satisfactory theoretical explanation for the resulting trust.

An alternative vision of the resulting trust is as an instrument of restitution. This alternative vision derives from the academic literature, rather than from the traditional discourse of equity. It involves the idea that the legal interest passes to the trustee and 'then' a resulting trust attaches to his legal interest to reverse the unjust enrichment which would otherwise arise. This idea was initially advanced by Birks[5] and has been vigorously developed by Chambers.[6] However, the repeated assertions in the cases and historical texts that the interest under a resulting use or trust is 'no new thing, but part of that which the owner of the land had'[7] appear damaging to the claim that there is a foundation in 'history and precedent' for the proposition that the resulting trust is an instrument of restitution. Furthermore, the arguments of principle against the retention idea, relied upon by Chambers in support of the restitution theory, appear on a closer analysis to be equally damaging to his view of the resulting trust.

In seeking a defensible theoretical basis for the automatic resulting trust, this chapter rejects both the retention and the restitution approaches and puts forward a different explanation (which does not require any modification of the existing substantive rules). Drawing on a consideration of the origins of the trust concept, it is argued that the key feature in the relevant situation is the fact that the settlor has transferred property to another person, reposing trust in that person to hold the property according to the

---

[5] P Birks, 'Restitution and Resulting Trusts' in S Goldstein (ed), *Equity and Contemporary Legal Developments* (Jerusalem, Hebrew University of Jerusalem, 1992) 335; P Birks, 'Trusts Raised to Reverse Unjust Enrichment: The *Westdeutsche* Case' [1996] *Restitution Law Review* 3; P Birks, *An Introduction to the Law of Restitution*, rev edn (Oxford, Clarendon Press, 1989) esp 54–73; P Birks, *Unjust Enrichment*, 2nd edn (Oxford, Clarendon Press, 2005) esp 150–52 and 304–07.

[6] Chambers (n 4); R Chambers, 'Resulting Trusts in Canada' (2000) 38 *Alberta Law Review* 378; R Chambers, 'Resulting Trusts' in A Burrows and Lord Rodger (eds), *Mapping the Law: Essays in Memory of Peter Birks* (Oxford, Oxford University Press, 2006) 247.

[7] *Samme's Case* (1609) 13 Co Rep 54, 56; 77 ER 1464, 1466.

settlor's instructions. This explanation requires a distinction to be drawn between the creation of a trust in this general sense and the creation of a particular trust in favour of specified beneficiaries. It is argued that, even if the beneficiaries are not validly specified, the trust does not truly 'fail'—it simply gives way to a resulting trust. Thus, the underlying reason for the creation of an automatic resulting trust is that the settlor intended to make the recipient of the property a trustee: to use Maitland's words, 'I have made A a trustee for somebody, and a trustee he must be—if for no one else then for me or my representatives.'[8]

Before moving on to consider the relevant arguments, it will be necessary, in the next section, to look briefly at the type of resulting trust on which this chapter will concentrate.[9] This section will give a sense of the theoretical work which is required in terms of justifying this class of resulting trusts. It will also anticipate the ultimate conclusion to be offered in the chapter.

B. 'AUTOMATIC' RESULTING TRUSTS

In a well-known statement of the law in *Re Vandervell's Trusts (No 2)*, Megarry J coined the term 'automatic resulting trust', explaining that:

> The second class of case is where the transfer to B is made on trusts which leave some or all of the beneficial interest undisposed of. Here B automatically holds on a resulting trust for A to the extent that the beneficial interest has not been carried to him or others.[10]

This type of resulting trust can arise in a variety of circumstances.[11] Although this would be curious thing for a settlor to do, he might in theory convey property to a trustee to hold 'on trust' without specifying particular beneficiaries (or to hold on trusts to be specified in the future). A more likely situation would be that the trusts which are specified by the settlor might, due to an oversight, fail to exhaust all the beneficial interest, for example if the settlor did not foresee a possible turn of events. Another possibility is that some or all of the trusts specified by the settlor might infringe a legal rule, failing, for example, because of the rule against perpetuities. It is undisputed that a resulting trust arises in these types of

---

[8] FW Maitland, *Equity: A Course of Lectures*, ed J Brunyate, rev edn (Cambridge, Cambridge University Press, 1936) 77.
[9] The other types of resulting trust are called 'presumed' resulting trusts (although terminology is controversial in relation to all forms of resulting trust), and arise upon a voluntary conveyance or where the claimant has advanced some or all of the purchase price for property which is conveyed into another's name.
[10] [1974] Ch 269, 294. Megarry J was summarising the position as established in the leading decision of the House of Lords in *Vandervell v IRC* (n 3).
[11] See eg Maitland (n 8) 75–77.

situation, so that the discussion in the literature focuses on the justification for the existing rules.

In a recent important contribution to the debate, Swadling[12] suggests that the term 'automatic' is misleading as a label for the relevant type of resulting trust because 'there is nothing "automatic" about the law. The ... resulting trust does not arise of its own volition, but because courts say it does.'[13] Swadling's objection appears to be to a tendency to assume that the law on this point is inevitable. Those sympathetic to the traditions of property or trusts law sometimes assert that the creation of this kind of resulting trust depends 'on a *simple* process of proprietary arithmetic; what I once had and have not granted away, I keep',[14] or that resulting trusts in general operate '*simply* as a series of default rules to locate the beneficial interest in property'.[15] In fact, the matter is not so straightforward because the ideas of 'locating' the beneficial interest, or engaging in 'proprietary arithmetic' concerning the beneficial interest, presuppose the existence of a separate beneficial interest under a subsisting trust.[16]

Taking a different view, Swadling considers that a trust 'fails' whenever, and to the extent that, the settlor has not validly specified a destination for the beneficial interest under an intended trust. For him, it is not clear why a resulting trust, seen as a new trust, should arise from the ashes of the 'failed trust'.[17] From a similar starting point, Chambers argues that the resulting

---

[12] Note also his earlier publications on the topic including W Swadling, 'A New Role for Resulting Trusts?' (1996) 16 *Legal Studies* 110; W Swadling, 'The Law of Property' in P Birks and F Rose (eds), *Lessons of the Swaps Litigation* (Oxford, Mansfield Press, 2000) 242; W Swadling, 'A Hard Look at *Hodgson v Marks*', in P Birks and F Rose (eds), *Restitution and Equity*, vol 1: *Resulting Trusts and Equitable Compensation* (London, Mansfield Press/LLP, 2000) 61.

[13] Swadling (n 4) 99. This criticism of Megarry J's choice of label may be misplaced, since it seems likely that Megarry J was merely concerned to emphasise that this type of resulting trust arises without reference to any presumption, a position accepted by Swadling: ibid, 94–99. The current author also sees no role for a presumption in the context of the kind of resulting trust under discussion. On the analysis favoured in this chapter, one is dealing with a situation where (i) the existence of a trust has been established and (ii) there has been no valid allocation of some or all of the beneficial interests under that trust. This means that, at a prior stage, one has ruled out the possibility that the settlor has filled the gap in the beneficial interest by allocating it to the trustee or to anyone else, including himself. Thus, there is no room for a presumption that the settlor intended to create a trust (since we already know that he did) nor is there room for a presumption that he validly allocated the relevant portion of the beneficial interest to anyone (since we already know that he did not).

[14] J Hackney, *Understanding Equity and Trusts* (London, Fontana, 1987) 153 (emphasis added).

[15] C Rickett and R Grantham, 'Resulting Trusts—A Rather Limited Doctrine' in *Restitution and Equity* (n 12) 39, 48 (emphasis added).

[16] It may be useful to mention that, in this chapter, the current author is using the terms 'equitable' interest and 'beneficial' interest interchangeably to refer to the interest of a beneficiary under a trust. A person is described as holding 'beneficially' when they hold outright as legal owner and there is no trust in existence.

[17] Contrast E O'Dell, 'The Resulting Trust' in C Rickett and R Grantham (eds), *Structure and Justification in Private Law: Essays for Peter Birks* (Oxford, Hart Publishing, 2008) 379, 389, referring to 'trusts which apparently fail'.

trust arising upon a 'failed trust' is restitutionary in nature (as are the other kinds of resulting trust), in that it arises to compel the trustee to 'give up' the enrichment he has acquired from the settlor.[18] Swadling responds to this by questioning why the response to the unjust enrichment should be proprietary in nature (to the prejudice of the trustee's creditors), in other words by asking why the law's response is not a personal remedy against the trustee.[19] It is unclear how this question is to be convincingly answered on Chambers's analysis. Swadling himself offers no answer, reaching the stark conclusion that this type of resulting trust 'still defies legal analysis'.[20]

However, it would be surprising if it were impossible to provide a theoretical justification for the rule under discussion, given that it seems an eminently sensible one. It is true that, as Swadling points out, the creation of a resulting trust is less advantageous to the trustee's creditors than the alternative approach of allowing the trustee to take the property beneficially, subject only to the possibility of a personal action in unjust enrichment.[21] However, without suggesting that this point is decisive in itself, it may be noted that there would be no question at all of the trustee's creditors having access to the value in question but for the circumstance (entirely fortuitous from their point of view) that something went wrong with the settlor's attempt to allocate the beneficial interests under the trust. The settlor, prior to creating the trust, had a power to make himself a beneficiary under the trust and, in its rules on the automatic resulting trust, equity is merely achieving what the settlor could have achieved himself by cautiously adding a proviso to the effect that any portion of the beneficial interest which has not been successfully allocated should belong to him. Looking at the question from the viewpoint of the settlor, a rule under which he becomes entitled under a resulting trust seems an entirely appropriate response to a failure in his attempt to allocate the beneficial interests; such a rule preserves the possibility of his making a renewed attempt to dispose of the beneficial interest.[22] It seems plausible to suggest that such a rule would reflect the legal response which settlors *as an abstract class* would be likely to prefer in the scenario under discussion (even if some settlors might, in individual sets of circumstances, prefer a rule that the trustee would take beneficially).[23] In devising the rules surrounding the

---

[18] Chambers (n 4) ch 2.
[19] Swadling (n 4) 99 and 101.
[20] Ibid, 102.
[21] Ibid, 99 and 101.
[22] On this occasion, there would be the legislative requirement under Law of Property Act 1925, s 53(1)(c) that the transfer of his existing beneficial interest must be in writing.
[23] One conceivable alternative rule would be that equity would allocate the beneficial interest on the basis of a guess as to what allocation the particular settlor would have made if he had realised that his intended allocation was invalid for some reason or if he had known that he had failed to provide for some contingency. However, it quickly becomes obvious that this kind of guesswork would not provide the kind of certainty necessary in the context of prop-

trust, an institution to which Equity gives its protection and approval, it seems clearly desirable to take an approach which facilitates those who make use of that institution and which does not punish them for any slip they may make.

The position, then, appears to be that one is faced with a fundamental preliminary question in relation to this class of resulting trusts. Does the trust 'fail' when the settlor has been unsuccessful in allocating the beneficial interests under an intended trust (in which case it is difficult to justify the creation of a resulting trust in its place) or does the trust survive, so that the consequent resulting trust only allocates the beneficial interest under a trust which the settlor has established? This chapter argues that, in order for 'automatic' resulting trusts to be justified, it is necessary to adopt the second answer. It will be suggested later in the chapter that this choice can be seen as dictated by the nature of a trust in Equity, as demonstrated by the origins of the concept. In any case, a choice must be made one way or another and a significant element in making this choice must be an assessment of the attractiveness of the consequences of each option. The view taken in this chapter is that the choice underlying the current rules is clearly the right one. It is important, though, to concede that the relevant rules reflect a particular choice which, like all choices, could conceivably have been made differently.

The discussion now moves on to a consideration of possible conceptualisations of the automatic resulting trust, beginning with the notion of retention.

C. THE IDEA OF RETENTION

In the leading case of *Vandervell v IRC*, Lord Upjohn argued that 'if the beneficial interest was in A and he fails to give it away effectively to another or others or on charitable trusts it must remain in him'.[24] Similarly, Lord Wilberforce insisted that 'the equitable, or beneficial interest, cannot remain in the air: the consequence in law must be that it remains in the settlor'.[25] These comments do not stand alone and it is relatively common for courts at the highest levels to refer to the retention of a beneficial interest in the context of resulting trusts.[26]

---

erty rights (and one would still need to develop a default rule which would apply where there was insufficient evidence to form the basis of any guess as to the hypothetical intentions of the individual settlor).

[24] *Vandervell v IRC* (n 3) 313.
[25] Ibid, 329. See also, in the same vein, ibid, 307–08 (Lord Reid).
[26] Examples include *Shephard v Cartwright* [1955] AC 431, 454 (Lord Reid); *Tribe v Tribe* [1996] 1 Ch 107 (CA) 129, 134 and 135 (Millett LJ); *Air Jamaica Ltd v Charlton* [1999] 1 WLR 1399 (PC) 1412 (Lord Millett); *Lavelle v Lavelle* [2004] EWCA 223, [2004] 2 FCR 418 [13] (Lord Phillips MR).

The retention approach favoured in *Vandervell* is criticised by Chambers in his influential monograph, where he argues that: 'The interest which the settlor has at the end of the story, as a beneficiary of a resulting trust, is an equitable interest which is different from the legal ownership he or she had at the beginning.'[27] Chambers goes on to quote the following remarks of Lord Browne-Wilkinson in the *Westdeutsche* case (made, interestingly, in the course of rejecting a version of the restitution thesis favoured by Chambers himself):

> A person solely entitled to the full beneficial ownership of money or property, both at law and in equity, does not enjoy an equitable interest in that property. The legal title carries with it all rights. Unless and until there is a separation of the legal and equitable estates, there is no separate equitable title.[28]

Swadling takes a similar view on the idea of retention:

> However, a theory based on 'retention' of an equitable interest does not work . . ., for the settlor generally has no equitable interest to retain. Suppose I convey my fee simple title to land to a friend to hold on trust for 'such objects of benevolence and liberality as he in his absolute discretion should most approve of.' The trust will fail for want of objects and the friend will hold the title for me on resulting trust. But I have 'retained' nothing. At the beginning of the story, I had a fee simple title to land. At the end of it, that title is held by my friend. What I now have is an interest under a trust, something I did not have before.[29]

Thus, the retention idea has been subjected to significant criticism in the recent literature. Later in this chapter, the merits of this criticism will be considered and it will be concluded that, although overstated to some degree, the criticism is essentially well founded at a theoretical level. However, it is unfortunate that the extent of the authority for the retention idea has been overlooked. The next part will attempt to set the historical record straight in this respect, before the discussion moves on to an assessment of whether the retention explanation can be sustained as a

---

[27] Chambers (n 4) 52. It might be argued that there can be no question of the retention of rights under a resulting trust because prior to the creation of the trust, the settlor—being the legal owner—had no rights recognised by equity: Chambers, ibid, 52, appearing to rely on this argument when quoting a passage from Hackney (n 14) 25. The premise of this particular argument, however, is false (note the criticism by Swadling 'Law of Property' (n 12) 265–7). It is standard for equity to recognise that X is the owner of certain property in a case where X holds that property beneficially (and there is no trust in existence). If this were not the case, how could equity ever have recognised a resulting trust consequent upon a voluntary transfer, since this involves equity taking note of the fact that the transferor was the owner prior to the transfer? See generally WN Hohfeld, 'The Relations Between Equity and Law' (1912–13) 11 *Michigan Law Review* 537, 553–54 (discussing instances of 'the concurrence of law and equity').

[28] *Westdeutsche* (n 1) 706.

[29] Swadling (n 4) 99. See also W Swadling, 'Property: General Principles' in A Burrows (ed), *English Private Law*, 2nd edn (Oxford, Oxford University Press, 2007) 272–74, making the point in more detail.

matter of principle (and then on to an examination of alternative explanations for the automatic resulting trust).

D. HISTORY OF THE RETENTION IDEA

As is well known, the earliest trusts were known as 'uses'. In Christopher St Germain's famous dialogue between *Doctor and Student* (1518), the student is asked to explain the origin of uses and responds as follows:

> [S]uch lands and goods as a man has, ought not to be taken from him but by his assent or by order of a law and then since it be so, that every man that has lands has thereby two things in him, that is to say, the possession of the land, which after the law of England is called the frank-tenement, or the freehold, and the other is authority to take thereby the profits of the land; wherefore it follows, that he that has land, and intends to give only the possession and freehold thereof to another, and keep the profits to himself, ought in reason and conscience to have the profits.[30]

The doctrine developed by the courts in relation to resulting uses reflects the same thinking. Sir Edward Coke explained the doctrine as follows:

> [W]hosoever is seized of land, hath not only the estate of the land in him, but the right to take profits, which is in the nature of the use, and therefore when he makes a feoffment in fee without valuable consideration to divers particular uses, so much of the use as he disposeth not, is in him as his ancient use in point of reverter.[31]

This passage makes clear the way in which the matter was visualised by Equity. An absolute owner of land (which is not subject to any use in favour of another person) was regarded as having, as one aspect of his ownership, the right to take the profits from the land,[32] and, when a resulting use was created, this pre-existing right was treated as remaining in him. Significantly, as well as being referred to as 'cestui que use', the beneficiary of a use was also known as the 'pernor of profits', that is, the taker of the profits.[33] The basic requirement of the trustee or feoffee to uses was simply

---

[30] C St Germain *Doctor and Student*, ed TFT Plunkett and JL Barton (Selden Society vol 91, 1974) Second Dialogue, ch 22 [54b].

[31] E Coke, *Institutes of the Lawes of England; or, a Commentary upon Littleton*, 4th edn (London, M Flesher et al, 1639) 23a, quoted by C Sweet, '"A Song of Uses": Some Reflections and a Moral' (1919) 35 *Law Quarterly Review* 127, 130. At the end of this passage, the word 'reverter' means 'reversion'.

[32] The word 'use' was sometimes used, in a broad sense, to refer to such a right of a landowner (though there was no equivalent of a trustee involved and a 'use' of this nature would not attract the operation of the Statute of Uses 1536). See N Jones, 'Uses, Trusts, and a Path to Privity' [1997] *Cambridge Law Journal* 175, 176–82 for discussion of the complex distinction between the 'conjoined use' and the 'separated use'. See also N Jones, 'Trusts in England after the Statute of Uses: A View from the Sixteenth Century' in RH Helmholz and R Zimmermann (eds), *Itinera Fiduciae* (Berlin, Duncker and Humblot, 1998) 190–92.

[33] See eg AWB Simpson, *A History of the Land Law* (Oxford, Oxford University Press, 1986) 174. The word 'pernor' is related to the French word 'prendre', meaning to take.

'the passive one of allowing the cestui que use to take the profits of the land'.[34] As a practical matter, where a settlor created a trust in his own favour, he would normally be able to continue his enjoyment of the land in the same manner as prior to the creation of the use, with no intervention on the part of the trustee being required. This reality lent plausibility to the proposition that the settlor in this case 'retained' rights over the land, notwithstanding the fact that he was no longer the legal owner.[35] Thus, it was explained in *Samme's Case*, decided in 1609, that '[a] use of land (which is but a pernancy of the profits) is no new thing, but part of that which the owner of the land had'.[36]

This view of the creation of uses had very important practical implications, particularly in the context of succession law. Formerly, the doctrine of descents was, in the words of Blackstone, 'a point of the highest importance; and . . . indeed the principal object of the law of real property in England'.[37] On intestacy, real property descended under the rules of heirship and a person's heir was traced from the most recent 'purchaser' of the land. The word 'purchaser' bore a technical meaning and did not assume, for example, that any value had been given by the purchaser. Essentially, a purchaser was someone who acquired land otherwise than by descent or inheritance. The crucial distinction, then, was between the acquisition of an estate by descent or by purchase.[38] Where an estate was acquired by purchase, 'the estate acquires a new inheritable quality, and is inheritable by the owner's blood in general as a feud of indefinite antiquity', that is, there were no restrictions on the heirs of the new owner who could inherit.[39] On the other hand, if an estate was acquired by descent, as for example when an eldest son took as heir on the intestacy of his parent, the estate retained its pre-existing inheritable quality. Thus, property which had descended to a person from his father's side (*ex parte paterna*) would continue to descend on intestacy to the heirs of the father, and property which had descended from the mother's side (*ex parte materna*) would

---

[34] Ibid. Beyond this, the feoffee's other responsibilities were to 'make estates' according to the direction of the cestui (ie to follow any instructions which the cestui might give requiring the land to be transferred to the cestui or anyone else) and to take any necessary steps to recover possession of the land if he had been disseised 'and so the feoffor disturbed'. See the description of the 'three parts' to a use in FW Sanders, *An Essay on Uses and Trusts*, ed GW Sanders and J Warner, 5th edn (London, Maxwell & Son, 1844) vol 1, 2.

[35] See further text to nn 56–62, discussing the fact that certain liberties are retained by the beneficiary under a resulting trust.

[36] *Samme's Case* (n 7) 13 Co Rep 56.

[37] W Blackstone, *Commentaries on the Laws of England*, 14th edn (London, A Strahan for T Cadell and W Davies, 1803) vol 2, 201.

[38] This 'great distinction' was also important because 'An estate by purchase will not make the person who acquires it answerable for the acts of his ancestors; as an estate by descent will': H Chitty, *A Treatise on the Law of Descents* (London, J Butterworth, 1825) 4; and see further Chitty, ibid, 324ff in relation to debts.

[39] Ibid, 4.

continue to descend to the mother's heirs.⁴⁰ If there were no heirs on the relevant side, then on intestacy the property would be lost by escheat and the heirs on the other side could not take.⁴¹

The inheritable quality of X's land would be changed if he conveyed it to Y who then conveyed it back to X. The rules of descent under discussion involve the proposition that when 'a person takes an estate which never vested . . . in [his] ancestor, he shall take by purchase'.⁴² In the example just given, X would take a new estate by purchase from Y, rather than the old estate which had descended to X originally, and so it would subsequently descend to X's heirs generally.

The question arose as to whether, when X conveyed the legal estate to Y and created a use in his own favour, this use constituted a new estate. If so, then it would be an estate that had never vested in X's ancestor, with the consequence that it could be inherited by the heirs on either side, even though the land in question had previously been inherited by X from (say) his mother's side. The answer to this question was absolutely clear: if a person who held land *ex parte materna* created a use in his own favour, that use would descend on intestacy to his heir *ex parte materna*. Precisely the same approach was taken in relation to resulting uses. The resulting use was not a new estate but merely the 'old use' which had previously resided in the grantor and which had originally come to him by descent. As Coke concluded, having explained the position in relation to resulting uses:

> So it is with lands of the part of the mother, the use shall goe to the heir of the part of the mother, which could not be, if it were not the old use, but a thing newly created.⁴³

After the Statute of Uses 1536, uses (including resulting uses) were executed, so that legal and beneficial ownership merged in the cestui que use. This meant that the person entitled under the resulting use would be entitled to the legal estate. Crucially, however, 'in the language of Lord Coke, he was in of the old use'.⁴⁴ As Sweet explained in 1919, '[a]t the present day, if a man conveys land to X and his heirs without consideration and without declaring any use', the conveyance would have absolutely no effect (including on changing the inheritable quality of the land) 'because owing to the doctrine of the old use and the operation of the Statute of Uses, the seisin goes around in a circle, returning to the place it started from'.⁴⁵

---

⁴⁰ Similarly, lands subject to the customary rules of gavelkind or borough-English would continue to descend according those rules.
⁴¹ This rule was finally altered by the Law of Property Amendment Act 1859, s 19, which allowed in the other class of heirs in the event of a total failure of heirs on the first side.
⁴² Chitty, (n 38) 4.
⁴³ Coke (n 31) 23a, quoted by Sweet (n 31) 130.
⁴⁴ Sweet (n 31) 131.
⁴⁵ Ibid, 130 n 5 (the point being that the circumstances would create a resulting use, which would be executed by the Statute of Uses).

Before discussing the position in relation to trusts, it may be useful to clarify the distinction between uses and trusts. There is not, in fact, 'any metaphysical difference in the essence of the things themselves'—'[a] use and a trust may essentially be looked upon as two names for the same thing'.[46] For convenience, the term 'trust' was used where a separate equitable interest continued to exist after operation of the Statute of Uses, while the term 'use' was reserved to describe interests which were executed by the Statute.[47] However, the terminology did not have any substantive significance, so that, for example, a conveyance 'to X on trust for Y' would have been executed by the Statute, in just the same way as a conveyance 'to X to the use of Y'. It is certainly true that the rules applied by equity in relation to trusts developed in various ways after the revival of trusts subsequent to the Statute of Uses. For example, the range of third parties bound by a trust was greater than those formerly bound by a use.[48] In this and certain other respects, 'equity has shaped [trusts] much more into real estates, than before when they were uses'.[49] The doctrine of the old use was already reflective of the principle that the use 'should be considered as the land, or as imitating the land'.[50] Therefore, it follows that the process of 'carrying the principle farther'[51] would not lead to any change in the doctrine.

That this was the case is confirmed by a number of nineteenth-century texts which are clear that the doctrine of the old use applied equally in relation to resulting trusts. For example, Preston states that 'the fee taken under a resulting use, or under a resulting trust, or under an express declaration of use; or under an express declaration of trust in favour of the former owner; will descend from the first purchaser under the former ownership' and that this rule 'depends altogether on the rules applied by courts of equity, anterior to the statute of uses'.[52] The rule had been stated

---

[46] *Burgess v Wheate* (1759) 1 Black W 123, 155; 96 ER 67, 81 (Lord Mansfield). See also ibid, 1 Black W 180 (Lord Henley): 'That [a] use and a trust are the same, seems adopted by all the great persons who have presided in this Court.'

[47] The statement in the text understates the complexity surrounding the usage of the terms 'use' and 'trust' before and after the Statute of Uses 1536. For detailed discussion, see Jones (1997) (n 32) 176–82.

[48] See eg Simpson *History of Land Law* (n 33) 181 (discussing the former distinction between those who came to the land *in the post* and *in the per*). Note that, since the term 'use' is used to refer to an interest which was executed by the Statute of Uses, thus ceasing to be an equitable interest, the question could never arise of the extent to which uses after the Statute would bind third parties as an equitable interest.

[49] *Burgess v Wheate* (n 46) 1 Black W 180 (Lord Henley).

[50] Ibid.

[51] Ibid.

[52] R Preston, *An Essay in a Course of Lectures on Abstracts of Title* (London, W Clarke & Sons, 1818) vol 2, 436. To similar effect is C Watkins, *An Essay on the Law of Descents*, ed J Williams, 4th edn (London, S Sweet, 1837) 243–44: 'as such use, whether expressly limited or resulting, was the ancient use . . . and so, as it were, a portion of the *old estate*, such trust, so limited or resulting, must be a portion of the old estate also'. See also G Gilbert, *The Law*

clearly in the 'great case'[53] of *Burgess v Wheate* in 1759. Lord Keeper Henley (speaking in the context of descent) stated the position as follows:

> [A] use, whether declared or resulting, must ensue [ie follow] the nature of the land, and retain the same quality; and whether it be expressed or resulting, makes no matter of difference. . . . Uses at common law, and trusts now, must ensue the nature of the land. . . . In the case of a resulting use, the true reason is, that 'tis never out of the grantor. In the case of trust, 'tis the same—'tis the old trust.[54]

The doctrine of the 'old use', although carrying the ancient authority of Lord Coke, continued to have real practical importance up to the end of 1925. Although reforming legislation in 1833 altered the rules of descent in relation to express uses and trusts, this legislation did not apply to resulting uses and trusts.[55] The Administration of Estates Act 1925, section 45 abolished the rules in relation to descent to heirs, except in relation to fees tail, although these rules continued to be important for a considerable time in relation to titles which depended on questions of descent arising before 1926. It may also be noted that section 51 of the 1925 Act (as amended) provides that the old rules of descent should continue to apply in the case of

> any beneficial interest in real estate [held at his death by] a person of unsound mind or defective living and of full age at the commencement of this Act, and unable, by reason of his incapacity, to make a will, who thereafter dies intestate in respect of such interest without having recovered his testamentary capacity.

This exception means that the rules under discussion would have had (limited) practical significance well into the second half of the twentieth century.

Thus, it will be seen that when Lords Upjohn, Wilberforce and Reid spoke in *Vandervell* of the beneficial interest under a resulting trust 'remaining' in the settlor, they were reflecting an approach which had consistently been adopted by Equity for four centuries. Having recognised the weight of historical authority in favour of this way of looking at the

---

of Uses and Trusts, ed E Sugden, 3rd edn (London, W Reed, 1811) 28, citing *Fawcet v Lowther* (1751) 2 Ves Sen 300, 28 ER 193; Chitty (n 38) 10 and 272; D Yale (ed), *Lord Nottingham's 'Manual of Chancery Practice' and 'Prolegomena of Chancery and Equity'* (Cambridge, Cambridge University Press, 1965) 245.

[53] Blackstone (n 37) vol 2, 246.

[54] *Burgess v Wheate* (n 46) 1 Black W 185. There is another crisp statement to similar effect in *Northen v Carnegie* (1859) 4 Drew 587, 593; 62 ER 225, 227 (Kindersley V-C).

[55] See the Inheritance Act 1833, s 3, which provided that in the future 'when any land shall have been limited . . . to the person or to the heirs of the person who shall thereby have conveyed the same land, such person shall be considered to have acquired the same as a purchaser by virtue of such assurance, and shall not be considered to be entitled thereto as his former estate or part thereof'. This reform did not affect the position in relation to resulting uses or trusts because in such cases the estate is not 'limited' to the grantor. See Sweet (n 31), 130 n 5; Watkins (n 52) 241.

resulting trust, the next section of the chapter considers whether the retention idea is satisfactory as a theoretical explanation.

E. ANALYSIS OF THE RETENTION IDEA

On a strict legal analysis, is there any plausibility in the retention idea? Or is Swadling correct to contend that when a resulting trust arises in my favour (over land in his example), I have '"retained" nothing'? Considering the matter in light of Hohfeld's classic analysis of rights, the owner of land does not simply have 'rights' but rather a 'complex aggregate' of claim-rights, liberties, powers and immunities.[56] The fee simple owner of land has certain claim-rights against each person in the world in respect of the land, for example that each of those persons should keep off the land. In respect of actually occupying and enjoying the land, the owner has a series of liberties against everyone else in the world, to occupy and enjoy the land in various ways, with the result that these other people have 'no right' to prevent this occupation or enjoyment.

When a resulting trust is created, it seems (looking at the position without reference to the complexity introduced by the Trusts of Land and Appointment of Trustees Act 1996)[57] that the settlor *does* retain these liberties against all the other persons in the world. The beneficiary under a bare trust has a liberty (in equity) as against the trustee to occupy and enjoy the land and the trustee has 'no right' (in equity) against the beneficiary that the beneficiary should refrain from doing those things. It is tempting to emphasise, as Hope JA did in *DKLR Holdings Co (No 2) Pty Ltd v Commissioner for Stamp Duties*, that 'at law a *cestui que trust* has no right to possession'.[58] However, as Hohfeld persuasively argued many years ago, in refuting the position of Maitland that there was no conflict, or virtually no conflict, between law and equity,[59] what is relevant is the 'net residuum derived from a "fusion" of law and equity'.[60] In other words, in cases

---

[56] See eg WN Hohfeld, 'Fundamental Legal Conceptions as Applied in Judicial Reasoning' (1916–17) 26 *Yale Law Journal* 710, 767.

[57] See C Harpum, S Bridge and M Dixon, *Megarry and Wade: The Law of Real Property*, 7th edn (London, Sweet & Maxwell, 2008) 477–81. Prior to the 1996 Act, it was clear that a beneficiary under a bare trust was entitled to occupy the land (ibid, 478). The statutory right of occupancy conferred on beneficiaries by the 1996 Act is subject to certain conditions, although such conditions cannot, in practice, be imposed by trustees in the case of a bare trust (ibid, 479–480). It seems reasonable to assume that the underlying nature of the resulting trust has not been altered by the recent introduction of this legislation in relation to land and the following discussion therefore focuses on the position at common law.

[58] [1980] 1 NSWLR 510 (NSWCA) 519.

[59] Note, for example, these famous comments of Maitland (n 8) 17: 'Equity had come not to destroy the law, but to fulfil it. Every jot and every tittle of the law was to be obeyed.'

[60] Hohfeld (n 56) 767. See also his comment ibid: '[many] substantive equitable rules . . . are in conflict with *so-called* legal rules,—the latter being *pro tanto* "repealed," and rendered as invalid as statutes that have been repealed by a subsequently enacted constitution.'

where equity gives a different answer to the common law, the answer that matters is the one given by equity. A common law court (if there were still any such courts in existence) would not see the beneficiary as having a liberty as against the trustee to occupy the land but this position would be overridden in equity and thus the position recognised by the legal system is that the beneficiary has the liberty in question.

It is true that, prior to the creation of the resulting trust, the settlor had claim-rights as against the other people in the world that they should stay off his land, and so on. Once the legal title has passed to the trustee, the settlor loses those claim-rights and as beneficiary he has 'no right' as against other people in respect of their occupying the land, and so on (although, in fact, if the beneficiary is in possession, his possession gives him claim-rights as against the other people in the world besides the trustee).[61]

However, he does acquire new claim-rights against the trustee that the trustee should enforce the trustee's claim-rights as legal owner against other people to ensure that they keep off the land, and so on. Thus, in this respect, the beneficiary under the resulting trust does not 'retain' his claim-rights—he loses them and they are replaced by claim-rights against the trustee. However, there is one important set of claim-rights which the beneficiary does retain, that is, his claim-rights (in equity) as against the trustee that the trustee should stay off the land, and so on. Since the trustee is the legal owner and therefore the most likely candidate, as a practical matter, to seek to exercise his liberties in a manner interfering with the beneficiary's enjoyment of the land, it is of obvious practical value to have this set of claim-rights against him.[62]

Thus, it would seem that the beneficiary under a resulting trust does 'retain' some of his pre-existing entitlements but it is also clearly true that he acquires other new entitlements and loses other pre-existing entitlements. This means that the idea of retention, although it does reflect the reality to some extent, is not fully accurate, notwithstanding the fact that aspects of the criticism of the retention point can be refuted. One might be tempted to gloss over the theoretical problems with the retention idea and to try to maintain the line that the beneficiary under a trust 'in substance' has the title to the property, so that it can be argued that in substance the retention idea holds true.[63] Unfortunately, when one is analysing the

---

[61] See Swadling (2007) (n 29) 273; *Mount Carmel Investments Ltd v Peter Thurlow Ltd* [1988] 1 WLR 1078.

[62] In addition, the beneficiary loses various powers in relation to the land (eg to convey the legal title to a third party) and these are replaced by claim-rights against the trustee. Also, the trustee acquires a power (but not a liberty) as against the beneficiary to convey the property to a third party in a manner which extinguishes the beneficial entitlement of the beneficiary.

[63] See Rickett and Grantham (n 15) 49 and 59. Note also Penner's argument in the present volume: chap 8, part D. One of the hypothetical examples Penner relies upon in support of the idea of retention 'in substance' involves an unregistered owner of land who subsequently obtains a registered title under the Land Registration Act 2002. Penner suggests that Chambers's and Swadling's positions would require them to contend that the landowner's registered

position as a matter of principle, rather than simply on the basis of authority, this is not fully satisfactory. The interest of a beneficiary under a trust is, in an important sense, 'not carved out of a legal estate but impressed upon it'.[64] Trying to uphold the retention thesis without offering a proper answer to this point involves an unnecessary fudging of the theoretical position and, if one is taking this kind of liberty in defence of one's own position, one cannot object to similar inconsistencies at the level of principle in competing theoretical positions. It will be necessary, therefore, in this chapter to look beyond the retention idea for a satisfactory theoretical explanation of the automatic resulting trust.

F. THE IDEA OF RESTITUTION

1. The Unjust Enrichment Theory

Chambers has argued that the concept of restitution underlies all resulting trusts. The resulting trustee has been unjustly enriched because 'the provider of the property did not intend to benefit the recipient'.[65] Chambers's categorisation of resulting trusts as restitutionary requires that they 'cause one person to give up something to another',[66] that something being an enrichment (or its value in money) which has been received at the expense of the other person.[67] His categorisation of resulting trusts would,

---

interest is a wholly new one, whereas Penner can more plausibly contend that the landowner's interest is substantially the same as before. The current author agrees that the landowner's interest in this example is not a completely new one, because many of his claim-rights, liberties, powers and liabilities are the same as before he registered his title. (Hohfeld's analysis of rights was used earlier in this Part to make the similar point that it is an exaggeration to suggest that a person who creates a trust in his own favour over land retains 'nothing': contrast Penner's view (chap 8, n 92) on the utility of Hohfeld's work in this context). On the other hand, the landowner's interest in the example is not truly identical to the one he had before, since some of his claim-rights, liberties, powers, and liabilities are different. Whether, in this example or in the context of the resulting trust, one can describe the person's past and present interests as 'substantially' the same depends on the meaning one wishes to ascribe to the slippery term 'substantially'. This chapter seeks to emphasise the historical significance of the retention idea in the context of resulting trusts (and it is relevant in other contexts also: compare W Swadling, 'The Vendor-Purchaser Constructive Trust' in S Degeling and J Edelman (eds), *Equity in Commercial Law* (Sydney, Lawbook Co, 2005) 463, 481–85). However, in seeking to counter the persistent argument that resulting trusts respond to unjust enrichment, an argument which appeals primarily to principle, it is essential to be as precise as possible. In my view, this requires recognition of the fact that, strictly speaking, the beneficiary under a resulting trust does not 'retain' his interest.

[64] *DKLR Holding Co (No 2) Pty Ltd v Commissioner for Stamp Duties* (1982) 149 CLR 431, 474 (Brennan J). See also *Re Transphere Pty Ltd* (1986) 5 NSWLR 309, 311 (McLelland J); Jones (1998) (n 32) 190 (suggesting that 'the creation of a trust is a process of cumulation, not of division').
[65] Chambers (n 4) 41.
[66] Ibid, 94.
[67] Ibid, 93–107.

therefore, be inappropriate if resulting trusts merely preserved a pre-existing entitlement of the settlor,[68] or if (which is a different proposition) such trusts did not involve the resulting trustee giving up any property received at the expense of the settlor.

If one wishes to see the trustee as being required to 'give up' or restore something to the beneficiary under the resulting trust, one is drawn towards a metaphorical conception of the creation of a resulting trust whereby the trustee takes the 'full' legal title, upon which equity 'then' fastens by creating a trust to effect restitution. The imperative to regard the trustee as taking a benefit, of which he can be stripped, leads to a visualisation in which the trust is created an imaginary instant *after* the trustee has taken legal title to the property. The reality, however, is that the trust is created neither before nor after the conveyance but at the same instant.

In the context of the restitution argument, an impression of a chronological progression may be created by looking first at the position 'at common law' and then shifting perspective to look to the position 'in equity'. This is an optical illusion, however, because the beneficiary's equitable rights come into being at the same time as the trustee's common law rights and there is never a moment when the trustee possesses the common law rights free of a trust. Obviously, in a hypothetical common law court, the trustee would be seen as having an unencumbered legal interest but that is simply to tell an incomplete story—the full story is that the common law view has been trumped by equity, leaving the trustee with just a 'bare' legal interest.[69]

In defending the restitution thesis, Chambers strongly rejects the 'retention' idea, suggesting that the retention reasoning in *Vandervell* is inconsistent with 'the true nature of the resulting trust itself'.[70] In light of the long pedigree of the retention argument, one must wonder as to the meaning of 'truth' in the context of this assertion. As a matter of authority, the law's approach in the context of descent seems to establish clearly that the interest held by the settlor under a resulting trust is not one which was ever held by the trustee. This seems damaging to Chambers's contention that the 'true' situation is that the trustee has been required to give up an interest to the settlor.

In terms of authority in relation to the idea of restitution, it is useful to consider the decision of the High Court of Australia in *DKLR Holding Co (No 2) Pty Ltd v Commissioner for Stamp Duties*:[71] 'That dreaded stamp

---

[68] Ibid, 102–04.

[69] It is sometimes contended that the trustee has the 'entire' legal interest, as does someone who owns beneficially, but *holds* this legal estate on trust for the beneficiary. However, this idea of 'holding' is revealed as a misleading metaphor when one thinks more precisely about ownership as an aggregate of jural relations—see Hohfeld's critique of Maitland's position on the relationship between law and equity: Hohfeld (n 56) 769–70. See further, text to nn 59–60.

[70] Chambers (n 4) 52.

[71] *DKLR* (HCA) (n 64).

duty case.'[72] Chambers relies on this case partly to combat the challenge from the retention idea and partly because it appears to offer some support for the conceptual basis of the restitution idea. Most useful to his position seems to be the remark of Aickin J in *DKLR*: 'It is of the nature of a resulting trust that it arises when the entire interest is vested in the transferee and at the very moment it becomes so vested.'[73] While even this *dictum* concedes the obvious truth that the resulting trust is created at the same instant when the trustee acquires his legal interest, the suggestion that the trustee acquires 'the entire interest' in the property seems to assist Chambers's argument.

The facts of *DKLR* were unusual. The case concerned the stamp duty implications of a voluntary transfer by a company called '29 Macquarie' to another company called 'DKLR Holding'. Given the intention of the transferring company, this transfer would (on one interpretation of the New South Wales registration of title legislation) have triggered a resulting trust. However, prior to the conveyance, DKLR had executed a declaration that it would hold the land on trust for 29 Macquarie. This added factor in the case made it more plausible to regard the equitable interest ultimately held by the settlor as, in a sense, coming from the trustee.[74] Interestingly, in his judgment in *DKLR*, Mason J (with whom Stephen J agreed) referred to the creation of 'a resulting trust of the equitable estate which has not been disposed of',[75] thus showing apparent support for the retention approach.

Finally, in terms of putting the *dicta* in *DKLR* into context, it is important to note the comments on the case by Deane J in the High Court of Australia in *Corin v Patton*. He stated that *DKLR*:

> turned upon the principle of stamp duties law that 'duty is levied on instruments, not on the underlying transactions to which they give effect'.[76] That principle of stamp duties law is to be contrasted with the general approach of equity to pay regard to substance rather than mere form.[77]

Deane J went on to state that:

> [A]s Mason J clearly recognized in the *DKLR Holding Co Case* (at p 450), equity permits an owner of property to convey it to another as bare trustee for himself or for a third party. In such a case, it is convenient to speak of the transfer as being of a bare legal estate. If more precise analysis is required, it is that the equitable rights of the beneficiary attach to the property at the instant of transfer

---

[72] So called by counsel in argument before the High Court of Australia in *Mary Metledge t/as Metledge & Associates v Koutsourais & Anor* [2005] HCATrans 425 (17 June 2005).
[73] *DKLR* (HCA) (n 64) 464.
[74] This point was certainly in the mind of Brennan J, who stated immediately after the passage quoted by Chambers (n 4) 53, that the 'charter of 29 Macquarie's interest was DKLR's declaration, not the memorandum of transfer' from 29 Macquarie: *DKLR* (HCA) (n 64) 474.
[75] *DKLR* (HCA) (n 64) 459.
[76] The internal quote is from Mason J in *DKLR* (HCA) (n 64) 449.
[77] (1990) 92 ALR 1, 28.

and the transferee receives the property subject to the equitable obligations of a bare trustee for the transferor or the third party . . . [and a transferee in such a position would not] have ever had any beneficial interest in the property transferred.[78]

As a matter of authority, therefore, *DKLR* does not take the restitution thesis very far. There remains for that thesis the difficulty of the line of authority discussed in part D which insists that the interest under a resulting trust is 'no new thing'[79] and bases important practical consequences on that conclusion.

2. Arguments of Principle

Turning from authority to principle, it seems that Chambers's argument against the retention idea contains the seeds of an argument against his own position. The reason why Chambers considers that the grantor 'retains' nothing after the creation of the resulting trust seems to be that, prior to its creation, he did not have a separate equitable title; what he has after the creation of the trust is an interest under a trust, which is different to the legal title which he held before.[80] But this same point seems to defeat the argument that, by giving a beneficial interest to the grantor, one is requiring the trustee to 'give up' an enrichment (or its equivalent in money) which he has received at the expense of the grantor. If ending up with a beneficial interest under a trust does not involve 'retaining' one's former legal interest, how does being given a beneficial interest under a trust amount to a restoration of that legal interest? Chambers emphasises that resulting trusts 'are normally bare trusts, meaning that the trustee's primary duty is to convey the property to (or at the direction of) the beneficiary'.[81] However, one cannot equate holding an interest under a trust with holding the property beneficially at law, simply by reference to the fact that the beneficiary's interest under the trust gives the beneficiary (amongst other rights) a power to call on the trustee to transfer the legal interest to him, so that he would ultimately end up holding beneficially. After all, if having a power to call on the trustee to convey the legal interest was equivalent to holding beneficially, one could fairly say that the grantor retains his interest when a resulting trust arises in his favour—initially, he held beneficially and, once the resulting trust has arisen, he holds an interest under a trust

---

[78] *Corin* (n 76) 28.
[79] *Samme's Case* (n 7) 13 Co Rep 56.
[80] Chambers (n 4) 52.
[81] Ibid, 94. Note that, if the object of the exercise were simply to put the recipient of the property under a duty to convey that property back to the settlor, this could most simply be achieved by means of an order of the court requiring the recipient to make such a conveyance—there would be no need to regard a trust as having come into existence at the time of the original transaction.

which allows him to call upon the trustee to convey the legal interest to him.

The problems with the retention idea also highlight another important difficulty with Chambers's thesis. For Chambers, '[a]ll resulting trusts come into being because the provider did not intend to benefit the recipient'.[82] The description of the basis of resulting trusts, which recurs frequently throughout his work on the subject, is a 'lack of intention to benefit the recipient'.[83] The resulting trust is 'equity's response to the receipt of property by someone who was not intended to have the benefit of that property'.[84] Chambers is at pains to emphasise that 'the essential fact of intention, common to all cases of resulting trusts' is not a 'positive' intention but rather an absence of intention. He explains that

> there is a difference between a presumption that the provider *did not intend* to benefit the recipient and a presumption that the provider *intended not* to benefit the recipient. Only the latter can explain all of the cases of resulting trust.[85]

This point is crucial in the scheme of Chambers's overall argument. His ultimate project is to establish the radical proposition that the resulting trust comes into existence in a far wider range of circumstances than the existing orthodoxy would accept, so that there would be a proprietary remedy in the form of a resulting trust 'in every case in which the provider is entitled to restitution on the basis of non-voluntary transfer'.[86] Thus, the resulting trust could arise, for example, in cases of mistaken payment or of undue influence or unconscionability or in suitable cases of 'failure of consideration'.[87] A difficulty in the way of this argument is the plausibility of the counter-argument that the traditional categories of resulting trust turn on an intention (which, in some cases, is proven through the operation of a presumption) on the part of the settlor to create a trust. If the resulting trust indeed turns on a positive intention to create a trust, then it cannot operate in the new categories of case which Chambers envisages, given that these new cases do not involve any intention on the part of the settlor to create a trust. Hence, Chambers's concern to establish the proposition that the basis for all resulting trusts is an absence of an intention to benefit the recipient.

In a recent critique of Chambers's position, Swadling finds it difficult to see when an 'absence of intention' could arise in practice, leading him to inquire 'if it really was the transferor's intention 'not to benefit' the trans-

---

[82] Ibid, 2.
[83] See eg Chambers (n 4) 21.
[84] Ibid, 33.
[85] Ibid, 21.
[86] Ibid, 113. This is subject to the requirements that '(i) the enrichment consists of assets capable of being the subject matter of a trust and (ii) the recipient does not obtain the unfettered beneficial ownership of those assets before the right to restitution arises'.
[87] Ibid, ch 5 ('Vitiated Intention') and ch 6 ('Qualified Intention').

feree, why did he make the transfer at all?'[88] It is true that, in the context of a transfer of property (on which Swadling's analysis in the relevant article tends to focus), it is at first sight difficult to see when there would be a total absence of intention to make the transfer, without a plea of *non est factum* being possible.[89] However, Chambers's argument relies for the most part on cases in the domain of the purchase money resulting trust. In that context, it is easy to envisage a person's money being used to fund the purchase of property in another's name without the first person's knowledge, such a case fitting well into the 'absence of intention' paradigm. Chambers places strong emphasis on the fact that certain older English cases which recognised that a trust should arise in this situation, including *Ryall v Ryall*,[90] referred to the relevant trust as 'resulting'.[91] Chambers categorises such cases as examples of the resulting trust and, emphasising the fact that these cases do not involve a positive intention to create a trust, he identifies the concept of 'absence of intention to benefit' as the feature which unites these examples with the other categories of resulting trust. This provides him with a basis to argue for the extension of the resulting trust to new situations which he regards as also satisfying the 'absence of intention to benefit' criterion.

On closer inspection, it appears that Chambers's argument essentially hinges on an ambiguity in the word 'benefit'. Chambers's reasoning runs into problems because the idea of an absence of intention to 'benefit' must, for the purposes of his position, cover two different situations: (i) an absence of intention to give any sort of interest to the recipient (to cover cases like *Ryall v Ryall*) and (ii) an intention to give the legal title to the recipient so that the recipient would hold on trust rather than taking beneficially (to cover the 'automatic resulting trust' and the other traditional examples of the resulting trust, excluding cases comparable to *Ryall v*

---

[88] Swadling (n 4) 93.

[89] It could arise, however, in a case triggering a right to rectification, as where the written conveyance included an interest in property which the transferor had not intended to be covered by it.

[90] (1739) 1 Atk 59, 26 ER 39. See also *Lane v Dighton* (1762) Amb 409, 27 ER 274; *Williams v Williams* (1863) 32 Beav 370, 55 ER 145.

[91] Chambers (1997) (n 4) 21–23. Chambers also discusses (at 22–23; see also 226–27) a handful of Canadian cases, by far the most recent of which is *Re Kolari* (1981) 36 OR (2d) 473. Given the development in Canadian law of the constructive trust as an instrument to remedy unjust enrichment (following *Pettkus v Becker* [1980] 2 SCR 834), it seems doubtful that the cases establish as a matter of authority that the current position in Canadian law is that a resulting trust, rather than a constructive trust, arises to remedy unjust enrichment in the situation under discussion. There is no assertion by Chambers that these are the only Canadian cases falling within the relevant fact pattern, so that it may be that only cases invoking the resulting trust have been cited. One case not mentioned is *Duff v Duff* (1988) 12 RFL (3d) 435 (Ontario Supreme Court) (cited in A Scott and W Fratcher, *The Law of Trusts*, 4th edn (Boston, MA, Little, Brown & Co, 1989) vol 5, §440.1) where, without her knowledge, a husband used his wife's share of the proceeds of sale of a house to purchase another property in his own name. Hoilett LJSC decided (ibid, 447–48) that the husband held the new property on a constructive trust for his wife.

Ryall). The second of these intentions involves a positive intention to create a trust, not merely an absence of intention to benefit the recipient. As Chambers is content to accept in the context of the 'retention' argument (and as is clearly established by *Westdeutsche*), it is a fallacy to suggest that a person who holds property beneficially holds a separate equitable interest alongside a separate legal interest.[92] Therefore, it is simply not tenable to suggest, as Chambers does,[93] that a person could intend to pass the legal interest but, without holding the positive intention of creating a trust giving rise to a separate equitable interest, could 'lack' an intention to pass the equitable interest. It would suit Chambers's argument if it could be said that such a person intends to give the recipient the legal title but has an absence of intention in respect of giving him 'the benefit' of the property. The trouble is that there is no such thing as 'the benefit' of the property as distinct from legal ownership or the equitable interest under a trust[94]—if one is to have any intention or absence of intention as to what will happen to the equitable interest, one must first intend to have a trust under which there will be a separate equitable interest. It should be stressed again that if there really were such a thing as the 'benefit' of the property, which the settlor possessed prior to the transfer and which he might fail to intend to transfer along with the legal title, then the retention thesis would be perfectly viable in principle.

The argument in the last paragraph suggests that Chambers's 'essential fact of intention' actually covers two distinct mental states, one an absence of intention to give any interest to the recipient of the property and the other a positive intention to have the recipient hold on trust rather than hold beneficially.[95] It is certainly possible to find words which describe the latter intention in terms of a mixture of positive and negative aspects, for example by stating it as a positive intention to create a trust coupled with an absence of intention to have the trustee take the beneficial interest under the trust. It is arguable that the negative aspect of this formulation adds nothing because the reference to a positive intention to make the recipient a trustee presupposes an intention to have a beneficiary or beneficiaries

---

[92] Lord Browne-Wilkinson's purpose in *Westdeutsche* (n 1) 706 in pointing out this fallacy was, in fact, to defeat an argument based on the conceptualisation of the resulting trust favoured by Chambers.

[93] See Chambers (2000) (n 6) 390, arguing that a resulting trust can arise in favour of someone who was aware that he was conveying the property to another person but 'simply failed to address [his] mind to the issue of beneficial ownership'.

[94] See the critique by Swadling (n 4) 90–93.

[95] Swadling (n 4) appears to assume that Chambers's idea of 'lack of intention to benefit' (and Birks's similar formula 'non-beneficial transfer', on which Swadling primarily focuses) must bear only one meaning. This leads him to struggle to pin down which meaning is intended. The current author differs from Swadling in concluding that the relevant formulations were intended by their authors to be sufficiently broad to cover both of the mental states identified in the text to this footnote (so that if either were present there would be a 'lack of intention to benefit' or a 'non-beneficial transfer').

other than the trustee (or to have a trust for a purpose) in respect of the portion of the beneficial interest under discussion. Furthermore, the formula 'an absence of intention to have the trustee take the beneficial interest' is overly inclusive in terms of identifying the cases where a resulting trust will come into existence, since it clearly covers cases of express trust.[96] Thus, when unpacked, the phrase 'lack of intention to benefit the recipient' is simply a short-hand for 'an absence of intention to give the recipient the legal title or a positive intention to make the recipient a trustee coupled with the absence of a valid allocation of the relevant portion of the beneficial interest to the trustee or anyone else or for any valid purpose'. This is far less convincing as a unifying principle for resulting trusts, which Chambers envisages as carrying a significant amount of weight in terms of justifying a radical expansion in the scope of such trusts. Unlike Chambers's preferred phrasing, this more detailed formulation emphasises the difference between cases involving an absence of intention and cases falling under the traditional categories of resulting trust. This encourages a straightforward riposte to Chambers's argument, which is to deny that the absence of intention cases are properly to be classified as examples of resulting trust (facilitating the argument, favoured by the present author, that the unifying feature of all resulting trusts is that they turn on the intention of the settlor to make the recipient of the property a trustee).[97]

One subset of absence of intention cases, including those where a trustee makes unauthorised use of trust money to make a purchase in his own name, appears to involve a standard application of tracing principles.[98] Following *Foskett v McKeown*, a case in this category 'does not involve any question of resulting or constructive trusts',[99] because the original express trust can be seen as covering the property which has been purchased using trust funds. It is not surprising, given the factual similarities between this aspect of the law of tracing and the purchase money resulting trust

---

[96] As pointed out by S Gardner, *An Introduction to the Law of Trusts*, 2nd edn (Oxford, Oxford University Press, 2003) 136. Gardner develops a concept of 'proprietary inertia' (ibid, 132–37) as an alternative basis for resulting trusts. However, it is difficult to see how the idea of 'inertia' provides a solution to the difficulty with the retention idea, especially when Gardner seems to be thinking in terms of the property 'remaining' with the settlor: ibid, 136.

[97] Although the voluntary conveyance and purchase money resulting trusts have not been analysed in detail in this chapter, it is submitted that they fit into the analysis advanced in the text. This chapter is part of a wider project which will involve the author in dealing specifically with these other types of resulting trust.

[98] See Swadling 'Property' (2000) (n 12) 254–56.

[99] [2001] 1 AC 102, 108 (Lord Browne-Wilkinson). See also Lord Millett's statement at 127 that 'A beneficiary of a trust is entitled to a continuing beneficial interest not merely in the trust property but in its traceable proceeds also.' Chambers does not agree: see generally R Chambers, 'Tracing and Unjust Enrichment' in J Neyers et al (eds), *Understanding Unjust Enrichment* (Oxford, Hart Publishing, 2004) 263.

G. AN ALTERNATIVE VIEW: REPOSING TRUST

This part seeks to develop a more satisfying theoretical rationalisation for the automatic resulting trust, drawing on equitable discourse on the nature of resulting trusts and also on the historical development of trusts generally.

1. Metaphorical Conceptions of the Resulting Trust in Equity

The word 'resulting' derives from the Latin 'resultare', meaning to spring or leap back. Its technical legal meaning seems closely related to a non-legal sense of the English word as meaning '[t]o recoil; to rebound or spring back' which, though now obsolete, seems to have been current at the time when the term was attached to trusts.[105] What is to be understood by the metaphor—implicit in the word 'resulting'—of springing or leaping back, or recoiling, or rebounding? Interestingly, it seems to constitute an alternative visualisation of the resulting trust in equity, existing alongside the idea of retention. Where a preference is expressed between them, it has tended to be for the notion of retention. Sweet,[106] for example, argued that the term 'resulting' is 'unfortunate, because it suggests the idea of returning or coming back' and he was adamant that using it in that sense would be 'an error' since it is inconsistent with the idea of retention (which, as has been discussed, had a solid basis in actual legal rules). Nonetheless, the 'springing back' or 'rebounding' metaphor seems likely to have explanatory value, given that is embedded in the very label applied to resulting trusts.

One way of looking at the relevant metaphor is to suggest that, by the act of conveying the property to the trustee to hold 'on trust', the settlor is seen as having separated the legal and the equitable interests and sent them off into the ether towards their intended recipients. The bare legal title is successfully projected on to the trustee but the equitable interest does not carry to anyone—it is 'in the air'[107] for an imaginary instant and, since it has no place to land, it springs 'back' to the settlor. This idea of the beneficial interest rebounding (as it were, against the brick wall it has come up against) does not involve the idea that it has come back *from* someone else. This point is conveyed by another metaphor to which equity has resorted—the idea contained in '[e]arly references to Equity, like Nature, abhorring a vacuum'.[108] This suggests the image of a physical template for a trust, with a space for the trustee (holding the bare legal title) and a space

---

[105] *The Oxford English Dictionary*, 2nd edn 1989; OED Online, Oxford University Press, 21 March 2009 <http://dictionary.oed.com/cgi/entry/50204534>, sv 'result v', giving examples from the sixteenth, seventeenth and eighteenth centuries.
[106] Sweet (n 31) 130.
[107] *Vandervell v IRC* (n 3) 329 (Lord Wilberforce).
[108] Ibid, 313 (Lord Upjohn) who regarded such references as 'delightful but unnecessary'.

for the beneficiaries (holding the beneficial interest). If there is a 'gap' in the ownership of the beneficial interest, the settlor is drawn in to fill this 'vacuum'—hence, in a sense, the settlor is drawn towards the beneficial interest, rather than the reverse as in the other metaphors.

The line of thought underlying these metaphors, although giving a useful flavour of the equitable rules in relation to resulting trusts, is insufficient to provide a full theoretical explanation of those rules. The difficulty does not lie in the concept of a trustee holding a 'bare legal title' since this is actually a coherent description of the interest of a trustee *in the eyes of equity* (which means in the eyes of our legal system).[109] The difficulty is instead that 'a bare legal title' is a relational idea—a trustee's rights are limited, as compared to someone who holds beneficially, because the trustee's aggregate of claim-rights, liberties, powers and immunities is altered *in relation to a particular beneficiary or beneficiaries*.[110] It is not truly coherent to say that a person holds a 'bare legal title' in the abstract, without reference to anyone else's position.[111] However, it must be remembered that this difficulty does not afflict the rule which proceeds from the metaphors under discussion. The trustee ends up having a bare legal title with the settlor as the beneficiary, so that there is never really a moment when the beneficial interest is in transit, unsuccessfully moving towards a beneficiary who cannot be reached; instead the beneficial interest instantly vests in the settlor. In fact, it may be helpful to regard the metaphors as illustrating the conceptual impossibility which the resulting trust is seen as avoiding. Equity says that the beneficial interest '*cannot* remain in the air' or that it will not countenance a vacuum in the beneficial interest—these things would make no sense and, so, cannot be.

It will be noticed, however, that the thinking which has just been discussed is dependent on a central assumption, namely that, where land has been conveyed 'on trust' to X, then X must hold as trustee even if the particular trusts on which he has been required to hold have failed. It could, naturally, be argued that this is a flaw in equity's approach and that the problem of a trustee without a beneficial interest could equally be solved by saying that there is no trust, so that the recipient never becomes a trustee and simply takes beneficially. The injustice which that would create could then be addressed by giving the settlor a personal claim in unjust enrichment against the intended trustee.[112] An account of the automatic

---

[109] See text to nn 59–60 above.

[110] The proposition in the text is not phrased so as to accommodate the possibility of charitable/purpose trusts but the existence of such trusts does not alter the substance of the point being made.

[111] Compare *Burgess v Wheate* (n 46), where the beneficiary under a trust died without heirs and, since the doctrine of escheat to the Crown was held not to apply and there was no beneficiary in whose favour to enforce the trust, the trustee was permitted to retain the property for his own benefit.

[112] See Swadling (n 4) 99 and 101.

resulting trust is, therefore, not complete without a justification for the assumption that a trust comes into existence in the circumstances under discussion. The following section attempts to provide this justification.

2. Why Does a Trust Come into Existence?

It is submitted that Equity concludes that a trust exists in the 'automatic resulting trust' situation because the settlor has created a trust. This explanation involves distinguishing between two different things (a distinction which is critical, it is submitted, to understanding all forms of resulting trust): (i) the creation of a trust through giving property to a trustee to be held on trust, thereby reposing trust in him; and (ii) the declaration of the particular trusts under which the trustee is to hold. The point is that what Chambers and Swadling call 'a trust which fails' does not truly fail for the purpose of the rules on resulting trusts. Equity does, of course, recognise the 'three certainties', without which an express trust will 'fail'.[113] For example, where property is conveyed to someone and the transferor imposes a purely moral duty on the recipient in respect of the property, no trust is created due to an absence of certainty of intention to create a trust and the recipient takes the property beneficially. However, 'failure' has a different meaning in the context of certainty of objects; it means, not that the intended trustee will take beneficially, but that there will be a resulting trust for the settlor. Where the other requirements for a valid trust are present but there is a failure in terms of certainty of objects, the trust in sense (i) above does not fail, it is only the particular trusts in sense (ii) above which fail.[114] Hence, there is a resulting trust for the settlor. As Megarry J put it in *Vandervell (No 2)*: 'Since ex hypothesi the transfer is on trust, the resulting trust does not establish the trust but merely carries back to A the beneficial interest that has not been disposed of.'[115]

Why then does equity regard a trust as having been created once property is given to a trustee 'on trust'? The point may be approached by looking back at the origins of the concept of a trust. Consider the following passage from Simpson's treatment of the question:

> In protecting the *cestui que use* the Chancellor most commonly proceeded by giving effect to the wishes, intention, or will (*volunt*) of the feoffor or settlor. His wishes might be declared either informally by parole, or they might be

---

[113] Compare Chambers (n 4) 44–45.
[114] Note that Chambers (ibid, 45) relies on a passage from Maitland ((n 8) 76) to demonstrate that 'the words, "on trust", do not create a trust'. It is submitted, however, that Maitland's emphasis in the relevant passage is on the fact that, while the settlor has made it clear that the recipient is to be a trustee, he 'has not saddled him with any *particular* trust' (emphasis added).
[115] *Vandervell (No 2)* (n 10) 294.

expressed formally either in writing or by a deed, such declarations being made on the occasion of the feoffment. Alternatively, the uses might be declared subsequently.[116]

Thus, the essential idea was of someone conveying land to another person to be held according to the first person's wishes. As it was put in one old case, uses were directed 'by the will of the owner of the lands: for the use is in his hands as clay in the hands of the potter'.[117] The 'most potent attraction of putting lands in use'[118] was that it allowed the settlor to acquire a power to devise his lands. A common way of doing this was making a conveyance to feoffees 'to the use of my will',[119] so that the first 'wills' simply consisted of the expression by the settlor of his intentions as to the property, often made when he was on his deathbed.[120] Simpson explains that:

> Such a transaction was not originally thought to . . . raise any issue different in principle to that raised by a feoffment to uses designed to create a settlement *inter vivos* . . . ; the basic policy was that the wishes and intention of the settlor, whatever they were, should be respected.[121]

Against this background, it is inconceivable that a trust would be regarded as 'failing' from the start in the case of a voluntary conveyance to a trustee to hold, for example, 'to the uses of my will'. Instead, this was a paradigmatic example of a trust, with land being transferred to be held according to the settlor's instructions. This illustrates the basic point that there was (and still is, it is submitted) a distinction between the creation of a trust—an arrangement under which the trustee was obliged to hold the property according to the settlor's expression of his will—and the expression of his will itself. This corresponds to the distinction contended for above, that is between the creation of a trust and the allocation of the beneficial interest to specific beneficiaries.[122]

In this context, the doctrine of resulting uses is readily comprehensible. Where property was conveyed to a trustee to hold to uses which were to be declared in the future, the question arose as to the fate of the land in the meantime. Given that a trust was clearly in existence, the only reasonable solution was to conclude that the land should be held to the use of the settlor, thus preserving his ability to determine subsequently what should

---

[116] AWB Simpson, *A History of the Common Law of Contract* (Oxford, Oxford University Press, 1987) 334.
[117] *Brent's Case* (1583) 2 Leonard 14, 16; 74 ER 319, 320 (Manwood J).
[118] Simpson (n 33) 182.
[119] Simpson (n 116) 334; R Megarry, 'The Statute of Uses and the Power to Devise' [1941] *Cambridge Law Journal* 354.
[120] Simpson (n 33) 182.
[121] Simpson (n 116) 334.
[122] Compare the comment of Maitland quoted as text to n 8: 'I have made A a trustee for somebody, and a trustee he must be.'

happen to the land. To allow the trustee to take the property beneficially would have been to ignore the trust which the settlor had reposed in the trustee. Equity's willingness to take account of this 'trust' (in the non-technical sense) has been crucial to equity's enforcement of trusts[123] and its associated willingness to prefer the rights of the beneficiaries over the trustee's creditors and to protect those rights against third parties other than bona fide purchasers for value. Therefore, if one asks why there should be a trust in the case of what is (misleadingly) termed a 'failed trust', the short answer is 'for the same reason as in the case of any trust'.

On this view, the automatic resulting trust is a hybrid. The creation of the trust itself is seen as arising from the decision of the settlor, while the allocation of the beneficial interest to the settlor is seen as occurring because of a rule of the law of equity devised to fill any gap in the beneficial interest under a trust. Adherents of Birks's taxonomy of causative events (in terms of 'consent', 'unjust enrichment', 'wrongs' and 'other events')[124] might ask to which category the causative event belongs. The rule creating a resulting trust in this situation can be seen as one of the background rules which are triggered when a person chooses to create a trust. It is part of a package of rules which cover matters which the settlor may not have consciously considered—such as, for example, the rules imposing various powers and duties on a trustee in terms of investment or the rules about liability for breach of fiduciary duty. In this sense, the allocation of the beneficial interest to the settlor in the context of an automatic resulting trust may be seen as resembling an implied term in a contract. Implied contractual terms are challenging for the Birksian taxonomy and, in some instances at least, might arguably be best placed outside the 'consent category' and allocated instead to the 'other events' category.[125] It may be that this categorisation would also be appropriate in the context of the approach advocated in this chapter, but this depends on one's understanding of the breadth of the 'consent' category.

H. CONCLUSION

This chapter has considered the justification for the 'automatic' resulting trust. It has been pointed out that, as a historical matter, the dominant explanation has been that the settlor 'retains' any beneficial interest of which he has not disposed. At the level of authority, this explanation provides a well-established justification for the existing rules. Since the

---

[123] See Jones (1998) (n 32) 193–94 for discussion of the personal element of trust and confidence which was central to the early idea of the trust.

[124] For recent discussion of this taxonomy, see Low (n 104).

[125] Ibid, 369–70. See also ibid, 357, noting the danger of assuming that the other three categories are somehow 'hierarchically superior' to the miscellaneous category.

view taken in this chapter is that these existing rules are satisfactory, this is not in itself an objectionable state of affairs. However, advocates of a radical expansion in the scope of operation of resulting trusts have argued that the retention idea is flawed at the level of principle, providing support for the idea that the existing rules should be altered to allow resulting trusts to operate as an instrument to reverse unjust enrichment in a wide variety of cases. The relevant issues have been investigated in this chapter and it has been concluded that the retention explanation, though deeply rooted in authority, is not fully satisfactory at the level of principle. It has also been noted that the proposition that all resulting trusts should be regarded as being based on unjust enrichment is not supported by authority and, at the level of principle, is vulnerable to some of the same criticisms as the retention idea.

This chapter has identified an alternative rationalisation of the existing rules (which does not involve any modification in the content of those rules). It has been suggested that, in the context of the 'automatic' resulting trust, equity is confronted with the question of what should happen when property is given on trust to a trustee but the particular trusts indicated do not exhaust the beneficial interest or are invalid. The rule chosen by equity in this situation, that there should be a resulting trust for the settlor, is difficult to fault as a matter of justice. It has been argued that it proceeds on the basis of a logically prior decision by equity that, once property has been conveyed to a trustee in whom the settlor has reposed trust to hold it according to the settlor's instructions, the trust will not 'fail', even where there is a failure in the particular trusts declared or a failure to declare any such trusts. Once one is willing to accept that a trust has been brought into existence by the conveyance to the trustee, so that someone must become entitled to the beneficial interest under that trust, it is difficult to justify anyone besides the settlor taking any unallocated beneficial interest. Although the existing rule is not the only conceivable option, it seems clearly preferable to the alternatives.[126] Thus, this chapter has sought to show that the automatic resulting trust does not truly 'def[y] legal analysis'[127] but is defensible as a matter of principle.

---

[126] See the discussion in the text following n 20.
[127] Swadling (2008).

8

Resulting Trusts and Unjust Enrichment: Three Controversies

JAMES PENNER*

A. INTRODUCTION

Recent work by William Swadling,[1] Robert Chambers[2] and Lord Millett[3] enables us to think seriously about whether it would be a good thing for the courts to recognise resulting trusts as 'restitutionary' trusts.[4]

This work has generated three distinct controversies. Two concern the presumption of resulting trust. The first controversy, perhaps of somewhat lesser moment than the other two, is over what a claimant needs to show in evidence before the presumption is raised: does he merely have to prove that he transferred title to the property to the defendant, or contributed to the purchase price of property title to which is transferred to the defendant, or must he also prove that the defendant provided no consideration in return? This issue is important, because on the former view the presumption arises to 'disambiguate' 'ambiguous transfers', which is Swadling's position, whereas on the latter view the presumption arises to reverse the effect of 'apparent gifts', which is the position taken by Chambers.

The second controversy is over how the presumption operates. Again,

---

*I would like to thank Robert Chambers and Bill Swadling for many illuminating discussions of the ideas discussed herein. I alone need own to any residual nonsense.

[1] W Swadling, 'Explaining Resulting Trusts' (2008) 124 *Law Quarterly Review* 72.
[2] R Chambers, 'Resulting Trusts' in A Burrows and Lord Rodger of Earlsferry (eds), *Mapping the Law: Essays in Memory of Peter Birks* (Oxford, Oxford University Press, 2006) 247; R Chambers and J Penner, 'Ignorance' in J Edelman and S Degeling (eds), *Unjust Enrichment and Commercial Law* (Sydney, Thomson LLP, 2008) 253; R Chambers, 'Two Kinds of Enrichment' in R Chambers, C Mitchell and J Penner (eds), *Philosophical Foundations of Unjust Enrichment* (Oxford, Oxford University Press, 2009) 240.
[3] Lord Millett, 'Proprietary Restitution' in S Degeling and J Edelman (eds), *Equity in Commercial Law* (Sydney, Thomson Lawbook Co, 2005) 309.
[4] A prospect which some of us find appalling: J Penner, 'Value, Property, and Unjust Enrichment: Trusts of Traceable Proceeds' in Chambers et al (n 2) 304.

our match-up is principally between Swadling and Chambers, although Millett has a look in here as well. Swadling argues that the presumption is evidentiary; it supplies a substitute proof where the evidence is exiguous. Moreover, the content of the presumption is that the transferor/contributor effectively declared a trust. Chambers's argument is that the presumption is a presumption of law. A resulting trust will arise by operation of law because the law presumes (rebuttably) that the transferor/contributor did not intend to make a gift. Getting this question right is vital, for if Swadling's view is the correct one, then 'presumed' resulting trusts are *express* trusts, and as such would have nothing to do with unjust enrichment. In the Birksian event/response categories, they would arise by consent, not as a response to unjust enrichment.

Peter Birks never advised me on my writing (which shows, I suppose), but Robert Chambers tells me that Birks advised him that an academic paper is not a whodunnit, and that there is no point in keeping the reader in suspense as to the outcome. I shall, therefore, give the following advance score on the resolution of these issues. Swadling beats Chambers on the first controversy. Chambers, however, gets his own back by (mostly) beating Swadling on the second.

The third controversy is over this question: even assuming that Chambers's view is substantially correct in that resulting trusts arise by operation of law in cases where a transferor/contributor does not intend to make a gift, do they do so as a response to the recipient's unjust enrichment? Here Millett argues, against both Chambers and Swadling, that resulting trusts arise by operation of law because 'what a man fails to give away, he keeps', not to reverse unjust enrichment. In my view Millett here wins against Chambers and Swadling, though I unhumbly claim to add some value in explaining precisely why.

B. THE FIRST CONTROVERSY

What must a claimant show to raise the presumption of resulting trust?

There are, as stated above, two views on this. The first, which I will attribute to Swadling,[5] is that in order for the presumption to 'kick in', all a claimant needs to show is that he transferred the property to the defendant or contributed to the purchase price (up to paying the entire price) of property transferred by the seller to the defendant. According to Swadling, these are 'ambiguous transfers', because the purpose in transferring or contributing in this way might be to make a gift or to constitute a trust or (in the case of contributing to the purchase price) may be by way of loan.

---

[5] I do not think Swadling ever quite puts it this way, but it is implicit, I think, in his discussion of ambiguous transfers: Swadling (n 1) 86.

Chambers, by contrast, argues that the presumption of resulting trust arises in cases of 'apparent gifts', that is, in cases in which the claimant transfers or contributes as above *for no consideration*. It would then seem to follow as a matter of logic that for a claimant to succeed he must establish both the transfer or contribution *and* that he received nothing of value in return, for only then would the claimant have established a case of an apparent gift.

It is submitted that Swadling has the better of this argument, for the simple reason that he has the cases on his side, though he is not as explicit about this as I now intend to be. The cases which make the point are those in which the application of the presumption determines the issue, that is, where evidence of the transferor's intentions is absent or unsatisfactory. Take, for example, *The Venture*.[6] The plaintiff, Percy Stone, proved that he had contributed to the purchase price of a yacht, title to which was transferred to his brother, Andrew, who had since died. Percy alleged he had paid in the capacity of a partner, his brother being intended to hold on trust for the two of them, but the judge at first instance found this evidence unsatisfactory and insufficient to establish an express trust of the yacht in his favour. Thus beyond the bare fact of Percy's contribution nothing was established on the evidence. Nevertheless, Percy succeeded. Farwell LJ, giving judgment for the Court of Appeal, said:

> [W]hen it is once proved that Percy Stone advanced 550l. of the 1050l. purchase-money for this yacht he thereupon became entitled to fifty-five 105ths. That being the presumption, it was, of course, open to the other side to displace that presumption, but it was not incumbent upon Percy Stone to prove more than that. It was for the other side to displace that presumption if they could, but they offered no evidence at all.[7]

Consider also the case of *Mehta Estate v Mehta Estate*.[8] The facts showed that a husband had purchased certain investments in the name of his wife, but again there was no proof of the intentions of the husband, or his wife, as both had perished in a plane crash and the issue had only arisen in a dispute between the representatives of their respective estates. The Manitoba Court of Appeal held that the presumption of advancement, though regarded in some quarters as out of date, still applied in Manitoba to transfers from husband to wife, and that this holding determined the issue in favour of the wife's personal representatives. There was no doubt, however, that had the presumption of advancement been abolished in the province, the husband's representatives would have succeeded though establishing no more than that the investments were purchased with the

---

[6] [1908] P 218.
[7] Ibid, 230.
[8] (1993) 104 DLR (4th) 24.

scenario, that they should sometimes be conflated.[100] However, this does not make them the same, especially since there is an important difference in the rules applicable to the two situations, in that a person whose money has, with his consent, been used to acquire property (so that he is entitled under a resulting trust) must take his proportionate share of the loss if the property goes down in value. In the tracing context, however, where the person's money has been used without consent, he is entitled to opt instead for a charge over the property reflecting the amount of his money which was used in the purchase.[101] In another subset of the absence of intention cases, where property is acquired on the basis of theft or fraud,[102] English authority indicates that the property acquired would be held on a constructive trust, rather than a resulting trust.[103]

To sum up, it is important to realise that Chambers's ambiguous phrase 'lack of intention to benefit' artificially ties together two distinct principles, one of which is based on a positive intention of the settlor to create a trust and another of which is not. The fact that in a limited number of early tracing cases the label 'resulting trust' was applied in a scenario involving an absence of intention proves relatively little, given that that usage has not generally been followed in the modern case law and runs counter to the approach of the House of Lords in *Foskett*. By grouping the two sets of cases together, Chambers is able to assemble a more secure foundation for his contention that the principles of resulting trusts could apply in a far wider range of circumstances than is currently accepted in the law. The argument is weakened significantly, however, if it is conceded that the mainstream categories of resulting trust actually turn on a positive intention to create a trust and so do not provide any support for an extension of the resulting trust to a greater range of cases which are said to involve an absence of intention.[104]

---

[100] Compare N Glover and P Todd, 'The Myth of Common Intention' (1996) 16 *Legal Studies* 325, 335, seeking to explain the purchase money resulting trust by reference to principles set out in the tracing case of *Re Hallett's Estate* (1880) 13 Ch D 696, 708 (Jessel MR)—rather than vice versa, as in Chambers's argument, where it seems that a tracing rule is being justified by reference to the doctrine of resulting trusts.

[101] See eg *Re Hallett's Estate* (n 101) 709. Compare Chambers (n 4) 190–91.

[102] See eg the facts of *Collings v Lee* [2001] 2 All ER 332 (CA).

[103] See *Westdeutsche* (n 1) 716 (Lord Browne-Wilkinson). The constructive trust solution is clearly established in US law in cases where one person's money is used without permission in the purchase of property, with the imposition of such a trust being seen as based on unjust enrichment. See Scott and Fratcher (n 91) vol 5, 145–48 (distinguishing this from the purchase money resulting trust).

[104] In fact, these other cases to which Chambers proposes to extend the resulting trust do not involve a true absence of intention but rather an intention which is, in some sense, 'qualified' or 'vitiated'. As a matter of principle, there is an important distinction between the claim that 'I was not even aware of this transfer' and, on the other hand, the claim that 'I did intend this transfer but'. See further KFK Low, 'The Use and Abuse of Taxonomy' (2009) 29 *Legal Studies* 355, 360–62.

husband's money; there was no need to show that there was an absence of any quid pro quo.

The nail in the coffin, however, is provided by *Tinsley v Milligan*.[9] There, it will be recalled, the defendant contributed to the purchase price of property transferred into the sole name of the plaintiff and later denied her contribution and thus her interest in the property in order to defraud the Department of Social Services. The House of Lords held 3:2 that the defendant could nonetheless establish her interest by way of the presumption of resulting trust. As Lord Browne-Wilkinson explained:

> Where the presumption of resulting trust applies, the plaintiff does not have to rely on the illegality. If he proves that the property is vested in the defendant alone but that the plaintiff provided part of the purchase money, or voluntarily transferred the property to the defendant, the plaintiff establishes his claim under a resulting trust unless either the contrary presumption of advancement displaces the presumption of resulting trust or the defendant leads evidence to rebut the presumption of resulting trust. Therefore, in cases where the presumption of advancement does not apply, a plaintiff can establish his equitable interest in the property without relying in any way on the underlying illegal transaction.[10]

There is nothing here about any further requirement of having to show that the recipient of the title to the property provided no consideration for it.[11] Indeed, if she did have to establish that there was no quid pro quo for her contribution the defendant may well have had to reveal the very circumstances of the transaction; that is, she might well have had to 'rely on the illegality' to establish her claim.

Together these cases are quite decisive. All that needs to be proved by a claimant in order to gain the benefit of the presumption of resulting trust is that the transfer or contribution was made to the benefit of the defendant. Hence the presumption applies to dispositions that could in reality be gifts, loans, transfers constituting trusts or transfers satisfying contractual obligations (where, of course, consideration could be shown to have been provided); that is, to ambiguous transfers. It is submitted that the courts' occasional references to the claimant's showing that the transfer or contri-

---

[9] [1994] 1 AC 340.
[10] Ibid, 371.
[11] Unfortunately, Lord Browne-Wilkinson then immediately diminished the clarity of the point just made by referring to the defendant's claim about the parties' common intentions, which were irrelevant to the application of the presumption. This is what he said about that: 'In this case Miss Milligan as defendant simply pleaded the common intention that the property should belong to both of them and that she contributed to the purchase price: she claimed that in consequence the property A belonged to them equally. To the same effect was her evidence in chief. Therefore Miss Milligan was not forced to rely on the illegality to prove her equitable interest. Only in the reply and the course of Miss Milligan's cross-examination did such illegality emerge: it was Miss Tinsley who had to rely on that illegality.' With respect this seems to confuse the facts that need to be proved to establish a common intention constructive trust with those necessary to invoke the presumption, and it is submitted that the former passage better represents the law and Lord Browne-Wilkinson's understanding of it.

bution was for no consideration is easily explained;[12] only an ill-advised claimant will try on the resulting trust argument where the transfer or contribution was obviously to meet a contractual obligation, since the presumption would then be trivially easy to rebut; the absence of consideration, then, will almost always be part of the surrounding factual circumstances, established without any difficulty by the claimant, though there would not, strictly speaking, be a burden upon him to do so.

The upshot is that to the extent that Chambers's theory of the nature of resulting trusts relies on any idea such as 'Equity is suspicious of gifts', then this reliance is misplaced, for the application by Equity of the presumption is not on the basis that the transaction reveals a gift, apparent or not.

C. THE SECOND CONTROVERSY

Is the presumption an evidentiary presumption or a presumption of law, and what is the content of the presumption?

It will take a little longer to get to the bottom of this controversy.

Trusts are traditionally divided into three categories: express, resulting and constructive trusts.[13] The latter two categories, resulting and constructive trusts, are traditionally distinguished from express trusts because they are trusts that arise by operation of law (TABOLs), whereas the former, express trusts, as their name indicates, arise because the settlor effectively exercised his power of disposition over property by sufficiently declaring a trust over it. The categorisation of resulting trusts as TABOLs is almost universally recognised in the texts.[14] One of the important claims of Swadling's theory is that in the case of one of the two traditional categories of resulting trust, presumed resulting trusts, this categorisation is wrong: according to Swadling, presumed resulting trusts are express trusts in which

---

[12] See eg *Re Vandervell's Trusts (No 2)* [1974] Ch 269, 294 (Megarry J), quoted in the text to n 39.

[13] This categorisation is respected by all the leading texts: J McGhee, *Snell's Equity*, 31st edn (London, Sweet & Maxwell, 2005) para 19-07 n 67; J Mowbray et al, *Lewin on Trusts*, 18th edn (London, Sweet & Maxwell, 2007) paras 1-37 and 1-38; D Hayton et al, *Underhill and Hayton: Law of Trusts and Trustees*, 17th edn (London, LexisNexis Butterworths, 2007) para 3.1; HAJ Ford and WA Lee et al, *Principles of the Law of Trusts* (Sydney, Thomson Lawbooks, 2006) paras 22.240–22.260. It is sometimes questioned whether there is a fourth category, 'implied' trusts. The concern to give this term meaning follows from its use in the Law of Property Act 1925, s 53(2), which states 'This section does not affect the creation or operation of resulting, implied, or constructive trusts.' It is, however, generally accepted that this means 'implied' in or by law, ie arising by operation of law, and since all trusts arising by operation of law are now considered to be resulting or constructive trusts, to the extent this category might once have had distinct content, that is no longer true, and so 'implied' trusts need not be separately addressed. See *Lewin*, ibid, para 7-04.

[14] *Snell* (n 13) paras 19-07, 19-08 and 23-01; *Lewin* (n 13) para 1-38; *Underhill* (n 13) para 3.1; *Ford & Lee* (n 13) para 21.000. An exception is JE Penner, *The Law of Trusts*, 6th edn (Oxford, Oxford University Press, 2008) ch 4, which aims to be neutral as between Swadling's and Chambers's theories.

an express intention operative to create a trust is proved by the application of an evidentiary presumption, that is, a legal presumption of fact.[15] Chambers and Millett, by contrast, seek to explain the traditional view that resulting trusts are TABOLs. In the course of doing so, they propose their own unorthodoxy, which is that the traditional boundary between constructive and resulting trusts is wrong. They both argue that the trust Equity imposes upon the third party recipient of property transferred in breach of trust (or the traceable proceeds thereof) is properly understood to be a resulting trust, not a constructive trust as on the traditional understanding.[16]

According to Chambers, all resulting trusts (1) arise by operation of law, and (2) do so because it is established, either on the facts alone or with the aid of a legal presumption of fact, that the person at whose expense the recipient receives an interest in property had *no intention to benefit* that recipient. The underlying rationale for the imposition of the resulting trust is to anticipate and prevent unjust enrichment. If Equity did not impose a resulting trust in these cases, then the recipient would be unjustly enriched at the transferor/contributor's expense. (3) Where the presumption of resulting trust applies, the fact presumed is that the transferor/contributor had no intention to confer a beneficial interest on the recipient. It is important to notice that this third element of the theory is distinct from the second, as it is perfectly possible to maintain that the trust arises by operation of law for the reason that the transferor/contributor had no intention to confer a beneficial interest on the recipient but that in the cases where the presumption applies this reason is established by the presumption that the transferor/contributor intended a trust, for if that presumption applies, namely that a trust was intended, it also follows that the transferor/contributor had no intention to confer a beneficial interest on the recipient. If that were the presumption, there would just be the practical result that more claims would be successfully rebutted, for it is easier to rebut a positive intention to create a trust than a negative intention, 'no intention to confer a benefit'. Once resulting trusts are understood in this way, as Chambers recommends, (4) certain trusts which have not been

---

[15] Swadling (n 1) 72–80.

[16] As long as the claimant can establish that the properties held by the defendant are the traceable proceeds of valuable rights which were beneficially the claimant's and which got into the defendant's hands because of a breach by the claimant's fiduciaries of their fiduciary obligations, he succeeds on equitable principles as a matter of trite law irrespective of whether the trust imposed by Equity is explained as a resulting or constructive trust: see *Agip (Africa) Ltd v Jackson* [1990] Ch 265, aff'd [1991] Ch 547 (CA); *El Ajou v Dollar Land Holdings plc* [1993] 3 All ER 717; rvs'd [1994] 2 All ER 685. This is most obviously shown by the traditional requirement that in order to trace in equity, the claimant must show that the property transferred away from him must have been held either on trust or by his fiduciary, ie that in order to trace in equity a precondition is the finding of a fiduciary relationship. See *Snell* (n 13) para 28-35; *Lewin* (n 13) para 41-11; *Ford & Lee* (n 13) paras 22.1020 and 22.10320ff.

recognised as resulting trusts, because they do not fall within the traditional categories, can be seen to be resulting trusts.

According to Swadling, resulting trusts arise in two basic circumstances. The first kind arises 'because of a legal presumption that a trust was declared by the transferor in his own favour'.[17] While formerly Swadling referred to the two traditional cases in which the presumption applies together as cases of 'presumed intention' resulting trusts,[18] he now refers to them separately as 'voluntary conveyance resulting trusts' (the case where the property is transferred directly from A to B inter vivos) and 'purchase-money resulting trusts' (where A pays C to convey property to B). The second kind of resulting trust, the 'failed trust' resulting trust, arises where a settlor transfers property to a trustee but the declared trusts fail, for example by reason of uncertainty of objects or perpetuity, to dispose of all or part of the beneficial interest in that property. In this case, the trustee holds the property on a trust which arises by operation of law in the settlor's favour.[19] While Swadling argues that the presumed intention resulting trust is convincingly explained as the court's recognition of the creation of an express trust,[20] he says there is no such convincing explanation for the 'failed trust' resulting trust, which in his opinion 'defies legal analysis'.[21]

Lord Millett offers something of a third way. He agrees with Robert Chambers that all resulting trusts arise by operation of law, and further that they arise on the basis of the transferor/contributor's absence of intention to benefit the recipient of the property (either transferred to him directly or purchased in his name). However, Lord Millett differs from Chambers as to the reason why resulting trusts arise. While he says that resulting trusts are cases of 'proprietary restitution', he denies that they arise as a response to, or in anticipation of, the defendant's unjust enrichment. Rather, they arise because in the view of Equity a person who transfers property with no intention to confer a beneficial interest upon the recipient, or whose property is transferred without their authority, fails to dispose of their beneficial interest. It therefore, in the eyes of Equity, remains with them. This latter view is sometimes referred to as the 'proprietary arithmetic' view,[22] or in the context of tracing, as the 'fiction of

---

[17] Swadling (n 1) 72.

[18] W Swadling, 'A New Role for Resulting Trusts?' (1996) 16 *Legal Studies* 110, 113.

[19] Or in favour of the settlor's successor(s) if deceased. If the trust that fails is a testamentary, there is no resulting trust; rather, the property just fails to be disposed of effectively under the provision in the will in question and the property will fall into residue.

[20] Swadling (n 1) 79–80. This is not to say that Swadling believes that proof of express trusts via the presumption should continue; indeed, at 84 and 102 he regards it as anachronistic.

[21] Ibid, 102.

[22] R Chambers, *Resulting Trusts* (Oxford, Clarendon Press, 1997) 51–5.

persistence'.[23] It is rejected by both Chambers[24] and Swadling[25] for the same reason, and we shall turn to it below in Part D.

According to Chambers all resulting trusts arise by operation of law on the same basis, which is that the person at whose expense the defendant receives an interest in property had 'no intention to benefit' the defendant. Such a view unifies the law governing the three traditional situations in which the resulting trust arises, that is, the gratuitous transfer presumed resulting trust (for example, *Re Vinogradoff*[26]), the purchase-money contribution presumed resulting trust (for example, *The Venture*[27]), and the so-called 'automatic' resulting trust that arises when express trusts failed to effectively dispose of the entire beneficial interest in the property transferred on trust (for example, *Vandervell v IRC*[28]). In presumed resulting trust cases, the fact presumed is that the transferor/contributor had no intention to benefit the recipient, whereas in the 'automatic' resulting trust cases this absence of intention to benefit the recipient (that is, the trustee) is established on the facts without the aid of any presumption, as the facts show that the recipient took as a trustee, that is, as one not intended to take any benefit from the property.

This theory contrasts with those that sharply distinguish the first two 'presumed' resulting trusts from the last 'automatic' resulting trust on the basis that the former arise for fundamentally different reasons than the latter. Megarry J was the first to draw a sharp distinction between the two (a distinction upon which Swadling firmly relies[29]) using the terminology of 'presumed' and 'automatic' resulting trusts, in *Re Vandervell's Trusts (No 2)*.[30] It is to be observed that the making of this supposedly fundamental distinction is very recent in view of the long history of the doctrine of resulting trusts. Chambers shows that the distinction has not been embraced in Australia, Canada or the United States.[31]

According to Megarry J, the distinction turns on one essential difference between the two cases. In the presumed resulting trusts cases, both the existence of the trust and the content of the trust need to be established, and '[the] presumption thus establishes both that B is to take on trust and also what that trust is'.[32] In the automatic resulting trust case, by contrast:

> The resulting trust here does not depend on any intentions or presumptions, but is the automatic consequence of A's failure to dispose of what is vested in him.

[23] Millett (n 3) 315–17.
[24] Chambers (n 22) 52–55.
[25] Swadling (n 1) 99–100.
[26] [1935] WN 68.
[27] [1908] P 218 (CA).
[28] [1967] 2 AC 291.
[29] Swadling (n 18) 113; Swadling (n 1) 73.
[30] [1974] Ch 269, 294; reversed on other grounds [1974] Ch 269 (CA) 316 ff.
[31] Chambers (n 22) 55–56.
[32] [1974] Ch 269, 294.

Since ex hypothesi the transfer is on trust, the resulting trust does not establish the trust but merely carries back to A the beneficial interest that has not been disposed of.[33]

The gist, then, of Megarry J's view is that what fundamentally distinguishes the cases is not that in the former a trust arises because of intention, whereas in the latter case a trust arises by operation of law. Rather, the cases differ *in terms of what needs to be proved, not in the sort of trust that arises*. As Chambers notices,[34] the issue of what needed to be proved was the issue that divided the Court of Appeal and the House of Lords in *Vandervell v IRC*:[35] the Court of Appeal relied upon the presumption, regarding the evidence as insufficient to determine what Vandervell intended; by contrast, in the House of Lords Lord Upjohn[36] and Lord Wilberforce[37] both felt that Vandervell's intention not to confer a beneficial interest upon his trustee company was sufficiently clear on the facts.

In view of this, does Megarry J's classification tell us anything significant about the content of the presumption? There does not appear to be much here to stand on, and yet it is typically assumed, even by Chambers,[38] that Megarry J held that the presumption that the law applies is a presumption that the transferor or contributor to the purchase price intended to create a trust in his favour. But a close examination of the passage in which Megarry J characterises the presumed resulting trust belies this. The passage describing presumed trusts in full is as follows:

> The first class of case is where the transfer to B is not made on any trust. If, of course, it appears from the transfer that B is intended to hold on certain trusts, that will be decisive, and the case is not within this category; and similarly if it appears that B is intended to take beneficially. But in other cases *there is a rebuttable presumption that B holds on a resulting trust for A*. The question is not one of the automatic consequences of a dispositive failure by A, but one of presumption: the property has been carried to B, and from the absence of consideration[39] and any presumption of advancement *B is presumed not only to hold the entire interest on trust, but also to hold the beneficial interest for A absolutely. The presumption thus establishes both that B is to take on trust and also what that trust is*. Such resulting trusts may be called 'presumed resulting trusts'.[40]

It is clear from the italicised passages that the presumption is not framed as a presumption as to what A (or A and B) *intended*, but rather what is

---

[33] Ibid.
[34] Chambers (n 22) 44.
[35] [1967] 2 AC 291.
[36] Ibid, 315–17.
[37] Ibid, 329.
[38] Chambers (n 22) 42–44.
[39] I realise this reference to the absence of consideration is against my determination of Issue 1; see the text accompanying n 12.
[40] [1974] Ch 269, 294 (emphasis added).

presumed by the law, that is, *what the law presumes*, on the given facts. Note that the first line of the passage states that the presumption applies where the transfer *is not made on any trust*; it does not state that the presumption applies where (1) a transfer is made and (2) there *fails to be evidence* of any trust. The second way of putting it is clearly not equivalent to the first and there is no justification for reading Megarry J's plain words as if it was. His statement of the law is only consistent with the view that the presumed resulting trust arises by operation of law in these circumstances—a transfer to the defendant or contribution to the purchase price of property put in the defendant's name for no consideration where there is no presumption of advancement—and not as an express trust effectively created by the transferor/contributor, proof of which is provided by a presumption. As far as this passage indicates, what is presumed is that B holds on trust for A, a presumption that can be displaced by contrary evidence; nothing in the passage states that B is presumed to hold on trust for A because A intended that he do so, much less that A not only intended to do so but expressed this intention sufficiently so as actually to create an express trust in his favour.

Swadling himself implicitly recognises this when he shows that more has to be said in order to find in Megarry's classification that the presumption is one of an intention to create a trust:

> We know from Megarry J's classic judgment in *Re Vandervell (No 2)* that there are two types of resulting trusts, automatic and presumed. . . . But it is misleading to label such a trust simply as 'presumed resulting trust'. Since what is being 'presumed' is an intention on the part of the transferor to create a trust, it is more accurately called a 'presumed intention resulting trust'. That 'presumed *intention* resulting trust' is the correct description of the type of trust in operation here will be demonstrated through an historical examination of such trusts.[41]

It is clear, therefore, that Swadling does not think Megarry J's judgment itself establishes that the presumption is a presumed intention to create a trust, but that this needs to be established by way of an examination of the preceding case-law. Be that as it may, Chambers argues that, however one interprets Megarry J's judgment, a number of different cases where a presumed resulting trust arose simply cannot be explained on the basis that the law rebuttably presumes an intention to create a trust, since in these cases the evidence established that the transferor or contributor had no such intention and yet the trust arose anyway.

Perhaps the best examples are the Canadian case of incapacity, *Goodfellow v Robertson*,[42] where the intention to create a trust might well have been impossible due to the contributor's unsound mind; *Hodgson v*

---

[41] Swadling (n 18) 113.
[42] (1871) 18 Gr. 572.

Marks,[43] where a woman transferred her house on an unenforceable oral trust; and two cases where the claimants at whose expense the defendant received the property were ignorant of the transfer: *Ryall v Ryall*[44] and *El Ajou v Dollar Land Holdings*.[45] In the former, an executor used assets from the estate to purchase assets in his own name; a resulting trust was declared in favour of the legatees. In *El Ajou*, Millett J held obiter that persons defrauded of money were entitled to rescind the transaction and trace their funds in equity on the basis that an 'old-fashioned institutional resulting trust' arose in their favour.[46]

Unfortunately, none of these cases is decisive since all can be undermined. As regards *Goodfellow v Robertson*, where a person lacking capacity properly to assent to a transaction purports to transfer property, the purported transfer is void: see for example *Re Beaney*.[47] In view of this, it can be argued that the judge in *Goodfellow* had no need to draw upon the presumption of resulting trust, as the entire disposition ought to have been found to be void. In reply, one might submit that one can, conceptually, distinguish between the capacity necessary to transfer property and that required to determine beneficial ownership in it, but I know of no authority for doing so besides *Goodfellow* itself. To the extent that it is possible for legal title to pass and yet the transferor to have limited capacity, intuitively the result in *Goodfellow* seems sound: the imposition of a resulting trust seems to be a proper exercise of the equitable jurisdiction. Therefore one might reply that while the judge erred in finding legal title to have passed in this situation, on the premise that it did, he was right to find the property to be held on resulting trust, and in order to do so this could not have been on any proof by evidence or presumption that the transferor intended a trust.

In *Hodgson v Marks*, Russell LJ, giving the unanimous judgment of the Court of Appeal, said the following:

> [T]he evidence is clear that the transfer was not intended to operate as a gift, and, in those circumstances, I do not see why there was not a resulting trust of the beneficial interest to the plaintiff, which would not, of course, be affected by section 53(1). It was argued that a resulting trust is based upon implied intention, and that where there is an express trust for the transferor intended and declared—albeit ineffectively—there is no room for such an implication. I do not accept that. If an attempted express trust fails, that seems to me just the occasion for implication of a resulting trust, whether the failure be due to uncertainty, or perpetuity, or lack of form. It would be a strange outcome if the plaintiff were to lose her beneficial interest because her evidence had not been

---

[43] [1971] 1 Ch 892.
[44] (1739) 1 Atk 59, 26 ER 39.
[45] [1993] 3 All ER 717.
[46] Ibid, 734.
[47] [1978] 1 WLR 770. I thank Bill Swadling for drawing this case to my attention.

confined to negativing a gift but had additionally moved into a field forbidden by section 53(1) for lack of writing.[48]

There is no question that this is the ratio of the Court of Appeal, and Chambers says the following in respect of it:

> This was not a case concerning the presumption of resulting trust, because there was proof of the transferor's intention. Her intention to create a trust was significant because it proved the lack of intention to transfer the beneficial interest. The court . . . identified the absence of intention to benefit the recipient as the essential element which gave rise to the resulting trust. The presumption of resulting trust cannot be of a different intention than that which, when proven, gives rise to the resulting trust.[49]

While Chambers's claim here is logical and compelling, the problem is that it can be forcefully argued[50] that the Court of Appeal erred in several ways. First, it confused the *unenforceability* of the trust by virtue of the Law of Property Act 1925, section 53(1)(b)—which requires only that trusts of land be 'manifested and proved' by writing not that they be made in writing (compare section 53(1)(c))—with the *validity* of the trust, that is, the effectiveness of the oral declaration. If the absence of writing merely made the trust unprovable and thus merely unenforceable, not void, then on the well-known principle usually associated with the case of *Rochefoucauld v Boustead*,[51] that Equity will not allow a statute intended to prevent fraud to be used as an instrument of fraud, the otherwise unenforceable oral trust in favour of the transferor could be proved, and no resort to resulting trust principles need have been made. This was the basis upon which Ungoed-Thomas J at first instance dealt with the trust issue.[52] Furthermore, given that the statute only makes the trust unenforceable, not void, there is no room for the court to impose a resulting trust in the transferor's favour, since she holds under a trust already. Finally, assuming that the trust fails, that is, is void rather than merely unenforceable for not being in writing, it seems wrong to draw an analogy between a failure due to 'lack of form' and a failure due to uncertainty or perpetuity. The former concerns the question whether a trust was effectively declared at all. The latter concerns the question whether a trust that is effectively declared fails in substance because of its particular provisions. Despite all of these criticisms, however, on the (mistaken) premise that section 53(1)(b) made the trust ineffective, the court's reasoning (bar the analogy with failure due to uncertainty or perpetuity) seems perfectly sound. If section 53(1)(b) ex

---

[48] *Hodgson* (n 43) 933.
[49] Chambers (n 22) 25.
[50] W Swadling, 'A Hard Look at *Hodgson v Marks*' in P Birks and F Rose (eds), *Restitution and Equity: Resulting Trusts and Equitable Compensation* (Oxford, Mansfield Press, 2000) 61.
[51] [1897] 1 Ch 196 (CA).
[52] [1971] 1 Ch 892, 907–09.

hypothesi did operate to make such a trust void, so that there could be no effective intention to create a trust, the imposition of a resulting trust on the basis that the transferor did not intend the recipient to take a beneficial interest seems entirely correct, and *Lewin* accepts the ratio of the case on this basis.[53]

As regards *Ryall v Ryall* and the dicta in *El Ajou*, the difficulty arises with their classification as resulting trusts. Strongly in Chambers's favour is the fact that the courts themselves identified them as such. However, trusts that arise by operation of law binding third party recipients of assets transferred in breach of fiduciary obligation or in consequence of fraud are generally regarded as constructive, not resulting trusts.[54] Both Chambers and Lord Millett argue that they are resulting trusts, and if they are, they clearly do not arise on the basis of a presumption that the plaintiffs entertained any intention to create a trust in their favour. The only remaining option is an absence of intention to benefit the recipient. We will consider their arguments for saying these trusts are resulting trusts in Part D.

We now turn to consider the contrary view that the intention presumed is an intention to create a trust, or at least a positive intention to retain a beneficial interest (a formulation which would especially apply in those cases, such as *Dullow v Dullow*,[55] where the transferor was unsophisticated and had no real understanding of the concept of the trust). Two arguments will be made here. The first argument will show that such an intention is insufficient to establish Swadling's theory. The second argument will show that even if this is the intention presumed, the basis for the court's imposition of the resulting trust must still be that the transferor/contributor lacked the intention to confer a beneficial interest.

As to the first argument, let it be assumed that the intention presumed is an intention on the part of the transferor/contributor to create a trust in his favour. This is clearly insufficient to take presumed resulting trusts out of the category of TABOLs and treat them as express trusts. Swadling fully recognises this, for a mere intention to create a trust is insufficient to create a trust. Any such intention must be sufficiently expressed. Swadling recognises this point in the following passage:[56]

> [I]n *Cook v Fountain*, Lord Nottingham LC spoke of trusts where the declarations
>
> > 'appear either by direct or manifest proof, or violent and necessary presumption. These last are commonly called presumptive trusts; and that is, when the Court, upon consideration of all the circumstances presumes there was a

---

[53] *Lewin* (n 13) para 7-02. *Underhill* (n 13) para 3.3 n 2 sits on the fence.
[54] Eg *Snell* (n 13) para 19-09; *Lewin* (n 13) paras 7-11 and 7-13; *Ford & Lee* (n 13) paras 22.1020 and 22.10320ff.
[55] (1985) 3 NSWLR 531.
[56] Swadling (n 1) 80 (emphasis added).

declaration, either by word or writing, though the plain and direct proof thereof be not extant'.

. . . It is important to appreciate that the fact proved by the presumption was, as Lord Nottingham makes clear, a declaration to uses, not merely that the feoffor possessed at the time of the transfer an unexpressed intention to create a use. Were it otherwise, *we would be dealing with a rule of substantive law, not procedure, for an unexpressed intention to create a trust when proved by evidence does not generate a trust*. As Megarry J said in *Re Vandervell's Trusts (No 2)*, 'the mere existence of some unexpressed intention in the breast of the owner of the property does nothing: there must at least be some expression of that intention before it can effect any result.' [Megarry J completes the thought by saying: 'To yearn is not to transfer.'[57]]

The corollary to this is that if all that is needed to establish a resulting trust is an unrebutted presumption that a trust was merely *intended*, as opposed to a presumption that a trust was *effectively declared*, then the trust arises by operation of law. Therefore, in order to establish the correctness of his theory Swadling has to show that the content of the presumption is not merely that the transferor/contributor intended a trust, but that he or she effectively created one.

This, however, I submit, Swadling fails to do. Besides the cited passage from *Cook v Fountain*, he cites the speeches of judges in only two cases, *Fowkes v Pascoe*[58] and the Canadian case of *Rathwell v Rathwell*,[59] as textual authority for the proposition that the presumption is that the transferor/contributor effectively declared a trust in his own favour,[60] but only one of these passages plausibly provides the support Swadling requires. The first quotation, from the decision of Mellish LJ in *Fowkes*, is as follows:

[I]f there is evidence to rebut the presumption, then . . . the Court must go into the actual facts. And if we are to go into the actual facts, and look at the circumstances of this investment, it appears to me utterly impossible . . . to come to any other conclusion than that the . . . investment was made for the purpose of gift and not for the purpose of trust. It was either for the purpose of trust or else for the purpose of gift; and therefore any evidence which shews that it was not for the purpose of trust is evidence to shew that it was for the purpose of gift.[61]

This passage suggests that the presumption is that the transfer was made 'for the purpose of trust' rather than for 'the purpose of gift'. 'Purpose' suggests merely (and no more than) the *intention* with which the transfer was made; it does not suggest that that intention was in any way made manifest or expressly declared.

[57] [1974] Ch 269, 294.
[58] (1875) LR 10 Ch App 343.
[59] (1978) 83 DLR (3d) 289.
[60] Swadling (n 1) 78 and 81–82.
[61] *Fowkes* (n 58) 353.

Swadling then cites the judgment of James LJ in the same case where he asks whether it was

> possible to reconcile with mental sanity the theory that [the deceased] put £250 into the names of herself and her companion, and £250 into the names of herself and the Defendant, as trustees upon trust for herself? What trust—what object is there conceivable in doing this? If this case were tried before a jury, no Judge could withdraw the facts of the contemporaneous purchases and of their repetition from the consideration of a jury, and, in my opinion, no jury would or could be found who would hesitate to say that the thing was done by way of gift and not trust.[62]

The phrase 'put £250 into the names of . . . as trustees upon trust for herself' is reasonably construed as posing the question in terms of the deceased having effectively declared a trust, as is the phrase in the last sentence that the transfer 'was *done* by way of gift and not trust' (my italics). Thus this passage does appear to support Swadling's contention.

Finally, Swadling cites[63] the following statement of Dickson J in *Rathwell*:

> Resulting trusts are as firmly grounded in the settlor's intent as are express trusts, but with this difference—that the intent is inferred, or is presumed as a matter of law from the circumstances of the case. [64]

Swadling continues by saying the following:

> Given that the only intention which counts is one which is expressed, for Dickson J at least, the content of the presumption in 1978 was still a declaration of trust.[65]

This passage provides no support for Swadling's theory; the passage says only that resulting trusts arise on the basis of the settlor's intention, not on the basis that the settlor effectively declared his intention (and indeed vis-à-vis the settlor's intention Dickson's reference to intention is entirely neutral as between an intention to create a trust and no intention to confer a beneficial interest, for both are equally matters of the settlor's intent). Swadling himself has to supplement the passage by stating his assumption that Dickson J shares his view that only an expressed intention counts.

So besides the passage in *Cook v Fountain* the only authority for the proposition that the presumption is one of an effectively declared trust is the passage from James LJ's judgment in *Fowkes*. There are, however, other cases concerning resulting trusts which show the proposition to be untenable.

We can begin with a case normally taken to favour Swadling's view, *Westdeutsche Landesbank Girozentrale v Islington LBC*,[66] which shows

---

[62] Ibid, 348–49.
[63] Swadling (n 1) 82.
[64] *Rathwell* (n 59) 303.
[65] Swadling (n 1) 82.
[66] [1996] AC 669.

that, whatever is presumed under the presumption, it is not an effective declaration of trust. No judge or lawyer advanced any argument that the presumption was that the transferor effectively declared an express trust in his favour. Furthermore, if any judge accepted that this was the presumption, then the case would have been open and shut, for on no account of the facts could it be said (whatever the intentions of the bank) that the bank declared an express trust of the money it transferred to the council. If the presumption is as Swadling says it is, then no judge or lawyer would have even considered making the resulting trust claim—it would have been ruled out *in limine* by the content of the presumption. That the case was argued at all, and that every member of the House of Lords decided against the bank but none did so on this basis, is extremely strong evidence that Swadling's theory has got the content of the presumption wrong.

Lord Browne-Wilkinson, who gave the majority's judgment, was actually ambiguous on the question of what the presumption actually is. In some sense he agreed with both Chambers and Swadling, as is apparent from this quotation:

> Under existing law a resulting trust arises in two sets of circumstances: (A) where A makes a voluntary payment to B or pays (wholly or in part) for the purchase of property which is vested either in B alone or in the joint names of A and B, *there is a presumption that A did not intend to make a gift to B*: the money or property is held on trust for A (if he is the sole provider of the money) or in the case of a joint purchase by A and B in shares proportionate to their contributions. It is important to stress that this is only a presumption, which presumption is easily rebutted either by the counter-presumption of advancement or by direct evidence of A's intention to make an outright transfer. . . . As the article by William Swadling, 'A new role for resulting trusts?' 16 Legal Studies 133 demonstrates *the presumption of resulting trust is rebutted by evidence of any intention inconsistent with such a trust, not only by evidence of an intention to make a gift*.[67]

On no reading, however, is it possible to read the presumption as one of an effective declaration of trust. Even when agreeing with Swadling, Lord Browne-Wilkinson says the resulting trust is rebutted by 'evidence of any intention inconsistent with such a trust', not any evidence which shows a trust was not effectively declared.

An even clearer case is *Re Vinogradoff*.[68] Here a resulting trust arose even though an effective declaration of trust was clearly impossible on the facts, since the resulting trustee was four years old, and any express declaration that the property was transferred to her to hold on trust would have been ineffective by virtue of the Law of Property Act 1925, section 20. Farwell J specifically held that the section 'did not operate to make any

[67] Ibid, 708 (emphasis added).
[68] [1935] WN 68.

difference to the presumption'.[69] While it is easy to criticise the case for relying upon the presumption rather than finding it was rebutted on any realistic appraisal of the facts, if the presumption is what Swadling says it is, then the case simply could not have been decided as it was.

However, the most obvious refutation of Swadling's theory lies in the court's understanding of the way the presumed resulting trust operates in the run-of-the-mill 'family home' case where a resulting trust arises on the basis of a contribution to the purchase price made by one or both cohabitees. In each of the following decisions the Court of Appeal considered the relevance of the intentions of a contributor to the purchase price of a shared home and in none can it possibly be argued that the fact 'presumed' or proved which gives rise to a resulting trust was that the contributor made an effective declaration of trust at all, much less a provable and thus *enforceable* declaration of trust, that is, one in writing so as to comply with the Law of Property Act 1925, section 53(1)(b).

Taking the cases in chronological order, we can begin with *Springette v Defoe*.[70] The Court of Appeal held that the presumption of resulting trust, which on the facts gave a woman a 75 per cent share based on her contribution, and her erstwhile partner a 25 per cent share, was not displaced in favour of a constructive trust of the house giving them an equal interest because the evidence was that there was no discussion between the parties of any kind, much less a discussion sufficient to establish a common intention to share the home equally. Nevertheless, this proof that no discussion of any beneficial interest took place did not rebut the presumption of resulting trust, which it would have done if the presumption was that an actual trust was declared. Dillon LJ put the point this way:

> [I]n the absence of an express declaration of the beneficial interests, the court will hold that the joint purchasers hold the property on a resulting trust for themselves in the proportions in which they contributed directly or indirectly to the purchase price.[71]

Notice that Dillon LJ does not say 'In the absence of evidence of an express declaration', but speaks of an absence of an express declaration itself. In the following passage Dillon LJ makes clear that this was not a case where there was insufficient evidence to determine whether an express declaration of trust was made: '[I]t is clear in the present case that there never was any discussion between the parties about what their respective beneficial interests were to be'.[72]

Clearly, then, there was never any express communication of any intended beneficial interest on the part of the contributors, much less an

---
[69] Ibid.
[70] [1992] 2 FCR 561.
[71] Ibid, 566 (emphasis added).
[72] Ibid, 567.

effective declaration. Nevertheless, Dillon LJ concluded, in terms, that the presumption of resulting trust was not displaced,[73] and therefore the presumption cannot be one of effective declaration of trust, for if that were the presumption, it would clearly have been rebutted on the facts.

In *Midland Bank plc v Cooke* [74] the Court of Appeal, affirming the trial judge's decision on this point,[75] held that the wife of the man in whose name the legal title to a house was registered acquired an interest in the house by way of a contribution to the purchase price. The money for the contribution was received by the husband as wedding gift from his parents. The court accepted that this was a joint gift to the couple, and therefore the wife took a proportionate beneficial interest in the house by way of purchase-contribution resulting trust even though it was accepted both by the trial judge and the Court of Appeal that there was no expression by the parties to each other in respect of their beneficial interests in the house whatsoever. If Swadling's theory is right, that the fact presumed is that a trust was effectively declared, then this was clearly rebutted on the evidence. Nevertheless, a resulting trust was found and no one, including Swadling, has argued that the case was wrongly decided on this point.[76]

Both *Springette* and *Midland Bank* were considered in detail in *Oxley v Hiscock*.[77] In *Oxley* the Court of Appeal preferred the reasoning in *Midland Bank* to the effect that where a party acquires an interest in property under a purchase-money contribution resulting trust, the court is not barred from determining a different share under a constructive trust simply because there was no express discussion between the parties of their respective beneficial interests; rather, the court may look to the entire course of dealing between the parties to award a share that is fair in all the circumstances. In rendering its decision the Court of Appeal clearly accepted that a resulting trust arises despite evidence that there was no express declaration of trust, evidence which would clearly rebut the presumption if it were as Swadling states it to be. The court's finding on this point is accurately reflected in the headnote to the Family Law Reports report as follows:

> In cases in which an unmarried couple bought property, intending to live together as husband and wife, each making a financial contribution to the purchase but purchasing the property in the sole name of one of them *and making no express declaration of trust*.[78]

---

[73] Ibid, 567.
[74] [1995] 4 All ER 562.
[75] Ibid, 568–70.
[76] The CA's decision that the wife was ultimately entitled to a 50 per cent share on the property via a constructive trust has been criticised (see eg Penner (n 14) 122–23), but its reasoning was later affirmed in *Oxley v Hiscock* [2004] EWCA Civ 546; [2004] 2 FLR 669, and in *Stack v Dowden* [2007] UKHL 17; [2007] 2 AC 432.
[77] *Oxley* (n 76).
[78] Ibid, 669 (emphasis added). See too Chadwick LJ's statement at 676 that the effect of the

The Court of Appeal's reasoning in Oxley was recently approved in its essentials by the House of Lords in *Stack v Dowden*.[79]

We can look finally at two further Court of Appeal decisions, cases in which the presumption of advancement figured. In *McGrath v Wallis*[80] the father (who was deceased at the time of the action) contributed 80 per cent of the purchase price of a property to be lived in by himself and his son, the son contributing 20 per cent by way of mortgage. The father's solicitor prepared a declaration of trust at the father's instruction in which the property was to be held in these proportions, but it was never executed. On the basis of all the surrounding circumstances, the Court of Appeal held that the presumption of advancement was rebutted, and that the father acquired an 80 per cent interest in the property by way of resulting trust. In *Lavelle v Lavelle*,[81] a father who was retiring to Spain purchased a flat in the name of his daughter, who claimed that she held the title for herself and her brother as a gift from her father; here again, there was also no evidence that the father at any time declared a trust of the flat in his favour. The Court of Appeal found that the evidence strongly spoke against the father's intention to give up the flat to his children, and that the presumption of advancement was rebutted, and that the daughter held the flat upon trust for her father.

Thus in both cases the court found that the fathers had made no effective declaration of trust in their own favour, but that on the evidence, neither had they any intention to confer the (entire) beneficial interest on their children. The presumption seems to be as Lord Phillips described it in *Lavelle*, where he summarised the law on 'Intentions and Presumptions' as follows: 'In these cases Equity searches for the *subjective* intention of the transferor.'[82]

The inescapable conclusion is that all these cases proceeded on the basis that the resulting trust arises by operation of law in reference to the intentions of the transferor/contributor, but not on the basis that an effective declaration of trust is or can be presumed.

This might appear to tip the scales in Chambers's and Lord Millett's favour decisively, but there is a third possibility, a variation on Swadling's theory perhaps more in keeping with his 1996 work, that Lord Browne-Wilkinson drew upon in *Westdeutsche*.[83] This is the idea that a resulting trust arises by operation of law to give effect to the transferor/contributor's positive intention that the property should be held beneficially in his

judge's findings was that there was no express agreement as to the parties' beneficial entitlements

[79] *Stack* (n 76).
[80] [1995] 2 FLR 114.
[81] [2004] EWCA Civ 223, [2004] 2 FCR 418.
[82] Ibid, [19] (emphasis added).
[83] Swadling (n 18).

favour. On this understanding of the resulting trust, the trust does not preserve for the transferor/contributor a beneficial interest in property which would otherwise be lost by him to the recipient, but is rather *perfectionary*, giving effect to the transferor/contributor's intention to set up a trust for himself even though he failed effectively to do so. While theoretically such a rationale could underlie the law's imposition of a resulting trust, there is nothing in the cases to support such a view. Furthermore, it is a maxim of Equity that 'Equity will not perfect an imperfect gift', which in general means that unless consideration is provided Equity will not treat as effective an ineffective disposition. There are, of course, exceptions to the maxim, such as the rule in *Re Rose*[84] or *Pennington v Waine*,[85] but no one has ever argued that resulting trusts should be understood in a similar way. The idea,[86] rather, is that in the presumed resulting trust cases, there seems to be no conceptual space between the statement 'Frank did not intend Margo to have the benefit of the property he transferred to her' and 'Frank intended to retain the benefit of the property he transferred to Margo, that is Frank transferred it to Margo intending that she would hold it for him.' Except in odd cases of mental incapacity such as *Goodfellow* discussed above, if a person has capacity to transfer property, then upon transferring it he must necessarily have intentions as to whom is to benefit from the property transferred. And, if he has those intentions, why on earth should the court, in the absence of evidence, act on a presumption as to what was absent from his mind ('no intention to benefit Margo'), rather than what was positively there (Frank's intention to benefit himself)? The answer, to hazard a guess, is that in an era where the presumption no longer makes regular sense as an accurate presumption as to what the transferor/contributor actually intended, it purports to apply, where it does, to remedy a failure on the part of the transferor/contributor to ensure that his intentions are sufficiently explicit. It coheres with the traditional assumption that underlies the presumed resulting trust that the usual reason for a gratutitous conveyance is to create a trust, either for oneself now or for others in the future or both. As John Mee makes clear in his chapter,[87] if the presumption is one of trust in the sense only of imposing a trust obligation upon the recipient, the presumption is essentially one of 'non-benefit' for the recipient, not of a positive benefit for the transferor/contributor. Our concern in such a case is with what he failed to do, or at least failed to do in the sense that there is insufficient evidence of what he did for a court to give effect to it.[88]

---

[84] [1952] Ch 499.
[85] [2002] EWCA Civ 227, [2002] 1 WLR 2075.
[86] With which I have some sympathy: J Penner, 'Lord Millett's Analysis' in W Swadling (ed), *Quistclose Trusts* (Oxford, Hart Publishing, 2004) 41.
[87] See ch 7.
[88] I hasten to say that nothing in this paragraph is meant to detract in any way from

I said earlier that Chambers 'mostly' beats Swadling on the second controversy, and now I can explain why the victory is not total. What the cases seem to show (particularly taking *Westdeutsche* on board) is that 'no intention to benefit' means a genuine absence of intention to confer a beneficial interest, either a positive state of mind that the recipient should hold the property for oneself, or no state of mind on the issue at all. There is nothing, nothing at all really, in these cases which suggests that an intention to confer a beneficial interest is something that can be 'vitiated' by a restitutionary unjust factor such as 'mistake'.[89] Thus, so far as the case law is concerned, while Chambers wins in that resulting trusts do arise on the basis he sets out, one can happily agree with all of that and, like Lord Millett,[90] deny that this indicates the recipient of a mistaken payment holds that payment on resulting trust; for in such a case there is no doubt on the facts that the mistaken payor did intend to confer on the recipient a beneficial interest. That is, the evidence in such a case clearly shows that the transferor (to employ a necessary but clumsy double negative) genuinely did not have no intention to benefit the recipient. And that brings us to our third controversy.

D. THE THIRD CONTROVERSY

Assuming resulting trusts arise by operation of law in cases where the transferor/contributor 'did not intend to benefit the recipient', do they arise to prevent unjust enrichments?

Lord Millett's theory of resulting trusts is essentially identical to Chambers's except in one significant aspect: Lord Millett regards the resulting trust as *restitutionary*, but he does not believe that it responds to unjust enrichment. Thus while Lord Millett accepts that the resulting trust arises by operation of law where A, the person at whose expense the property was received, has no intention that B, the recipient, should receive a beneficial interest, he does not conceive of this as a case of reversing unjust enrichment. Rather, he regards this as a case where Equity regards A as retaining his beneficial interest because he did not effectively dispose of it;

Swadling's criticisms of *Hodgson v Marks*, discussed briefly above in the text accompanying n 50; in cases where it is clear that a transferor/contributor effectively declared a trust of land, he creates an express trust of land, and following Swadling's argument in his chapter in this volume (ch 3), the most conceptually coherent way of understanding the court's enforcement of such a trust (ie on a showing only of the facts of the transfer and declaration in the absence of proof of further factors such as detrimental reliance) is the court's enforcement of the express trust despite the strictures of the statute.

[89] I have discussed elsewhere that the language and conceptual structure both as regards the cause of actions and the remedies available sharply differentiate resulting trust cases from cases of restitution for unjust enrichment. See Penner (n 4) 329–34.

[90] Lord Millett, 'Review Article: Resulting Trusts' [1998] *Restitution Law Review* 283, 284.

therefore, it remains with him in the eyes of Equity and the consequence is that B holds the property on resulting trust.

In order to show that Lord Millett has the better view most effectively, one would need, first, to show support for the 'retention' conception in the historical judicial treatment of resulting trusts, and second, to show why there is nothing conceptually awry with the idea. Happily, John Mee's contribution to this volume has carried out the first task more than admirably.[91] He demonstrates that the retention 'idea', as he calls it, constitutes the overwhelmingly dominant conceptual perspective on the resulting trust. As for the second task, he also provides a particular conceptual perspective on why the idea of retention, perhaps more precisely 'rebounding', makes sense of the law. I leave the reader, nay strongly encourage him, to examine Mee's essay in detail at his leisure.[92] My task here will be to show that the retention 'idea' is not merely metaphorical. Rather, I shall say that the concept of retention is the superior substantial explanation of the logic behind resulting trusts.

An understanding of the resulting trust as the law's recognition of the transferor/contributor's 'retention' of his beneficial interest is most clearly in evidence in the way that judges explain the operation of the resulting trust in cases where a settlor fails to dispose of the entire beneficial interest under an express trust. In *Vandervell v IRC* Plowman J, Lord Upjohn, and Lord Wilberforce all revealed this understanding of the resulting trust. At first instance Plowman J said:

> As I see it, a man does not cease to own property simply by saying 'I don't want it.' If he tries to give it away the question must always be, has he succeeded in doing so or not?[93]

Of course Vandervell had succeeded in transferring the *legal* right to the valuable option into the hands of the trustee company—the resulting trust arose because he had failed effectively to give away the beneficial interest in it in the eyes of Equity. Lord Upjohn put it this way:

> A, the beneficial owner, informs his trustees that he wants forthwith to get rid of his interest in the property and instructs them to hold the property forthwith upon such trusts as he will hereafter direct; that beneficial interest, notwithstanding the expressed intention and belief of A that he has thereby parted with

---

[91] See ch 7.
[92] While I would say that I am in broad agreement with Mee about the nature of the conceptual underpinnings of the resulting trust, I do not find, as he does, much use in the Hohfeldian way of putting things. To my mind Hohfeldian analysis undermines any workable distinction between substance and form upon which both the retention and rebounding conceptions depend; an interest can only be substantially the same as another if the congeries of Hohfeldian jural relations is in substance the same, but Hohfeld's analysis is disintegrative in principle, and in principle would oppose the identification of congeries of jural relations as meaningful 'substances'.
[93] [1966] Ch 261, 275.

his whole beneficial interest in the property, will inevitably remain in him for he has not given the property away effectively to or for the benefit of others.[94]

Lord Upjohn then continued by expressly adopting the words of Plowman J quoted above. Likewise, Lord Wilberforce said:

> The conclusion, on the facts found, is simply that the option was vested in the trustee company as a trustee on trusts, not defined at the time, possibly to be defined later. But the equitable, or beneficial interest, cannot remain in the air: the consequence in law must be that it remains in the settlor.[95]

Lord Millett clearly thinks that Chambers's theory and this 'retention of beneficial interest' understanding of Equity's imposition of the resulting trust work together; in the following passage in his Privy Council advice in *Air Jamaica Ltd v Charlton* he says:

> Like a constructive trust, a resulting trust arises by operation of law, though unlike a constructive trust it gives effect to intention. But it arises whether or not the transferor intended to retain a beneficial interest—he almost always does not—since it responds to the absence of any intention on his part to pass a beneficial interest to the recipient. It may arise even where the transferor positively wished to part with the beneficial interest, as in *Vandervell v Inland Revenue Commissioners* [1967] 2 AC 291. In that case the retention of a beneficial interest by the transferor destroyed the effectiveness of a tax avoidance scheme which the transferor was seeking to implement. The House of Lords affirmed the principle that a resulting trust is not defeated by evidence that the transferor intended to part with the beneficial interest if he has not in fact succeeded in doing so. As Plowman J had said in the same case at first instance [1966] Ch 261, 275: 'As I see it, a man does not cease to own property simply by saying "I don't want it." If he tries to give it away the question must always be, has he succeeded in doing so or not?' Lord Upjohn [1967] 2 AC 291, 314 expressly approved this.[96]

It can now be seen why Lord Millett thinks trusts imposed by law on a recipient of property transferred in breach of trust or fiduciary obligation are resulting trusts. In these cases, the beneficial owner of the property, the beneficiary or principal, has not disposed of his beneficial interest in the eyes of Equity—his trustee or principal ex hypothesi has acted without authority in disposing of the assets in this way, and without effective authority, in the eyes of Equity such transfers cannot dispose of the beneficiary's or principal's beneficial interest. That interest therefore remains with him, and Equity gives effect to this via the imposition of a resulting trust in his favour. The following (admittedly long) quotation shows the steps in Lord Millett's reasoning. He begins with the right a beneficiary under a trust has to the traceable proceeds of his property:

---

[94] [1967] 2 AC 291, 313–14.
[95] Ibid, 329.
[96] [1999] 1 WLR 1399, 1412.

> How did we arrive at the rule [that the owner of a thing can claim ownership of its traceable proceeds]? Not by way of unjust enrichment. Equity took the authorised disposition of trust property as its starting point. A trust fund is not a res. The beneficiaries' interests in a trust fund are proprietary interests in the assets from time to time comprised in the fund subject to the trustees' overriding powers of managing and alienating the trust assets and substituting others. . . . This is the 'fiction of persistence', except that it is not a fiction. The beneficiaries' interests in the new assets are exactly the same as their interest in the old. They have a continuing beneficial interest which persists in the substitute.
>
> Now suppose that the disposal is unauthorised. The trustee sells a trust investment in breach of trust and uses the proceeds to buy shares for himself. The beneficiaries have a continuing proprietary interest in the original investment but they cannot recover it from the purchaser if he is a bona fide purchaser of the legal title without notice of the breach. But they can instead claim a proprietary interest in the shares which the trustee bought for himself. He bought them with trust money, and the beneficiaries are not bound to challenge the sale of the trust shares or the purchase of the new shares as a breach of trust. . . .
>
> It is often said that wrongfully substituted assets are held on constructive trust. I do not think they are. I think that they continue to be held on the same trusts throughout. If the claimant was the beneficiary under an express trust, the substituted assets are held on the same express trust. If he was an absolute beneficial owner, they are held on resulting trust for him. It is sometimes said that the resulting trust is a response to unjust enrichment. In this context it is a response to the disposal of property without the owner's consent. This gives us a principled basis for proprietary restitution. I have long argued that the resulting trust provides a sound basis, indeed the only basis, for proprietary restitution.[97]

To summarise: because Equity views the beneficial interest as persisting through a substitution of assets, in cases where A's property is disposed of without A's consent, A retains his beneficial interest, and this interest will subsist not only in the asset non-consensually disposed of, but in any substitute asset acquired in exchange for it.

This reasoning also formed the basis of Lord Millett's analysis of tracing in *Foskett v McKeown*,[98] the most important decision on the law of tracing since *Re Hallett's Estate*[99] and *Re Oatway*[100] were decided a century before. Writing the majority opinion, Lord Millett said this:

> The transmission of a claimant's property rights from one asset to its traceable proceeds is part of our law of property, not of the law of unjust enrichment. There is no 'unjust factor' to justify restitution (unless 'want of title' be one,

---

[97] Millett 'Proprietary Restitution' (n 3) 315–16. For previous expression of Lord Millett's views, see: 'Book Review' (1995) 111 *Law Quarterly Review* 517; 'Review Article' [1998] *Restitution Law Review* 283; 'Equity's Place in the Law of Commerce' (1998) 114 *Law Quarterly Review* 214; 'Restitution and Constructive Trusts' (1998) 114 *Law Quarterly Review* 399.
[98] [2001] 1 AC 102.
[99] (1880) 13 Ch D 696.
[100] [1903] 2 Ch 356.

which makes the point). The claimant succeeds if at all by virtue of his own title, not to reverse unjust enrichment. Property rights are determined by fixed rules and settled principles. They are not discretionary. They do not depend upon ideas of what is 'fair, just and reasonable'. Such concepts, which in reality mask decisions of legal policy, have no place in the law of property.

A beneficiary of a trust is entitled to a continuing beneficial interest not merely in the trust property but in its traceable proceeds also, and his interest binds everyone who takes the property or its traceable proceeds except a bona fide purchaser for value without notice. In the present case the plaintiffs' beneficial interest plainly bound Mr Murphy, a trustee who wrongfully mixed the trust money with his own and whose every dealing with the money (including the payment of the premiums) was in breach of trust. It similarly binds his successors, the trustees of the children's settlement, who claim no beneficial interest of their own, and Mr Murphy's children, who are volunteers. They gave no value for what they received and derive their interest from Mr Murphy by way of gift.[101]

Lord Millett holds that the ground of restitution in these cases is 'want of title', that is, that because the property in question was transferred without the beneficial owner's consent the recipient cannot have acquired the beneficial title in the eyes of Equity. Lord Millett coined this usage specifically to oppose the view of unjust enrichment theorists such as Birks and Burrows that restitution arose in these cases to reverse an unjust enrichment where the 'unjust factor' was 'ignorance' or 'powerlessness'.[102] Having set out Lord Millett's views, we can now tackle the reason given by Chambers and Swadling (and Birks and others) for rejecting Lord Millett's view that proprietary restitution gives effect to the plaintiff's continuing beneficial interest in property in the eyes of Equity.

The reason that Lord Millett must be wrong, claim Chambers[103] and Swadling,[104] is that there is nothing that A *retains* in circumstances where he traces into a substitute asset, or where Equity imposes a resulting trust on B in A's favour, whether by operation of a presumption or because A's false fiduciary transfers property which is beneficially A's to B. In each of these cases, the trust A enforces is a different interest from the one that he began with. In the tracing case, A begins with an equitable interest in one property but enforces an equitable interest in the substitute. In the presumption and false fiduciary cases, A begins with a legal title to an item

---

[101] *Foskett* (n 98) 127.
[102] See Millett, 'Review Article' (n 97) 285; Millett, 'Restitution and Constructive Trusts' (n 97) 409 and 416; Millett, 'Proprietary Restitution' (n 3) 317–18. Robert Chambers and I have recently argued (Chambers and Penner (n 2)) that 'ignorance' and 'powerlessness' are unworkable 'unjust factors'; we go on to consider 'want of authority' as the ground of restitution, although we would maintain that as a ground of restitution it should be regarded as an unjust factor and so Chambers maintains his view that the resulting trust arises to reverse unjust enrichment.
[103] Chambers (n 22) 51–55.
[104] Swadling (n 1) 99–100.

of property, but as the legal title is transferred to the recipient, A does not *retain* that; the equitable title which A enforces is wholly new; *that* is A's equitable interest under the resulting trust which *arises*—it did not exist before.

If I may put it this way, this is a very *theoretical* objection to the concept of 'beneficial title', based on the (true) distinction between *legal* and *equitable* title. As Lord Browne-Wilkinson correctly stated in *Westdeutsche*:

> A person solely entitled to the full beneficial ownership of money or property, both at law and in equity, does not enjoy an equitable interest in that property. The legal title carries with it all rights. Unless and until there is a separation of the legal and equitable estates, there is no separate equitable title. Therefore to talk about the bank 'retaining' its equitable interest is meaningless. The only question is whether the circumstances under which the money was paid were such as, in equity, to impose a trust on the local authority. If so, an equitable interest arose for the first time under that trust.[105]

This point, however, does not decide the issue in favour of Chambers and Swadling against Lord Millett. It would only do so if 'beneficial' needs to be treated as a synonym for 'equitable', and it does not.[106]

It seems perfectly conceptually feasible to recognise a continuing beneficial interest in property even though the legal structure under which it is held changes. Consider three straightforward examples. A transfers his painting to B to hold on bare trust for him. It is true that A now holds his beneficial interest in a different way than before, and his beneficial interest is secured by a title with different incidents; for example, now that the property is held on trust, A's interest is liable to be defeated by sale to a bona fide purchaser, which was not true of his legal title to the painting. Nevertheless, it would be absurd to say that A has not held the beneficial interest in the painting throughout: no one else has during this time held any beneficial interest, nor could it be seriously contended that A simultaneously destroyed and created his beneficial interest in the painting when he transferred it on trust. Yet Chambers's and Swadling's theoretical objection to Lord Millett's explanation of resulting trusts requires us to say something like this. (I am, of course, taking the orthodox view that an interest under a trust is a kind of property interest, but I think that is common ground between us.)

Or consider the case where A makes a contract with B to lease B's land. As we know from *Walsh v Lonsdale*[107] this will give rise immediately to a lease in equity; that is, A will immediately be beneficially entitled to the leasehold interest in equity. Now A and B formally execute a lease by deed.

---

[105] *Westdeutsche* (n 66) 706.

[106] Indeed, in many contexts it must not. Consider, for example, the reach of the Law of Property Act 1925, s 53(1)(c) if one treated 'equitable' as synonymous with 'beneficial'.

[107] (1882) 21 Ch D 9

Now A is entitled to the leasehold interest at law. Again, Chambers and Swadling must contend that A now has a different beneficial interest in the land, not just that A's beneficial interest is now better protected by the legal title to it.

Consider one last case which operates wholly at law: let us say that A holds title to Blackacre by deeds. Under the Land Registration Act 2002, section 3, A can apply to the Registrar and acquire the registered title. This will give rise to a change in the incidents of A's legal title (for example, registration will give rise to a different regime under which A might lose the land by adverse possession). There is no reason to say in this case that A's legal beneficial ownership has been at once extinguished and recreated in a different form, rather than saying that A's legal beneficial interest in Blackacre is the same, though now held under a different, more secure, legal structure. A had the same beneficial fee simple interest before and after registration.

What these examples show is that there is a perfectly conceptually acceptable alternative to the position adopted by Swadling and Chambers, that is, that a 'beneficial' interest cannot continue to exist through a change in the legal form by which that beneficial interest is secured. Of course it can; all one needs to do is maintain a distinction between form and substance. My interest in Blackacre is substantially the same before and after my registration of title in the last example. Any tenant I had prior to registering my title would be the same tenant afterwards, and we all understand that. Chambers and Swadling need to explain why, on their view, the right to register a title voluntarily would not also be the right to unilaterally destroy a lease.

Swadling has objected[108] to the use (in this case by Chambers) of the term 'beneficial interest'. The gist of Swadling's objection is that while 'beneficially' is a respectable adverb in English legal usage—it is perfectly all right to say that I hold my fee simple in Blackacre beneficially (as opposed to on trust for someone else)—it is wrong to say that I am the 'beneficial' owner of Blackacre, or that I have a beneficial interest in Blackacre (for example, if I am the beneficiary of Blackacre under a bare trust). It seems to me the latter two 'adjectival' uses of 'beneficial' are perfectly respectable, indeed common. To take several examples: we have seen both Megarry J and Lord Upjohn use 'beneficial interest' in their *Vandervell* judgments,[109] and the term was used by counsel and the bench throughout the 1857 case of *Childers v Childers*.[110] The root of Swadling's objection appears to be that there is no notion of a beneficial interest in our legal system which is not *also* either an equitable or legal interest. He therefore

---

[108] Swadling (n 1) 90–91.
[109] Text to nn 39 and 94, respectively.
[110] (1857) 1 De G & J 482, 44 ER 810.

might argue that I assume what I seek to prove, that is, that there is such a thing as a beneficial interest separate from either an equitable or legal interest.

To make such an objection would be to misunderstand the point I am making and the use I intend to make of my examples. The point of the examples is not to show that one can have a beneficial interest which is somehow distinct from an equitable or a legal interest, in the sense that one could have a beneficial interest without having either a legal or equitable interest. The idea is rather that it is perfectly sensible and correct in law to conceive of different sorts of titles as different *formal* or *technical* ways of holding the *same* interest in *substance*. The final example (in which an equitable interest does not figure), the case of the fee simple holder who voluntarily registers his ownership of Blackacre, makes that clear. The claim was not that prior to registration, A had a legal interest evidenced by deeds, which was therefore subject to certain legal incidents, *plus* a beneficial interest, whereas after registration A had a different legal interest, evidenced by entry on the register and therefore subject to certain other legal incidents, *plus* the same beneficial interest that he had before. Rather my claim was that A held the absolute fee simple interest in the land throughout, and therefore had the beneficial fee simple interest in the land throughout, though upon registration the legal incidents of that title changed (for example, liability to defeat of the title by adverse possession was much reduced following registration). To hold otherwise would be to hold that A's interest in Blackacre was extinguished upon registration, whereupon an entirely new legal interest in Blackacre arose; that A now has an entirely different legal right to the land following registration; and that it is incorrect to say, even 'adverbally', that A has held Blackacre beneficially throughout, for on such a view there is *no interest* that A has held 'throughout', beneficially or otherwise. I find this way of conceiving the situation implausible, as, apparently, do judges at the highest level.

As far as I can tell, on Swadling's and Chambers's analysis, an alteration of any kind in the incidents of any right entails that the right has wholly changed, since there is no legal concept of the 'substance' of an interest. Thus if a statute were passed altering the rules governing damages for breach of contract, all the contractual rights now existing would be extinguished and immediately replaced by new rights arising by operation of law which were identical to the pre-existing ones except that they incorporated the new incident introduced by the statute. Again, I find such a way of looking at things implausible. Once the law's recognition of a substantive beneficial interest in property is acknowledged, there is no need to find a reason such as the prevention of unjust enrichment to explain why resulting trusts arise in the cases when they do. They arise because the 'settlors' did not effectively dispose of their beneficial interest (whether by effectively transferring legal title to someone to hold absolutely or by declaring a trust that fully disposes of the beneficial interest), and the rule is that what you fail effectively to dispose of, you keep, just as the judges say it is.

As I understand it, the motivating force behind Swadling's objection to the retention conception is that transferring legal title, say, to a painting to a friend to hold on trust for me effects a radical change in my legal situation. Prior to the transfer, I had the right to possess the painting, and rights against anyone who interfered with that possession. Afterwards, I did not. But in reply, one has to say that all depends on the terms of the trust. True, if I transfer the painting by delivery, then I am now out of possession, but if the terms of the trust are that I have the right to possess the painting, then I can take it right back. I might have effected the same thing by way of deed. And the objection is clearly most vivid in the case of tangible property, and has very little bite in the case of the sorts of property—shares, bank balances, and so on—which largely populate the funds of modern trusts. To say all of this is not to deny in any way that such transactions have legal consequences, very significant ones. If the law teaches us anything, it is that form matters. But to acknowledge that is not to require oneself to deny that the law has concepts, 'beneficial interest' being a perfect example, which is a substantive concept, not a formal one.

One final point, which shows, I think, that the 'retention model' is actually necessary even to make sense of Swadling's and Chambers's positions, and here I happily give credit to John Mee for the point.[111] Let me put the point in my own words, and add a thought, so the reader can judge whether we are actually expressing the same idea. Restitution for unjust enrichment, if successful *as* restitution for unjust enrichment, requires the defendant to give up to the claimant the very enrichment or gain he has received.[112] Conceived as an increase in his wealth, that is, as a abstract enrichment of monetary value, a money payment by the defendant effects restitution perfectly. In the case of proprietary restitution, perfect restitution can only be effected by the return of the very property rights received (or, if one believes in a fund analysis of property held on trust,[113] the traceable proceeds thereof). Therefore Chambers's and Swadling's denial that the law conceives of a substantive beneficial interest entails that imposing a trust on the property the recipient receives does not effect restitution. Or, if it does, that is, if the interest under the resulting trust is *as good as* the original legal title for the purpose of effecting restitution, they must explain why is it not *as good as* the original legal title for the purposes of the retention argument. How can Chambers and Swadling deny that the

---

[111] See ch 7, 224.
[112] Subject to defences, of course.
[113] See Penner (n 4); JE Penner, 'Duty and Liability in Respect of Funds' in J Lowry and L Mistelis (eds), *Commercial Law: Perspectives and Practice* (London, LexisNexis Butterworths, 2006) 207.

transferor/contributor essentially *retains* 'just what he had before' but then argue that the trust effects restitution, *giving* him 'just what he had before'? It is only by treating the resulting trust as a *substantive* equivalent to the interest transferred away that the restitutionary argument makes any sense.

A last thought. Parenthetically a few sentences back I mentioned trusts of traceable proceeds. It seems to me that Mee's insight on the issue of substantive beneficial interests is a powerful one. Assuming that a beneficiary's claim to the traceable proceeds acquired by a third party beneficiary of trust assets transferred in breach of trust effects restitution is to assume a doctrine of substantial equivalents that goes beyond anything the retention argument claims, for in the absence of something like a fund analysis of trust property,[114] upon which so far as I know no restitution-for-unjust-enrichment argument relies, it cannot be the case that a claim that the third party recipient holds the case of wine he received in exchange for the money he received in breach of trust effects proprietary restitution.

[114] Ibid.

9
Is There a Presumption of Resulting Trust?

ROBERT CHAMBERS

A. INTRODUCTION

The presumptions of resulting trust and advancement have been part of the law of trusts for perhaps as long as we have had a law of trusts. It is not certain how much time passed between the end of the resulting use in 1536 and the emergence of the resulting trust,[1] but the presumptions were operating in the seventeenth century.[2] So why in the twenty-first century would anyone with some familiarity with the subject ask if there is a presumption of resulting trust? There is no shortage of modern cases invoking the presumptions, and so this is not a situation in which a legal concept has fallen into disuse and ought to be given a decent burial.[3] While it is suggested below that the presumptions have outlived their usefulness and could easily be dispensed with, the central question addressed in this chapter is not whether there should be a presumption of resulting trust, but whether the phenomenon we call the presumption of resulting trust is really a presumption.

In a recent essay, William Swadling said that the presumption of resulting trust is 'a legal presumption that a trust was declared by the transferor in his own favour', while the presumption of advancement was not really a presumption, but 'only a situation where the resulting trust presumption does not apply'.[4] Presented here is the view that the converse is true, that the presumption of advancement is a presumption of an intention to give, while the resulting trust is not a true presumption after

---

[1] J Baker, *The Oxford History of the Laws of England*, Vol VI: *1483–1558* (Oxford, Oxford University Press, 2003) 675 and 683–86.
[2] *Cook v Fountain* (1676) 3 Swans 585, 36 ER 984; *Grey v Grey* (1677) 2 Swans 594, 36 ER 742.
[3] Cf J Penner, 'Decent Burials for Dead Concepts' (2005) 58 *Current Legal Problems* 313.
[4] W Swadling, 'Explaining Resulting Trusts' (2008) 124 *Law Quarterly Review* 72, 72–73.

all, but only a situation in which the presumption of advancement does not apply.

The significance of this debate is not how it affects the operation of the presumptions of resulting trust and advancement. They do not much matter as evidentiary devices, since they rarely determine the outcome of cases, and it is regrettable when they do. Its real significance is what it might tell us about the nature of the resulting trust and its relationship to unjust enrichment.

B. SIGNIFICANCE OF THE PRESUMPTIONS

The presumptions of resulting trust and advancement are called upon in cases that have been described as 'apparent gifts'[5] and also as 'ambiguous transfers'.[6] These are cases in which one person has received an interest in an asset at another person's expense, and there is no apparent explanation for the transaction. The recipient appears to be a donee of that interest, having not provided valuable consideration for it. Another person has either transferred it to the recipient gratuitously or paid the purchase price for it. These cases are often divided into two separate categories of 'voluntary conveyance and purchase-money resulting trusts',[7] but the problem is the same in both: it appears that one person has been enriched at the expense of another and there is no explanation for it.

While often called upon, the presumptions rarely ever provide the explanation. As Lord Upjohn said in *Vandervell v IRC*, the 'presumption of a resulting trust is no more than a long stop to provide the answer when the relevant facts and circumstances fail to yield a solution'.[8] This will only occur when there is no evidence of the relevant intention or that evidence is inadmissible due to illegality. The absence of evidence is now so rare that the presumptions really matter only in cases of illegality.

1. No Evidence

Apart from cases involving illegality (discussed below), there will be very few cases in which the choice of presumption affects the outcome. Judges have been able to find the relevant facts based on the slimmest of evidence. For example, in *Lohia v Lohia*,[9] the defendant and his father purchased a house as joint owners in 1955. In 1965, title was transferred to the father as the sole registered proprietor, and he died intestate in 1971. In 2000, the

---

[5] R Chambers, *Resulting Trusts* (Oxford, Clarendon Press, 1997) ch 1.
[6] Swadling (n 4) 86.
[7] Ibid, 73.
[8] [1967] 2 AC 291, 313.
[9] [2001] WTLR 101; affd [2001] EWCA Civ 1691.

defendant claimed that a resulting trust had arisen when his father acquired sole title in 1965. The judge rejected the defendant's evidence that the 1965 conveyance was a forgery, leaving no evidence about the transaction except that it had not been for valuable consideration. The judge concluded that the transfer had probably been intended to benefit the father as part of some family arrangement which the defendant had been unwilling to explain. This was affirmed by the Court of Appeal. Mummery LJ said:

> On the basis of the very limited amount of solid information, the judge had to decide on the civil standard of proof what was the more probable explanation of how and why the father came to be registered as sole proprietor. It cannot be said, in the light of his assessment of the appellant's evidence, that the judge's inference from the available material as to the probable explanation for the transfer to the father was unsupported by any evidence or was against the weight of the evidence or was an inference which no reasonable court could have made in all the circumstances.
>
> The judge's finding as to a family arrangement under which the property was transferred to the father is also sufficient to rebut any presumption of resulting trust to the appellant which might arise from the voluntary nature of the transfer.[10]

Courts often speak in terms of unrebutted presumptions, but normally do so when the presumption is consistent with the evidence available. In *Mehta Estate v Mehta Estate*,[11] a husband and wife both died in a plane crash. His estate claimed that several investments he had purchased in her name were held on resulting trust. The Manitoba Court of Appeal applied the presumption of advancement, but it is doubtful that it would have reached a different conclusion even if it had started instead with the presumption of resulting trust. Huband JA said:

> The husband was the major provider for the family. The wife's employment was part-time and generated modest income. Her major role was as homemaker and mother. Under these circumstances, it is entirely understandable that a loving husband should put assets in the name of his wife with the intent that they should be hers as gifts.[12]

In *Antoni v Antoni*,[13] a father of three adult children was the beneficial owner of all five shares issued by a company he controlled. He arranged for three of those shares to be transferred: one share each directly to two of his children and a third share to a trustee in trust for his third child. The father later divorced and remarried, and after his death, his widow claimed that those shares had been held on resulting trust for him. The Privy Council advised that the presumption of advancement applied to the transaction and had not been rebutted, but there was sufficient evidence that the father

---

[10] Ibid, [20]–[21].
[11] (1993) 104 DLR (4th) 24.
[12] Ibid, [34].
[13] [2007] UKPC 10, [2007] WTLR 1335.

had intended to transfer beneficial ownership of the shares to his children. There was no need to rely on a presumption to decide the case.

In the absence of direct evidence, courts are prepared to draw inferences of intention from the nature of the transaction and the nature of the relationship between the parties to it. If the presumptions did not exist and judges were required to determine on the balance of probabilities whether or not a gift had been intended, there would be difficult cases, but it seems likely that all of them could be decided properly. The lack of a presumption would not increase the number of cases or costs of litigation. In other words, the presumptions do not fill a necessary function.

Not only are the presumptions almost completely unnecessary, they can be undesirable as well. We are not entirely happy whenever the application of a presumption actually determines the outcome of a case. For example, in *Re Vinogradoff*,[14] a grandmother purchased stocks for herself and her infant granddaughter as joint owners. After her death, her estate successfully claimed the stocks on the basis of an unrebutted presumption of resulting trust. If there had been no presumption and the judge had been required to decide the issue based on the available evidence, he might well have concluded that the circumstances of the transaction and relationship between the parties indicated that the grandmother had intended a gift of a joint interest (possibly subject to a life interest for herself). Perhaps the case was wrongly decided. It seems likely that it would be decided differently today. The point is that we do not want the outcome to be determined by a presumption whenever that would differ from the outcome based on the admissible evidence. We do not need the presumptions and would be better off without them.

2. Illegality

The one situation in which the presumptions continue to matter is when evidence of intention is inadmissible because it is connected to an illegal purpose. Again, no one is happy when a presumption actually affects the outcome (except the lucky claimant or defendant). In *Tinsley v Milligan*,[15] the claimant and defendant purchased a house in the claimant's name and lived in it together as their family home. They pretended to the Department of Social Security that the defendant was a lodger with no interest in the house so that she could fraudulently claim benefits to which she was not entitled. Both parties were guilty of fraud and had benefited from it. After they separated, the defendant claimed her interest in the house.

---

[14] [1935] WN 68. Also see *Re Muller* [1953] NZLR 879, and see JE Penner, *The Law of Trusts*, 6th edn (Oxford, Oxford University Press, 2008) 90: '*Re Vinogradoff* is an atrocity of a decision.'
[15] [1994] 1 AC 340.

According to the majority led by Lord Browne-Wilkinson, the evidence that the parties had intended a trust was inadmissible because of their illegal purpose for making that arrangement. However, the defendant needed only to show that she had contributed to the purchase to raise the presumption of resulting trust and take advantage of it. No evidence of intention was necessary. The operation of the presumption happened to coincide with the parties' intentions, and so no harm was done to either party in this particular case, but no one finds the prospect of a mismatch palatable.[16]

The same trust would have existed even if the presumption of resulting trust had not applied, but the defendant would have been prevented from establishing its existence. It would be difficult to justify reaching a different outcome solely because the parties were in a relationship to which the presumption of advancement applied or because the same arrangement had been created in a different way. If instead of contributing to the purchase price, the defendant had transferred her interest in the house to the claimant, the presumption of resulting trust might have been precluded by the Law of Property Act 1925, section 60(3).[17] Yet, in substance, the same event has occurred in all these situations: one person has obtained an interest in land at the expense of another to facilitate a fraud committed by both parties. The choice of presumption and thus the winner has nothing to do with any substantial reasons for either allowing or denying recovery. As Peter Birks said:

> Where the litigation concerns the assertion of proprietary rights the courts thus seem prepared to watch the parties play an amoral game of cards, in which the party who turns over the illegality card loses.[18]

The illegality cases provide the last refuge in which the presumptions are allowed to affect people's lives, and to our shame we seem to be using them only to shuffle the cards to be dealt to the parties. In the absence of a presumption, courts would have had to deal squarely with the issue of how illegality should affect the right to enforce trusts. The choice of presumption provides no meaningful way to distinguish one case of resulting trust from another, nor does it explain why resulting trusts should be treated

---

[16] See the comments in *Tribe v Tribe* [1996] Ch 107, 116, 118, 122 and 134, and in *Collier v Collier* [2002] EWCA Civ 1095, (2002) 6 ITELR 270 [106]. In *Q v Q* [2008] EWHC 1874 (Fam); [2009] 1 FLR 935, a father was not permitted to rebut the presumption of advancement because his apparent gift of land to his sons had been for an illegal purpose of evading tax. However, this matched the desired outcome produced by proprietary estoppel and constructive trust.

[17] See *Lohia* (CA) (n 9) [21]–[26]; *Ali v Khan* [2002] EWCA Civ 974 [24]; Law Commission, *The Illegality Defence: A Consultative Report* (LCCP No 189, 2008) paras 6.34–6.36.

[18] P Birks, 'Recovering Value Transferred Under an Illegal Contract' (2000) 1 *Theoretical Inquiries in Law* 155, 166. Also see *Tribe* (n 16) 134, where Millett LJ said of *Tinsley*: 'But the primary rule, as it has emerged from that decision, does not conform to any discernible moral principle. It is procedural in nature and depends on the adventitious location of the burden of proof in any given case.'

differently from constructive or express trusts.[19] What if the defendant in *Tinsley* had contributed not to the purchase of the house but in other substantial ways in reliance on a common intention of sharing it equally? What if the parties had simply declared the trust in writing in compliance with the Law of Property Act 1925, section 53(1)(b) (without reference to their illegal purpose) and hidden the declaration from the Department of Social Security? While the presumption of resulting trust might appear to be useful in this situation, it is detrimental because it allows courts to avoid the important issues that ought to determine the outcome of cases.

3. Choice of Presumption

In cases of illegality, the choice of presumption can have arbitrary effects that have nothing to do with the reasons for choosing one presumption over the other. This unhappy situation is not improved by an examination of those reasons, for the choice itself seems more or less arbitrary. It is not based on any important or immutable principle, but changes from time to time and varies from place to place. The reasons given are never fully convincing.

At one time, the presumption of advancement was firmly grounded in the father's moral duty to advance his children in life, and would not apply if that duty had already been performed. According to Lord Nottingham LC in *Elliot v Elliot*:

> [I]f the Father purchase Land in the Name of a Son, and pay for it, or convey Land to his Son, it shall be taken not to be a Trust *ut supra*, but to be an Advancement or Provision for the Son, because the Father is under an Obligation of Duty and Conscience to provide for his Child in such Case; but after he hath provided for him, he is under no further Obligation to provide more than for a Stranger, and else no Father could trust his Child.[20]

The existence of the father's duty of advancement provided the reason to apply the presumption of advancement to apparent gifts from persons standing *in loco parentis*,[21] and its absence was the reason for not applying it to apparent gifts from mothers.[22] However, as the years passed, the choice of presumption came to depend less on duty and more on altruism. In *Nelson v Nelson*,[23] the High Court of Australia held that the presumption of advancement applied to apparent gifts from mothers because there

---

[19] See *Barrett v Barrett* [2008] EWHC 1061 (Ch).
[20] (1677) 2 Ch Cas 231, 232; 22 ER 922, 922; also see *Grey v Grey* (1677) 2 Swans 594, 600–01, 36 ER 742, 744. And for discussion see ch 10 below.
[21] *Ebrand v Dancer* (1680) Chan Cas 26, 22 ER 829.
[22] *Bennet v Bennet* (1879) 10 Ch D 474.
[23] [1995] HCA 25, (1995) 184 CLR 538. Also see *Brown v Brown* (1993) 31 NSWLR 582 (NSWCA).

was no longer any reason to treat them differently from apparent gifts from fathers. Both parents now owe the same legal and moral duties to their children and are equally likely to intend gifts. Almost everyone agrees that there is no reason to treat men and women differently in this situation,[24] but it is curious that the choice of presumption would be modified without clearly identifying the reasons for making that choice.

The Supreme Court of Canada recently decided to alter the choice of presumption. The presumption of advancement now applies to apparent gifts from fathers or mothers to their minor children, while the presumption of resulting trust applies to apparent gifts to their adult children. The court also returned to the concept of duty to justify the choice. In *Pecore v Pecore*, Rothstein J said:

> First, given that a principal justification for the presumption of advancement is parental obligation to support their dependent children, it seems to me that the presumption should not apply in respect of independent adult children. . . . [P]arental support obligations under provincial and federal statutes normally end when the child is no longer considered by law to be a minor: see eg Family Law Act, s 31. Indeed, not only do child support obligations end when a child is no longer dependent, but often the reverse is true: an obligation may be imposed on independent adult children to support their parents in accordance with need and ability to pay: see eg Family Law Act, s 32. Second, . . . it is common nowadays for ageing parents to transfer their assets into joint accounts with their adult children in order to have that child assist them in managing their financial affairs. There should therefore be a rebuttable presumption that the adult child is holding the property in trust for the ageing parent to facilitate the free and efficient management of that parent's affairs.[25]

It might be regarded as an indication of the continued vitality and importance of the presumptions that both the High Court of Australia and the Supreme Court of Canada have in recent years taken time to consider them. However, there are two factors indicating that the opposite might be true. First, in none of these cases did the choice of presumption actually affect the outcome, since the declaration of trust or gift depended on evidence of intention and not a presumption. It is perhaps ironic that these pronouncements are obiter dicta, but it is doubtful that a change to the choice of presumptions would ever form part of the ratio decidendi, except in a case where all evidence of intention was excluded by reason of illegality. This is a sure sign that the presumptions no longer have practical value.

Secondly, it is notable that the choice of presumption may now be

---

[24] But see L Sarmas, 'A Step in the Wrong Direction: The Emergence of Gender "Neutrality" in the Equitable Presumption of Advancement' (1994) 19 *Melbourne University Law Review* 758; and ch 10 below.
[25] [2007] SCC 17, [2007] 1 SCR 795 [36]. Also see *Saylor v Madsen Estate* [2007] SCC 18, [2007] 1 SCR 838.

different depending on whether an apparent gift is made in New South Wales or Nova Scotia. There is no reason to assume that Australian mothers are more generous than their Canadian counterparts, or owe more onerous duties towards their children. If the choice of presumption was linked to anything of substance, one might expect that similar social conditions would lead to similar choices being made. Fortunately, the choice does not really matter, and so these inexplicable differences are of little consequence.

Courts in England have not yet addressed the unequal treatment of fathers and mothers in this context, although in *Laskar v Laskar*,[26] Neuberger LJ did suggest that the presumption of advancement might apply between mother and daughter (but would have been rebutted if it did). When giving the advice of the Privy Council in *Antoni v Antoni*,[27] Lord Scott said that the presumption of advancement 'applies when a *parent* places assets in the name of a child and assumes that the *parent* intends to make a gift to the child'.

The unequal treatment of men and women in this context seems to violate the European Convention on Human Rights. According to Article 5 of the Seventh Protocol: 'Spouses shall enjoy equality of rights and responsibilities of a private law character between them, and in their relations with their children, as to marriage, during marriage and in the event of its dissolution.'

In 2006, a private member's bill was introduced in the House of Commons partly to address this problem. It would have abolished the presumption of advancement between husbands and wives and engaged couples, but did not deal with the unequal treatment of fathers and mothers. It did not receive a second reading.[28]

The choice of presumption in cases involving apparent gifts between cohabiting couples may have been changed by *Stack v Dowden*, where Baroness Hale said: 'The burden will therefore be on the person seeking to show that the parties did intend their beneficial interests to be different from their legal interests, and in what way.'[29] Lord Hope added:

> Where the parties have dealt with each other at arms length it makes sense to start from the position that there is a resulting trust according to how much each party contributed. . . . But cohabiting couples are in a different kind of relationship. . . . A more practical, down-to-earth, fact-based approach is called for in

---

[26] [2008] EWCA Civ 347, [2008] 1 WLR 2695 [20].

[27] *Antoni* (n 13) [20] (emphasis added).

[28] Family Law (Property and Maintenance) Bill 2005, no 73, s 2. See Law Commission, *The Presumption of Advancement: Does It Have Any Effect in Practice?*' (London, Law Commission, 2006) paras 1.10–1.12; Tey Tsun Hang, 'Reforming the Presumption of Advancement' (2008) 82 *Australian Law Journal* 40.

[29] [2007] UKHL 17, [2007] 2 AC 432 [68]. Also see [56]. It is not clear whether the *Stack* presumption that equity follows the law applies to other relationships, such as parent and child: *Laskar* (n 26) [15]–[17].

their case. . . . So in a case of sole legal ownership the onus is on the party who wishes to show that he has any beneficial interest at all, and if so what that interest is. In a case of joint legal ownership it is on the party who wishes to show that the beneficial interests are divided other than equally.[30]

Perhaps the claimant can meet that onus merely by showing that her or his contribution to the purchase price substantially exceeds her or his share of the legal estate, in which case the presumption of resulting trust still applies. However, except for Lord Neuberger's dissent,[31] the speeches seem to indicate otherwise. It does seem unlikely that the House of Lords would modify the choice of presumption in this context without clearly stating their intention to do so, but this may be yet another indication of the relative unimportance of that choice.

One might pause to reflect how this change would affect the outcome in a case such as *Tinsley v Milligan*.[32] Assuming the 'amoral game of cards' is still played the same way,[33] can the sole legal owner of the house now play the 'cohabiting couple' card and thereby shift the onus to the other party 'to show that the parties did intend their beneficial interests to be different from their legal interests',[34] a task that would surely require turning over the illegality card?

Except in cases of illegality, the choice of presumption should rarely ever matter. If a presumption is needed as a long stop,[35] it is a very long stop indeed and the ball should rarely travel that far. What should the law do in the unlikely case that there is no available evidence of intention other than the apparent gift itself and no clues available from the circumstances surrounding the transaction or relationship between the parties? Should it require some justification for the enrichment of one person at the expense of another or some good reason to interfere in the manner in which people have voluntarily chosen to order their affairs? Perhaps there is no legal principle at stake at this point, but merely a preference for one adage over another: 'better safe than sorry' or 'let sleeping dogs lie'?

Ambivalence over the choice of presumption should not be mistaken for a waning interest in the resulting trust. There is a world of difference between the presumption of resulting trust and the trust itself. When a resulting trust arises, it almost always responds to evidence of intention rather than a presumption of intention. The abolition of the presumption of resulting trust would have little or no effect on the resulting trust, which continues to be an important part of the law of trusts and (I believe) unjust enrichment. As Lord Millett wrote (extra-judicially), 'the development of a

---

[30] Ibid, [3]–[4].
[31] Ibid, [110].
[32] *Tinsley* (n 15).
[33] Birks (n 18) 166.
[34] *Stack* (n 29) [68] (Baroness Hale).
[35] *Vandervell* (n 8) 313.

coherent doctrine of proprietary restitution for subtractive unjust enrichment is impossible unless it is based on the resulting trust as traditionally understood'.[36]

The presumptions of resulting trust and advancement are important because of what they reveal about the resulting trust. What we are presuming clearly has a great deal to tell us about why the resulting trust arises.

C. WHAT IS BEING PRESUMED?

After considering why the presumptions do not (or at least should not) matter, it is now time to consider why they do. What is being presumed when one of the presumptions applies? The presumption of resulting use probably began as a presumption of a declaration of resulting use. When a court encountered a feoffment for no apparent consideration, it assumed that the feoffor had declared a use for himself. William Swadling has argued that the presumption of resulting trust operates on the same basis,[37] but this is disputed below.

1. Declaration of Trust

It is doubtful that the presumption of resulting trust began life as a presumption of a declaration of trust, but even if it did, that approach was soon foreclosed by the Statute of Frauds 1677. The presumption of a declaration of use had probably ceased to be the true basis of the resulting use before the Statute of Uses came into force in 1536. By then, the resulting use operated as a formal rule of law responding to an absence of consideration. It would arise and be executed by the statute (thus nullifying the transaction) unless there was a declaration of use in favour of the transferee or some other consideration, such as kinship or a bargain and sale. When we see the presumptions of resulting trust and advancement emerging in the seventeenth century, the courts are proceeding by analogy to the resulting use as a response to an absence of consideration. However, there were then two different kinds of trusts at work: presumed and implied. The former was created by act of the parties and the latter arose by operation of law.

In *Cook v Fountain*, Lord Nottingham LC spoke of a 'presumptive trust' in which the court 'presumes there was a declaration', but he regarded this as a subcategory of the express trust:

> All trusts are either, first, express trusts, which are raised and created by act of

---

[36] P Millett, 'Restitution and Constructive Trusts' (1998) 114 *Law Quarterly Review* 399, 410.
[37] Swadling (n 4) 84.

the parties, or implied trusts, which are raised or created by act or construction of law; again, express trusts are declared either by word or writing; and these declarations appear either by direct and manifest proof, or violent and necessary presumption. These last are commonly called presumptive trusts; and that is, when the Court, upon consideration of all circumstances presumes there was a declaration, either by word or writing; though the plain and direct proof thereof be not extant. In the case in question there is no pretence of any proof that there was a trust declared either by word or in writing; so the trust, if there be any, must either be implied by the law, or presumed by the Court.[38]

Cook v Fountain concerned two leases and a rent charge that Cook had granted to his friend, Fountain. After Cook's death, his estate claimed that they had been held on trust for Cook. Lord Nottingham LC presumed a trust of the leases because Cook had continued to behave as landlord after the conveyance, receiving rents, repairing, and dealing with trespassers and requests for renewals. The rent charge caused more difficulty, but on balance he decided there was no trust, primarily because it was unlikely that someone would want to create a trust of it:

> Leases are often made upon trust to indemnify sureties, and for other like purposes, but who ever heard of a rent-charge created *de novo*, and then granted in trust? Certainly nothing can be more unnatural and unusual.[39]

Lord Nottingham LC dealt with *Cook v Fountain* as a case of express trust, considering whether it was reasonable to presume that the parties had actually declared one. A year later in *Grey v Grey*,[40] he took a very different approach when asking whether a father's purchase of an estate in the name of his eldest son was a trust for the father or an advancement for the son. After deciding that it was not possible to presume a declaration of trust, he considered whether a trust could be implied by law. In other words, there was no express trust, but that did not foreclose the possibility of an implied trust:

> Upon these facts, the law will best appear by these steps. 1. Generally and *prima facie*, as they say, a purchase in the name of a stranger is a trust, for want of a consideration, but a purchase in the name of a son is no trust, for the consideration is apparent. 2. But yet it may be a trust, if it be so declared antecedently or subsequently, under the hand and seal of both parties. 3. Nay, it may be a trust, if it be so declared by parol, and both parties uniformly concur in that declaration. 4. The parol declarations in this case are both ways; the father and son sometimes declaring for, and sometimes against, themselves. 5. *Ergo*, there being no certain proof to rest on as to parol declarations, the matter is left to construction and interpretation of law. 6. And herein the great question is, whether the law will admit of any constructive trust at all between father and son?[41]

[38] (1676) 3 Swans 585, 591; 36 ER 984, 987.
[39] Ibid, 3 Swans 597.
[40] (1677) 2 Swans 594, 36 ER 742.
[41] Ibid, 2 Swans 597.

There were then two avenues of inquiry open to the court when dealing with an apparent gift: was there a declaration of express trust (either proved or presumed), or did an implied trust arise by operation of law in response to an absence of consideration? While Swadling would like to trace the modern resulting trust back to the former branch, it is much more likely that it sprang from the latter.

It is notable that *Grey v Grey* was decided on 26 March 1677, just three months before the Statute of Frauds came into force. Then, a parol declaration of trust of land would give rise to an enforceable trust. This was no longer possible after the Statute of Frauds came into force on 24 June 1677:

> AND bee it further enacted by the authoritie aforesaid That from and after the said fower and twentyeth day of June all Declarations or Creations of Trusts or Confidences of any Lands Tenements or Hereditaments shall be manifested and proved by some Writeing signed by the partie who is by Law enabled to declare such Trust or by his last Will in Writeing or else they shall be utterly void and of none effect.
>
> PROVIDED alwayes That where any Conveyance shall bee made of any Lands or Tenements by which a Trust or Confidence shall or may arise or result by the Implication or Construction of Law or bee transferred or extinguished by an act or operation of Law then and in every such Case, such Trust or Confidence shall be of the like force and effect as the same would have beene if this Statute had not been made. Any thing herein before contained to the contrary notwithstanding.

This put an end to the possibility of presuming a declaration of trust in the absence of writing signed by the party making the declaration. The statute left an exception for Lord Nottingham LC's second category of implied trusts, and it is in this category that the modern resulting trust belongs. This prohibition and exception have been preserved in subsections 53(1)(b) and 53(2) of the Law of Property Act 1925, respectively. When a modern court deals with the resulting trust there is no doubt that it is dealing with a trust excepted under section 53(2), that is, a trust arising or resulting by the implication or construction of law, and not because of a presumed declaration of trust.

This dichotomy is well demonstrated by *Hodgson v Marks*.[42] The plaintiff had been induced by fraud to transfer her house to her lodger, Mr Evans, who had orally agreed to hold it in trust for her, but then sold it on to the innocent Mr Marks. There were two possible ways for her to establish an enforceable equitable interest in the house: either as an oral declaration of express trust, which was enforceable despite section 53(1) because of the fraud, or as a resulting trust excepted under section 53(2), which arose because she had not intended to make a gift. There was no

---

[42] [1971] Ch 892.

third possibility of enforcing a presumed declaration of trust. Russell LJ said:

> I turn next to the question whether section 53(1) of the Law of Property Act 1925 prevents the assertion by the plaintiff of her entitlement in equity to the house. Let me first assume that, contrary to the view expressed by the judge, Mr Marks is not debarred from relying upon the section, and the express oral arrangement or declaration of trust between the plaintiff and Mr Evans found by the judge was not effective as such. Nevertheless, the evidence is clear that the transfer was not intended to operate as a gift, and, in those circumstances, I do not see why there was not a resulting trust of the beneficial interest to the plaintiff, which would not, of course, be affected by section 53(1). It was argued that a resulting trust is based upon implied intention, and that where there is an express trust for the transferor intended and declared—albeit ineffectively—there is no room for such an implication. I do not accept that. If an attempted express trust fails, that seems to me just the occasion for implication of a resulting trust, whether the failure be due to uncertainty, or perpetuity, or lack of form. It would be a strange outcome if the plaintiff were to lose her beneficial interest because her evidence had not been confined to negativing a gift but had additionally moved into a field forbidden by section 53(1) for lack of writing. I remark in this connection that we are not concerned with the debatable question whether on a voluntary transfer of land by A to stranger B there is a presumption of a resulting trust. The accepted evidence is that this was not intended as a gift, notwithstanding the reference to love and affection in the transfer, and section 53(1) does not exclude that evidence. . . .
>
> On the above footing it matters not whether Mr Marks was or was not debarred from relying upon section 53(1) by the principle that the section is not to be used as an instrument for fraud.[43]

It was clear that section 53(1) applied to the plaintiff's declaration of trust, unless the fraud of Mr Evans prevented Mr Marks from relying on that section. The effect of that fraud would not have been an issue if a presumed declaration of trust was effective to give rise to a trust even in the absence of fraud. The plaintiff's declaration produced a resulting trust only indirectly because it provided evidence that she did not intend to make a gift. The resulting trust was a response to that intention and not a direct response to her declaration of trust.

Swadling wrote that 'an unexpressed intention to create a trust when proved by evidence does not generate a trust'.[44] It is true that an unexpressed intention will not be effective to create an express trust. There must be some manifestation of that intention in the required form, even if it is as simple as saying, 'This money is as much yours as mine.'[45] However, when it comes to trusts arising by operation of law, the intentions of the

---
[43] Ibid, 933.
[44] Swadling (n 4) 80.
[45] *Paul v Constance* [1977] 1 WLR 527 (CA).

parties can be relevant even when not declared or not involving a declaration of trust.

If the presumption of resulting trust really was a presumption of a declaration of trust, we would be left with three surprising consequences. The first would be the court's willingness to completely disregard Parliament's statutory requirement of form right from the beginning, without even debating the point. The issue did not arise because courts believed they were dealing with trusts arising by implication or construction of law and not with presumed trusts.[46] Secondly, it would mean that all resulting trusts of personal property are really express trusts. Since writing is not required, if a declaration of trust is presumed as a fact, it would be effective to create the intended trust directly.

Thirdly, it would mean that a large number of cases have been decided incorrectly. If the court presumed a declaration of trust, and it was that fact which gave rise to the resulting trust, then it ought to be rebutted by evidence that a trust had not been declared. Conversely, if the presumption of advancement was merely a situation in which there was no reason to presume a declaration of trust, then it should only be rebutted by evidence that a trust had been declared. This is demonstrably not true. The courts ask whether a gift was intended. While this is often rebutted by showing that a trust was probably intended, the courts do not require proof that a trust has been declared, and any evidence which negates an intention to give is sufficient to give rise to a resulting trust. This is discussed below.

2. Absence of Consideration

The modern resulting trust is the descendant of Lord Nottingham LC's implied trust. His presumptive trust became extinct when the Statute of Frauds 1677 required that all declarations of trust must be proved in writing. Then a trust could arise by implication or construction of law for several different reasons, but this trust arose in response to an absence of consideration. The modern cases do not speak in the same terms, and so the question becomes whether the presumption of resulting trust has evolved into a presumption of intention (or perhaps even a presumption of declaration).

Absence of consideration remained the key for at least the next two centuries. At the end of the eighteenth century, Lord Eyre CB said in *Dyer v Dyer*:

---

[46] *Lloyd v Spillet* (1740) 2 Atk 148, 150; 26 ER 493, 494 (Lord Hardwicke LC): 'I am now bound down by the statute of frauds and perjuries, to construe nothing a resulting trust, but what are there called trusts by operation of law.'

The clear result of all the cases, without a single exception, is, that the trust of a legal estate, whether freehold, copyhold, or leasehold; whether taken in the names of the purchasers and others jointly, or in the name of others without that of the purchaser; whether in one name or several; whether jointly or successive, results to the man who advances the purchase-money. This is a general proposition supported by all the cases, and there is nothing to contradict it; and it goes on a strict analogy to the rule of the common law, that where a feoffment is made without consideration, the use results to the feoffor. It is the established doctrine of a Court of equity, that this resulting trust may be rebutted by circumstances in evidence.[47]

In the late nineteenth century, Stuart VC said in *Sayre v Hughes*:

If stock be found standing in the names of two persons, the presumption of law is that it is their property. But if there be evidence that one of them purchased the stock, and that the name of the other was used without any consideration proceeding from that person, *the want of consideration induces the Court to presume a resulting trust*. The more simple case, and that generally referred to in the reported decisions, is the case of a purchase by one person in the name of another. As soon as you have the fact of the purchase in evidence, and shew that the purchase-money was paid by a person other than the person to whom the conveyance was made, *the fact of want of consideration almost necessarily creates the presumption of a resulting trust*.[48]

If there has been any major change to the presumptions, it must have taken place in the twentieth century. Of course, the choice of presumption has changed recently in Australia and Canada, as discussed above, but this does not mean that the presumptions themselves have changed. Can we point to anything in the twentieth century that might indicate a shift from a presumption based on an absence of consideration to one based on an intention to create a trust?

The most significant twentieth-century development has been the rise of the common intention constructive trust of the family home, in close association with the resulting trust, and partly in reaction to its limitations. Courts wanted to go beyond the resulting trust based on a direct contribution to the purchase price and give effect to detrimentally relied upon intentions to share the home. The search for a common intention to share beneficial ownership of the home in this context (that is, an intention to create a trust) may well have obscured the basis on which the presumption of resulting trust operates. It begins perhaps with Lord Diplock's famous statement in *Gissing v Gissing*:

A resulting, implied or constructive trust—and it is unnecessary for present purposes to distinguish between these three classes of trust—is created by a transaction between the trustee and the cestui qui trust in connection with the

---

[47] (1788) 2 Cox 92, 93; 30 ER 42, 43.
[48] (1868) LR 5 Eq 376, 380 (emphasis added).

acquisition by the trustee of a legal estate in land, whenever the trustee has so conducted himself that it would be inequitable to allow him to deny to the cestui qui trust a beneficial interest in the land acquired. And he will be held so to have conducted himself if by his words or conduct he has induced the cestui qui trust to act to his own detriment in the reasonable belief that by so acting he was acquiring a beneficial interest in the land.[49]

This may have led Lord Browne-Wilkinson to say in *Westdeutsche Landesbank Girozentrale v Islington LBC* that resulting trusts 'are traditionally regarded as examples of trusts giving effect to the common intention of the parties'.[50] The waters were muddied further in *Stack v Dowden*, where only Lord Neuberger (in dissent)[51] thought there was any reason to distinguish resulting trusts from constructive trusts when resolving disputes over ownership of the family home. Baroness Hale said:

> The presumption of resulting trust is not a rule of law. According to Lord Diplock in *Pettitt v Pettitt* [1970] AC 777, 823h, the equitable presumptions of intention are 'no more than a consensus of judicial opinion disclosed by reported cases as to the most likely inference of fact to be drawn in the absence of any evidence to the contrary'. Equity, being concerned with commercial realities, presumed against gifts and other windfalls (such as survivorship). But even equity was prepared to presume a gift where the recipient was the provider's wife or child. These days, the importance to be attached to who paid for what in a domestic context may be very different from its importance in other contexts or long ago. . . .
>
> There is no need for me to rehearse all the developments in the case law since *Pettitt v Pettitt* [1970] AC 777 and *Gissing v Gissing* [1971] AC 886. . . . The law has indeed moved on in response to changing social and economic conditions. The search is to ascertain the parties' shared intentions, actual, inferred or imputed, with respect to the property in the light of their whole course of conduct in relation to it.[52]

It was Lord Diplock's speech in *Gissing* that led the Supreme Court of Canada to invent the common intention resulting trust in *Rathwell v Rathwell*,[53] and then perhaps ironically, to reject the search for 'phantom intent' in favour of a constructive trust based on unjust enrichment in *Pettkus v Becker*.[54] So, while the common intention resulting trust is no longer used in Canada, the confusion over *Gissing* may have had a lasting effect on the Canadian law of resulting trusts. However, there are signs that this is not the case. In *Hollett v Hollett*, Green J said:

> Argument in the instant case was directed to establishing evidence of a 'common intention' of the parties as forming the basis of a resulting trust. Reference was made in this context to the comments in such cases as *Rathwell v Rathwell*.

---

[49] [1971] AC 886, 905.
[50] [1996] AC 669, 708.
[51] *Stack* (n 29) [110].
[52] Ibid, [60].

Proof of a common intention is not, however, the basis of resulting trust in purchase money resulting trust situations. The basis of the resulting trust in such cases is that, because persons who pay for property generally expect to get value in return, equity presumes that the person furnishing the purchase money does not intend to make a gift of the property to the grantee and therefore the grantee is presumed to hold the property (or a proportionate part thereof) on resulting trust for the payor. Proof of a common intention cannot be the basis of such a resulting trust because that would be tantamount to allowing proof of an express trust which, by section VII of the Statute of Frauds, is required to be evidenced in writing, where the subject matter is land. Resulting trusts are exempt from the writing requirements of the Statute of Frauds under Section VIII because of the very point that expression of a trust intention is not their basis. Equity supplies that which is not expressed, namely a presumed intention, and concludes that in view of the relationship of the parties, their acts express an intent to have a trust even though they did not use language to that effect.[55]

Since the presumptions of resulting trust and advancement no longer have the significance they once had, and almost every case can be decided based on available evidence (illegality aside), there are no modern cases which set out definitively the modern basis for the presumptions. Their true nature can only be revealed by examining the evidence which is able to rebut each presumption.

Evidence of no intention to give will rebut the presumption of advancement, but evidence of no intention to declare a trust will not rebut the presumption of resulting trust. While the courts no longer speak in terms of want of consideration, that remains the real basis on which the presumptions operate. An intention to give provides the consideration or reason for the transaction which displaces the resulting trust. That intention can be established by evidence or presumption. When that intention is absent, and there is no other reason for the transaction, the resulting trust arises in response to that absence of consideration.

There are numerous cases in which a resulting trust arose in favour of people who clearly had no intention to declare a trust, either because they were unaware of the transaction,[56] lacked the mental capacity to declare a trust[57] or simply failed to consider the issue.[58] While all are consistent with a presumption of resulting trust based on absence of consideration, none are consistent with a presumed declaration of trust.

---

[53] [1978] 2 SCR 436.
[54] [1980] 2 SCR 834, 843 (Dickson J).
[55] (1993) 31 RPR (2d) 251, 264–65.
[56] *Ryall v Ryall* (1739) 1 Atk 59, 26 ER 39; Amb 413, 27 ER 276; *Lane v Dighton* (1762) Amb 409, 27 ER 274; *Williams v Williams* (1863) 32 Beav 370, 55 ER 145; *Merchants Express Co v Morton* (1868) 15 Gr 274 (Ont Ch); *Sharp v McNeil* (1913) 15 DLR 73 (NSSCAD) 75; affd (1915) 70 DLR 740 (SCC); *Re Kolari* (1981) 36 OR (2d) 473.
[57] *Goodfellow v Robertson* (1871) 18 Gr 572 (Ont Ch).
[58] *Lattimer v Lattimer* (1978) 82 DLR (3d) 587 (Ont); *Brown v Brown* (1993) 31 NSWLR 582 (NSWCA); *Laskar* (n 26) [8], [21] and [29].

Conversely, a presumption of advancement will be rebutted by evidence that no gift was intended. It is not necessary to establish an intention to declare a trust. In *Brown v Brown*,[59] a mother contributed to the purchase of a house in the names of her two sons. The New South Wales Court of Appeal decided that the presumption of advancement applied, but was rebutted because the mother 'did not have any intention concerning the potential ownership of the' house and therefore 'did not intend to make a gift (or a loan) to her sons'.[60] Proof of no intention rebuts the presumption of advancement because it is a presumption of a positive intention to give and not merely a situation in which the presumption of resulting trust does not apply. Once rebutted, there is no consideration for the transaction at the mother's expense and a resulting trust arises by operation of law in response.

This is precisely how the presumptions operated in previous centuries. In *Sayre v Hughes* (quoted above), after saying that 'the fact of want of consideration almost necessarily creates the presumption of a resulting trust', Knight VC went on to say:

> In the case, however, of a father purchasing property in the name of a son, and having the conveyance made to the son—the father paying the purchase-money—the circumstance of relationship raises a presumption of benefit intended for the son which rebuts the notion of a resulting trust.[61]

The presumption of resulting trust responds to the apparent absence of consideration, and when the presumption of advancement applies, it operates to provide an apparent consideration, being the intention to make a gift.

3. A True Presumption

Swadling was correct to point out that the presumption of resulting trust as explained above is not a true presumption.[62] He described a true presumption as follows:

> [P]roof by evidence of one fact, the 'basic' or 'primary' fact, gives that party to the litigation the benefit of another fact, the 'secondary' fact, without any need to adduce evidence in proof. In such cases, the fact is proved by presumption. The burden then lies on the other party to adduce evidence to rebut the presumption.[63]

The presumption of resulting trust arises when one person acquires an

---

[59] (1993) 31 NSWLR 582 (NSWCA).
[60] Ibid, 587 and 591 (Gleeson CJ).
[61] *Sayre* (n 48) 380.
[62] Swadling (n 4) 89.
[63] Ibid, 74.

asset at the expense of another and there is no apparent reason for the transaction. However, those are exactly the same facts that give rise to the resulting trust itself when proved by evidence. In other words, there is no 'secondary' fact being presumed.

In contrast, the presumption of advancement is a true presumption. Proof of the relationship between the parties gives rise to a presumption that the apparent gift was intended as such. The intention to give is the secondary fact which displaces the resulting trust because it provides an apparent reason (or consideration) for the transaction.

It is noteworthy that rebuttal of the presumption of advancement will not lead to a resulting trust if the evidence disproving the intention to give establishes another reason for the transaction, such as a loan. On the other hand, proof of a loan will also rebut the presumption of resulting trust by providing a consideration for the transaction. The presumptions are not mirror images of each other, nor is it true that one is merely the absence of the other. The presumption of resulting trust arises in response to an apparent absence of consideration, while the presumption of advancement is a presumption of one possible consideration: an intention to make a gift.

In *Bennet v Bennet*,[64] a mother borrowed £3,000 and paid that amount to her son. After his death, she was allowed to claim for that amount against his estate because the evidence established that it was intended as a loan. Jessel MR held that the presumption of resulting trust applied to apparent gifts from mothers to their children, but could easily be rebutted because mothers are inclined to make such gifts. Evidence of the intention to make a loan meant there was neither trust nor gift. If the presumption of advancement had applied, the outcome would have been the same.

D. CONCLUSION

As Swadling correctly pointed out, the presumption of resulting trust, as explained in *Resulting Trusts*,[65] is not a true presumption. However, that does not invalidate the explanation. It merely removes an unnecessary element, which is that the presumption of resulting trust is a presumption of a secondary fact that 'the provider did not intend to benefit the recipient'.[66] The resulting trust responds to the absence of a reason for the transaction. The absence of evidence of a reason is not the same as evidence of the absence of a reason. The former is sufficient to produce a resulting trust. There is no need to infer the latter.

The presumption of resulting trust is simply a situation in which there is no apparent reason (or consideration or basis) for the transfer of assets to

[64] (1879) 10 Ch D 474.
[65] Chambers (n 5) 19.
[66] Ibid, 38.

the recipient at the expense of another. Evidence of a reason, such as an intention to give, rebuts the presumption because it fills a gap in the evidence and not because it displaces a presumed fact. The presumption of advancement, on the other hand, is a true presumption because it is an inference of the existence of a secondary fact, that the provider had an intention to give.

In very many cases, the evidence establishes that the real reason for the transaction was the apparent donor's intention to create a trust for herself or himself. No doubt this rebuts the presumption of advancement. It must also displace the presumption of resulting trust even though it leads to the same end. How does the law respond to that intention? The intended trust matches the trust that would have been imposed by law in the absence of any explanation for the transaction. This is probably the reason why the presumption of resulting trust is often mistaken for a presumption of an intention to create a trust. However, the resulting trust is only one of at least four possible responses to this situation.

First, if the intention amounts to a proper declaration of trust, there is no reason not to give direct effect to it as an express trust. Often this is not possible because the intention was never properly expressed, either at all or in the form required for a trust of an interest in land. If lack of writing is the obstacle, then a second but rarely available option might be to ignore the writing requirement because of the trustee's own fraud.[67] Thirdly, detrimental reliance on common intentions or reasonable expectations might provide a sufficient reason to perfect that intention by imposing a constructive trust. If none of these options is available, then a resulting trust should arise.

There is an important difference between a resulting trust and these other responses. Unlike the express trust and perfectionary constructive trust, a resulting trust does not operate by giving effect to the intention to create a trust. As explained in *Hodgson v Marks*,[68] discussed above, proof of that intention negates the possibility of a gift or any other consideration that would justify the defendant's retention of the benefit. It is almost always preferable to give effect to the parties' intentions, but when that is impossible, the resulting trust fulfils the very important function of ensuring that unintended benefits are returned.

Unlike the resulting trust, the presumptions of resulting trust and advancement are not that important, and could (and perhaps should) be dispensed with completely. However, a proper understanding of them is important for a proper understanding of the resulting trust, and this is essential if we are to make sense of the divisions between express, constructive and resulting trusts. The classification of trusts does matter

---

[67] *Rochefoucauld v Boustead* [1897] 1 Ch 196 (CA), discussed in ch 3.
[68] *Hodgson* (n 42).

(despite the trend to the contrary begun in *Gissing v Gissing*[69] and continued in *Stack v Dowden*).[70] Each kind of trust is pursuing a different goal, and we should be asking whether it is possible to achieve the most desirable goal. Can we give direct effect to the intentions of the parties (through an express trust)? If not, can we fulfil any detrimentally relied upon intentions and expectations (through a constructive trust)? If not, can we return any unintended benefits (through a resulting trust)? There is a very important distinction between perfection and restitution.[71]

While researching and writing *Resulting Trusts*, I came to believe that all resulting trusts arise in response to unjust enrichment. I still believe this to be true. Then I struggled with a very difficult issue, which was how to relate the resulting trust to the recognised list of factors that make enrichments unjust. It was not an easy fit. Perhaps I was struggling in vain. In hindsight, it might have been better to explain the law of unjust enrichment in terms of absence of basis rather than trying to explain the resulting trust in terms of unjust factors.

---

[69] *Gissing* (n 49) 905.
[70] *Stack* (n 29).
[71] These terms are used by G Elias in *Explaining Constructive Trusts* (Oxford, Clarendon Press, 1990). Also see Chambers (n 5) 220–33; R Chambers, 'Constructive Trusts in Canada' (1999) 37 *Alberta Law Review* 173; reprinted (2001) 15 *Trust Law International* 214 and (2002) 16 *Trust Law International* 2.

10

The Presumption of Advancement

JAMIE GLISTER*

A. INTRODUCTION

The presumption of advancement operates to allocate the burden of proof in disputes over the voluntary transfer of property. In the usual case of a transfer of full legal title for no consideration equity will presume that the recipient holds on trust for the donor.[1] However, if the parties to the transaction stand in a particular relationship, then that presumption changes and instead equity assumes that an outright transfer was indeed intended.[2]

Unfortunately, this description of the effect of the presumption of advancement obscures several difficult issues. Most importantly, it is not always clear exactly which relationships are 'advancement' relationships. This problem is compounded by uncertainty about why we have the presumption and by confusion regarding the usefulness of evidence as to the parties' actual relationship. On a more theoretical level there is doubt about what intention is necessary to rebut the presumption, and this in turn is linked to the wider question of why resulting trusts arise.[3]

---

*I am very grateful to Stephen Gilmore for his helpful discussions about the material in part C. Of course, I remain responsible for any errors.

[1] On the question whether a lack of consideration must be shown before the presumption of resulting trust may be invoked, or whether the presence of consideration simply rebuts an existing presumption of resulting trust, see ch 8.

[2] In fact equity goes a step further and presumes that the recipient was to receive a gift. Evidence that a loan was intended will consequently rebut the presumption of advancement even though full legal title will still pass to the recipient and there will be no trust. See *Re Whitehouse* (1888) 37 Ch D 683, a case that essentially involved a loan from father to son with no consideration, cited in R Chambers, *Resulting Trusts* (Oxford, Clarendon Press, 1997) 31. The two presumptions of advancement and resulting trust are therefore not quite mirror images of each other.

[3] Full discussion of the theoretical points is beyond the scope of this paper, but in a nutshell the point is this: in order to establish that he retains an interest, does the donor in an advancement relationship only need to show a lack of intention to benefit the recipient or does he need to show a definite intention to retain the benefit himself? Chambers argues that the

Despite these interesting questions, the current enquiry should be put into a realistic context. The presumptions of resulting trust and advancement are rarely determinative because in most cases there is enough actual evidence to support a real finding of intention.[4] Still, this is not always the case: evidence may be unavailable because of illegality,[5] witnesses might be unreliable and obviously self-serving, or the parties to the relevant transaction may all be dead.[6] Here the questions of which presumption to apply, and how to apply it, will be very important. The presumptions are also one of the few areas where gender differences remain, and for this reason alone they are worthy of discussion.

In this paper I focus on the parental presumption of advancement and contend that the true reason for having this presumption has not been properly understood for a long time. I think that the reasoning behind recent extensions of the presumption relationships is mistaken and I argue that any change should be consistent with the original purpose of the presumption. I do not come to a definite conclusion about which (if any) relationships should be advancement relationships, but I try to identify the right question to ask: who is under an obligation to establish their child as an independent economic actor, able to contribute to society? This question is not answered by pointing to identical parental obligations to maintain an infant child.

B. THE GENERAL NATURE OF PRESUMPTION OF ADVANCEMENT RELATIONSHIPS

It is important to keep separate the questions of which presumption to apply and whether that presumption has been rebutted. The presumption of advancement applies to transfers between parties who stand in a particular relationship. The list of advancement relationships is short, and even within these relationships the presumption only applies in one direction: in England and Wales a presumption is currently applied to transfers from fathers to children, from those *in loco parentis patris* to their children, from husbands to wives, and from fiancés to fiancées. Clearly not all such transfers will actually be intended as gifts, and so the presumption is rebuttable. The analysis should go like this: first, are the parties in a

---

former position is correct (see ch 9), but in *Damberg v Damberg* [2001] NSWCA 87, (2001) 52 NSWLR 492 [44], Heydon JA said that a 'definite intention to retain beneficial title' is required.

[4] See *Vandervell v IRC* [1967] 2 AC 291, 313 (Lord Upjohn): 'in reality the so-called presumption of a resulting trust is no more than a long stop to provide the answer when the relevant facts and circumstances fail to yield a solution'.

[5] *Tinsley v Milligan* [1994] 1 AC 340; cf *Nelson v Nelson* (1995) 132 ALR 133 (HCA).

[6] *Hepworth v Hepworth* (1870) LR 11 Eq 10; *Re a policy no 6402 of the Scottish Equitable Life Assurance Society* [1902] 1 Ch 282.

relationship where the law presumes that a voluntary transfer of property is an advancement? Second, if the parties are in such a relationship, do the evidential circumstances of the actual case reinforce or rebut the initial conclusion of the presumption? The second question may be difficult, but the first—with the occasional exception of *in loco parentis* cases—should be easy.

In *Cheung v Worldcup Investments Inc*,[7] the Hong Kong Court of Final Appeal found that a presumption of advancement applied to transfers from a man to his long-term partner. The matter was complicated by a Chinese customary law concept of 'concubine', to which a presumption of advancement may apply in Hong Kong, but the position should still be clear: either the woman in question was in a relationship that gave rise to a presumption of advancement or she was not. If she was not, then evidence as to the duration and nature of the parties' relationship might still demonstrate that a gift was probably intended and the presumption of resulting trust might then be rebutted. However, it is respectfully argued that the following comment of Litton NPJ was mistaken:

> In the present case, [the judge below] says that because Madam Chin had not proved that she was either 'wife' or 'concubine' according to Chinese customary law, she had failed to establish that she was 'within the category of persons in whose favour a presumption of advancement would arise'. In my respectful view this misstates the position. The legal pigeon-hole into which a party is put is not determinative of the issue.[8]

In my view the judge below was correct: the issue is what general relationship the parties stand in. This answers the first question and is indeed determinative of the presumption that then applies. The specifics of that relationship go to the rebuttal of the presumption and are relevant to answering the second question.

Certain evidence may commonly displace a presumption, but we should be wary of formalising this by changing the presumption that applies in the first place. In *Pecore v Pecore*,[9] a majority of the Supreme Court of Canada thought that the presumption of advancement should no longer apply to transfers from parents to their adult children. Considering transfers to adult children who are still dependent on their parents, Rothstein J said:

> As compelling as some cases might be, I am reluctant to apply the presumption of advancement to gratuitous transfers to 'dependent' adult children because it would be impossible to list the wide variety of the circumstances that make

[7] [2008] HKCFA 78.
[8] Ibid, [8]. Lord Scott of Foscote NPJ also thought that the specifics of the relationship had a bearing on the presumption that applied: ibid, [44]. Also note *Edwards v Bradley* [1957] SCR 599, where Kerwin CJ and Taschereau J thought that no presumption of advancement would apply because, inter alia, the child lived a long distance away from the parent.
[9] [2007] SCC 17, [2007] 1 SCR 795.

someone 'dependent' for the purpose of applying the presumption. Courts would have to determine on a case-by-case basis whether or not a particular individual is 'dependent', creating uncertainty and unpredictability in almost every instance.[10]

In the *Pecore* case itself a transfer was made by a father to his dependent adult daughter. The presumption of resulting trust was applied but was rebutted by, amongst other things, evidence of the daughter's dependency. It is argued that this is exactly right: the general father–child presumption relationship can be altered to father–minor child if desired.[11] But a category of father–dependent child would be too subjective; it would conflate the first and second questions.[12]

C. LEGAL OBLIGATIONS TO MAINTAIN AND SUPPORT

A popular justification for presuming advancement is that the donor is under a recognised duty to provide for the recipient. A court of equity will presume, so the argument goes, that any transfer of property is intended to be in furtherance of that obligation. However, the occasions when a duty of maintenance is actually owed do not coincide with the occasions when equity applies a presumption of advancement. If some kind of donor obligation can be used to justify the presumption of advancement, then this obligation needs further investigation and explanation. First we need to sketch an outline of the legal obligations to maintain and support.[13]

Much of the relevant material is from the public law sphere.[14] When statutes provided that a parent had a duty to maintain a child (for example), the effect was to permit the poor law authorities to charge the

---

[10] Ibid, [40].

[11] In *Pecore* the reason given for restricting the presumption of advancement to minor children was the common practice of parents putting their assets into the joint names of themselves and their children so that the children could help the parents in the management of the assets: *Pecore* (n 9) [36]. Compare the exactly opposite reasoning in the English case of *McDonnell v Loosemore* [2007] EWCA Civ 1531, quoted below at n 103.

[12] It follows that, in my view, the correct presumption to apply in the *in loco parentis* cases should be the presumption of resulting trust, but with the fact of the donor being *in loco parentis* available as strong evidence to rebut that presumption. This is not the law, but the exception of the *in loco* cases does not mean that the general point—about separating the objective, legally categorised relationship from the subjective circumstances—is invalid.

[13] The following discussion of private and public law duties to maintain is very superficial. For an excellent summary, see N Wikeley, *Child Support: Law and Policy* (Oxford, Hart Publishing, 2006) chs 2 and 3.

[14] It might now be the case in England and Wales that child support is entirely public-law based, following the decision of the House of Lords in *R (Kehoe) v Secretary of State for Work and Pensions* [2005] UKHL 48, [2006] 1 AC 42. In that case a majority of the House of Lords found that the Child Support Act 1991 had removed a wife's right to sue her husband directly for child support. The case has been strongly criticised in notes by N Wikeley [2006] *Child and Family Law Quarterly* 287 and S Gilmore (2006) 28 *Journal of Social Welfare & Family Law* 180.

parent for costs incurred by the parish in supporting the child. The statutory obligations could not be relied upon or invoked by the poor relatives themselves. Under the Poor Relief Act 1601 people were required to maintain their poor parents, children and grandchildren, and following the Married Women's Property Acts of 1870 and 1882 the authorities could also recover maintenance costs from a married woman having separate property. The Married Women's Property Act 1870 provided in section 14 that a 'married woman having separate property shall be subject to all such liability for the maintenance of her children as a widow is now by law subject to for the maintenance of her children'.[15] In 1882 this obligation was extended to 'all such liability for the maintenance of her children and grandchildren as the husband is now by law subject to for the maintenance of her children and grandchildren'.[16]

Section 1 of the National Assistance Act 1948 repealed the existing poor law and provided that parents were no longer liable to maintain children over the age of 16.[17] Under section 42 a man was liable to maintain his wife and his children, and a woman was liable to maintain her husband and her children. This remains the position today under the Social Security Administration Act 1992.[18] In short, as far as public law is concerned, spouses have long owed duties of support to each other and to their children. However, there has been no general liability to maintain adult children since 1948.

The advancement context involves direct transfers of property between people, and so we would be more concerned with a private law obligation to maintain a spouse or child. Perhaps this could be the obligation that equity presumed was being fulfilled. However, such duties are difficult to pinpoint: any private law duties appear to have been virtually impossible to enforce and this raises the question of whether the obligation truly existed at all. In the context of wives, the common law obligation to maintain was unenforceable until the mid-nineteenth century because the ecclesiastical courts had jurisdiction but canon law did not provide an effective remedy.[19] In relation to children, Ward J said in *Re C (A Minor) (Contribution Notice)*:

---

[15] Under s 13 a married woman with separate property would also be liable to the parish for the maintenance of her husband. This provision was re-enacted as the Married Women's Property Act 1882, s 20.

[16] Married Women's Property Act 1882, s 21. A married woman's duties to maintain her husband and her children and grandchildren were later combined into the same section: Poor Law Act 1927, s 41 and Poor Law Act 1930, s 14.

[17] National Assistance Act 1948, s 64(1).

[18] Under the Social Security Administration Act 1992, s 78(6)(d) liability to maintain a child ends at 16 (or at 19 if one of the parents is receiving income support in respect of the child).

[19] See the discussion and sources cited in Wikeley (n 13) 72–73. The position was changed by the Matrimonial Causes Act 1857 and subsequent legislation: *Kehoe* (n 14) [58] (Baroness Hale).

The strange state of our law is that there may be a so-called common law duty to maintain, but when one analyses what that duty is it seems effectively to come to nothing. Like so many rights, the right extends only so far as the remedy to enforce it extends. There is no longer any agency of necessity and the common law has no remedy. The remedies to enforce a duty to maintain are the statutory remedies which are variously laid down in numerous statutes.[20]

It is true that a lack of effective enforcement in a primary sense would not automatically mean that the obligation could not be recognised by equity and presumed in a secondary sense, but in fact there is authority for saying that there was never any common law duty at all. In *National Assistance Board v Wilkinson*, Lord Goddard CJ said:

> [A]s is well known a father was under no civil liability apart from the Poor Law to maintain his children. True if he failed to do so he would become amenable to the criminal law, but a child never had the right to pledge the father's credit as the wife could her husband's, and there is no doubt, anomalous as it may seem, a father is not by the civil law liable for a child's maintenance.[21]

Similarly in *Thomasset v Thomasset*, Lindley LJ commented that 'as regards maintenance, the parents' obligations were measured both at law and in equity by the Poor Laws. I know of no case in which a father has been ordered by a Court of Equity to maintain his child.'[22] Hall concluded that there was no obligation of maintenance outside statute, and Wikeley recently called this the 'traditional understanding of family lawyers'.[23]

On the other hand, Baroness Hale found in *Kehoe* that there was indeed a common law obligation to maintain one's children. She recognised that this obligation was unenforceable, but found that the duty was 'reinforced and expanded'[24] by two kinds of statutory obligation: first, the public law duties outlined above; and second, the statutory requirement to pay sums ordered by the courts under various private law systems.[25] In Baroness Hale's view, and in apparent contrast to the majority of the House of

---

[20] [1994] 1 FLR 111, 116–17. See also *Huxley v Child Support Officer* [1999] EWCA Civ 3015, [2000] 1 FLR 898 [51]–[54] (Hale LJ).

[21] [1952] 2 QB 648 (Div Ct) 657. His Lordship said the same in *Stopher v National Assistance Board* [1955] 1 QB 486 (Div Ct) 495.

[22] [1894] P 295 (CA) 299.

[23] Wikeley (n 13) 71, referring to JC Hall, *Sources of Family Law* (Cambridge, Cambridge University Press, 1966) 271. Wikeley further argues at 70 that in the 'Victorian period societal norms were such that the notion that husbands should be subject to an enforceable private law duty to support their legitimate children would simply have been fanciful.'

[24] *Kehoe* (n 14) [65].

[25] Ibid, [58]: 'These were the origins of the four private law systems under which one parent might be ordered to make payments to or for the benefit of a child being looked after by another: (i) as an ancillary to matrimonial causes, which until 1967 were always in the High Court; (ii) in matrimonial proceedings in magistrates' courts; (iii) in Guardianship of Minors Act proceedings in the High Court, county courts or magistrates' courts; and (iv) in affiliation proceedings in magistrates' courts, which were until 1987 the only means of obtaining support from the father of an illegitimate child.'

Lords,[26] this underlying common law obligation was not removed by the Child Support Act 1991.

Baroness Hale referred to the *father's* obligation throughout the historical part of her speech, but her Ladyship concluded by referring to 'children's civil rights to be properly maintained by their parents'.[27] A lack of gender distinction would be appropriate: Baroness Hale was firm in her view that the case was actually about children's rights, and it would be very odd if under the present common law a child's right to support from a non-resident parent depended on which parent was absent. As we have seen, Baroness Hale also recognised that the content of the private law obligation was influenced by the surrounding public law duties, and so the gender-neutrality of the public law duties must also be relevant. In short, it is argued that if Baroness Hale's arguments in support of a subsisting common law duty are valid, then those arguments require that a maternal obligation also exists (and has done for some considerable time).

It is very difficult to state definite conclusions about the obligations to maintain and support. However, some points can be made that will enable a comparison between the actual maintenance duties and the times when equity presumes advancement. First, it seems clear that the duties were mainly owed and enforced at a public law level, and in this area women have owed duties to their husbands and children since at least the time of the Married Women's Property Acts. Second, although private law responsibilities would be more relevant to the advancement context, there must be real doubt about whether any such obligations actually existed. Third, even if private law obligations did exist, the duty to maintain only ever applied to minor children[28] and it must surely have extended to mothers at some point long before now.

D. THE ADVANCEMENT RATIONALE: EARLY CASES

1. Obligation and Affection

In the older cases two distinct justifications are given for the application of a presumption of advancement: the obligation and affection rationales. The

---

[26] This must be stated tentatively. Only Lord Brown explicitly found that neither Mrs Kehoe nor her children retained any rights outside of the CSA scheme: *Kehoe* (n 14) [79]. However, this conclusion does seem to be implicit in the opinions of Lord Bingham, Lord Hope and Lord Walker.

[27] *Kehoe* (n 14) [76]. Also at [71]: 'it is clear to me that children have a civil right to be maintained by their parents which is such as to engage article 6 of the European Convention on Human Rights. Their rights are not limited to the rights given to the parent with care under the Child Support Act. The provisions of that Act are simply a means of quantifying and enforcing part of their rights.'

[28] N Lowe and G Douglas, *Bromley's Family Law*, 10th edn (Oxford, Oxford University Press, 2007) 916.

first approach sees the father or husband as being under a duty to provide for his child or wife, with the presumption of advancement arising because equity assumes that a relevant transfer of property is made in furtherance of that obligation. The second approach sees the relationship itself as important: the natural love and affection that flows from husbands to their wives and from parents to their children justifies an exception to equity's normal approach. I will argue that the obligation model has more judicial support, but it must immediately be admitted that in fact the majority of cases simply do not examine the rationale of the presumption of advancement at all. As Freedman points out, it was never the basis of the enquiry: the point was to decide what was actually intended in the case at hand.[29] This is why many of the cases appear to turn principally on their actual facts, in the sense that they would have been decided in the same way if either presumption had applied.

In *Grey v Grey*, a case where a father purchased land in the name of his son but the rents were paid over to the father, Lord Nottingham said:

> The great question is, whether the law will admit of any constructive trust at all between father and son? For the natural consideration of blood and affection is so apparently predominant, that those acts which would imply a trust in a stranger will not do so in a son. [At law] a feoffment to the son without other consideration raised no use by implication to the father, for the consideration of blood settled the use in the son, and made it an advancement. How can this Court justify itself to the world, if it should be so arbitrary as to make the law of trusts differ from the law of uses in the same case?[30]

There is a plain reference to affection here, and there were clearly close parallels between the resulting use at law and the resulting/constructive trust in equity.[31] But the Lord Chancellor went on to say:

> [The reason why the law does not presume a trust here is] from moral philosophy, *quia amor descendit non ascendit*, and from divinity, because fathers are bound to provide for their children, but children do not provide for the fathers; therefore, when a father, according to his duty, hath provided for his son, it were hard to take away that provision by a constructive trust.[32]

---

[29] CD Freedman, 'Reassessing Gratuitous Transfers by Parents to Adult Children' (2005) 25 *Estates, Trusts & Pensions Journal* 174, 191. Of course it should also be noted that the available case reports are not always reliable.

[30] (1677) 2 Swans 594, 598; 36 ER 742, 743.

[31] A similar comparison to the common law use was made by Eyre CB in *Dyer v Dyer* (1788) 2 Cox 92, 94; 30 ER 42, 43: 'natural love and affection raised a use at common law; surely then it will rebut a trust resulting to the father'. Cf *Baylis v Newton* (1687) 2 Vern 28, 23 ER 628, where the father's conveyance of land 'for natural love and affection' to the use successively of himself, his wife, and his child did not automatically dispose of the trust question.

[32] *Grey* (n 30) 2 Swans 594. Similarly in *Elliot v Elliot*, his Lordship noted the father's 'obligation of duty and conscience to provide for his child': (1677) 2 Chan Cas 231, 232; 22 ER 922, 923.

This is the language of obligation and duty rather than affection. Indeed, the argument that some kind of paternal obligation was the basis for the presumption can also be made in a more subtle way. Several cases discuss the issue of whether the recipient had already been advanced, yet this would have no bearing on a father's love and affection and could only be relevant to the satisfaction of an obligation.

In *Grey* Lord Nottingham said that if a father purchased property in the son's name, then this was generally and prima facie an advancement. Even if the rents were paid to the father, this would not necessarily rebut the presumption because it could be seen as merely reverence and good manners on the part of the son. The age of the son was not material of itself, but any existing provision was relevant:

> Lastly, the difference I rely upon is this; where the son is not at all or but in part advanced, and where he is fully advanced in his father's lifetime. . . . [I]f the son be married in his father's lifetime, and by his father's consent, and a settlement be thereupon made, whereby the son appears to be fully advanced, and in a manner emancipated, there a subsequent purchase by the father in the name of such a son, with perception of profits, etc, by the father, will be evidence of a trust; for all presumption of an advancement ceases.[33]

A few months later Lord Nottingham confirmed the position and based his decision in *Elliot v Elliot* on the distinction between an advanced and an unadvanced son.[34] His Lordship said that after a father has provided for his son 'he is under no further obligation to provide more than for a stranger, and else no father could trust his child'.[35] In a similar vein the Lord Chancellor thought in *Ebrand v Dancer* that where a grandfather put investments in his grandchild's name it was relevant whether or not the father was still alive and still able to advance his child himself.[36] The death of a natural father would obviously be relevant to the question of whether someone else was *in loco parentis* for certain purposes, but it should not affect the love and affection of a grandfather.

The distinction between advanced and unadvanced children was followed and applied by later judges,[37] and although it was eventually abandoned this was for pragmatic reasons that were unconnected to any affection rationale.[38] For present purposes the distinction is relevant because it

---

[33] Ibid, 2 Swans 600–01.
[34] (1677) 2 Chan Cas 231, 232; 22 ER 922, 923.
[35] Ibid, 2 Chan Cas 232.
[36] (1680) 2 Chan Cas 80, 22 ER 829.
[37] *Shales v Shales* (1701) 2 Freeman 252, 22 ER 1151; *Lamplugh v Lamplugh* (1709) 1 P Wms 111, 24 ER 316; *Pole v Pole* (1747–48) Ves Sen Supp 54, 28 ER 454. See also *Stileman v Ashdown* (1742) 2 Atk 477, 26 ER 688, where the judge stated the role of the presumption very narrowly, specifically that a transfer from a father to a younger son was presumed to be an advancement and the older brother could not argue that the younger was a trustee. Again, this is far removed from an affection rationale.
[38] See the discussion below around nn 48–49.

shows that the judges were thinking in terms of obligations rather than love and affection.

Of course, in many cases the rationale for the presumption was not considered at all, and even when it was there would rarely be a conflict between an obligation model and an affection model. However, cases involving transfers from mothers to their children are an important exception: a mother might not owe the same duties to her child, but surely her affection for the child would be the same as her husband's? In *Garrett v Wilkinson* the judge thought that the presumption of advancement 'probably' applied to mothers,[39] and in *Sayre v Hughes* the presumption of advancement was found to apply where a widowed mother transferred stock into the name of her daughter.[40] In the latter case Stuart V-C commented that 'maternal affection, as a motive of bounty, is, perhaps, the strongest of all' and said that 'it is not easy to understand why a mother should be presumed to be less disposed to benefit her child in a transaction of this kind than a father'.[41] Weaker authority can also be found in *Batstone v Salter*,[42] where the conclusion appeared to be a simple finding of the mother's actual intention to give, but where the judge also expressly distinguished between a son-in-law and a complete stranger. In sum, until *Bennet v Bennet* was decided in 1879, as discussed in the next section, it was possible to argue that the presumption of advancement applied to transfers from mothers to their children.[43] However, this argument would have been made on the basis of love and affection, which was not the reason given for the paternal presumption of advancement.

2. Source and Extent of the Obligation

Although the obligation model probably had more judicial support, the source and the extent of the relevant obligation were not clearly identified. In terms of the extent of the obligation, we have seen that Lord Nottingham in *Elliot* thought that it ended once full provision for the child had been made. *Shales* specifically mentions children unprovided for,[44] and the report of *Pole v Pole* even refers to children *unprovided for* in original italics.[45] In his *Vendors and Purchasers of Estates*, Sugden was strongly of

[39] (1848) 2 De G & Sm 244, 246; 64 ER 110, 111. In that case the son acted as the mother's solicitor, which 'neutralise[d] or prevent[ed] the application of the general rule'. This means that the presumption was seen as inapplicable, rather than rebutted, which strictly means that the comments of Knight Bruce V-C were obiter.
[40] (1868) LR 5 Eq 376.
[41] Ibid, 381.
[42] (1874) LR 19 Eq 250.
[43] See A Dowling, 'The Presumption of Advancement between Mother and Child' [1996] *Conveyancer and Property Lawyer* 274, 275.
[44] *Shales* (n 37).
[45] (1747–48) Ves Sen Supp 54, 55; 28 ER 454, 454. In that case the father had already given substantial amounts to the oldest son and still had several other sons unprovided for.

the view that the child in question must be unadvanced for the presumption to apply, simply because the obligation was to advance him.[46] On the other hand, in *Dyer v Dyer* Eyre CB found the distinction drawn in relation to emancipated sons to be 'not very solidly taken'.[47] Which view prevailed?

It would seem sensible for equity to stop presuming the fulfilment of an advancement obligation once that obligation had actually been fulfilled. However, although this sounds attractive in theory, in practice it would be difficult for a court to judge the adequacy of a father's provision for his son.[48] It would therefore be difficult to know when the obligation had been satisfied and so when to stop applying a presumption of advancement. Many advancements took place through marriage settlements, and so one option might have been to draw an arbitrary line whereby the presumption of advancement would cease to apply on marriage. But of course this would have brought its own problems, and in fact no arbitrary line was drawn.[49] Indeed, after *Dyer v Dyer* the distinction between advanced and unadvanced children rather disappeared in the context of deciding which presumption to apply, although of course it remained relevant in the context of rebutting the presumption.

In terms of the source of the obligation, it is clear even in the early cases that the obligation was not legal in the sense of being imposed or recognised by statute or common law. In *Elliot* Lord Nottingham called it an 'obligation of duty and conscience',[50] and in *Murless v Franklin* Lord Eldon referred to a 'species of natural obligation to provide'.[51] The nature of the obligation can also be shown by the determining feature of the *in loco parentis* cases being the *intention* to place oneself in the father's position.[52] Yet the duty was of something more than a merely moral character. As Page Wood V-C explained in *Soar v Foster*, there may be many occasions when a man owes a moral duty to provide for someone, but this duty would not of itself mean that a purchase in joint names should be presumed an advancement.[53] The relevant obligation was therefore rather hard to define. It was not obviously legal in the sense of being found in statute or in

---

[46] EB Sugden, *Practical Treatise on the Law of Vendors and Purchasers of Estates* (London, Butterworth, 1805) 326.

[47] (1788) 2 Cox 92, 94; 30 ER 42, 44. See also the discussion in *Re Grimes (deceased)* (1937) IR 470, 476.

[48] As Eyre CB noted in *Dyer* (n 47) 2 Cox 94.

[49] The two recent Canadian cases of *Pecore* (n 9) and *Madsen Estate v Saylor* [2007] SCC 18, [2007] 1 SCR 838 limit the presumption to infant children. See the discussion around nn 102–04.

[50] *Elliot* (n 34) 2 Chan Cas 232.

[51] (1818) 1 Swans 13, 17; 36 ER 278, 280.

[52] *Powys v Mansfield* (1837) 3 My & Cr 359, 40 ER 964, and *Pym v Lockyer* (1841) 5 My & Cr 29, 41 ER 283, although strictly double portion cases, show that a person may stand *in loco parentis* even if the child lives with and is maintained by his father. As Freedman (n 29) puts it at 190–91, the principle was 'liberally applied to a wider class of people that would not be the object of any enforceable legal obligation'.

[53] (1858) 4 K & J 152, 161; 70 ER 64, 68. The case involved a widower purporting to

300 *The Presumption of Advancement*

common law. It apparently was legal in the sense of being recognised by courts of equity, but at the same time there was no question of an unadvanced son bringing an action against his father solely on the ground that his father had failed to fulfil an obligation recognised by equity.[54]

3. A Moral–Legal Obligation

The 1879 case of *Bennet v Bennet* decided the question of which presumption to apply to mother–child transfers and also attempted to explain the source of the advancement obligation.[55] Mrs Bennet borrowed £3,000 and gave it to her adult son Philip. At first Philip paid the interest instalments on the loan but he later died insolvent. After her son's death Mrs Bennet took over paying the premiums herself and later claimed to be a creditor for £3,000 on Philip's estate. Although the surrounding evidence in favour of an intended loan was so strong that the mother would have been able to prove the debt regardless of the presumption that applied,[56] Sir George Jessel MR explained that there was no presumption of advancement from mothers to children because equity did not recognise a relevant obligation that the mother would be presumed to fulfil. The Master of the Rolls therefore applied a model based on obligation (or a lack of obligation) and disapproved of the affection justification. As to the source of the duty, Jessel MR said:

> But in our law there is no moral legal obligation—I do not know how to express it more shortly—no obligation according to the rules of equity—on a mother to provide for her child: there is no such obligation as a Court of Equity recognises as such.[57]

None of the cases prior to *Bennet* that had suggested that a presumption of advancement might apply to mothers had done so on the basis of obligation. Instead the justification for presuming advancement had been the equal maternal and paternal love and affection. So it might not have been surprising that in adopting an obligation model Jessel MR at the same

---

marry his dead wife's sister, but this was prohibited by statute and the marriage was void ab initio. The other examples given include cohabiting partners and a bigamist who deceives a woman into marrying him.

[54] *Thomasset* (n 22) 299 (Lindley LJ): 'I know of no case in which a father has been ordered by a Court of Equity to maintain his child.'

[55] (1879) 10 Ch D 474.

[56] It is important to note that the mother was not the beneficiary of a resulting trust. The presumption of resulting trust was rebutted, meaning that full legal title in the property passed to the son. The son owed a contractual liability to repay, and so his mother could prove this debt against his estate. Any presumption of advancement would also have been rebutted in the sense that the son was not intended to take the property as a gift, but this would not have affected the son's receipt of full legal title as a matter of property law.

[57] *Bennet* (n 55) 478.

time rejected the application of the presumption to mothers. But in fact the Master of the Rolls went further than that: he expressly stated that there was no relevant obligation recognised in the case of mothers. This is interesting because, as we have seen, mothers did owe public law duties to maintain and support their children.

It is true that the relevant transactions in *Bennet* took place before the Married Women's Property Act 1870 came into force, but the case was decided in 1879 and in any event the 1870 Act referred to *existing* obligations on widowed mothers.[58] If the obligation of maintenance was really in question then it should have been a short case: Mrs Bennet was widowed, and widows owe duties to maintain their children. Indeed, in the 1872 edition of Snell's textbook the author noted the provisions of the 1870 Act and predicted that a presumption of advancement should in future apply to transfers from mothers to their children.[59] In short, if duties to maintain and support children really were relevant to the presumption of advancement, then *Bennet* should have been reasoned differently.

Instead much of the analysis in the case focused on whether Mrs Bennet had placed herself *in loco parentis* to her son. Given that she was a widow and therefore already owed duties to maintain her son, this question must have been irrelevant unless the obligation in question was something different. Put simply, the reasoning in *Bennet* demonstrates that the equitable obligation to advance and the legal obligation to maintain were not considered parallel. Indeed, the Snell prediction was soon reversed: in the 1878 edition, after referring to a case where the court refused to apply a presumption of advancement to maternal transfers, the new author wrote that 'the decision of the court would probably be the same still, notwithstanding . . . the Married Woman's Property Act 1870'.[60] In the fifth edition, published the year after *Bennet* was decided, the author deleted the word 'probably' and added a reference to the case.[61] He did not explain why he thought that the 1870 Act had no effect, but it seems that he simply thought it irrelevant to the advancement obligation.[62]

---

[58] Married Women's Property Act 1870, s 14: 'A married woman having separate property shall be subject to all such liability for the maintenance of her children *as a widow is now by law subject to* for the maintenance of her children' (emphasis added).

[59] EHT Snell and JR Griffith, *The Principles of Equity*, 2nd edn (London, Stevens & Haynes, 1872) 101 n 5.

[60] EHT Snell and A Brown, *The Principles of Equity*, 4th edn (London, Stevens & Haynes, 1878) 125.

[61] EHT Snell and A Brown, *The Principles of Equity*, 5th edn (London, Stevens & Haynes, 1880) 128. Cf W Ashburner, *Principles of Equity* (London, Butterworth & Co, 1902) 148.

[62] In later editions of *Snell* it is said that statute does not affect the question 'as it is merely an equitable obligation' (20th edn, 1929, 117; 27th edn, 1973, 176; 29th edn, 1990, 180). In the two most recent editions it is said that 'a different result would probably be reached today': J McGhee, *Snell's Equity*, 30th edn (London, Sweet & Maxwell, 2000) 208; and 31st edn (London, Sweet & Maxwell, 2005) 574. On this see the discussion in the text to n 98 of *Re Zielinski (deceased)* [2007] WTLR 1655 and *Laskar v Laskar* [2008] EWCA Civ 347, [2008] 1 WLR 2695.

E. DEVELOPMENTS SINCE *BENNET V BENNET*

1. Widowed Mothers

Although Jessel MR stated in *Bennet* that the presumption of advancement did not apply to mothers, he did say that in the case of a widowed mother it would be very easy to rebut a presumption of resulting trust. Putting this together with the possibility of widowed mothers placing themselves *in loco parentis patris*, it would only have been an incremental step for a higher court to find that the presumption of advancement could apply generally to widowed mothers. Some obiter comment was made to this effect by Isaacs J in the Australian case of *Scott v Pauly*,[63] and in the Irish case of *Re Grimes (deceased)* the matter was decided by Johnston J.[64] In the latter case the judge followed *Sayre v Hughes*, and with respect to the conflict with *Bennet*, he commented that any obligation 'might reasonably be regarded as resting upon the shoulders of a widowed mother as well as upon the shoulders of a father'.[65] For Johnston J, the inclusion of widows could be justified by reference to the moral–legal obligation and did not depend on natural love and affection.

However, the decision in *Re Grimes* survived for less than two years before it was overruled in *McCabe v Ulster Bank Ltd*.[66] Murnaghan J found that 'neither natural affection nor moral obligation has been consistently relied upon to found the presumption', and concluded that it must be based upon 'the obligation to make provision which a Court of Equity recognises'.[67] Meredith J expanded this argument in his separate reasons: it might be that equity was wrong (1) to see an obligation on certain people to do more than merely support and maintain their children as required by law; and (2) to distinguish between fathers and mothers or widowed mothers in the recognition of this obligation. However, the point was that courts of equity did both of these things, and this was the basis of the presumption. He continued:

> Once duty is out of the case nothing remains in but natural expectation founded on the relationship. However strong this presumption may be it still only leaves the presumption of a resulting trust one to be rebutted, in the case of mother and child, on the strength of the evidence and not as a rule of law on the presumption of an advancement.[68]

---

[63] (1917) 24 CLR 274, 282: 'In case of his death the inference called a presumption as to the mother might well be different from that where the father was still alive'.
[64] [1937] IR 470.
[65] Ibid, 474.
[66] [1939] IR 1.
[67] Ibid, 15.
[68] Ibid, 18–19.

So a relationship of natural love and affection may be of great weight in rebutting a presumption of resulting trust, but as a matter of law that does not mean that a presumption of advancement applies—and equity simply did not regard women as being bound by the relevant advancement obligation in 1939. Assuming that Meredith J was not saying the advancement obligation could *never* apply to women, his reasoning is highly convincing. In fact it is disappointing that this case has not received more attention because it is respectfully suggested that Meredith J's judgment is by far the clearest explanation of why the presumption arises.

2. Australian Cases and a 'Greater Prima Facie Probability'

Bennet and *McCabe* confirmed that a relationship of affection alone did not justify the presumption of advancement and that instead the presumption was based on an obligation that a court of equity was prepared to recognise if not actively enforce. In *Wirth v Wirth*,[69] an Australian case involving an engaged couple, Dixon CJ commented that it would not be characteristic of equity to see the advancement categories as closed for merely historical reasons. The Chief Justice then applied a presumption of advancement to gifts from a fiancé to his fiancée.[70] Given that the other majority judge preferred not to decide the question, Dixon CJ's comments are strictly obiter, but they are particularly interesting because they point to a revision of the presumption, and, in effect, an alternative basis for its application:

> While the presumption of advancement doubtless in its inception was concerned with relationships affording 'good' consideration, it has in the course of its growth obtained a foundation or justification in the greater prima facie probability of a beneficial interest being intended in the situations to which the presumption has been applied.[71]

This construction seems, at first sight, to be very attractive. The probability reasoning can both justify the presumption and be the test of when the presumption applies. In the 1984 case of *Calverley v Green*, Gibbs CJ expressly approved the passage and called the approach both intelligible and likely to lead to a just result.[72] However, none of Mason, Brennan or Deane JJ endorsed this probability approach.[73] Unlike Gibbs CJ, their

[69] (1956) 98 CLR 228.
[70] Ibid, 238. McTiernan J agreed, giving separate reasons. Taylor J dissented and, at 248, clearly did not favour an expansion of the presumption to engaged couples.
[71] Ibid, 237.
[72] (1984) 155 CLR 242, 249–50. His Honour found that the presumption should apply 'when the relationship between the parties is such that it is more probable than not that a beneficial interest was intended to be conferred', whether or not any duty of support was owed.
[73] Murphy J favoured the abolition of all presumptions and argued that we should see legal

Honours would not apply a presumption of advancement to gifts from a de facto husband. It might be argued that those judges simply took a different view as to the probable intention of parties to a de facto relationship,[74] but unfortunately their objections cannot be explained away so easily. Mason and Brennan JJ would only apply the presumption as between parties to a 'lifetime relationship',[75] and also thought it important that judges had no discretion to reorder property rights on the failure of a de facto relationship, whereas this power did exist on divorce. In their view, the existence of this power in the Family Law Act 1975 (Cth) meant that 'special rules affecting the title to property of husband and wife can have no application in the present case'.[76] Deane J strictly reserved his position but said that he found the reasons of Mason and Brennan JJ in this regard to be convincing.[77]

It is argued that Gibbs CJ probably did go too far in finding a presumption of advancement to apply in the case of de facto spouses, given the difficulties of precisely defining that relationship and therefore of constructing a general exception to the normal presumption of resulting trust. It would be more appropriate for a de facto relationship to be viewed as evidence available to rebut a presumption of resulting trust. But this alone should not mean that the probability model is ignored or discarded: there are many relationships that can be precisely defined.

The probability model received a rather lukewarm reception in *Brown v Brown*,[78] a case about mother–son transfers heard by a strong New South Wales Court of Appeal. All three judges agreed that the presumption of advancement should apply to such transfers, but Gleeson CJ and Cripps JA differed from Kirby P as to the reason why it should apply. In his analysis Gleeson CJ cited the probability passage from *Wirth* but he also mentioned the obligation model and did not express a preference between the two.[79]

---

title as complete unless there are good reasons to the contrary: (1984) 155 CLR 242, 264. This view later received explicit support from Kirby P in *Stivactas v Michaletos (No 2)* (NSWCA, 31 August 1993) and *Brown v Brown* (1993) 31 NSWLR 582 (NSWCA) 595, and McHugh J appeared to agree with the intended result if not the intended means in *Nelson* (n 5) 184. In any case, given the decisions in *Brown* and *Nelson* it is clear that the Australian courts have considered themselves able to expand (although not abolish) the presumption relationships.

[74] *Calverly* (n 72) 260 (Mason and Brennan JJ): 'An assumption that the parties [in a de facto relationship] intend to maintain independent control of money and property and to retain a testamentary power to dispose of assets in which they have an interest is more likely to coincide with reality than an assumption of joint ownership.'

[75] Ibid, 259. Their Honours cited marriage as an example before accepting that this lifetime union is often defeated and without mentioning the presumption of resulting trust that applies to gifts from wives to husbands.

[76] Ibid, 261.

[77] Ibid, 268.

[78] (1993) 31 NSWLR 582.

[79] Gleeson CJ noted that there was disagreement as to the precise reason for the presumption of advancement: ibid, 590. Ultimately his Honour may have preferred a probability

In contrast, Kirby P spoke of 'the ordinary experience of human existence' and 'modern social norms and understandings'.[80] It seems clear that his Honour was applying a probability test even if much of his reasoning concerned the slightly different point that gender neutrality is desirable in law.

The welcome given to the probability model was even cooler in the High Court case of *Nelson v Nelson*, where none of the judges used probability reasoning alone to justify the inclusion of gifts from mothers to children. Dawson J thought that the presumption should apply whether the basis was a moral obligation or the reflection of actual probabilities,[81] three judges simply ignored the probability model, and Toohey J expressly disapproved of it by calling it open-ended and question-begging.[82]

Given its reception in *Nelson* it is perhaps not surprising that the probability approach has fallen out of favour in Australia. Instead the courts have gone back to the established categories, with only the single new addition of mother–child transfers. There have been two recent cases involving relationships that might be thought to warrant some kind of examination (cases involving transfers between siblings and transfers from parents to their children-in-law), but in neither was the probability test seriously applied. In *McGregor v Nichol*, Davies AJ did quote from Gibbs CJ's judgment in *Calverley* but his Honour then concluded without analysis that 'the relationship between the [brother and sisters] was not such as to raise that presumption'.[83] This, with respect, rather begs the question about the probability of transfers between siblings generally: it may well be that the parties in *McGregor* had a distant relationship, evidence of which would have rebutted a presumption of advancement, but that is beside the point. Further, in the most recent case at appellate level the probability model was completely ignored. *Z v Z* was a decision of the Full Family Court of Australia and the point at issue was whether a presumption of advancement would apply between a father and his daughter-in-law. Coleman and Boland JJ said:

> The law relevant to the presumption of advancement is well settled and applies only to a limited range of relationships. The presumption was explained by

---

approach because he found a presumption of advancement to apply while at the same time noting at 591 that 'Mrs Brown had no moral obligation to make such provision for her sons at the expense of her estate.' But the weight of that comment is really in the 'at the expense of her estate' part, rather than in the mention of moral obligation. The mother had transferred practically all of her property into her sons' names despite being relatively young and despite also having two daughters. It was therefore thought unlikely that the transfer was meant as a gift to the sons.

[80] Ibid, 599. In fact Kirby P would have preferred to abandon presumptions altogether, like Murphy J in *Calverley*, but he recognised that he was bound to apply them.
[81] *Nelson* (n 5) 163.
[82] Ibid, 171.
[83] [2003] NSWSC 332 [4].

Gibbs CJ in *Calverley* at 247 as arising 'when a husband makes a purchase in the name of his wife, or a father in the name of his child or other person to whom he stands loco parentis.' The presumption also applies between a mother and child (*Nelson*) and to a purchase by a man in the name of his fiancée (*Wirth v Wirth*).

It is well settled law that the presumption of advancement could arise between the husband's father and the husband and his brother, subject to rebuttal by contrary intention. An extension of the presumption to a daughter in law is not within the category of relationships recognised by the law.

We accept that the doctrine of presumption of advancement is one which could properly, on the existing state of the law, be applied to the husband and his brother. We agree with counsel for the husband and counsel for the wife that the presumption should not be extended to the wife. To do so would be contrary to recent judicial consideration of the doctrine which seeks to limit its applicability rather than to extend categories of relationships to which it could apply.[84]

This is rather startling. In *Calverley* Gibbs CJ commented that 'the principle on which these decisions have been rested is not altogether satisfactory', and went on to adopt the probability model from Dixon CJ in *Wirth*. Coleman and Boland JJ cited the part of Gibbs CJ's judgment that he was using to demonstrate the failings of the current law, but their Honours cited it in favour of the opposite position.[85] Of course, that is not to say that Gibbs CJ would automatically have found a presumption to exist between fathers and daughters-in-law, but his Honour would have asked what the general likelihood of intention would be.

It must be accepted that the precedent status of the probability model is weak: only Dixon CJ commented on it in *Wirth* and no other judges agreed with Gibbs CJ on the point in *Calverley*. Since then the model has been accorded varying (and perhaps descending) degrees of respect in Australia, and it does not appear to have gained a footing in other jurisdictions.[86] However, it is still rather surprising that the approach has not been given more of a chance. It does have the advantage of simplicity of theory when compared to a justification that involves a hybrid legal–moral obligation of undetermined provenance and uncertain modern relevance. One objection is that the probability model will prove inefficient in practice: until a case (or several cases if we are to be strict about *rationes*) with appropriate facts reaches the highest level, then much court time will be taken up with arguing about what the probable intention might be in any given relation-

---

[84] [2005] FamCA 996 [143]–[146]. At [32] Finn J reserved his position on the presumption of advancement.

[85] It should be noted that the point was not the subject of dispute between the parties to the case, but nevertheless their Honours clearly felt able to express concluded views on the matter. The passage from *Z v Z* was also cited in *Sikorski v Sikorski* [2007] FamCA 487 [69], where Burr J treated it as 'confirming' the law.

[86] It was recently mentioned by Litton NPJ in the context of whether a presumption of advancement applied to de facto wives: *Cheung* (n 7) [9].

ship. Perhaps the conclusion of the probability analysis is also worrying: to most observers it would probably seem natural to assume that people mean to do what they actually do.[87] After all, evidence may be introduced to reverse this and we already have doctrines of undue influence and relief against unconscionable transactions to protect against the exploitation of the vulnerable.[88] What role, then, for the general presumption of resulting trust in law? These points have merit and it is understandable why a court would not wish to open Pandora's Box in that way. Moreover, any clamour to change will have been quietened now that the presumption is not so sexually discriminatory.[89] But one of the other arguments against change—that parties will have structured their affairs according to the current law—is less convincing.[90] Presumptions in this context are important when actual evidence is weak or unavailable and it is highly unlikely that people will intentionally rely on a basic presumption and will then demonstrate this intentional reliance by remaining silent about it. At all events, it now seems clear that in Australia the presumption includes mothers but that any further development will be slow, incremental and only made if absolutely necessary.[91]

3. Other Jurisdictions

In England and Wales the presumption has been explored and to some extent re-evaluated in the context of family home trusts and transfers for an illegal purpose. In both it has been the effect of the presumption that has been the subject of inquiry: it has a determinative but arbitrary effect in cases of illegality,[92] and is arguably unhelpful in shared home cases.[93] In

---

[87] Note Swadling's suggestion that a presumption of resulting trust may have no place in a society where people rarely declare trusts for themselves: WJ Swadling, 'Explaining Resulting Trusts' (2008) 124 *Law Quarterly Review* 72, 84. Swadling's view is that it operates as a strict presumption of declaration of trust (and for that reason is rebutted by any evidence inconsistent with a trust). Chambers would argue that even if the presumption of resulting trust were to be abandoned the resulting trust itself would still be available on proof of a lack of intention to benefit: Chambers (n 2) and also ch 9 in this book.

[88] For a comparison of the presumption of resulting trust and the doctrine of undue influence, see Swadling (n 87) 88.

[89] Or, at least, not as importantly so: the marital presumption still only applies in one direction, but like many jurisdictions its effect has been lessened in Australia by legislation enabling courts to reorder property rights on divorce: Family Law Act 1975 (Cth), s 79.

[90] See *Nelson* (n 5) 141 (Deane and Gummow JJ): 'the presumptions are interrelated and entrenched "landmarks" in the law of property. Many disputes have been resolved and transactions effected on that foundation' (citation in original omitted).

[91] See *Calverley* (n 72) 268 (Deane J): 'Any adjustment of those relationships must however, be made by reference to logical necessity and analogy and not by reference to idiosyncratic notions of what is fair and appropriate.'

[92] See *Tinsley v Milligan* [1994] 1 AC 340, 372 (Lord Browne-Wilkinson); *Tribe v Tribe* [1996] Ch 107 (CA) 118 (Nourse LJ). This has led the Law Commission to call for reform in this area: *The Illegality Defence: A Consultative Report* (LCCP No 189, 2009) Part 6.

[93] *Pettitt v Pettitt* [1970] AC 777, 793 (Lord Reid), 811 (Lord Hodson), 815 (Lord Upjohn)

neither line of cases has the extent of the presumption relationships been examined.[94] Indeed, even where some relatively recent cases would have lent themselves to a reappraisal—because the transfer was from a mother to her daughter[95] or from a father to his adult child[96]—the orthodox position has been accepted apparently without argument. In the 2008 case of *Laskar v Laskar*, Lord Neuberger suggested that he would have applied a presumption of advancement to a transfer from a mother to a daughter, but the comment appears to be obiter and it was not supported by analysis.[97] Only a year or so earlier, *Re Zielinski (deceased)*[98] had followed *Bennet* in finding that no presumption of advancement applied to mothers.

In *Pettitt v Pettitt*, Lord Diplock commented that a 'presumption of fact is no more than a consensus of judicial opinion disclosed by reported cases as to the most likely inference of fact to be drawn in the absence of any evidence to the contrary'.[99] This looks like English authority for a probability approach, but in fact his Lordship was speaking in a very specific context: he was pointing out that the presumptions of advancement and resulting trust were no longer helpful tools in ascertaining or imputing the intentions of married couples as to the ownership of their property. The speech does not mention the presumption of advancement in the context of transfers from parents to their children and, apart from one case involving a home shared by father and son,[100] it appears not to have been referred to outside the context of couples sharing homes.[101]

Two recent decisions of the Supreme Court of Canada appear to have settled the presumption questions there in relation to transfers from

and 824–25 (Lord Diplock); *McGrath v Wallis* [1995] 2 FLR 114 (CA). The real question in this line of cases was whether the court had discretion to reorder the property rights of separating unmarried couples in the same way as it has that authority on divorce.

[94] Although note the comment of Robert Walker LJ in *Lowson v Coombes* [1999] Ch 373 (CA) 385: 'the presumption has been cogently criticised both as out of date . . . and as being uncertain in its scope (especially in relation to transfers by wives and mothers)'.

[95] *Sekhon v Alissa* [1989] 2 FLR 94.

[96] *Lavelle v Lavelle* [2004] EWCA Civ 223, [2004] 2 FCR 418.

[97] *Laskar* (n 62) [20]–[21]. In the event there was enough actual evidence of an intended joint business venture.

[98] *Zielinski* (n 62).

[99] *Pettitt* (n 93) 823–24. Lord Diplock made similar comments in *Gissing v Gissing* [1971] AC 886, 907: '[the presumption of advancement] could seldom have any decisive part to play in disputes between living spouses in which some evidence would be available in addition to the mere fact that the husband had provided part of the purchase price of property conveyed into the name of the wife'.

[100] *McGrath v Wallis* [1995] 2 FLR 114 (CA) 115 where Nourse LJ (with whom Hirst LJ and Sir Ralph Gibson agreed) said that the effect of the decision in *Pettitt* was to reclassify the presumption of advancement as 'a judicial instrument of last resort' in shared home cases.

[101] It has been referred to in several shared home cases where the parties were unmarried. Both presumptions are considered equally unhelpful in shared home cases: *Stack v Dowden* [2007] UKHL 17, [2007] 2 AC 432 [60]; *Vajpeyi v Yusaf* [2003] EWHC 2788 (Ch), [2004] WTLR 989 [73]; *Burns v Burns* [1984] Ch 317 (CA). Compare *Re Hogg deceased* (Ch D, 11 July 1983).

mothers and transfers to adult children. Interestingly, all three of the obligation, affection and probability models were applied in the cases. *Pecore v Pecore* and *Madsen Estate v Saylor* both involved transfers from fathers to their adult children and in each case the Supreme Court held that the correct presumption was one of resulting trust.[102] Although transfers from parents to children would normally be covered by the presumption of advancement, the court held that this presumption ceases to apply when the child becomes an adult. Rothstein J, delivering the reasons of the majority in *Pecore*, said:

> First, given that a principal justification for the presumption of advancement is parental obligation to support their dependent children, it seems to me that the presumption should not apply in respect of independent adult children. . . . [P]arental support obligations under provincial and federal statutes normally end when the child is no longer considered by law to be a minor. . . . Second, it is common nowadays for ageing parents to transfer their assets into joint accounts with their adult children in order to have that child assist them in managing their financial affairs. There should therefore be a rebuttable presumption that the adult child is holding the property in trust for the ageing parent to facilitate the free and efficient management of that parent's affairs.[103]

Rothstein J therefore used both an obligation and probability model to justify restricting the presumption to minor children. Although the second justification was framed as a positive reason for having a presumption of trust, we can equally well state it like this: if experience tells us that the most common reason for transferring property into the joint names of parents and adult children is the greater ease of administering that property, then there is no compelling reason to depart from the general position of resulting trust. Of course, the evidence in individual cases may establish a rebuttal of that presumption. In contrast, Abella J in separate reasons adopted the affection model and therefore saw no reason to limit the presumption of advancement to minor children.[104]

Several recent cases in Singapore have considered the rationale for the presumption, and the preferred view in that jurisdiction seems to be that the presumption arises because of an obligation to maintain and support.[105]

---

[102] *Pecore* (n 9) and *Madsen* (n 49). In both decisions the majority included McLachlin CJ, Bastarache, Binnie, LeBel, Deschamps, Fish, Charron and Rothstein JJ. Abella J gave different reasons in each case: in *Madsen Estate* her Honour dissented, whereas in *Pecore* she concurred in the result.

[103] *Pecore* (n 9) [36]. Compare *McDonnell v Loosemore* [2007] EWCA Civ 1531 [33] (Toulson LJ): 'It is not unusual for a person of advancing years and in poor health to decide to pass on his capital assets to his family immediately, trusting that they will behave honourably towards him by not letting him become homeless and destitute. . . . that is sufficient to rebut a presumption of a resulting trust.'

[104] Ibid, [89].

[105] In addition to the cases mentioned in the text, see *Ang Toon Teck v Ang Poon Sin* [1998] SGHC 67 [48]; *Low Geok Khim (administratrix of the estate of Low Kim Tah, deceased) v*

For example, in *Re Estate of Chong Siew Kum*, Andrew Ang JC justified the inclusion of mothers by referring to legislation that required both parents to maintain and support a child.[106] Likewise in *Low Gim Siah v Low Geok Khim* the Court of Appeal found that 'a dependency relationship was the original basis of the presumption of advancement', and quoted *Bennet* in support of that finding.[107]

F. COMPARING DUTIES TO ADVANCE AND DUTIES TO SUPPORT

In cases where the presumption has been extended to mothers the justification has often been that mothers and fathers are under the same legal duties to maintain and support their children. With few exceptions,[108] the equal love and affection argument has not been used as the main justification since before *Bennet v Bennet*.[109] Yet the discussion of legal duties to maintain and support in the context of the obligation model is argued to be beside the point: the issue has never been the legal obligation to maintain or support a child, but is instead the obligation recognised by equity to advance him.[110] Several cases justify departing from *Bennet* on the basis that there was no obligation on a mother to provide for her children when *Bennet* was decided. For example, in the *Chong Siew Kum* case, the judge commented that the 'absence of such an obligation on the part of a mother was apparently the reason why in *Bennet v Bennet* Jessel MR favoured the

Low Geok Bian [2006] SGHC 41 [42]–[47]; *Shih Shin Wang-Liu* [2006] SGHC 196 [48]. For a comprehensive review, see TH Tey, 'Singapore's Muddled Presumption of Advancement' [2007] *Singapore Journal of Legal Studies* 240.

[107] [2005] SGHC 41 [18].

[107] [2006] SGCA 45 [29].

[108] In *Pecore* (n 9) [89]–[98] Abella J applied the affection model in her separate reasons. As authority she cited *Sidmouth v Sidmouth* (1840) 2 Beav 447, 48 ER 1254; *Scawin v Scawin* (1841) 1 Y & CCC 65, 62 ER 792; and *Hepworth v Hepworth* (1870) LR 11 Eq 10; however, it is respectfully submitted that she placed undue weight on these cases. In both *Sidmouth* and *Scawin* the comments about the age of the children being immaterial were made in the specific context of whether adulthood was positive evidence in favour of a trust in the same way that infancy was evidence against an intended trust. In both cases this was decided in the negative: adulthood was not important one way or the other. In *Hepworth* the judge applied a presumption of advancement when the aged father was actually dependent on the child, but Malins V-C still used an obligation justification: he simply applied the argument that only a father can be the judge of when and how much to advance his child.

[109] It is common for natural love and affection to be mentioned alongside a discussion of legislative and socio-economic change: see eg *Re Wilson* (1999) 27 ETR (2d) 97 (Ont Gen Div) [50] (Fedak J): 'Taking into consideration the natural affection between a mother and child, legislative changes requiring mothers to support their children, the economic independence of women and the equality provisions of the Charter.' Similarly in *Fong v Sun* [2008] HKCU 730 [19] the judge mentioned a 'very close family or blood relationship', but then also mentioned the obligation and probability models.

[110] It was usually a 'him', as someone who would be expected to become head of his own household.

traditional view'.[111] The same point has been made in cases decided in Canada[112] and Hong Kong.[113] But if we are talking about a common law obligation, then Mr Bennet would not have owed any duty to his adult son either; and if we are talking about a public law duty, then the widowed Mrs Bennet did indeed owe an obligation of support. Moreover, if the problem in *Bennet* truly was the lack of any relevant legal obligations on women, then it is very surprising that the Married Women's Property Act 1870 is not mentioned anywhere in Jessel MR's judgment.

If the equitable obligation to advance was the same as a private common law obligation to maintain, then the presumption would not have applied in relation to adult children. If the relevant legal duties were found in public law, then the presumption would not have applied to adults since around 1948, and it would have been extended to mothers sometime soon after the Married Women's Property Acts of 1870 and 1882. That this did not happen cannot simply be explained on the grounds of legal inertia and the rigid application of *stare decisis*: all of the modern cases refer to reams of family law and social security legislation, whereas in the older cases statutes (even when they existed) are hardly mentioned at all. Perhaps it is not surprising that pre-1870s courts of equity did not refer to common law duties, but this rather strengthens the point that the duties were not the same: it was not as simple as equity presuming the fulfilment of a common law duty.

Instead it is argued that the obligation in question was an obligation to advance and set up in life. This is an equitable private law duty that is unknown to the common law, and the content and scope of the equitable duty differ from those of a maintenance obligation. It is true that the presumption applies regardless of existing provision, even though the equitable obligation ends once provision has been made.[114] But the reason for this is stated in *Dyer v Dyer*: it is difficult for a court to determine when someone is sufficiently advanced already, so the law leaves it up to the father.[115] The contrast with the legal duty to maintain is clear: in cases like

---

[111] *Chong* (n 106) [18].

[112] *Dagle v Dagle Estate* (1990) 70 DLR (4th) 201 (Prince Edward Island CA) [22].

[113] *Fong v Sun* [2008] HKCU 730 [14]: '*Bennet v Bennet* was decided 129 years ago at a time when women had no independent financial means and no obligation to provide for their children. . . . Mrs Margaret Thatcher became the first woman prime minister of the United Kingdom and a woman president of the United States is probably in the making.'

[114] Despite early authority to the effect that the presumption ends when provision has been made: *Elliot* (n 34) 2 Chan Cas 232: 'after he hath provided for him, he is under no further obligation to provide more than for a stranger, and else no father could trust his child'.

[115] *Dyer* (n 47) 2 Cox 94. Also *Sidmouth v Sidmouth* (1840) 2 Beav 447, 456; 48 ER 1254, 1258 (Lord Langdale MR): 'The parent may judge for himself when it suits his own convenience, or when it will be best for his son, to secure him any benefit which he voluntarily thinks fit to bestow upon him, and it does not follow that because the reason for doing it is not known, there was no intention to advance at all.' This passage was cited with approval in *Hepworth v Hepworth* (1870) LR 11 Eq 10, 13, a case where the aged father was actually dependent on the son but where the presumption of advancement still applied.

Grey v Grey, *Elliot v Elliot* and *Dyer v Dyer* it was the issue of the son's existing provision that caused difficulty, not whether he had reached a certain age or not. Indeed, the possibility of reversing the presumption when the child reached majority does not seem to have occurred to judges before the twentieth century.

Binion v Stone provides a further illustration of how the age of the recipient was viewed.[116] In contrast to some modern decisions that see dependency as important, in *Binion* the very young age of the child (five years) was actually evidence that an advancement had *not* been intended, and so the court presumed a trust for the father. So why was advancement still presumed in the case of minors? Because, as Freeman wrote in the report of *Binion v Stone*, even if it was surprising to see an advancement for a five-year-old it was surely even more unlikely that the father intended the infant to be a trustee.[117] This is similar to the question of existing advancement: ideally advancement would not be presumed unless the child was of an age where he could make use of it, and neither would it be presumed where it had already occurred. In fact the presumption *was* applied both to minors and to those already advanced, but this was for the reasons just outlined and it should not obscure the true nature of the obligation.

G. CONCLUSION

It may be that the welfare state, free education, and the freer acquisition and disposition of land mean that it is no longer incumbent upon a father to establish his children in the world. Similarly, if women and men are economic equals, then any advancement obligation should apply to mothers too.[118] If either of these is true, then the answer is easy: abolish the presumption in relation to both parents or extend it to include both parents.[119]

---

[116] (1663) 2 Freeman 169, 22 ER 1135.

[117] (1663) 2 Freeman 169, 169; 22 ER 1135, 1136.

[118] Note Sarmas's view that the presumption of advancement should not be applied to wife–husband transfers, given women's disadvantaged economic position in relation to men: L Sarmas, 'A Step in the Wrong Direction: The Emergence of Gender "Neutrality" in the Equitable Presumption of Advancement' (1994) 19 *Melbourne University Law Review* 758, 765. Sarmas does appear to support the inclusion of mother–child transfers. See the discussion in R Graycar and J Morgan, *The Hidden Gender of Law*, 2nd edn (Sydney, Federation Press, 2002) 44–48.

[119] Another possibility is that the presumption is changed for an unconnected reason. For example, the UK Government currently proposes to ratify the seventh protocol to the ECHR, Art 5 of which provides that 'spouses shall enjoy equality of rights and responsibilities of a private law character between them, and in their relations with their children'. The presumption of advancement would need changing before ratification could occur. In November 2005 the Family Law (Property and Maintenance) Bill was published and by clause 2 it sought to abolish the presumption of advancement between spouses and engaged couples (although nothing was said about the parental presumption). The Bill never made any progress and was not re-

But the question must be asked in the right way; the problem is not solved by pointing to equal obligations to support spouses or minor children. Despite the fact that equity appears to have acted independently of the law in this regard, duties to maintain and support were not the source of the obligation and should not be used to enlarge it. The point of an advancement was not merely to enable the recipient to support themselves; it was to enable them to live their life and contribute to society.[120]

In part this might be a rather academic plea for correct legal analysis, but it is also more than that: there may be occasions where legal duties to maintain and support children apply equally to mothers, but where the economic position of women is such that mothers could not generally be expected to establish their children in life. The problem can be illustrated by two recent cases from Singapore.[121] In the first, *Re Estate of Chong Siew Kum*, Andrew Ang JC extended the presumption of advancement to mothers and commented that 'where once [women] were mere dependants, they now often assume equal importance as providers for the family'.[122] A year later, in *Low Gim Siah v Low Geok Khim*, the Court of Appeal said:

> We find it difficult to accept an argument that in modern Singapore, fathers and husbands have somehow changed their paternal or marital obligations so radically that the presumption is no longer applicable or should not be applied. There is no doubt that many married women in Singapore are financially independent of their husbands. But there are also many of them who are not or who choose to be housewives in order to look after their husbands, their children and their homes.[123]

It might be thought inconsistent for one case to retain a presumption by pointing to women's financial vulnerability and for another case to extend a presumption by pointing to women's financial independence. In this context it should not automatically be assumed that mothers will owe the same duty to establish their children in life, even if they are under the same obligations to maintain and support.[124] If the relative economic positions of the sexes are such that it would be wrong to see an equal advancement obligation applicable to both parents, then it follows that a general

---

introduced in the next Parliamentary session. For general discussion, see G Andrews, 'The Presumption of Advancement: Equity, Equality and Human Rights' [2007] *Conveyancer and Property Lawyer* 340.

[120] *Ward v Snelling* (CA, 20 April 1994) (Dillon LJ): 'the obligation recognised by courts of equity on a father to provide for establishing his children in life'.

[121] Similar reasoning can be found in *Fong v Sun* [2008] HKCU 730 [13]–[17], where the judge extended the presumption to women based upon equal statutory obligations to maintain and the fact that a mother's financial contribution to the household is often indispensable. It seemed to be assumed that the father's contribution is always indispensable.

[122] *Chong* (n 106) [18]. His Honour also referred to s 68 of the Women's Charter (ch 353, 1997 rev ed), which imposes a duty of maintenance on both parents.

[123] *Low* (n 107) [44].

[124] Contrast *Brown* (n 78) 599 (Kirby P).

presumption of advancement should not apply to mothers. The specifics of a particular relationship (a rich and generous mother) can always be taken into account when rebutting a presumption of resulting trust.

11

Intention, Mistakes and Resulting Trusts

CHARLIE WEBB*

A. INTRODUCTION

The debate surrounding the basis of resulting trusts is well known. Until now the arguments have largely focused on the question of which view better fits the cases. In this chapter I shall leave this to one side and instead focus on some of the conceptual and justificatory arguments that have been made. My primary focus will be an argument recently made by William Swadling, which seeks to demonstrate that the view that resulting trusts arise to prevent or reverse unjust enrichment should be rejected not simply because it fails to fit the cases but, more fundamentally, because it is conceptually incoherent.[1] If this is correct, we do not need to worry about the authorities: the unjust enrichment view *cannot* be true. However, as I hope to show, this argument fails. Nonetheless, we may learn something useful from it, for, in seeing where the argument falls down, we reveal an important truth about the basis of claims in respect of defective transfers.

B. UNJUST ENRICHMENT AND NON-BENEFICIAL TRANSFERS

The claim that unjust enrichment explains resulting trusts appears a simple one.[2] The standard and central cases of unjust enrichment are transfers

---

*My thanks to Neil Duxbury, John Mee and Irit Samet for their comments.

[1] W Swadling, 'Explaining Resulting Trusts' (2008) 124 *Law Quarterly Review* 72.
[2] For full statements of this argument, see P Birks, 'Restitution and Resulting Trusts' in S Goldstein (ed), *Equity and Contemporary Legal Developments* (Jerusalem, Hebrew University of Jerusalem, 1992) 335, reprinted as Appendix 1 of P Birks and F Rose (eds), *Restitution and Equity*—Vol 1: *Resulting Trusts and Equitable Compensation* (Oxford, Mansfield Press, 1998); P Birks, *Unjust Enrichment*, 2nd edn (Oxford, Oxford University Press, 2005) 180–98;

made by mistake or where the claimant's consent is absent or in some other way defective. Consistently with this we might say that such cases involve situations in which the transferor has no proper or effective intention to benefit the recipient, or, more succinctly, non-beneficial transfers. The claim then is that the situations in which resulting trusts are conventionally recognised are instances of non-beneficial transfers and hence of unjust enrichment, and that the trust is imposed precisely to reverse that unjust enrichment.

Now, as a matter of jurisdictional history, this account may turn out to be untrue. It may be that, on closer examination, the cases reveal that the courts have had something else in mind when developing and applying the law on resulting trusts. But, whatever the answer to this question, the unjust enrichment account at least appears *possible*, in the sense of being analytically coherent, a position that a legal system *could* plausibly and rationally adopt. Indeed, this appears to have been assumed on both sides of the debate. Now, though, Swadling has challenged not only the historical accuracy of the unjust enrichment account but its very possibility.

Swadling's argument goes like this.[3] When I transfer title to an asset to you, I must intend, broadly, one of two things.[4] Firstly, I may intend an outright transfer. In other words, my intention is that you should not only receive the asset and the set of claims, powers, privileges and immunities that title entails, but that you should then, through their exercise, be free to use that asset for your ends and your own benefit. Secondly, I may intend that you hold the asset on trust. Here too I intend that you should take over the claims, powers, privileges and immunities entailed by legal title, but this time you are not to exercise them in pursuance of your own ends but rather for the exclusive benefit of someone else, the trust beneficiary. If we want to talk in terms of 'beneficial' and 'non-beneficial' transfers, the former are clearly beneficial, the latter not (so far as you, the transferee, are concerned).

But, on this basis, the standard instances of unjust enrichment are not in fact examples of non-beneficial transfer. If I pay you money, mistakenly believing that I owe it to you, I do not intend that you hold that money on trust, whether for me or for any other person. On the contrary, when actually handing over the money, my intention is that you take it outright. Of course, my mistake enables me to say that *had I known the truth* I

R Chambers, *Resulting Trusts* (Oxford, Oxford University Press, 1997); R Chambers, 'Resulting Trusts' in A Burrows and Lord Rodger (eds), *Mapping the Law: Essays in Memory of Peter Birks* (Oxford, Oxford University Press, 2006) 247. I summarise the arguments in C Webb and T Akkouh, *Trusts Law* (Basingstoke, Palgrave MacMillan, 2008) 208–13.

[3] Swadling (n 1) 90–93 and 101. See too W Swadling, 'Policy Arguments for Proprietary Restitution' (2008) 28 *Legal Studies* 506, 529.

[4] In fact Swadling (n 1) 90–91 and 101 also mentions a third possibility—transfers by way of security—but these can be safely left to one side for present purposes.

would not have paid you and I would not have intended to pay you. But I did not know this and (so the argument goes) it is simply a fiction to say that I had any other intention but to benefit you at the time I made the payment. (Indeed if the 'had I known' argument works to establish that the claimant had no intent to pay, then why not allow the claimant to go a stage further and say: 'Had I known that the money wasn't due I would have intended that you hold any money I did mistakenly pay on trust for me'? If we reject this 'in hindsight' intention to create a trust as a fiction, then surely we must by the same measure reject the equally 'in hindsight' absence of intention to benefit?)

If this argument is correct, it has far-reaching implications. In the first instance, it means that the argument that resulting trusts arise in the event of non-beneficial transfers cannot support its intended conclusion—that a resulting trust should be recognised in cases of mistaken[5] transfers—for the very reason that these are not in fact instances of non-beneficial transfer.[6] More fundamentally, however, it appears to question any account of the law of unjust enrichment that seeks to explain liability in cases of mistake by reference to the claimant's lack of intent to benefit the defendant. That is because, whatever reason we may have for recognising a claim *of any kind* (that is, whether personal or proprietary), it cannot be that the claimant did not intend the benefit he conferred, again for the reason that, at the time, he *did* intend this.

So have unjust enrichment theorists got things so badly wrong? I do not think so. Nonetheless Swadling's challenge is important and demonstrates that we need to take a little more care in explaining exactly how mistakes impact upon a claimant's intentions.

It is common among unjust enrichment writers to describe mistakes as

---

[5] I am focusing on mistakes for the sake of simplicity, though the point equally stands with respect to what have been variously described as 'future mistakes', 'mispredictions' and 'failures of consideration'. Things are less straightforward in relation to transfers made under duress. There is, I think, a clear sense in which a claimant who makes a transfer under duress can claim that his intention to benefit the recipient was impaired, if not absent. However, the way coercion impacts on the claimant's decision-making process and hence the way in which his intention is affected is plainly different to the way things work in cases of mistake. I leave these cases to one side. Swadling's argument does not bite on cases of ignorance, since there the claimant can say that at no time and in no sense did he intend to benefit the defendant (see further n 6), and so I shall leave these aside too (though the argument made in the second half of this paper shows how we may view cases of mistake and ignorance as materially alike: see text to n 19).

[6] Much the same position is taken by Lord Millett, who, though aligning himself with Chambers's view that resulting trusts arise where the claimant does not intend to benefit the defendant, would deny any role for resulting trusts in mistaken transfers on the ground that in these cases the claimant's intention *is* to benefit the defendant. Hence he sees the 'no intention to benefit' argument as applying only in cases of ignorance. See P Millett, 'Resulting Trusts' [1998] *Restitution Law Review* 283, 284; P Millett, 'Restitution and Constructive Trusts' (1998) 114 *Law Quarterly Review* 399, 401–02; cf *Air Jamaica Ltd v Charlton* [1999] 1 WLR 1399 (PC) 1412.

having the effect of 'vitiating' a claimant's intention.[7] The implication is that, in some sense, the claimant's mistaken belief nullifies or destroys the relevant intention. But this seems an odd claim. A person's intentions—as with all states of mind—are matters of fact.[8] Accordingly, the suggestion that intentions can somehow be erased or nullified looks unreal. Either the claimant had a particular intention at a particular point in time or he did not have this intention. If he did, then to proceed as though he did not is to resort to fiction; if he did not there is nothing to nullify or vitiate in the first place. What we need is an account of the operation of mistakes that does not deny (or appear to deny) the reality of the defendant's state of mind at the time he transferred the asset to the defendant. For this, we must first take a closer look at how intentions operate in our practical reasoning.

C. INTENTIONS AND CONDITIONS

All intentional action is directed towards the achievement of some end or set of ends. The agent formulates both a state of affairs that he wishes to see realised and a plan or proposal for its realisation, which he then seeks to effectuate through his actions. All aspects of the proposal—both the end state of affairs and the various chosen steps or means to the achievement of that end—are intended.[9]

Let us say I am thinking about what I shall do this evening. Having weighed up various possibilities, I settle on going to the cinema. To bring this about, I know I must take various steps. So I resolve to do the following: check the cinema listings to see what is on, walk to the cinema, stop off at a cash machine on the way, buy a ticket for the film, take my seat and so on. Indeed, each of these steps can themselves be broken down into smaller proposals. To get money from the cash machine, I walk up to the cashpoint, take my wallet from my pocket, insert my bank card, key in my PIN code, etc. Similarly, my objective of watching the film can itself be understood as just one step in a broader, often longer-term plan directed towards some ulterior or more basic end—say, to take my mind off work or

---

[7] See eg P Birks, *An Introduction to the Law of Restitution*, rev edn (Oxford, Clarendon Press, 1989) 100–101 and 147; P Birks and R Chambers, *The Restitution Research Resource* (Oxford, Mansfield Press, 1997) 3; A Burrows, *The Law of Restitution*, 2nd edn (London, Butterworths, 2002) 71. See too Burrows, ibid, 130, where it is stated that a mistake 'negatives the voluntariness' with which the claimant made the transfer.

[8] *Edgington v Fitzmaurice* (1885) 29 Ch D 459 (CA) 483 (Bowen LJ). I know that the purely factual or descriptive status of intentions is disputed. However, this is an assumption on which this essay proceeds.

[9] See generally J Finnis, 'Intention and Side-effects' in R Frey and C Morris (eds), *Liability and Responsibility: Essays in Law and Morals* (Cambridge, Cambridge University Press, 1991) 32.

to give me something to talk about with my friends.[10] Again, all these things—all these states of affairs which are either my chosen ends or my chosen means to those ends—I direct my actions towards and so intend.

Next, note that various parts of proposal may be explicitly provisional or conditional. I may resolve, consciously, when forming my plan, that if it rains I will catch the bus rather than walk to the cinema; or that, if one cashpoint is not working, I shall go on to the next. This is no less true of the proposal as a whole. I may decide that I shall not go to the cinema if my friend, Dan, calls up to suggest going for a drink instead. In such cases, a full statement of my proposal—and hence of my intentions—would need to make references to these contingencies. So, though, if you ask me what my plans are for the evening, I may still say—for simplicity and anticipating the more likely sequence of events—'I intend to go to the cinema', this is no longer a fully accurate statement of my relevant intention. A complete statement would be 'I intend to go to the cinema unless Dan calls', and we can go on, 'in which case I intend to go for a drink'.

Now let us imagine that, when forming my proposal to go the cinema, I give no thought to the question of what I shall do if it rains or if Dan calls. These possibilities never come to mind or, though they do, I disregard them without committing myself one way or another. In these cases, I cannot say that I intend to catch the bus if it rains or that I intend to go for a drink with Dan if he calls. I do not intend these things because they are not plans I have decided upon and committed myself to—though it may well be true that, had you raised these possibilities or had I taken the time to think them through, I would have modified my proposal accordingly; that is to say, this is what *I would have intended*. (We can note here that this is why we are correct not to view unjust enrichment claims as founded on and giving effect to the claimant's intentions, notwithstanding that in the vast majority of cases a return of the relevant asset or enrichment is precisely what the claimant would have intended had he been alerted to the possibility that the payment was not due, etc.)

But neither is it correct to say in such circumstances that my intention to walk or to go to the cinema is entirely unconditional. Here we must distinguish two different ways in which an intention may be conditional or unconditional. When we say my intention is unconditional we may simply mean that I have not consciously formulated and attached any explicit limits or qualifications to it. That is the case here when I have not considered events which may alter my plan of going to the cinema. However, if by saying my intention is unconditional we mean that my intention is that I shall go to the cinema *come what may* or *in all events*, then this is not (or

---

[10] Although I think there must be a limit to this process of abstraction, since we would lose sight of the genuine diversity of our objectives and values if we viewed all these specific proposals and ends, and hence all chosen action, as ultimately directed towards a single life-defining end, such as 'happiness' or 'fulfilment'.

at least need not be) true. Just as I have not resolved *not to* go to the cinema and instead to go for a drink with Dan if he calls, nor have I resolved *to go* to the cinema even should he call. My proposal simply does not embrace or provide for this contingency. So, just as it would wrongly describe my state of mind to say that my intention is not to go to the cinema if Dan suggests a drink, it would likewise be a misdescription to say that I do intend still to go even in this eventuality. Rather, on this question, there is a gap.[11] I have no relevant intention one way or the other.[12]

There is also an important midway point between the situation just described—where my proposal makes no provision whatsoever in respect of a particular contingency (it rains, Dan calls, etc)—and the situation set out before—where my proposal explicitly provides for what I shall do in that event (catch the bus, go for a drink). Say, when formulating my plan to go to the cinema, I consciously resolve to walk *unless it rains*, but then do not take the further step of deciding what I shall do in that case—whether I shall get the bus or the tube or a taxi. In this case, though I have no intention in respect of how I shall (positively) travel if it rains, I do have an intention *not* to walk in that event. There is still a gap here, but not so great a gap as if I had made no decision whatsoever in respect of what I shall do if it rains.

This also brings out another possible source of confusion when we talk about intentions. Take the following sentence: 'I don't intend to walk if it rains.' This statement is consistent with either of two different states of mind or dispositions. The first is that I have positively resolved not to walk in the event of it raining (whether or not I have also gone on to decide what I shall do in that event). The second is that I have made *no* resolution

---

[11] The idea of intentions and voluntary undertakings having gaps is well-established in contract scholarship: see eg C Fried, *Contract as Promise: A Theory of Contractual Obligation* (Cambridge, MA, Harvard University Press, 1981) 57–63; cf B Langille and A Ripstein, 'Strictly Speaking—It Went Without Saying' (1996) 2 *Legal Theory* 63. I think the gaps in intentional transfers are likely to be greater than they are in contracts, where both voluntary negotiated risk-allocation and the possibility of genuine consent to the law's default rules of risk-allocation will often result in many such gaps being filled. These possibilities do not apply, at least not in the same way, to (non-contractual) transfers.

[12] We may note that the conclusion that my intentions are conditional in the sense of being limited or incomplete does not depend on how I would answer the question of whether consideration of the unprovided for contingency would have led to me modifying my plans. So, we can say that my intention to go to the cinema is conditional, in this sense, even before we address the question of whether I would have altered my plans had I properly considered the possibility of my friend suggesting a drink. Rather it is simply the fact that I have not factored this in one way or another—that my proposal makes no provision for this eventuality—that makes my intention conditional or, better, incomplete. Now, of course, the likelihood is that consideration of some of these unconsidered eventualities would have led me to change my plans. This may well be significant when we turn to the question of mistakes and the claims they may support. However, for now, the point I want to make is simply that intentions, even where not explicitly conditional, will invariably have gaps, irrespective of whether those gaps turn out to be significant. For more on which contingencies can be understood as creating gaps in proposals for action, see n 13.

one way or another as to whether I shall walk if it rains—it is something I have not considered or factored into my plans. So the first interpretation of the statement corresponds to 'I intend not to walk if it rains', the second 'I have no intention as to whether (or not) I shall walk if it rains.' The distinction here is between the presence of a particular intention (not to do something) and the absence of intention—a distinction masked by formulations of the kind 'I do not intend . . .'—and, though this distinction is fine, it will occasionally be important.

This is only a brief account of intentions and conditions and I shall expand on some of these points later on. For now, the point I would like to stress is that an intention to X (go to the cinema, catch the bus, etc) need not, indeed generally will not, be an intention to X *come what may* or *in all events*. This is clearest where the intention is explicitly conditional, that is, where I consciously formulate a contingency or set of contingencies to which my commitment to bring about my chosen end is subject, such as where I resolve to go to the cinema unless my friend calls. However, even in the absence of such explicit conditions, intentions will usually, perhaps always, be limited in their scope in so far as there are contingencies to which they do not extend, for the simple reason that there will be material eventualities or factors which I have not considered and cannot meaningfully be said to have provided for when forming my proposal. In respect of such contingencies there is simply a gap in my intentions. So, even where the terms in which I express my intention to myself and to others appear absolute and unconditional—as where I would simply say 'I am going to the cinema'—my intention is (at the very least) unlikely to be an intention to do this in all events.

Given this, whenever I form an intention to X, there remains a question as to whether this intention extends to a relevant contingency, C.[13] To this question there are three possible answers:

---

[13] I should say what I mean by relevant contingencies. This may also answer a possible challenge to the account of intentions and conditions which I present here. I shall set out the challenge first. If, as I claim, intentions are conditional even where the agent does not consciously formulate or explicitly attach limits to their application wherever he fails to provide for a particular contingency, does this not reduce intentions to vanishing point? After all, there are infinite contingencies which in no sense do I factor into my proposal. So, when planning to go to the cinema, I give no thought to the possibility of Dan calling and what I intend in that event. But nor do I give any thought to the question of what Dan is having for lunch today, or what the Bishop of Ely is having for lunch today, or yesterday, or five years ago, etc. If my intentions are not only silent but absent on all such issues, then the actual content of my intentions recedes to almost nothing. But that is not all. If what Dan (or the Bishop of Ely or anyone else) has for lunch today (or any other day) is a contingency to which my intention is or could be subject, then it follows that I have no intention to go to the cinema in the event of Dan having, say, a croque-monsieur for lunch as this is something which my plan does not provide for. But equally I have no intention to go to the cinema in the event of him *not* having a croque-monsieur for lunch, since again I have not taken this into account. Yet one or other of these contingencies will inevitably apply which then leaves my intention with no scope at all.

One, though I suspect not the only, way around these difficulties is to consider why we

1. Yes, I intend to X (even) if C.
2. No, I do not intend to X if C.
3. I have no intention either to X or not to X if C—in other words, my intention does not provide for contingency C either way.

A final observation before we turn to the question of mistakes: though the focus till now has been the operation of conditions at the stage of intention formation—when I first decide to set myself towards some end and devise a proposal towards its realisation—the content of intentions does not change simply by their being put into action. Although agents can change their minds and intentions can be revoked or amended, it would be wrong to think of intentions as essentially interim or (temporally) provisional plans up until the time comes for their implementation, at which point they become fixed—as if every agent before every intended action resembles an uncertain parachutist who must decide whether to take the leap. In no meaningful sense are most actions immediately preceded by a final decision to commit. Rather, typically, we just go ahead and act according to the pre-existing plan.

This is no different for intentions which are explicitly conditional. If my intentions were explicitly conditional or otherwise limited in their scope when I first formed them, then, unless I reopen my earlier decision and revise my intentions accordingly, they will remain so when I later act on them. If I have a conditional intention to walk to the cinema, it does not mean I am undecided. On the contrary, it means that I *have* decided to walk to the cinema so long as certain facts obtain. So, conditional intentions are, by their nature, no less firm and are no more requiring of pre-implementation revision or supplement than intentions which are, at least explicitly, unconditional.[14] Of course, it would sound odd for me to

---

form (explicitly) conditional intentions. Our intentions are driven and determined by our reasons for action. I form the intention to go to the cinema because I want, say, to relax or to take my mind off things and I believe that watching a film will achieve this. Conditions I attach to this proposed course of action will similarly be determined by my reasons for action, whether they are connected to the desirability of my chosen end or the availability of that end or my chosen means to that end. So, my intention to go to the cinema *unless Dan calls* reflects the fact that though I desire to watch a film, my preference would be to have a drink with Dan, whilst acknowledging that the latter option may not be available. The contingency of Dan calling connects to and affects my reasons for going to cinema. This is not true of the question of what Dan has for lunch. Hence for me to intend to go to the cinema *unless Dan has a croque-monsieur for lunch*, would be not simply unlikely but incoherent. Most contingencies not only do not but *cannot* have an impact on the substance of my intentions. Where this is the case, we should not think that there is a gap where an agent's intentions make no provision for their occurrence. For further discussion of the sorts of contingencies which can form the basis of a conditional intention see D Davidson, *Essays on Actions and Events*, 2nd edn (Oxford, Clarendon Press, 2001) 92–95; C Moya, *The Philosophy of Action—An Introduction* (Cambridge, Polity Press, 1990) 154–57.

[14] See further J Cartwright, 'Conditional Intention' (1990) 60 *Philosophical Studies* 233; J Finnis, 'On Conditional Intentions and Preparatory Intentions' in L Gormally (ed), *Moral*

say, as I am strolling down the street in glorious sunshine, that I (still) have no intention of walking to the cinema in the rain. That contingency simply never arose. Nonetheless it remains true that my walking to the cinema was and is conditional on it not raining, and hence my intention did not and does not extend to walking in the rain.

D. MISTAKES

How does this all relate to mistakes and unjust enrichment? Let us move away from cinema trips and consider what tends to be treated as the central case of liability in unjust enrichment: the mistaken payment.

Say I believe I owe you £100. Because it is important for me to meet my liabilities, I resolve to pay you this sum. I therefore decide that I shall go to the bank, take out £100 in cash and then hand this over to you in person. I do all this. I later discover that in fact I was under no such liability—I made a mistake.

Now, it is plainly true that when I handed you the £100, I had a, very real, intention to transfer legal title to that money to you. To this extent, Swadling is clearly right. However, as we have seen, it does not follow that my intention was that you should have the money in all events, and, in particular, that it extended to the contingency of the money not being due.

My proposal to pay you was directed towards the end of discharging the liability I believed I was under. My paying you was a means to that end. Hence it is clear that my intention to pay you was conditional on my owing you that money. Indeed, here the conditionality and so the limit of my intent to pay you is even clearer than in the case of my intent to go to the cinema. There is no incompatibility between my plan of going to the cinema and my friend suggesting a drink instead—the *offer* of the drink does not make going to the cinema impossible or unachievable. It just so happens that I would have resolved to abandon my plan of going to the cinema in favour of going for the drink if offered. By contrast, my not owing you the money is flatly inconsistent with my desired end of discharging my debt to you. I cannot achieve that end unless that debt is in fact due. Hence my intent to pay you—given that this is simply one element of my broader intention of discharging my (perceived) liability—is necessarily conditional on my actually owing you the money. So, even if I do not accompany my handing over the money to you with a running monologue saying 'I am paying you only because I believe this money is due'—and so even if the possibility that this money is not due *has never crossed my mind*—it is clear that, right there and then, my intention to pay you only extends to the

---

Truth and Moral Tradition: Essays in Honour of Peter Geach and Elizabeth Anscombe (Dublin, Four Courts Press, 1994) 163.

situation where that money is due. In the event that I do not owe you that money, my intention to pay runs out.

Though one way I can bring out my mistake and call for relief is to say 'Had I known the truth, I wouldn't have paid you', my claim does not depend on any such appeal to hindsight or some imagined parallel universe where I keep better tabs on to whom I owe what. I am not saying that I have changed my mind. Rather I am appealing to the reality of my intentions, my state of mind, at the very time I made the payment and can say, genuinely, this is not what I intended. So, when resolving to pay you that money, it would not have been impossible for me to have formed the intention that you should have that money even in the event that the money is not due. In this situation my intention would be of the form 'I intend X [to pay you £100] (even) if C [the money is not owing].' But clearly this is not what most mistaken payers intend. And if we ask whether an intention to pay off a (perceived) debt with no thought given to the possibility of the money not owing is equivalent to this, again the answer is clearly 'no'. They are plainly different intentions, different states of mind. Now, the question is whether anything changes when I put my intentions into effect and actually hand you the money. Here too the answer must be 'no'. At the point of handing over the money, I do not suddenly revise my previous intention and resolve that you should have the money even if it turns out not to be due. I simply act on my original intentions as they apply to the facts as I, wrongly, believe them to be

Importantly, my claim that I had no applicable intention to pay you in no way denies or contradicts the clear fact that, when I handed over the money, it was indeed with an intention to pay you. There is no contradiction here because there is no contradiction between intending to pay you money I owe and not intending to pay you money I do not owe. The positive intention and 'negative' (or really absence of) intention cover different ground.

Of course, the same analysis extends outside liability mistakes. Provided I can point to some relevant factor which I misunderstood or overlooked when resolving to transfer the asset to you, I can say that my intention to make that transfer does not and never did extend to these conditions.[15] We

---

[15] One question this analysis raises is why we require a claimant to show that he would not have made the transfer but for his mistake. In other words, if we can establish that the claimant was mistaken and hence that his intention to transfer the asset to the defendant did not extend to the situation in which the relevant facts were not as the claimant assumed, why do we need to go further to justify recovery? Why isn't it enough for the claimant to show that his intentions simply did not provide, one way or the other, for the possibility that the facts were other than he believed them to be, and hence that he never had an intention to make the transfer in these circumstances? (Cf the example described earlier when I simply do not consider, and so do not factor in, the possibility of my friend suggesting a drink when I form my proposal of going to the cinema.) I think the answer to this is that, while a mistaken claimant can indeed establish that he lacked an applicable intention to make the transfer without going

can also now see that the significance of mistakes is not that they reveal the claimant's reasoning and choices to be faulty or in some way defective, but that they mark out contingencies to which the claimant's intentions do not extend. Indeed, to say that the claimant's intention when making the transfer was defective is, I think, strictly inaccurate. A truer description would be simply to say that there was no *applicable* intention at all, for whatever intention the claimant *did* have was conditional upon a state of affairs which did not obtain. So, what is defective is my understanding of my circumstances or some part of the world, and this misunderstanding is significant only in so far as it provides a basis for identifying a contingency to which my intentions did not extend.

This also suggests that we should not worry ourselves too much about being able to offer a precise definition of what 'counts' as a mistake or even what particular mistake the claimant was labouring under in a particular case.[16] What matters is that it can be shown—whether through proof of a causative mistake or otherwise—that he had no intent to make the transfer in the relevant circumstances. Take a case like *Nurdin & Peacock plc v DB Ramsden & Co Ltd*.[17] Nurdin made ten overpayments of rent to its landlord, Ramsden. The first five overpayments resulted from Nurdin having overlooked the fact that the rent had fallen to a lower sum and, therefore, having failed to notify its accounts department of the revised rent. By the time of the sixth overpayment, Nurdin had realised that it was most likely paying more than it in fact owed. However, Nurdin had received legal advice to the effect that it would be safer to continue paying the higher sum until the matter was resolved and that any overpayment would in any case be recoverable. It, therefore, made its sixth overpayment. Nurdin commenced legal proceedings, seeking a return of the overpayments or a set off against future rent payments. While these proceedings were ongoing, Nurdin made a further four overpayments, but only after having written to Ramsden stating that 'obviously the [further] overpayment will be refundable if [Nurdin] is successful at trial'. Ramsden's solicitors wrote back saying that Nurdin's comments as to these further payments had been 'noted'.

Neuberger J held that Nurdin made the first five overpayments under a mistake of fact—its failure to note that the rent had fallen for review prior

---

on to show that he would not have made the transfer but for this mistake, unless he can *also* show that a correct understanding of the fact would have made a difference to the decision he would have reached, he cannot establish any injustice or hardship sufficient to justify the law insisting on a reversal of that transfer.

[16] Or rather this should not matter in principle. I accept that while, for example, limitation statutes make reference to claims based on mistakes, correctly identifying mistakes remains important. The implication of the argument I am making here, however, is that—at least in relation to claims to reverse transfers—we should not have rules (of liability or limitation) which treat mistakes differently to other situations in which the claimant's intention to transfer is absent.

[17] [1999] 1 WLR 1249.

to the first overpayment and the subsequent failure to ensure that its accounts department was instructed to pay at a lower rate. This could not be said of the last five payments, however, since, by then, Nurdin strongly suspected, at the very least, that it had been overpaying Ramsden. Hence it was impossible to say that the later payments were made under the same mistake of fact for the simple reason that Nurdin was no longer, in that respect, mistaken. Nonetheless, Nurdin was able to recover the final four overpayments on the basis that Ramsden, through the letter from its solicitors, had agreed to repay the money if it later turned out not to have been due. The sixth payment was the most problematic. Nurdin could not rely on its earlier mistake of fact since it now knew (or strongly suspected) the truth, nor could it recover on the basis of an agreement to repay since it was only after this payment that Nurdin informed Ramsden that it expected any further overpayments to be refunded. Neuberger J held, however, that Nurdin could recover here too, this time on the basis that it paid under a mistake of law. Nurdin had believed that if it made the sixth payment it would be able to recover the overpayment if it turned out not to have been due. In fact, since it was now no longer mistaken as to its liability to pay, and hence could not recover the sum on that (or any other) basis, this was a mistake of law—a mistake as to the law as to the recoverability of payments known or suspected not to be due. With the mistake of law bar having recently been removed,[18] this mistake was sufficient to ground recovery, notwithstanding the 'logical paradox' that allowing recovery then refuted the premiss that Nurdin's belief as to the recoverability of the overpayment was actually mistaken.

So, in the end, all ten overpayments were held to be recoverable. This result is, I think, plainly correct. But getting there was a lot more difficult than it should have been. It is clear that at no time did Nurdin ever intend anything other than to pay Ramsden the money it owed. In other words, Nurdin never had any intention of paying Ramsden anything more than the money properly due under the lease. That was clear before it learnt that it had in fact been overpaying Ramsden, it was even clearer later on. Hence it should not have been necessary to construct an undertaking on Ramsden's part to repay the final four overpayments or to get tangled up in a self-refuting mistake of law to justify recovery. So, though I am not saying that Nurdin remained mistaken as to the extent of its liability even after it learned that the lower rent was due, I would argue that recovery of all ten payments is plainly justified and, in all cases, for the same reason: Nurdin's (real) lack of intention to pay anything more than the sum it owed. Or to put the same point another way, Nurdin's intention to pay the additional sum was conditional on that sum being properly owing and so did not extend to the situation in which it was not due.

---

[18] In *Kleinwort Benson Ltd v Lincoln City Council* [1999] 2 AC 349.

The upshot of this is that mistakes are important for what they tell us about the claimant's intention when making the transfer—that it did not extend to the relevant contingency and so was, in the circumstances, absent. But then what is important and what actually justifies recovery is not that the claimant was mistaken but the fact that he had no applicable intention to transfer the asset to the defendant. Establishing a mistake is just a means to that end. But, as cases like *Nurdin* show, that end can also be established—indeed more clearly established—in other ways and even where we cannot say that the claimant was mistaken.

Another example is provided by cases of ignorance, that is, cases where the claimant is entirely unaware that the asset to which he is entitled is being transferred to (or taken by) the defendant. A number of unjust enrichment lawyers have argued that these cases are not just analogous to but a fortiori of mistaken transfers, since here the claimant can say that any intention to transfer that asset on their part was wholly absent rather than merely defective or vitiated. In fact, on the argument made here, we can see ignorance and mistake as being even more closely connected, since in *both* cases there is no applicable intention to make the transfer. Of course, where the claimant is mistaken, 'alongside' his lack of intention to make the transfer on the facts as they stand is a positive intention to make a transfer if events had been different. But in such cases, *on the facts as they stand*, the claimant no more intends the transfer than if the asset had been taken from him without his knowledge.[19] So, while it may well be that English law deals with cases of ignorance differently to cases of mistake,

---

[19] My claim here is that no material difference between these two cases exists in respect of the claimant's intent to pay the defendant. I am not suggesting that we cannot identify other (potentially) material differences between cases of mistake and ignorance. For instance, in the case of a mistaken transfer the claimant bears a responsibility for the transfer which he does not, at least typically, in cases of ignorance. Although this is insufficient reason for denying a claim (see eg *Kelly v Solari* (1841) 9 M & W 54, 152 ER 24), it may be relevant, for example, to determining who, as between claimant and defendant, should bear any losses resulting from the transfer; cf *Dextra Bank & Trust Co Ltd v Bank of Jamaica* [2002] 1 All ER (Comm) 193 (PC). This also allows us to see why conditional intentions have a different significance in the law of restitution than they do in the criminal law, and so answers another possible challenge to the account I have set out here. The challenge: if, as I claim, the significance of mistakes is that they identify contingencies to which my intent to X (go to the cinema, pay you £100) does not extend, then why is it not a defence to a defendant charged with murder that he killed the victim mistakenly thinking that the victim was, say, carrying lots of money? Can't that defendant also say his intention to kill the victim did not extend to the situation where the victim was in fact penniless? In the context of payments and other property transfers, we are concerned with establishing an claimant's intentions so that (all things being equal) they can be given effect. So we are right to ask whether the claimant's intentions extended to the situation at hand, since we want to know whether upholding the transfer would implement or defeat his intentions. By contrast, in the criminal law we inquire into intentions not so as to give them effect but in order to establish responsibility for harm. A defendant who kills in pursuance of a plan to kill a man and take his money has and seeks to implement an intention to kill. This establishes his responsibility for the killing, notwithstanding that he can truly say that it was never his intention to kill someone penniless. The fact that made a choice to kill and then did kill is enough.

any suggestion that there is not a factual and legal 'problem' of ignorant transfers which is analogous to the 'problem' of mistaken transfers is, I think, plainly false.[20] And, to the extent that these two sorts of problems are fundamentally, materially alike, the law *should* deal with them in the same way.

E. RESULTING TRUSTS AND MISTAKEN TRANSFERS

The short answer to Swadling's objection therefore is that there is no incoherence or inconsistency in arguing that resulting trusts arise in the event of non-beneficial transfers and that this then supports the imposition of such a trust in cases of mistaken transfers. Mistaken payers *do* intend to benefit the defendants they pay. But these intentions only go so far and the circumstances as to which the claimant is mistaken identify one contingency to which his intention does not extend.

I think this understanding of the effects and significance of mistakes also sheds light on the basis of claims arising from mistaken transfers and the role resulting trusts might play in their reversal. The first point is the most important: when I pay you, mistakenly thinking the money is due, it is not simply my intention to *benefit* you which is contingent and so, in present circumstances, absent, but my intention to *pass title*. It is my intention to pay you—to pass title to the money to you—which I am saying is conditional and which does not extend to the situation where the money is not owing. So, to describe the issue as one of unjust *enrichment* is in a sense inaccurate, in that it implies that the injustice relates to a question of abstract enrichment or benefit rather than the specific question of entitlement to the asset transferred from claimant to defendant.

Of course, it is true that in the majority of mistaken transfers legal title is held to pass to the defendant in spite of the claimant's mistake and recovery is limited to the asset's monetary value. This makes it look like we are concerned with reversing a transfer of (abstract) value rather than the transfer of (title to) a particular asset. But whatever reasons there may be for prioritising this form of response, this cannot be justified by reference to the claimant's intentions or the nature and implications of his mistake. In the cases we are dealing with here there exists no intention to benefit the defendant which is separate to or separable from the claimant's intention to pass title and which we can view as defective or absent in a way that his intention to pass title is not.[21] So, though it is the claimant's mistake which

---

[20] Cf W Swadling, 'Ignorance and Unjust Enrichment: The Problem of Title' (2008) 28 *Oxford Journal of Legal Studies* 627.
[21] See C Webb, 'Property, Unjust Enrichment, and Defective Transfers' in R Chambers, C Mitchell and J Penner (eds), *Philosophical Foundations of the Law of Unjust Enrichment* (Oxford, Oxford University Press, 2009) 335, 358–59.

grounds his claim, the typical form and scope of such claims fail to reflect the nature of that mistake or the substance of his intentions.

Now, the second key point: we can see now that the imposition of a (resulting) trust over the transferred asset would be more consistent with—and give truer effect to the substance of—the claimant's intentions and the implications of his mistake. It is that asset, and not some abstract quantum of wealth or value, to which the claimant held legal title; it is the transfer of that asset and his title to it which the claimant, given his mistake, did not intend. Although legal title would still be held to pass to the defendant, through the recognition of a trust the claimant would then be entitled to demand both the return of the asset and a revesting of the title he lost.

Now, it does not follow from this alone that imposing a resulting trust over the relevant asset is (always, ever) a justified response to mistaken transfers. The claimant's interest in recovering 'his' asset is not the only interest recognised and protected by the law and there may be competing principles and interests that provide reasons for confining the claimant to a personal claim to its value. Nonetheless, a truer characterisation of the claimant's intentions and of the significance of his mistake—and so a better understanding of the basis of his claim—provides a surer starting point for consideration of how exactly the law should respond to that claim. In particular, it puts the standard arguments made in respect of, and the objections raised to, recognising trusts in cases of mistaken transfers in their proper context.

Take the question of priority in insolvency—or, if you prefer, whether the mistakenly transferred asset should form part of the defendant's estate available for distribution among his creditors in the event of his insolvency.[22] Typically analysis of this issue has centred on the impact such 'priority' would have on the defendant's other creditors. If the claimant is able to claim that the asset is held on trust for him, it removes that asset from the pool available for distribution amongst those other creditors. This at the same time advantages the claimant and disadvantages the defendant's other creditors, which seems at odds with the basic principle underlying much of insolvency law, that of *pari passu* distribution, which holds that, all things being equal, all creditors should bear a proportionate share of the losses resulting from the defendant's insolvency.

Those who have argued for priority to be accorded to claims in respect of misapplied assets have, therefore, sought to show how such claimants

---

[22] Such 'priority' in insolvency is clearly not the only, nor necessarily the most important, consequence or feature of proprietary claims (on which see generally Swadling (n 3) 512–14). However, substantially the same arguments as I make here in respect of insolvency apply or can be extended to justify these other consequences of 'granting' proprietary relief to mistaken transferors, such as claims against remote recipients and entitlement to increases in the asset's value.

may be distinguished from other creditors, so as to justify their exemption from the *pari passu* regime. These attempts have often fallen short. For instance, it has been argued that such claimants deserve priority on the basis that they have not chosen to take the risk of the defendant's insolvency.[23] However, even where true, this can be countered by showing that there are other creditors who likewise cannot be said to have accepted this risk, but who nonetheless fall within the application of the *pari passu* principle.[24] A second argument is that, without such priority, the defendant's other creditors would receive a windfall.[25] This is closer to the mark, but to be convincing requires some explanation as to why the gain which would be made by the other creditors if they were to have access to the asset is better viewed as an undeserved windfall rather than a legitimate and fair reduction of the losses which they would otherwise suffer as a result of the defendant's insolvency.[26]

A better approach requires that we pay closer attention to the basis of claims following mistaken transfers.[27] As I have argued thus far, the significance of the claimant's mistake is that it highlights a contingency to which his intention to transfer the asset does not extend. This enables him to say that, given these circumstances, he lacks an intention not simply to *benefit* the defendant but to *pass title* to the asset to him. Consequently, what the claimant's mistake calls into question is not (just) the abstract gains the defendant has derived from his receipt and use of the asset but the very transfer of that asset and the defendant's entitlement to it.

More broadly, the claimant's intention matters here precisely because, at the point of transfer, it is *his* asset, *his* title. This title means that, so far as it extends, it is for him to determine the disposition of the asset and hence who may receive, use and benefit from it. Unless, therefore, the claimant has given his consent, others are not at liberty to make use of the asset. The insolvency 'priority' accorded by proprietary claims is just one consequence of this: the claimant's asset should not be available to meet the defendant's liabilities. Now this clearly covers situations where the asset is taken from the claimant's possession without his knowledge and so where there is no consent whatsoever to any transfer. But a better understanding of the implications of mistakes shows us how a claimant who has mistakenly trans-

---

[23] See eg G Jones, Note [1980] *Cambridge Law Journal* 275, 276; D Paciocco, 'The Remedial Constructive Trust: A Principled Basis for Priorities over Creditors' (1989) 68 *Canadian Bar Review* 315.

[24] W Swadling, 'Property and Unjust Enrichment' in J Harris (ed), *Property Problems: From Genes to Pension Funds* (London, Kluwer Law International, 1997) 130,142–43; Swadling (n 3) 517 and 525–27.

[25] See eg W Goodhart and G Jones, 'The Infiltration of Equitable Doctrine into English Commercial Law' (1980) 43 *Modern Law Review* 489, 500.

[26] Cf Swadling (n 24) 143; Swadling (n 3) 527.

[27] See generally Webb (n 21).

ferred his asset to the defendant can make the same argument. Whatever consent he did give to the transfer, and hence to his title passing, was contingent upon certain facts being present. In their absence, he has no intention to make the transfer and gives no consent to the asset passing to and being used by the defendant. Now, as before, the claimant should therefore be entitled to recover the asset and his title to it, and the asset should not be made available for the satisfaction of claims of the defendant's creditors.

It is no good to object that cases of ignorance and mistake are not truly analogous on the basis that only in the former does the claimant retain his title to the asset. Plainly, we cannot take the rules on title as a given without begging the very question we are seeking to answer: whether resulting trusts should have a role in reversing mistaken transfers. Moreover, any attempt to argue that the claimant *really did* intend the transfer must provide an account of the operation of mistakes which not only backs this up but which can also explain why we *do* say that the defendant's enrichment is unjust and must be given up. In other words, if we are to claim that the intention *to pass title* is unaffected (or insufficiently affected) by the claimant's mistake—and so the passing of title to the defendant is not open to challenge—then we bear the onus of showing how we can say, at the same time, that that same mistake nonetheless denies or sufficiently impairs the claimant's intention *to benefit* the defendant so as to justify a personal claim to the recovery of that enrichment. Given the indivisibility of these intentions—or, more accurately, given that there are not two intentions here but one[28]—any such argument is, I think, hopeless.[29]

Similarly, any concerns that it is unfair to the defendant's other creditors to let the claimant recover the asset must address the question of why this should be considered unfair *now* given that there would have been no question of it being unfair to deny them access to the asset prior to the mistaken transfer. Once again, we would need to offer an account that could explain why the mistaken transfer makes a difference to our view of the fairness of according such 'priority' which is consistent with both the reality of the claimant's intentions and the imposition of liability *of some*

---

[28] See Webb (n 21) 358–59.
[29] An example: some argue that unjust enrichment claims are rooted in respect for the claimant's autonomy. Now, in itself, this argument is not hopeless, though it is seriously deficient unless and until some attempt is made to identify when and why the claimant's autonomy requires or merits legal protection (as clearly not all of an individual's choices and preferences support a legal entitlement). However, the argument becomes untenable if one is also to take Swadling's view that mistaken payers *do*, straightforwardly and unconditionally, intend to pay (and so to benefit) their payees. If the claimant unquestionably intends to pay—to pass title to and so to benefit—the defendant, his autonomy is protected by giving effect to the transfer and seeing that it is upheld. Any claim to recover the asset or the enrichment it generates would defeat this intention and so denies rather than respects the claimant's autonomy when making that transfer.

kind on the defendant in respect of his receipt of the asset. Again, I think the search for such an account will be in vain.

F. CONCLUSION

Justifying claims in respect of mistaken transfers requires that we can say why the basic facts of (1) a transfer of an asset from claimant to defendant and (2) a mistaken belief held by the claimant without which he would not have made the transfer give us reason to impose liability on the defendant. The same goes if we want to know not only why there is liability but what precise form or measure this liability should take. To do this, we need, I think, a clearer understanding of the significance of mistakes and what they tell us about the claimant's intentions when making the transfer. This is what I have sought to do in the first half of this chapter.

Two important points emerge. The first is that mistakes are significant in that they demonstrate that the claimant's intention to make the transfer is conditional or contingent, in the sense that there are situations or circumstances to which it does not extend. In such circumstances, the claimant can say, genuinely, that he has no intention to make the transfer. The second is that the claimant's mistake denies not simply his intention to benefit the defendant but his very intention to make the transfer and hence to pass title to him. Indeed, in such cases, there is no intention to benefit which is separate to or separable from the claimant's broader intention to pass title. Armed with a clearer understanding of mistakes and their significance, we can not only deal with Swadling's specific objection—that we cannot explain claims arising out of mistaken transfers on the basis that the claimant has no intent to benefit the defendant—but we are better positioned to see the merits of the claim that recipients of mistakenly transferred assets should hold them on trust for their transferors.

The arguments I have offered here only go so far. As I noted earlier, though recognising trusts here would better protect the claimant's interest in determining the disposition of his assets—the interest which, I suggest, justifies his claim and to which that claim seeks to give effect—there may be other principles and interests equally deserving of the law's attention which justify limiting the claimant to some other, lesser form or measure of recovery. I have not addressed this question save to note that such arguments will not be found in the potential 'unfairness' to the defendant's other creditors, and by implication remote recipients, of according the claimant proprietary relief. Nor have I addressed the question of defences, in particular how, if at all, change of position operates here and whether it should exist alongside or in place of the rule protecting bona fide purchasers. There are also important points to make about the operation of these principles in cases where the mistaken or conditional transfer is made in fulfilment of a contractual obligation owed to the defendant or some third party. I leave these all for another time. For now it is enough to note that consideration of the principles and interests which operate to deny or restrict claims arising out of mistaken and other defective transfers is premature until we have a better understanding of why such claims are or may be justified in the first place.

12
Locus Poenitentiae: Repentance, Withdrawal and Luck

IRIT SAMET

A. LEGAL BACKGROUND

1. Introduction

The parties in *Tinsley v Milligan*[1] were a lesbian couple, Stella Tinsley and Kathleen Milligan. In 1986 they decided to buy a house together, but the property was put into Tinsley's sole name. Although it was clear from the start that ownership of the property was to be shared, they wanted to hide this fact from the world. This would enable Milligan to continue claiming social security benefits to which she would lose her entitlement once she became the (part-)owner of a house. In 1988, Milligan went to the Department of Social Security (DSS) and confessed that she had made false benefit claims over the previous two years. The authorities apparently 'did not regard the situation with any alarm'.[2] Afterwards the couple fell out, and Milligan was left with nothing but an oral agreement with Tinsley that ownership of the property should be shared—not a cheerful position to be in, unless she could show (by evidence or presumption) that Tinsley held the property on resulting trust for both of them.

Leaving the court's actual decision in the case to one side, the facts of *Tinsley* illustrate some of the issues that can arise when property is transferred between the parties to an illegal scheme. If the court held that Milligan had an equitable proprietary interest in the house, then this would

---

*I am grateful to William Edmundson, Timothy Macklem, Ben McFarlane, Charles Mitchell, Jeremy Waldron and Lorenzo Zucca; also to the other participants at the Conference on Analytic Legal Philosophy held at King's College London in May 2009, at which a draft of this chapter was discussed.

[1] [1994] 1 AC 340.
[2] Ibid, 353 (Lord Goff).

have amounted to condoning the parties' conspiracy. But if it refused to help her, then Tinsley, who was equally implicated in the benefit fraud, would have got the whole house. Should it have been a relevant consideration that Milligan repented of her own free will? Should it have mattered if instead she confessed her fraud because of fear, rather than guilt over her wrongdoing? What difference might it have made if the women had won the lottery before any benefits were claimed, so that they never needed to carry through their plan to defraud the DSS? The aim of this chapter is to offer a theoretical framework within which questions of this kind can be answered in a systematic and informed way.

2. Illegal Agreements

The parties to an illegal contract clearly cannot expect the courts to enforce their contract for them,[3] but it is less clear whether the courts will correct any injustice that ensues from the contract's invalidity. As levels of state regulation grow, so too do the chances that a contract will be tainted with illegality, and so too does the need for the courts to work out a proper response to situations where the parties enter such contracts. The problem with which this chapter is concerned derives from the convergence of two well-established rules in English law: (1) ownership in property can pass under an illegal contract;[4] and (2) the courts will leave the parties to illegal contracts to their own devices and will not reverse property transfers between them even where the basis for the transfer has failed—for example, when the agreed consideration for the property has not been paid. The latter rule can produce injustice, since it can prevent the transferor from recovering her property from a recipient who was equally guilty of planning to break the law.[5] In such cases the courts often say that the policy of the rule rendering the contract illegal outweighs the need to do justice between the parties.[6] Nevertheless allowing the recipient to profit from her wrongdoing is most unpalatable.

---

[3] At least when the illegality is not negligible. Similar rules can be found in other common law jurisdictions, in Roman law and in the European systems which follow it.

[4] *Singh v Ali* [1960] AC 167, 177: 'The parties to the fraud are, of course, liable to be punished for the part they played in the illegal transaction, but nevertheless the property passes to the transferee.' However, if it is illegal for the transferee to be in possession of the property, then title will not pass; cf *Costello v Chief Constable of Derbyshire Constabulary* [2001] EWCA Civ 381, [2001] 1 WLR 143.

[5] If the recipient is convicted in a criminal trial for performing his part of the contract, the property may be confiscated in accordance with the Proceeds of Crime Act 2002, s 6(4)(c). S 240 of the same Act introduces the possibility of civil confiscation that can be imposed even in cases where no criminal proceedings take place. However, it is likely that the majority of the cases to which the illegality rule applies will be insufficiently serious to merit the procedure: Law Commission, *The Illegality Defence: A Consultative Report* (LCCP No 189, 2008) 166.

[6] Cf *Holman v Johnson* (1775) 1 Cowp 341, 343; 98 ER 1120, 1122 (Lord Mansfield); *Tinsley* (n 1) 72 (Lord Browne-Wilkinson).

Two ways of dealing with the general rule against recovery have emerged in English legal discourse. The first is essentially technical—the *Bowmaker* test,[7] which was thought by the majority of the court to underpin earlier authorities on the issue,[8] allows the transferor to reclaim the property, provided that her claim can be established without relying on evidence of the parties' illegality. This test produces formalistic and arbitrary distinctions between cases with essentially identical facts. Moreover, to escape from the injustices produced by the *Bowmaker* rule, the courts have sometimes felt compelled to bend and distort neighbouring doctrines, as in the leading case on the topic of repentance, *Tribe v Tribe*.[9] As we shall see, the *Bowmaker* rule and the presumption of advancement converged to produce a clear injustice in *Tribe*, to avoid which the court adopted a crude interpretation of the *locus poenitentiae* doctrine.

A second way of dealing with the injustice of the general rule against recovery, suggested by the Law Commission, is to give the courts discretion whether to enforce illegal contracts or award remedies to the parties. The Law Commission wrote:[10]

> We consider that the best way of overcoming this injustice is to replace the present strict rule with a discretionary approach under which the courts would be able to take into account such relevant issues as the seriousness of the illegality involved, whether the plaintiff was aware of the illegality and the purpose of the rule which renders the contract illegal.

The Commission'a final recommendation was that 'only when depriving the claimant of his or her rights is a proportionate response based on the relevant illegality policies, should the defence succeed'.[11] In other words,

---

[7] *Bowmakers Ltd v Barnet Instruments Ltd* [1945] KB 65 (CA). Although *Bowmakers* concerned a common law claim for conversion, the same principles have also been applied in equity. See *Tinsley* (n 1) 371 (Lord Browne-Wilkinson): 'English law has one single law of property made up of legal and equitable interests. . . . If the law is that a party is entitled to enforce a property right acquired under an illegal transaction, in my judgment the same rule ought to apply to any property right so acquired, whether such right is legal or equitable.'

[8] Probably mistakenly: M Halliwell, 'Equitable Property Rights, Discretionary Remedies, and Unclean Hands' [2004] *Conveyancer and Property Lawyer* 439, 444.

[9] [1996] Ch 107 (CA).

[10] Law Commission, *Illegal Transactions: The Effect of Illegality on Contracts and Trusts* (LCCP No 154, 1999) 91. See too LCCP No 189 (n 5) 148, which concludes that, except in the case of trusts, such a discretionary approach can be developed even without legislative intervention. For a comparison with law reform proposals in New Zealand, Canada and Australia, see RA Buckley, 'Illegal Transactions: Chaos or Discretion?' (2000) 20 *Legal Studies* 155. See also the Israeli Contracts (General Part) Law (1973) which confers discretionary power on the court (under s 31) while prescribing (under s 21) that as a general rule 'each party shall restore to the other party what he has received under the contract or . . . pay him the value'.

[11] Ibid, s 3.142. In distinction to the open-ended 'public policy test' developed by the Court of Appeal in *Tinsley v Milligan* [1992] Ch 310, the Law Commission has called for a structured discretion. For the operation of a wide discretion in Australia, see *Nelson v Nelson* (1995) 132 ALR 133 (HCA).

one of the reasons for developing a flexible approach is to avoid the harsh results that would flow from refusing to enforce contracts in cases of trivial illegality. With this in mind, the following account will only discuss agreements which are aimed at a substantially illegal purpose, of a kind that a court could justifiably refuse to enforce. The parties whose position is considered are those, like Milligan, who intended to engage in serious illegality.

3. The Denial of Recovery Justified

If A gratuitously transfers her property to B where no gift is intended, or where the basis for the transfer later fails, the court will normally help A to recover the property. This rule echoes our most basic intuitions about the reversal of unjust enrichment. Why, then, does the fact that A and B enter an illegal agreement justify a departure from this fundamental principle of justice? Why should the fact that the two women in *Tinsley* intended to cheat the social security authorities affect their proprietary rights against one another?

Two very different considerations support the view that recovery should be denied on the ground of illegality: the first is that claimants who disregard the law when it suits them should not be entitled to the law's help once they run into trouble; the second is that allowing recovery will encourage other people who contemplate entering, or who are already parties to, an illegal agreement. These considerations should also determine the extent to which the *locus poenitentiae* rule is invoked to mitigate the harshness of the rule against recovery. But to gain a better understanding of this doctrine, we should start by considering the reasons for the general rule against recovery, in the absence of special circumstances such as mistake, power gaps between the parties or, indeed, repentance.

First, though, a word of caution is needed. Historically, English law has responded in two different ways to claims for the recovery of gratuitously transferred property where no gift was intended: by recognising a resulting trust in equity and by ordering restitution at common law.[12] In principle, however, the issues presented by illegality and repentance should be treated in the same way in both classes of case, since both reflect the same basic consideration, namely that if you do not intend to transfer property gratuitously, then you should get it back.[13] Hence, while the discussion which

---

[12] The question whether resulting trusts are established on the basis of a negative intention not to make a gift, or on a positive intention to create a trust is beyond the scope of this paper, but for examples of these two opposing views, see R Chambers, *Resulting Trusts* (Oxford, Clarendon Press, 1997) and W Swadling, 'Explaining Resulting Trusts' (2008) 124 *Law Quarterly Review* 72; and for general discussion see ch 8 above.

[13] Although it is unclear whether illegality is an independent head of restitution, or just a defence to claims which are based on other unjust factors: AS Burrows, *The Law of Restitution* (London, Butterworths, 2002) 425; P Birks, *An Introduction to the Law of Restitution*

follows takes place within the conceptual and terminological framework of equity, the arguments should apply mutatis mutandis to repentance as a ground for restitution at common law.

Let us look, then, at the reasons that have been offered for withholding recovery in cases where the claimant has engaged in an illegal transaction. The idea that a claimant's behaviour can disentitle him to the court's assistance has long historical roots in English law. The maxim of Equity which prescribes that 'he who comes to equity must come with clean hands' can be traced back to the early seventeenth century.[14] The common law, for its part, adopted the Roman law maxim that *ex turpi causa non oritur actio* (no action arises from a tainted cause). Right from the start these rules were expressed in the language of uncleanliness and impurity. Thus, we find Lord Wilmot CJ refusing to hear the claim of a party to an illegal contract on the ground that 'no polluted hand shall touch the pure fountains of justice'.[15] In a similar vein we find the New York State Supreme Court talking of the 'unworthiness of the plaintiff to approach the altar of justice', Lord Mansfield's reference to the 'pure fountains' from which the plaintiff must draw his remedy, and Luxmoore LJ's quotation of Virgil's line, '*procul este profani*' ('begone ye uninitiated').[16] From the law's point of view, compliance with legal obligations is a moral duty, and so illegal activity can be frowned upon as an immorality.[17] But if such statements are meant to convey the court's moral abhorrence of illegality, why is this abhorrence expressed in the amoral language of uncleanliness and defilement? One essential feature of these primordial categories may hint at the answer: unlike moral fault, impurity is contagious—it can contaminate *others* through contact.[18] Perhaps, then, these statements express the courts' concern that by adjudicating on a dispute between the parties to illegal dealings, they might themselves become tainted with the parties' immorality. Perhaps, too, this explains why the courts raise the issue of illegality of their own initiative, even if none of the parties use it in their arguments.

(Oxford, Clarendon Press, 1989) 299–303 and 424–32, and his amended view in P Birks, 'Recovering Value Transferred Under an Illegal Contract' (2000) 1 *Theoretical Inquiries in Law* 155, 191.

[14] For an abridged history of the maxim, see Halliwell (n 8) 441–44. Another closely related maxim prescribes that 'he who seeks equity must do equity'. On the relationship between the two maxims, see PH Pettit, 'He Who Comes to Equity Must Come with Clean Hands' [1990] *Conveyancer and Property Lawyer* 416, 418.

[15] *Collins v Blantern* (1767) 2 Wils KB 347, 350; 95 ER 850, 852. This statement was later cited in a long line of cases: JW Wade, 'Benefits Obtained under Illegal Transactions–Reasons For and Against Allowing Restitution' (1946) 25 *Texas Law Review* 31, 38.

[16] *Meech v Stoner* 19 NY 26, 28 (1859); *Lowry v Bourdieu* (1780) 2 Doug 468, 470; 99 ER 299, 301; *Parker v Mason* [1940] 2 KB 590 (CA) 602.

[17] J Raz, *The Authority of Law* (Oxford, Oxford University Press, 1979) chs 1 and 2; J Finnis, *Natural Law and Natural Rights* (Oxford, Clarendon Press, 1980) chs 1 and 11.

[18] P Ricoeur and E Buchanan, *The Symbolism of Evil* (Boston, MA, Beacon Press, 1969) 25–40.

Following a careful examination of the clean hands maxim, Murphy J in the US Supreme Court found that:

> It is a self-imposed ordinance that closes the doors of a court of equity to one tainted with inequitableness or bad faith relative to the matter in which he seeks relief, however improper may have been the behaviour of the defendant. That doctrine is rooted in the historical concept of a court as a vehicle for affirmatively enforcing the requirements of conscience and good faith.[19]

Murphy J's criteria of 'conscience' and 'good faith' may well make more sense than the language of 'purity' and 'cleanliness' because a substantial body of equitable doctrine now exists which uses 'unconscionability' as the courts' yardstick for the parties' conduct in various contexts. The way in which the metaphors of purity and defilement might be interpreted by a court is mysterious. But concepts such as 'conscience' are more helpful because they simply require the court to apply moral categories to the case at hand, to decide whether particular conduct is legally acceptable.[20] Thus, it can be said that a claimant who relies on the *locus poenitentiae* rule must not have acted so unconscionably as to make her unworthy to appear before the court. And that seems just right. A robber who is cheated by her accomplice when it comes to the distribution of the loot should not qualify for the court's assistance; nor should a person who pays for child pornography and does not get the merchandise. While other considerations may sometimes outweigh the consideration that a claimant has behaved unconscionably, this fact will always be most relevant to the question whether recovery should be allowed.[21]

---

[19] *Precision Instrument Manufacturing Co v Automotive Maintenace Machinery* Co 324 US 806, 814 (1945). For a discussion in terms of the court's 'dignity' and 'integrity', see LCCP No 189 (n 5) 14ff. This language is no more precise than the historical language of 'purity'.

[20] In England, 'conscience' is undergoing a renaissance as a key concept in the resolution of cases argued in Equity: eg *Gillett v Holt* [2000] EWCA Civ 66, [2001] Ch 210; *Oxley v Hiscock* [2004] EWCA Civ 546, [2005] Fam 211. For supporting commentary, see N Hopkins, 'Conscience, Discretion and the Creation of Property Rights' (2006) 26 *Legal Studies* 475. In Australia, the courts have always been inclined to interpret the category of conscience as a wide ethical principle: eg *Commercial Bank of Australia v Amadio* (1983) 151 CLR 447. For appraisals of 'conscience' as a device for injecting moral norms and standards into the courts' appraisal of relationships, see M Halliwell, *Equity and Good Conscience in Contemporary Context* (London, Old Bailey Press, 1997); M Macnair, 'Equity and Conscience' (2007) 27 *Oxford Journal of Legal Studies* 659.

[21] Cf Birks (2000) (n 13) 162: 'revulsion from turpitude . . . can be ignored in almost all cases of illegality'. Instead of analysisng them in terms of a search for innocence, Birks tries to interpret the cases on illegality as answering a completely different question, namely whether allowing restitution will make nonsense of the law's refusal to allow action on the contract itself: ibid, 173. However, his analysis of the *locus poenitentiae* cases is based on the distinction between claimants who went through a 'change of heart' and those who did not. As we shall see, the differences between what he calls 'genuine withdrawal' and abandonment that is forced by the retraction of the accomplice indeed implies different deterrence considerations. But the essential distinction between such claimants lies in their level of innocence. The 'evaluation of the parties' conduct and deserts' cannot be avoided as Birks wishes, for it forms the basis for all of the behaviour-directing factors that he identifies as determinative.

B. REPENTANCE

As for the wickedness of the wicked, he shall not fall thereby in the day that he turneth from his wickedness; . . . None of his sins that he hath committed shall be mentioned unto him: he hath done that which is lawful and right; he shall surely live.[22]

The idea that repentance can restore the moral status of offenders is fundamental to the way that humans stand before God in the Jewish and Christian traditions. Maimonides writes in his *Law of Repentance*: 'Nothing undermines the opportunity to repent . . . All evil, criminals, apostates and the like, who repent are accepted [back].'[23] The *locus poenitentiae* doctrine is not so generous. The basic case in which the doctrine operates is clear and well established: a claimant who transfers property under an illegal contract can recover the property if she *freely* abandons the contract *before* any part of her illegal purpose has been carried out. So, unlike repentance in the religious and moral contexts, the *locus poenitentiae* rule enables the claimant to retrieve her property only if she pulls out in time, that is, before any violation of the law has taken place. Repentance is therefore possible only in relation to the act of entering an agreement with an illegal purpose in mind, and not with regard to committing the offence itself. On the other hand, as we shall see, the law is more relaxed about the claimant's motive for repudiating the illegal contract, since it does not require that complete change of heart which characterises religious or moral repentance.

The difference between what is required of a moral or religious repentance, and what is needed for a claimant to take advantage of the *locus poenitentiae* rule, derives from the fact that behaviour-guiding considerations operate differently in each context. Theology is interested mainly in the moral status of the transgressor vis-à-vis her victim, the wider community and God; the lawmaker is concerned about these things, but is also concerned about the effect of allowing recovery on other members of society.

To be sure, deterrence considerations have a place in the religious and moral context too. An over-generous approval of repentance may encourage some people to taste the sweetness of sin while relying on repentance to return them to a prelapsarian state of innocence once they have had enough. 'He who says I will sin and repent, sin and repent, is debarred from repenting.'[24] However, the goals of the *locus poenitentiae* doctrine

---

[22] Ezekiel 12:16.
[23] Moses Maimonides, *The Law of Repentance* (Jerusalem, Mamre Institute, 2009) 3:26–27 (my translation). See also St Thomas Aquinas, *Summa Theologiae*, trans English Dominicans (London, Burns, Oates, and Washbourne, 1912–36) part 3, question 86, art 1.
[24] Mishna, Yoma, 8:9. See also Maimonides (n 23) 4:1. Notice the repetition, which may indicate that a thought like 'I will sin and repent' is tolerated once, but is unpardonable the second time.

are more ambitious. In formulating the general rule against recovery and the exceptions to it, lawmakers must consider their effect on people who contemplate entering an illegal transaction, but they must also consider their effect on those who have already done so. Moreover, it is argued by many that in formulating and applying legal rules we can give more weight to the effect that they will have on society as a whole, than we would when resolving other moral issues.[25] In examining which kinds of repentance should exceptionally entitle a repentant claimant to recover, we will therefore look first into the claimant's innocence, and then into the question of whether, and if so, to what extent, recovery is likely to influence the behaviour of others.

The different situations in which the *locus poenitentiae* rule can be invoked are summarised in the following table:

The date of the intended lawbreaking

		Before	After
Motive	**Internal**	Atonement	Renunciation
	External	Abandonment	Withdrawal

These are all situations in which the claimant has abandoned her illegal purpose before any law was violated.[26] But they differ from one another with respect to two components: the motivation behind the decision to stop and the timing of this decision—and more specifically, the question whether the decision precedes the date when the harmful event was supposed to take place (for example, the date of a meeting at which creditors were to be deceived, or a tax inspection that was to be subverted). In 'Atonement' situations the claimant withdraws out of a sincere change of heart regarding the illegality, before the harm anticipated by the violated law took place. In 'Abandonment' again the claimant pulls out in time but in this case the withdrawal is not motivated by an insight into the normative impropriety of the plan, but by self-interest. 'Renunciation' and 'Withdrawal' situations, in contrast, arise when claimants are lucky in that no violation of the law takes place even without any action on their part (for example, because the house that A pays B to burn is demolished by an earthquake). In 'Withdrawal' situations the question arises whether

[25] For the view that directing future behaviour is not a legitimate consideration in private law, see L Smith, 'The Motive, Not the Deed' in J Getzler (ed), *Rationalizing Property, Equity and Trusts* (London, LexisNexis Butterworths, 2003) 53, 60–61. But see the sources cited in M Conaglen, 'The Nature and Function of Fiduciary Loyalty' (2005) 121 *Law Quarterly Review* 452, 453 n 7; LCCP No 189 (n 5) 000.

[26] This assumes that no law was violated when the parties entered their agreement. When the act of entering the agreement is itself illegal (as in eg *Parkinson v College of Ambulance* [1925] 2 KB 1) there is no room for the *locus poenitentiae* doctrine to apply.

recovery should be granted simply on the basis that the claimant has pulled out of the deal, without undergoing any change of heart. In 'Renunciation' situations, however, the claimant can show that she sincerely regrets the illegal nature of the arrangement, and that she meant to renounce her part in it even before a change in circumstances made that unnecessary (for example, because she sent a letter to the other party asking him to stop, but it never arrived as the new postman put it in the neighbours' letterbox).

C. ATONEMENT

1. Guilt

Nietzsche considered that repentance is nothing but 'a second piece of stupidity adding to the first'.[27] But even for those who are more optimistic about the prospect of repentance, wiping one's moral slate clean is still an ambitious project, and the requirements are correspondingly tough: 'What is repentance?' asks Maimonides. 'It is when the sinner abandons his sin... and resolves never to return to it again, and feels penitence over the transgression... and the Omniscient testifies that he will never repeat this inequity.'[28] The ideal repentance, says Maimonides, comprises four elements: (1) recognition of the sinful nature of one's conduct; (2) abandonment of the sin; (3) feelings of regret (shame and guilt); and (4) commitment never to return to the sinful path. However, the precise nature of these elements and the relationship between them are far from clear.

For the purposes of the present discussion, a number of issues arise in connection with the question whether repentance should entitle the claimant to recovery. Perhaps the most important of these goes to the relationship between the first and the second requirements. To what extent should the claimant have been led to abandon her illegal scheme because she recognised that her intended lawbreaking would be morally wrong? Should abandonment be enough in itself, or is something more required? These questions are addressed below in part D, and in this part the discussion is focused on clear 'atonement' cases, where the claimant recognises the wrongful nature of her intention to engage in illegal conduct, and decides for this reason to abort her plan. Such changes of heart can be triggered by a newly acquired value, or reflect a shift in the claimant's internal hierarchy of values, in which values such as respect for the law are promoted to a higher, more influential place in her thinking. Her new way of thinking leads her to feel a strong repugnance for lawbreaking that

[27] F Nietzsche, 'The Wanderer and His Shadow' in *Human, All Too Human*, trans RJ Hollingdale (Cambridge, Cambridge University Press, 1996) s 323.
[28] Maimonides (n 23) 2:3. For a comprehensive analysis, see J Watkins, 'Forgiveness and its Place in Ethics' (2005) 71 *Theoria* 59, 70.

causes her to pull out of a scheme which she previously thought would work to her advantage, because the price to be paid in terms of moral integrity now seems too high. Should the law recognise this move as an undoing of the claimant's past commitment to illegality? If so, then her newly acquired innocence should enable her to retrieve any property that was transferred under the illegal scheme.

The claimant who decides to pull out of a profitable arrangement because it is illegal, exhibits the right causal connection between the first and second stages of repentance (that is, consciousness and abandonment). But what about the third requirement, for penitence? Must the claimant feel guilt or shame? To emerge from her 'impure' state she must regain her innocence. But negative emotions such as guilt and shame are not an indispensible part of the process by which innocence is reacquired. To see why, we must examine the function of self-castigation, and consider whether it is an integral part of repentance, or merely has an instrumental value in ensuring the proper functioning of the other three stages. For those who see an intrinsic value in penitence, feelings of guilt and shame function as a punishment, that is, as an evil which the evildoer must suffer in order to purify herself from sin; in St Augustine's words, 'Penance is the vengeance of the sorrowful, ever punishing in them what they are sorry for having done.'[29] But the kind of purity which can only be gained through such self-imposed punishment is surely a matter for God and/or one's conscience, and not for the court. Such a level of personal propriety cannot possibly be the threshold for the right to the court's assistance.

Apart from the obvious evidential difficulties that would arise if the court had to test the authenticity of a claimant's external expressions of regret, 'sorrow or sadness' over the intended illegality are in any case an unnecessary accompaniment to a genuine change of heart. It is true that many people feel remorse and anguish over past actions which they later come to see as wrongful. Yet some can see themselves as embarking on a new path in which the past is securely left behind, to such an extent that guilty feelings are out of place.[30] Spinoza thought that this was the way in which a reasonable person handles past wrongdoing: '[H]e who repents what he did is twice wretched, or lacking in power.'[31] Others may think

---

[29] Cited by Aquinas (n 23) part 3, question 85, art 3. According to Michael Moore, the emotion of guilt is an acknowledgement of the right to inflict the suffering of punishment on the sinner and so it can have an intrinsic value in the context of criminal law: M Moore, 'The Moral Worth of Retribution' in F Schoeman (ed), *Responsibility, Character, and the Moral Emotions: New Essays in Moral Psychology* (Cambridge, Cambridge University Press, 1987) 179.

[30] R Bittner, 'Is It Reasonable to Regret the Things One Did?' (1992) 89 *Journal of Philosophy* 262, 272.

[31] B Spinoza *Ethics*, trans and ed GHR Parkinson (Oxford, Oxford University Press, 2000) part IV, proposition 54: 'for first he suffers himself to be conquered by evil desire, and then by sadness'.

that penitence is merely conceit or self-indulgence. But whatever the truth of that, guilty feelings should only matter to the extent that they indicate the claimant's motive for abandoning the scheme, since genuine recognition of the wrongfulness of one's conduct, leading to a complete change of heart, can be present even in those who feel no shame or guilt.

Of course, feelings of shame and guilt can also be good indicators that the fourth element of repentance is firmly in place. Aquinas explains that 'man should always be displeased at having sinned, for if he were to be pleased thereat, he would for this very reason fall into sin and lose the fruit of pardon'. And this is why, when there is no risk of future misconduct nor doubt about the agent's innocence, penitence is unnecessary: 'after this life the saints . . . will be displeased at, without sorrowing for, their past sins'.[32] This leads us to the fourth element of repentance: the commitment not to perform similar acts in the future. It is interesting to see that in explaining this final requirement, Maimonides actually resorts to a quasi-legal setting in which the Almighty testifies (to whom?) about the immaculate future conduct of the repentant; surely He knew better than to leave such matters to be decided on the basis of a flimsy commitment of the human heart. Unfortunately, though, the courts cannot see into the future, and their engagement with the possibility of relapse is naturally more limited. When formulating the *locus poenitentiae* rule we can only ensure that restitution is awarded to claimants who are unlikely to fall back into similar behaviour in the future.

It is important to note that the question of relapse is always either external to the process of repentance, or instrumental to one of its four elements. For, even in the religious and moral context it is unclear why a sinner's future behaviour should influence the way that she is judged in reference to her sin now. Commitment is one thing, actual (divine) knowledge that the repentant will live up to her intentions, is another. When repentance is sincere it should be accepted and the slate wiped clean; in the future, the sinner may sin again, but this should not retroactively undo her repentance.[33] It is true that subsequent misconduct may show that her repentance was not as sincere as it seemed, in which case the relapse has an instrumental value as evidence of the profundity of the first and second elements of repentance (recognition and abandonment). It may show that the shift in the repentant's value system was instable. But even so, that does not mean that property recovered under the *locus poenitentiae* rule should be taken away again in the case of a relapse (and, for example, given to the Crown). For there is always a chance that a claimant's repentance was sincere, and that she simply lacked the strength of will to carry out her

---

[32] Aquinas (n 23) part 3, question 84, art 8.
[33] Ibid, question 88.

good intentions, in which case the basis for allowing recovery at the time of her repentance still holds good.

If entry into the illegal agreement is thought to contaminate the parties, how can atonement reverse this result? How can it undo the past? Repentance, explains Swinburne, can indeed remove both 'the harm caused . . . [and] the purposive attitude of the wrongdoer towards the victim manifested in the causing of the harm'.[34] In cases where no part of the illegal plan has been executed, any harm caused is minimal, if it exists at all. However, 'the consequences of the act are not merely such harm but the fact that the wrongdoer has by doing the act made himself someone who has harmed the victim'. Although this piece of the past cannot be changed, the wrongdoer can do something about it: 'he can distance himself from it by privately and publicly disowning the act'.[35] Thus, repentance enables the claimant to distance herself from the person who chose to participate in the forbidden conduct. If her conscience leads her to withdraw from a profitable scheme, then in this crucial respect she is no longer identical with the person who embarked on the illegality.

When the courts help a repentant claimant to retrieve her property they are no more implicated in her previously intended illegality than they would be in a case of duress or mistake. This is especially clear where the result of allowing recovery is substantially different from the result that would follow from enforcement of the contract. In returning the repentant to the pre-contract stage (that is, with her property in hand, with no contractual rights or obligations) the court is actually helping an innocent party to repudiate her unconscionable intentions, a move which clearly does not implicate the court in her previously intended wrongdoing. Indeed, the power of repentance is so great that it can put a repentant claimant on the same footing as an innocent party who was forced into the illegal contract and therefore retained her innocence throughout. And even where the *locus poenitentiae* rule is successfully invoked to generate a remedy that resembles performance of the contract (for example, where the court declares a resulting trust over a smuggled asset), there is still an important conceptual difference between allowing an innocent party to escape from the ramifications of an illegal contract, and the enforcement of an illegal transaction. Only in the latter case will the court be seen to condone illegality; in the former case, repentance breaks the continuity between the person who entered the illegal scheme and the person who asks the court to retrieve her property, with the result that ordering restitution does not undermine the court's antipathy towards the original transaction.

In abandoning the illegal contract and asking for the court's help, the claimant shows that she no longer sees her personal interests as superior to

---

[34] R Swinburne, *Responsibility and Atonment* (Oxford, Clarendon Press, 1989) 81.
[35] Ibid, 81. See also N Richards, 'Forgiveness' (1988) 99 *Ethics* 77, 88.

the social values which are protected by the law.³⁶ Moreover if the distressing experience of repentance causes her to change her ways on a more general level—for example, to abandon any 'grey area' practices—then there is a serious sense in which the past has acquired a new *meaning* for her (from a simple case of wrongdoing into a transformative event for good).³⁷ It must be noted, however, that there is no necessary overlap between the change of heart which is needed for the purposes of the *locus poenitentiae* rule, and *moral* regeneration. There could be circumstances in which the claimant believes that her moral duty required her to act illegally, and in vowing to abide by the law the next time, she commits herself to act against her conscience. In a mostly just legal system, such a situation would be rare, as illegal transactions are usually motivated by one's private good, rather than by high moral values. However, when such unusual situations come about, the *locus poenitentiae* doctrine and the concept of repentance will pull in different directions.

One should not forget, however, that atonement is not identical to repentance. One major difference between a wrongdoer who asks her victim to pardon her, and a claimant who invokes the *locus poenitentiae* rule, is that the latter claims a *right*, whereas the former must seek, if not beg for, forgiveness. In some interpersonal situations, withholding forgiveness can be a wrong in itself (depending, for instance, on the severity of the wrong, on the time that has elapsed and the nature of the relationship that preceded the wrong), and testify to character flaws (for example, an inclination to hold grudges and inflated self-esteem);³⁸ but in other cases, a person who has been wronged might legitimately hold hard feelings towards the wrongdoer. The court's willingness to allow recovery by applying the *locus poenitentiae* rule has many parallels with forgiveness as a response to repentance. Perhaps the most prominent is the re-establishment of intimacy and trust in the wake of forgiveness which is echoed in the court's renewed willingness to assist the claimant and restore her to a prelapsarian state. Nevertheless, invoking the *locus poenitentiae* rule to award restitution differs from personal forgiveness. Unlike the human victims of wrongful behaviour, courts do not need to forgo hard feelings towards claimants who have intended to act illegally. Hence there is no

---

[36] According to Jean Hampton, the point of punishment is to demolish the offender's view according to which her interests are superior to those of her victim, a view that is both expressed and affirmed by the crime: J Hampton, 'The Retributive Idea' in JG Murphy and J Hampton (eds), *Forgiveness and Mercy* (Cambridge, Cambridge University Press, 1988) 111.

[37] See L Radzik, *Making Amends* (Oxford, Oxford University Press, 2009) 3.4, 3.5.

[38] So much so that: 'if his friend (whom he wronged) does not want to forgive he should send three of his friends to beg him to forgive [and if after three times he is still unforgiving] he can leave him alone, and the person who did not forgive is the sinner', for 'a person should not be cruel and refuse to make up' (Maimonides (n 23) 2:13–14). See also Swinburne (n 34) 86–87, who distinguishes between the removal of guilt that is up to the sinner and forgiveness that is always up to the victim; see too Richards (n 35) 90–91.

need to recognise a space in which such hard feelings are understandable even in the face of a sincere repentance. When the conditions of atonement are in place, the claimant can therefore *demand* that her pre-illegality relationship with the court should be reinstated, and that her claim to recover the property should be heard.[39]

2. Deterrence

Let us turn to the effect which allowing recovery in atonement situations might have on other people's behaviour. On the face of it, allowing recovery on withdrawal from an illegal transaction at any point before its purpose is accomplished, from *whatever* motive, can have a positive deterrent effect. Such a lenient rule means that people who enter illegal agreements take upon themselves an extra risk (in addition to the risk that they will be caught and punished), namely that the other party will, at any time before completion, call off the contract without losing any property that she has transferred. The thought might be that a substantial number of people who contemplate achieving their goals in an illegal manner will take that additional risk into account and consequently decide against this course. If that does not work and the illegal contract does go ahead, then the possibility of getting her property back will at least encourage each party to abandon the deal once she has second thoughts about its cost-effectiveness.

We need to keep in mind, though, that (presumably) the parties have compelling reasons to go along with the illegality in the first place, and so, unless some significant counter-consideration becomes apparent, there is no reason why they would want to return to their starting point. The problem with a *locus poenitentiae* rule that takes no heed of the parties' motivation is that it will also have the opposite effect of encouraging a hesitating party to go along with the illegal scheme, calculating that she can always withdraw at a later stage (and at least be able to retrieve her property, even if she cannot avoid any sanctions from the law-enforcement authorities). An automatic right to retrieve property before the illegal contract has been fully performed will also have the perverse effect of encouraging the recipient to perform her part as quickly as possible in order to get the contract beyond the last point at which withdrawal is possible.[40] It seems

---

[39] In that the court is more akin to God who can change His attitude to the repentant at one fell swoop: 'Yesterday he [the repentant] was hated by the Lord, detested, distant and abominated. And today he is loved and pleasant, close and companion' (Maimonides (n 23) 7:7). This allows him to develop a detailed protocol for divine forgiveness according to which the fulfilment of certain conditions ensures divine pardon for most offences (cf Maimonides (n 23) 1:8–12).

[40] Birks (1989) (n 13) 119; Wade (n 15) 50.

therefore that behaviour-directing considerations cannot conclusively support or undermine a motivation-neutral *locus poenitentiae* rule.

However, within the more specific context of atonement we can see more clearly how deterrence considerations might operate. A requirement for a 'change of heart' will dramatically reduce the risk that those who hesitate will nevertheless 'test the water' and then fall back on the *locus poenitentiae* doctrine if they find it too cold. This is because such transformations of moral outlook are inherently spontaneous; the change often feels as if it overpowers the agent who experiences it – as if a part of the self that cannot bear to engage in the illegality defeats another (perhaps more calculating) part which pushed the agent to engage in the illegal scheme. Perhaps she was initially reckless about the illegal nature of the deal, or perhaps she only comes to recognise her status as a wrongdoer when she takes a first substantial step towards realising the forbidden purpose. But once the atoning claimant realises the effect which her participation will have on her moral integrity, the risk that she will get involved in a similar scheme in the future is probably quite low (or, at least lower than it is for claimants in withdrawal situations, discussed in the next part).

The 'testing the water' argument also has hardly any force in the context of atonement cases. For it would be quite unusual for a claimant to embark on a course about which she feels terribly guilty in the belief that if guilt overpowers her she can always withdraw. Such a calculating approach is unlikely to be found in cases of sincere repentance. Compare that with the case of a person whose indecisiveness regarding the illicit deal is rooted in fear, or doubts about its economic viability. When she decides to go ahead with the plan, she will do so in the hope that at least if new factors come up, she can always respond to them and withdraw; a rule which ensures that she will indeed be able to undo the deal can therefore play an important role in her decision to go ahead. But a thought of the kind 'let's see how guilty I am going to feel once I really start to break the law, and if it's too much I will quit' reflects poorly on the sincerity of the repentance; hence, once we require a genuine change of heart, we can assume that hesitating agents will find no encouragement in the *locus poenitentiae* rule.

Of course, there is always the chance that people will try to present a self-serving withdrawal as one which was motivated by atonement. However, as we shall see in the next part, the courts have been asked to decide evidential problems of exactly this kind in criminal law (both at the conviction and at the sentencing stages), and it can be assumed that they have the means to distinguish real and false atonements. Moreover, the risk of false claims of atonement is reduced, in comparison with criminal law, as the burden of proof lies with the claimant, rather than the prosecution.[41]

---

[41] Cf AP Simester and GR Sullivan, *Criminal Law: Theory and Doctrine*, 3rd edn (Oxford, Hart Publishing, 2007) 319, suggesting that the defendant should be allowed to bring evidence to prove a parallel defence in criminal law.

D. ABANDONMENT

In *Taylor v Bowers*[42] Taylor returned from America to find that his son, who had been running his business while he was away, was in debt. Fearing that his business creditors would seize his machinery, Taylor assigned it to his nephew for a fictitious consideration. He calculated that once the creditors were convinced that he had nothing to give them, his nephew would return the machines. However, his nephew had different plans. Instead of keeping the machines for his uncle, he transferred them to a third party (who was not in good faith). Two creditors' meetings were called, but only one minor creditor turned up, and Taylor then realised that the risk of losing his property was probably much smaller than he had feared. So he asked for his machines back, knowing that once they were openly back in his possession, he would be exposed to the risk that creditors would appear and demand them—that is, he would be back at square one, with no illegality having been committed (since no creditors were ever deceived) and with no special protection for his property. The court held that since 'nothing has been done to carry out the . . . illegal object beyond the delivery of the goods . . . and before anything was done . . . the plaintiff repudiated the whole transaction . . . we think that the plaintiff is entitled to recover back his goods'.[43]

This part concerns claimants who, like Taylor, abandon an illegal scheme for reasons other than repentance and who wish to recover their property. Note that if such claims are allowed, then this would be on the basis that the claimant *never* intended to make a gift to the recipient, and not on the basis that she *changed her mind* regarding the viability of the transaction. A party to a valid agreement who recalculates her position is of course debarred from reneging on her promise on that basis alone. But claimants like Taylor are in a different position: they seek to enforce their *original* intention, for example, to form a trust for their own benefit (and not to transfer the property outright).[44]

To decide whether abandonment should entitle such claimants to invoke the *locus poenitentiae* rule, we must first be clear about the relationship between the illegal contract and its actual outcome. Imagine a ball that is pushed from the top of a hill in order to hit a target at the bottom. What happens if the person who set the ball in motion decides to prevent it from hitting the target? Should we care about the motivation behind this 'stop act' (as criminal lawyers would call it)? For the moment, let us ignore the question whether the act was successful in diverting the ball. The significance of this will be discussed in the next part. The present discussion is

---

[42] (1876) 1 QBD 291 (CA).
[43] Ibid, 295.
[44] *Tribe* (n 9) 133.

focused on the decision to stop the ball and the relevance of the motivation behind it. Again, we can divide this discussion in two: first, we will ask whether a self-interested stop act should be capable of restoring a claimant's innocence to the extent that she is entitled to the court's help; secondly, we will consider the likely effect of a motivation-neutral formulation of the *locus poenitentiae* rule on people who are considering whether to enter an illegal contract or to withdraw from one.

1. Guilt

On finding that 'it is impossible to reconcile all the authorities on the circumstances in which a party to an illegal contract is permitted to withdraw', Millett LJ decided in *Tribe* that although 'it is clear that [the claimant] must withdraw voluntarily', 'genuine repentance is not required'.[45] In Millett LJ's view, therefore, there is a material distinction between voluntary and involuntary withdrawals that does not map onto the distinction between atonement and abandonment. In his rendering of the *locus poenitentiae* rule, when a claimant is forced to withdraw because her plan is discovered, or her accomplice refuses to co-operate, her abandonment is involuntary and recovery is denied, but if she discovers that the whole plan is pointless, she can 'voluntarily' pull out and ask for her property back.[46] Apparently, therefore, Millett LJ believes that a person who finds out that her illegal scheme was unnecessary can still *choose* to go along with it, so that she should be entitled to recover her property is if she chooses instead to repudiate the contract.

As *Tribe* itself illustrates, however, the voluntary/involuntary distinction drawn by Millett LJ is a vacuous one. Tribe worked all his life to establish and develop a prosperous business. Upon retirement, he planed to leave the business to his four children in equal parts. Unfortunately, two of his shops ran into some trouble and he feared that the creditors would take over the entire business. Hence he transferred all his shares in the company to one of his sons on the agreed understanding that when the threat was lifted the son would reassign the shares to his father. Eventually, it transpired that Tribe's fears were largely exaggerated and no real threat hung over the business. He therefore asked the son to return the shares to him. Tribe junior refused. Since the rebellious assignee was his son, a legal presumption arose according to which property transferred from a father to son is meant as a gift (the 'presumption of advancement').[47] In order to rebut this presumption, Tribe had to rely directly on the illegal nature of the transaction when giving evidence, and explain that he did not mean to make a

[45] Ibid, 135.
[46] Ibid.
[47] For discussion of this rule, see ch 10 above.

gift but rather to cheat his creditors. Evidence of this kind was legally inadmissible, but the court helped the father to get his shares back by declaring that the son held the shares on a resulting trust for his father. In this way, the father's position was on a par with the position of other claimants, who fell outside the scope of the presumption of advancement, and could therefore base their claim on the *Tinsley/Bowmakers* 'reliance rule'.

It is clear why the court wanted to reach this result. But we need to ask whether the scope of the general rule against recovery can sensibly be determined by the distinction drawn in *Tribe* between situations where the claimant can decide to proceed with an illegal scheme and situations where she cannot. Once an illegal scheme has become completely pointless, an act of withdrawal from the scheme becomes a mere formality. Indeed, it is not even clear in what sense the claimant in *Tribe* repudiated the arrangement with his son—the whole purpose of the transfer was to shelter the property while it was at risk, so that once it was no longer at risk, the shares would be returned to the father. In asking for the shares to be reassigned to him the father can therefore be seen as asking the son to perform his part of the deal, rather than abandoning it. There was no space in which he could have chosen otherwise, so as to render his decision 'voluntary'. No creditor was ever cheated, and leaving the property in the hands of his son would have been a brutal violation of the principle that one should not gain from one's own wrong. But this had nothing to do with Tribe's mental state, and his 'choice' made no difference.

There are, however, other situations where the claimant does have a real choice between withdrawing and continuing with the scheme, and where she chooses to withdraw for self-interested reasons. An example would be a case where a claimant recalculates the risks and benefits of continuing with the scheme and arrives at an inconclusive result. Think of A, who gives money to B so that he can bribe a government official who has the authority to take a decision in which A has an interest. Before any bribe money is paid to the official, A realises that her interest in the matter to be decided is not that great, and that it may well be that paying the bribe is not worth the risk of discovery and punishment. If A then decides to call B and cancel the agreement, then this certainly reflects a real choice, for it would not be totally unreasonable of her to proceed with the scheme despite her misgivings. But should such a decision entitle A to the court's help in retrieving her money from B?

Some interesting discussion of a similar question can be found in the literature on criminal attempts. Section 1 of the Criminal Attempts Act 1981 provides that 'If, with intent to commit an offence to which this section applies, a person does an act which is more than merely preparatory to the commission of the offence, he is guilty of attempting to commit the offence.' Section 4 stipulates that the defendant is 'liable on conviction on indictment to any penalty to which he would have been liable on conviction on indictment of that offence'. The US Model Penal Code (MPC) also recommends that a person should be convicted of attempt if he 'purposely engages in conduct that would constitute the crime if the attendant circumstances were as he believes them to be' (section 5.01(a)). The law governing withdrawal from illegal agreements has some deep structural similarities to the law of criminal attempts as reflected in these sections. In both cases the initial step on the way to an illegal action is isolated from the act as a whole, so as to become an independent sanction-bearing action.[48] This focus on the first step as a stand-alone segment which ought to be treated independently of the way the action as whole transaction has unfolded is motivated by a respect for agency as definitive of the human. In other words, it reflects the belief that people are morally responsible only for what it is in their power to do or avoid; that what is outside their control can neither be attributed to them for the purposes of allocating blame, nor diminish their responsibility for what *is* under their control. Thus, if a person intended to do wrong and acted to bring it about, that is enough to attract the sanction for this wrong, even if, for reasons that are independent of the agent, the harm never materialised. To give a simple example: if C puts a miscarriage-inducing drug in a woman's cup, but the doctors manage to save the pregnancy, C will be punished just as severely as B who was successful in killing a foetus by the same method.

This outline of the reasoning behind the criminalisation of attempts should suffice to demonstrate its relevance to the current discussion of claimants who intend to carry out an illegal purpose, but who never actually violate the law. The question raised by such cases is very similar: should the court treat the act of contracting to engage in future illegality as a step that is sufficiently substantial to debar the claimant from recovery even when the agreement comes to nothing? We could argue that entering the agreement is an unequivocal expression of disregard for the law which should generate the harsh response of withholding restitution. But if we accept this argument, then a similar question will arise for both criminal and private law: how should we treat cases where the harm was prevented by the agent's decision to stop after she crossed the threshold of attempt/ illegal agreement?

Unlike the Criminal Attempts Act 1981, the MPC includes a *locus poenitentiae* exception. Subsection (4) on 'Renunciation of Criminal Purpose' stipulates that 'when the actor's conduct would otherwise constitute an attempt . . . it is an affirmative defence that he abandoned his effort to commit the crime . . . under circumstances manifesting a complete and

---

[48] The question just how 'initial' can it be is heavily debated in criminal law; but for our purposes signing the contract surely parallels an 'act that is more than merely preparatory'. On recent developments in this area, see Simester and Sullivan (n 41) 306–09.

voluntary renunciation of his criminal purpose'. Here, as in English private law, only stop acts that are 'voluntary' have the power to reverse the sanction. However, it is already clear from the wording of the section that when using the term 'voluntary' the draftsman had in mind something quite different from the sense in which Millett LJ used this word in *Tribe*. To qualify as 'voluntary' for the purposes of the 'renunciation' defence, the stop act must not be 'motivated . . . by [unexpected] circumstances . . . that increase the probability of detection or apprehension or that make more difficult the accomplishment of the criminal purpose'.[49] In considering as involuntary any withdrawal from the most common self-interested motivations, namely (re)calculation of the risk of punishment and/or the chances of success, the MPC takes atonement as the paradigm case of voluntary abandonment. Many courts interpreted the statutes that followed the MPC in a strict way which virtually identified the 'voluntary' requirement with moral regeneration. Even defendants who refused to continue with a crime when induced to do so were denied the defence, on the ground that they did not stop out of the right motivation.[50]

However, this pietistic approach to the renunciation defence has been forcefully criticised. According to Shachar, while the criminalisation of attempts was 'one of the most important steps in the humanization of criminal law', by limiting a defendant's opportunity to undo an attempt to cases of 'moral regeneration', 'we have lost sight of the delicate relations between [the offender's inner world of intentions and perception] and reality itself'.[51] In his view, then, the ideal of framing criminal responsibility so that it covers what, and only what, is under the agent's control, cannot justify the almost automatic application of the criminal sanction once the first (substantial) step towards the offence is taken. If stop acts can only exonerate a defendant once they are done in conditions of atonement, an unjustified asymmetry is thereby created, for the choice to go ahead need not be motivated by a desire to engage in illegality per se: 'the same respect for human dignity that has put the individual, as is, in the mirror territory [ie judge him according to his intention], requires respect for his decision to remove himself from it, as is, on the same terms of entry'.[52]

If we apply the same rationale to private law, then the test for the *locus*

---

[49] The MPC has had a substantial influence on state legislation of a Renouncement defence: see ET Lee, 'Cancelling Crime' (1997) 30 *Connecticut Law Review* 117, 120 n 15. According to Simester and Sullivan (n 41) 319, the 1981 Act did not introduce a similar defence because of the evidential difficulty of distinguishing between voluntary and involuntary desistance.

[50] See the examples in Simester and Sullivan (n 41) 148–50, and the conclusion in Lee (n 49) 151 that 'the courts have uniformly insisted on nothing less that a genuine moral conversion to establish a valid abandonment'. See too Y Shachar, 'Wresting Control from Luck: The Secular Case for Aborted Attempts' (2008) 9 *Theoretical Inquiries in Law* 140, 149–51 and 142–49 for a similar tendency in Israel.

[51] Ibid, 154.

[52] Ibid, 154.

poenitentiae rule should follow Millett LJ's suggestion in *Tribe*: as long as the abandonment of the illegal contract is initiated by the claimant, she can ask for her property to be returned (with the possible exception of cases where carrying out the agreement has become pointless). However, I believe that at least in the context of the *locus poenitentiae* rule in private law, there is a good reason for introducing an asymmetry between the motivation behind the claimant's act of repudiating the illegal contract and her reasons for entering the contract in the first place. The reasons why a person chose to enter an illegal agreement are irrelevant, and the no-recovery sanction ought to be in place even if the claimant deeply regretted the illegal nature of the deal. We clamp down on contracts to engage in future illegality because in entering them the parties express such contempt for the law that it disqualifies them from the court's help when things go wrong. If withdrawal from the contract is to return the claimant to a state of innocence that entitles her to the court's assistance, then it must encapsulate a rejection of the mind-set from which it was made: that is, of the attitude which led her to prioritise her own interests over the public interest as embodied in the law. In atonement situations such a reversal of outlook is fully achieved. The past act of signing the contract cannot be undone, but the claimant's state of mind can be, and that should be enough to entitle her to be readmitted to the courtroom. In contrast, the stop act of a claimant who becomes too scared, or too uncertain about the viability of the agreement, should not be enough, since she may still hold the same disgraceful attitude that prioritised her private interest over the demands of the law.

There is a line of thought which holds that *all* those claimants who choose to stop should be able to retrieve their property, regardless of their motivation, provided that the expected harm has not materialised.[53] According to this line of thought, self-interested abandoners should be able to get their property back because it is a mistake to focus exclusively on the claimant's action in entering an illegal agreement, ignoring the effect that this action has actually had in the world. In the next part, we will examine the significance of the way in which things eventually turn out. But even if we conclude there that the outcome of the parties' actions should affect the

[53] One of the arguments in *Q v Q* [2008] EWHC 1874 (Fam) was that since the illegal scheme was put to an end while the father was still alive, so that the purpose of cheating on inheritance tax never materialised, he had a right to recover his proprietary rights in the house. In an obiter remark (at [30]), Black J rejected the claim and warned that the illegal purpose 'should not be too narrowly defined'. Since the father's actions went 'beyond the mere creation of authentic looking documents . . . and moved into the realm of actually presenting a false picture to the taxman', he had partly carried the illegal purpose into effect, and thus 'deprived himself of the chance of withdrawing'. But cf *21st Century Logistic Solutions Ltd (in liq) v Madysen Ltd* [2004] EWHC 231 (QB) [19] where it was held that a mere intention by the seller eventually to evade VAT was too remote from the sale contract to render it unenforceable for illegality.

claimant's right to recovery, that will be for reasons that are independent of the question whether this outcome can be attributed to the claimant's choice or to pure chance; unless, that is, her choice to stop was motivated by atonement. If a case cannot be made for taking the outcome into account, then the rule against recovery should apply even when a self-interested stop act failed to prevent the illegality from happening. Thus, in the bribe example given above, if the claimant A decides to call B and order him to return the money, A's self-interested decision to withdraw should not entitle her to the court's help if B refuses to comply.

The rationale for focusing exclusively on the question whether the claimant has made a substantial step towards illegality, and ignoring the effects of her actions, is that her decision to take this step reflects a dangerous disrespect for the law. However, the links between attitudes and sanctions should be treated with utmost care. A disdainful attitude to the law is not enough in itself to disentitle the claimant from the court's assistance. If an anarchist is assaulted in the course of a stormy anti-globalisation rally she can take legal action against her attacker. Only an attitude that is embodied in a specific agreement to engage in illegality will lead the court to refuse its assistance. Unlike criminal law, where the dangerous *character* of the offender can be a reason for locking her up as soon as this character is sufficiently expressed in an attempt to commit a crime, a denial of restitution is a response only to the specific agreement and the contempt towards the law that it embodies.[54]

2. Deterrence

A straightforward argument in favour of recognising abandonment as a reason for recovery is that this will incentivise the parties to illegal agreements to renege on their promises and thus prevent the intended law-breaking from ever taking place. When one party is considering whether to go along with the illegal plan or to put an end to it, the knowledge that if she opts for the latter option she will be able to retrieve her property will make this option much more attractive. However, such a motivation-neutral view of stop acts could have adverse effect on choices that are made at the pre-contract stage, as well as on the post-abandonment situation.

The MPC is very explicit in regard to the post-abandonment situation: section 5.01(4) expresses the concern that self-interested abandonment will also be accompanied by 'a decision to postpone the criminal conduct until a more advantageous time or to transfer the criminal effort to another but similar objective or victim'. Since the inner constitution of the attempter did not change, there is every reason to believe that if and when more

---

[54] On the problems of the 'dangerous character' rationale for the criminalisation of attempt, see Lee (n 49) 145; A Duff, *Criminal Attempts* (Oxford, Clarendon Press, 1996) ch 7.

favourable external circumstances arise she will try again. Without a dramatic change in her attitude towards her obligation to obey the law, she will ignore it again as soon as her interests conflict with its requirements. Therefore, if we look beyond the specific stop act, and adopt a more forward-looking perspective, we will see that there is little point in letting the claimant off the hook just because external circumstances pushed her to abandon the scheme. However, when applied to private law, this argument carries less force. In the criminal context the renunciation defence encourages the offender to abandon the plan at a stage when her intentions can still go unnoticed, and so it can be argued that in many cases the motivation-neutral defence is no more than an incentive to stop now and try again later when the chances for success will be better. In contrast, the *locus poenitentiae* rule encourages people to renege on their promise by helping them to recover their property in court, that is, in a way that will force them to bring their intended illegality out in the open. This exposure is likely to reduce their willingness to engage in illegal activities in the future if only because from now on, the authorities, such as HMRC, for example, will pay a special attention to their activities. For the more conscientious person, the shame of being exposed as a would-be criminal will also have a deterrent effect. But that should be balanced against the risk that the power to ask for recovery will just be used by the transferor to put pressure on the transferee to return the property *outside* court in order to avoid any criminal sanctions that exposing the deal might attract.

The ramifications for the pre-contract stage for recognising abandonment as a reason for recovery are more worrisome. For reasons that have been discussed already, only atonement can ensure that the *locus poenitentiae* rule will not tip the balance in favour of illegality in the case of a hesitant would-be party. And there is also the danger that if abandonment is recognised as a basis for recovery, the party who is interested in going along with the deal will hasten to perform his part in order to push it beyond the point when withdrawal is possible.[55] It seems therefore that the effect of allowing recovery in abandonment cases on future conduct is hard to make out. Encouraging stop acts regardless of motivation may dissuade people from performing a promised illegality, but allowing recovery in cases where there is no atonement may have bad effects at the pre-contract stage.

E. WITHDRAWAL

In *Bigos v Boustead*[56] Bousted's young daughter had tuberculosis. In order

---

[55] R Merkin, 'Restitution by Withdrawal from Executory Illegal Contracts' (1981) 97 *Law Quarterly Review* 420.
[56] [1951] 1 All ER 92 (CA).

to recover she went with her mother to Italy. The illness persisted, but their money ran out. Bousted sought to transfer some money to his wife and daughter, but he tried to do so in a way that breached the exchange control regulations: he asked Bigos to supply the women with £150 worth of lire in return for a payment in sterling. As a security, the father gave Bigos a share certificate. The lire were never supplied, the women had to return home early, and Bigos refused to return the share certificate. Hence the question arose whether Bousted should be granted the assistance of the court in retrieving it? There is no question that he never meant to give the certificate as a gift to Bigos, and that although their contract enshrined a promise to break the law, no illegal action ever took place because Bigos never performed her part of the deal. If the court allowed the loss to lie where it fell, then one party who was just as guilty as the other of involvement in the agreement would get a windfall at his expense in circumstances where no illegality came to pass. Nevertheless Pritchard J decided that since 'this case falls within the category of cases which I call the frustration cases', that is, cases where the illegal purpose did not materialise because the other party chose to withdraw, no restitution could be ordered.[57] In his view, apparently, the fact that the harm against which the exchange regulations were directed never occurred was not enough in itself to entitle the claimant to recovery: only a (successful) stop act initiated by the claimant would suffice.

And why indeed should we distinguish between two claimants who enter an illegal agreement from which they do nothing to withdraw, where the only difference between them is that in one case the purported illegality materialises and in the other it does not? Such a distinction would subordinate the legal result to the vagaries of circumstances that are beyond the claimants' control, and therefore introduce a hefty dose of 'legal luck' into this area of the law.[58]

'Legal luck' can be contrasted with 'moral luck', that is, the idea that the moral status of an action can turn upon its random outcome. Thus, says Nagel, if you leave a baby in the bath in order to answer the phone, perhaps the moral status of this foolish misjudgement will depend on whether the baby drowned or just went on splashing in the water.[59] But

[57] Ibid, 100. In an obiter dictum in *Parker* (n 16) 602, the CA reached the same conclusion.

[58] 'To insist that there is no legal luck is to insist that an agent's legal status . . . supervenes on what is under that agent's control': D Enoch, 'Luck Between Morality, Law, and Justice' (2008) 9 *Theoretical Inquiries in Law* 23, 28. For a detailed discussion of the arguments for and against legal luck, see J Feinberg, *Problems at the Roots of Law: Essays in Legal and Political Theory* (Oxford, Oxford University Press, 2003) ch 4.

[59] T Nagel, 'Moral Luck' in *Mortal Questions* (Cambridge, Cambridge University Press, 1979) 24. For a review of many of the arguments for the view that moral assessment is dependent on actual wrongdoing, and a criticism of them, see MS Moore, 'The Independent Moral Significance of Wrongdoing' (1994) 5 *Journal of Contemporary Legal Issues* 237, 241–52.

many will argue that 'moral luck' is an incoherent concept because moral responsibility cannot be dependent on factors over which the agent has no control. Surely, the question whether the baby died or not will have an enormous significance to her family and community, but the fact that you feel less guilty if she survives does not reflect a real difference in the moral value of the two possible outcomes; your natural relief to find her alive and kicking in the water does not mean that you are any less of a wrongdoer than you would have been if she had happened to die.

The claim that moral responsibility is not a function of chance outcomes has a powerful intuitive appeal and it is considered by many to be the bedrock of their moral convictions. Taking its roots from Kant's treatment of the good will as the foundation of morality,[60] the rejection of moral luck has developed into a sophisticated array of arguments which bear upon fundamental issues such as free will and the nature of action. In this chapter I will try to steer clear of these murky waters. Instead, I will accept that *moral* responsibility for actions does not depend on any outcome over which the agent had no control.[61] However, that rejection of moral luck does not entail that the existence and scope of *legal* responsibility ought to be similarly insulated from chance. If we find that the legal significance of a party's actions must not turn on outcomes over which she has no control, then the rule against recovery should apply equally to all parties to illegal contracts, regardless of the question whether their illegal objectives were achieved (unless the different end-result can be attributed to a claimant's atonement). In other words, two claimants who both enter an illegal agreement under which they transfer property, and then sit quietly to wait for the lawbreaking to happen, should prima facie be subjected to the same sanction, irrespective of whether a violation of the law ever actually happens. In what follows I will show that there are good, even if not decisive, reasons to hold that the application of rule against recovery can be limited to cases where a breach of the law did ensue from the agreement.

In the previous parts, on atonement and abandonment, the discussion considered the issues of guilt and deterrence in turn. Here, though, the discussion will be divided along slightly different lines: under the heading of 'guilt' I will discuss the view that the outcome of the parties' agreement can make a difference at the level of legal blameworthiness, and that it can (and should) be reflected in the way legal sanctions are applied. A thorough discussion of these arguments is well beyond the scope of the present

---

[60] Although his argument does not imply that moral agency is a totally luck-free zone: J Gardner, 'The Wrongdoing that Gets Results' (2004) 18 *Philosophical Perspectives* 53, part 3.

[61] I am referring here only to 'outcome luck', ie to the way the results of our choices are dependent on factors that are outside our control. That is to be distinguished from 'situational', or 'constitutive' luck, which refer to the way other aspects of out lives and personality are determined by chance. The distinction can already be found in Nagel (n 59) 28. For the view that 'moral luck' is not a real problem at all, see eg Nagel (n 59) part 5 and Moore (n 59) part 4.

paper, but I will present them briefly and examine their applicability to our issue. Another set of arguments takes a different route to the same conclusion (ie that cases can understandably be treated differently according to whether any lawbreaking occurred): instead of challenging the claim that this is a case of legal luck, these arguments seek to show that even if we adopt an anti-legal-luck policy we need not be too worried about the outcome dependency aspect of the present rule against recovery. These arguments will naturally focus more on the rule against recovery and its context, and less on the moral status of the parties, and I will discuss them under the heading of 'legal luck in illegal contracts'.

1. Guilt

In his discussion of the relationship between culpability and luck, Anthony Duff asks:

> Should (or can) our judgements of culpability or blameworthiness, and the response that they structure, depend purely on the question of what the agent can claim moral credit for, or of what we can properly regard as being to her moral discredit?[62]

His answer is 'no'. In contrast with what he dubs the 'subjectivist' view of attempts,[63] he believes that the objective outcome of the attempt, that is, its actual success or failure, should be taken into consideration when deciding how to punish successful attempt. A complete offence, he argues, should be punished more severely than a failed one. This is because in his view 'the cosmic ledger' in which our moral blameworthiness is calculated purely on the basis of factors that are under our control is appropriate only 'to a detached god-like observer of the human scene. We however . . . are participants in the human scene . . . acting, thinking and responding to each other within a human social life.'[64] One can reject the idea of moral luck, says Duff, without being committed to a project of cleansing the criminal law of all the ways in which fortuitous outcomes determine the legal result. Differences in punishment between complete offences and the attempts to commit them can be justified even in regard to cases of 'complete attempt', that is, where the last act that is necessary to complete the action was done (for example, by pulling the trigger). This is because the attempter

> has not in fact (even though it may be a matter of luck) fully engaged himself in

---

[62] Duff (n 54) 343.

[63] For a thoroughly subjectivist view, see A Ashworth, 'Criminal Attempts and the Role of Resulting Harm under the Code, and in the Common Law' (1988) 19 *Rutgers Law Journal* 726.

[64] Duff (n 54) 344.

the world as the perpetrator of serious harm to his victim; and that fact . . . should be marked in the conviction and sentence which he receives.[65]

This is because in criminal law, blameworthiness is determined not by the degree of control over the outcome which the agent possessed, but by the proximity of the outcome to the normal course of events that is to be expected to result from the agent's action. The doctrine of 'proximal causation' stipulates that agents are responsible for those outcomes which are not too freakish, that is, which do not fall too far from what would normally follow from the agent's actions.[66] Thus, if you hit A hard enough you will be held responsible for A's death even if you had no control over his already frail health, or over the doctors' (unsuccessful) efforts to save his life. But if A happened to be the only specialist who could save B's eyesight, you will not be held legally responsible for B's loss; this harm is too far from what one could expect to follow from beating A. At least when it comes to legal responsibility, the 'freakish result' test for blameworthiness does a better job than the 'control' test (according to which an act is criminal only when the agent was in control of the factors that are necessary for the result). For, as Duff and Moore show, it is very difficult to find a definition of chance-clean act. That I managed to get to the scene, that it was not too muddy, that my hand obeyed my mind's command to shoot the red deer – these are all events that are in a serious sense out of my control. So even if we try to abstract from 'killing a red deer' and leave it with 'shooting', or even with 'aiming a gun at', we are still far from a luck-free definition of the act.[67] If we adopt the control test, the definition of crimes will have to be reduced to purely mental acts like 'forming the intention to shoot a deer', with the requirement of some actual act for evidential purposes.[68]

Is that a convincing perception of criminal responsibility? Sometimes the underlying personality and the virtues or vices of the agent play such a crucial role in determining his responsibility that the difference between trying and succeeding evaporates. This typically happens in intimate relationships of love and friendship, and indeed, in any relationship where trust and confidence are crucial, such as those between a fiduciary and her principal or a political candidate and the voters.[69] However, many would

---

[65] A Duff, 'Auctions, Lotteries, and the Punishment of Attempts' (1990) 9 *Law and Philosophy* 1, 35. On the way in which outcome responsibility is crucial to our self identity, see T Honoré, 'Responsibility and Luck: The Moral Basis of Strict Liability' in *Responsibility and Fault* (Oxford, Hart Publishing, 1999) 14, and J Gardner, 'Obligations and Outcomes in the Law of Torts' in P Cane and J Gardner (eds), *Relating to Responsibility* (Oxford, Hart Publishing, 2001) 111, esp part 5.
[66] Moore (n 59) 256–58.
[67] Ibid, 272–74; Duff (n 54) 290–92.
[68] Eg D Enoch and A Marmor, 'The Case Against Moral Luck' (2007) 26 *Law & Philosophy* 405, 415.
[69] B Zipursky, 'Two Dimensions of Responsibility in Crime, Tort, and Moral Luck' (2008) 9 *Theoretical Inquiries in Law* 97, 118; Duff (n 54) 341.

say that the relationship between the state and the citizen is essentially different in this respect, and that therefore legal responsibility ought to fasten directly to actual wrongdoing rather than to mental states (like intentions). In law, an outcome-sensitive concept of responsibility will therefore be preferable to outcome abstracting one.

Unfortunately, I do not have the space to assess these views here, but I do want to say something about the possible application of the result-embracing concept of action to our issue, namely recovery of property transferred under illegal agreements. Let us assume that, as Gardner, Moore and Perry have argued, there is a sound basis for attributing responsibility for any foreseeable outcome of action where the agent had control over the *initial* step, and where she was under a duty not to take this step because of its potential harmful results.[70] If so, then a claimant A who enters an illegal agreement which ripens into an actual breach of law cannot complain if she is denied recovery (for example, on the ground that the other party B's performance is only partial), even if she has had no control over the sequence of events that have led from the agreement to the actual lawbreaking (for example, if A becomes seriously ill after transferring the money to B so that she cannot stop B from offering (part of it) as a bribe). Moreover she will not be heard to say that she ought to get the same treatment as C who signed an illegal contract that, for reasons that are beyond C's control, never led to lawbreaking (for example, because the government official was sacked before B managed to bribe him).

The problem is that in criminal law, even if we do not treat the attempt and the complete offence in exactly the same way (as the 'subjectivist' would), we have a way of expressing our discontent with the fact that the defendant tried to commit an offence: we can convict her for attempt and inflict on her a punishment that will fit the measure of her culpability as a person who came close to injuring another but never quite made it.[71] In other words, we have the means to express the culpability-basis of the guilt, even when the wrongdoing-basis is absent. In contrast, the rule against recovery of property transferred under an illegal agreement does not leave room for such discretion: it is an either/or response; the claimant's wish to retrieve her property can be granted or denied, but there is no middle way of allowing her to take, say, only half of what she transferred. Therefore, if we allow a claimant to recover her property whenever the illegal purpose fails we will be treating her as if she was innocent. For the purposes of private law, the only difference that the illegality will have on her position is that the contract itself will be unenforceable, but otherwise her position

---

[70] SR Perry, 'Responsibility for Outcomes, Risk, and the Law of Torts' in GJ Postema (ed), *Philosophy and the Law of Torts* (Cambridge, Cambridge University Press, 2001) 73; Gardner (n 60); Moore (n 59).

[71] For Simester and Sullivan (n 41) 322, the flexibility in punishment plays a particularly important role in justifying outcome-sensitive punishment in criminal law.

will be identical to that of any party to a failed (benign) contract. No middle ground parallel to the offence of attempt can be fitted into the scheme. This failure to differentiate the innocent from the culpable will also send a very problematic message to the public.[72] And moreover, in some cases—most prominently in trusts that are aimed at hiding the asset—granting recovery will have a similar effect to that of enforcing the contract, and the only difference between the 'attempter' and the innocent (that is, the unenforceability) will become irrelevant. Those who believe that the law should employ the outcome-embracing concept of action can of course bite the bullet and accept this result as an unfortunate side-effect of applying their superior view of legal responsibility to this area of private law.

2. Legal Luck in Illegal Contracts

Even its most staunch opponents admit that in some instances legal luck can be introduced, or at least, be allowed to stay.[73] The following arguments in favour of taking the chance outcome of the illegal contract into account are supposed to occupy this conceptual space; that is, they should work even if the actual lawbreaking makes no difference whatsoever to a claimant's blameworthiness. We can divide them into two kinds: one examines the role of legal luck in the area of illegal contracts in general; and the other examines some intuitions we have about certain cases of contemplated illegality in order to extrapolate the version of the rule which these intuitions reflect.

It is plain to see that our private law is in fact saturated with legal luck. Even if we ignore the question of situational luck and focus only on outcome luck, we find it wherever we look—it often influences, if not determines, our liability for tortious actions, the amount we have to pay as compensation for damages in contract, and the amount of profits we have to pay (for example, as wrongdoing fiduciaries). But let us look more closely at the prevalence of legal luck in the specific set of rules that make up the law of illegal contracts. The following argument is not meant to *justify* the subjection of parties to such contracts to fortuitous circumstances—the question still remains 'whether we should reform our legal doctrines so . . . that legal status supervenes on what is under the relevant agent's control'.[74] What it can show is that if we wish to eradicate legal

---

[72] J Feinberg, 'The Expressive Function of Punishment' in *Doing and Deserving: Essays in the Theory of Responsibility* (Princeton, NJ, Princeton University Press, 1970) 96, 98.

[73] Eg J Feinberg, *Problems at the Roots of Law: Essays in Legal and Political Theory* (Oxford, Oxford University Press, 2003) 78: 'if the law is arbitrary in some respect, then provided we can improve it in that respect, at a reasonable cost in other values, we should improve it'.

[74] Enoch (n 58) 28.

luck from this body of law, we will have to reform it from top to bottom, and that restricting the sanction of illegality only to cases where the illegal purpose was actually achieved is hardly the worst incident of legal luck in this area.

One serious manifestation of legal luck in the way the law treats illegal agreements is the disconnection between the severity of the sanction imposed and the gravity of the contemplated illegality (unless this falls below the minimum threshold that is required for the invocation of the sanction). In some cases, like paying for another party to commit a criminal offence, the payment will presumably reflect the risk, so that an assassin will charge higher fees than a burglar, and the claimant's loss if she cannot recover the money will be accordingly higher. But this is not necessarily so, and cases where the claimant purports to hide her assets from creditors are usually good examples of legal luck: the injurious potential of the sanction is dependent on the value of the assets that the claimant had to hide, and not on the gravity of the offence. An example is provided by *Chettiar v Chettiar*.[75] Chettiar conveyed part of his field to his son in order to circumvent the Malayan Rubber Regulations (1934). When the son refused to give it back, the father's loss was dependent solely on the size of the field, even though, for the purposes of the illegality itself it did not matter whether he transferred two acres, or forty (as he did). The damage suffered by claimants who are denied recovery is therefore often a function of their wealth and not of their blameworthiness.

The outcomes produced by application of the rule against recovery are a notorious example of legal luck not only because of the harm that this rule wreaks on the claimant, but also because of the windfall it brings to the defendant. Although the courts insist that they are not doing recipients any favours, their refusal to intervene has the outrageous result of allowing the recipient to keep property that she was never meant to take as a gift. One way of dealing with this unpalatable result is to introduce a mechanism by which the property can be confiscated by the state.[76] But until such a solution is in place, the application of the general rule against recovery is so infested with legal luck that the complaint about the dependence of the sanction on actual outcome seems rather weak. If we are to eradicate legal luck from the law of illegal contracts, the withdrawal exception to the rule against recovery is hardly the most obvious place to start.

A different kind of strategy is to examine some intuitions about specific situations in order to show that allowing recovery in withdrawal cases has a significant intuitive appeal.[77] 'Suppose, for example, that in *Bigos* . . .

---

[75] [1962] 1 All ER 494 (PC).

[76] For the mechanism in the Proceeds of Crime Act 2002, s 240, see n 5.

[77] Some writers believe that if these intuitions are strong enough, the values of democracy mean that they have to be reflected in the law, because the law should not go beyond the 'sensibilities of common people': Ashworth (n 63) 748. But for the opposite view, see Feinberg

exchange control had been abolished before the foreign currency was made available: it is absurd to suppose that the plaintiff should have been denied restitution.'[78] Perhaps 'absurd' would be taking it too far, but there is a serious sense in which we will find it hard to put a label of 'illegality' on an act that is no longer against the law even if it was illegal at the time of the agent's act. Similarly, it would be odd if a contract that was never against the law would be considered as illegal just because the parties thought by mistake that it was.[79] It seems that the intuition in favour of recovery will be particularly strong in cases like *Bigos* where the illegality is less central to the transaction, that is, where the direct aim of the transaction—here, transferring money to Italy—could have been achieved by legal means. Compare this with contracts that are directly aimed at illegality, like an artificial transfer of property in order to make the balance sheet of the recipient look better, or in order to evade tax. In these cases, the transaction can turn out to be legitimate after all because, for example, the tax laws were changed, but since the whole raison d'être of the contract was to commit an offence, the court may justly find it harder to ignore the original intention of the parties.

And what about cases where the act, as it was conceived by the parties, was indeed illegal, but it turned out that a large gap stretched between reality and the picture they had in their mind? To change the facts of *Tribe* slightly, what if it transpires that the father had no creditors at all? In such cases there was never even a possibility of bringing about the harm from which the law is supposed to protect us. The sanction, if it is applied, will attach to intentions that are completely removed from any concrete possibility of harm.[80] True, the contract is a manifestation of the parties' indifference to the law, but we may well find it too harsh to withhold recovery from a claimant whose action never posed the slightest threat to anyone.

The picture that emerges from these intuitions seems to be that it should matter whether wrongdoing actually took place. In fact, we may well find it hard to accept that the rule against recovery must apply according to the parties' unconscionable intentions, regardless of any actual violation of the

---

(n 73) 84–85 and 92–94; Y Shachar, 'The Fortuitous Gap in law and Morality' (1987) 6 *Criminal Justice Ethics* 12.

[78] *Tribe* (n 9) 135 (Millett LJ).

[79] On this question in the criminal law context, see Duff (n 54) 92–96. If the opposite happens, ie if the claimant mistakenly thought that the transaction was permissible, then it may be that he can escape the 'no recovery rule': *Mohamed v Alaga & Co (a firm)* [2000] 1 WLR 1815. It is well established that a mistake in fact argument will defeat an illegality claim: Burrows (n 13) 574–77.

[80] The Criminal Attempts Act 1981, s 1(3)(b) provides that 'if the facts of the case had been as he believed them to be, his intention would be so regarded, then . . . he shall be regarded as having had an intent to commit that offence'. On the interpretation of this section and on impossible attempts in general see Duff (n 54) ch 3; Simester and Sullivan (n 41) part 9.4

law. But perhaps this fact only testifies to the strong grip which pre-moral conceptions of harm-based responsibility still have on us.[81] It would then be the job of the law reformer to clean the law of such contorted perceptions, in the hope that the public conscience will follow suit.

F. RENUNCIATION

Under the category of renunciation we find those claimants whose mental attitude can be described as atonement, but their inability to halt the illegal scheme puts them on the same footing as in the withdrawal cases. Situations of renunciation will most likely involve some (innocent) ignorance about the last date at which the illegal scheme can be undone. For example, suppose that a claimant regrets her entry into a tax evasion scheme, and calls the tax inspector, only to discover that a decision about her assessment has already been taken on an altogether different basis; or, suppose that a claimant is driven by guilt to call her friend and ask her not to transfer the bribe money after the official who agreed to take the bribe has already been sacked. Again, since the burden of proof lies with the claimant, we need not worry too much about the possibility of self-interested motivation masquerading as a true atonement. Obviously, if we decide that recovery should be allowed on the ground of withdrawal alone, then the claimant's morally admirable motivation will make no difference in these cases. But, if we decide that withdrawal is not enough in itself to generate a right of recovery, then the question arises, whether a sincere change of heart (that could not lead to abandonment) should tip the scale in favour of recovery?

The difference between renunciation and atonement is that there is no stop act in the latter case (besides the mere formality of the repudiation). But as we have already discussed in part D, on 'abandonment', the stop act cannot, on its own, determine the claimant's right to recovery. The crucial consideration can be either the motivation behind the decision to call off the deal, or the occurrence of lawbreaking. The stop act has only a limited role in atonement situations, as evidence of the claimant's regret. When calling off a deal that he otherwise deems profitable, the claimant shows that a sincere shift in his attitude towards the requirements of the law took place, and that he therefore deserves to be helped by the court. However, if he missed the opportunity to cancel the agreement, then that fact alone should not stand in his way to argue that he deserves to be readmitted to the court. It may well be harder for him to convince the judges of his regained innocence, but if he can bring evidence to that effect (for example, a letter that purports to cancel an otherwise successful deal when,

---

[81] See Shachar (n 77) for a discussion of the way in which incidents of legal luck contribute to the widespread tendency in society to formulate moral judgement according to outcome, rather than intentions and choices of the agent.

unbeknown to him, it was no longer relevant), his plea for recovery should be heard.

At this point, one may well wonder what is the difference between 'renunciation' and a case where atonement took place after the contract *did* result in a violation of the law? Unlike criminal, or even tort law, in the context of contracts, there will be many cases where any damage that the violated law was designed to prevent can be fully corrected by monetary means—*Tinsley* would be a good example, for the claimant confessed her benefit fraud while it was still successfully ongoing. And since the question whether the contract led to actual lawbreaking is one of chance, there is a place to argue that a 'legal luck'-free concept of the *locus poenitentiae* rule should be totally neutral about actual harm, and allow nothing but the claimant's motivation to determine the result even when harm did occur. English law, however, has always taken the view that the *locus poenitentiae* doctrine applies only to cases where no actual law-breaking took place, and the question of whether this can be justified will have to wait for another day.

G. CONCLUSION

The *locus poenitentiae* doctrine tests our intuitions about a kind of situation that occurs in many areas of the law, where an agent never really violates the law, but seems to come close enough to justify a sanction. In seeking to delineate the limits of the law's response to an agent's first substantial move towards a prohibited end, the doctrine touches on some basic questions about legal responsibility. To what extent does the rule relate to the agent's inner world of intentions and motivations? How important is the occurrence of real harm? Can intentions be undone? Blameworthiness is not the only relevant issue, however. Any decision about the precise limits of the doctrine must also take account of the effect that the rule is likely to have on other people's conduct. These two considerations—turpitude and deterrence—can at times lead to different conclusions and call for another principled decision about the proper relationship between them.

In contrast to the sanctions for criminal attempts, or dangerous conduct in tort, the sanction to which the *locus poenitentiae* rule in private law relates does not embody the response of the harmed person or the aggrieved community. Instead, it is a unique expression of the courts' reluctance to engage with claims that are tainted by the unconscionable behaviour of the litigants who make them. The courts' refusal to respond to claims that are tainted by illegality is readily understandable, and the burden of proof lies on those who seek to justify the *locus poenitentiae* rule as an exception to the general recovery bar. It is clear that in its present version, as presented in *Tribe*, the rule is deformed by the need to make up for some serious flaws in the area of illegal contracts. And since it is now widely recognised by the courts, academics and the Law Commission that these faults should be amended, this seems to be a good time to rethink the theoretical foundation of the *locus poenitentiae* rule.

We saw that claimants who atone for taking the first step towards illegality ought to be given the opportunity to undo the agreement and recover their property from the other party. A person who eradicates her disgraceful attitude towards the law is in a unique position, not only because her actions will dismantle the hostility of the court, but also because deterrence considerations will support the decision to grant her the recovery. In contrast, claimants who actively put an end to an illegal scheme because it serves their own interests to do so should not be favoured over parties to an illegal contract which never came to an actual violation of the law. A self-interested stop act cannot restore the claimant's relationship with the court, and recognising such acts as a reason for allowing recovery will not help to promote general obedience to the law. However, a case may be made for a more comprehensive *locus poenitentiae* rule in which recovery will be allowed whenever the illegal purpose of the contract was never achieved.

The question whether we ought to introduce such a sharp distinction between cases where the intended harm has occurred, and cases where it has not, depends on one's views about legal luck. Since the no-recovery sanction is an all or nothing measure, such a distinction would basically mean that an illegality which is embedded in a contract that failed to achieve its purpose will be ignored by the court, and the parties to it will be treated as if they were innocent. Some intuitions that we seem to have about the way parties to illegal contracts ought to be treated support a rule which only denies recovery where an actual violation of the law has taken place. Against this, however, a formulation of the *locus poenitentiae* doctrine which is permeated with legal luck goes against the grain of a rule which originated in an acknowledgement of our ability to regain our lost innocence through the act of repentance.